Jaguar & Daimler Owners Workshop Manual

J H Haynes
Member of the Guild of Motoring Writers
and Peter G Strasman

Models covered
Jaguar XJ6, XJ & Sovereign and Daimler Sovereign
Saloon and Coupe, Series 1, 2 and 3
2.8, 3.4 and 4.2 litre

*Covers long wheelbase and Vanden Plas models
Does not cover XJ-S 3.6, 12-cylinder models or new range
introduced October 1986*

(242-7S6)

Haynes Group Limited
Haynes North America, Inc

www.haynes.com

Acknowledgements

Thanks are due to the Champion Sparking Plug Company Limited who supplied the illustrations showing the spark plug conditions, to Holt Lloyd Limited who supplied the illustrations showing bodywork repair, and to Duckhams Oils who provided lubrication data. Thanks are also due to Sykes-Pickavant Limited who supplied some of the workshop tools and to Jaguar Cars Limited for their assistance in the provision of technical information.

We are indebted to Reg Hawkins who was kind enough to lend his car for the project, and of course, to all those people at Sparkford who helped in the production of this manual.

A book in the **Haynes Owners Workshop Manual Series**

ISBN **978 0 85733 963 8**

British Library Cataloguing in Publication Data
Strasman, Peter G.
  Jaguar/Daimler 6-cyl (XJ type) owners
  workshop manual.–(Owners Workshop Manual).
  1. Jaguar automobile
  I. Title   II. Series
  629.28'722   TL215.J3
  ISBN 1-85010-178-7

Contents

About this manual

Its aim

The aim of this manual is to help you get the best value from your vehicle. It can do so in several ways. It can help you decide what work must be done (even should you choose to get it done by a garage), provide information on routine maintenance and servicing, and give a logical course of action and diagnosis when random faults occur. However, it is hoped that you will use the manual by tackling the work yourself. On simpler jobs it may even be quicker than booking the car into a garage and going there twice, to leave and collect it. Perhaps most important, a lot of money can be saved by avoiding the costs a garage must charge to cover its labour and overheads.

The manual has drawings and descriptions to show the function of the various components so that their layout can be understood. Then the tasks are described and photographed in a step-by-step sequence so that even a novice can do the work.

Its arrangement

The manual is divided into thirteen Chapters, each covering a logical sub-division of the vehicle. The Chapters are each divided into Sections, numbered with single figures, eg 5; and the Sections into paragraphs (or sub-sections), with decimal numbers following on from the Section they are in, eg 5.1, 5.2, 5.3 etc.

It is freely illustrated, especially in those parts where there is a detailed sequence of operations to be carried out. There are two forms of illustration: figures and photographs. The figures are numbered in sequence with decimal numbers, according to their position in the Chapter – eg Fig. 6.4 is the fourth drawing/illustration in Chapter 6. Photographs carry the same number (either individually or in related groups) as the Section or sub-section to which they relate.

There is an alphabetical index at the back of the manual as well as a contents list at the front. Each Chapter is also preceded by its own individual contents list.

References to the 'left' or 'right' of the vehicle are in the sense of a person in the driver's seat facing forwards.

Unless otherwise stated, nuts and bolts are removed by turning anti-clockwise, and tightened by turning clockwise.

Vehicle manufacturers continually make changes to specifications and recommendations, and these, when notified, are incorporated into our manuals at the earliest opportunity.

Whilst every care is taken to ensure that the information in this manual is correct, no liability can be accepted by the authors or publishers for loss, damage or injury caused by any errors in, or omissions from, the information given.

Introduction to the Jaguar XJ6 and Daimler Sovereign

The car was originally introduced as the Jaguar XJ6 in 1968 with a six cylinder (type XK) twin overhead camshaft engine, which was offered in 2.8 or 4.2 litre capacity.

The transmission was a four-speed manual gearbox with optional overdrive or three-speed automatic transmission.

Power steering was standard on de-luxe models but optional on standard models.

In October 1972, a long wheelbase model was introduced. This had the 4.2 litre engine and was known as the XJ6L and provided extra space in the rear passenger compartment.

In September 1973, the Series 2 range was introduced offering only the 4.2 litre engine, the 2.8 litre version being discontinued. The new car included ventilated front brake discs, laminated windscreen and revised interior and instrumentation. Overdrive could be specified as a standard fitting and full air-conditioning was offered as an option.

In January 1974, the Series 2, two door coupe was launched and designated the XJ6C.

In April 1975, a 3.4 litre version of the XJ6 was introduced, having an engine which had a re-designed cylinder block which was torsionally stronger. Overdrive or automatic transmission was offered at no extra cost.

The Daimler range has followed closely the Jaguar model introductions and as the car differs only in detail (such as the radiator grille), it is designed to cater for the brand loyalty which exists among Daimler owners.

There is a great difference in equipment between early cars and Series 2 models, also there is a wide variation in accessories and emission control systems according to the model, the date of production and the territory for which the car is destined.

Generally, the overhaul and repair operations are not difficult to carry out but many of them are rather protracted due to the number of components which have to be removed. This is to be expected on such a well constructed, lavishly equipped car.

Refer to Chapter 13 for Series 3 models.

General dimensions, weights and capacities

For modifications, and information applicable to later models, see Supplement at end of manual

Dimensions (early cars)
Overall length	15 ft 9½ in (4.812 m)
Overall width	5 ft 9 ¾ in (1.762 m)
Overall height	4 ft 8 7/8 in (1.44 m)
Wheelbase	9 ft 0 7/8 in (2.765 m)

Weights (early cars)
2.8 litre (manual)	30¼ cwt (1536.8 kg)
2.8 litre (overdrive)	30½ cwt (1549.5 kg)
2.8 litre (automatic)	30¼ cwt (1536.8 kg)
4.2 litre (manual)	30¾ cwt (1562.2 kg)
4.2 litre (overdrive)	31 cwt (1574.9 kg)
4.2 litre (automatic)	31½ cwt (1600.3 kg)

Dimensions (Series 2)
	XJ6	XJ6L (LWB)	XJ6C (Coupe)
Overall length *	190.7 in (4.844 m)	194.7 in (4.945 m)	190.7 in (4.844 m)
Overall width	69.7 in (1.760 m)	69.7 in (1.760 m)	69.7 in (1.760 m)
Overall height	54.1 in (1.374 m)	54.1 in (1.374 m)	54.1 in (1.374 m)
Wheelbase	109.1 in (2.771 m)	113.1 in (2.873 m)	109.1 in (2.771 m)

Weights (Series 2)
	XJ6	XJ6L (LWB)	XJ6C (Coupe)
3.4 litre	3717 lb (1686 kg)	—	—
4.2 litre	3867 lb (1754 kg)	3907 lb (1772 kg)	3879 lb (1759 kg)
4.2 litre (N. American Specification) **	4074 lb (1848 kg)	—	4086 lb (1853 kg)

* Add 4.2 in (107 mm) for impact bumpers   ** Includes automatic transmission and air-conditioning.

Capacities
Fuel tank:
Not N. America	Each tank 12 Imp. gals. (54.6 litres/14.5 US gals.)
N. America	11 Imp. gals. (50 litres/13.2 US gals.)
Series 2 cars	10.5 Imp. gals. (47.75 litres/12.6 US gals.)

Cooling system (including heater):
2.8 and 3.4 litre	30 Imp. pints (17 litres/36 US pints)
4.2 litres	32 Imp. pints (18 litres/38 US pints)
Gearbox (without overdrive) - early cars	2½ Imp. pints (1.5 litres/3 US pints)
Gearbox (with overdrive) - early cars	4 Imp. pints (2.25 litres/4¾ US pints)
Gearbox (without overdrive) - later cars	3 Imp. pints (1.6 litres/3¼ US pints)
Gearbox (with overdrive) - later cars	4½ Imp. pints (2.4 litres/5 US pints)

Automatic transmission (from dry): *
Model 8	16.5 Imp. pints (9.4 litres/19.8 US pints)
Model 12	16.5 Imp. pints (9.4 litres/19.8 US pints)
Model 35	16.5 Imp. pints (9.4 litres/19.8 US pints)
Model 65	14.5 Imp. pints (8.2 litres/17.4 US pints)
Rear axle	2¾ Imp. pints (1.5 litres/3¼ US pints)
Engine (including new filter)	14½ Imp. pints (8.25 litres/17½ US pints)

*At service refill use only ¾ of quantities shown

Safety first!

Professional motor mechanics are trained in safe working procedures. However enthusiastic you may be about getting on with the job in hand, do take the time to ensure that your safety is not put at risk. A moment's lack of attention can result in an accident, as can failure to observe certain elementary precautions.

There will always be new ways of having accidents, and the following points do not pretend to be a comprehensive list of all dangers; they are intended rather to make you aware of the risks and to encourage a safety-conscious approach to all work you carry out on your vehicle.

Essential DOs and DON'Ts

DON'T rely on a single jack when working underneath the vehicle. Always use reliable additional means of support, such as axle stands, securely placed under a part of the vehicle that you know will not give way.

DON'T attempt to loosen or tighten high-torque nuts (e.g. wheel hub nuts) while the vehicle is on a jack; it may be pulled off.

DON'T start the engine without first ascertaining that the transmission is in neutral (or 'Park' where applicable) and the parking brake applied.

DON'T suddenly remove the filler cap from a hot cooling system – cover it with a cloth and release the pressure gradually first, or you may get scalded by escaping coolant.

DON'T attempt to drain oil until you are sure it has cooled sufficiently to avoid scalding you.

DON'T grasp any part of the engine, exhaust or catalytic converter without first ascertaining that it is sufficiently cool to avoid burning you.

DON'T allow brake fluid or antifreeze to contact vehicle paintwork.

DON'T syphon toxic liquids such as fuel, brake fluid or antifreeze by mouth, or allow them to remain on your skin.

DON'T inhale dust – it may be injurious to health (see *Asbestos* below).

DON'T allow any spilt oil or grease to remain on the floor – wipe it up straight away, before someone slips on it.

DON'T use ill-fitting spanners or other tools which may slip and cause injury.

DON'T attempt to lift a heavy component which may be beyond your capability – get assistance.

DON'T rush to finish a job, or take unverified short cuts.

DON'T allow children or animals in or around an unattended vehicle.

DO wear eye protection when using power tools such as drill, sander, bench grinder etc, and when working under the vehicle.

DO use a barrier cream on your hands prior to undertaking dirty jobs – it will protect your skin from infection as well as making the dirt easier to remove afterwards; but make sure your hands aren't left slippery. Note that long-term contact with used engine oil can be a health hazard.

DO keep loose clothing (cuffs, tie etc) and long hair well out of the way of moving mechanical parts.

DO remove rings, wristwatch etc, before working on the vehicle – especially the electrical system.

DO ensure that any lifting tackle used has a safe working load rating adequate for the job.

DO keep your work area tidy – it is only too easy to fall over articles left lying around.

DO get someone to check periodically that all is well, when working alone on the vehicle.

DO carry out work in a logical sequence and check that everything is correctly assembled and tightened afterwards.

DO remember that your vehicle's safety affects that of yourself and others. If in doubt on any point, get specialist advice.

IF, in spite of following these precautions, you are unfortunate enough to injure yourself, seek medical attention as soon as possible.

Asbestos

Certain friction, insulating, sealing, and other products – such as brake linings, brake bands, clutch linings, torque converters, gaskets, etc – contain asbestos. *Extreme care must be taken to avoid inhalation of dust from such products since it is hazardous to health.* If in doubt, assume that they *do* contain asbestos.

Fire

Remember at all times that petrol (gasoline) is highly flammable. Never smoke, or have any kind of naked flame around, when working on the vehicle. But the risk does not end there – a spark caused by an electrical short-circuit, by two metal surfaces contacting each other, by careless use of tools, or even by static electricity built up in your body under certain conditions, can ignite petrol vapour, which in a confined space is highly explosive.

Always disconnect the battery earth (ground) terminal before working on any part of the fuel or electrical system, and never risk spilling fuel on to a hot engine or exhaust.

It is recommended that a fire extinguisher of a type suitable for fuel and electrical fires is kept handy in the garage or workplace at all times. Never try to extinguish a fuel or electrical fire with water.

Note: *Any reference to a 'torch' appearing in this manual should always be taken to mean a hand-held battery-operated electric lamp or flashlight. It does NOT mean a welding/gas torch or blowlamp.*

Fumes

Certain fumes are highly toxic and can quickly cause unconsciousness and even death if inhaled to any extent. Petrol (gasoline) vapour comes into this category, as do the vapours from certain solvents such as trichloroethylene. Any draining or pouring of such volatile fluids should be done in a well ventilated area.

When using cleaning fluids and solvents, read the instructions carefully. Never use materials from unmarked containers – they may give off poisonous vapours.

Never run the engine of a motor vehicle in an enclosed space such as a garage. Exhaust fumes contain carbon monoxide which is extremely poisonous; if you need to run the engine, always do so in the open air or at least have the rear of the vehicle outside the workplace.

If you are fortunate enough to have the use of an inspection pit, never drain or pour petrol, and never run the engine, while the vehicle is standing over it; the fumes, being heavier than air, will concentrate in the pit with possibly lethal results.

The battery

Never cause a spark, or allow a naked light, near the vehicle's battery. It will normally be giving off a certain amount of hydrogen gas, which is highly explosive.

Always disconnect the battery earth (ground) terminal before working on the fuel or electrical systems.

If possible, loosen the filler plugs or cover when charging the battery from an external source. Do not charge at an excessive rate or the battery may burst.

Take care when topping up and when carrying the battery. The acid electrolyte, even when diluted, is very corrosive and should not be allowed to contact the eyes or skin.

If you ever need to prepare electrolyte yourself, always add the acid slowly to the water, and never the other way round. Protect against splashes by wearing rubber gloves and goggles.

When jump starting a car using a booster battery, for negative earth (ground) vehicles, connect the jump leads in the following sequence: First connect one jump lead between the positive (+) terminals of the two batteries. Then connect the other jump lead first to the negative (–) terminal of the booster battery, and then to a good earthing (ground) point on the vehicle to be started, at least 18 in (45 cm) from the battery if possible. Ensure that hands and jump leads are clear of any moving parts, and that the two vehicles do not touch. Disconnect the leads in the reverse order.

Mains electricity and electrical equipment

When using an electric power tool, inspection light etc, always ensure that the appliance is correctly connected to its plug and that, where necessary, it is properly earthed (grounded). Do not use such appliances in damp conditions and, again, beware of creating a spark or applying excessive heat in the vicinity of fuel or fuel vapour. Also ensure that the appliances meet the relevant national safety standards.

Ignition HT voltage

A severe electric shock can result from touching certain parts of the ignition system, such as the HT leads, when the engine is running or being cranked, particularly if components are damp or the insulation is defective. Where an electronic ignition system is fitted, the HT voltage is much higher and could prove fatal.

Jaguar Series Two XJ6 Coupe (UK Specification)

Buying
spare parts and vehicle identification numbers

Buying spare parts

Spare parts are available from many sources, for example: Jaguar garages, other garages and accessory shops, and motor factors. Our advice regarding spare parts is as follows:

Official appointed Jaguar garages - This is the best source of parts which are peculiar to your car and otherwise not generally available (eg; complete cylinder heads, internal gearbox components, badges, interior trim etc). It is also the only place at which you should buy parts if your car is still under warranty; non-Jaguar components may invalidate the warranty. To be sure of obtaining the correct parts it will always be necessary to give the storeman your car's engine and chassis number, and if possible, to take the old part along for positive identification. Remember that many parts are available on a factory exchange scheme - any parts returned should always be clean! It obviously makes good sense to go to the specialists on your car for this type of part for they are best equipped to supply you.

Other garages and accessory shops - These are often very good places to buy material and components needed for the maintenance of your car (eg; oil filters, spark plugs, bulbs, fan belts, oils and grease, touch-up paint, filler paste etc). They also sell general accessories, usually have convenient opening hours, charge lower prices and can often be found not far from home.

Motor factors - Good factors will stock all of the more important components which wear out relatively quickly (eg; clutch components, pistons, valves, exhaust systems, brake cylinders/pipes/hoses/seals/shoes and pads etc). Motor factors will often provide new or reconditioned components on a part exchange basis - this can save a considerable amount of money.

Vehicle identification numbers

When buying spare parts, always quote the car model, chassis or engine number, as necessary, to the partsman. This will ensure that the correctly fitting item is supplied for your particular car.

The *engine and car numbers* are located on a plate attached to the left-hand wing valance within the engine compartment.

On cars destined for operation in *North America,* the *chassis number* is repeated on the top of the fascia panel just inside the windscreen.

Engine and car number index plate

Fixings (late Series 2 and Series 3)

Nuts and bolts used throughout the car may be to metric (ISO) or UNF standards. Metric bolts are identified by ISOM or M and strength grade numbers stamped onto their heads. Metric nuts have the strength grade marked on one of their flats and some also include the symbol M.

Unified bolts have a circular depression on their heads whilst the nuts have an unbroken line of circles on one flat.

Hydraulic brake fittings are to metric standards and components must never be interchanged with earlier threaded (UNF) parts.

The hydraulic components for the power steering gear still retain threads to UNF pattern, even on the latest models.

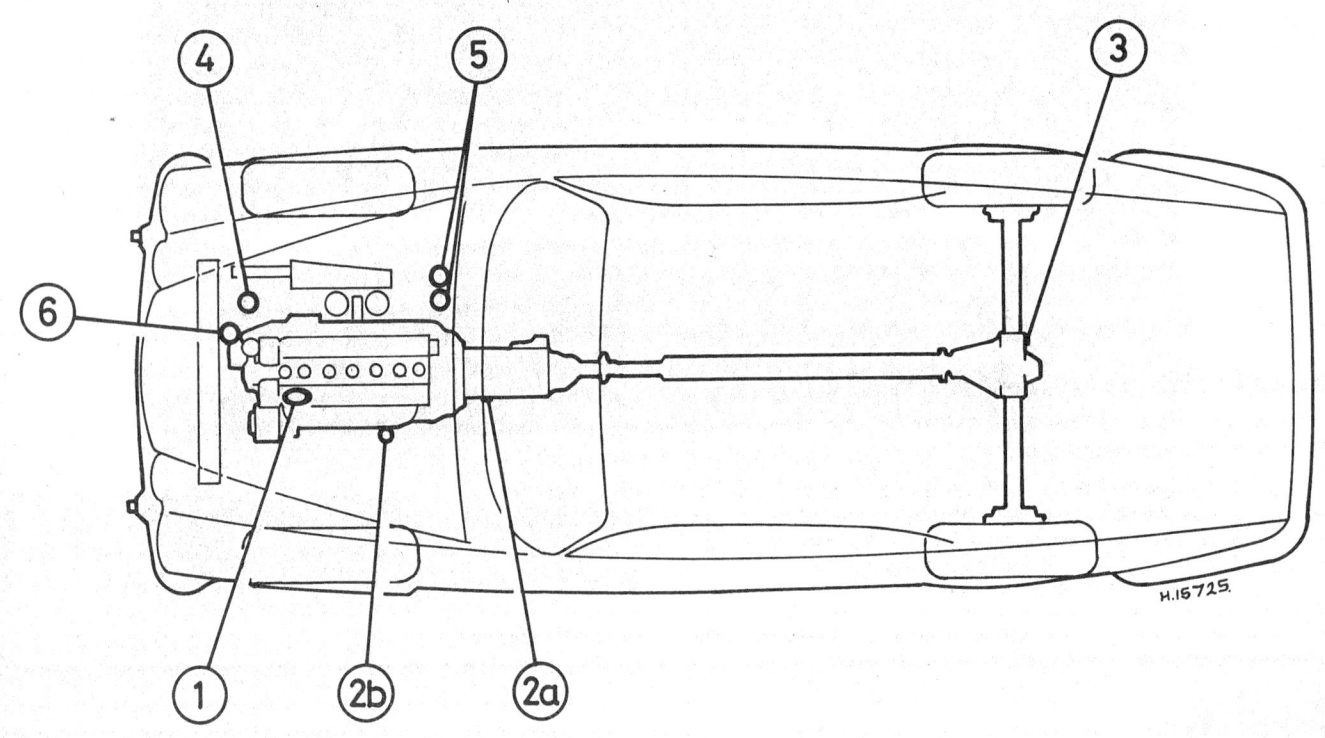

Recommended lubricants and fluids

Component or system	Lubricant type/specification	Duckhams recommendation
1 Engine	Multigrade engine oil, viscosity range SAE 10W/40 to 20W/50, to BLS-0L-02 or API SE/CC	Duckhams QXR, Hypergrade, or 10W/40 Motor Oil
2A Manual Gearbox*		
4-speed	Hypoid gear oil, viscosity SAE 90EP	Duckhams Hypoid 90
5-speed (drain and refill)	Hypoid gear oil, viscosity SAE 75	Duckhams Hypoid 75
5-speed (top-up only)	Hypoid gear oil, viscosity SAE 80EP	Duckhams Hypoid 80
2B Automatic transmission	ATF to M2C 33G	Duckhams Q-Matic
3 Final drive		
Standard	Hypoid gear oil, viscosity SAE 90EP	Duckhams Hypoid 90S
Limited slip (drain and refill)	Powr-Lok approved gear oil, viscosity SAE 90	Duckhams Hypoid 90DL
Limited slip (top-up only)	Hypoid gear oil, viscosity SAE 90EP	Duckhams Hypoid 90S
4 Power assisted steering	ATF to M2C 33G	Duckhams Q-Matic
5 Brake and clutch hydraulic systems	Hydraulic fluid to SAE J1703D	Duckhams Universal Brake and Clutch Fluid
6 Cooling system	Antifreeze to BS 3150, 3152 or 6580	Duckhams Universal Antifreeze and Summer Coolant

*Note: *If baulking problems are experienced with 5-speed gearboxes, it is permissible to drain the oil and refill with Dexron II type ATF (Duckhams D-Matic) – see Chapter 13*

Routine maintenance

For modifications, and information applicable to later models, see Supplement at end of manual

Maintenance is essential for ensuring safety and desirable for the purpose of getting the best in terms of performance and economy from the car. Over the years the need for periodic lubrication - oiling, greasing and so on - has been drastically reduced if not totally eliminated. This has unfortunately tended to lead some owners to think that because no such action is required the items either no longer exist or will last for ever. This is a serious delusion. It follows therefore that the largest initial element of maintenance is visual examination. This may lead to repairs or renewals.

Every 250 miles (400 km) or weekly

Brakes
Check reservoir fluid level (photo).
Check foot and handbrake movement for increased travel or falling off in efficiency.

Engine
Check oil level (photo).
Check coolant level (photo).
Check battery electrolyte level.

Lights
Check for operation.
Clean lenses.

Steering
Check tyres for pressure and wear characteristics.

General
Clean windscreen.
Check and, if necessary, top up the water reservoir adding a screen wash such as Turtle Wax High Tech Screen Wash.

At first 1000 miles (1600 km) - new cars only

Brakes
Check fluid level in reservoir.
Check travel of footbrake and handbrake lever.

Engine
Check torque of cylinder head nuts.
Check for oil, water or fuel leaks.
Top-up carburettor dampers.
Top-up battery.

Topping-up the brake master cylinder reservoir

Check coolant level in header tank or expansion tank.
Drain and refill engine oil.
Check tension of all drivebelts.
Check contact breaker gap and ignition timing.

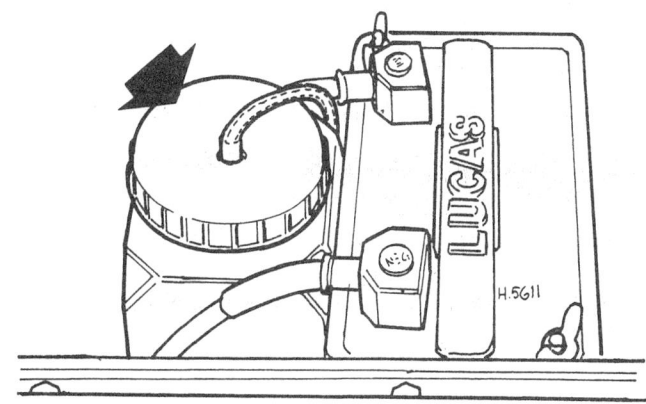
Windscreen washer reservoir

Steering/suspension
Check level of power steering reservoir fluid.
Check all suspension bolts and nuts.
Check wheel alignment.
Check tyre pressures.
Grease all suspension nipples.

Transmission
Check clutch fluid level.
Check clutch free-movement.
Check gearbox (or automatic transmission) fluid level.
Adjust rear brake band (model 12 automatic transmission only).
Adjust front brake band (model 8 and 35 automatic transmission only).
Check oil level in final drive unit.

General
Check all lights and headlamp alignment.
Check locks and controls and adjust, if necessary.
Top-up screen washer reservoir.
Lubricate locks, hinges and controls.

Every 3000 miles (4800 km)

Brakes
Check disc pad wear.
Check handbrake and foot pedal travel.
Check fluid lines for leaks.

Engine
Check drivebelt tension.
Check exhaust system for leaks.
Top-up carburettor dampers.

Steering
Check condition of steering joints and gaiters.

Every 6000 miles (9600 km)

Clutch
Check reservoir fluid level.
Check free-movement.

Engine
Change engine oil and filter element.
Renew fuel filter.
Clean carburettor gauze filters (SU type only).
Clean and adjust contact breaker points.
Clean and re-gap spark plugs.
Check ignition timing.
Lubricate distributor.
Clean automatic enrichment device (AED) filter. SU - HS8 carburettor only.
Check and adjust carburettors and lubricate linkage.
Adjust upper timing chain (if necessary).
Check all fuel injection system connections.

Steering
Check power steering fluid level.
Lubricate grease nipples on trackrod ends and rack and pinion assembly.

Transmission
Check fluid level in manual gearbox or automatic transmission.
Check fluid level in final drive unit.

Suspension
Lubricate all grease nipples including those on wheel bearings.

Topping-up the engine oil level

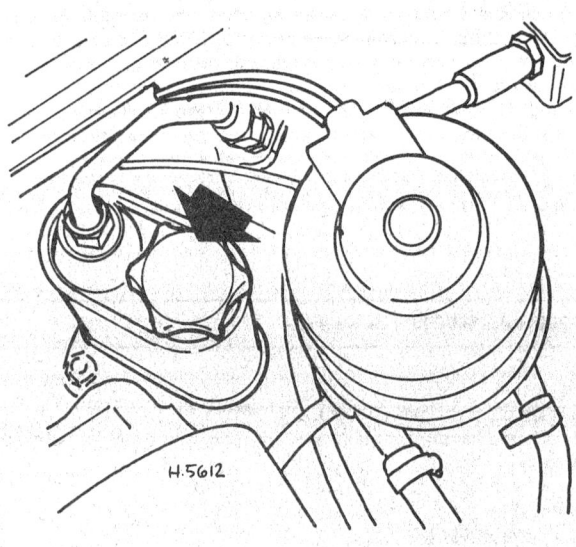

Clutch fluid reservoir

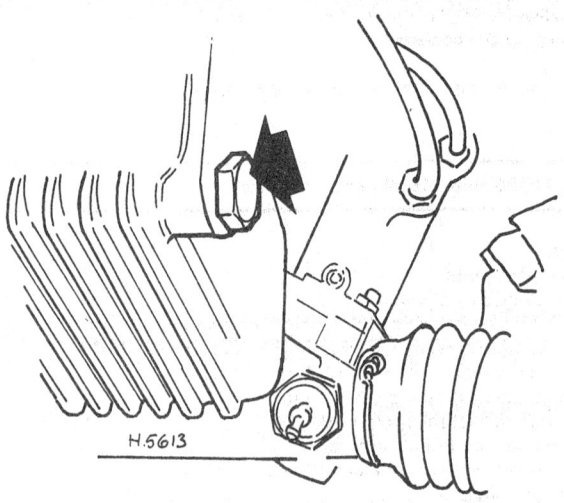

Location of engine drain plug

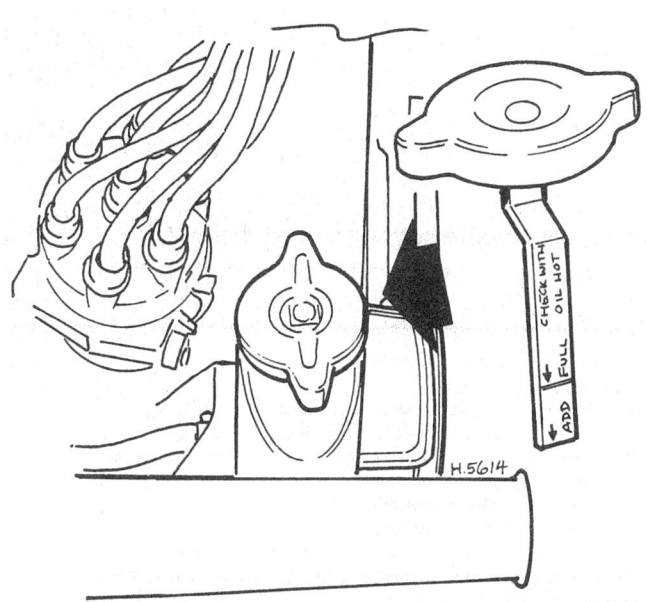

Location of power steering fluid reservoir

Topping-up the coolant

Every 12000 miles (19300 km)

Engine
Renew spark plugs.
Renew air cleaner element .
Clean EGR system orifice of carbon (emission control systems only).
Renew contact breaker assembly (mechanical distributor).
Lubricate distributor (electronic distributor).
Check tightness of cylinder head nuts.
Check tightness of manifold nuts.
Clean crankcase ventilation filter.
Check exhaust system for leaks or deterioration.
Renew fuel filter.

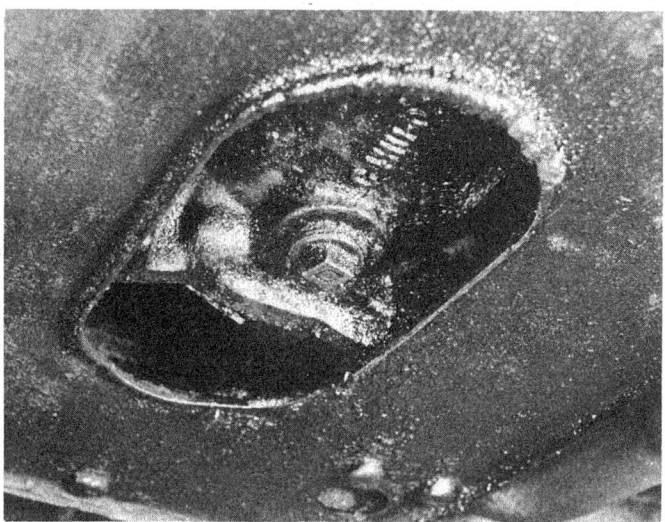

Final drive unit drain plug

Steering/suspension
Check front wheel alignment and security of all steering and suspension nuts and bolts.
Check front hub bearing endfloat.

Transmission
Change final drive unit oil (use special oil if limited slip differential).
Change manual gearbox/overdrive oil.
Clean overdrive unit filter.

Fuel injection
Renew oxygen sensor (N. America only).

General
Check headlamp alignment.

Every 24000 miles (38600 km)

Brakes
Drain hydraulic system, flush and refill with new fluid.

Engine
Renew charcoal canister (fuel evaporative control system).
Check fuel filler cap seal and renew if defective.

Every 30 000 miles (48 000 km)

Transmission
Adjust rear brake band (model 12 automatic transmission only).
Renew fluid, clean filter.

Every 48000 miles (77200 km)

Brakes
Drain hydraulic system and renew all seals. Refill with fresh fluid and bleed.

Every two years

Renew coolant with fresh antifreeze mixture.

Chapter 1 Engine

For modifications, and information applicable to later models, see Supplement at end of manual

Contents

Specifications

Engine (general)

Number of cylinders	...	...	...	...	...	...	...	...	6

	2.8 litre	3.4 litre	4.2 litre
Bore	3.2677 in (83.0 mm)	3.2677 in (83.0 mm)	3.625 in (92.07 mm)
Stroke	3.3857 in (86.0 mm)	4.1732 in (106.0 mm)	4.1732 in (106.0 mm)
Cubic capacity	170.38 cu in (2792 cc)	210 cu in (3442 cc)	258.43 cu in (4235 cc)

Compression ratio ... ... 8 : 1 (L), 7.81 : 1 (S3/3.4), 9 : 1 (S), 8.4 : 1 (Series 2 and 3)

Firing order ... ... 1 — 5 — 3 — 6 — 2 — 4 (No. 1 cylinder at rear)

Camshaft

Number of bearings	4 per shaft
Journal diameter	1.00 in (25.4 mm)
Running clearance	0.0005 in to 0.002 in (0.013 to 0.05 mm)
Endfloat (maximum)	0.004 to 0.006 in (0.10 to 0.15 mm)

Connecting rods

	2.8 litre	3.4 litre, 4.2 litre
Length (centre to centre)	5 5/8 in (14.28 cm)	7 3/4 in (19.68 cm)
Big-end bearing bore	2.2330 to 2.2335 in (56.72 to 56.73 mm)	
Big-end bearing running clearance	0.0015 to 0.0033 in (0.037 to 0.083 mm)	

Big-end side clearance ... ... 0.0058 to 0.0087 in
(0.15 to 0.22 mm)

Small end bush bore diameter ... ... 0.875 in (+ 0.0002 in)
(22.22 mm + 0.005 mm)

Crankshaft

Number of main bearings	7
Journal diameter	2.75 to 2.7505 in (69.85 to 69.86 mm)
Thrust washer thickness	0.092 in ($\pm$ 0.001 in) (2.33 $\pm$ 0.025 mm)
	0.096 in ($\pm$ 0.001 in) (2.43 $\pm$ 0.025 mm)
Endfloat	0.004 to 0.006 in (0.10 to 0.15 mm)
Main bearing running clearance	0.0025 to 0.0042 in (0.063 to 0.106 mm)
Crankpin diameter	2.086 + 0.0006 in (52.98 + 0.015 mm)
Regrind undersizes	0.010, 0.020, 0.030, 0.040 in (0.25, 0.51, 0.76, 1.02 mm)
Minimum journal diameter after regrind	2.05 in (52.07 mm)

Cylinder block

Material ... ... Cast-iron

Cylinder head

Material ... ... Aluminium alloy
Valve seat angle ... ... 45°

Gudgeon pin

Type ... ... Fully floating
Outside diameter:
    Green ... ... 0.8750 to 0.8751 in (22.225 to 22.228 mm)
    Red ... ... 0.8751 to 0.8752 in (22.228 to 22.230 mm)

Pistons and piston rings (except Series 2)

Type	Alloy, solid skirt
Skirt clearance in bore	0.0007 to 0.0013 in (0.018 to 0.032 mm)
Number of piston rings	2 compression, 1 oil control
Ring width (compression)	0.0770 to 0.0780 in (1.97 to 2.00 mm)

Ring thickness:
    2.8 litre, 3.4 litre compression ... ... 0.124 to 0.130 in (3.15 to 3.30 mm)
    4.2 litre compression ... ... 0.151 to 0.158 in (3.775 to 3.95 mm)
Ring end-gap:
    Compression ... ... 0.015 to 0.020 in (0.38 to 0.51 mm)
    Oil control ... ... 0.015 to 0.033 in (0.38 to 0.82 mm)
Ring side-clearance:
    Compression ... ... 0.0025 in (0.064 mm)
    Oil control ... ... 0.004 in (0.102 mm)

Pistons and piston rings (Series 2)
As for other models except:

Compression ring width	0.0781 in (2.0 mm)
Compression ring thickness	0.171 to 0.188 in (4.35 to 4.60 mm)
Compression ring side-clearance in groove	0.0015 to 0.0035 in (0.038 to 0.089 mm)
Top compression ring end-gap	0.015 to 0.020 in (0.38 to 0.51 mm)
Second compression ring end-gap	0.009 to 0.014 in (0.23 to 0.35 mm)
Oil control ring end-gap	0.015 to 0.045 in (0.38 to 1.14 mm)

Tappets

Material ... ... Cast-iron
Outside diameter ... ... 1.3738 to 1.3742 in (34.89 to 34.90 mm)
Running clearance ... ... 0.0008 to 0.0019 in (0.02 to 0.048 mm)

Timing chains and sprockets

Type	Duplex
Pitch	3/8 in (9.5 mm)

Number of pitches:
    Top chain 100
    Lower chain 82
Crankshaft sprocket (teeth) 21
Intermediate sprocket (teeth) ... ... Outer 28, Inner 20
Camshaft sprocket (teeth) 30
Idler sprocket 21

Valve timing

Inlet valve opens ... ... 17° BTDC
Inlet valve closes ... ... 59° ABDC
Exhaust valve opens ... ... 59° BBDC
Exhaust valve closes ... ... 17° ATDC

Valves

Material:	
Inlet	Silicon chrome steel
Exhaust	21 – 4 – NS
Valve head diameter:	
Inlet	1.75 in $\pm$ 0.002 in (44.45 $\pm$ 0.05 mm)
Exhaust	1.625 $\pm$ 0.002 in (41.28 $\pm$ 0.05 mm)
Valve stem diameter (inlet and exhaust)	0.3125 in (7.94 mm)
Valve lift	0.375 in (9.53 mm)
Valve clearance (cold) - inlet and exhaust	0.012 to 0.014 in (0.30 to 0.35 mm)

Valve springs

Free-length, except Series 2	(Inner) 1 21/32 in (42.0 mm); (Outer) 1 15/16 in (49.2 mm)
Free-length, Series 2	(Inner) 1.734 in (44.04 mm); (Outer) 2.103 in (53.42 mm)

Valve guides

Material	Cast-iron
Length:	
Inlet	1.86 in (47.24 mm)
Exhaust	1.95 in (49.53 mm)
Inside diameter:	
Inlet	5/16 in (7.94 mm)
Exhaust	5/16 in (7.94 mm)
Interference fit in cylinder head	0.0005 to 0.0022 in (0.013 to 0.055 mm)

Valve seat inserts

Material	Sintered iron
Inside diameter:	
Inlet	1½ + 0.003 in (38.1 + 0.076 mm)
	– 0.001 in 0.025 mm.
Exhaust	1.379 to 1.383 in (35.03 to 35.13 mm)
Interference (shrink) fit in cylinder head	0.003 in (0.076 mm)

Lubrication system

Pump type	Eccentric rotor
Lobe to lobe tip clearance (max.)	0.006 in (0.15 mm)
Rotor to body clearance (max.)	0.010 in (0.25 mm)
Rotor end-clearance (max.)	0.0025 in (0.06 mm)
Oil pressure (hot) at 3000 rev/min	40 lb/sq in (2.81 kg/sq cm)
Oil type/specification	Multigrade engine oil, viscosity range SAE 10W/40 to 20W/50, to BLS-0L-02 or API SE/CC (Duckhams QXR, Hypergrade, or 10W/40 Motor Oil)
Oil capacity (including new filter)	14½ Imp. pints (8.25 litres/17½ US pints)
Oil filter type (3.4 litre up to 1977 only)	Champion A101

Torque wrench settings

	lb ft	Nm
Cylinder head nuts	54	73
Camshaft bearings	9	12
Main bearing bolts	72	98
Connecting rod nuts	37	50
Flywheel bolts	67	91
Oil filter centre bolt	20	27
Torque converter to driveplate bolts	30	41
Driveplate to crankshaft	67	91
Torque converter housing to engine bolts	35	48
Clutch to flywheel bolts	20	27
Clutch bellhousing to engine bolts	35	48
Oil filter bolt	20	27
Rear mounting bracket to body:		
Small bolts	18	25
Large bolts	32	44
Front mounting bracket to crossmember	18	25
Rear mounting peg	30	41
Rear flexible mounting pads	32	44

1 General description

1 The engines fitted to the models covered by this manual are very similar in design but vary slightly in the style of some small components.

2 All engines are of six cylinder twin overhead camshaft design and may be of high or low compression ratio.

3 The cylinder block is of cast-iron construction while the cylinder head is of aluminium alloy. The cylinder block on Series Two, 4.2 litre engines is of modiified, torsionally stronger construction with dry type cylinder liners.

4 The crankshaft is supported in seven main bearings.

5 Duplex camshaft chains are used and the camshafts have four bearings each.

6 Pressure lubrication is by means of an eccentric rotor type pump.

2 Major operations possible with the engine in the car

1 The following operations can be carried out without removing the engine from the car:

  Removal and installation of the cylinder head.

  Removal and refitting of the sump (after first withdrawing the front suspension - see Chapter 11).

  Removal and installation of the piston/connecting rod assemblies (after having first removed cylinder head and sump).

  Removal and refitting of the timing gear (after first having removed cylinder head and sump).

  Removal of the engine mountings (weight of engine supported on a hoist).

  Renewal of main bearing shells (not recommended).

3 Major operations only possible with the engine removed from the car

1   The following operations can only be carried out after the engine has been removed from the car:
   Removal and refitting of the main bearings and crankshaft.
   Removal and refitting of the flywheel

4 Method of engine removal

1   The engine should be removed from the car complete with manual gearbox or automatic transmission and the two units separated afterwards.
2   The power train is hoisted upwards from the engine compartment and in view of its weight, a substantial hoist or lifting tackle must be employed.

5 Engine/manual gearbox - removal

1   Remove the bonnet, as described in Chapter 12.
2   Remove the crossbraces from the engine compartment bulkhead and inner wings (photos).
3   Disconnect the lead from the battery negative terminal.
4   Drain the cooling system and remove the radiator as described in Chapter 2. *On cars equipped with full air-conditioning,* the condensor must be unbolted and carefully supported before the radiator can be withdrawn. On no account disconnect any of the air-conditioning system hoses.
5   Drain the engine oil.
6   Remove the air cleaner.
7   Disconnect the lead from the starter motor solenoid.
8   Disconnect the right-hand engine wiring harness at the plug and socket connector.
9   Disconnect the high tension and low tension cables from the ignition coil.
10 Disconnect the brake vacuum servo pipe from the underside of the inlet manifold. Refer to Section 26, Chapter 3 for disconnection details of manifold used with Stromberg carburettors.
11 Disconnect the flexible hoses from the power steering pump and plug the hoses.
12 Release the power steering pump adjuster nuts and push the pump as far as it will go towards the engine.
13 Disconnect the heater flow and return hoses from the nozzles on the engine compartment rear bulkhead.
14 Close the fuel tap and then disconnect the fuel inlet pipe from the carburettor.
15 Detach the throttle cable from the accelerator pedal, release the nut on the cable conduit and pull the assembly through the engine compartment rear bulkhead. Disconnect the choke cables or leads from the starter device.
16 Disconnect the leads from the alternator.
17 Disconnect the exhaust downpipes from the exhaust manifold.
18 *On cars fitted with air-conditioning,* unbolt the compressor and pull it to one side of the engine compartment and tie it securely. Move the receiver/dryer to one side (two bolts under right-hand wheel arch). **On no account disconnect any of the air-conditioning system hoses.**
   Warning. If the various components of the air conditioning system (condenser, receiver/dryer, compressor) cannot be moved far enough to avoid obstruction during engine removal due to the limitation of their flexible connecting hoses, *the system must be discharged by your dealer or a refrigeration engineer before disconnecting any of the system pipelines.* This also applies to the fuel cooler attached to the air cleaner brackets on fuel injection models (see Chapter 13).
19 Disconnect the leads to the overdrive switch (where fitted) and remove the gearshift control lever knob.
20 Disconnect the remaining gearbox electrical leads.
21 Unbolt the clutch slave cylinder from the clutch bellhousing and tie it up out of the way. There is no need to disconnect the clutch hydraulic lines.
22 Attach a suitable hoist to the engine and take its weight.
23 Remove the engine rear mounting. To do this, place a jack under the mounting and then remove the four setscrews. Lower the jack until the tension in the mounting spring plate is released. Extract the

5.2A Engine compartment rear bulkhead brace attachment

5.2B Engine compartment wing valance brace attachment

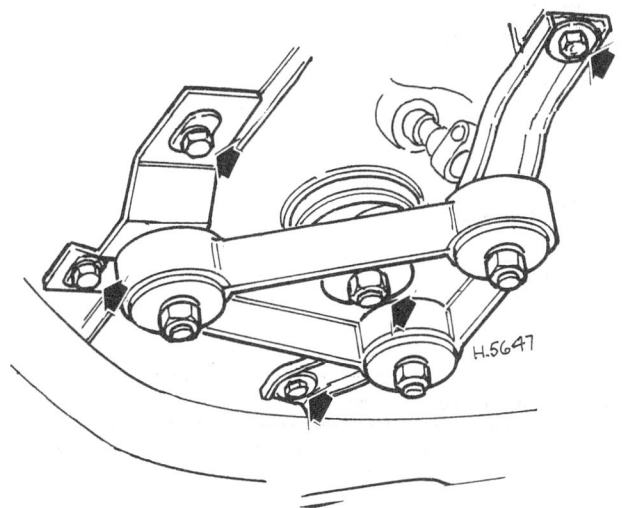

Fig. 1.1. Engine rear mounting (earlier cars) (Sec. 5)

Fig. 1.2. Engine rear mounting (later cars) (Sec. 5)

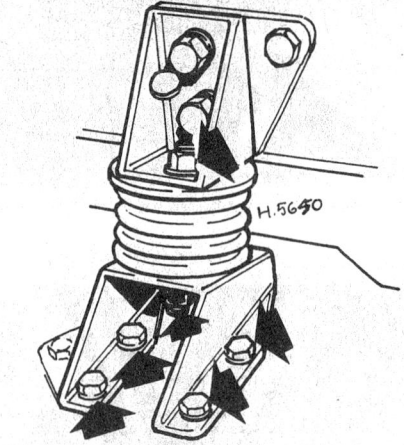

Fig. 1.3. Engine front mounting (Sec. 5)

mounting components which include four spacers which are located between the body and the mounting. Two types of engine rear mounting may be encountered but the removal procedure is identical. (Figs. 1.1 and 1.2).
24 Disconnect the propeller shaft at its front flange and tie it carefully to one side.
25 Remove the engine front mountings by unscrewing the top and bottom nuts which secure the flexible components. (Fig. 1.3)
26 Disconnect the speedometer cable.
27 Lower the rear of the engine/gearbox until the gearshift control lever clears the console grommet and then hoist the engine/gearbox forward and up and out of the engine compartment at a steeply inclined angle.

6 Engine/automatic transmission - removal

1 The procedure is similar to that described in the preceding Section but carry out the following operations as substitutes for those concerning the clutch and gearshift knob.
2 Disconnect the kick-down cable from the carburettor.
3 Disconnect the speed selector cable from the lever on the side of the transmission housing.
4 Disconnect the speed selector cable clamp from the torque converter housing.
5 Disconnect vacuum pipes and electrical leads (refer to Chapter 6, Part 2).
6 Disconnect and plug the fluid cooler pipes.

7 Engine/manual gearbox - separation

1 Unbolt and withdraw the bolts which secure the clutch bellhousing to the engine.
2 Pull the gearbox from the engine in a straight line, supporting the weight of the gearbox to prevent strain or distortion to the clutch components while the gearbox primary shaft is still in engagement with the clutch driven plate. The use of a trolley jack will facilitate this operation. If the overdrive must be removed, refer to Chapter 6.

8 Engine/automatic transmission - separation

1 Unbolt and remove the semi-circular plate from the lower half of the torque converter housing.
2 Unbolt and remove the starter motor.
3 Unscrew and remove each of the four setscrews which retain the torque converter to the driveplate. These are accessible through the starter motor aperture but the crankshaft will have to be turned (by applying a spanner to the crankshaft pulley bolt) to bring each of the torque converter screws into view in sequence.
4 Unscrew and remove the bolts which secure the torque converter housing to the engine and then withdraw the automatic transmission. Be prepared for some loss of fluid and keep the torque converter pressed towards the transmission to prevent its disengagement from the oil pump drive tangs.
5 In view of the weight of the transmission, the use of a trolley jack will be an advantage during the foregoing operations.

9 Engine ancillaries - removal

1 With the engine removed from the car and separated from the transmission unit, remove the following external components before attempting to dismantle the engine:
   The alternator (Chapter 10)
   The distributor (Chapter 4)
   The clutch (Chapter 5)
   The water pump (Chapter 2)
   The starter motor (Chapter 10)
   The emission control equipment (Chapter 3).

10 Preparation for dismantling the engine

1 During the dismantling process, the greatest care should be taken to keep the exposed parts free from dirt. To that end, thoroughly clean down the outside of the engine, removing all traces of oil and congealed dirt. Use paraffin or proprietary solvent. The latter will make the job much easier for after the solvent has been applied and allowed to stand for a time a vigorous jet of water will wash off the solvent with all the dirt. If the dirt is thickly and deeply embedded, work in the solvent with a stiff brush.
2 Finally wipe down the exterior of the engine with rag and only then when the engine is quite clean, should the dismantling process begin. As the engine is stripped, clean each part in a bath of paraffin or solvent.
3 Never immerse parts with oilways (for example the crankshaft) in the cleaning bath. To clean such items, carefully wipe down with a clean paraffin soaked rag and then wipe dry. Oilways can be cleaned out with wire or blown through with an air blast.
4 Re-use of old engine gaskets, copper washers etc is false economy and will, in all probability, lead to oil or water leaks. Always use new items throughout.
5 Retain the old gaskets until the job is finished - for it sometimes happens that a replacement is not always immediately available and in such cases the old one will come in handy for use as a template.
6 When stripping the engine it is best to work from the top down - the underside of the crankcase, when supported on wooden blocks, makes a firm base from which to work. We always recommend, therefore, that the sump is removed at an early stage.
7 Whenever possible, replace nuts, bolts and washers finger tight from wherever they were removed. This helps to avoid loss and muddle later; if they cannot be replaced lay them out in such a fashion that it is clear from whence they came.

11 Cylinder head (engine in car) - removal

1 Disconnect the lead from the battery negative terminal.
2 Remove the two bulkhead to inner wing braces.
3 Drain the cooling system.
4 Remove the air cleaner and the backplate which is secured to the carburettor flanges.
5 Close the fuel tap and disconnect the fuel inlet pipe from the carburettor.
6 Disconnect the high tension leads from the coil and from the spark plugs and then unclip the distributor cap and remove it to one side of the engine compartment.

7 Disconnect the vacuum pipe from the distributor and from the front carburettor.

8 Disconnect the accelerator cable from the pedal and draw the cable into the engine compartment.

9 Release the power steering pump adjustment bolt, push the pump towards the engine and remove the drivebelt. Now pull the pump away from the engine as far as possible.

10 Disconnect the heater hose from the connection on the water pump.

11 Disconnect the heater hoses from the nozzles on the engine compartment rear bulkhead.

12 Disconnect the brake servo vacuum pipe from the inlet manifold.

13 Disconnect the lead from the carburettor solenoid.

14 Disconnect the lead from the thermostatic switch on the inlet manifold water jacket.

15 Disconnect the carburettor overflow pipe support brackets from the engine sump.

16 Remove the top coolant hose and the bypass hose from the front of the inlet manifold water jacket.

17 Disconnect the exhaust manifold from the cylinder head.

18 Disconnect the two camshaft oil supply pipe unions from the rear of the cylinder head.

19 Remove the spark plugs.

20 Remove the dome nuts (and countersunk screw on 4.2 litre) from each camshaft cover and then lift off the covers.

21 Remove the four nuts which secure the breather housing to the front of the cylinder head and withdraw the housing.

22 Release the tension on the camshaft chain by slackening the nut on the eccentric idler sprocket shaft, depressing the spring-loaded stop peg and rotating the serrated adjuster plate in a clockwise direction (viewed from the front of the engine).

23 Cut the locking wire (later models have lock tabs) on the two setscrews which secure each of the sprockets to their camshafts. Extract one setscrew from each sprocket and then rotate the crankshaft to bring the remaining bolts into view. Unscrew and remove these bolts. (photos)

24 Slide the camshaft sprockets up the slots in their support brackets. Do not turn the crankshaft once the camshaft sprockets have been disconnected.

25 Working in a diagonal pattern from the centre outwards, remove the fourteen dome nuts and six ordinary nuts (these are at the front of the cylinder head). If the car is equipped with an air-conditioning system, the compressor and mounting bracket will have to be unbolted and moved to one side to gain access to the cylinder head nuts. **On no account disconnect the air-conditioning system hoses.**

26 Lift the cylinder head complete with inlet manifold and carburettors from the cylinder block.

27 Peel off the old gasket and discard it.

28 Support the cylinder head on blocks of wood to prevent damage to the open valves.

12 Cylinder head (engine out of car) - removal

1 The operations are identical to those described in the preceding Section, paragraphs 18 to 28.

13 Cylinder head - dismantling

1 Unbolt and remove the inlet manifold and carburettors (refer also to Chapter 3, Section 26).

2 Remove the four bearing caps from the camshaft, noting their mating marks for refitting in their original locations (Fig. 1.6).

3 Lift out the camshafts and their shell bearings (photo).

4 Make up a suitable tray or rack with compartments so that the valve components can be stored in order for refitting in their original locations (no. 1 cylinder at flywheel end).

5 Withdraw the hollow tappets and extract the adjustment shims. These may be stuck to the end of the valve stem or to the inside of the tappet by the adhesion of the lubricating oil. Keep the components in their original order, making sure not to mix them up (photo).

6 Insert a small wooden block into the combustion chamber at the front of the cylinder head and lay the cylinder head face down on a bench. The block will prevent the valves being displaced when the valve springs are compressed.

7 Using a valve spring compressor, compress the first valve spring

11.23A Cutting camshaft sprocket locking wire

11.23B Unscrewing camshaft sprocket bolt

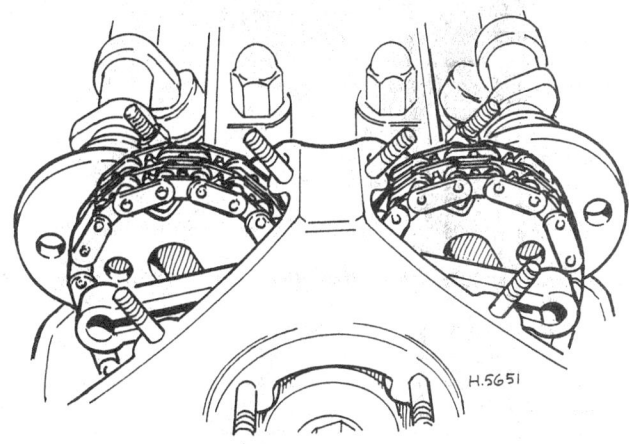
Fig. 1.4. Camshaft sprockets disconnected (Sec. 11)

Fig. 1.5.

H.5646

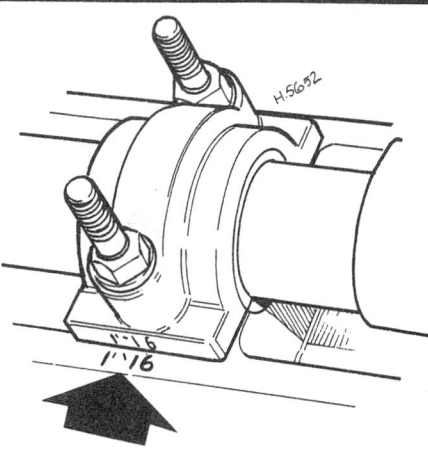

Fig. 1.6. Camshaft bearing marks (Sec. 13)

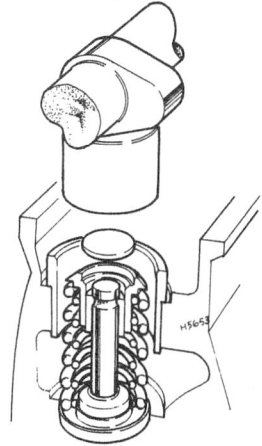

13.3 Extracting camshaft bearing shell

Fig. 1.7. Camshaft, tappet, shim and valve arrangement (Sec. 13)

Fig. 1.5. Exploded view of the cylinder head (Sec. 13)

1 Cylinder head	18 Inlet valve	33 Plug	49 Banjo bolt	65 Sealing ring
2 Stud	18a Seal	34 'O' ring	50 Washer	66 Inlet manifold
3 Dowel	19 Exhaust valve	35 Seal	51 Breather housing cover	67 Gasket
4 Core plug	20 Valve spring (inner)	36 Plug	52 Flame trap	68 Stud
5 Washer	21 Valve spring (outer)	37 'O' ring	53 Gasket	69 Stud
6 Valve guide	22 Valve spring seat	38 Setscrew	54 Dome nuts	70 Adaptor
7 Valve guide circlip	23 Valve spring collar	39 Washer	55 Spring washers	71 Washer
8 Inlet valve insert	24 Split cotters	40 Camshaft cover	56 Breather pipe	72 Manifold starting pipe
9 Tappet guide	25 Tappet	41 Gasket	57 Hose	73 Manifold starting pipe
10 Cylinder head gasket	26 Valve adjusting shim	42 Camshaft cover	58 Clip	74 Manifold starting pipe
11 Stud	27 Inlet camshaft	43 Gasket	59 Exhaust manifold	75 Neoprene tube
12 Stud	28 Exhaust camshaft	44 Dome nut	60 Exhaust manifold	76 Clip
13 Stud	29 Camshaft bearing	45 Washer	61 Gasket	77 Water outlet pipe
14 Stud	30 Oil thrower	46 Oil filler cap	62 Gasket	78 Gasket
15 Stud	31 Setscrew	47 'O' ring	63 Thermostat housing	79 Thermostat
16 Setscrew	32 Washer	48 Oil pipe	64 Stud	80 Automatic choke thermostat
17 Lifting lug				81 Gasket

13.5 Extracting valve adjustment shim

13.7A Removing valve spring collar

13.7B Removing valve springs

13.8 Method of removing valve split cotters without compressor

collar and extract the split collets. Release the compressor and withdraw the collars, springs and spring seats (photos).

8   The inlet valves are fitted with valve stem oil seals and these should be removed, discarded and new ones obtained at time of major overhaul. An alternative method of dismantling the valves is to place a piece of tubing on the end of the valve collar and strike it hard in order to compress the spring and eject the split cotters (photo).

14 Sump and oil pump - removal

The sump can be removed with the engine still in the car but the front suspension assembly must first be withdrawn, as described in Chapter 11.

1   Drain the engine oil.

2   Slacken the clip and disconnect the oil return hose at the base of the oil filter. Disconnect the oil cooler pipe clips (automatic transmission).

3   Remove the setscrews and nuts which secure the sump to the crankcase. Note the location of the short screw at the right-hand front corner of the sump.

4   Withdraw the sump and peel or scrape off the gasket.

5   Remove the four nuts which secure the sump baffle plate and withdraw the plate.

6   Disconnect the filter screen and then unbolt the oil return pipe by unscrewing the two flange nuts.

7   Disconnect the suction and delivery pipes from the oil pump.

8   Flatten the lockplates on the bolts which secure the oil pump to the front main bearing cap.

9   Withdraw the oil pump and catch the coupling sleeve at the top of the pump driveshaft.

15 Oil filter - renewal of element

1   The oil filter is located on the right-hand side of the engine.

2   To gain access to it, remove the air cleaner and the support plate which retains the front carburettor overflow pipe to the sump and then detach the pipe from the carburettor float chamber.

3   Working from underneath the car, disconnect the flexible hose from the oil filter relief valve return pipe.

4   Unscrew the filter centre bolt and lift away the canister complete with element.

5   Discard the old element and sealing ring, wipe the interior of the canister clean and then install the new element.

6   Locate the new sealing ring (supplied with the element) in the groove in the filter base and then refit the canister and screw in and tighten the centre bolt (photo).

16 Piston/connecting rod - removal and dismantling

If the engine is in the car, the sump, oil pump and cylinder head will first have to be removed as previously described. (Sections 11 and 14).

1   Check that the connecting rods and big-end caps are numbered from 1 to 6 (from the flywheel end). The numbers should be adjacent and note to which side of the engine they face. If no marks are visible, dot

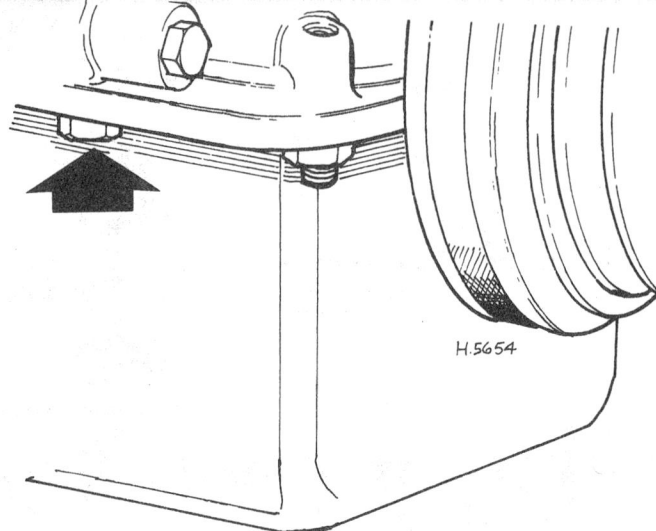

Fig. 1.8. Location of sump short securing setscrew (Sec. 14)

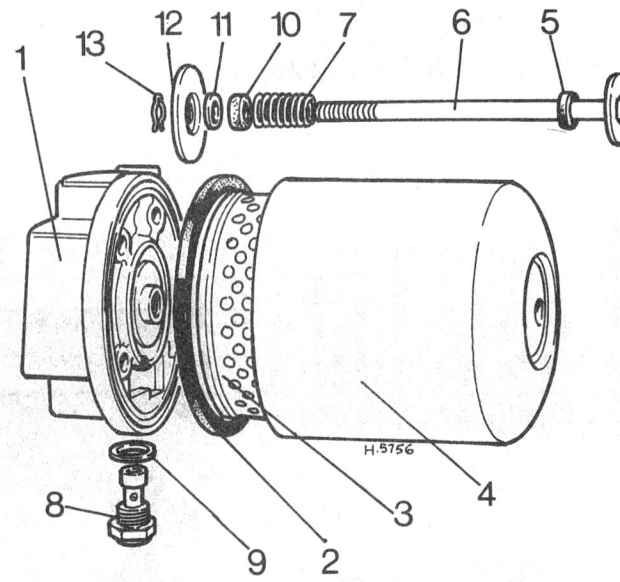

Fig. 1.9. Exploded view of the oil filter (Sec. 15)

1	Base	8	Relief valve
2	Sealing ring	9	Seal
3	Element	10	Felt washer
4	Canister	11	Washer
5	Sealing washer	12	Plate
6	Centre bolt	13	Spring clip
7	Spring		

15.6 Extracting oil filter canister sealing ring

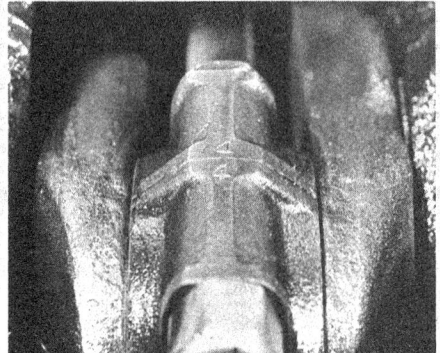

16.1 Connecting rod and big-end cap markings

16.3 Withdrawing piston/connecting rod

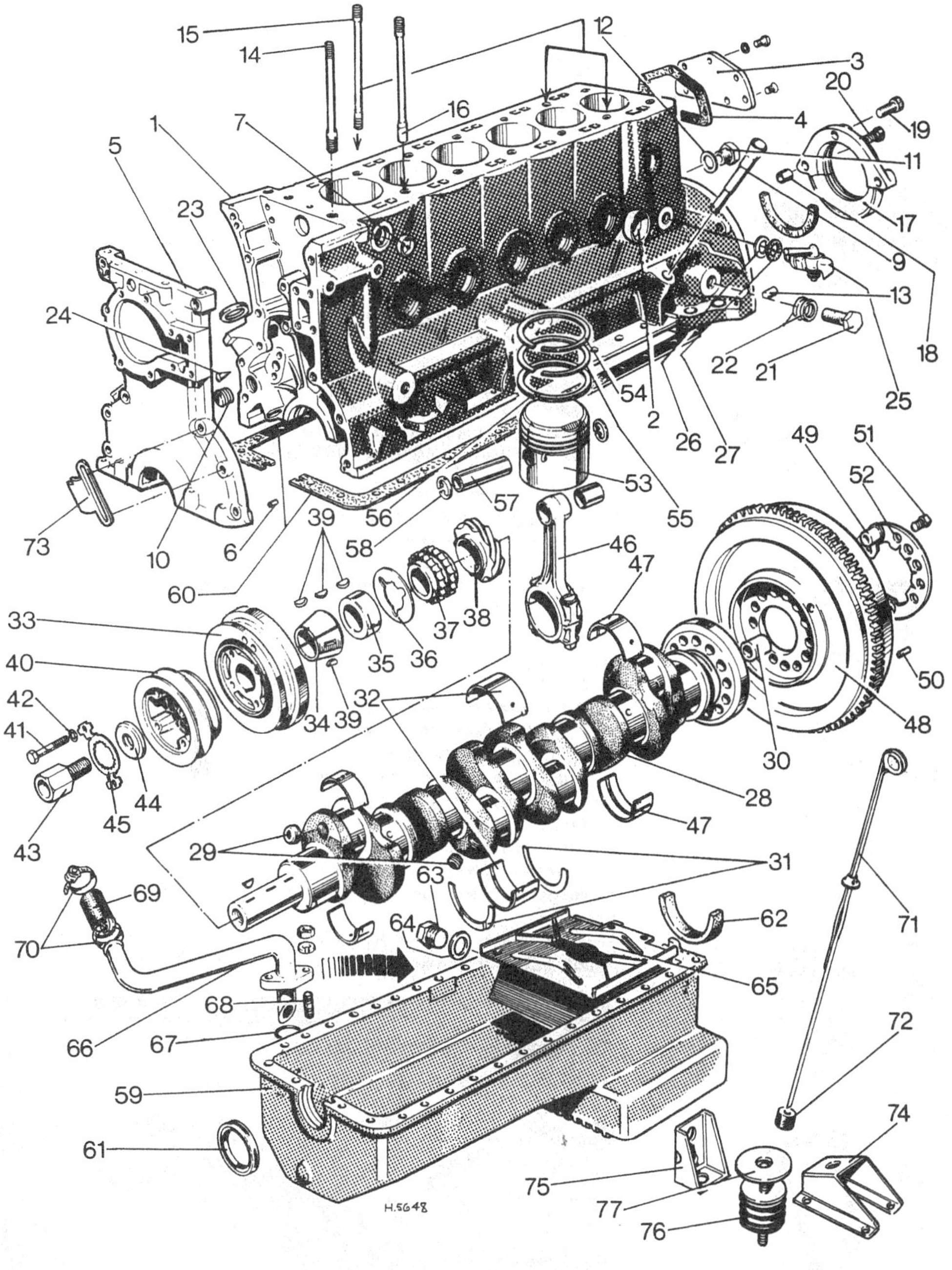

Fig. 1.10. Crankcase and cylinder block components (Sec. 16)

1. Cylinder block
2. Core plugs
3. Blanking plate
4. Gasket
5. Timing cover
6. Dowel
7. Core plug
9. Dipstick guide tube
10. Plug
11. Hexagon plug
12. Copper washer
13. Dowel
14. Stud
15. Stud
16. Dowel stud
17. Rear oil seal cover
18. Dowel
19. Socket headed screw
20. Socket headed screw
21. Banjo bolt
22. Copper washer
23. Sealing ring
24. Filter gauze
25. Drain tap
26. Copper washer
27. Fibre washer
28. Crankshaft
29. Plug
30. Bush (clutch pilot)
31. Thrust washer
32. Main bearings
33. Damper
34. Cone
35. Distance piece
36. Oil thrower
37. Crankshaft sprocket
38. Oil pump drive gear
39. Woodruff key
40. Pulley
41. Bolt
42. Lockwasher
43. Bolt
44. Washer
45. Lockplate
46. Connecting rod
47. Big-end shell bearing
48. Flywheel
49. Dowel
50. Dowel
51. Setscrew
52. Lockplate
53. Piston
54. Top compression ring
55. Lower compression ring
56. Oil control ring
57. Gudgeon pin
58. Circlip
59. Sump
60. Gasket
61. Crankshaft front oil seal
62. Crankshaft rear oil seal (part)
63. Drain plug
64. Copper washer
65. Baffle assembly
66. Oil pump pipe
67. 'O' ring
68. Stud
69. Hose
70. Hose clip
71. Dipstick
72. Ferrule
73. Ignition timing pointer
74. Engine mounting bracket
75. Engine mounting bracket
76. Flexible mounting pad
77. Washer

punch both cap and rod before removal (photo).

2   Turn the crankshaft until the first connecting rod is at the lowest point of its travel and then unscrew the self-locking nuts from the big-end bolts.

3   Pull off the cap complete with its shell bearing and then push the piston/rod assembly up and out of the top of the cylinder bore. If there is a wear ridge at the top of the bore, this should be scraped away before attempting to remove the piston but take great care not to damage the surfaces of the bore (photo).

4   If the original bearing shells are to be refitted, mark them with tape or spirit pen in respect of both cylinder number and whether located in rod or cap.

5   Repeat the removal operations on the remaining five piston/rod assemblies.

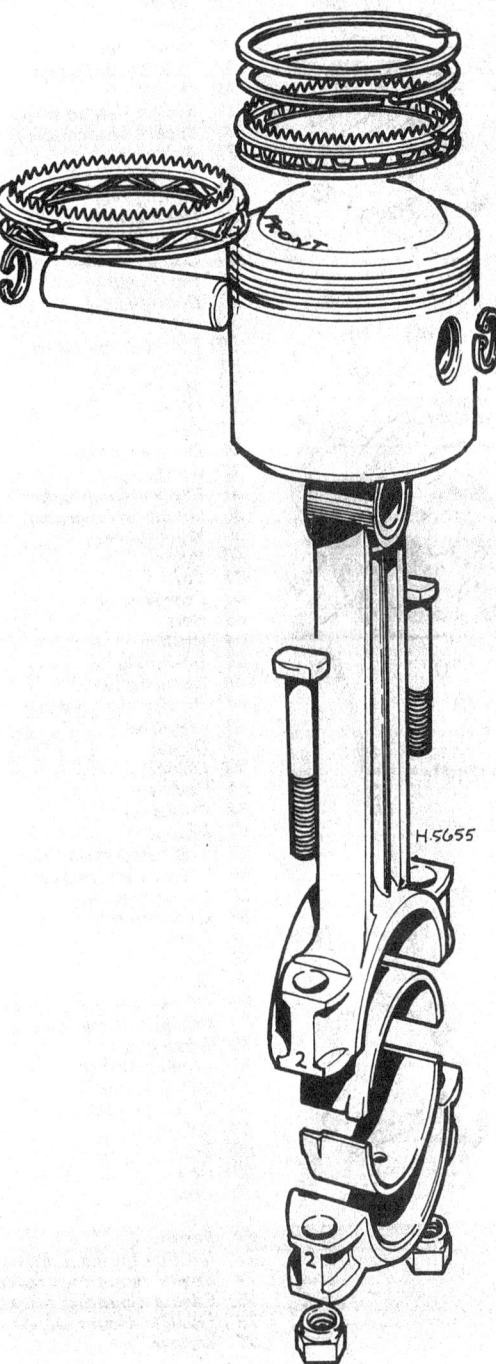

Fig. 1.11. Exploded view of a piston/connecting rod assembly
Note alignment of piston (front) mark and rod numbers (Sec. 16)

This illustration also shows two types of oil control rings which are available

6   The piston rings can be removed using a twisting action. Two or three old feeler blades slid behind the rings at equidistant points will prevent the rings dropping into an empty groove as they are withdrawn.

7   The gudgeon pins are a push fit in the piston and connecting rod small end. To dismantle the piston from the connecting rod, extract the circlips from both ends of the gudgeon pin and then stand the piston in hot or boiling water. The gudgeon pin can then be pushed out with thumb pressure.

17 Crankshaft damper - removal

If the engine is still in the car, remove the steering pump and cooling fan drivebelts, also the alternator drivebelt and (if fitted) the compressor pump belt for the air-conditioning system.

1   Bend the tabs flat on the crankshaft damper bolt lockplate and extract the two setscrews which retain the lockplate. Mark the relationship of the damper to the pulley as they are balanced as an assembly and then extract the two remaining pulley bolts and withdraw the pulley from the damper assembly.

2   Unscrew and remove the large crankshaft damper bolt and extract the washer from behind it. In order to prevent the crankshaft turning as the bolt is unscrewed, place a block of wood between a crankshaft web and the crankcase wall (engine out of car) or jam the starter ring gear with a large screwdriver (engine in car). Alternatively, place a ring spanner or socket wrench on the bolt and strike it a sharp blow rather than attempting to lever the bolt undone.

3   Insert two levers behind the damper and lever it from the split cone. If necessary, give a sharp blow to the end of the cone to free the damper.

4   Remove the cone, spacer, oil thrower and keys.

18 Timing gear - removal and dismantling

If the engine is in the car, remove the cylinder head, the sump, header tank, cowl, fan and radiator also the water pump and crankshaft damper assembly.

1   Remove the setscrews and withdraw the timing chain cover. Note that it is located by two dowels. Remove the crankshaft oil thrower.

2   Withdraw the hexagon plug from the end of the bottom timing chain tensioner and insert an Allen key into the tensioner cylinder. Turn the Allen key clockwise until the cylinder is fully retracted and the timing chain tension released.

3   Unbolt the chain tensioner body and withdraw the tensioner complete with cone-shaped gauze which is located in the tensioner oil feed hole (photo).

4   Unscrew the four setscrews from the timing gear mounting bracket but do not remove them completely.

5   Remove the setscrews from the timing chain guides and remove the guides.

6   Now lift the complete timing gear from the cylinder block, disconnecting the lower chain from the teeth of the crankshaft

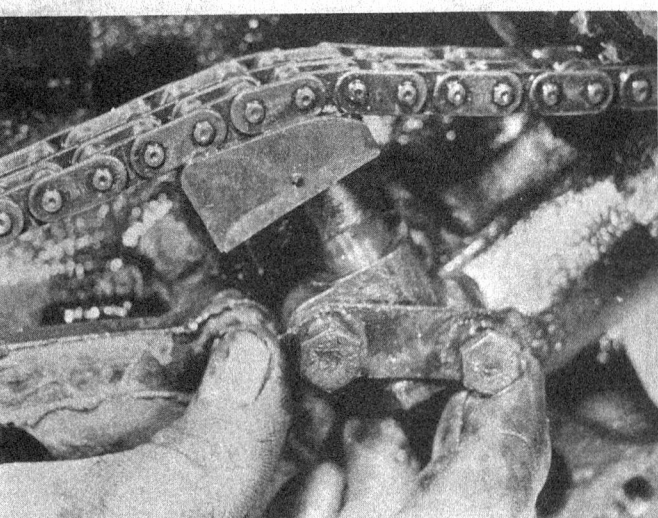

18.3 Timing chain tensioner

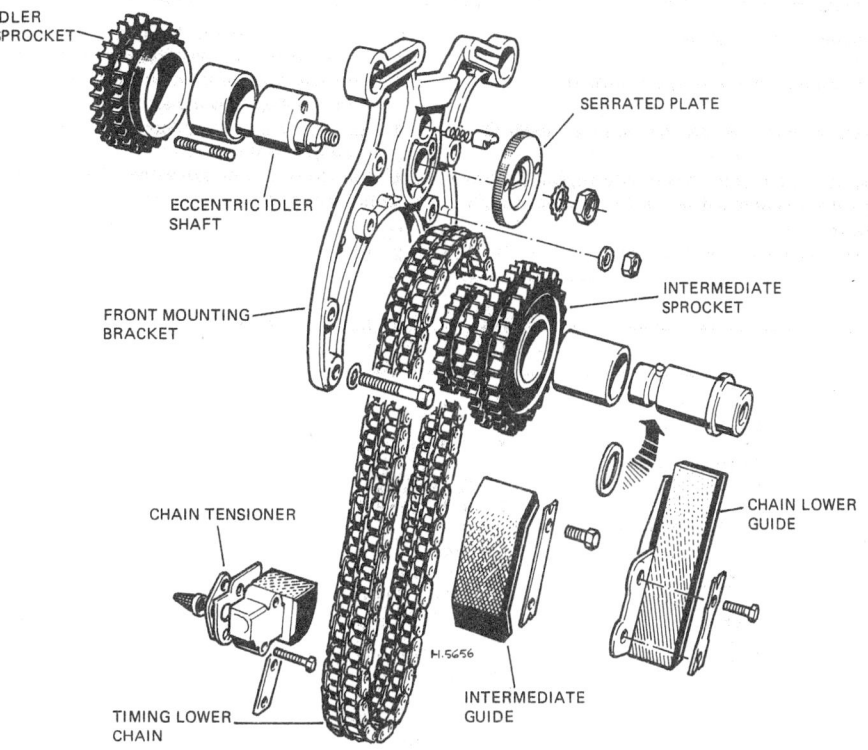

IDLER SPROCKET

SERRATED PLATE

ECCENTRIC IDLER SHAFT

FRONT MOUNTING BRACKET

INTERMEDIATE SPROCKET

CHAIN TENSIONER

CHAIN LOWER GUIDE

H.5656

TIMING LOWER CHAIN

INTERMEDIATE GUIDE

Fig. 1.12. Timing lower chain and gears (Sec. 18)

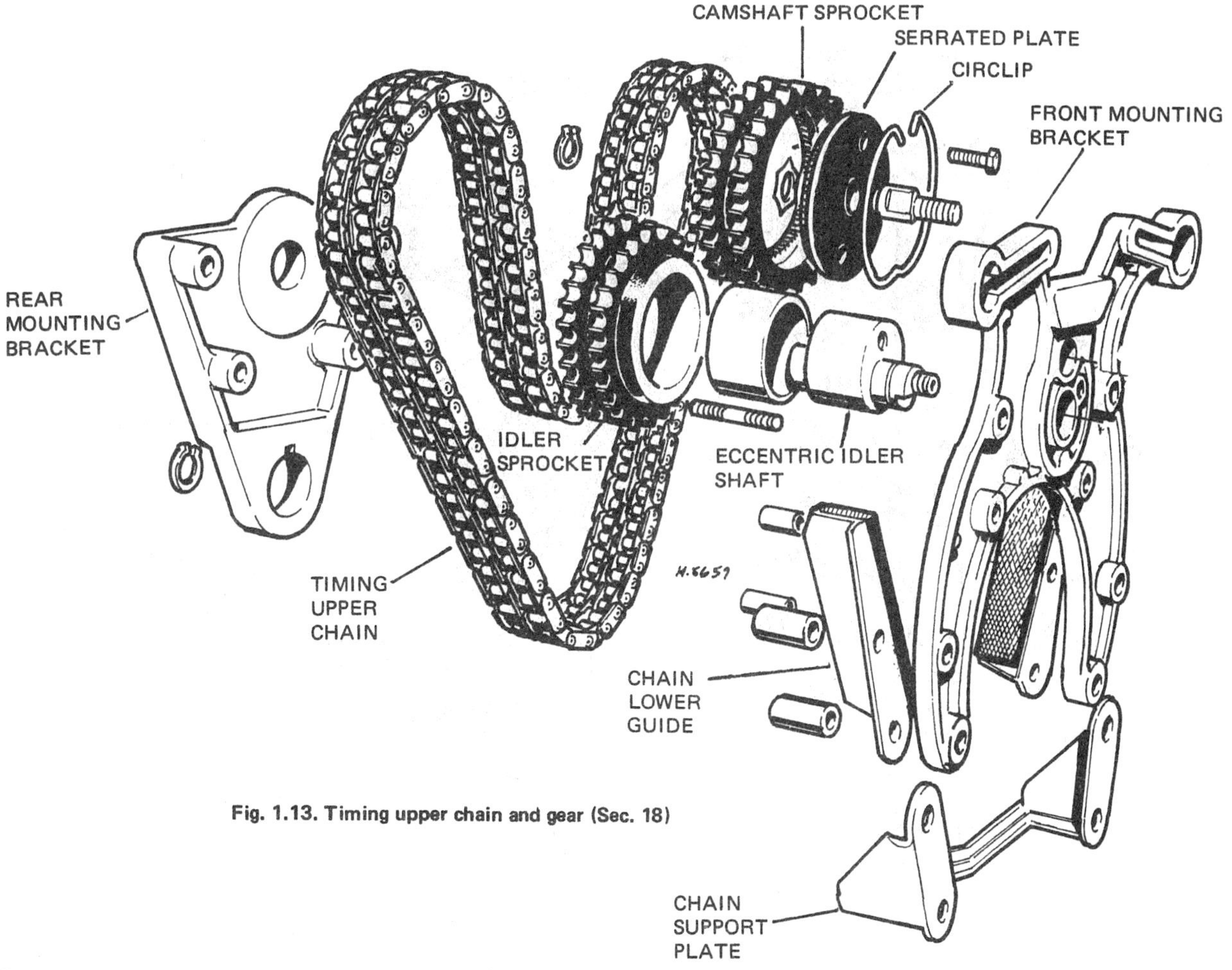

CAMSHAFT SPROCKET

SERRATED PLATE

CIRCLIP

FRONT MOUNTING BRACKET

REAR MOUNTING BRACKET

IDLER SPROCKET

ECCENTRIC IDLER SHAFT

H.5657

TIMING UPPER CHAIN

CHAIN LOWER GUIDE

Fig. 1.13. Timing upper chain and gear (Sec. 18)

CHAIN SUPPORT PLATE

sprocket as the assembly is withdrawn. Pull the sprocket forward if necessary.

7 Remove the nut and serrated washer from the idler shaft and extract the plunger and spring.

8 Remove the four nuts which secure the front mounting bracket to the rear bracket.

9 Detach the lower timing chain from the intermediate sprocket.

10 Extract the circlip from the end of the intermediate sprocket shaft and press the shaft from the bracket.

11 Withdraw the two camshaft sprockets and upper chain.

19 Distributor drive - removal

1 With the oil pump already removed as described in Section 14,

flatten the tab of the lockplate and unscrew the distributor drive gear nut. Remove the nut and the special washer.

2 Carefully tap the squared end of the distributor driveshaft upwards out of the helical driven gear.

3 Remove the helical driven gear and thrust washer and then withdraw the driveshaft (photo).

4 The drive gear on the front of the crankshaft can be removed if required after first pulling off the crankshaft timing sprocket (photo).

20 Flywheel (or driveplate - auto. transmission) - removal

1 Flatten the tabs of the securing bolt lockplates.

2 Mark the relationship of the flywheel to the crankshaft flange.

3 Unscrew and remove the flywheel bolts and lift the flywheel from

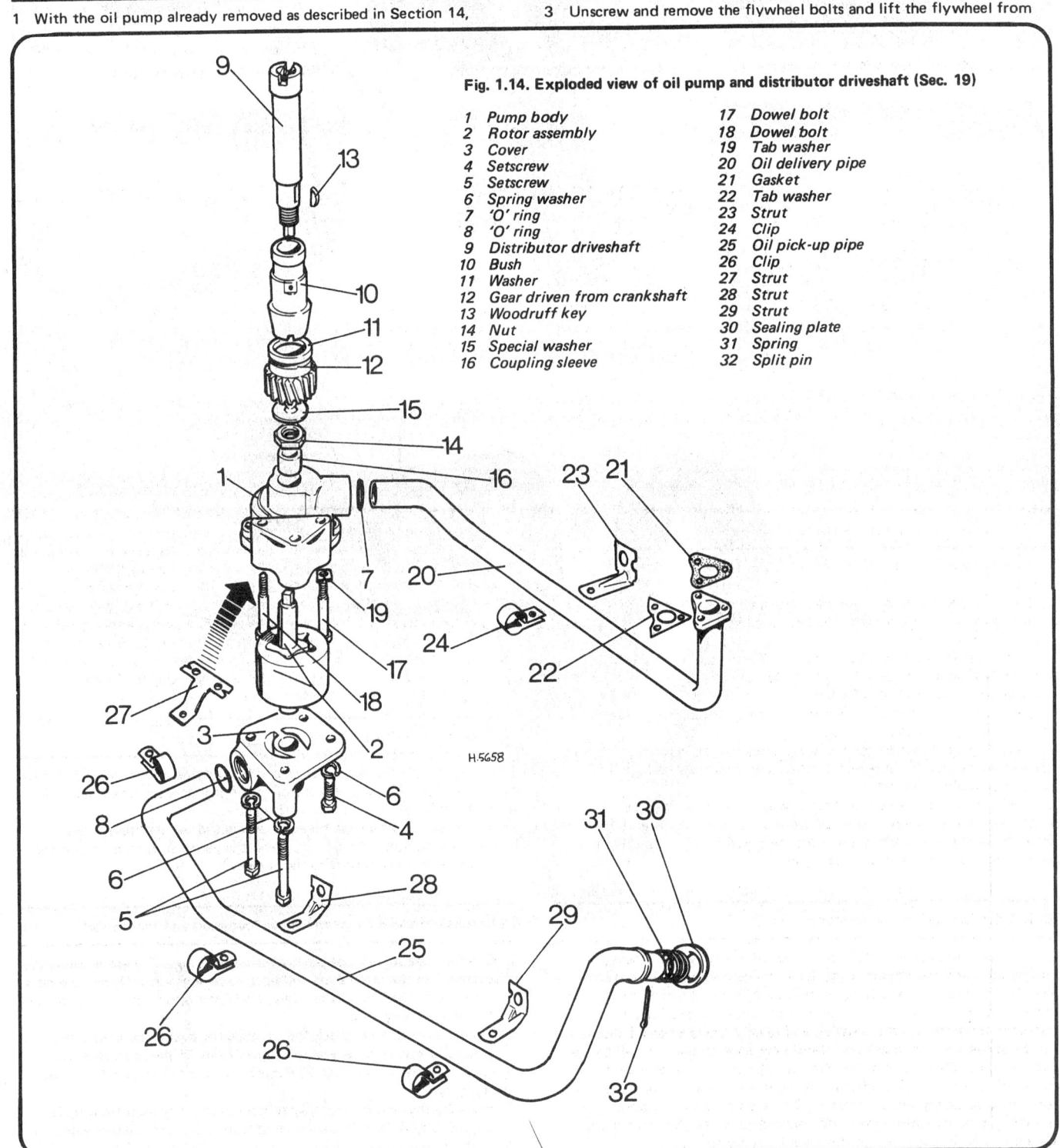

Fig. 1.14. Exploded view of oil pump and distributor driveshaft (Sec. 19)

1	Pump body	17	Dowel bolt
2	Rotor assembly	18	Dowel bolt
3	Cover	19	Tab washer
4	Setscrew	20	Oil delivery pipe
5	Setscrew	21	Gasket
6	Spring washer	22	Tab washer
7	'O' ring	23	Strut
8	'O' ring	24	Clip
9	Distributor driveshaft	25	Oil pick-up pipe
10	Bush	26	Clip
11	Washer	27	Strut
12	Gear driven from crankshaft	28	Strut
13	Woodruff key	29	Strut
14	Nut	30	Sealing plate
15	Special washer	31	Spring
16	Coupling sleeve	32	Split pin

H.5658

19.3 Distributor driven gear and thrust washer

19.4 Distributor drive gear on front of crankshaft

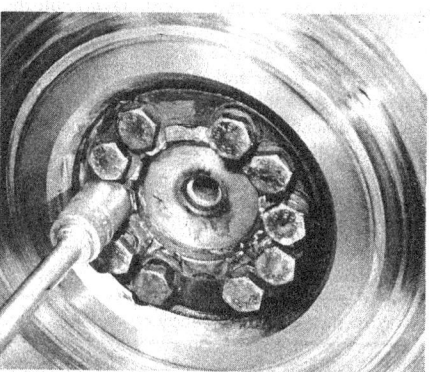

20.3A Unscrewing flywheel bolts

20.3B Removing flywheel

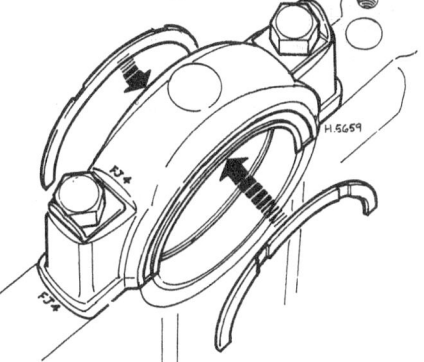

Fig. 1.15. Crankshaft thrust washers (Sec. 21)

21.5 Removing socket headed screw from crankshaft rear oil seal

its mounting flange (photos).

21 Crankshaft and main bearings - removal

1   Knock back the tab washers securing the fourteen main bearing cap bolts.
2   Note the corresponding numbers stamped on the caps and on the bottom face of the crankcase. The caps must be correctly identified if they are not marked.
3   Undo the bolts and remove the main bearing caps. If a main bearing shell does not come away with its cap, remove it from the crankshaft and keep it with its cap.
4   Note the thrust washers fitted in the recess at each side of the centre main bearing cap.
5   Detach the bottom of the crankshaft rear oil seal cover by removing the two Allen securing screws (photo). Note that the two halves are located by hollow dowels.
6   The crankshaft can now be lifted away from the crankcase.
7   Collect the remaining halves of the main bearing shells and, if they are to be refitted, identify them with the position from which they were removed using tape or a spirit pen.

22 Lubrication system - description

A force feed system of lubrication is employed with oil being circulated round the engine from the sump below the cylinder block. The level of the oil in the sump is indicated by the dipstick located on the left-hand rear side of the engine. High and Low level of oil is indicated by marks on the dipstick and ideally the level of oil should not be above the high mark and should never be allowed to fall below the low mark. Oil is replenished via the filler cap in the left-hand camshaft cover. The oil is circulated round the engine by an eccentric rotor type oil pump which consists of five main parts: the body, the driving spindle with the inner rotor pinned to it the outer rotor and the cover which is secured to the main body by four bolts.

Oil is drawn from the sump and is then passed under pressure by the pump to the filter on the right-hand exterior of the crankcase and thence through drillings to the big-end and main bearings; the camshaft bearings are fed via an external oil pipe. A longitudinal drilling through the connecting rod feeds the small end and the gudgeon pin with oil and a small hole in each connecting rod throws a small jet of oil to the cylinder wall with each revolution. The oil filter is of the full flow type with a replaceable element. The filter base incorporates a removable oil pressure relief valve and a balance valve which provides a safeguard against the possibility of the filter element becoming so choked as to prevent oil reaching the bearings. Oil which passes the oil pressure relief valve is returned to the engine sump by an external rubber hose.

23 Crankcase ventilation system

1   Extraction of crankcase fumes and blow-by gases is accomplished by means of a breather on the front of the engine and a connecting hose to the air filter attached to the carburettor.
2   Periodically, unbolt the breather and withdraw the flame trap (gauze) and disconnect the hose. Clean the gauze and hose, renew the breather gaskets and refit it to the engine.

24 Crankshaft and main bearings - examination and renovation

1   Examine the surfaces of the crankshaft journals, if there is evidence of scoring then the crankshaft will have to be reground. If the bearing surfaces are in good condition, always take the opportunity of renewing the bearing shells (photo).
2   Using a micrometer, check the journals for ovality by measuring the journal diameter at several different points. If the journal is oval or worn in excess of 0.003 in (0.8 mm), again the crankshaft will have to be reground.
3   Provided the original crankshaft is suitable for reconditioning, it can be exchanged for a factory reconditioned one at a Jaguar agent. Undersize bearings are available in steps of 0.010 in (0.25 mm), 0.020

24.1 Typical scored crankshaft journal

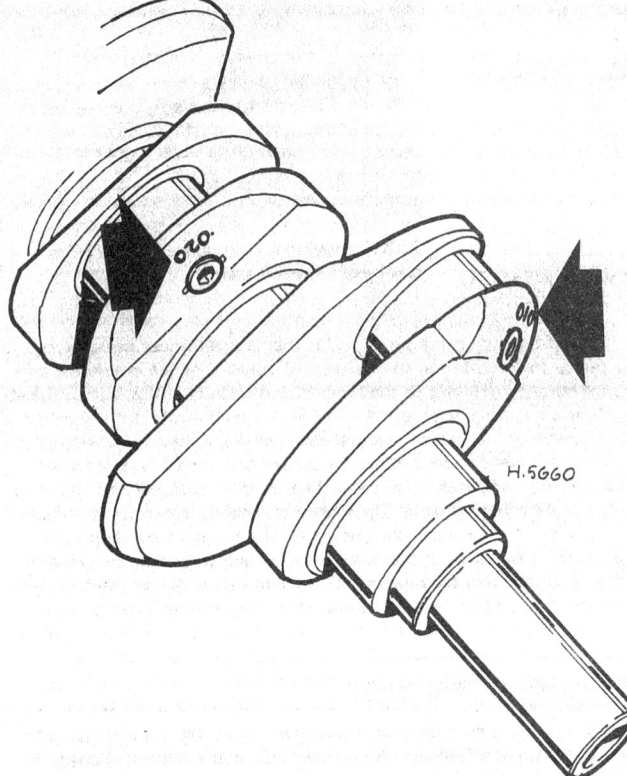

H.5660

Fig. 1.16. Location of crankshaft regrind undersize (Sec. 24)

in (0.51 mm), 0.030 in (0.76 mm) and 0.040 in (1.02 mm). If the crankshaft has already been exchanged for one with undersize main bearings, the undersize will usually be found stamped on the crankshaft webs (Fig. 1.16).

4   If the original crankshaft is re-ground at an engineering works then the undersize bearings will be supplied to be compatible with the reground diameter of the main bearing journals.

5   Examine the pilot bush which is installed in the flywheel mounting flange at the rear end of the crankshaft. If it is worn, it must be renewed. To do this, either tap a thread into it and screw in a bolt to extract the bush or fill the bush with grease and drive in a close fitting mandrel. The hydraulic pressure created by the latter method will eject the bush. The new bush should be soaked in engine oil for 24 hours before pressing it into position.

6   To ensure that the crankshaft oil passages are clear, remove the socket screws from the crankshaft webs and clean out the passages with wire or compressed air.

7   Refit the screws and stake them securely in position.

8   The thrust washers which fit either side of the centre main bearing should normally be renewed at the time of major overhaul. However, when the crankshaft is installed, its endfloat must be checked, as described in Section 41, and new thrust washers of different thicknesses may be required to bring the endfloat within the specified tolerance.

25 Big-end bearings and connecting rods - examination and renovation

1   Examine and check the crankshaft crankpins in a similar manner to that described for the journals in the preceding Section.

2   If the crankshaft is renewed on an exchange basis or if it is reground, then undersize big-end shell bearings will be supplied.

3   If the crankpins are in good condition, take the opportunity of renewing the big-end bearing shells in any event.

4   Any wear in the connecting rod small end bush can be overcome by pressing out the worn bush and pressing in a new one but as the bush will then have to be reamed to the specified diameter this is a job best left to your dealer.

5   Should a connecting rod have to be renewed because of damage or distortion, make sure that its weight does not vary by more than 3.5 grammes when compared with the other rods.

6   It is recommended that new big-end bolts and nuts are used on reassembly.

26 Crankshaft pulley and damper - examination and renovation

1   Check that the rubber of the damper has not deteriorated; if it has, renew the damper.

2   The drivebelt should not bottom in the Vee of the pulley; if it does, try renewing the belt but if this new belt still bottoms, then the pulley will have to be renewed as well.

27 Cylinder bores - examination and renovation

1   The cylinder bores must be examined for taper, ovality, scoring and scratches. Start by carefully examining the top of the cylinder bores. If they are at all worn a very slight ridge will be found on the thrust side. This marks the top of the piston ring travel. The owner will have a good indication of the bore wear prior to dismantling the engine, or removing the cylinder head. Excessive oil consumption accompanied by blue smoke from the exhaust is a sure sign of worn cylinder bores and piston rings.

2   Measure the bore diameter just under the ridge with a micrometer and compare it with the diameter at the bottom of the bore, which is not subject to wear. If the difference between the two measurements is more than 0.006 in (0.15 mm) then it will be necessary to fit special pistons and rings or to have the cylinders rebored and fit oversize pistons. If no micrometer is available remove the rings from a piston and place the piston in each bore in turn about 1 in (25.4 mm) below the top of the bore. If an 0.0012 in (0.030 mm) feeler gauge slid between the piston and the cylinder wall requires less than a pull of between 1.1 and 3.3 lbs (0.5 and 1.5 kg) to withdraw it, using a spring balance, then remedial action must be taken. Oversize pistons are available as listed in Specifications.

3   These are accurately machined to just below the indicated measurements so as to provide correct running clearances in bores bored out to the exact oversize dimensions.

4   If the bores are slightly worn but not so badly worn as to justify reboring them, then special oil control rings and pistons can be fitted which will restore compression and stop the engine burning oil. Several different types are available and the manufacturer's instructions concerning their fitting must be followed closely.

5   If new pistons are being fitted and the bores have not been reground, it is essential to slightly roughen the hard glaze on the sides of the bores with fine glass paper so the new piston rings will have a chance to bed in properly.

6   Reboring beyond 0.030 in (0.76 mm) should not be carried out and when this stage is reached, the only remedy is to have liners fitted with standard pistons.

7   Series 2 and later engines are originally fitted with dry liners and these will have to be pressed out so that they emerge from the top of the block and new ones fitted.

28 Pistons, piston rings and gudgeon pins - examination and renovation

1 The method of removing the gudgeon pin and piston rings has already been described in Section 16.

2 Clean carbon from the head of the piston using worn emery cloth and paraffin. Do not use a scraper or any tool that may score the head.

3 Do not use an abrasive to clean the outside of the piston despite the discolouration that may be present; a wipe with a cloth and paraffin will suffice.

4 Examine the lands for burrs as these may prevent freedom of movement of the ring, rectify as necessary using fine emery cloth.

5 Clean all dirt out of the grooves especially in the corners. A broken piston ring is a handy tool for this job but be careful not to dig in or remove metal.

6 Examine the skirt for fractures at the extremity of the split.

7 When a new piston ring is brought into use its gap, when sprung out in the cylinder bore, must be measured and adjusted as necessary. If the gap is too small seizure will result when the ring expands, if the gap is too great compression pressure will be lost.

8 Push the new ring down the bore as far as possible using a piston; this will ensure that the ring is square in the bore.

9 Measure the piston ring end-gap which should be in accordance with the tolerance listed in Specifications for the appropriate ring and engine type.

10 Repeat the check on each ring in turn in its respective bore.

11 Check the ring to groove clearance again using a feeler gauge. The clearance should be as specified. If the ring is tight, it can be eased by rubbing it on a sheet of emery cloth held on a piece of plate glass. If the ring is excessively tight then the groove will have to be machined out.

12 Check the gudgeon pin for wear in the piston and the connecting rod small end bush. Any slackness can only be overcome by renewal of the components concerned.

29 Flywheel and starter ring gear - examination and renovation

1 If the starter ring gear is worn or the teeth are chipped, then the flywheel should be renewed complete.

2 If the surface of the flywheel is badly scored or small cracks are visible, it should be renewed; machining or surface grinding is not recommended (photo).

3 The flywheel and clutch are balanced and if a new flywheel is fitted, then before installation, have the components re-balanced by your Jaguar dealer.

4 *On cars equipped with automatic transmission,* examine the bolt holes of the driveplate for cracks and the starter ring gear for wear. If these conditions are evident, renew the driveplate complete.

30 Camshaft and camshaft bearings - examination and renovation

1 The camshafts and bearings normally give a very long life but there are always exceptions to the rule. The photograph shows a camshaft which has failed due to a breakdown in the surface hardening of the cam lobe; it is estimated that the engine from which this shaft was removed had done well over 100,000 miles (160,000 km). This type of fault is not so common as general wear on the lobes, this point can be checked by making a comparison with a new shaft although a good estimate of their condition can be obtained by comparing one lobe with another and with those on the other camshaft (photo).

2 Scoring on the bearing surfaces is a more likely fault to be found. It may be possible to remove slight score marks by gently rubbing down with fine emery cloth or an oilstone but this must not be overdone as undersize bearings are not supplied. Therefore, if the scoring cannot be rectified, or if wear on the lobes is found, the shaft should be scrapped.

3 Examine the shell bearings for scoring, pitting and general signs of wear. It is advisable to fit new bearings if there is any doubt as to their condition.

31 Valves and seats - examination and renovation

1 Examine the heads of the valves for pitting and burning, especially the exhaust valves.

2 If the valves appear serviceable re-use after grinding to their seats in the cylinder head, scrape all the carbon away and carefully clean the stem of the valve. Clean the valve guide in the cylinder head and fit the valve to its guide.

3 With the valve about threequarters of its way in the guide, check it for sideways movement. If the movement appears to be excessive, remove the valve and measure the diameter of the stem, this should be not less than specified. If the stem diameter is satisfactory it means that the valve guide is worn and remedial action as indicated in Section 33 will have to be taken.

4 If no wear is present, check the valve stem for distortion by moving the valve up and down in its guide and at the same time rotating it, no restriction to movement should be felt.

5 Grinding the valves to their seats is easily carried out. First place the cylinder head upside down on the bench resting on a block of wood at each end to give clearance for the valve stems.

6 Smear a trace of coarse carburundum (photo) on the seat face and apply a suction grinding tool to the head of the valve. With a semi-rotary action, grind the valve to its seat (photo), lifting the valve occasionally to re-distribute the paste. When a continuous ring of dull matt even finish is produced on both the valve seat and the valve, then wipe off the coarse paste and repeat the process with a fine paste, lifting and turning the valve as before. A light spring placed under the head of the valve will assist in the lifting operation. When a smooth unbroken ring of light grey matt is produced on both valve and valve seat faces, the grinding operation is complete. Be very careful during the grinding operation not to get the abrasive paste on the stem of the valve, do not handle the valve stem once you have started to use the paste because it will be transferred from the fingers to the stem and the result will be rapid wear of the valve guide. Trouble is often experienced with the suction tool not gripping the valve head, this can be overcome if the valve head and the tool are kept free of oil and grease at all times

7 When grinding is completed, thoroughly clean the cylinder head to remove any trace of carburundum as this can cause a lot of damage

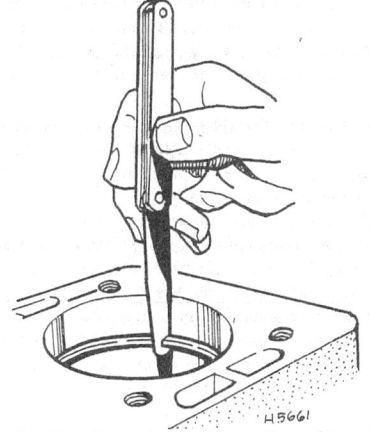
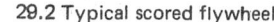

Fig. 1.17. Checking piston ring end-gap (Sec. 28)

29.2 Typical scored flywheel

30.1 Typical pitted camshaft lobe

31.6A Applying grinding paste to a valve

31.6B Grinding in a valve

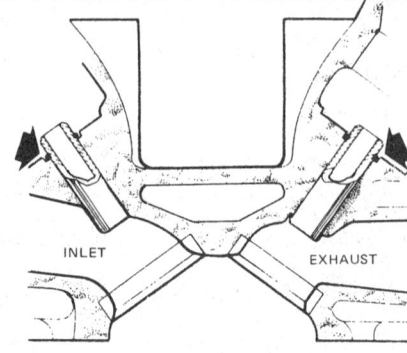

INLET   EXHAUST

Fig. 1.18. Valve guide fitting diagram (Sec. 33)

after first start up of the engine.
8 If a valve seat is too badly burned to be renovated by grinding, it
should be re-cut or renewed by your Jaguar dealer.

32 Valve springs - examination and renewal

1 The valve springs should be renewed as a matter of course if they
have been in use for 25,000 miles (40,000 km) or more.
2 If they have been in use for a shorter period, check their free
lengths against Specification. If they have been compressed excessively
when compared with a new spring, renew them.

33 Valve guides - renewal

1 The valve guides are of cast-iron construction differing in length
between inlet and exhaust types. The guides are secured by circlips
and those for the inlet valves incorporate valve stem oil seals.
2 If the guides are found to be worn as a result of testing, as described
in Section 31, renew them in the following way.

3 Immerse the cylinder head in boiling water for thirty minutes
and then using a suitable drift drive out the old guide from the
combustion chamber end of the head.
4 The old valve guide must now be examined to establish its size
which represents external diameter.
   No external groove - 0.501 to 0.502 in (12.70 to 12.725 mm)
   One external groove - 0.503 to 0.504 in (12.776 to 12.801 mm)
   Two external grooves - 0.506 to 0.507 in (12.852 to 12.877 mm)
   Three external grooves - 0.511 to 0.512 in (12.979 to 13.005 mm)
The new valve guide should be an oversize. Where the original guide did
not have a groove, install a new guide with one groove. If the old guide
had one groove, install a new guide with two grooves and if it had two
grooves previously, install a new guide with three grooves. When
installing a new guide which has one groove, no reaming will be
necessary. If installing a new valve guide with two grooves which
previously had one groove, ream the cylinder head to 0.505 in (12.83
mm) diameter to accept (interference fit) the new valve guide. If
installing a new guide with three grooves which previously had two
grooves, ream the cylinder head to 0.510 in (12.95 mm) to accept
(interference fit) the new valve guide.
5 To fit the new guide, keep the cylinder head at high temperature
in boiling water and then smear the guide with graphite grease and
drive in the guide from the top face of the cylinder head until the
guide circlip registers.

34 Tappets and shims - examination and renovation

1 Examine the bearing surface of the tappet on which the camshaft
bears. Any indentation on this surface or any cracks indicate serious
wear and the tappet must be renewed.
2 It is unlikely that the sides of the tappet will be worn, but if the
tappet can be rocked in its guide in the cylinder head it should be
established by measurement which item is at fault; details of
dimensions are given under Specifications at the beginning of this

Chapter.
3 The tappet should also be checked to see that it moves freely in its
guide, the most likely cause of restriction is dirt but rectify as necessary.
4 Clean and examine the valve adjusting shims. After a considerable
mileage the valve stem will probably have made an indentation on its
face. In this case the shim should be renewed but where the valves
have been ground in, shims of alternative thickness will probably be
required (refer to Section 48).

35 Timing gear and chains - examination and renovation

1 Clean the sprockets and chains in a paraffin bath and dry them on
a non-fluffy rag.
2 Examine the teeth of the sprockets for wear. Each tooth forms an
inverted 'V' with the periphery of the sprocket and, if worn, the side
of the tooth under tension will be slightly concave in shape when
compared with the other side of the tooth. If any wear is present the
sprocket should be renewed.
3 Examine the links of the chain for side slackness and renew the
chain if any slackness is noticeable when compared to a new chain. It
is sensible to replace the chain if the engine is stripped for overhaul and
when the cylinder head is removed for decarbonisation or some other
purpose, if it is known that the chain has been in use for a considerable
time.
4 The chain tension slipper and the rubbing surfaces of the guides
should be examined for grooves or deterioration and renewed, if
necessary.

36 Cylinder head - decarbonising and examination

1 With the cylinder head removed, use a blunt scraper to remove all
trace of carbon and deposits from the combustion spaces and ports.
Remember that the cylinder head is aluminium alloy and can be
damaged easily during the decarbonising operations. Scrape the
cylinder head free from scale or old pieces of gasket or jointing
compound. Clean the cylinder head by washing it in paraffin and take
particular care to pull a piece of rag through the ports and cylinder
head bolt holes. Any dirt remaining in these recesses may well drop
onto the gasket or cylinder block mating surface as the cylinder head
is lowered into position and could lead to a gasket leak after reassembly
is complete.
2 With the cylinder head clean, test for distortion if a history of coolant
leakage has been apparent. Carry out this test using a straight edge and
feeler gauges or a piece of plate glass. If the surface shows any warping
in excess of 0.039 in (0.1015 mm) then the cylinder head will have to
be resurfaced which is a job for a specialist engineering company.
3 Clean the pistons and top of the cylinder bores. If the pistons are
still in the block then it is essential that great care is taken to ensure
that no carbon gets into the cylinder bores as this could scratch the
cylinder walls or cause damage to the piston and rings. To ensure this
does not happen, first turn the crankshaft so that two of the pistons
are at the top of their bores. Stuff rag into the other four bores or seal
them off with paper and masking tape to prevent particles of carbon
entering the cooling system and damaging the water pump.
4 Rotate the crankshaft and repeat the carbon removal operations

on the remaining pistons and cylinder bores.

5   Thoroughly clean all particles of carbon from the bores and then inject a little light oil round the edges of the pistons to lubricate the piston rings.

37 Oil pump - examination and renovation

1   With the oil pump removed, as described in Section 14, remove the bottom cover (four bolts) from the pump body.

2   Withdraw the rotors from the pump body but do not attempt to separate the inner rotor from the driveshaft.

3   If the rotors or body show signs of scoring or wear it will probably be best to renew the oil pump complete. The need for individual replacement parts can be determined by checking for wear in the following manner.

4   Using a feeler blade, check the clearance between the inner and outer rotors. This should not exceed 0.006 in (0.15 mm).

5   Check the clearance between the outer rotor and the oil pump body. This should not exceed 0.010 in (0.25 mm).

6   Check the rotor endfloat by measuring the gap between the rotor endfaces and a straight-edge placed across the body. This should not exceed 0.0025 in (0.06 mm).

7   Reassembly is a reversal of dismantling.

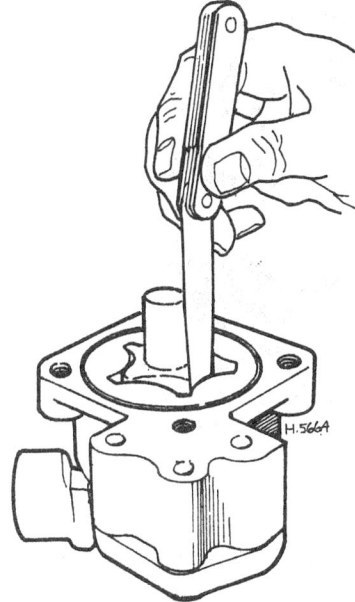

Fig. 1.19. Checking oil pump rotor tip clearance (Sec. 37)

38 Oil seals - renewal

1   At time of major overhaul always renew engine oil seals even if they appear in good condition.

2   Renew the crankshaft front and rear oil seals and the 'O' rings on the oil pump suction and return pipes.

39 Engine - preparation for reassembly

1   To ensure maximum life with reliability from a rebuilt engine, not only must everything be correctly assembled but all components must be spotlessly clean and the correct spring or plain washers used where originally located. Always lubricate bearing and working surfaces with clean engine oil during reassembly of engine parts.

2   Before reassembly commences, renew any bolts or studs the threads of which are damaged or corroded.

3   As well as your normal tool kit, gather together clean rags, oil can, a torque wrench and a complete (overhaul) set of gaskets and oil seals.

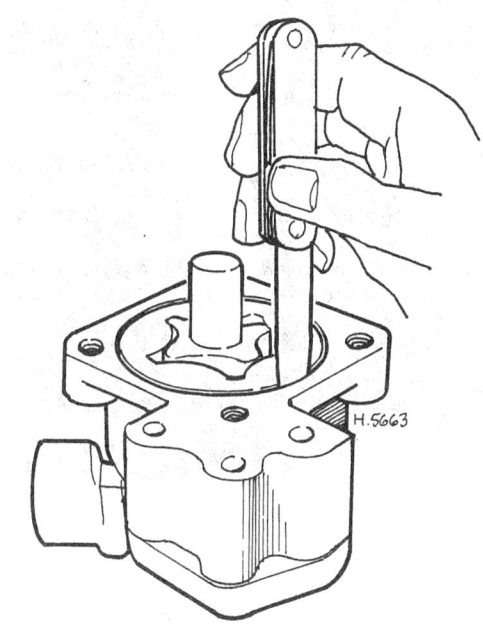

Fig. 1.20. Checking oil pump outer rotor to body clearance (Sec. 37)

40 Engine reassembly sequence

1   If the engine has been complete dismantled then the following reassembly sequence is recommended:

Crankshaft and main bearings.
Flywheel (or driveplate - automatic transmission).
Distributor drive.
Piston/connecting rods.
Timing chains and gear.
Oil pump and sump.
Camshaft and valve clearance adjustment.
Cylinder head.

41 Crankshaft and main bearings - installation

1   Fit the top half of the rear oil seal cover assembly and then fit the top half of the oil seal. First prepare the new oil seal by carefully tapping it on its side face to narrow the section. Apply a thin coat of permanent jointing compound (red Hermetite or similar) to the seal housing grooves, coating only the first inch (25 mm) of the leading edge of each half. Fit the seal to the housing and press into the groove, using a hammer handle, until the seal does not protrude from the ends of the housing. **Do not** cut the ends off the seal if they do protrude but continue pressing into the groove until both ends are flush. Using a knife or similar tool, press all loose ends of asbestos into the ends of the groove so that they will not be trapped between the two halves of the housing when assembled. Fit the asbestos seal to the bottom half of the cover assembly in the same manner as described above (Fig. 1.22).

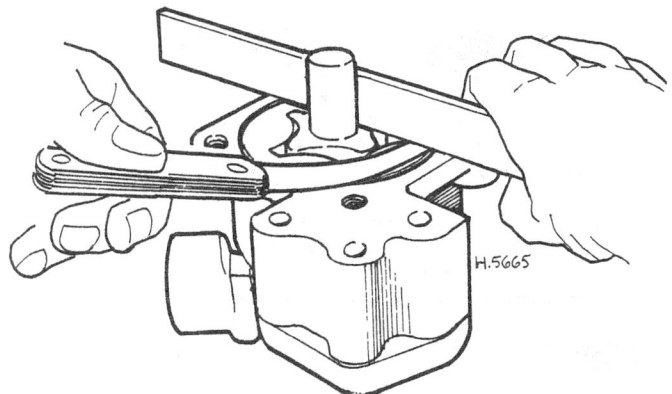

Fig. 1.21. Checking oil pump rotor endfloat (Sec. 37)

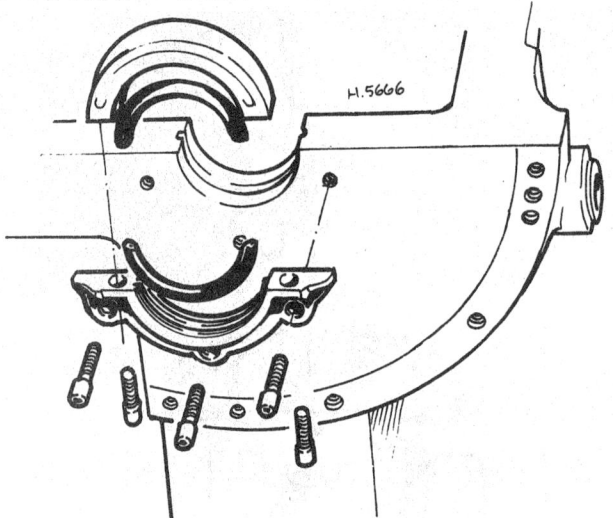

Fig. 1.22. Crankshaft rear oil seal assembly (Sec. 41)

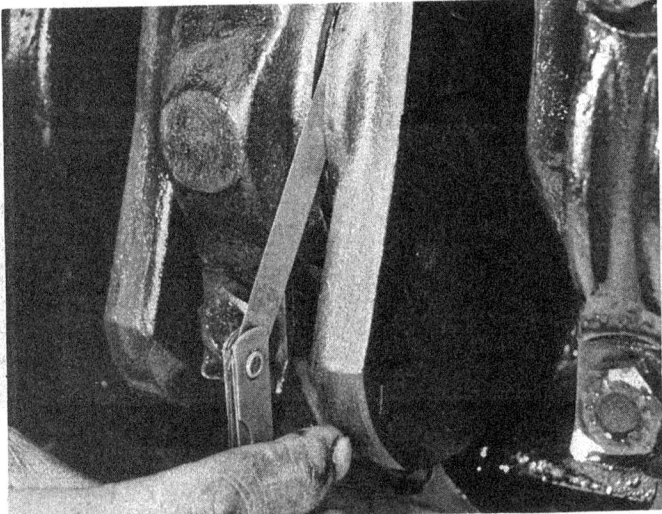

41.5 Checking crankshaft endfloat

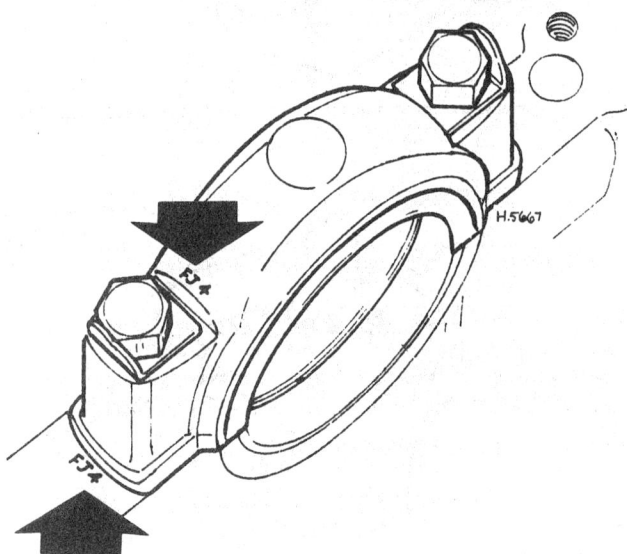

Fig. 1.23. Crankshaft main bearing numbers (Sec. 41)

2 Clean the locations for the half main bearing shells in the crankcase and fit the half bearing shells. Lubricate the shells liberally.
3 Smear some engine oil or (preferably) colloidal graphite on the inside surfaces of the rear oil seal halves. If the official sizing tool JD 17B is available, temporarily assemble the oil seal halves to the crankcase and use the tool to pre-size the seal. Remove the tool and separate the oil seal halves.
4 Fit the crankshaft in the crankcase and assemble the rear oil seal halves around it.
5 Fit the centre main bearing cap with a new thrust washer, white metal side outwards, in the recess at each side of the cap. Tighten down on the cap and check the crankshaft endfloat (photo), this should be 0.004 in to 0.006 in (0.10 to 0.15 mm). The thrust washers are supplied in two thicknesses, standard and 0.004 in (0.10 mm) oversize and should be selected to bring the endfloat within permissible limits. There is no objection to the use of a standard and an oversize washer on the same shaft. The oversize washers are stamped +0.004 (0.010) on the steel face.
6 Fit the main bearing caps and shells to the crankshaft. But do make sure that the numbers stamped on the caps correspond with those stamped on the crankcase and are adjacent.
7 Fit the main bearing cap bolts and tab washers and tighten down to specified torque. The tab washers for the rear main bearing bolts are longer than the remainder and the plain ends should be tapped down round the bolt hole bosses.
8 Test the crankshaft for freedom of rotation. If there is no undue restriction to movement of the crankshaft, knock up the tab washers to secure the bolts.
9 Fit the Woodruff key to the inner slot.

42 Flywheel (or driveplate - auto. transmission) - refitting

1 Install the flywheel to the crankshaft mounting flange so that the alignment marks are correctly mated.
2 Fit a new lockplate and screw in the bolts and tighten to the specified torque.

43 Distributor drive - refitting

1 If the drive gear on the front of the crankshaft was removed, drive it into position using a suitable piece of tubing so that the thicker boss is to the rear. Make sure that the Woodruff key is fitted.

44 Piston/connecting rod - installation

1 If the piston was removed from the connecting rod by pushing out the gudgeon pin, reassemble the piston to the connecting rod so that with the word 'FRONT' on the piston crown towards the crankshaft pulley, the mating numbers on the connecting rod and cap will be in alignment and on the left-hand side when looking towards the crankshaft pulley from the rear of the engine. Fit new circlips to the ends of the gudgeon pin.
2 The piston ring gaps will have been checked as described in Section 28, now fit them to the pistons. The top and second compression rings are tapered and must be fitted so that the word 'TOP' is uppermost. Do not remove any red coating from these rings.
3 The oil control ring is of three section type incorporating two rails and an expander. The assembly is usually supplied, held together with adhesive for ease of installation. Make sure that the expander has its ends butted together when installed and not overlapping.
4 Wipe the cylinder bores clean with a non-fluffy rag, and then liberally lubricate the walls of each.
5 The pistons, complete with connecting rods must be fitted to their respective bores, from the top of the cylinder block. As each piston is inserted in the bore, make sure that it is the correct assembly for that bore by checking the number stamped on the connecting rod (no. 1 cylinder is at the rear of the engine).
6 Ensure that the pistons are the correct way round in the cylinder, the piston crown is marked 'Front' to aid correct assembly.
7 Check that the piston ring gaps are not in alignment to cause gas blow-by.
8 Compress the piston rings in a clamp. Guide the piston into the bore until it reaches the ring compressor. Gently tap the piston into

the bore with a wood or hide faced hammer.

9 Do not try to fit the pistons without a ring compressor as the chance of breaking a ring and scoring the bore is very high.

10 Wipe the connecting rod half of the big-end bearing location and the underside of the shell bearing clean. Fit the shell bearing in position with its locating tongue engaged with the corresponding groove in the connecting rod.

11 Wipe clean and then generously lubricate the crankpin journals with engine oil. Turn the crankshaft to a handy position for the connecting rod to be drawn onto it and for the connecting rod cap to be fitted.

12 Fit the bearing shell to the connecting rod cap in the same manner as with the connecting rod itself.

13 Generously lubricate the shell bearing and offer up the cap to the connecting rod, ensure that the numbers are mating.

14 Fit the connecting rod bolts (it is advisable to use new nuts and bolts), fit the nuts and tighten down to the specified torque.

45 Distributor driveshaft and timing gear - refitting

1 To the front of the crankshaft fit the timing chain sprocket, but do not push it fully home at this stage. Fit the Woodruff key, oil thrower and distance piece (photo).

2 Fit the eccentric idler shaft to the hole in the front mounting bracket.

3 Fit the spring and plunger into the bracket and locate the serrated plate onto the shaft. Secure the plate loosely with the washer and nut.

4 Fit the idler sprocket (21 teeth) to the idler shaft.

5 Fit the intermediate sprocket (20/28 teeth), so that the larger gear is towards the front of the engine, onto the intermediate shaft. Fit the shim in the rear mounting bracket making sure that the roll pin engages in the slot. Secure the shaft with its circlip.

6 Engage the upper (longer) timing chain with the smaller of the two intermediate sprockets.

7 Engage the lower timing chain with the larger intermediate sprocket.

8 Loop the upper chain under the idler sprocket and secure the upper mounting bracket to the rear mounting bracket using the four nuts and lockwashers.

9 Screw in the four long setscrews and lockwashers to the front mounting bracket and fit the lower guides, chain support plate and distance pieces.

10 Equalize the loops of the upper timing chain and then engage the camshaft sprockets in the loops.

11 Turn the eccentric idler shaft until the idler sprocket is at its highest point between the camshaft sprockets.

12 Engage the lower timing chain under the crankshaft sprocket and tap the sprocket fully home using a piece of tubing as a drift. Tighten the four setscrews to retain the timing gear assembly to the cylinder block.

13 Fit the lower (C) and intermediate (A) timing chain guides but do not tighten the securing bolts on the intermediate guide at this stage (Fig.1.24B).

45.1 Refitting crankshaft sprocket

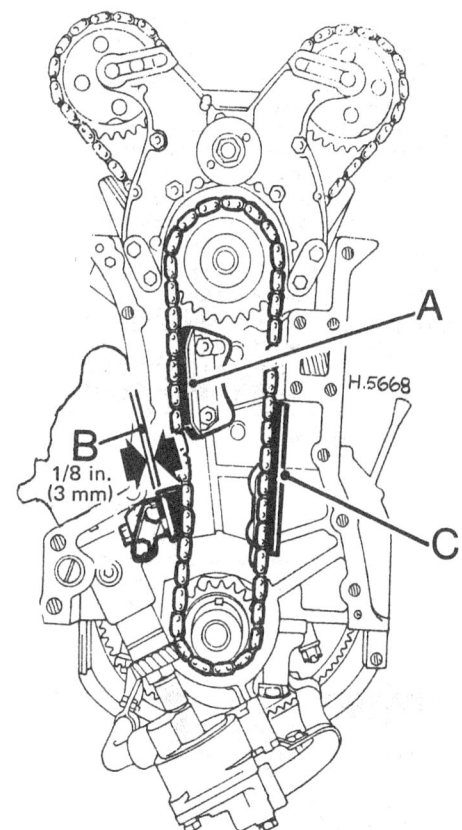

Fig. 1.24B. Timing chain tensioning diagram (Sec. 45)

A Intermediate guide
B Slipper to body clearance
C Lower guide

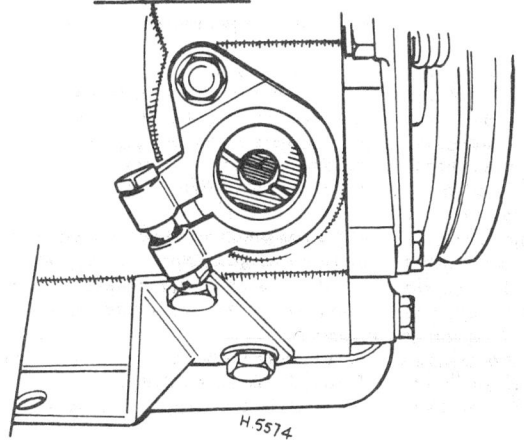

Fig. 1.24A. Distributor driveshaft installation diagram (Sec. 45)

14 Fit the conical filter to the hole in the cylinder block.
15 Screw the chain tensioner slipper into the tensioner body until there is a gap (B) between the slipper and body of 0.125 in (3.17 mm).
16 Fit the tensioner to the cylinder block using shims as necessary under the tensioner backplate to ensure that the chain runs centrally on the slipper. Secure the tensioner with the two setscrews and lockplate.
17 Insert a packing piece (or the card supplied with a new tensioner) between the body and slipper so that the clearance set (see paragraph 15) will be maintained during the following operation.
18 Move the intermediate guide (A) so that it just contacts the chain. Tighten the securing setscrews and bend up the lockplates.
19 Extract the packing piece and tap the slipper to release it from its ratchet.
20 Refit the distributor driveshaft in the following way. Turn the crankshaft until Nos 1 and 6 pistons are at TDC.
21 Push the distributor driveshaft into its hole so that the offset slot in the end of the shaft is as shown (Fig.1.24A). Holding this slot alignment, withdraw the shaft just enough to be able to fit the Woodruff key, the thrust washer and the driven gear.
22 Press the driveshaft downward so that the drivegears mesh without altering the slot alignment at the top end of the shaft.
23 Fit the pegged tab washer and secure the shaft with its nut.
24 Now check the shaft endfloat. This should be between 0.004 and 0.006 in (0.10 and 0.15 mm). If no clearance exists at all, the drivegear should be renewed. As a second best alternative, rub down the thickness of the thrust washer.
25 With a new oil seal fitted, install the timing cover having smeared the joint faces with gasket cement.
26 Fit the crankshaft damper assembly by reversing the removal operations.

46 Oil pump and sump - refitting

1 Fit the coupling shaft between the squared end of the distributor drive shaft and the driving gear of the pump.
2 Secure the oil pump to the front main bearing cap by the three dowel bolts and tab washers. Check that there is appreciable endfloat of the short coupling shaft.
3 Fit the oil delivery pipe from the oil pump to the bottom face of the crankcase with a new 'O' ring and gasket.
4 Fit the suction pipe with a new 'O' ring at the oil pump end and secure to its clip on the main bracket cap.
5 The oil sump may be refitted at this stage or, if it desired to use the base of the cylinder block on which to rest the engine for further assembly work, it may be left until later. However, to refit the sump:
6 Clean the mating faces of the sump and the crankcase. Although not really necessary, they may be treated with jointing compound if desired.
7 Fit a new sump gasket to the bottom face of the crankcase.
8 Fit the oil seal to the recess in the rear main bearing cap.
9 Fit the sump to the crankcase and secure with the twenty-six set screws and the four nuts and washers. Remember that the short set screw goes at the right-hand front corner of the sump.
10 Fit the sump strainer in position using new gaskets.

47 Cylinder head - reassembly and refitting

1 With the cylinder head standing on the bench, oil the first two valve stems and then insert the valves into their guide making sure that each valve is returned to its original location, or if new valves have been fitted, to the seats into which they have been ground.
2 Install a small wooden block into the combustion chamber so that when the cylinder head is placed face down on the bench, the two valves will not drop out.
3 When looking down on the head from the crankshaft pulley end, the inlet valves are on the left and the exhaust valves are on the right. Remember that oil seals must be fitted to the inlet valve stems.
4 To the first valve fit the valve spring seat, the double valve springs (close coils nearer cylinder head) and the valve spring collar. Compress the valve springs, using either a conventional compressor or a tube made up to a design similar to the one shown with a cut-out for inserting the split collets (photo).
5 Insert the split collets, retaining them in position if required, with a dab of thick grease. Release the compressor.
6 Repeat the operations on the remaining 11 valves.
7 Install the shim and tappet to each valve. If the valves have been ground in or new valves have been installed, the valve clearances must be checked and adjusted, as described in Section 48.

48 Camshaft installation and valve clearance adjustment

1 Clean the location in the cylinder head for the camshaft bearing shells. Fit the half bearing shells to the head.
2 Clean the bearing location in the camshaft bearing caps and fit the half shell bearings.
3 Fit one camshaft to the cylinder head making sure that the correct shaft is being offered to the correct set of valves. Check the numbers on the caps to that shaft and the corresponding numbers on the cylinder head and fit the caps in their correct position. Fit the nuts and 'D' washers to the bearing studs (photo).
4 Tighten down on the nuts to a torque of 9 lb/ft (12 Nm).
5 Rotate the camshaft to bring the back of a cam to the valve tappet. Measure, and record, the clearance between the cam and the tappet. Repeat for all the valves in that bank. The clearances should be between 0.012 and 0.014 in (0.304 and 0.355 mm) for all valves (photo).
6 Adjusting pads are available rising in 0.001 in (0.03mm) sizes from 0.085 in to 0.110 in (2.16 to 2.79 mm) and are etched on the surface with the letter 'A' to 'Z', each letter indicating an increase in size of 0.001 in (0.03 mm).
7 Should any valve clearance require adjustment, remove the camshaft, the tappet and adjusting pad.
8 Observe the letter stamped on the adjusting pad and should the recorded clearance for this valve have shown, say, 0.002 in (0.05 mm) in in excess of the correct value, select a new adjusting pad bearing a letter two higher than the original pad.
9 After all the adjusting pads have been changed as may be required, reassemble the camshaft and carry out a final check to ensure that the clearances are indeed correct. Remove the camshaft or slacken all the nuts to relieve all pressure on the valves.
   When checking the valve clearances the camshafts must be fitted

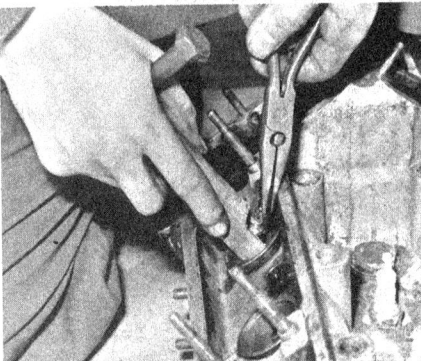
47.4 Refitting split cotters after compressing valve spring with tubular tool

48.3 Fitting a camshaft 'D' washer

48.5 Checking a valve clearance

one at a time as, if one camshaft is rotated when the other shaft is in position, fouling is likely to take place between the inlet and exhaust valves. When checking of the clearances of one set of valves is completed, the shaft must either be removed or the bearing cap bolts must be slackened to the extent of relieving all pressure on the valves.

10 Repeat the foregoing to check the valve clearances for the other set

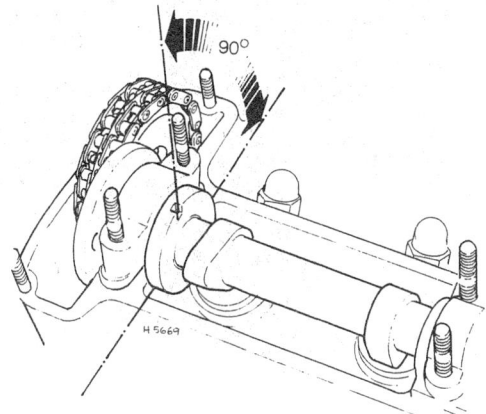

Fig. 1.25. Camshaft alignment (Sec. 48)

of valves. When satisfied that the clearances are correct, check the security of the nuts and turn the camshaft so that the square slot in the shaft at the rear of the front bearing is at 90° to the camshaft cover face.

11 Fit the other camshaft and position it so that its slot is also at 90° to the camshaft cover face. Fit the nuts to the studs and tighten them down to a torque of 9 lb/ft (12 Nm).

12 From now on, the camshafts must not be rotated independently of each other, otherwise the valves may impinge on each other and bend.

49 Cylinder head - installation

1 Turn the crankshaft so that no. 6 piston (the one nearest the crankshaft pulley) is at TDC. This can be ascertained by checking that the 'O' mark on the crankshaft damper is opposite the pointer on the crankcase.

2 Make sure that the mating surfaces of cylinder head and block are absolutely clean and position a new gasket on the cylinder block so that the word 'TOP' on the gasket is visible.

3 On no account move the camshafts from their previously set position (see Section 48).

4 Lower the cylinder head carefully into position complete with inlet manifold assembly.

5 Fit the spark plug lead carrier to some of the studs on the right-hand side and the 'D' washers to the remaining ones.

6 Tighten the cylinder head dome nuts, half a turn each at a time to the

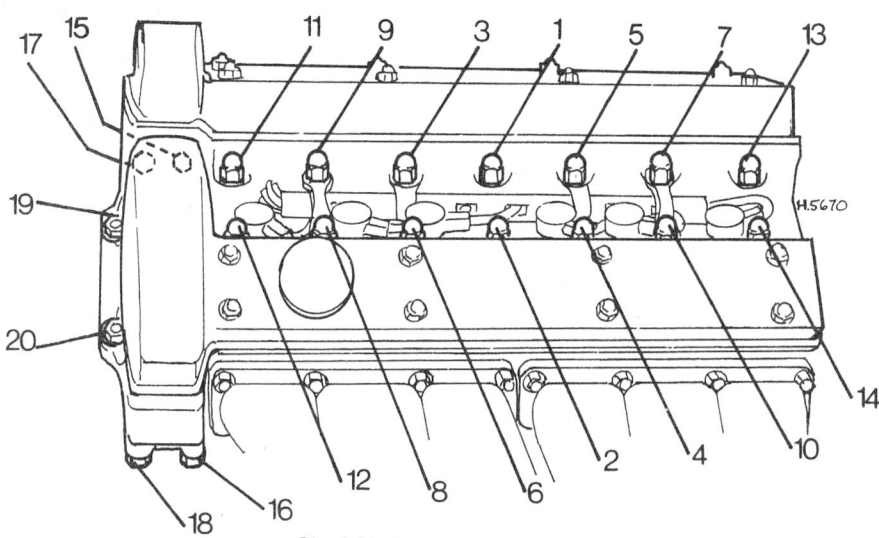

Fig. 1.26. Cylinder head nut tightening sequence (Sec. 49)

Fig. 1.27. Ignition timing marks on crankshaft damper (Sec. 50)

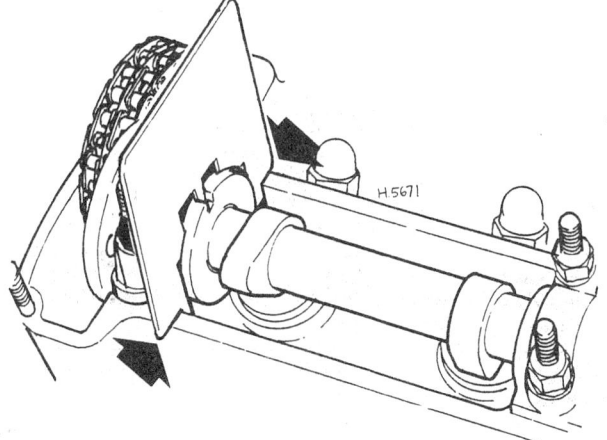

Fig. 1.28. Camshaft setting gauge (Sec. 50)

specified torques in the sequence shown in Fig. 1.26. Tighten the six nuts at the front of the cylinder head.

7   If the cylinder head was removed while the engine was still in the car, reverse all the operations described in paragraphs 1 to 21, of Section 11.

50 Valve timing

1   Check that no. 6 piston is at TDC ('O' mark on crankshaft damper opposite pointer on crankcase).
2   Check that the notches in the camshaft sprocket flanges are at 90° to a line touching the two rocker cover mating surfaces of the cylinder head. A gauge can be made up as shown in Fig.1.28 to set the camshaft position.
3   Withdraw the circlips which retain the adjusting plates to the camshaft sprockets. Pull the adjusting plates forward until the serrations disengage.
4   Fit the sprockets to the camshaft flanges and then align the bolt holes. If these holes are not in exact alignment, turn the adjuster plates through 180°. On no account attempt to force a bolt in otherwise the camshaft position will be altered.
5   Fit the circlips to the sprocket and insert one bolt into its hole in each of the adjuster plates. Turn the crankshaft until the two other bolt holes are accessible and insert the two remaining bolts.
6   Now tension the timing chain by pressing the stop peg (plunger) inwards and rotating the serrated plate anticlockwise. A special tool will be needed to carry out this operation (tool no. JD 2B) or one can be made up to the dimensions shown in Fig. 1.29 (photo).
7   When correctly tensioned, there should be slight flexibility of the chain below the camshaft sprockets. The chain must not be absolutely taut. Release the locking plunger and securely tighten the locknut on the idler shaft.
8   Turn the engine until the 'O' mark on the crankshaft damper is again opposite the pointer and use the gauge to check the setting of both camshafts. If all is correct, lock the camshaft sprocket bolt heads with new wire (Fig.1.30) or lockplates (later models).
9   Use new gaskets and refit the camshaft covers.
10 Refit the breather housing to the front of the cylinder head.
11 Refit the water pump (Chapter 2).

51 Engine ancillaries - refitting

1   Refit the alternator and drivebelt (Chapter 10).
2   Refit the clutch having centralised it, as described in Chapter 5.
3   Refit the distributor as described in Chapter 4.
4   Refit the starter motor (Chapter 10).

52 Engine to transmission - reconnection

1   This is a reversal of operations described in Sections 7 or 8.
2   Where the car is equipped with automatic transmission, make sure that the torque converter is fully engaged with the tangs of the oil pump before offering up the transmission to the engine.

53 Engine/transmission - installation

1   Refer to Section 5 or 6, and reverse the removal operations.
2   Make sure that wires and controls are well out of the way before the engine/transmission is lowered into position.
3   With the engine installed, check that all drain plugs have been refitted and tightened and that the oil filter has been renewed and that drivebelts have been correctly adjusted.
4   Refill the cooling system (with antifreeze mixture), the engine sump and check and top-up the transmission oil level.

54 Initial start-up after major overhaul

1   Refer to Chapter 3 and follow the instructions for initial setting of the carburettors, and follow the instructions in Chapter 4 for timing of the ignition.

50.6 Tool for tensioning upper timing chain

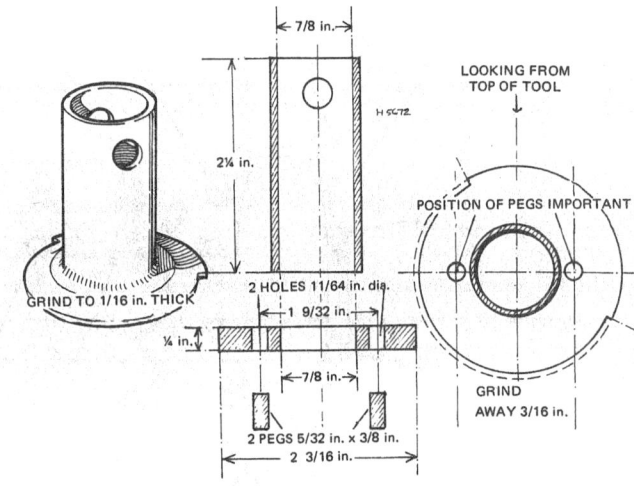

Fig. 1.29. Timing chain adjusting tool diagram (Sec. 50)

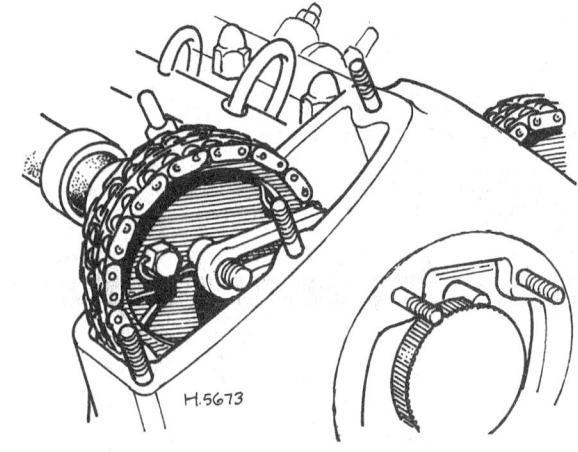

Fig. 1.30. Camshaft sprocket showing bolts locked with wire (Sec. 50)

2 Make sure that the battery is fully charged and that all lubricants and fuels are replenished.

3 Switch on the ignition and allow the petrol pump time to fill the carburettor float chambers.

4 Start the engine, as soon as it fires and runs, keep it going at a fast tickover only (no faster). Watch the oil pressure gauge, after a very short wait, whilst the oil filter is being filled, it should register around 40 lbs per sq. in. If, after about 30 seconds, no oil pressure is registered, switch off the engine and investigate the cause; it may be that you have not fully tightened a union or the filter canister is not correctly seated on the rubber sealing ring in the head of the filter.

5 Bring the engine up to its normal working temperature, as it warms up there will be odd smells and some smoke from parts getting hot and burning off oil deposits. Look round carefully for water and oil leaks.

6 When the engine running temperature has been reached adjust the carburettors as described in Chapter 3.

7 Stop the engine and wait a few minutes to see if there are any water or oil leaks.

8 Before road testing the car it is advisable to have an assistant listening to the brake servo, run the engine for a few minutes and then operate the foot brake. If the brake servo connections are satisfactory the exhaust from the servo will be plainly heard.

9 Road test the car to check that the timing is correct and is giving the necessary smoothness and power. Do not race the engine. If new bearings or pistons or rings have been fitted, it should be treated as a new engine and run in at reduced revolutions for the first 500 miles (800 km).

55 Fault diagnosis - engine

Symptom	Reason/s
Engine fails to turn over when starter switch operated	Flat or defective battery. Loose battery leads. Defective starter solenoid or switch or broken wiring. Engine earth strap disconnected. Defective starter motor.
Engine turns over but will not start	Ignition system damp or wet. Ignition leads to spark plugs loose. Shorted or disconnected low tension leads. Dirty, incorrectly set, or pitted contact breaker points. Faulty condenser. Defective ignition switch. Ignition leads connected wrong way round. Faulty coil. Contact breaker point spring earthed or broken. No petrol in petrol tank. Vapour lock in fuel line (in hot conditions or at high altitude). Blocked float chamber needle valve. Fuel pump filter blocked. Faulty fuel pump. Too much choke allowing too rich a mixture to wet plugs. Float damaged or leaking or needle not seating. Float lever incorrectly adjusted.
Engine stalls and will not start	Ignition failure - sudden. Ignition failure - misfiring preceding total stoppage. Ignition failure - in severe rain or after traversing water splash No petrol in petrol tank. Petrol tank breather choked. Sudden obstruction in carburettor(s). Water in fuel system. Ignition leads loose. Battery leads loose on terminals. Battery earth strap loose on body of attachment point.
Engine misfires or idles unevenly	Engine earth lead loose. Low tension leads to SW and CB terminals on coil loose. Low tension lead from CB terminal side to distributor loose. Dirty, or incorrectly gapped plugs. Dirty, incorrectly set, or pitted contact breaker points. Tracking across inside of distributor cover. Ignition too retarded. Faulty coil. Mixture too weak. Air leak in carburettor. Air leak at inlet manifold to cylinder. Incorrect valve clearances. Burnt out exhaust valves. Sticking or leaking valves. Weak or broken valve springs. Worn valve guides or stems. Worn pistons and piston rings.

Symptom	Reason/s
Lack of power and poor compression	Burnt out exhaust valves. Sticking or leaking valves. Worn valve guides and stems. Weak or broken valve springs. Blown cylinder head gasket (accompanied by increase in noise). Worn pistons and piston rings. Worn or scored cylinder bores. Ignition timing wrongly set. Too advanced or retarded. Contact breaker points incorrectly gapped. Incorrect valve clearances. Incorrectly set spark plugs. Carburation too rich or too weak. Dirty contact breaker points. Fuel filters blocked causing fuel starvation. Distributor automatic balance weights or vacuum advance and retard mechanisms not functioning correctly. Faulty fuel pump giving top end fuel starvation.
Excessive oil consumption	Badly worn, perished or missing inlet valve stem oil seals. Excessively worn valve stems and valve guides. Worn piston rings. Worn pistons and cylinder bores. Excessive piston ring gap allowing blow-up. Piston oil return holes choked. Leaking oil filter gasket. Leaking camshaft cover gasket. Leaking timing case gasket. Leaking sump gasket. Loose sump plug.
Unusual noises from engine	Worn valve gear (noisy tapping from top cover). Worn big-end bearing (regular heavy knocking). Worn main bearings. Worn camshaft chains.

Chapter 2 Cooling system

For modifications, and information applicable to later models, see Supplement at end of manual

Contents

Specifications

System	Thermo-syphon with radiator and water pump. Belt driven fan with fluid coupling
Fan	12 blades
Fluid coupling slip commences	1500 to 1900 rev/min
Pressure cap rating	13 lb/sq in (0.9140 kg/sq cm)

Thermostat

Standard	Opens 159°F (70.5°C); Fully open 165°F (74°C)
Special (extreme cold)	Opens 174°F (78.8°C); Fully open 179°F (82°C)
Coolant type/specification	Antifreeze to BS 3150, 3152 or 6580 (Duckhams Universal Antifreeze and Summer Coolant)

Coolant capacity

	Up to 1977	1978 on
2.8 litre engine	30 Imp pints (17 litres/36 US pints)	—
3.4 litre engine	30 Imp Pints (17 litres/36 US pints)	32 Imp pints (18 litres/38.5 US pints)
4.2 litre engine	32 Imp pints (18 litres/38.5 US pints)	32 Imp pints (18 litres/38.5 US pints)

Torque wrench settings

	lb ft	Nm
Radiator mounting bolts	26	35
Retainer to radiator crossmember	18	25
Expansion tank to wing valance	18	25
Fan cowl upper bracket to body	7	10

1 General description

1 The cooling system incorporates a crossflow radiator with a header tank which is pressurised and thermostatically flow controlled.
2 The header tank on smaller engined cars is mounted above the radiator matrix while on larger cars it is attached to the inlet manifold. With larger engined models, an expansion tank is mounted on the left-hand wing valance.
3 Coolant circulation is assisted by an impeller type pump driven by a belt from the crankshaft pulley.
4 The cooling fan is driven through a fluid coupling which slips at a pre-determined speed.
5 A pressure type cap is fitted to the header tank on smaller engined cars also to the expansion tank of larger models while a plain cap is fitted to the header tank of the larger engined models (Figs. 2.1 and 2.2).

2 Cooling system - draining

1 The engine cooling system is provided with two drain taps, one located in the base of the radiator and the other positioned on the rear left-hand side of the cylinder block below the exhaust manifold. A drain plug is located in the bottom water pipe. The expansion tank can be drained by disconnecting the pipe at its base.

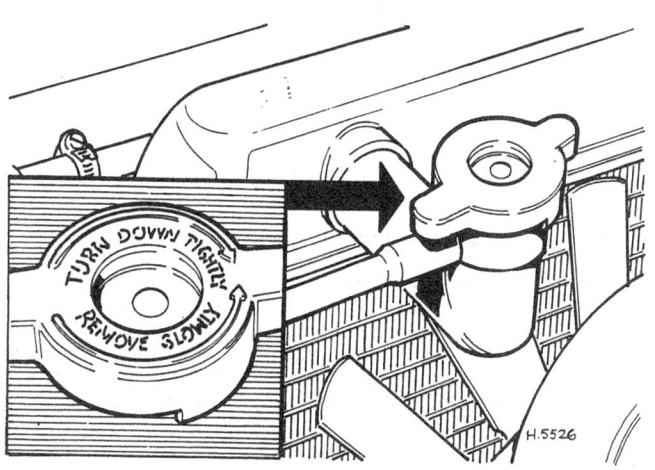

Fig. 2.1. Header tank filler cap on smaller capacity engines (Sec. 1)

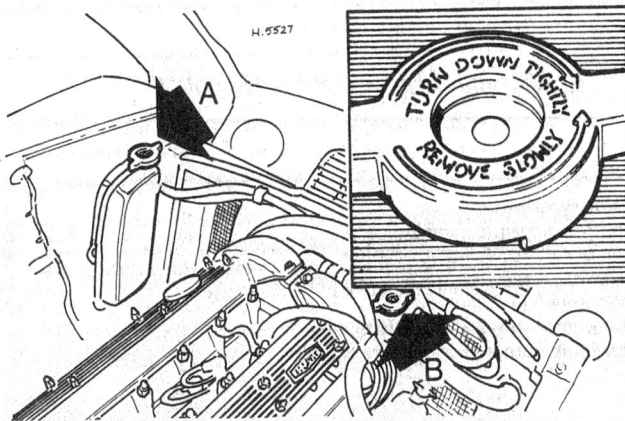

Fig. 2.2. Expansion tank cap (A) and header tank cap (B) on larger capacity engines (Sec. 1)

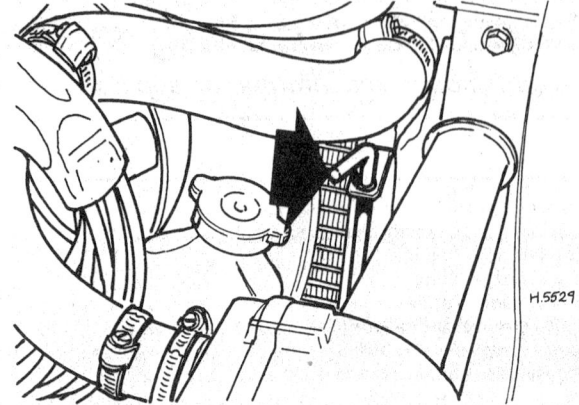

Fig. 2.3. Radiator drain tap remote control rod (Sec. 2)

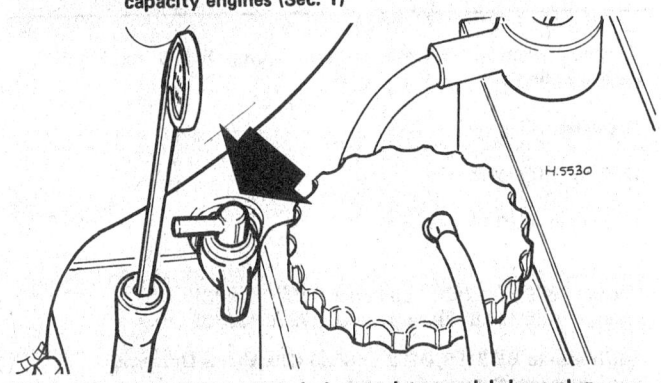

Fig.2.4. Cylinder block drain tap - later models have plug (Sec. 2)

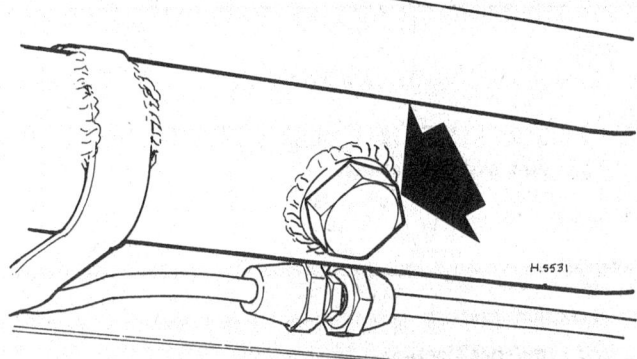

Fig. 2.5. Drain plug in bottom water pipe (Sec. 2)

2 Place the car on level ground.

3 If possible, wait until the engine is cold. Unscrew and remove the header tank/expansion chamber filler cap. **Remember** the system is pressurised so **do not** remove the cap whilst the engine is hot without taking precautions to prevent injury to yourself by the hot liquid which will be thrown out when the pressure is released. If any liquid containing anti-freeze mixture comes into contact with painted surfaces remove it immediately by washing with clean water otherwise the surface will be damaged.

4 Place the heater control at 'HOT'.

5 Open the radiator drain tap. It sometimes happens that this tap becomes blocked with sludge accumulated in the bottom of the radiator and it may be possible to clear the tap by poking with a piece of wire but if this is not successful, the tap will have to be removed. To do this, first disconnect the tap remote control rod by extracting the split pin from the forked end of the rod.

6 Open the cylinder block drain tap. This tap may also be blocked by scale and sludge in the cylinder block passages; if poking with wire fails to clear it, remove it by unscrewing with a spanner. Again take precautions if the engine is hot.

7 Unscrew and remove the plug from the bottom water pipe.

3 Cooling system - flushing

1 After prolonged use it is possible that the cooling system will gradually deteriorate in efficiency as the radiator becomes choked with rust scale, deposits from the water and other sediment. The symptom of deterioration is boiling of the engine or high operating temperatures which cannot be accounted for by fuel, ignition and other faults. These conditions are unlikely to arise if the coolant is renewed regularly as specified in 'Routine Maintenance.'

2 To flush the cooling system, remove the filler caps and open the radiator and cylinder block drain taps and remove the plug from the bottom water pipe. Place a cold water hose in the filler neck of the radiator header tank and let the water run until it is clear in appearance. If, after a reasonable period the water still does not run clear, the

radiator can be flushed with a good proprietary cleaning system such as Holts Radflush or Holts Speedflush.

3 In severe cases of contamination, place the hose in the lower of the two radiator matrix hose connections and reverse flush the matrix until the water runs clear from the neck of the header tank.

4 Remove the hose, reconnect any hoses which were disconnected and close the two drain taps and refit the plug to the bottom water pipe.

4 Cooling system - filling

1 Check that all drain plugs and taps are closed.

2 Place the heater control in the 'HOT', 'HI' or 'DEF' position.

3 Pour in two or three pints of water (preferably rain water or softened water) and then pour in the specified quantity of antifreeze product. Continue to pour in more water until the coolant level reaches the filler neck of the header tank. Fit the cap to the header tank.

4 Where an expansion tank is fitted, pour in coolant (mixed in similar proportions to the main quantity of coolant) until the tank is filled and then fit the cap.

5 Always fill the cooling system slowly and when filled, run the engine for a few minutes and then check the coolant level again when the engine has had a chance to cool down.

On cars without an expansion tank, the coolant level should be at the bottom of the header tank filler neck.

On cars with expansion tank, top-up the coolant level to the base of the expansion tank filler neck - do not remove the header tank cap.

5 Antifreeze mixture

1 Plain water should never be used in the cooling system as apart from not providing protection against adverse climatic conditions, the internal metal surfaces of the water passages will also corrode. The inhibitors found in good quality antifreeze mixtures protect iron and aluminium against corrosion for periods not exceeding twelve months.

2 In conditions where antifreeze is not required make sure that a

suitable corrosion inhibitor is used in the coolant.

3   The following table gives a guide to the proportion of antifreeze required for various levels of protection:

Antifreeze volume	Protection to
25%	$-15^{\circ}F\ (-26^{\circ}C)$
35%	$-38^{\circ}F\ (-39^{\circ}C)$
40%	$-42^{\circ}F\ (-41^{\circ}C)$
50%	$-53^{\circ}F\ (-47^{\circ}C)$

4   When carrying out routine topping-up of the cooling system, always use coolant which has been mixed in the same proportion as the original coolant.

6   Radiator - removal and installation

1   Drain the cooling system as previously described, retaining the coolant if required for further use.

2   Disconnect the coolant hoses from the radiator (photos).

3   Remove the two setscrews with their plain and lock washers which secure the top half of the fan cowl to the body upper cross panel (photo).

4   Remove the two setscrews and their washers which secure the upper cowl to the lower cowl and detach the upper cowl.

5   Remove the eight setscrews with their washers and withdraw the body upper cross panel complete with header tank.

6.2A Removing radiator upper hose clip

6.2B Releasing header tank hose clip

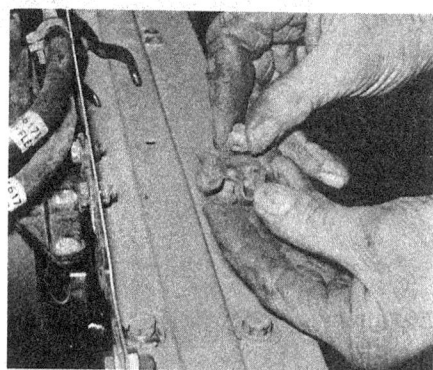

6.3 Removing radiator upper shroud bolt

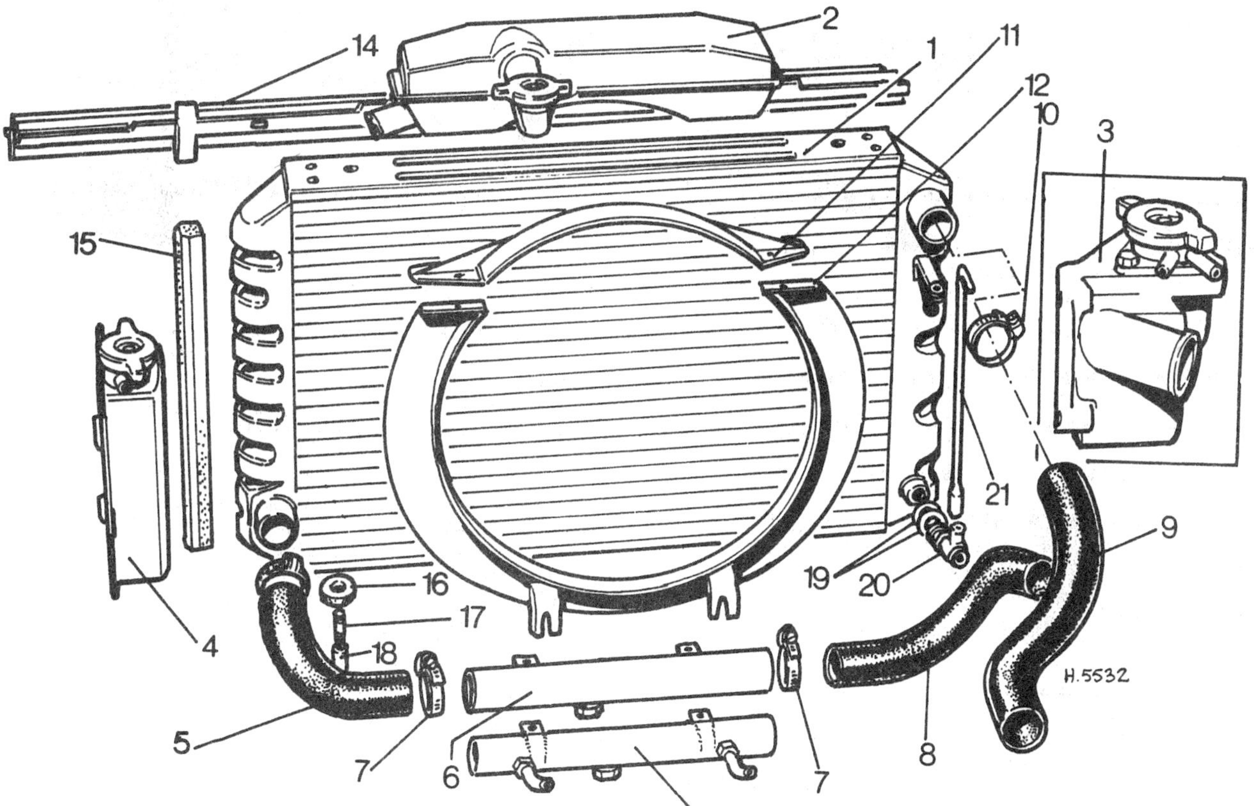

H.5532

Fig. 2.6. Radiator components (Sec. 6)

1 Matrix	6 Bottom water pipe (manual gearbox)	10 Hose clip	15 Sealing strip
2 Header tank (smaller engine)	7 Hose clip	11 Radiator cowl (top section)	16 Mounting rubber
3 Header tank (larger engine)	8 Radiator	12 Radiator cowl (bottom section)	17 Stud
4 Expansion tank (larger engine)	9 Radiator top hose	13 Bottom water pipe (automatic transmission)	18 Distance piece
5 Radiator hose		14 Upper cross panel	19 Fibre washer
			20 Drain tap
			21 Tap remote control

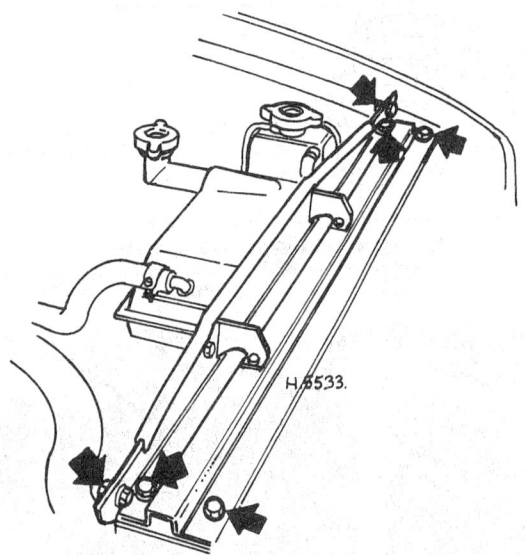

Fig. 2.7. Radiator upper mounting points (Sec. 6)

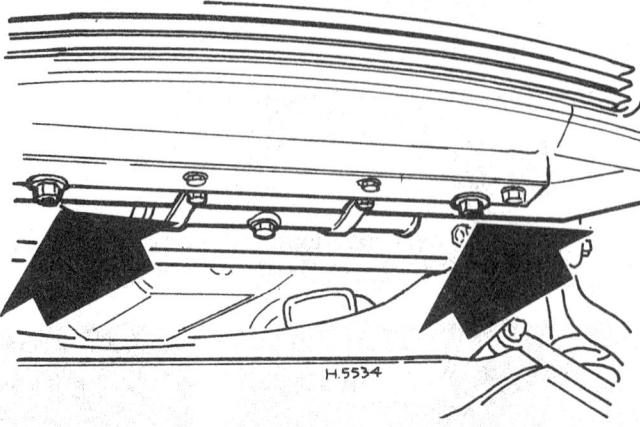

Fig. 2.8. Radiator lower mounting points (Sec. 6)

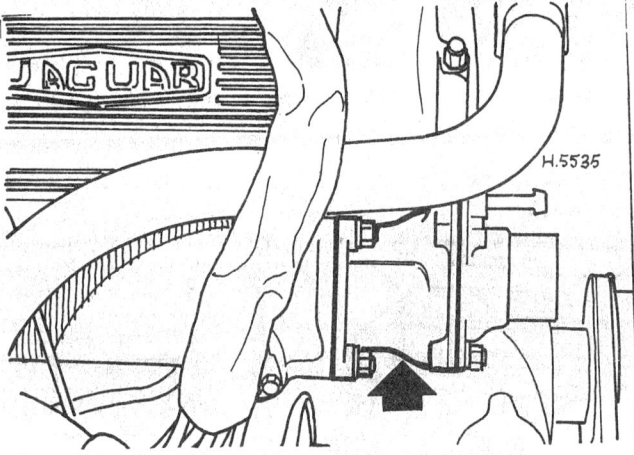

Fig. 2.9. Location of thermostat (Sec. 9)

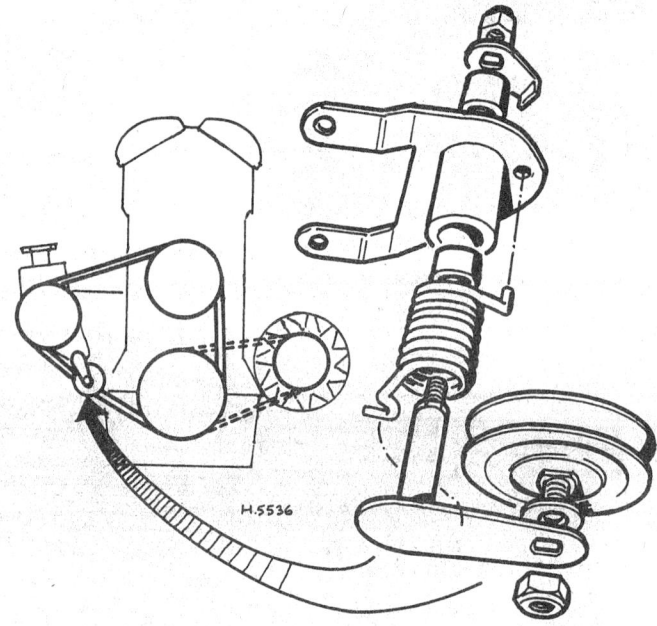

Fig. 2.10. Fan/steering pump jockey pulley (Sec. 10)

6   The header tank can be detached from the panel by the removal of two setscrews.

7   Extract the split pin and withdraw the radiator drain tap remote control rod.

8   Remove the radiator lower mounting setscrews and extract the mounting rubbers.

9   If the car is equipped with air-conditioning equipment, the setscrews must be withdrawn from the condenser mounting brackets at this stage. The condenser must then be supported away from the radiator **but on no account must any pipe be disconnected within the air-conditioning system circuit.**

10 Lift the radiator matrix clear from its side mounting cradle and collect the foam insulator.

11 Installation is a reversal of removal.

7   Bottom water pipe - removal and refitting

1   The rigid section of water pipe which is located below the radiator need normally only be removed if the flexible coolant hoses are being renewed.

2   The water pipe is fitted with a drain plug and acts as a cooler for the automatic transmission fluid on cars equipped with this type of transmission.

3   To remove the pipe, drain the cooling system and disconnect the flexible hoses from the radiator.

4   On cars with automatic transmission, disconnect the fluid pipe unions from the water pipe and plug them to prevent loss of fluid or entry of dirt.

5   Installation is a reversal of removal but with automatic transmission, check the fluid level in the transmission after the car has been driven a few miles and top-up as necessary.

8   Radiator - inspection and cleaning

1   Examine the top and bottom tanks for damage and leaking, especially at the seams. Any leaks or possible weakness can be repaired with a proprietary compound such as Holts Radweld. The application of heat to the radiator, soldering for instance, is not recommended for the home enthusiast as this may result in breaking other soldered seams.

2   Examine the core for damage and corrosion. It may be possible to repair leaks from physical damage temporarily but if leaks are present due to corrosion it is best to renew the radiator as any repair that is made will only effect a temporary remedy. A replacement radiator can be obtained from your Jaguar agent on an exchange basis.

3   When the radiator is out of the car it is advantageous to reverse flush it in the manner described in Section 3. Clean the outside of the radiator by hosing down the matrix with a strong jet of water to clean away road dirt, dead flies etc.

4   Inspect the radiator hoses for cracks, internal and external perishing and cuts on the exterior from the hose clips. Change the hose if its condition is at all doubtful. Examine the hose clips for rust and damage and renew as necessary.

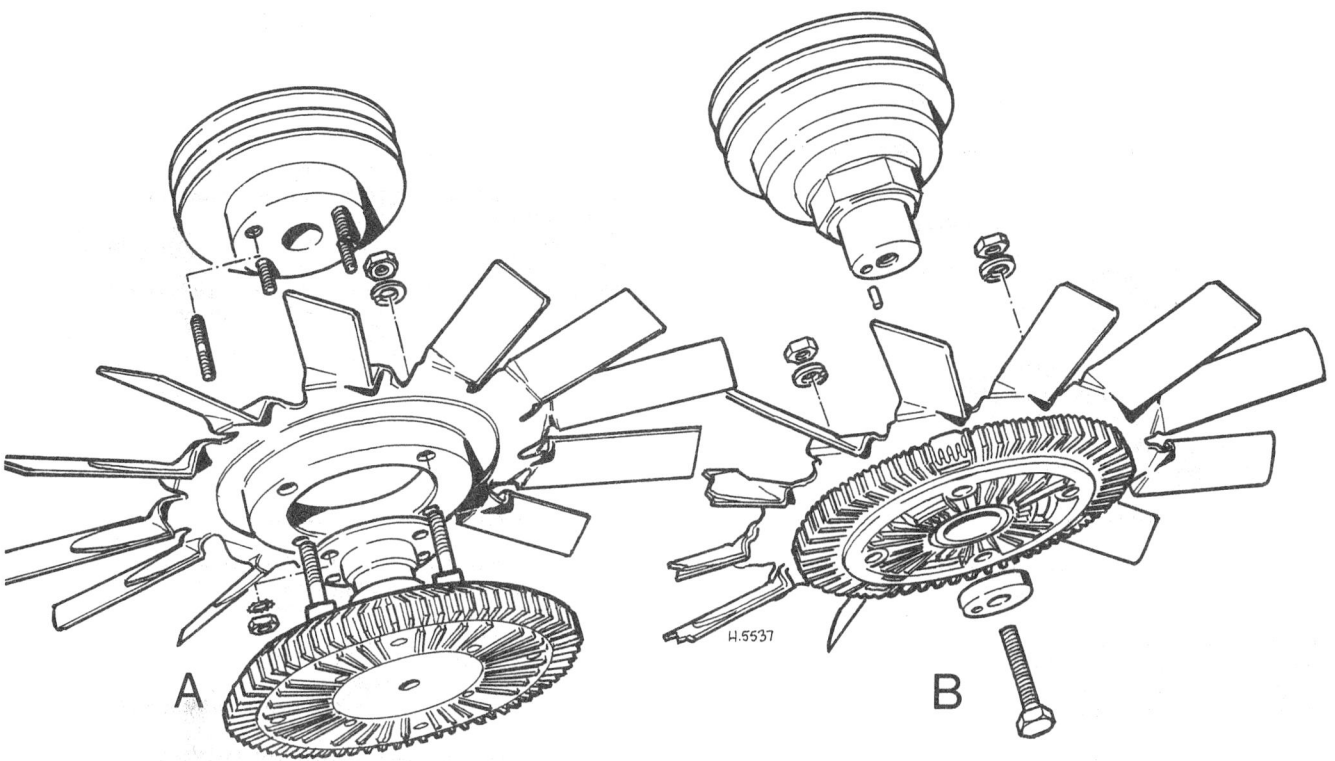

Fig. 2.11. Dismantling fan and fluid coupling (A) early cars (B) later cars (Sec. 11)

11.3 Removing fan/fluid coupling

small screwdriver will be necessary but do not lever on the circular valve which will be seen on the top face of the thermostat.
6   Clean the thermostat and ensure that the small hole on the valve is clear. If the valve is open it indicates that the thermostat is unserviceable and should be renewed with one of similar operating temperature, this figure will be seen on the top side of the thermostat.
7   If correct operation of the thermostat is in doubt test it by immersing it together with a 0 to 212°F (0 - 100°C) thermometer in a container of cold water. Heat the water, keeping it stirred, and observe if the operation of the valve is in close agreement to the temperature marked on the body of the thermostat. Allow the water to cool down and check that the valve closes correctly.
8   If the operation is satisfactory, the thermostat may be refitted in the reverse order to the above. A new gasket should be fitted between the elbow pipe and the thermostat housing.

10 Fan belt - removal and refitting

1   Release the bolt on the power steering pump adjustment strap and press the pump in towards the engine.
2   Press against the spring of the jockey pulley and ease the fan belt from the pulley and over the tips of the fan blades.
3   Refitting the belt is a reversal of removal. Adjustment of belt tension is automatic.

11 Fan unit - removal and refitting

1   On early cars, slacken the steering pump adjustment link and disconnect the drive belt. Unscrew and remove the four nuts which secure the fan to the fluid coupling.
2   Slide the fan up the hub of the pulley to expose the four nuts which secure the fluid coupling to the pulley.
3   Withdraw the fan and fluid coupling (photo).
4   On later cars, remove the top section of the fan cowl then the four nuts which secure the fan to the fluid coupling. Allow the fan to rest in the cowl.
5   Remove the centre bolt and special washer from the fluid coupling and tap the coupling off the pulley spigot. Remove the coupling and the fan.

9 Thermostat - removal, testing and refitting

1   The thermostat is located on the right-hand side at the front of the cylinder head above the steering pump.
2   To remove the thermostat first partially drain the system, approx: 8 Imp. pints (4.5 litres) will be sufficient, collect the coolant in a suitable container if it is desired to re-use it.
3   Slacken the clip securing the hose to the thermostat housing and remove the hose.
4   Remove the three nuts securing the elbow pipe to the housing and remove the pipe and gasket. The thermostat will now be visible in its housing.
5   Remove the thermostat from its housing, it is possible that it will be securely held in place by scale in which case careful levering with a

6 The fluid coupling is a sealed unit and it should be renwed if faulty, not dismantled.

7 Refitting is a reversal of removal.

12 Water pump - removal and refitting

1 Drain the cooling system by opening the radiator and cylinder block taps.

2 Remove the radiator header tank, fan, fluid coupling and the drivebelt and pulley (use an extractor for the latter).

3 Remove the power steering pump adjuster bolt.

4 If the car is equipped with air-conditioning, remove the compressor front mounting bracket.

5 Disconnect all heater hoses.

6 Remove the nuts and screws which secure the water pump to the engine front cover and withdraw the pump.

7 Clean away all traces of the old gasket.

8 Refitting is a reversal of removal but use a new gasket to which jointing compound has been applied.

13 Water pump - overhaul

1 In the event of a water pump leaking or becoming noisy in operation, undoubtedly the best way to overcome the problem is to install a new or factory reconditioned pump.

2 However, where a repair kit can be obtained, the unit can be overhauled in the following way.

3 Remove the pump and withdraw the pulley as described in the preceding Section.

4 Slacken the locknut (4) and remove the screw (3) (Fig. 2.12).

5 Press the spindle/impeller assembly from the pump. To do this, apply pressure by placing a piece of tubing against the bearing. On no account apply pressure to the end of the spindle or the bearing will be

ruined.

6 The impeller must then be supported and the spindle pressed from it.

7 Remove the seal and thrower.

8 The components cannot be further dismantled and any which are worn must be renewed as assemblies.

9 Commence reassembly by installing the spindle/bearing assembly into the pump body from the rear making sure to align the hole in the bearing with the tapped hole in the pump body. Insert the lock screw and locknut.

10 Place the rubber thrower in its groove on the spindle and in front of the seal.

11 Apply jointing compound to the outside of the brass seal housing and install the seal into the recess in the pump body.

12 Support the end of the spindle and press on the impeller to its opposite end until the gap between the impeller and the body is as shown, when measured with a feeler blade (Fig. 2.13).

13 Refit the pump pulley.

14 Water temperature gauge and transmitter

1 The water temperature gauge operates on the thermal principle using a bi-metal strip surrounded by a heater winding.

2 The transmitter unit is mounted in the inlet manifold water jacket adjacent to the thermostat.

3 Failure of the gauge to register correctly may be due to a loose connection or faulty wiring insulation.

4 Testing of the gauge or transmitter cannot be undertaken without special equipment.

5 Removal of the gauge can be carried out, as described in Chapter 10.

6 If the fuel contents gauge and the water temperature gauge both become faulty at the same time, then the instrument voltage stabilizer may be the cause.

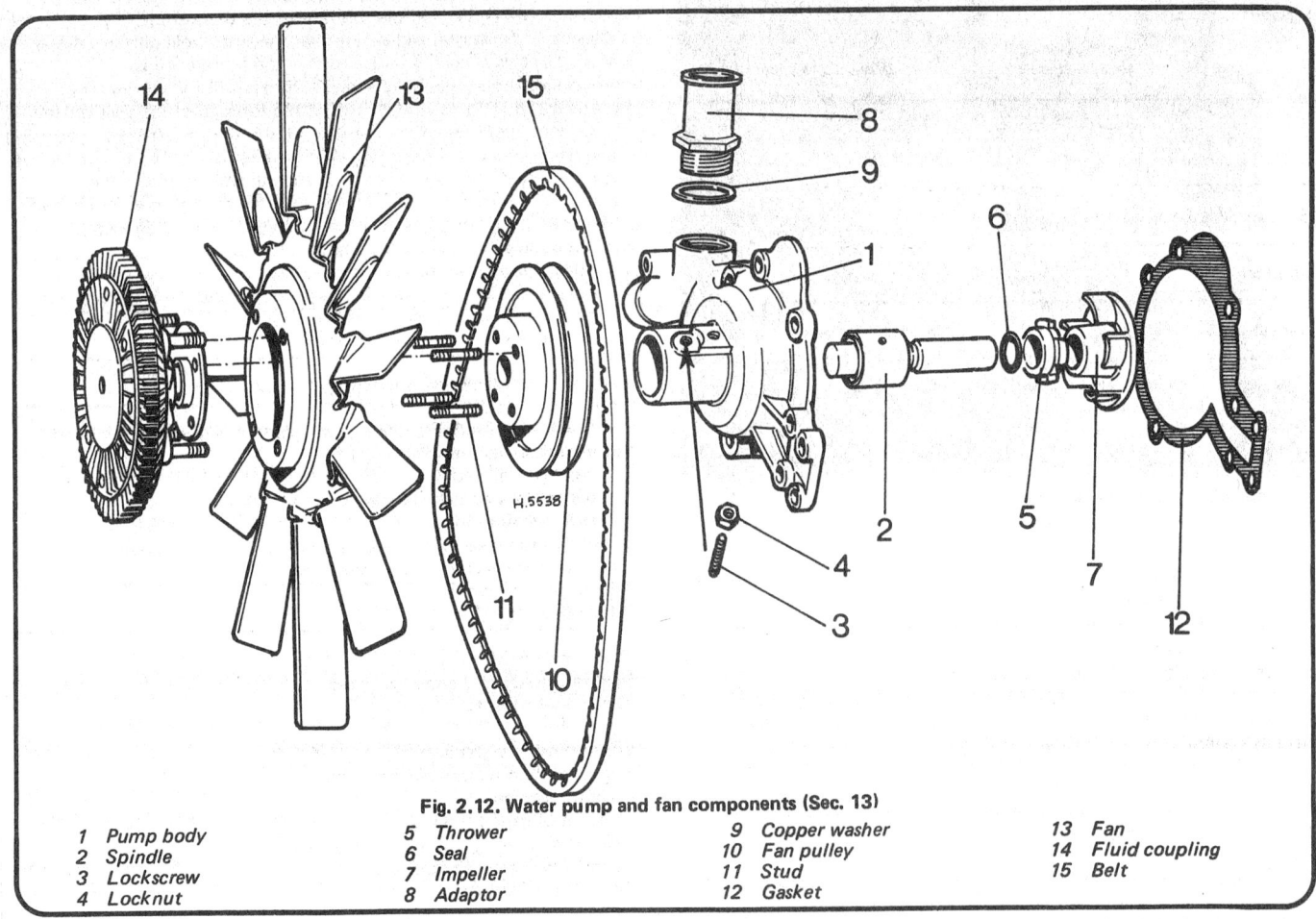

Fig. 2.12. Water pump and fan components (Sec. 13)

1	Pump body	5	Thrower	9	Copper washer	13	Fan
2	Spindle	6	Seal	10	Fan pulley	14	Fluid coupling
3	Lockscrew	7	Impeller	11	Stud	15	Belt
4	Locknut	8	Adaptor	12	Gasket		

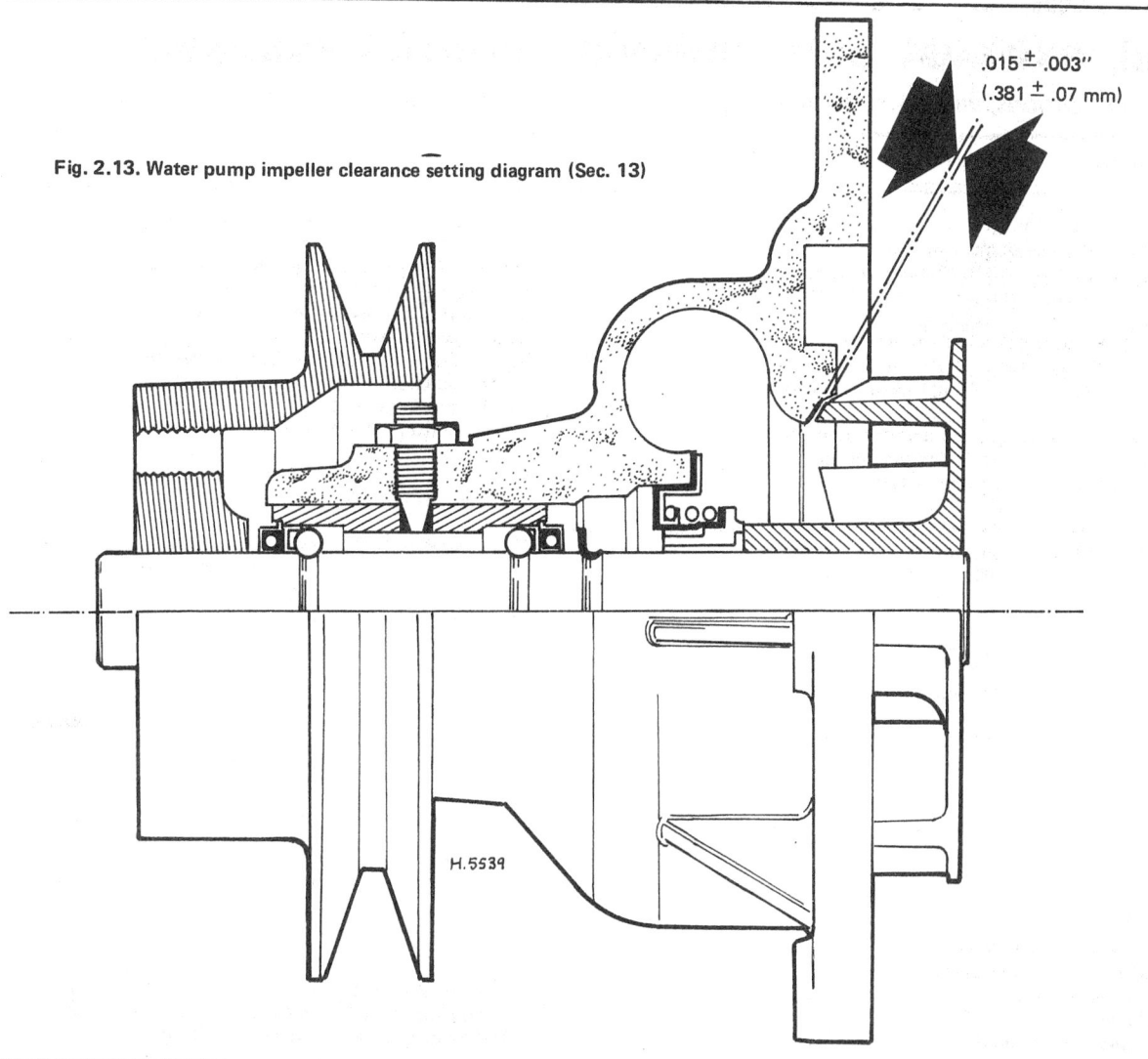

Fig. 2.13. Water pump impeller clearance setting diagram (Sec. 13)

.015 ± .003″
(.381 ± .07 mm)

H.5539

15 Fault diagnosis - cooling system

Symptom	Reason/s
Overheating	Insufficient water in cooling system.
	Fan belt slipping.
	Radiator core blocked or radiator grille obstructed.
	Thermostat not opening properly.
	Ignition advance and retard incorrectly set (accompanied by loss of power and perhaps misfiring).
	Incorrect fuel/air mixture.
	Exhaust system partially blocked.
	Oil level in sump too low.
	Blown cylinder head gasket (water/steam being forced down the radiator overflow pipe under pressure).
	Engine not yet 'run-in'.
	Brakes binding.
Engine running 'cold'	Thermostat jammed open.
	Incorrect grade of thermostat fitted.
	Thermostat missing.
Leaks in system	Loose clips on water hoses.
	Top or bottom water hoses perished.
	Radiator leaking.
	Thermostat gasket leaking.
	Pressure cap spring worn or seal ineffective.
	Cylinder wall or head cracked.
	Core plug corroded.

Chapter 3 Carburation;
fuel, exhaust and emission control systems

For modifications, and information applicable to later models, see Supplement at end of manual

Contents

Specifications

System	Dual rear mounted fuel tanks, twin electric fuel pumps and twin carburettors
Air cleaner element	Champion U510

Fuel capacity (each tank)
All models except Series 2 and 3:

Except N. America	12 Imp. gals. (54.6 litres)
N. America	11 Imp. gals. (50.0 litres/13.2 US gals.)
Series 2 and 3 (each tank)	10.5 Imp. gals. (47.75 litres/12.6 US gals.)

Fuel pumps

3.4 litre engine	Two AC Delco electric submerged
4.2 litre engine	Lucas electric roller cell with integral relief and non-return valves

Carburettors (application)
Except N. America:

Early cars	Twin SU HD8
Later cars	Twin SU HS8
N. America	Twin Stromberg 175 CD2SE (in conjunction with emission control system)

Fuel octane requirement

Low compression engines	94 octane minimum
Standard compression engines	98 octane minimum
N. America (with catalytic converter) low compression	91 octane minimum

Carburettor specification (SU HD8)

Size	2 in (5.08 cm)
Needle	UM (4.2 litre), UVV (2.8 litre)
Jet	0.125 in (3.17 mm)
Auxiliary carburettor needle	425/8

Carburettor specification (SU HS8)

Needle *	BAW (4.2 litre); BCX (3.4 litre); BAU (2.8 litre)

* Later cars with air intake temperature control BBK or BCC

Carburettor specifications (Stromberg 175 CD2SE)

Needle **	B1BT (early cars)

** Later cars B1CG (fixed orifice EGR); B2AZ (variable orifice EGR)

CO content (Stromberg carburettors with air pump delivery hose disconnected)	Not exceeding 4½%		

Idling speeds
SU HD8 carburettors:
   Manual gearbox (in neutral) ... ...   700 rev/min
   Automatic transmission (in N or P) ... ...   600 rev/min
SU HS8 carburettors:
   Manual gearbox (in neutral) ... ...   750 rev/min
   Automatic transmission (in N or P) ... ...   650 rev/min
Stromberg 175 CD2SE carburettors:
   Manual gearbox (in neutral) ... ...   750 rev/min
   Automatic transmission (in N or P) ... ...   650 rev/min

Torque wrench settings

	lb ft	Nm
Fuel tank drain plug:		
Large	28	38
Small	25	34
Fuel pipe banjo union bolts	25	34
Exhaust downpipes to manifold	25	34
Exhaust mounting to crossmember	18	25

1 General description

1 The fuel system incorporates two rear mounted fuel tanks, dual electrically-operated fuel pumps and twin carburettors.
2 Emission control equipment is fitted to later cars but only the most comprehensive systems are installed on cars destined for operation in North America.
3 The make and type of carburettors depends upon the date of production of the car and the type of emission control system with which it is equipped.
4 For cars equipped with fuel injection, refer to Chapter 13.

2 Air cleaner - renewal of element

Non-emission control type
1 Raise the toggle type clips, detach the front cover of the air cleaner and withdraw the disposable paper element (photo).
2 Wipe out the air cleaner casing and check the condition of the rubber sealing gaskets. Renew them if they are deformed or have perished.
3 If for any reason the air cleaner backplate must be removed, it can be unbolted from the carburettor flanges. Always renew the backplate gaskets before refitting.
4 Insert the new element, refit the air cleaner front cover making sure that the bottom edge of the cover engages with the lip on the backplate before locking the toggle clips.

Emission control type
5 Slacken the nut which secures the inner end of the stay to the mounting bracket (Fig. 3.2).

6 Remove the nut and bolt which secure the outer end of the stay to the mounting bracket and swing the outer end of the stay away from the air cleaner.
7 Slacken the clip and disconnect the flexible inlet pipe.
8 Slacken the clip and disconnect the air duct flexible pipe.
9 Disconnect the vacuum pipe from the vacuum capsule.
10 Release the toggle clips and withdraw the air cleaner cover.
11 Lift out and discard the filter element, wipe out the interior of

2.1 Air cleaner element

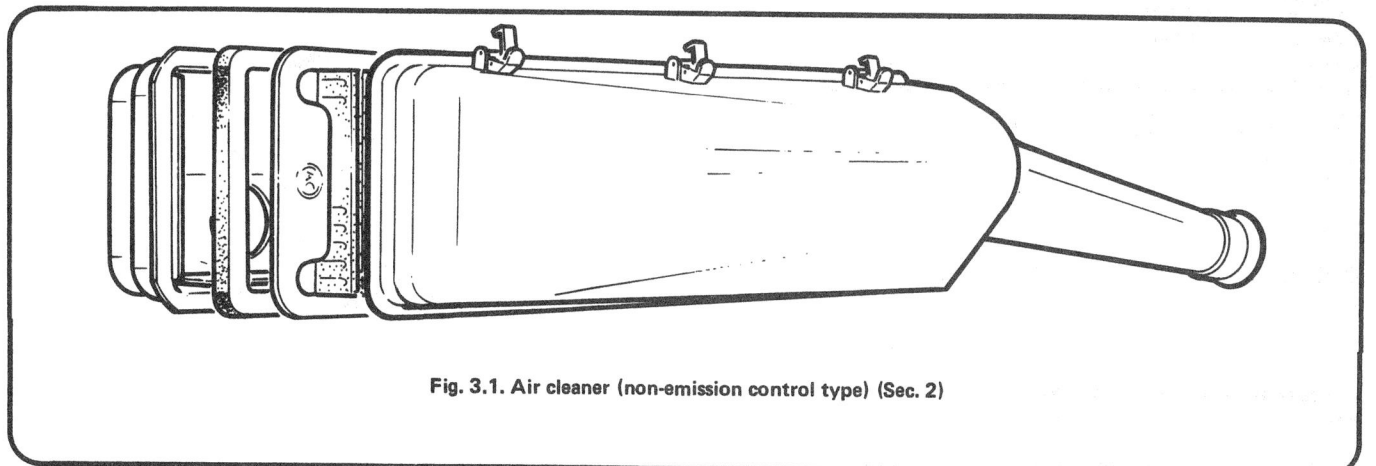

Fig. 3.1. Air cleaner (non-emission control type) (Sec. 2)

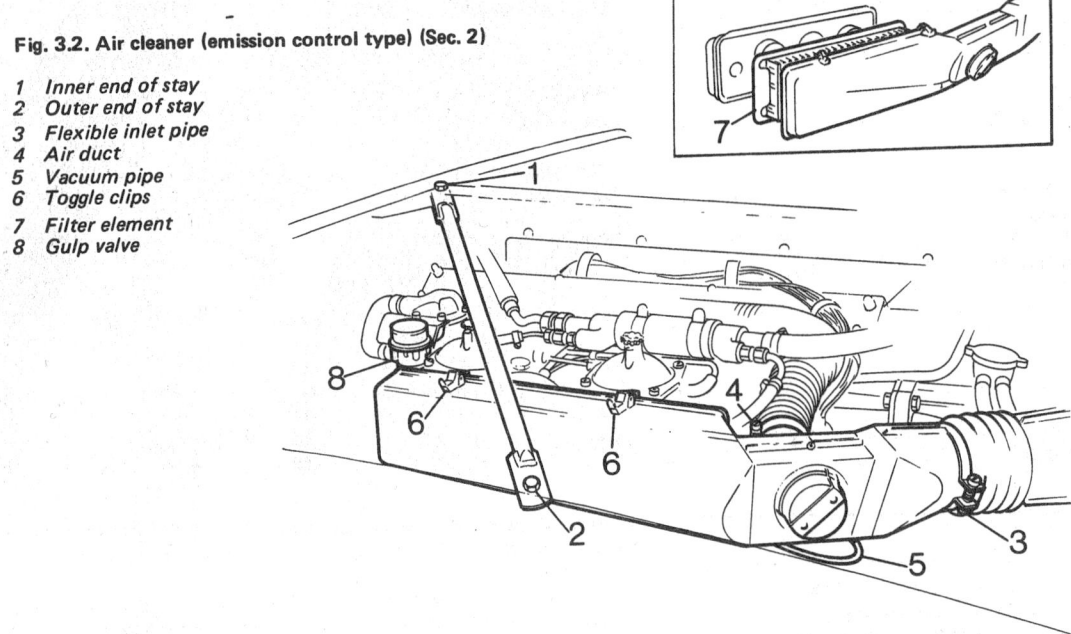

Fig. 3.2. Air cleaner (emission control type) (Sec. 2)

1   Inner end of stay
2   Outer end of stay
3   Flexible inlet pipe
4   Air duct
5   Vacuum pipe
6   Toggle clips
7   Filter element
8   Gulp valve

the casing and refit the new element by reversing the removal operations.

12 If the air cleaner backplate must be removed for any reason, first withdraw the element as just described and then prise the gulp valve hose from the backplate. Unbolt the backplate, withdraw it from the carburettor flanges and disconnect the vacuum pipe from the thermal sensing switch.

13 Refit by reversing the removal process using new flange gaskets.

3   Fuel line filter (up to 1973) - renewal of element

1   On cars built up until 1973, a disposable element glass bowl type filter is located on the wing valance within the engine compartment.

2   At the specified maintenance intervals, close the fuel tap on top of the filter by turning it fully clockwise.

3   Slacken the locknut and swing the retaining clip to one side so that the filter bowl can be removed.

4   Discard the element and wipe out the bowl (photo).

5   Check that the sealing washers are in good condition, otherwise renew them.

6   Insert the new filter element and refit the bowl and turn the fuel tap anticlockwise.

4   Fuel line filter (1973 on) - renewal of element

1   The filter is located on one side of the spare wheel recess.

2   In the interest of safety, disconnect the lead from the battery negative terminal.

3   Remove the spare wheel.

4   Fit a clamp on the fuel inlet pipe. A pair of self-locking grips will serve this purpose provided that the pipe is protected by wrapping something round it first.

5   Place a suitable container underneath the filter and then unscrew the centre bolt which retains the filter bowl.

6   Discard the filter element and wipe out the bowl and then check that the seals are in good condition.

7   Install the new element and refit the filter bowl but do not overtighten the centre bolt.

8   Remove the container and pipe clamp, reconnect the battery and start the engine and check for leaks from the filter.

9   Refit the spare wheel into its recess.

5   Carburettor fuel filters - cleaning

1   On cars with SU carburettors, a small gauze filter is located in the fuel inlet union on each of the carburettor float chambers.

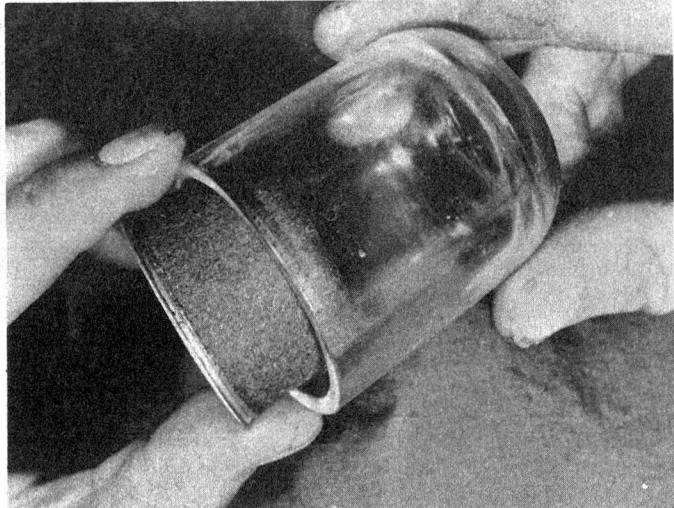

3.4 Fuel filter element

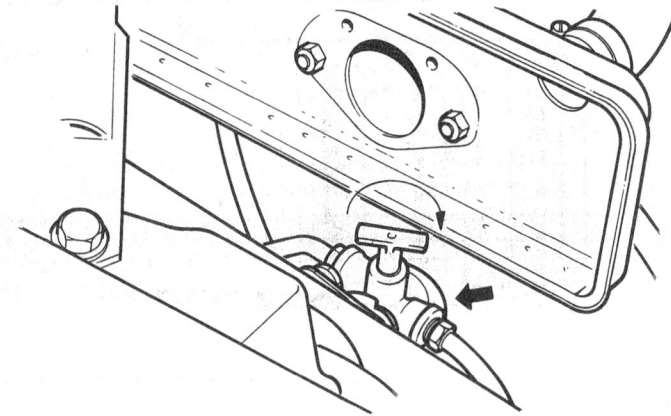

Fig. 3.3. Fuel line filter (up to 1973) (Sec. 3)

Fig. 3.4. Fuel line filter (1973 onwards) (Sec. 4)

3   *Fuel pipe temporary clamp*   7   *Filter centre bolt*

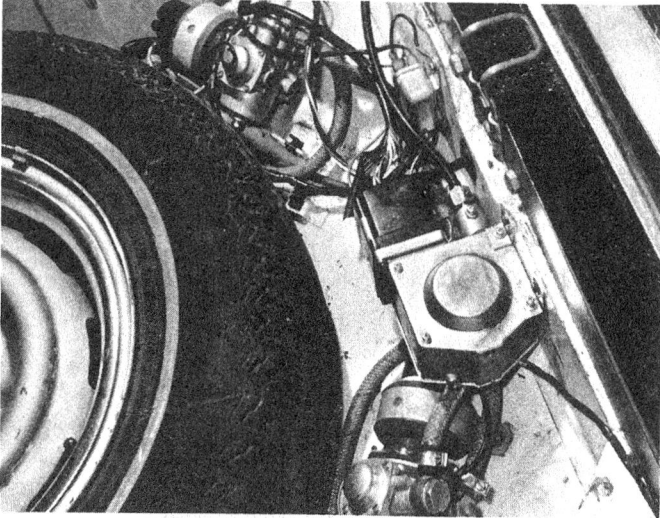

6.1 Location of electric fuel pumps

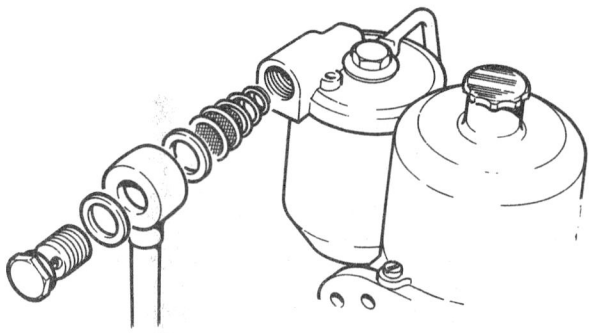

Fig. 3.5. S.U. fuel inlet filter (Sec. 5)

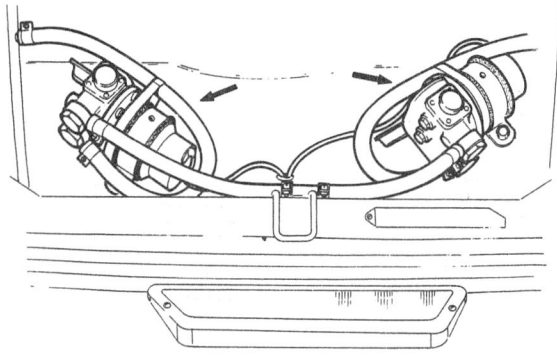

Fig. 3.6. Location of fuel pumps (Sec. 6)

2   At the specified maintenance intervals, remove the hollow bolts from the banjo unions and extract the filter and spring.
3   Clean the filter gauze using a small brush and some clean fuel and then refit by reversing the dismantling operation. Make sure that a fibre washer is located each side of the banjo union.

6   Fuel pumps - removal and refitting

1   The dual fuel pumps are located in the spare wheel recess below the luggage compartment floor panel (photo).
2   Remove the floor panel and the spare wheel.
3   Remove the pump protective covers.
4   Either drain the fuel tank or clamp the inlet hose to prevent loss of fuel when the pump which is to be removed is disconnected.
5   Disconnect the lead from the battery negative terminal.
6   Disconnect the leads from the pump which is going to be removed.
7   Disconnect the fuel pipes and the pump mounting clamp and lift the fuel pump from its location.
8   Refitting is a reversal of removal but make sure that the rubber insulated mounting studs have not deteriorated otherwise excessive pump noise can occur.

7   Fuel pump - overhaul

1   With the pump removed from the car unwind the tape and remove the band.
2   Remove the insulating sleeve, nut, connector and washer and lift off the end cap.
3   Mark the relationship of the pump body to the coil housing and then extract the coil housing screws and lift off the housing.

4   Unscrew and remove (anticlockwise) the diaphragm and spindle. Do not try to dismantle the diaphragm/spindle.
5   Extract the contact blade securing screw and the pedestal securing screws and lift off the condenser.
6   Remove the washer, terminal nut, contact and terminal tag.
7   Lift off the pedestal complete with rocker assembly.
8   Extract the pin and detach the rocker assembly.
9   Extract the two crosshead screws and lift off the clamp plate, valve caps, valves, sealing washers and filter.
10 Extract the screws which secure the flow smoothing device cover and lift off the cover, 'O' ring, diaphragm and support ring.
11 Remove the inlet air bottle cover and gasket.
12 Renew any worn components and all gaskets and seals.
13 Commence reassembly by fitting the rocker assembly to the pedestal.
14 Fit the terminal stud, spring washer, terminal, terminal tag, nut and seal.
15 Install pedestal and condenser.
16 Fit impact washer and the spring to the diaphragm spindle.
17 Fit the diaphragm and then screw the spindle into the trunnion until the rocker will not throw over.
18 Fit the plastic armature guide (flat face towards diaphragm) and then unscrew the diaphragm spindle until the rocker will just throw over then unscrew it to its nearest hole plus a further 2/3rds of a turn. This is the correct diaphragm setting.
19 Refit the valves into the body, fit the clamp plate but do not overtighten the screws.
20 Fit the flow smoothing diaphragm, the 'O' ring and the cover.
21 Fit the air bottle cover and the gasket, making sure not to overtighten the centre screw.
22 Connect the coil housing to the pump body making sure that they are in their original relative positions, insert the screws and tighten

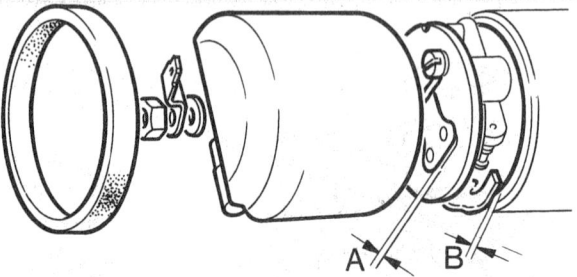

Fig. 3.8. Fuel pump contact setting diagram (Sec. 7)

A 0.030 to 0.040 in (0.77 to 1.03 mm)
B 0.065 to 0.075 in (1.67 to 1.93 mm)

diagonally.
23 Fit the contact blade.
24 Now using a feeler blade, check the two gaps shown in Fig. 3.8. If necessary, bend the stop finger to achieve the specified clearances.
25 Install the end cap, seal and cover joint. Tape the joint with fresh tape.

8 Fuel tanks - removal, servicing and installation

1   A fuel tank is located in each of the rear wings. Each tank has its own filler cap and level transmitter.
2   Certain models have a fuel evaporative emission control device (see Section 28) but the following operations still apply except that additional pipework is connected to the tank.
3   Disconnect the rear number plate lamp and remove the rear bumper.
4   Remove the fuel tank cover panel (fifteen screws).
5   Remove the drain plug and drain the fuel into a clean container.
6   Remove the exhaust tail pipe.
7   Unscrew and remove the four setscrews and detach the fuel filler assembly from the body.
8   Disconnect the flexible hose from the overflow pipe.
9   Disconnect the fuel pump feed pipe from the union at the base of the tank.
10 Remove the cover plate from the rear of the wheel arch and disconnect the two electrical leads from the tank transmitter unit. Mark the leads so that they can be correctly reconnected.
11 Unscrew and remove the tank securing bolts. These are accessible in the following positions:
   Wheel arch.
   Side panel within luggage compartment.
   Lower rear edge of fuel tank accessible through aperture from which exhaust tail pipe has been removed.
   Self-locking nut on support rod at the front lower edge of tank.
12 Carefully lower the tank and remove it.
13 If the tank contains sediment, remove the transmitter unit (Section 9) and shake the tank vigorously using several changes of fuel.
14 If the tank has a leak, never be tempted to repair it by soldering or welding but leave it to professional repairers. A fuel tank must be steamed out for several hours before risk of explosion can be eliminated. A temporary repair can be made using a proprietary compound.
15 Installation is a reversal of removal.

9 Fuel tank transmitter and level gauge

1   A fuel contents transmitter unit is installed in each fuel tank.
2   In the event of a fault developing, first check all the connecting wires and terminals for security.
3   Refer to Chapter 2, Section 14.
4   Remove the cover plate and disconnect the transmitter electrical leads.
5   On later models, remove the rear lamp cluster for better access.
6   Removal of a tank transmitter unit can be carried out using two levers to rotate the securing ring.
7   Always use a new rubber sealing ring when installing the transmitter unit.

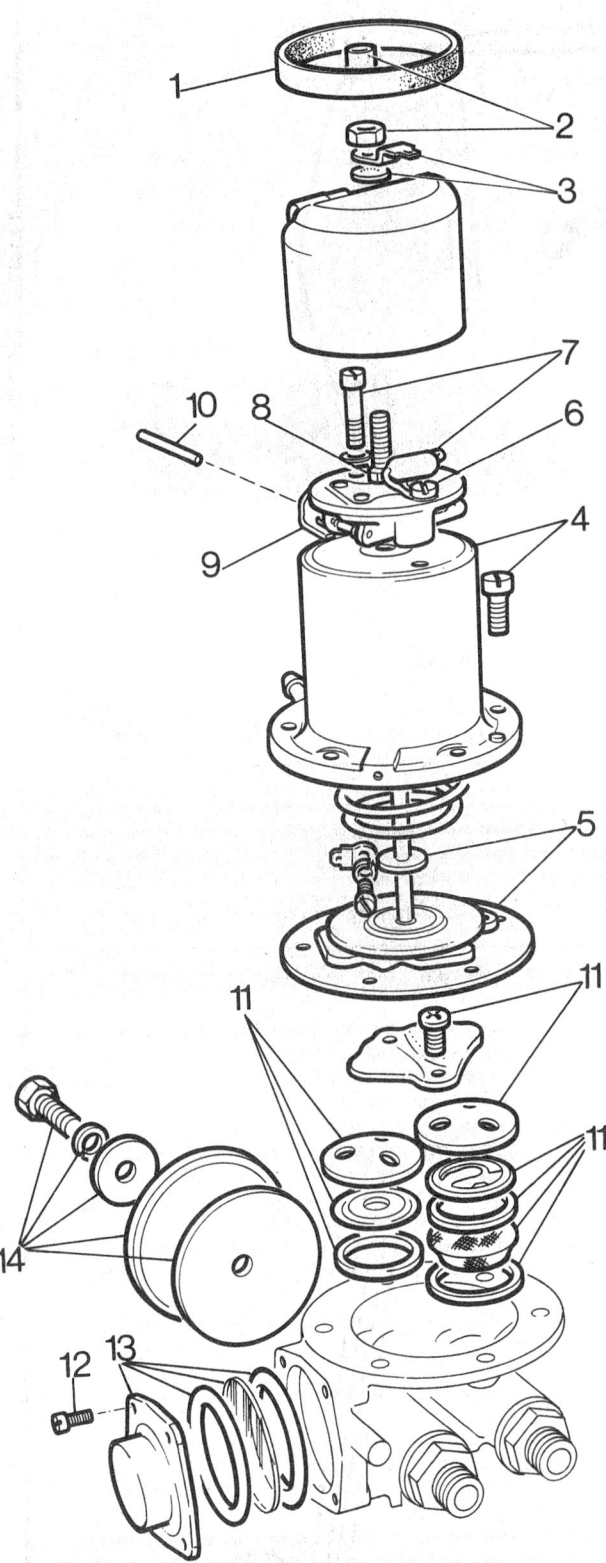

Fig. 3.7. Exploded view of a fuel pump (Sec. 7)

1	*Seal*	*8*	*Terminal nut*
2	*Sleeve, nut*	*9*	*Pedestal/rocker assembly*
3	*Washer and connector*	*10*	*Rocker assembly pin*
4	*Coil housing*	*11*	*Clamp plate, valves and filter*
5	*Diaphragm and spindle*	*12*	*Screw*
6	*Contact blade screw*	*13*	*Flow smoothing device*
7	*Pedestal screws and condenser*	*14*	*Inlet air bottle*

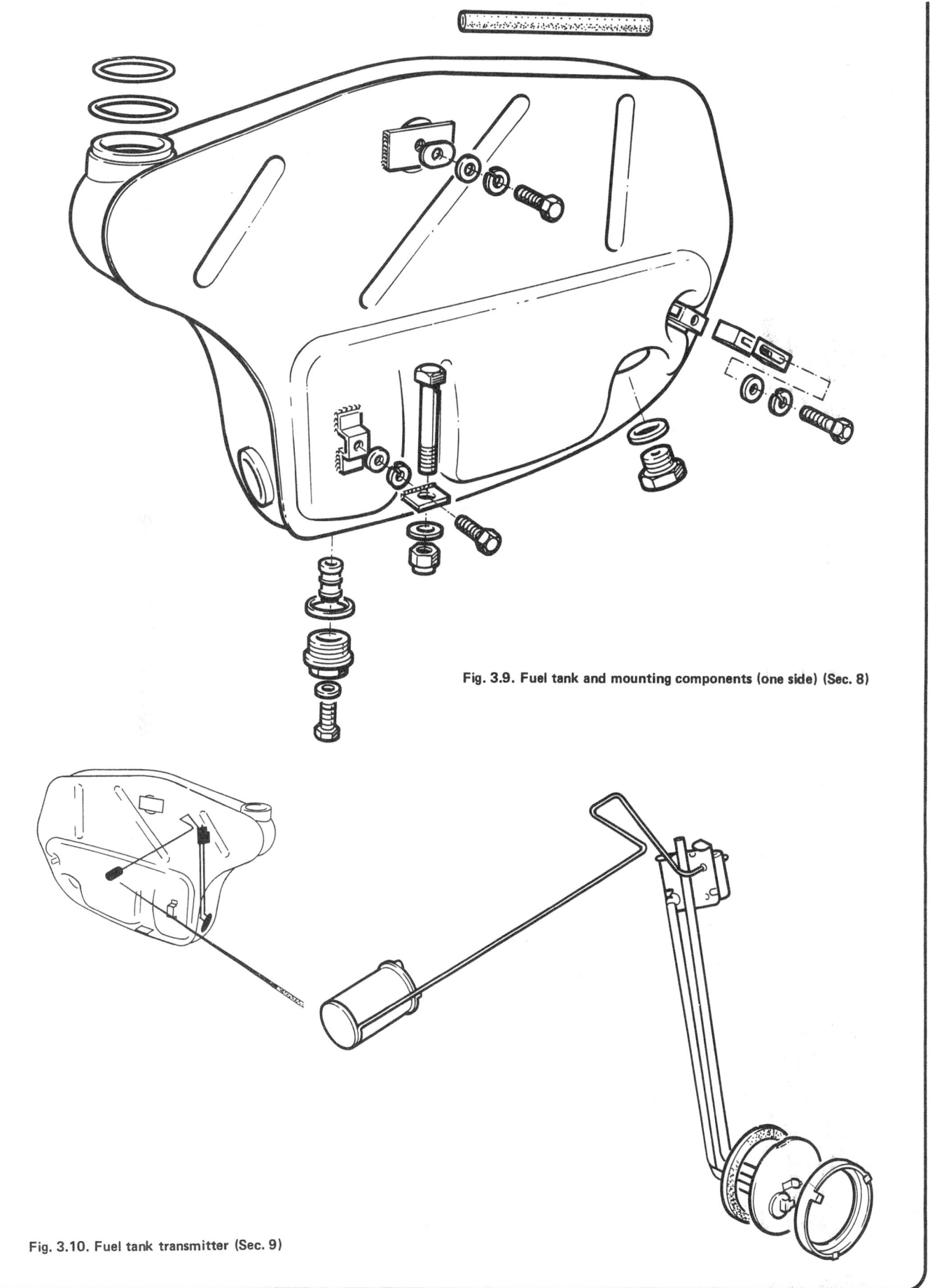

Fig. 3.9. Fuel tank and mounting components (one side) (Sec. 8)

Fig. 3.10. Fuel tank transmitter (Sec. 9)

10 Carburettors - description and maintenance

1   A twin carburettor arrangement is fitted to all models but the carburettors, although of variable choke design, differ in type and make according to engine size and operating territory.

2   The only regular maintenance required is to clean the fuel filter gauze on SU carburettors and to check and top-up the oil in the dampers on all models.

3   To top-up the damper, unscrew the piston cap and withdraw the piston assembly. Inject SAE 20 engine oil into the hollow piston and then refit the piston. When sufficient oil has been injected, the piston should require a firm downward pressure to install it.

11 SU carburettor (HD8) - adjustment and tuning

1   It is useless to attempt carburettor tuning until the cylinder compressions, valve clearances, spark plug gaps and contact breaker gaps have been tested, checked and adjusted as necessary. The distributor centrifugal advance mechanism and vacuum advance

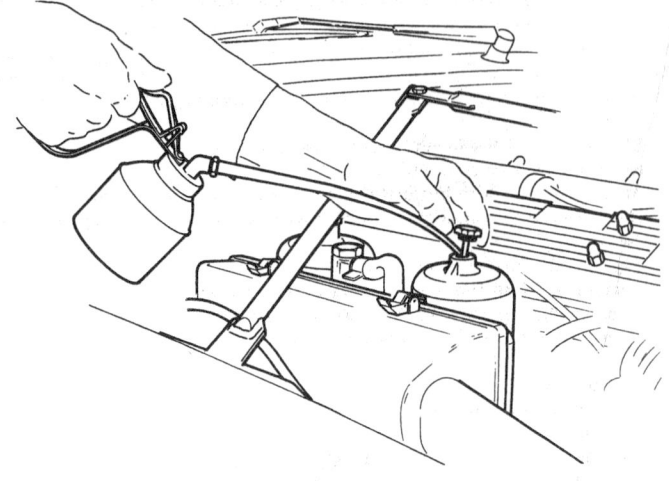

Fig. 3.11. Topping up a carburettor damper (Sec. 10)

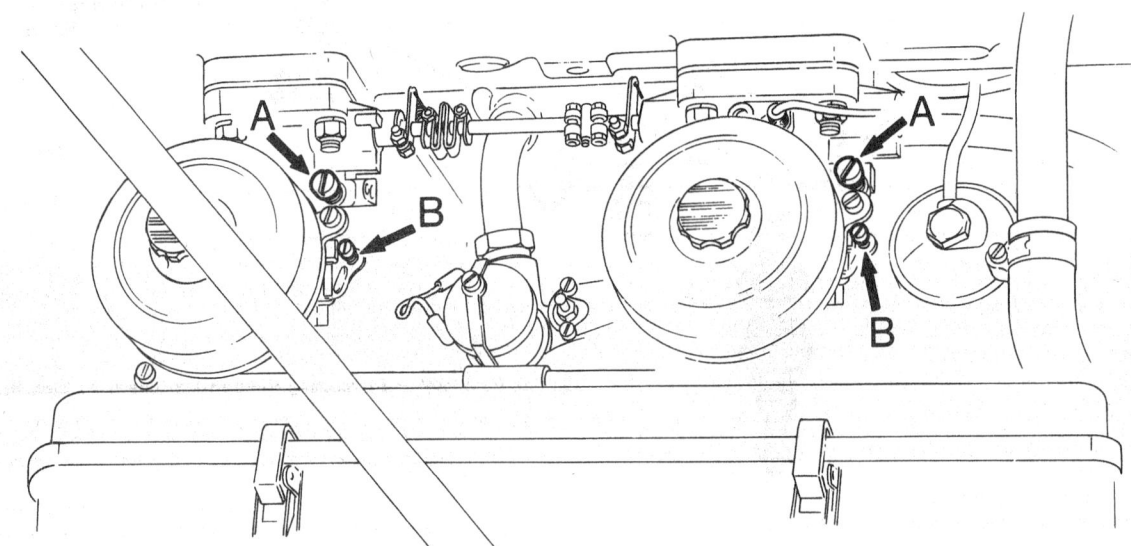

Fig. 3.12. SU - HD8 carburettor adjustment screws (Sec. 11)

A   Slow-running volume screws   B   Mixture adjusting screws

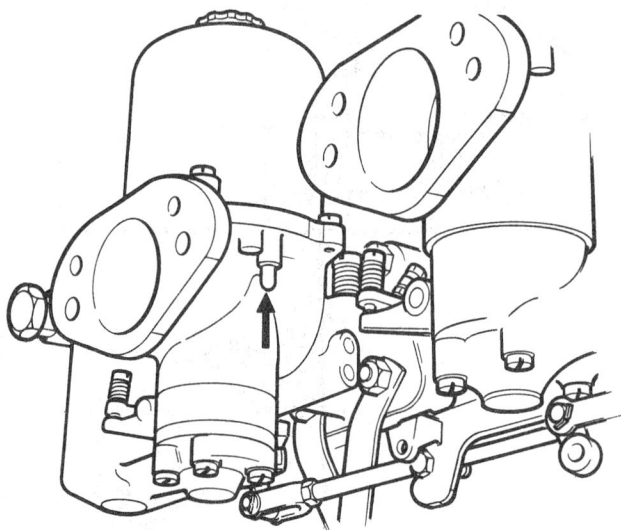

Fig. 3.13. Piston lifting pin (SU carburettor) (Sec. 11)

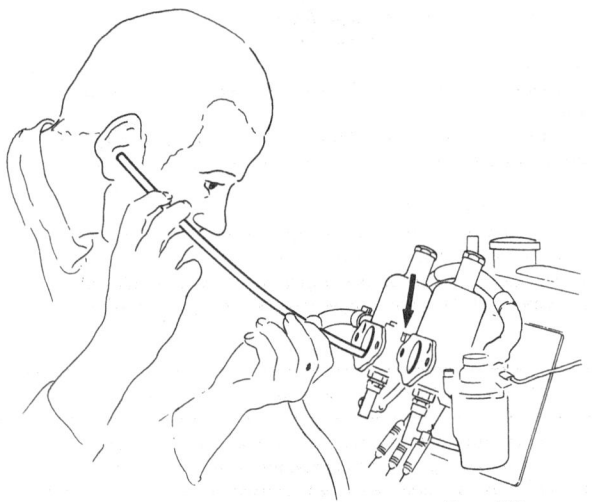

Fig. 3.14. Synchronising SU carburettors (Sec. 11)

operation should be checked and ignition timing set to the correct figure. The ignition timing is important since if retarded or advanced too far the setting of the carburettors will be affected. Check that petrol filters are clean.

2 Run the engine to normal operating temperature and then remove the air cleaner.

3 Slacken one of the pinch bolts on the coupling which is located between the throttle spindles.

4 Make sure that both butterfly valve plates are fully closed by rotating the throttle spindles clockwise when viewed from the front of the car.

5 Tighten the coupling pinch bolt.

6 Screw in each of the slow-running volume screws (A) until they are fully seated then unscrew each screw exactly two turns (Fig. 3.12.)

7 Remove the piston and suction chambers and unscrew each of the mixture adjusting screws (B) until each jet is flush with the bridge of its carburettor.

8 Refit the pistons and suction chambers and then check that each piston falls freely by pressing the small lifting pin upwards and letting the pistons fall onto their bridges. A distinct 'clunk' should be heard.

9 Turn each of the screws (B) down 2½ turns and then top-up the piston dampers with SAE 20 oil.

10 Start the engine and adjust each of the volume screws (A) by an equal amount until the engine idling speed is 600 rev/min for cars equipped with automatic transmission or 700 rev/min for cars with manual transmission. To make sure that both carburettors are synchronised, use a length of tubing placed between the carburettor intake and the ear and adjust screws (A) fractionally until the hiss from both units is similar. Alternatively, use a balancing device (flowmeter) in accordance with its manufacturer's instructions.

11 When the carburettors have been correctly synchronised, screw the mixture screws (B) up or down by a similar amount until the fastest idling speed is obtained consistent with even firing. If necessary, readjust the volume screws (A) until the specified idling speeds are again obtained.

12 Now check the mixture strength. With the engine idling raise the piston on the front carburettor by about 1/32 in (0.8 mm) using the lifting pin. One of the following conditions will occur:

The engine speed increases and continues at this higher speed indicating a rich mixture.

The engine speed drops and may even stall indicating a weak mixture.

The engine speed momentarily increases slightly then resumes its previous level. This indicates that the mixture is correct.

13 Repeat the mixture strength tests on the rear carburettor and then recheck the front one again as the carburettors are interdependent.

12 SU carburettors (HD8) - removal and installation

1 Remove the air cleaner, including the backplate and filter element (see Section 2).

2 Close the tap on the fuel filter and disconnect the fuel line banjo unions from the carburettor float chambers.

3 Remove the distributor vacuum advance pipe.

4 Disconnect the fuel feed pipe from the auxiliary starting carburettor.

5 Disconnect the throttle cables and the leads from the choke solenoid.

6 On cars equipped with automatic transmission, remove the spring clip which secures the kick-down link at the rear of the rear carburettor.

7 Disconnect the throttle return springs.

8 Remove the four nuts which secure each carburettor to the inlet manifold and lift the carburettors away.

9 Installation is a reversal of removal but always renew the gaskets or 'O' rings located on the flanges whichever type of sealing device is used.

13 SU carburettor (HD8) - examination, overhaul and adjustment

1 The SU carburettor, generally speaking is most reliable and it is very rarely that you would have to completely dismantle it. However, after a long period of use some deterioration must be expected, therefore when the time arrives for a major overhaul of the engine, serious

consideration should be given to replacing the carburettors with factory reconditioned items.

2 Thoroughly clean the outside of the carburettor.

3 Clean down the top of the bench, it is advisable to lay out a sheet of paper on which all parts can be placed as they are removed.

4 Unscrew the damper and remove it together with its washer.

5 Using a small file or scriber, mark the suction chamber so that it can be refitted in its original position.

6 Remove the three suction chamber securing screws and remove the chamber from the body leaving the piston in position. Be careful when lifting off the suction chamber not to apply side loads to the piston otherwise the piston needle may be bent.

7 Lift the piston spring from the piston noting which way round it is fitted.

8 Remove the piston and invert it over a container to allow the oil in the damper bore to drain out. Place the piston in a safe place so that the needle will not be damaged or that the piston will not roll onto the floor. It is suggested that the piston is placed in a suitably sized jar with the needle inside, so acting as a stand.

9 It is recommended that, unless absolutely necessary, the needle is not separated from the piston. However, if the needle must be removed, slacken the retaining screw in the side of the body and remove the needle.

10 Mark the position of the float chamber lid in relation to the body. Undo the cap nut and remove it together with the washer. Lift off the float chamber lid.

11 Withdraw the pin from the float chamber lever and remove the lever. You will find that the pin is serrated and can be removed in one direction only.

12 Using the correct sized spanner, unscrew the brass valve body and remove it together with the float needle.

13 Lift the float out of the float chamber and place it in a position where it will not be damaged.

14 Remove the four setscrews securing the float chamber to the body.

15 Separate the float chamber from the body and this will free the jet spring, the jet and diaphragm and the jet housing which may now be lifted out of the body.

16 Unscrew the jet bearing nut and lift out the jet bearing.

17 Unscrew the slow running control valve from the body and collect the spring and the gland washers. Note the position of the gland washers for reassembly.

18 No further dismantling of the carburettor is necessary, indeed, it is rarely that dismantling beyond the stage decided in paragraph 13 will ever be required.

19 Reassembly is the reverse of the above. Fit new washers throughout and, if you removed the jet needle, install it in the piston so that the shoulder of the needle is flush with the base of the piston.

20 The jet will almost certainly require centring in the following way.

21 Using a ring spanner, slacken the jet locking nut approximately half a turn.

22 Refer to Fig. 3.17. Replace the jet and diaphragm assembly. Push

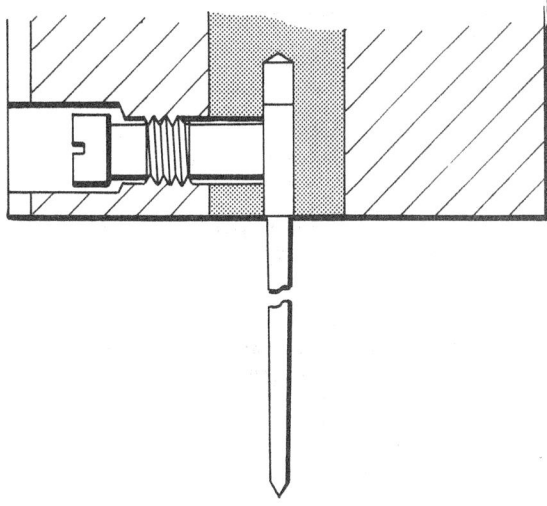

Fig. 3.15. Jet needle setting diagram (SU carburettor) (Sec. 13)

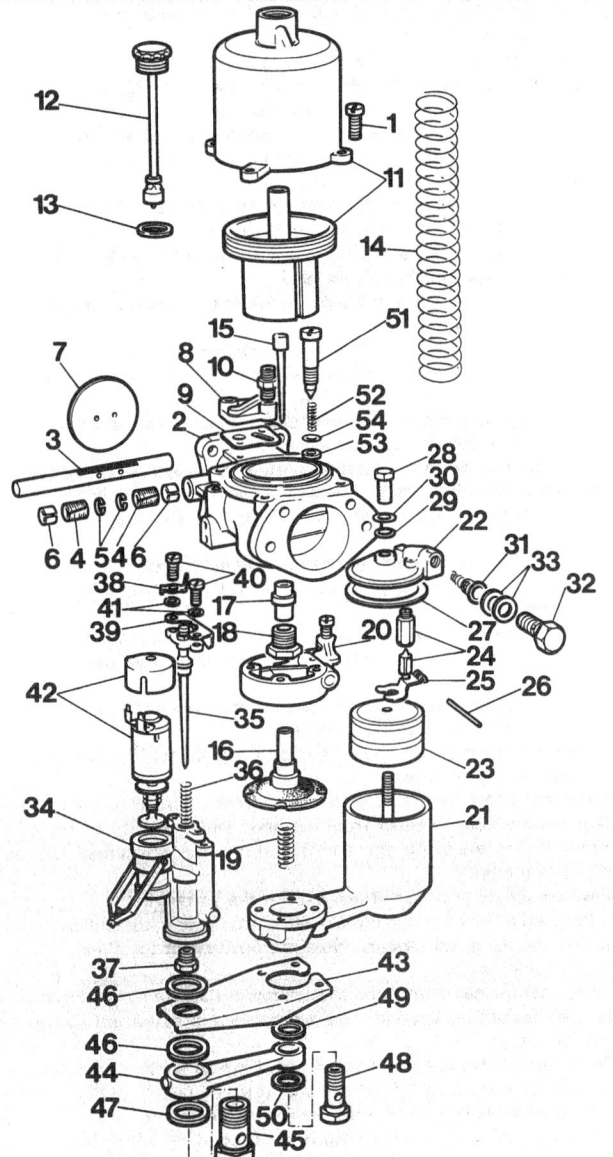

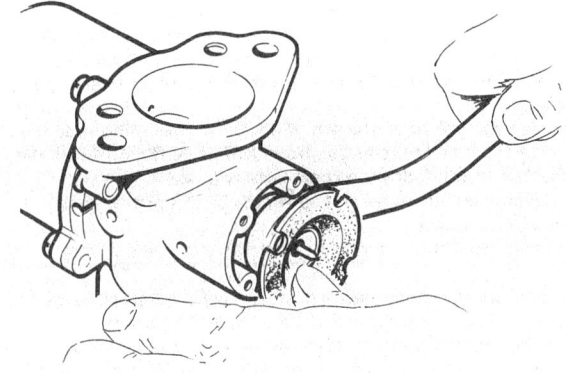

Fig. 3.17. Centring the jet (SU carburettor) (Sec. 13)

the jet and diaphragm assembly as high as possible with hand pressure and at the same time press the piston down onto the jet bridge, using a pencil or a piece of rod for this. Centralisation will be helped by lightly tapping on the side of the carburettor body.

23 Tighten the jet locking nut.

24 The actual centring must be carried out with the setscrew holes in the jet diaphragm and carburettor in alignment. After tightening the jet locking nut the jet diaphragm must be kept in the same position relative to the carburettor body and to do this it is advisable to mark one of the corresponding jet diaphragm and carburettor setscrew holes with a soft pencil. Centring will be upset if the diaphragm is moved radically after tightening the jet nut.

25 The jet is correctly centred when the piston falls freely and hits the jet 'bridge' with a metallic click. Check if there is any difference in the sound of the piston hitting the bridge with the jet in its highest and lowest positions. If there is any difference in the sound, the procedure for centralising the jet will have to be repeated.

26 The float level should be checked, particularly if flooding of the carburettor has been encountered during operating conditions. To do this, invert the float chamber lid and check that a bar 7/16 in (11.1 mm) in diameter will just slide between the float lever fork and the lid as shown. Any correction must be carried out by bending at the junction of the curved and straight sections of the lever (Fig. 3.18).

27 Finally, and before fitting the suction chamber, fill the piston damper bore to within ¼ in (6.35 mm) of its top with SAE 20 engine oil, wipe any spillage off the outside of the piston. After fitting the

suction chamber, raise the piston by means of the lifting pin and check that it falls back smartly on to the upper face of the body. Any sluggishness, assuming all other factors to be correct, will probably be due to oil on the outside of the piston.

28 Whenever a carburettor has been overhauled and refitted to the engine, carry out the adjustments described in Section 11.

14 SU carburettor (HD8) - auxiliary starting carburettor - adjustment

1 Run the engine to normal operating temperature.

2 Adjust the stop screw until the mixture has a tendency towards richness. This stage should be evident by the emission of black gases from the exhaust when lower temperature engine running is artificially created by energising the solenoid by short circuiting the terminal of the thermostatic switch directly to earth with a screwdriver and flicking open the throttles. Actuation of the auxiliary starting carburettor will be evident by a pronounced hissing noise (photo).

3 The stop screw should be turned in an anticlockwise direction to enrich the mixture. Ideally turn the screw to the point where any further movement would cause the engine to idle roughly under conditions where the thermostatic switch is being short circuited.

4 If for any reason the thermostatic switch must be removed, loss of water from the cooling system will be minimised if the radiator filler cap is kept securely tightened.

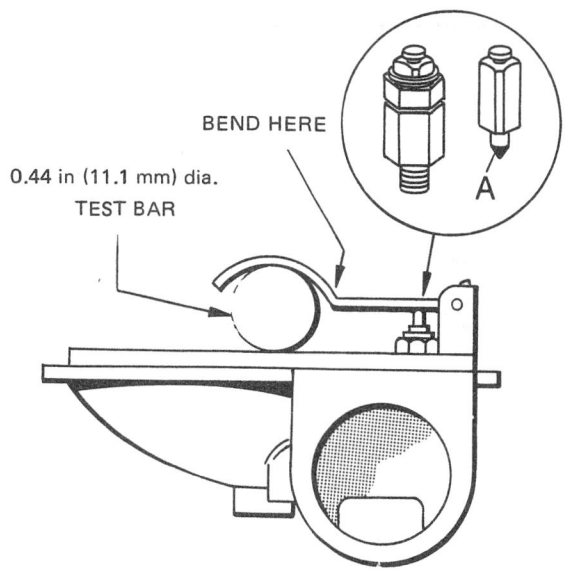

BEND HERE

0.44 in (11.1 mm) dia.
TEST BAR

A

Fig. 3.18. Float lever setting diagram (SU carburettor) (Sec. 13)

A   Coned end of needle valve

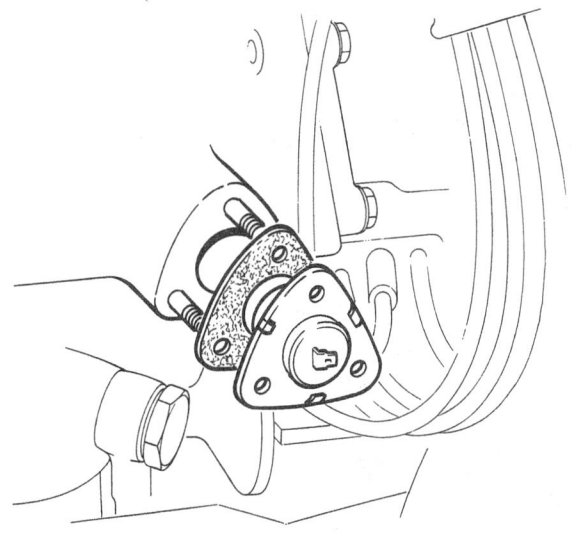

Fig. 3.20. Thermostatic switch - SU auxiliary starting carburettor
(Sec. 14)

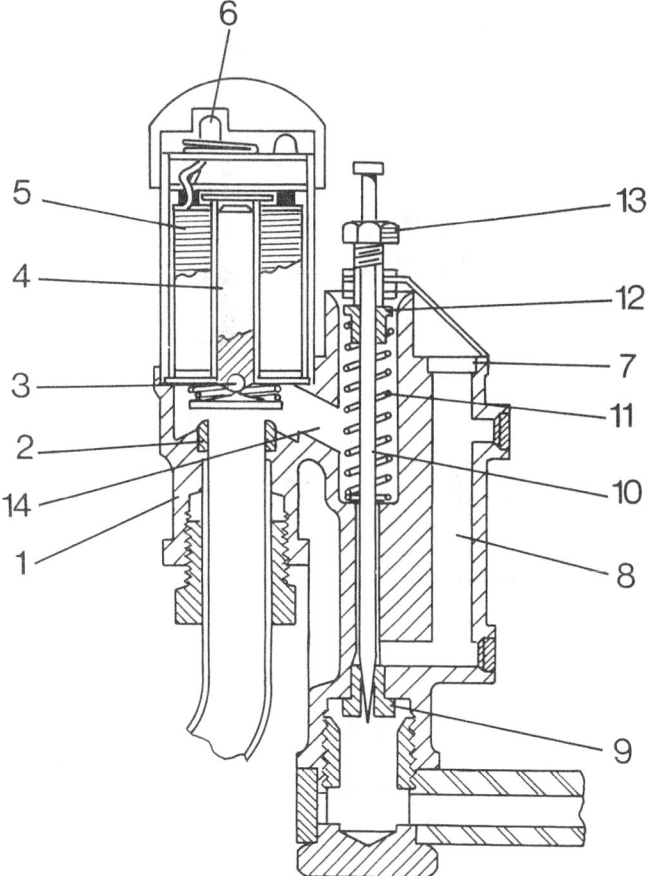

Fig. 3.19. Sectional view of auxiliary starting carburettor (SU) (Sec. 14)

1 Body	8 Connecting passage
2 Valve seating	9 Jet
3 Valve	10 Needle
4 Iron core (solenoid)	11 Spring
5 Solenoid winding	12 Disc
6 Solenoid terminals	13 Adjustable stop
7 Air intake	14 Connecting passage

(Refer also to Fig. 3.16).

14.2 Auxiliary starting carburettor (SU HD8)

15 SU carburettor (HS8) - adjustment and tuning

1   The twin carburettor installation of this type incorporates an automatic enrichment device (A.E.D.) which is essentially an auxiliary carburettor which increases the fuel/air mixture ratio when the engine is below normal operating temperature.

Slow-running adjustment

2   Make sure that ignition and all other engine adjustments are correct.
3   Run the engine to normal operating temperature and check that the mixture delivery pipe is warm.
4   Screw both the throttle speed adjusting screws back until they no longer contact the throttle levers. **On no account disturb the mixture screws,** these are preset in production (Fig. 3.21.)
5   Check that the throttle butterfly valve in each carburettor is fully closed.
6   Screw the throttle speed screws in until they just make contact with the throttle levers and then turn them a further 1½ turns inwards.
7   Remove the air cleaner cover and the element.

8 Balance the carburettors by one of the methods and in a similar way to that described in Section 11, paragraph 10. The correct idling speed is:

650 rev/min cars with manual gearbox
750 rev/min cars with automatic transmission

9 It is recommended that a final check is made using an exhaust gas analyser to ensure that the level of CO emission is within the specified limit (under 4½%).

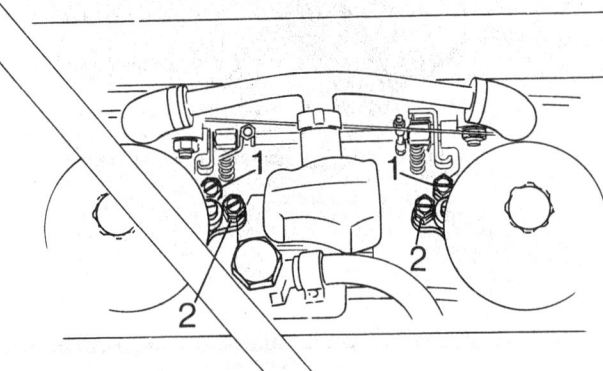

Fig. 3.21. Adjustment screws (SU - HS8 carburettor) (Sec. 15)

1   Slow-running screws   2   Pre-set mixture screws

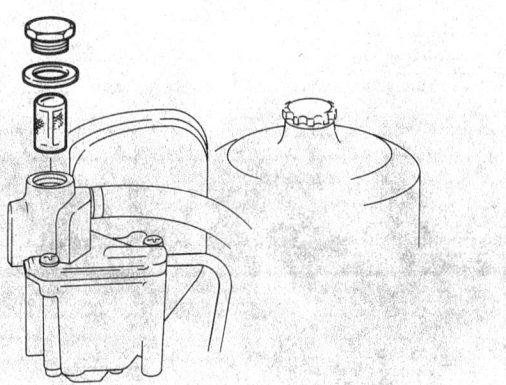

Fig. 3.22. Automatic enrichment device (A.E.D.) filter (Sec. 16)

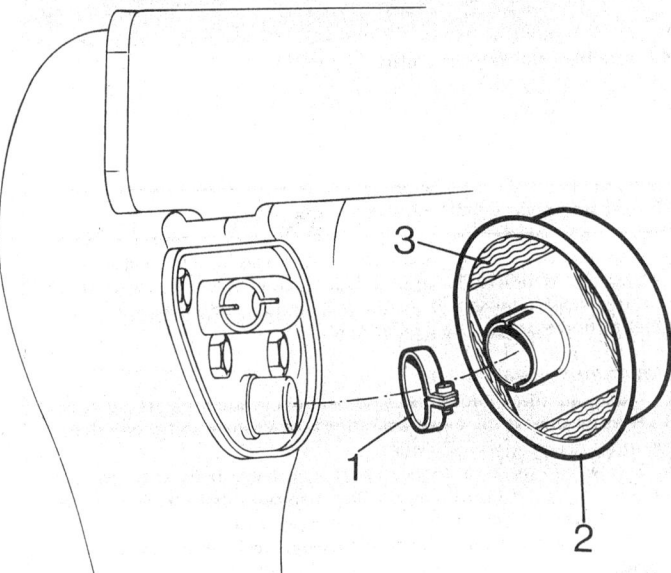

Fig. 3.23. Hot air pick-up unit filter (SU - HS8 carburettor) (Sec. 17)

1   Clip   2   Filter   3   Filter mesh

16 SU carburettors (HS8) - servicing of automatic enrichment device (A.E.D.)

1 At the recommended internals specified in 'Routine Maintenance',

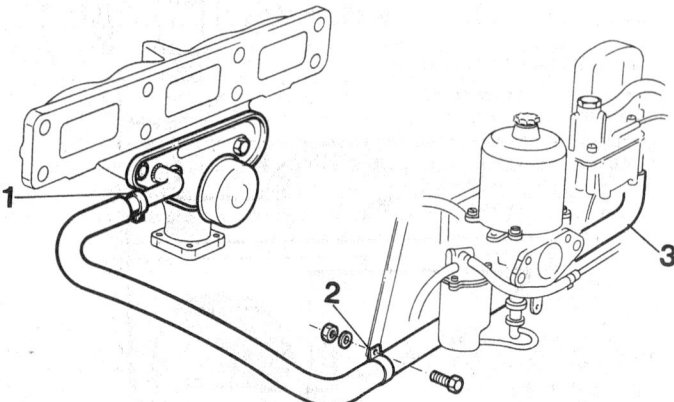

Fig. 3.24. Hot air pick-up unit air delivery pipe (SU - HS8 carburettor (Sec. 17)

1   Clip   2   Support   3   Pipe to A.E.D.

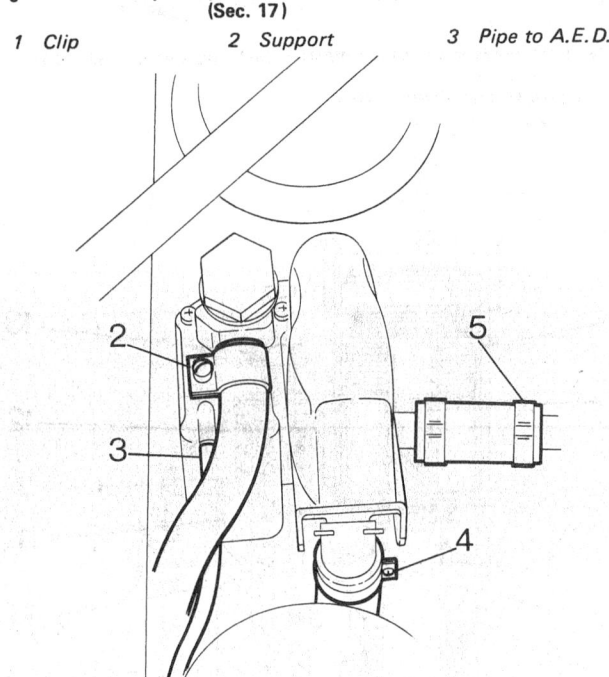

Fig. 3.25. Automatic enrichment device (A.E.D.) connections (Sec. 18)

2   Fuel inlet pipe   4   Air delivery pipe
3   Fuel overflow pipe   5   Mixture delivery pipe

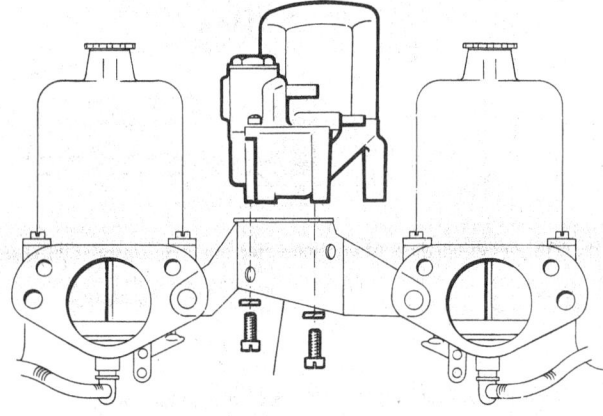

Fig. 3.26. Automatic enrichment device (A.E.D.) mounting components (Sec. 18)

remove the plug and aluminium washer from the float chamber of the automatic enrichment device.

2 Withdraw the filter gauze, clean with fuel and dry with air from a tyre pump and refit.

17 SU carburettors (HS8) - hot air pick-up unit, servicing and removal and refitting

1 At the intervals specified in 'Routine maintenance' slacken the clamp, move the filter towards the cylinder block and withdraw it.

2 Clean the filter in fuel, dry it and then lightly apply engine oil to the filter gauze.

3 If required, the hot air unit can be removed from the exhaust manifold after disconnecting the air delivery tube and withdrawing the two securing bolts.

4 Refitting is a reversal of removal.

18 SU carburettor (HS8) - removal and refitting of automatic enrichment device (A.E.D.)

1 Disconnect the lead from the battery negative terminal.

2 Disconnect the fuel inlet pipe.

3 Disconnect the fuel overflow pipe.

4 Disconnect the air delivery pipe.

5 Disconnect the mixture delivery pipe.

6 Unbolt and remove the securing bolts and lift off the automatic enrichment device.

7 Refitting is a reversal of removal.

19 SU carburettors (HS8) - removal and refitting

1 Remove the automatic enrichment device as described in the preceding Section.

2 Disconnect the crankcase breather pipe from the carburettors.

3 Disconnect the fuel inlet and the overflow pipes from the carburettor float chambers.

4 Disconnect the mixture delivery pipes.

5 Disconnect the vacuum pipe from the rear carburettor.

6 Slacken the slow-running adjustment screws until they are no longer contacting the throttle levers.

7 Mark the relative position of the throttle rod to the clamping bracket.

8 Slacken the clamping bracket pinch bolt and slide the bracket along the throttle rod until it is disengaged from the carburettor linkage.

9 Withdraw the throttle rod from the hollow nut by pressing the rod towards the engine compartment rear bulkhead.

10 Remove the carburettor securing nuts and lift the carburettor assembly from the inlet manifold complete with throttle lever return springs and brackets.

11 Peel off the flange gaskets and discard them.

12 Slacken the clamp pinch bolt and withdraw the front carburettor from the throttle link rod.

13 Commence installation by placing new flange gaskets on the inlet manifolds.

14 Fit the carburettors and tighten the flange nuts in diagonal sequence.

15 Make sure that both throttle butterfly valve plates are closed and then tighten the clamp pinch bolt.

16 Locate the throttle rod in the hollow nut and engage the clamp

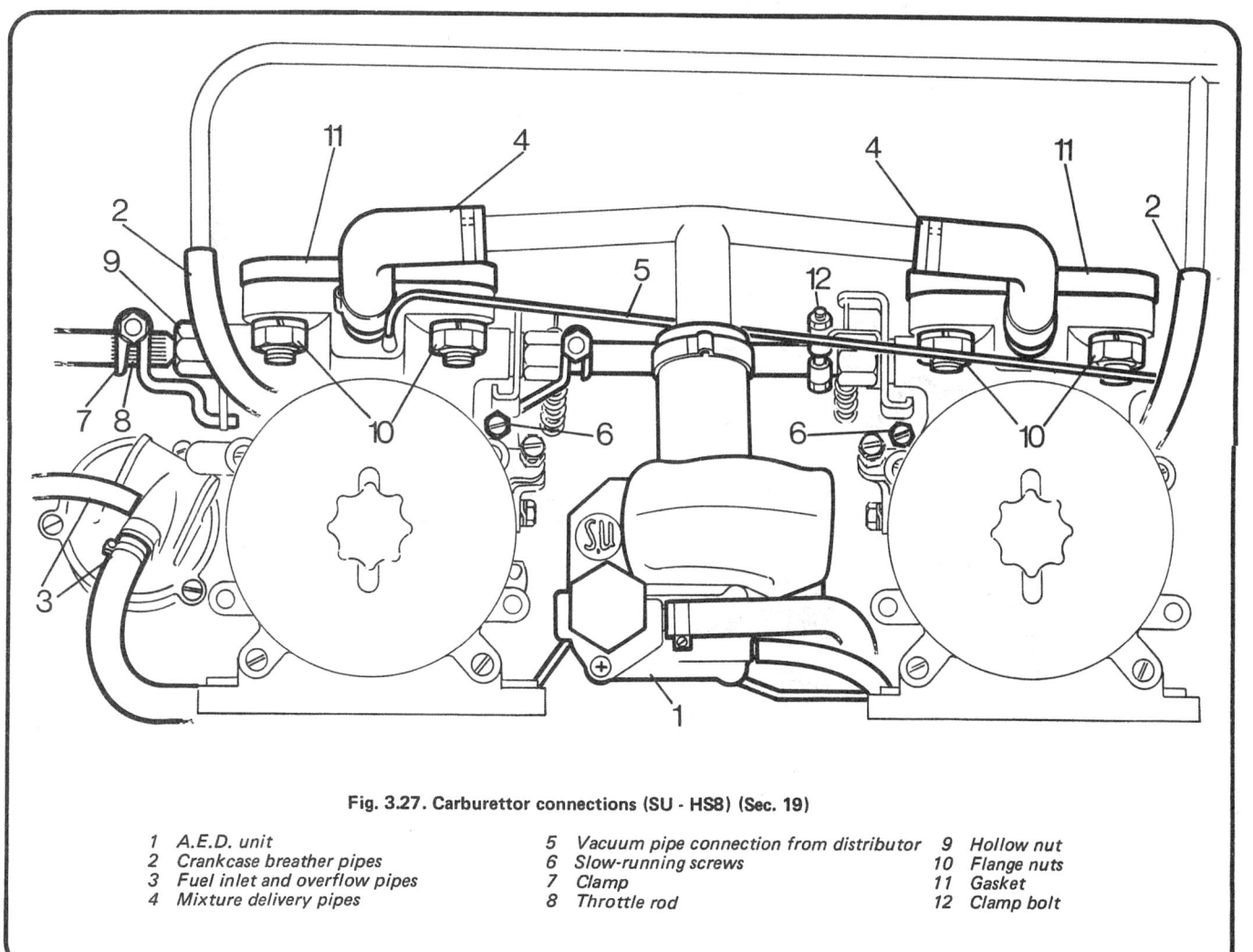

Fig. 3.27. Carburettor connections (SU - HS8) (Sec. 19)

1 A.E.D. unit	5 Vacuum pipe connection from distributor	9 Hollow nut
2 Crankcase breather pipes	6 Slow-running screws	10 Flange nuts
3 Fuel inlet and overflow pipes	7 Clamp	11 Gasket
4 Mixture delivery pipes	8 Throttle rod	12 Clamp bolt

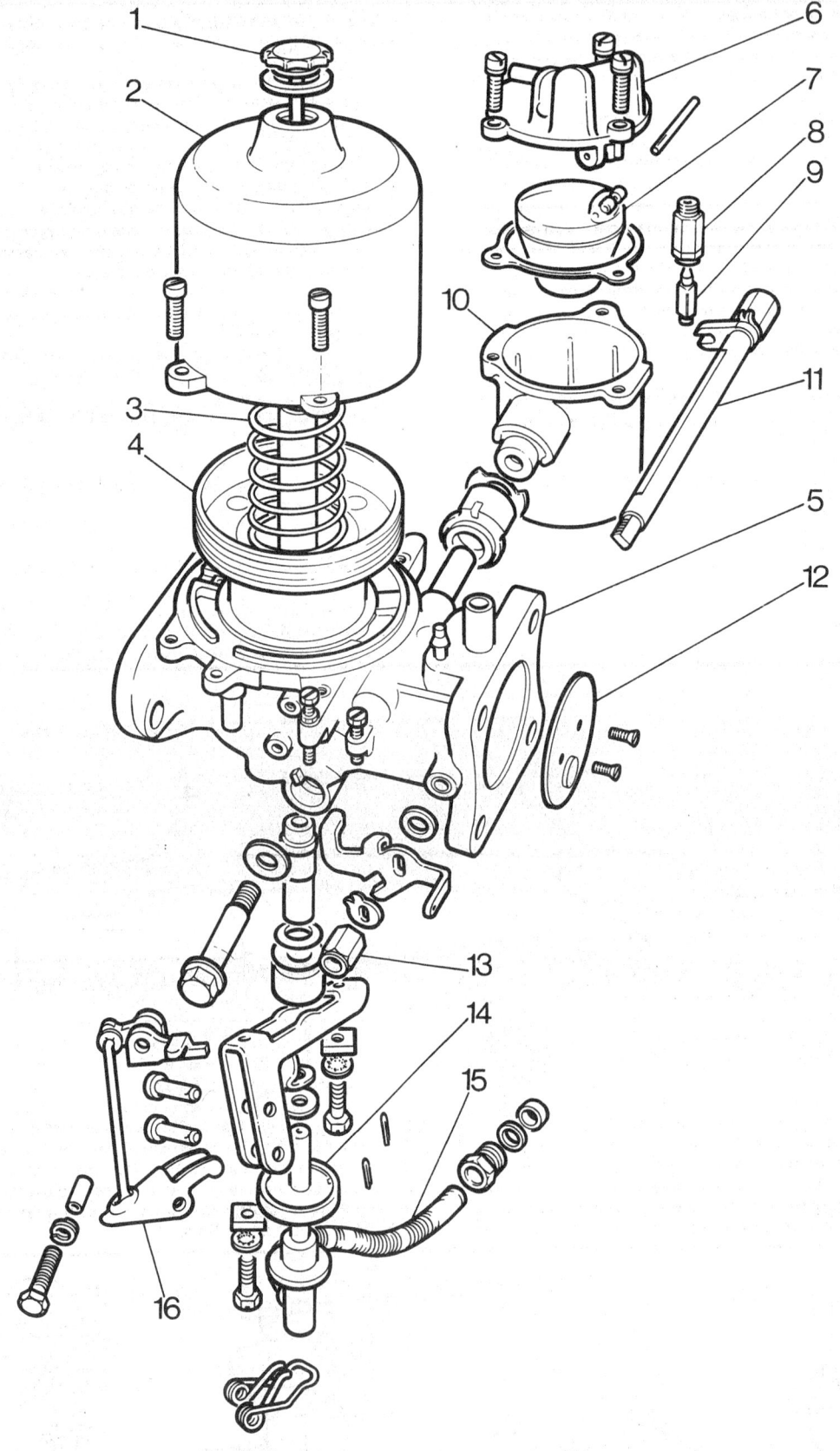

Fig. 3.28. Exploded view of SU - HS8 carburettor (Sec. 20)

1	Damper piston	5	Body	9	Fuel inlet needle valve	13	Hollow nut
2	Suction chamber	6	Float chamber lid	10	Float chamber	14	Jet assembly
3	Spring	7	Float	11	Throttle valve spindle	15	Flexible pipe
4	Piston/needle	8	Fuel inlet valve seat	12	Throttle butterfly valve plate	16	Jet fork

bracket with the carburettor linkage.

17 Place a spanner on the hollow nut and so keep the throttle butterfly valve plates closed. Now rotate the throttle rod until the reference marks on the rod and clamping bracket are in alignment. Tighten the clamp pinch bolt.

18 Reconnect all pipes to the carburettors and then refit the automatic enrichment device.

19 Adjust the carburettor slow-running, as described in Section 15.

20 SU carburettor (HS8) - examination, overhaul and adjustment

1 With the carburettors removed from the engine as described in the preceding Section, clean all dirt from their external surfaces.

2 Unscrew and remove the damper and washer.

3 Mark the relationship of the suction chamber and the carburettor body, extract the suction chamber screws and lift the chamber from the body.

4 Remove the piston spring and withdraw the piston and needle assembly.

5 Unscrew and remove the needle locking screw and then withdraw the needle from the piston complete with bias sleeve and spring.

6 Extract the split pins which retain the jet spring anchor pin and the jet fork pivot pin. Withdraw the pins and spring.

7 Withdraw the jet fork from its bracket.

8 Remove the bolt, washer and bush which secure the link arm to the carburettor body.

9 Unscrew the nut which secures the flexi-pipe to the float chamber, withdraw the pipe and the washer and the gland.

10 Withdraw the jet assembly together with the bi-metal sensor, washer and spacer.

11 Remove the bolts, washer and spacers which secure the fork bracket to the carburettor body.

12 Withdraw the jet bearing together with spacer and concave washers.

13 Bend back the tabs and unscrew the throttle lever securing nut, withdraw the lever and plain washer.

14 Only dismantle the throttle butterfly valve plate from its spindle if essential. To dismantle, extract the securing screws and discard them.

15 Mark the relationship of the float chamber lid to the float chamber and then extract the screws and lift off the lid and gasket.

16 Remove the fuel inlet needle from the lid and using a close fitting spanner, unscrew the fuel inlet valve seating.

17 Extract the float hinge pin. The pin is serrated at one end and should be driven out by applying a drift to the serrated end. Remove the float.

18 Remove the bolt which secures the float chamber to the carburettor body. Detach the float chamber and remove the flexible coupling and steel backing washer.

19 Clean all components in fuel and examine for wear or damage. Obtain a repair kit which will contain all the necessary gaskets and other renewable items.

20 If the throttle valve and spindle were dismantled, commence reassembly by inserting the spindle into the carburettor body.

21 Insert the butterfly valve plate into the slot in the spindle and insert two new securing screws but tighten them only finger tight at this stage. Note that the 'pip' on the valve plate should be below and on the same side as the countersunk screw holes in the throttle spindle.

22 Adjust the valve plate until it closes smoothly and fully and then

tighten the two screws fully and spread their split ends to lock them.

23 Screw in the fuel inlet valve seating, insert needle valve so that the coned end enters first.

24 Refit the float and pivot pin and then invert the float chamber lid and check the float level. The gap between the closest point of the float and the lid should be between 1/8 and 3/16 in (3.2 and 4.7 mm) (A in Fig. 3.29). If this is not so, a new float or needle valve will be required as there is no provision for adjustment.

25 Fit a new gasket to the float chamber lid.

26 Refit the lid and gasket to the float chamber in the original relative position and tighten the securing screws in diagonal sequence.

27 Insert the float chamber bolt into the carburettor body, refit the flexible coupling, washer and float chamber.

28 Install the bias sleeve and spring to the needle in the position shown. Screw in the needle securing screw and check that the needle is free to move (Fig. 3.30).

29 Check that the suction piston key is securely fitted, lightly oil the piston and install it into the carburettor body.

30 Fit the piston spring.

31 Install the suction chamber, aligning the marks made before dismantling and insert and tighten the securing screws in diagonal sequence.

32 Fit the jet bearing with concave washers and spacers.

33 Install the fork bracket, spacers and bolts.

34 Locate the jet fork in the bracket, insert the pivot pin and lock with a new split pin.

35 Locate the bush in the link arm, securing with bolt and double spring washer.

36 Locate the bi-metal sensor, copper washer and spacer on the jet assembly and slide the assembly into the jet bearing. The spacer must be positioned as shown in the diagram (Fig. 3.31).

37 Fit the jet spring, insert the anchor pin and secure it with a new split pin.

38 Slide the nut onto the flexi-pipe followed by the steel washer and a new gland.

39 Locate the flexi-tube in the bottom of the float-chamber and fit the nut but do not overtighten it.

40 Fit the plain washer, throttle lever, a new tab washer and nut to the throttle butterfly valve spindle. Hold the valve plate closed while tightening the nut and then secure the nut by bending over the lock tabs.

41 After installing the carburettors, top-up the dampers and tune them as described in Section 15.

21 Throttle kick-down switch (auto. transmission with SU-HS8 carburettor) - testing and adjustment

1 Any fault occurring in the kick-down function such as delay or too early an actuation may be due to the switch being out of adjustment.

2 Disconnect the red/black lead from the switch.

3 Connect a test lamp between the switch terminal and earth.

4 Switch on the ignition and depress accelerator pedal to the kick-down position when the test lamp should illuminate. If it does not, gently raise the spring steel lever on the switch until a 'click' is heard. The test lamp should now illuminate. If it does, adjust the position of the switch by releasing the securing screws. If it does not, the switch is faulty and must be renewed.

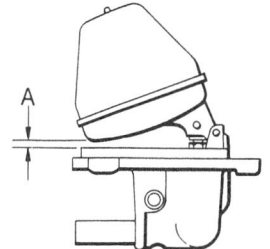

Fig. 3.29. Float level checking diagram (SU - HS8 carburettor) (Sec. 20)

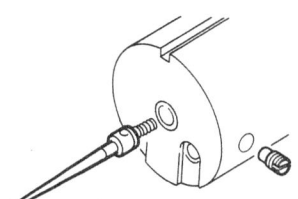

Fig. 3.30. Piston and needle components (SU - H.S.8 carburettor) (Sec. 20)

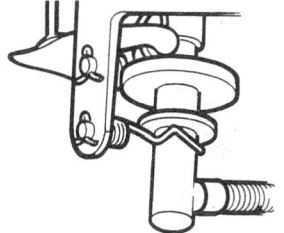

Fig. 3.31. Jet assembly (SU - HS8 carburettor) (Sec. 20)

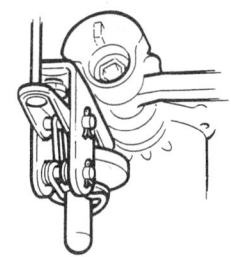

Fig. 3.32. Jet spring and anchor pin arrangement (SU - HS8 carburettor) (Sec. 20)

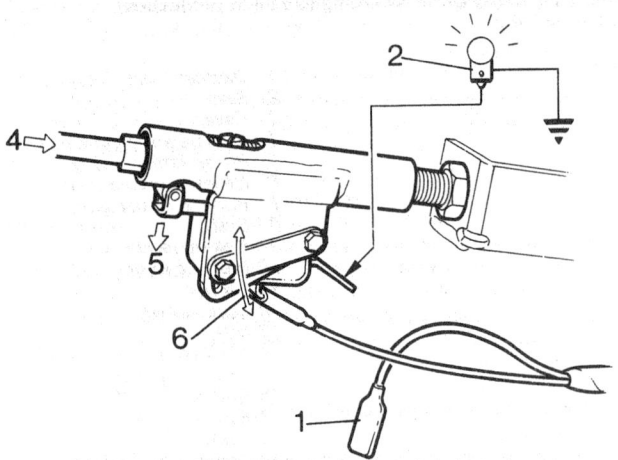

Fig. 3.33. Automatic transmission kick-down switch test (Sec. 21)

1 Red/black lead
2 Test lamp
4 Accelerator pedal rod

5 Spring steel lever
6 Switch adjustment travel

22 Stromberg 175CD2SE carburettors - adjustment and tuning

1 This carburettor has been specially developed to meet the most exacting emission control requirements and operations should therefore be limited to those described.
2 Make sure that ignition and engine adjustments are correctly set.
3 Run the engine until normal operating temperature is reached. Switch off the engine and remove the air cleaner cover and element.
4 Check and top-up if necessary, the oil in the carburettor dampers.
5 Slacken each of the two idle speed screws until they no longer contact the throttle levers.
6 Slacken the choke inner cable clamp bolts, check that the choke valve plates are fully open and then retighten the bolts.
7 Slacken the throttle spindle clamp bolts, check that the throttle valve plates are are fully closed and then retighten the clamp bolts.
8 Screw in the idle speed screw on the rear carburettor until it just

contacts the throttle lever.
9 Start the engine and adjust the idle speed screw on the rear carburettor until the engine idling speed is as follows:
  750 rev/min - cars with manual gearbox (in neutral)
  650 rev/min - cars with automatic transmission (in 'N' or 'P')
10 On some carburettors an idle trim screw is fitted adjacent to the temperature compensator cover. This screw is normally only adjusted to compensate for engine stiffness which is apparent at start-up of a new engine. When the initial stiffness wears off, the screw may be screwed in slightly to offset the weak mixture necessary in stiff engines.
11 On some carburettors, a throttle bypass valve is installed. This is a vacuum-operated valve actuated by manifold depression which during periods of engine overrun when the throttle is closed, allows fuel to feed to the downstream side of the primary throttle. This arrangement causes the gases in the engine combustion chambers to become enriched to a combustible level.
12 The throttle bypass valve is preset and normally requires no adjustment but it is possible for particles of dirt to become trapped under the valve seating. In the event of this happening and the valve action becoming unsatisfactory, remove the valve cover and carefully clean the valve and its seat.
13 The fast idle setting does not normally require altering. With the choke fully released (control knob fully in) the gap between the head of the fast idle screw and the cam should be 0.067 in (1.6 mm). If necessary, release the screw locknut and turn the screw in or out to obtain the correct gap.
14 A 'Summer' and 'Winter' position can be selected for the choke. If the pin on the knurled brass plunger is lying horizontally in its slot, this is the 'Winter' setting. To move it to 'Summer' position, depress the plunger and turn it through 90°.
15 Check the CO emission level is below 4½% using an exhaust gas analyser to prove that your adjustments have been carried out correctly. The air pump delivery hose should be disconnected for the test.

23 Stromberg 175CD2SE carburettors - removal and installation

1 Remove the air cleaner as described in Section 2.
2 Disconnect the crankcase breather pipe from each carburettor.
3 Disconnect the vacuum pipe from each bypass valve.
4 Slacken the clip and disconnect the fuel inlet pipe from the Tee-piece.

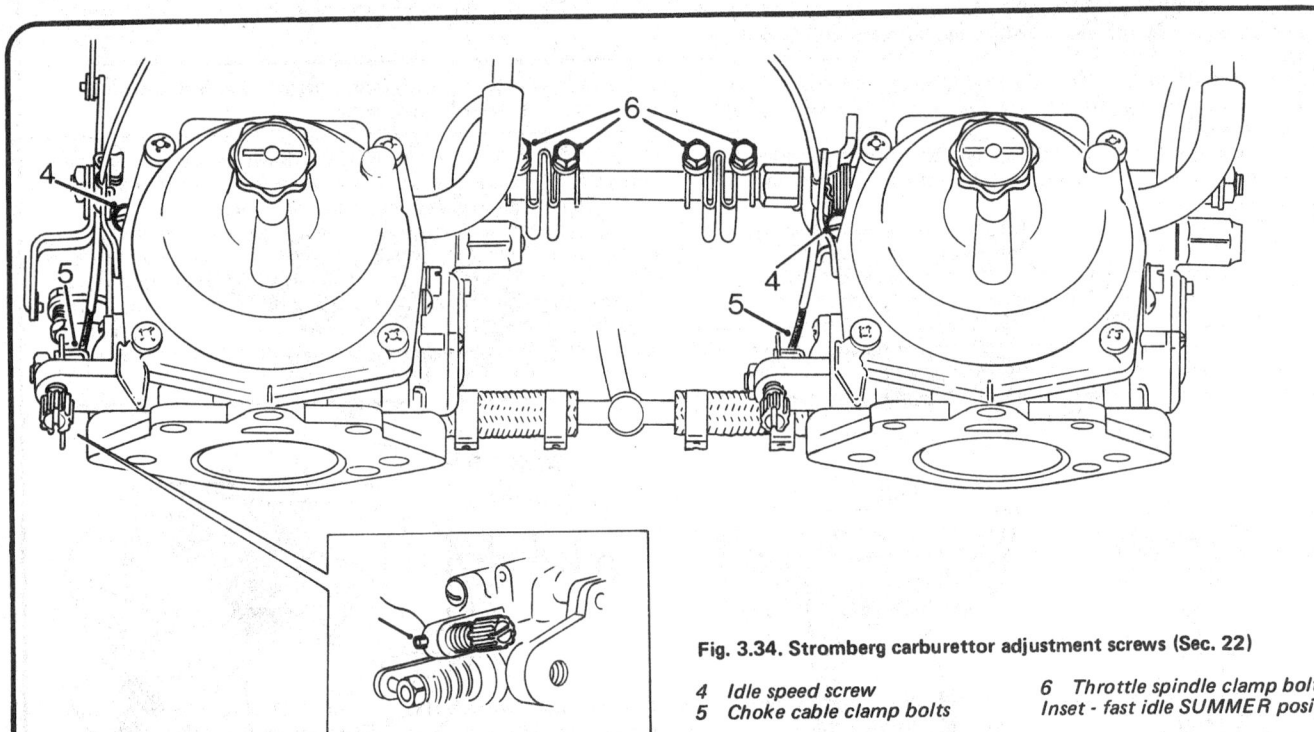

Fig. 3.34. Stromberg carburettor adjustment screws (Sec. 22)

4 Idle speed screw
5 Choke cable clamp bolts

6 Throttle spindle clamp bolts
Inset - fast idle SUMMER position

Fig. 3.35. Exploded view of Stromberg carburettor (jet cover arrangement may differ according to date of production)
Inset - Location of idle trim screw (arrowed) and throttle by-pass valve (A)

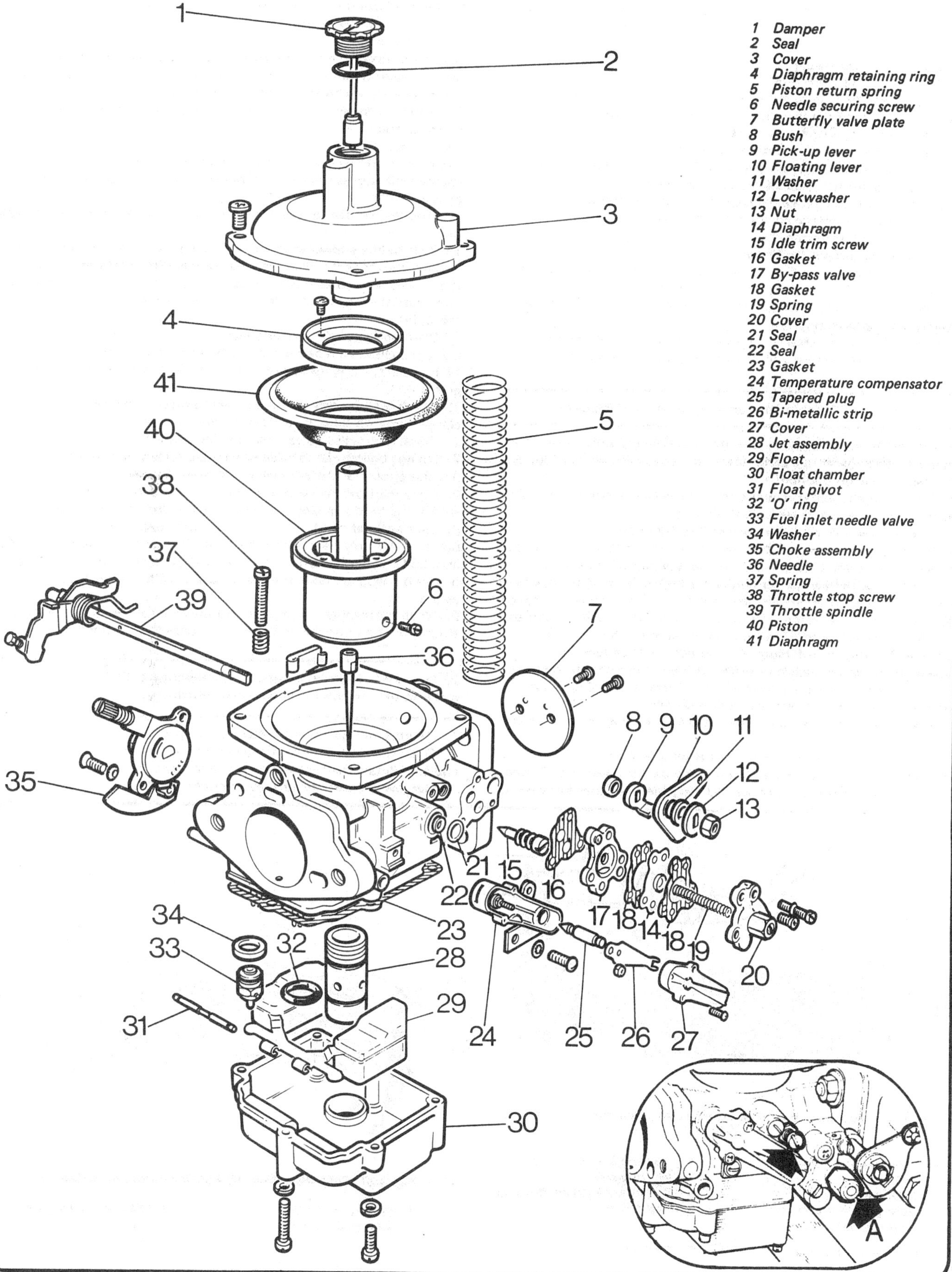

1 Damper
2 Seal
3 Cover
4 Diaphragm retaining ring
5 Piston return spring
6 Needle securing screw
7 Butterfly valve plate
8 Bush
9 Pick-up lever
10 Floating lever
11 Washer
12 Lockwasher
13 Nut
14 Diaphragm
15 Idle trim screw
16 Gasket
17 By-pass valve
18 Gasket
19 Spring
20 Cover
21 Seal
22 Seal
23 Gasket
24 Temperature compensator
25 Tapered plug
26 Bi-metallic strip
27 Cover
28 Jet assembly
29 Float
30 Float chamber
31 Float pivot
32 'O' ring
33 Fuel inlet needle valve
34 Washer
35 Choke assembly
36 Needle
37 Spring
38 Throttle stop screw
39 Throttle spindle
40 Piston
41 Diaphragm

5 Slacken the clamp bolts and withdraw the choke inner cables. Disconnect the choke outer cables from their clips.
6 Prise off the spring clip which secures the front throttle lever to its connecting link. Do not disconnect the lever from the link at this stage.
7 Prise off the spring clip which secures the rear throttle lever by following the same procedure.
8 On cars equipped with automatic transmission, release the spring clip and disconnect the kick-down rod from the throttle lever.
9 Remove the nuts and spring washers which secure the carburettor assembly to the secondary throttle housing.
10 Withdraw the carburettors enough to be able to disconnect the front and rear throttle levers from their connecting links. Remove the carburettors completely. On later models with emission control and coolant heated automatic choke, refer to Chapter 13 and disconnect the coolant hoses from the choke housing.
11 Peel off and discard the flange gaskets.
12 Mark the relative position of the throttle spindles to the connecting rod and then slacken one bolt on each connecting clamp.
13 Remove the clips which secure the T-piece to the carburettors and separate the carburettors.
14 Installation is a reversal of removal but always use new flange gaskets and once installed, adjust them as described in Section 22.

24 Stromberg 175CD2SE carburettor - examination and overhaul

1 Dismantle one unit at a time so that components will not become interchanged between the carburettors as many parts are individually matched during production.
2 With the carburettors removed from the engine as described in the preceding Section, clean away all external dirt.
3 Prise out the soft plug from one of the cover screws.
4 Mark the relationship of the cover to the carburettor body, remove the four cover screws, lift off the cover and withdraw the spring.
5 Carefully withdraw the piston/diaphragm assembly. If the diaphragm is split or has hardened, remove the screws which secure the diaphragm retaining ring to the piston. Lift off the ring and discard the diaphragm.
6 Do not remove needle locking screw or needle. This is selected and positioned during manufacture. If the needle must be renewed because it has become worn or distorted, then it can only be renewed complete with piston as an assembly. The needle size is B1BT and it should appear biased to one side - this is correct.
7 Remove the float chamber screws and lift the float chamber from the carburettor body.
8 Do not remove the jet cover unless absolutely essential in which case bend back the retaining lugs and withdraw the cover and 'O' ring. On reassembly, renew the jet cover, 'O' ring and float chamber gasket.

9 Disconnect the float pivot pin and detach the float.
10 Unscrew the fuel inlet needle valve.
11 Remove the nut, serrated and plain washers which secure the throttle lever to the throttle spindle. Withdraw the throttle lever, bush and actuating link.
12 Do not dismantle throttle valve plate unless essential in which case mark its relative position to the spindle, remove the securing screws and slide the plate from the slot in the spindle.
13 Withdraw the spindle having noted the position of the spindle return spring.
14 Remove the screws and lockwashers which secure the bypass valve and cover to the carburettor body, discard the joint gasket. Do not separate the bypass valve cover from the body or its adjustment will be lost.
15 Prise the throttle spindle seals from the carburettor body and discard them.
16 Remove the screws which secure the temperature compensator to the carburettor body, withdraw the compensator and discard the seals. If a countersunk brass screw is observed adjacent to the compensator, make sure that this is fully tightened otherwise an air leak can occur at this point.
17 Clean and examine all components, renewing any that are worn or damaged. Obtain a repair kit for each carburettor - part no. JS478.
18 Reassembly is a reversal of dismantling but observe the following points.
19 Check that the tapered plug is free to move in the temperature compensator housing. If it sticks, renew the assembly.
20 Fit all new seals and gaskets supplied in the kit.
21 Do not tighten the throttle valve plate screws until smooth and positive closure of the valve plate has been checked.
22 Once the float has been reassembled, invert the carburettor body so that the float arm closes the needle valve and then check the distance between the face of the carburettor body and the highest point on the visible surface of the float. This should be between 0.650 and 0.670 in (16.5 and 17.0 mm). Any adjustment should be carried out by bending the float arm. Make sure both floats are equal in height.
23 When reassembly is complete and the carburettors are installed to the engine, tune and adjust them, as described in Section 22.

25 Secondary throttle housing (in conjunction with Stromberg carburettor) - removal, overhaul and refitting

1 Remove the cap from the radiator header tank.
2 Open the radiator drain tap and drain off about one (US) gallon of coolant. Retain the coolant for replenishment.
3 Remove the carburettors, as described in Section 23.

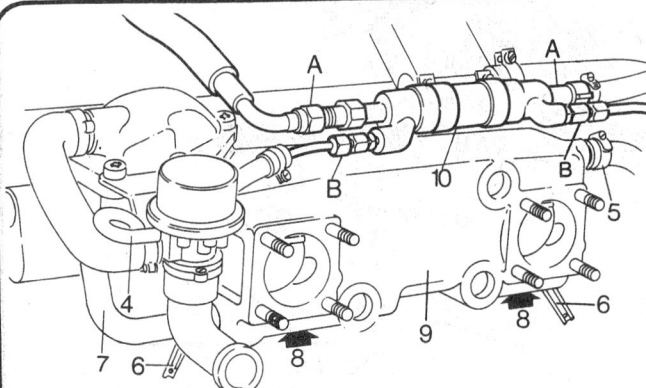

Fig. 3.36. Secondary throttle housing (with Stromberg carburettor) (Sec. 25)

4	Inlet manifold hose from gulp valve	8	Housing and anchor bracket securing nuts
5	Inlet water hose	9	Secondary throttle housing
6	Spring anchor brackets	10	Fuel cooler
7	Water outlet hose		
A	Refrigerant pipes	B	Fuel lines

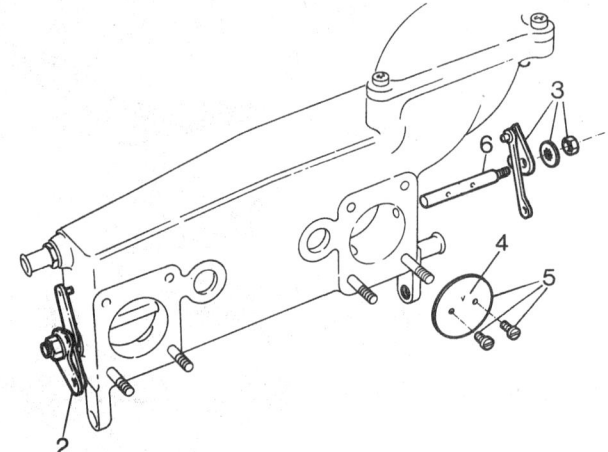

Fig. 3.37. Secondary throttle housing components (Sec. 25)

2	Bellcrank (front)	4	Throttle valve plate
3	Bellcrank (rear)	5	Screws
		6	Spindle

4 Disconnect the inlet manifold hose from the gulp valve.
5 Slacken the clip and disconnect the water inlet hose.
6 Detach the secondary throttle return springs having first noted into which anchor bracket holes they are secured.
7 Slacken the clip and disconnect the water outlet hose.
8 Remove the nuts which secure the secondary throttle housing and spring anchor brackets to the inlet manifold and withdraw the housing and gulp valve. Discard all gaskets.
9 To dismantle the secondary throttle housing, remove the nut and

washer which secure the bellcrank to the front secondary throttle spindle, withdraw the bellcrank.
10 Repeat these operations to remove the rear bellcrank.
11 If the throttle plates are to be removed from their spindles then mark the relationship of the valve plates to the spindles and the spindles to the housing.
12 Remove the valve plate screws, withdraw the spindles and prise out the spindle seals.
13 Reassembly is a reversal of dismantling, use new spindle seals.

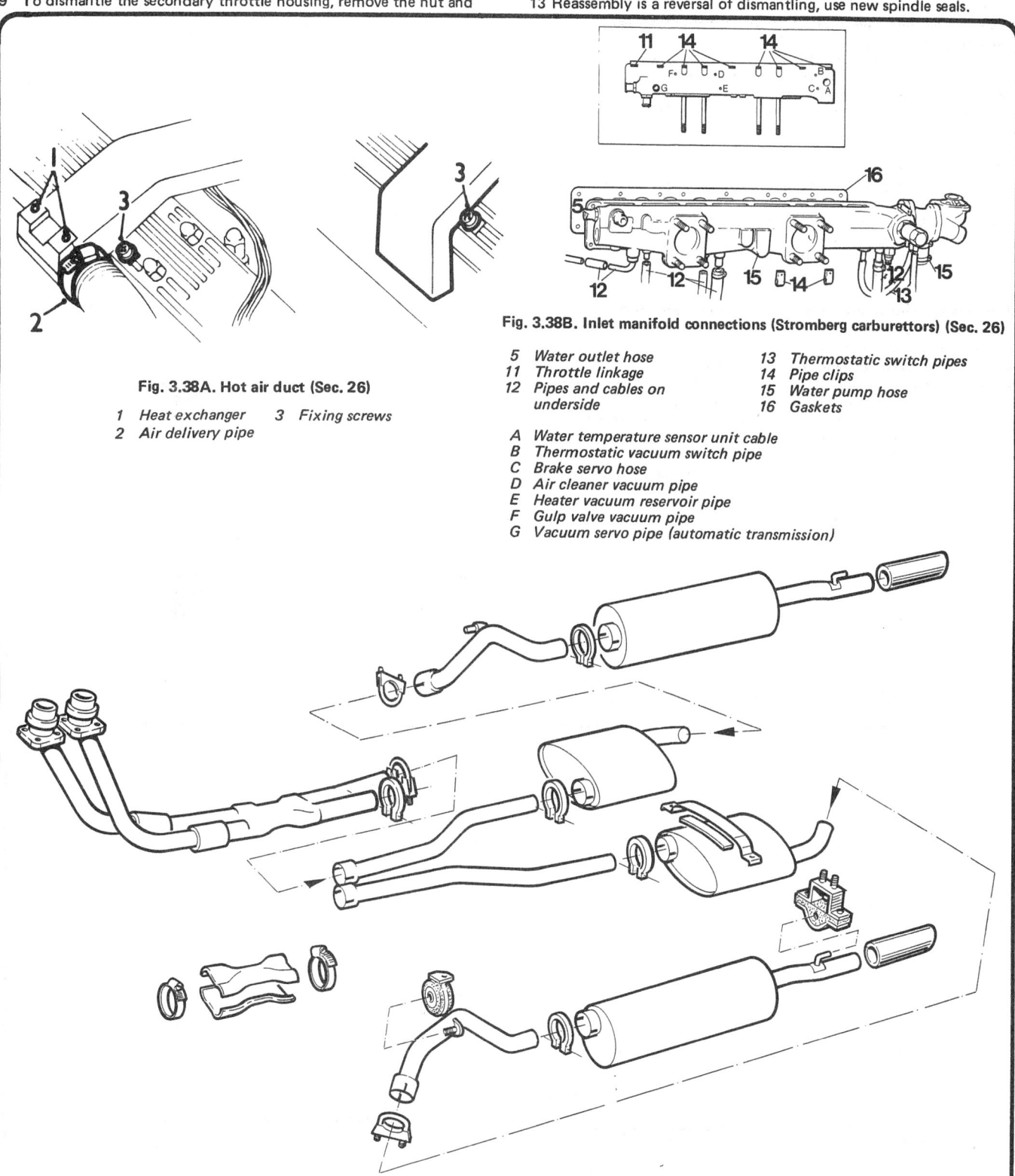

Fig. 3.38A. Hot air duct (Sec. 26)

1 Heat exchanger   3 Fixing screws
2 Air delivery pipe

Fig. 3.38B. Inlet manifold connections (Stromberg carburettors) (Sec. 26)

5   Water outlet hose   13 Thermostatic switch pipes
11 Throttle linkage   14 Pipe clips
12 Pipes and cables on   15 Water pump hose
    underside   16 Gaskets

A Water temperature sensor unit cable
B Thermostatic vacuum switch pipe
C Brake servo hose
D Air cleaner vacuum pipe
E Heater vacuum reservoir pipe
F Gulp valve vacuum pipe
G Vacuum servo pipe (automatic transmission)

Fig. 3.39. Exhaust system (typical) (Sec. 26)

26 Manifolds and exhaust system

1   The inlet and exhaust manifolds fitted to all cars with SU carburettors are secured in a straightforward way with studs and nuts. Always use new joint gaskets when refitting a manifold.

2   The inlet manifold fitted to cars which have Stromberg carburettors is much more complicated and the following removal procedure should be followed.

3   Remove the cap from the radiator header tank, open the radiator drain tap and drain about one (US) gallon of coolant. Retain the coolant for replenishment purposes.

4   Remove the secondary throttle housing, as described in Section 25.

5   Remove the air duct which runs across the top of the camshaft covers.

6   Disconnect the water outlet hose.

7   Detach the crankcase breather pipe from its retaining clips and withdraw the pipe from the elbow.

8   Disengage the HT leads from their retaining clip.

9   Disconnect the radiator upper hose.

10 Disconnect the hoses from the radiator header tank filler neck.

11 Slacken the clip that secures the water pump hose to the header tank.

12 Withdraw throttle linkage and support in its frame (three nuts).

13 Disconnect pipes and water temperature transmitter lead from the underside of the inlet manifold.

14 Disconnect the pipes from the thermostatic switch.

15 Note the position of the two pipe clips and then remove the nuts which secure the inlet manifold to the cylinder head.

16 Withdraw the inlet manifold far enough to be able to disconnect the water pump hose from the underside of the radiator header tank. Lift away the inlet manifold and discard the old gaskets.

17 The following points should be observed when removing the exhaust manifold.

Cars with emission control

18 Unbolt the hot air duct from the camshaft covers and exhaust manifold heat shield.

19 Remove the air pipe from the exhaust manifold heat shield, detach the air pump belt and pull the air pump away from the cylinder head.

20 Release the nut securing the EGR pipe.

21 Pull the hot air pipe from the AED hot air pick-up unit (SU carburettors only).

22 Remove the steering pinion heat shield (LHD only).

23 Remove the exhaust manifold heat shields.

24 Remove the compressor heat shield (air conditioned models only).

25 Remove the hot air pick-up unit from the rear of the exhaust manifold.

26 Installation is a reversal of removal, always use new gaskets.

27 The exhaust system is of dual type having twin downpipes and then left and right-hand intermediate rear silencer and tailpipe assemblies. The flexible sections of the exhaust pipes may be renewed independently by cutting and brazing.

28 Depending upon the date of car production, the design of the exhaust system may vary slightly.

29 Examination of the exhaust pipe and silencers at regular intervals is worthwhile as small defects may be repairable with products such as Holts Flexiwrap or Holts Gun Gum. Holts Flexiwrap is an MOT approved permanent exhaust repair. If left, such defects will almost certainly require renewal of one of the sections of the system. Also, any leaks, apart from the noise factor, may cause poisonous exhaust gases to get inside the car which can be unpleasant, to say the least, even in mild concentrations. Prolonged inhalation could cause sickness and giddiness.

30 As the sleeve connections and clamps are usually very difficult to separate it is quicker and easier in the long run to remove the complete system from the car when renewing a section. It can be expensive if another section is damaged when trying to separate a bad section from it.

31 Refitting should be carried out after connecting the sections together. De-burr and grease the connecting socket and make sure that the clamp is in good condition and slipped over the front pipe but do not tighten it at this stage.

32 Connect the system to the manifold and connect the rear support. Now adjust the attitude of the silencers, so that they are properly aligned and will not knock against any part of the bodyframe when deflected to the limit of travel on their flexible mountings. When alignment is correct, tighten the pipe clamps.

33 The tailpipe trims are retained by socket-headed grub screws.

27 Emission control systems - description

1   The emission control systems are designed to reduce (i) the emission of fumes from the engine crankcase which are generated by blow-by past the piston rings, (ii) fumes which are the result of evaporation of fuel stored in the fuel tank and the carburettor float chambers and (iii) noxious gases which are emitted from the exhaust pipes and which are the result of the normal combustion cycle within the engine.

2   The crankcase ventilation system is described in Chapter 1, Section 23.

3   The exhaust emission control systems are undoubtedly the most complex and a very comprehensive layout is employed in conjunction

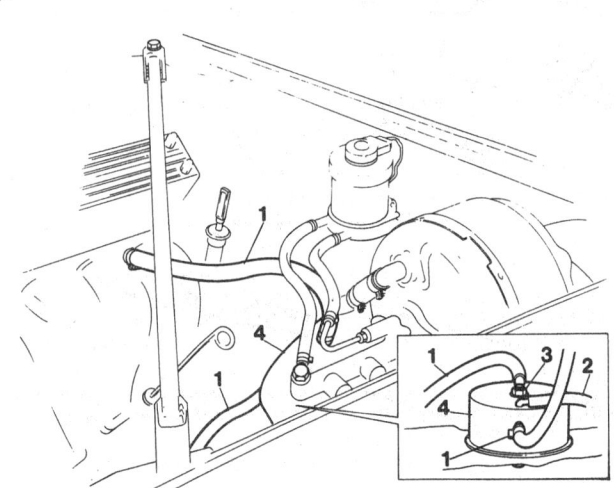

Fig. 3.40. Fuel evaporative control system (earlier cars) - charcoal canister attachments and under-bonnet location (Sec. 28)

1   Outlet hoses   3   Canister securing bolt
2   Inlet hose   4   Canister

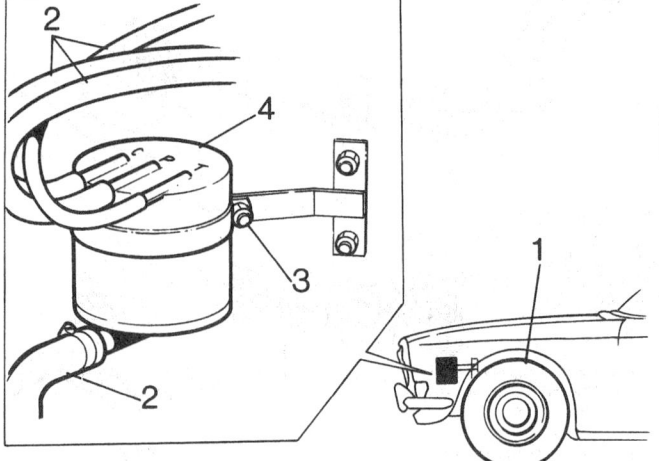

Fig. 3.41. Fuel evaporative control system (later cars) - charcoal canister attachments and under front wing location (Sec. 28)

1   Front roadwheel   3   Securing clamp
2   Pipes   4   Canister

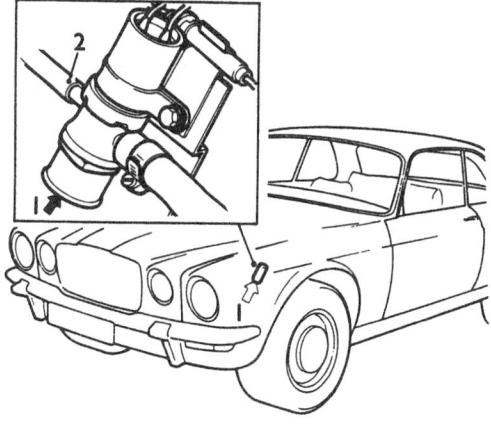

Fig.3.42. Anti-run-on valve (Sec. 29)

1   Valve plunger   2   Vacuum pipe

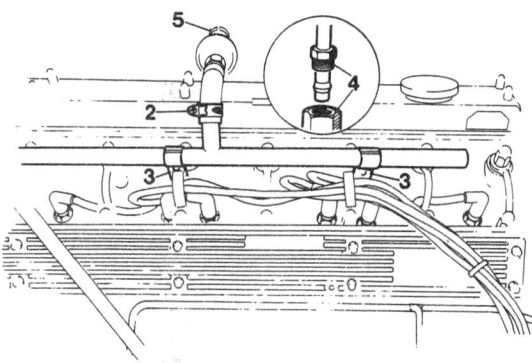

Fig. 3.43A. Air injection system pipework (Sec. 30)

2   Non-return valve hose   4   Air injection pipe cylinder
3   Air delivery pipe   head union
    brackets   5   Non-return valve

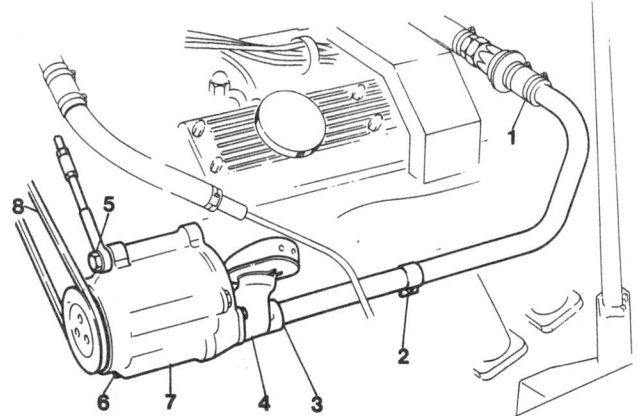

Fig. 3.43B. Air injection system air pump (Sec. 30)

1   Air pump delivery pipe   5   Adjustment rod
2   Pipe clip   6   Pump lower mounting
3   Pump outlet elbow   7   Air pump
4   Pump elbow   8   Drivebelt

with Stromberg carburettors on cars destined for operation in North America.

4   It must be emphasised that the condition and adjustment of the engine components (valve clearances, air filter etc.) and the setting of the ignition and carburettors are all essential factors in meeting the requirements of emission regulations quite apart from the function of the emission control equipment itself.

28 Fuel evaporative control system - description and maintenance

1   The system is designed to store vapour from the fuel tank and carburettor float chambers in a charcoal-filled canister during periods when the engine is not running. When the engine is running, the vapour is drawn from the charcoal canister into the engine crankcase emission control system and burned in the engine combustion chambers.

2   At the intervals specified in 'Routine Maintenance' the charcoal canister should be renewed. The canister design and connections vary according to the date of production of the car and particular care should be taken to identify the pipe connection on later models.

29 Anti-run on valve - description, testing and renewal

1   This valve is fitted to later cars to prevent any tendency to run-on when the engine is switched off. The system comprises a solenoid valve, an extra oil pressure switch and an additional contact in the ignition switch. When the ignition switch is turned off, voltage is applied to a solenoid valve in the evaporative control canister purge line, closing the line to atmosphere. The valve is connected electrically to an oil pressure switch which is closed while oil pressure exists. The solenoid valve at the same time applies manifold depression through the medium of the canister to the interior of the float chambers to equalise pressure on both sides of the carburettor jet and so prevents any fuel flowing past the metering needle. The foregoing action is applied only momentarily while the oil pressure still exists after the engine is switched off. Once the oil pressure drops, the pressure switch opens to de-actuate the solenoid valve and the canister purge line is re-opened to atmosphere.

2   If the system is suspected of being faulty, first check the fuse below the fascia panel on the driver's side.

3   If the fuse is sound, check the vacuum pipe between the inlet manifold and the solenoid valve which is located on the wing valance within the engine compartment.

4   Remove the air cleaner filter element and then pull the lead from the oil pressure switch which is located to the left-hand side of the oil filter. Start the engine and short the oil pressure switch lead to the engine block. Switch off the engine, if the engine does not run on, renew the oil pressure switch.

5   If the engine does run on, the switch is satisfactory and continue with the final test.

6   Check the security of all electrical connections making sure that 12 volt is present at the solenoid valve when the ignition switch is off. If it is then the solenoid must have an internal fault and should be renewed.

30 Air injection system - description and maintenance

1   This system was fitted to certain North American models in order to reduce the level of noxious gases from the exhaust pipes. It is a method of injecting air into the exhaust ports in order to oxidise the combustion gases before they are emitted from the exhaust system. Clean air is drawn through a small filter, compressed by a belt-driven pump and injected through a system of pipes and a non-return valve.

2   Periodically check the tension of the air pump drivebelt. The centre point of the upper run of the belt should have a deflection of ½ in (12.7 mm). If adjustment is required, slacken the pump mounting bolts and adjust the effective length of the rod by releasing the locknuts.

31 Exhaust gas recirculation (E.G.R) system - description and maintenance

1   This system is fitted to later cars as a substitute for the air injection

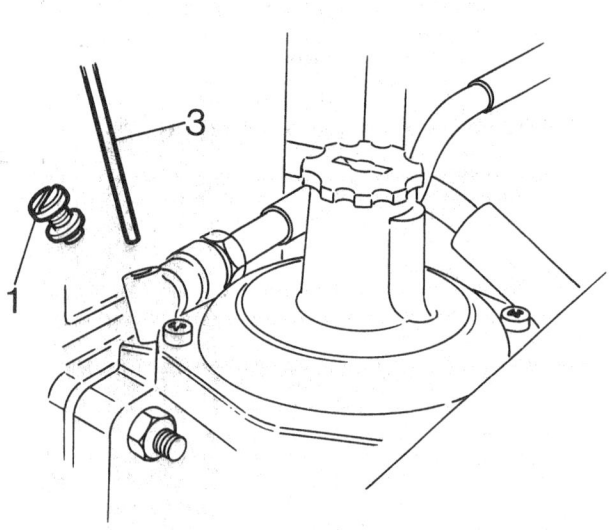

Fig. 3.44. Removing inlet drilling carbon deposits (E.G.R. system) (Sec. 31)

1 Blanking screw   3 Mild steel rod

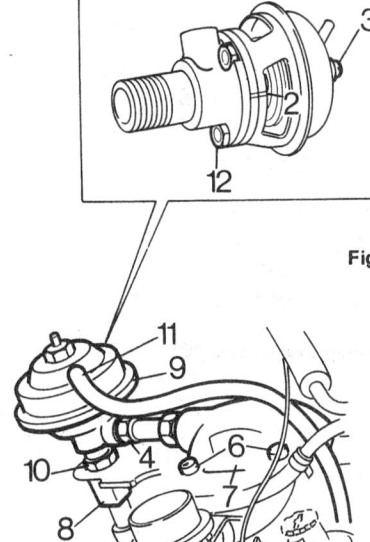

Fig. 3.45. Location of E.G.R. valve and unit securing nuts (Sec. 31)

2 Alignment marks
3 Adjuster screw and locknut
4 Valve delivery port
6 Secondary throttle housing cover screw
7 Secondary throttle housing cover
8 Pillar nut
9 E.G.R. valve
10 Valve bracket
11 Vacuum pipe
12 Securing nuts
13 Gulp valve

system. It operates by tapping off a predetermined volume of exhaust gas and injecting it into the carburettor inlet. The admission of this exhaust gas reduces the combustion temperature and so helps to minimise the level of noxious gases produced during the normal engine combustion cycles.

All cars except series 2 models

2 At the intervals specified in 'Routine maintenance' remove the blanking screw from the top of the left-hand carburettor mounting flange.
3 Hold the throttle fully open and then remove any carbon deposits from the inlet drilling using a piece of mild steel rod 8 in long x 1/8 in diameter (203 mm x 3.2 mm). Refit the blanking plug.
4 Repeat the operations on the second carburettor.
5 The connecting 'Y' piece and restrictor should also be decarbonised. To do this, unscrew the union nut which secures the outlet pipe to the adaptor. Remove the carburettors and withdraw the restrictor from the adaptor.
6 Clean the 'Y' piece and restrictor with a wire brush and then blow through with air from a tyre pump.
7 Refit all components using new gaskets.

Series 2 cars

8 A variable orifice E.G.R. system is used on these cars which incorporates a diaphragm type recirculation valve.
9 At regular intervals, mark the relationship of the diaphragm unit to the valve body by scribing a mark across the flange joint. Remove the three securing nuts and separate the diaphragm unit from the valve body. On no account disturb the adjuster screw and locknut on the top of the diaphragm unit.
10 Clean all components free from carbon deposits using a wire brush and air from a tyre pump and check the condition of the valve head, shaft and seat, also the diaphragm for wear. If the components are faulty, the complete valve/diaphragm assembly must be renewed.

32 Fuel cut-off inertia switch

1 In the interest of safety, this device is fitted to most Series 2 cars. It is located below the fascia panel on the passenger side and is secured in

spring clips.
2 To remove the switch, disconnect the leads and pull it from the clips. Refit by reversing the removal procedure, the leads can be connected to either terminal. When installed, depress the plunger and fit the cover.

33 Accelerator pedal linkage

1 This comprises an 'organ' type pedal and a mixed system of rods and cables.
2 Dismantling and reassembly is quite straightforward, the cable and rods being disconnected after removal of circlips or split pins and clevis pins.
3 There are minor differences in design of components used in the various models and whether left or right-hand steering.
4 When a new cable is fitted always check that the throttle valve plates are closed when the pedal is released and that an almost imperceptible amount of slack exists in the cable to allow for engine rocking.
5 Check that the throttle valve plates are fully open with the pedal depressed, but do not allow the cable to be strained by over-depression of the pedal. A floor-mounted stop bolt is provided to limit the downward travel of the pedal.
6 On cars equipped with automatic transmission, refer to Section 21.

34 Fuel feed line heat exchanger (cars with air-conditioning)

1 On cars equipped with an air-conditioning system, a small fuel cooler (see Fig.3.36) is mounted in the fuel supply line above a heat shield on the induction side of the engine. Its purpose is to prevent a fuel vapour lock occurring in exceptionally hot operating conditions and the design utilises some of the cooling action which takes place as fuel passes through a jacket which surrounds the air-conditioning system suction pipe.
2 **On no account disconnect the refrigerant pipes from the heat exchanger unless the air-conditioning system has first been discharged.** This is a job for your Jaguar dealer or a professional refrigeration engineer.

35 Fault diagnosis - carburation and fuel systems

Symptom	Reason/s
Excessive fuel consumption	Air filter choked. Leakage from pump, carburettor or fuel lines or fuel tank. Float chamber flooding. Distributor capacitor faulty. Distributor weights or vacuum capsule faulty. Mixture too rich. Contact breaker gap too wide. Incorrect valve clearances. Incorrect spark plug gaps. Tyres under inflated. Dragging brakes.
Insufficient fuel delivery or weak mixture	Fuel tank air vent or pipe blocked or flattened. Clogged fuel filter. Float chamber needle valve clogged. Faulty fuel pump valves. Fuel pump faulty. Fuel pipe unions loose. Inlet manifold gasket or carburettor flange gasket leaking. Incorrect adjustment of carburettor.
Rough idling	Sticking piston. Split diaphragm (Stromberg). Faulty temperature compensator (Stromberg). Perforated vacuum pipes.

36 Fault diagnosis - automatic enrichment device (AED)

Symptom	Reason/s
Engine fails to fire when cold	Lack of fuel to AED. Lack of fuel from AED to inlet manifold.
Engine fires when cold but fails to keep running	Sticking or faulty needle valve or float. Faulty air flap valve on AED air inlet elbow. Inadequate fuel supply.
Engine warm or hot; fails to start or keep running	Leaks in system pipes. Sticking or faulty needle valve or float. Faulty AED unit.

37 Fault diagnosis - emission control systems

Symptom	Reason/s
Fault in air injection system	Slack pump drivebelt. Perforated or loose connecting hoses. Choked air pump air filter.
Fault in EGR system	Choked inlet drilling, restrictor or 'Y' piece. Clogged EGR valve (cause of backfire).

Chapter 4 Ignition system

For modifications, and information applicable to later models, see Supplement at end of manual

Contents

Specifications

System ... ... 12 volt, negative earth, battery coil and crankshaft driven distributor

Distributor

Type:

2.8 litre	Lucas 25D6 - 41275
3.4 litre	Lucas 45D6
4.2 litre	Lucas 22D6 - 41060A (later models - Lucas 45D6)
Rotation	Anticlockwise
Contact breaker points gap	0.014 to 0.016 in (0.36 to 0.41 mm)
Dwell angle	$35^o \pm 3^o$
Firing order	1 − 5 − 3 − 6 − 2 − 4 (No 1 cylinder at rear)

Ignition timing

	2.8 litre	3.4 litre	4.2 litre
Static:			
7.8 : 1 compression ratio	—	8° BTDC	—
8 : 1 compression ratio	12° BTDC	—	8° BTDC
8.4 : 1 compression ratio	—	8° BTDC	8° BTDC
9 : 1 compression ratio	12° BTDC	—	8° BTDC
9 : 1 compression ratio (N. America)	—	—	10° BTDC
Dynamic (with stroboscope) Vacuum pipe disconnected, where applicable:			
7.8 : 1 compression ratio	—	18° BTDC @ 1500 rev/min	—
8 : 1 compression ratio	22° BTDC @ 1000 rev/min	—	20° BTDC @ 1700 rev/min
8.4 : 1 compression ratio	—	18° BTDC @ 1500 rev/min	20° BTDC @ 1700 rev/min
9 : 1 compression ratio	22° BTDC @ 1000 rev/min	—	20° BTDC @ 1700 rev/min
9 : 1 compression ratio (N. America)	—	—	TDC @ 650 rev/min

Spark plugs

Type:

2.8 litre	Champion N7YCC or N7YC
3.4 litre	Champion N12YCC or N12YC
4.2 litre (carburettor):	
UK models	Champion N11YCC or N11YC
US models	Champion 2404 or N12YC
Electrode gap:	
'YC' and 2404 spark plugs	0.025 in (0.6 mm)
'YCC' spark plugs	0.032 in (0.8 mm)

Torque wrench settings

	lb ft	Nm
Spark plugs	18	25

1 General description

The ignition system is based on the supply of low tension voltage from the battery to the ignition coil where it is converted into high tension voltage. The high tension voltage is powerful enough to jump the spark plug gap in the cylinders under high compression pressures - provided that the ignition system is in good working order and that all adjustments are correct.

The ignition system comprises two individual circuits known as the low tension (LT) and the high tension (HT) circuits. The LT circuit which is sometimes referred to as the primary circuit, comprises the battery, the lead to the control box, the lead to the ignition switch and from there to the low tension or primary coil windings of the coil (terminal SW), and the lead from the low tension coil windings (terminal CB) to the contact breaker points and condenser in the distributor.

The HT circuit consists of the high tension or secondary coil windings, the heavy ignition lead from the centre of the coil to the centre position in the distributor cap and thence via a carbon brush to the rotor arm and then through the spark plug leads to the spark plugs.

The system functions as follows. Low tension voltage is changed in the coil into high tension voltage by the opening and closing of the contact breaker points in the low tension circuit. HT voltage is then fed via the carbon brush in the centre of the distributor cap to the rotor arm of the distributor. The rotor arm revolves inside the distributor cap and each time it comes into line with one of the six metal segments in the cap, which are connected to the spark plug leads, the opening and closing of the contact breaker points causes the HT voltage to build up, jump the gap from the rotor arm to the appropriate metal segment and so via the lead to the spark plug, where it finally jumps the spark plug gap before going to earth. The contact breaker points consist of one fixed and one free point. The free point bears on the shaft which carries the rotor arm and movement of this point is governed by the shape of the shaft which is hexagonal at the position where the point bears. As the shaft revolves the free contact breaker point moves over one of the humps of the hexagon and is so brought out of contact with the fixed point.

The ignition is advanced and retarded automatically to ensure that the spark occurs at the right moment for the particular load at the prevailing engine speed.

The ignition advance is controlled both mechanically and by a vacuum operated system. The mechanical system comprises two lead weights, which act in the same manner as a governor, and which due to centrifugal force, move out from the distributor shaft as the engine speed rises. As they move outwards they rotate a cam relative to the distributor shaft and so advance the spark. The weights are held in position by two light springs and it is the tension of the springs which is largely responsible for correct spark advancement.

The vacuum control consists of a diaphragm, one side of which is connected via a small bore tube to the inlet manifold and the other side to the contact breaker plate. Depression in the inlet manifold, which varies with engine speed and throttle opening, causes the diaphragm to move carrying with it the contact breaker plate and thus advancing or retarding the spark. A fine degree of control is achieved by a spring in the vacuum assembly. It will be seen from the specification at the beginning of the Chapter that the type of distributor used varies with the model of the car. There is little or no outward difference in either of them and the above description and the following sections apply to each.

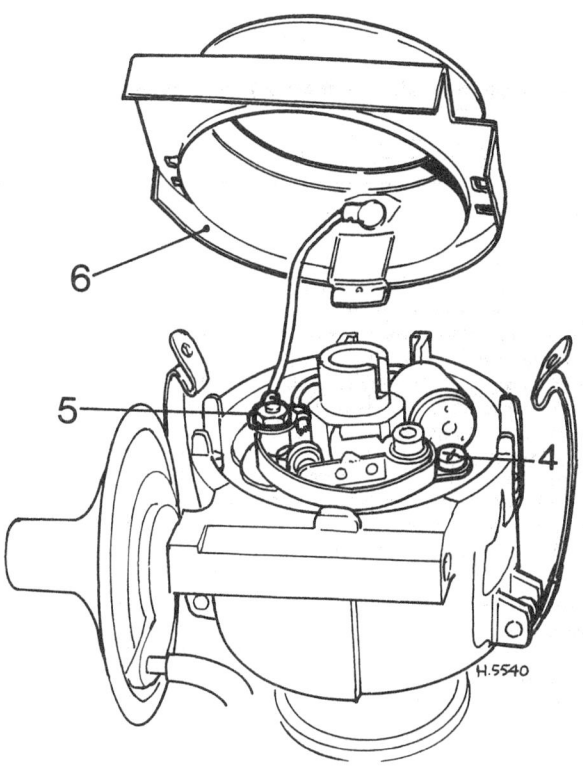

Fig. 4.1. Waterproof cover fitted to some distributors (Sec. 2)

4   Condenser securing screw   6   Waterproof cover
5   Contact terminal nut

2   Contact breaker points - adjustment

1   At intervals of 6000 miles (9600 km) check the contact breaker gap in the following way. This check should also be carried out at the end of the first 1000 miles (1600 km) after new points have been fitted as the plastic heel of the movable contact arm will probably have bedded in and the gap will have been decreased.
2   Slip back the spring clips from the distributor cap, remove the cap and pull off the rotor arm. Later models have a waterproof cover which can be removed after the condenser securing screw and the contact arm terminal nut have been removed.
3   Turn the crankshaft until the plastic heel of the movable contact arm is in one of the high points of the cam. The crankshaft can be turned by applying a spanner to the crankshaft damper bolt or on cars with a manual gearbox, by engaging top gear and pushing the car. It will be found easier with either method if the spark plugs are first removed.
4   Check the points gap with a feeler blade, it should be between 0.014 and 0.016 in (0.36 and 0.41 mm).
5   If the gap requires adjusting, release the screw which secures the fixed contact breaker plate and turn the breaker plate by inserting a screwdriver in the two small slots which are provided for the purpose in contact plate and baseplate.
6   Retighten the contact breaker plate screw.
7   It is emphasised that if the points are pitted or one of them has a 'pip' on it which is the result of extended service, then a false reading will be obtained using the feeler blades. In this case, the points should either be renewed or removed and dressed as described in the following Section.
8   Check the dwell angle (see Section 4).

3   Contact breaker points - removal and refitting

1   If on examination, the contact breaker points are seen to be pitted or eroded, or one of the points has a 'pip' on it, then the contact breaker arms must be removed.
2   Unscrew and remove the small nut from the anchor post to which

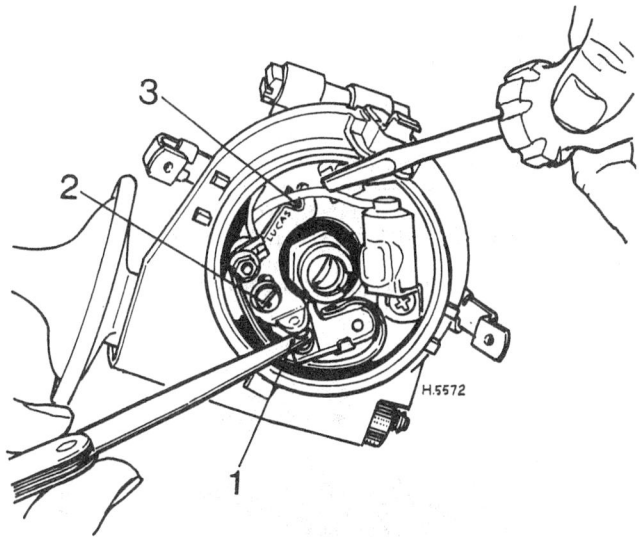

Fig. 4.2. Adjusting distributor contact points (Sec. 2)

1   Feeler blade   3   Adjustment leverage
2   Fixed breaker arm screw   notch

the spring arm of the movable contact is attached, extract the insulating bush and the low tension wire terminal tag and the condenser lead tag.
3   Prise up the spring arm and lift the movable contact from its pivot post.
4   Unscrew and remove the screw from the fixed contact breaker arm and lift the arm from the distributor baseplate.
5   If the points are only lightly pitted, dress them smooth on an oilstone, keeping their faces quite square. If they are deeply pitted,

then they should be renewed.

6   Clean the faces of the points, before installing them, with solvent or methylated spirit.

7   Refit the contact breaker arms and adjust the gap as described in the preceding Section.

8   Apply lubricant to the distributor at the points indicated, refit the rotor arm and distributor cap (Fig. 4.3.)

9   Check the dwell angle (Section 4) and the ignition timing (Section 8).

4   Dwell angle - description and checking

1   The setting of the contact breaker points gap using a feeler blade must be regarded as an initial adjustment only and wherever possible the dwell angle must be checked as soon as possible thereafter. This is particularly important with engines which are equipped with full emission control systems.

2   The dwell angle is the number of degrees through which the distributor cam turns during the period between the instants of closure and opening of the contact points. It can only be checked with a dwell meter. If the dwell angle is found to be too large, increase the points gap, if the dwell angle is too small, reduce the size of the points gap.

5   Condenser (capacitor) - removal, testing and refitting

1   The condenser ensures that with the contact breaker points open, the sparking between them is not excessive to cause severe pitting. The condenser is fitted in parallel and its failure will automatically cause failure of the ignition system as the points will be prevented from interrupting the low tension circuit.

2   Testing for an unserviceable condenser may be effected by switching on the ignition and separating the contact points by hand. If this action is accompanied by a blue flash then condenser failure is indicated. Difficult starting, missing of the engine after several miles running or badly pitted points are other indications of a faulty condenser.

3   The surest test is by substitution of a new unit.

4   The condenser is secured to the distributor baseplate by a single screw and its head is attached to the top of the contact breaker spring arm anchor post.

6   Distributor - removal and installation

1   The distributor is driven by a shaft which is an upper extension of the oil pump driveshaft, both of which are gear driven from the crankshaft.

2   To remove the distributor, pull off the low tension wire from the terminal block on the side of the distributor body.

3   Prise back the spring clips and remove the distributor cap. Extract the condenser screw and contact breaker terminal nut and remove the waterproof cover (later models only).

4   Pull off the vacuum tube from the distributor vacuum capsule.

5   Mark the position of the distributor body in relation to the clamp plate, release the pinch bolt on the clamp plate and pull the distributor straight upwards from its recess.

6   The distributor is driven by an offset dog (large and small segments) and if no further dismantling of the distributor drive is carried out then the distributor can be installed simply by pushing it back into its recess so that the offset dog mates with its slot. Set the distributor in its original relative position to the clamp plate and tighten the pinch bolt.

7   Time the ignition, as described in Section 8, whenever the distributor has been removed and installed.

7   Distributor - overhaul

1   Remove the distributor from the car as described in Section 6.

2   Refer to Fig. 4.5. which shows an exploded view of the distributor.

3   Remove the contact breaker points as described in Section 2 and remove the condenser as described in Section 5.

4   Remove the two screws securing the baseplate and earth lead. Disconnect the link to the vacuum control unit and lift off the baseplate.

5   Before proceeding any further, take careful note of the relative positions of the rotor arm slot located above the cam and of the offset driving dog. It is possible to assemble these items 180° out on reassembly, which means that the distributor would have to be rotated 180° in order to obtain correct timing of the engine and connections cannot be made with the distributor so located.

6   Remove the cam retaining screw and remove the cam.

7   Lift out the automatic timing control weights and their springs. Note how these are fitted.

8   Remove the circlip securing the knurled advance and retard adjustment nut. Remove the adjusting nut and spring. The vacuum unit can now be withdrawn.

9   Remove the clamp plate by undoing the pinch bolt and sliding the plate off the base of the distributor.

10 To remove the driving dog, knock out the taper pin and lift off the dog and thrust washer. The shaft may now be lifted upwards.

11 Thoroughly wash all mechanical parts in petrol and wipe dry using a clean non-fluffy rag.

12 Check the contact breaker points as described in Section 2.

13 Check the distributor cap for signs of 'tracking' which will be indicated by a thin black line between the segments. Renew the cap if this defect is noted.

14 Ensure that the carbon brush in the cap is free to move in its holder

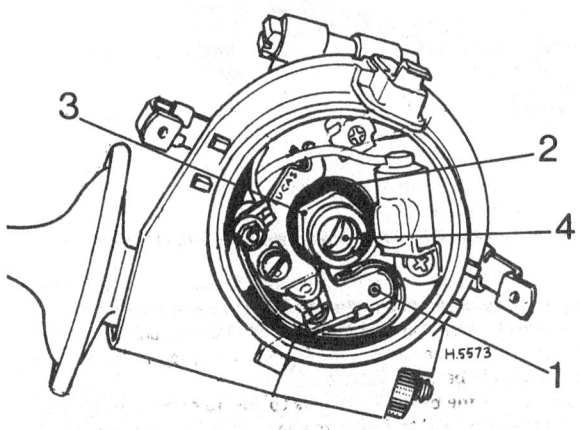

Fig. 4.3. Distributor lubrication points (Sec. 3)

1   Pivot post (engine oil)
2   Baseplate cut-out (engine oil)
3   Cam high points (grease or petroleum jelly)
4   Centre screw (engine oil)

6.8 Crankshaft damper timing marks and timing cover pointer

and is not worn down. Do not remove the brush needlessly as the spring is usually a tight fit in the holder and will be badly stretched as you pull the brush out.

15 If the metal portion of the rotor arm is badly burned or is loose, renew the arm. Slight burning can be rectified with a piece of fine 'wet-and-dry' paper but maintain the face square.

16 Examine the fit of the contact breaker plate on the baseplate and check the breaker arm pivot for looseness or wear. Renew the plate if necessary.

17 Examine the centrifugal weights and pivot pins for wear and renew the weights or cam assembly if a degree of wear is found.

18 Examine the shaft and the fit of the cam assembly on the shaft. If the clearance appears to be excessive, compare with new items and renew either or both if they show excessive wear.

19 If the shaft is a loose fit in a distributor bush and can be 'rocked', we suggest that a reconditioned distributor is obtained.

20 Reassembly is a straightforward reversal of the dismantling process. Note in addition:

21 Lubricate the centrifugal weights and other parts of the mechanical advance mechanism with thin machine oil. Lubricate the distributor shaft with clean engine oil and smear the cam face with engine oil or petroleum jelly. Do not be too lavish with the oil.

22 Check the action of the weights in the fully advanced and retarded positions, make sure they are not binding.

23 Adjust the micrometer advance and retard adjusting nut to bring the mechanism to the mid position of the timing scale.

24 Finally set the contact breaker points as described in Section 2.

8 Ignition timing

1 It is recommended that the static ignition timing is set initially using a test bulb and then checked with a stroboscope with the engine running.

2 Set the vernier adjuster to the centre of its scale.

3 Remove the no. 6 (front) spark plug and turn the crankshaft until compression can be felt being generated when the finger is placed over the plug hole.

4 Continue turning the crankshaft until the appropriate BTDC mark (see Specifications) is exactly opposite the pointer on the crankcase (Fig. 4.6).

5 Connect a 12v test lamp between the CB (−) terminal of the coil and a good earth.

6 Slacken the distributor clamp plate pinch bolt until the distributor will turn stiffly.

7 Switch on the ignition and turn the distributor one way or the other, until the test lamp just lights up which indicates that the contact points are just open.

8 Switch off the ignition and tighten the pinch bolt without disturbing the setting of the distributor.

9 Fine adjustment may be carried out from this setting to accommodate variations in fuel and operating conditions by turning the vernier adjuster screw not more than six 'clicks' in either direction.

10 The ignition timing should now be checked with a stroboscope in the following manner.

11 Run the engine to normal operating temperature then switch off the ignition and disconnect the vacuum pipe from the distributor and plug the pipe.

12 Connect a stroboscope in accordance with the manufacturer's instructions (usually between no. 6 spark plug and the end of no. 6 spark plug lead)..

13 Start the engine and let it idle at the specified speed shown in Specification Section. Point the stroboscope at the crankshaft damper, the appropriate degree mark should then appear stationary opposite the crankcase pointer. If it is not opposite, adjust the distributor until the mark and pointer coincide. This can usually be achieved by using the vernier adjuster provided the static setting was carried out correctly.

14 If the timing mark and pointer are difficult to see, paint them with a dab of white paint.

15 Remove the stroboscope, reconnect the spark plug lead and reconnect the vacuum pipe to the distributor.

9 The coil

1 High tension current should be negative at the spark plug terminals.

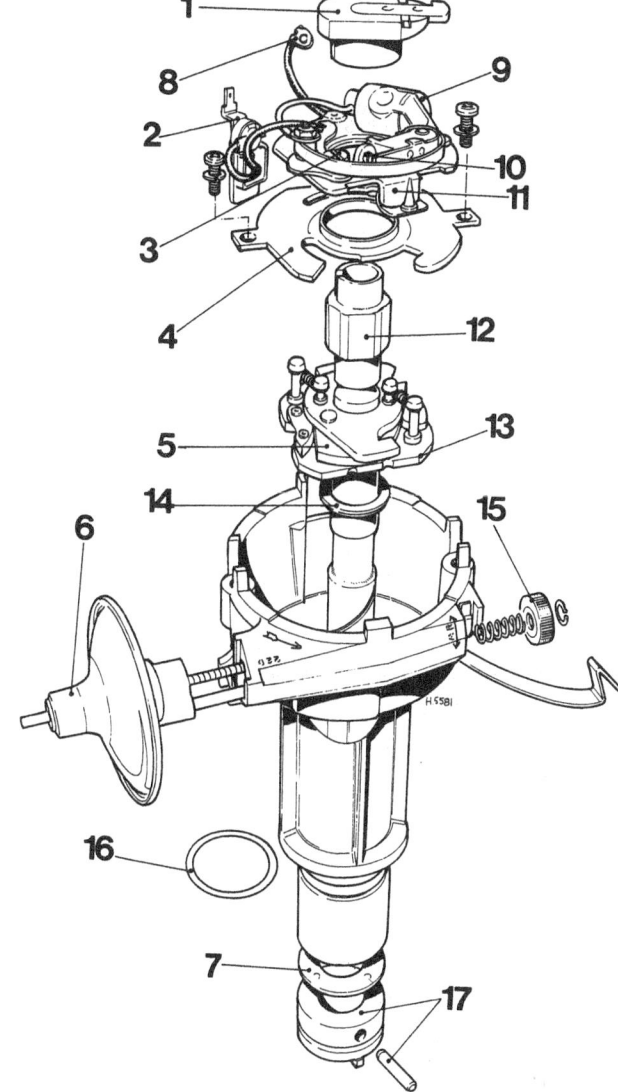

Fig. 4.4. Exploded view of type 22D6 distributor (Sec. 7)

1 Rotor	10 Contact points
2 LT terminal	11 Moving baseplate
3 Fixed contact securing screw	12 Cam
4 Baseplate	13 Action plate
5 Centrifugal counterweights	14 Collar
6 Vacuum capsule	15 Vernier adjuster knurled
7 Thrust washer	nut
8 Earth bond	16 'O' ring
9 Condenser	17 Offset dog and pin

To ensure this, check the LT connections to the coil are correctly made.

2 The LT wire from the distributor must connect with the (−) negative terminal on the coil.

3 The coil (+) positive terminal is connected to the ignition/start switch.

4 An incorrect connection can cause as much as a 60% loss of spark efficiency and can cause rough idling and misfiring at speed.

5 Earlier models were fitted with a standard 12 volt ignition coil while later models have a ballast resistor ignition system. The coils are not interchangeable between systems.

6 The purpose of the ballast resistor is to ensure maximum efficiency at high engine speeds and to facilitate engine starting at low ambient temperature conditions. The ballast resistor prevents the voltage applied to the coil from falling during the period when the starter motor is cranking the engine. This is normally the case in systems without this device, due to the starter motor load conditions.

7 The ballast resistor is mounted on early cars in conjunction with the

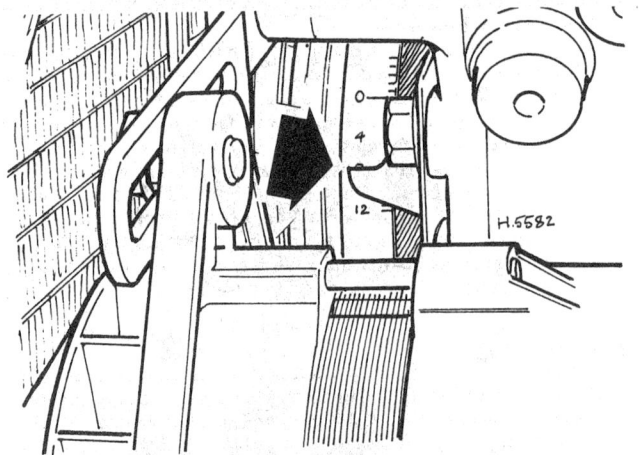

Fig. 4.5. Ignition timing marks on crankshaft damper (Sec. 8)

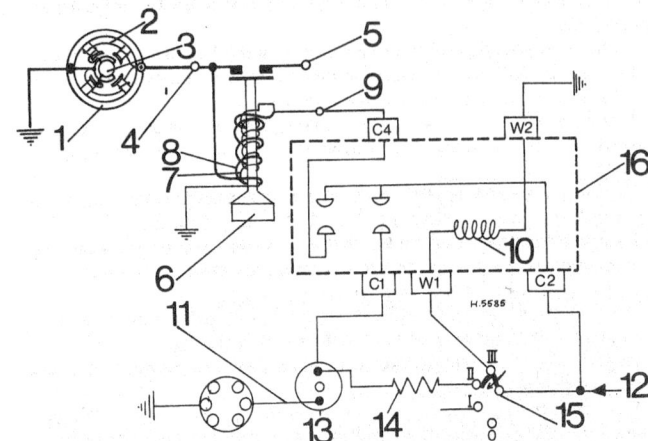

Fig. 4.6. Ballast ignition system circuit diagram (Sec. 9)

1 Starter motor	9 Solenoid terminal
2 Field windings	10 Relay coil
3 Armature	11 LT lead
4 Solenoid terminal 'STA'	12 Ignition supply lead
5 Battery supply terminal	13 Coil
6 Solenoid core	14 Ballast resistor
7 Solenoid shunt winding	15 Ignition/starter switch
8 Solenoid series winding	16 Relay

coil on the right-hand wing valance at the front of the engine compartment. On later cars, the coil and ballast resistor are mounted on a plate on the right-hand side of the engine.

10 Spark plugs and high tension (HT) leads

1   The correct functioning of the spark plugs is vital for the correct running and efficiency of the engine. It is essential that the plugs fitted are appropriate for the engine, and the suitable type is specified at the beginning of this Chapter. If this type is used and the engine is in good condition, the spark plugs should not need attention between scheduled replacement intervals. Spark plug cleaning is rarely necessary and should not be attempted unless specialised equipment is available as damage can easily be caused to the firing ends.

2   At intervals of 12000 miles (19300 km) the plugs should be renewed even if they appear in good condition, as they will almost certainly have a low efficiency when sparking under compression in combustion chamber conditions after this length of service. Renew with plugs of currently specified type.

3   The appearance of a spark plug will tell much about the overall condition of the engine, for example, if the insulator nose of the spark plug is clean and white, with no deposits, this is indicative of a weak mixture, or too hot a plug. (A hot plug transfers heat away from the electrode slowly - a cold plug transfers it away quickly).

4   If the top and insulator nose is covered with hard black looking deposits, then this is indicative that the mixture is too rich. Should the plug be black and oily, then it is likely that the engine is fairly worn, as well as the mixture being too rich.

5   If the insulator nose is covered with light tan to greyish brown deposits, then the mixture is correct and it is likely that the engine is in good condition.

6   The spark plug gap is of considerable importance, as, if it is too large or too small the size of the spark and its efficiency will be seriously impaired. Set the spark plug gap to the figure specified at the beginning of this Chapter.

7   To set it, measure the gap with a feeler gauge, and then bend open, or close, the out plug eceltrode until the correct gap is achieved. The centre electrode should never be bent as this may crack the insulation and cause plug failure, if nothing worse.

8   When replacing the plugs, remember to use new plug washers and replace the leads from the distributor in the correct firing order which is 1-5-3-6-2-4. Number 1 cylinder being at the rear of the engine and number 6 being nearest the radiator (Fig. 4.8).

9   Occasionally wipe the plug leads free from dirt and grease.

11 Ignition system - fault diagnosis

Failures of the ignition system will either be due to faults in the HT

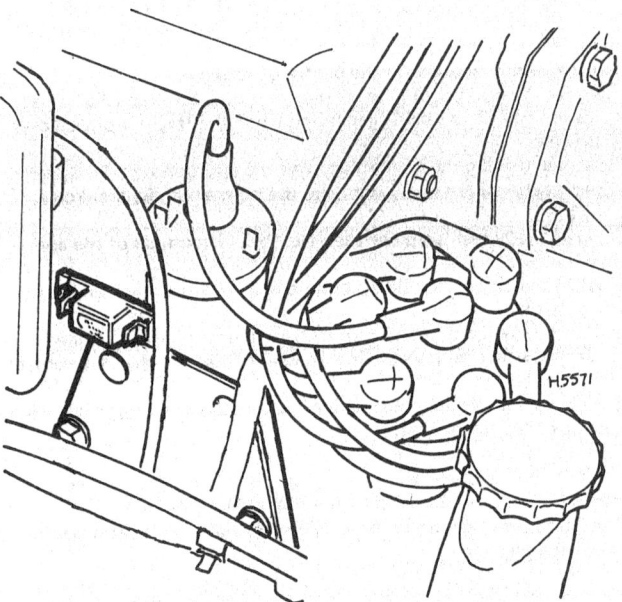

Fig. 4.7. Coil and ballast resistor (later cars) (Sec. 9)

or LT circuits. Initial checks should be made by observing the security of spark plug terminals, Lucar type terminals, coil and battery connection. More detailed investigation and the explanation and remedial action in respect of symptoms of ignition malfunction are described in the following sub-Sections.

Engine fails to start

1   If the engine fails to start and the car was running normally when it was last used, first check there is fuel in the fuel tank. If the engine turns over normally on the starter motor and the battery is evidently well charged, then the fault may be in either the high or low tension circuits. First check the HT circuit. **Note:** If the battery is known to be fully charged; the ignition light comes on, and the starter motor fails to turn the engine **check the tightness of the leads on the battery terminals** and also the secureness of the earth lead to its **connection to**

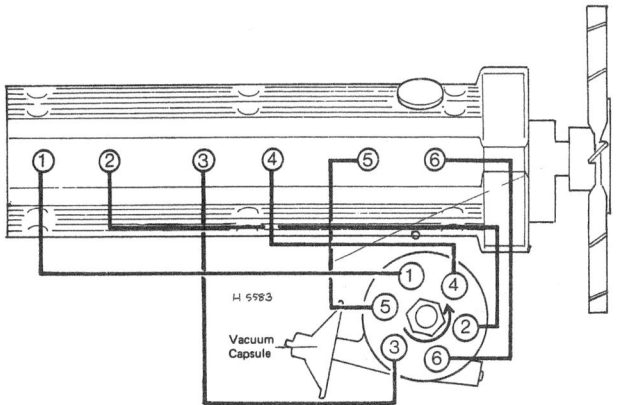

Fig. 4.8. Spark plug lead connection diagram (Sec. 10)

the body. It is quite common for the leads to have worked loose, even if they look and feel secure. If one of the battery terminal posts gets very hot when trying to work the starter motor this is a sure indication of a faulty connection to that terminal.

2   One of the commonest reasons for bad starting is wet or damp spark plug leads and distributor. Remove the distributor cap. If condensation is visible internally, dry the cap with a rag and also wipe over the leads. Replace the cap. A moisture dispersant, such as Holts Wet Start, can be very effective in these situations. To prevent the problem recurring Holts Damp Start can be used to provide a sealing coat, so excluding any further moisture from the ignition system. In extreme difficulty, Holts Cold Start will help to start a car when only a very poor spark occurs.

3   If the engine still fails to start, check that current is reaching the plugs, by disconnecting each plug lead in turn at the spark plug end, and hold the end of the cable about 3/16th inch (5.0 mm) away from the cylinder block. Spin the engine on the starter motor.

4   Sparking between the end of the cable and the block should be fairly strong with a regular blue spark. (Hold the lead with rubber to avoid electric shocks). If current is reaching the plugs, then remove them and clean and regap them. The engine should now start.

5   If there is no spark at the plug leads take off the HT lead from the centre of the distributor cap and hold it to the block as before. Spin the engine on the starter once more. A rapid succession of blue sparks between the end of the lead and the block indicate that the coil is in order and that the distributor cap is cracked, the rotor arm faulty, or the carbon brush in the top of the distributor cap is not making good contact with the spring on the rotor arm. Possibly the points are in bad condition. Clean and reset them as described in this Chapter.

6   If there are no sparks from the end of the lead from the coil, check the connections at the coil end of the lead. If it is in order start checking the low tension circuit.

7   Use a 12v voltmeter or a 12v bulb and two lengths of wire. With the ignition switch on and the points open test between the low tension wire to the coil (it is marked (+) and earth. No reading indicates a break in the supply from the ignition switch. Check the connections at the switch to see if any are loose. Refit them and the engine should run. A

reading shows a faulty coil or condenser, or broken lead between the coil and the distributor.

8   Take the condenser wire off the points assembly and with the points open, test between the moving point and earth. If there now is a reading, then the fault is in the condenser. Fit a new one and the fault is cleared.

9   With no reading from the moving point to earth, take a reading between earth and the (—) terminal of the coil. A reading here shows a broken wire which will need to be replaced between the coil and distributor. No reading confirms that the coil has failed and must be replaced, after which the engine will run once more. Remember to refit the condenser wire to the points assembly. For these tests it is sufficient to separate the points with a piece of dry paper while testing with the points open.

Engine misfires

10   If the engine misfires regularly run it at a fast idling speed. Pull off each of the plug caps in turn and listen to the note of the engine. Hold the plug cap in a dry cloth or with a rubber glove as additional protection against a shock from the HT supply.

11   No difference in engine running will be noticed when the lead from the defective circuit is removed. Removing the lead from one of the good cylinders will accentuate the misfire.

12   Remove the plug lead from the end of the defective plug and hold it about 3/16 inch (5 mm) away from the block. Restart the engine. If the sparking is fairly strong and regular the fault must lie in the spark plug.

13   The plug may be loose, the insulation may be cracked, or the points may have burnt away giving too wide a gap for the spark to jump. Worse still, one of the points may have broken off. Either renew the plug, or clean it, reset the gap, and then test it.

14   If there is no spark at the end of the plug lead, or if it is weak and intermittent, check the ignition lead from the distributor to the plug. If the insulation is cracked or perished, renew the lead. Check the connections at the distributor cap.

15   If there is still no spark, examine the distributor cap carefully for tracking. This can be recognised by a very thin black line running between two or more electrodes, or between an electrode and some other part of the distributor. These lines are paths which now conduct electricity across the cap thus letting it run to earth. The only answer is a new distributor cap.

16   Apart from the ignition timing being incorrect, other causes of misfiring have already been dealt with under the section dealing with the failure of the engine to start. To recap - these are that:

a)   *The coil may be faulty giving an intermittent misfire*
b)   *There may be a damaged wire or loose connection in the low tension circuit.*
c)   *The condenser may be short circuiting*
d)   *There may be a mechanical fault in the distributor (broken driving spindle or contact breaker spring).*

17   If the ignition timing is too far retarded, it should be noted that the engine will tend to overheat, and there will be a quite noticeable drop in power. If the engine is overheating and the power is down, and the ignition timing is correct, then the carburettor should be checked, as it is likely that this is where the fault lies.

Chapter 5 Clutch

For information applicable to Series 3 models, see Supplement at end of manual

Contents

Specifications

Type	Diaphragm spring with hydraulic actuation
Make	Borg and Beck 9.5 in
Release bearing	Graphite

Free-movement at withdrawal lever

Except Series 2	1/16 in (1.5 mm), at pedal ¼ in (6.35 mm)
Series 2	0.125 in (3.2 mm)

Clutch fluid type/specification	Hydraulic fluid to SAE J1703D (Duckhams Universal Brake and Clutch Fluid)

Torque wrench settings

	lb ft	Nm
Clutch cover bolts	20	27
Clutch bellhousing to gearbox bolts	42	57
Clutch bellhousing to engine bolts	35	48
Slave cylinder bolts	25	34

1 General description

1 The clutch fitted to all models is of Borg and Beck diaphragm spring type.
2 The diaphragm spring is riveted inside the pressure plate cover and has two fulcrum rings interposed between the shoulders of the rivets and the cover. The diaphragm spring pivots on these rings and depression of the clutch pedal actuates the release bearing causing the diaphragm spring to deflect and pull the pressure plate from the driven plate (friction disc) thus freeing the clutch.
3 Clutch actuation is hydraulic.

2 Clutch - adjustment

1 The clutch is virtually self-adjusting and the correct free-movement will normally be maintained throughout the life of the clutch driven plate.
2 However, on early models with a threaded pushrod, after overhaul or renewal of any of the actuating components, check that there is specified free-movement at the point of connection of the operating rod and withdrawal lever. This can be felt more easily if the return spring is first unhooked.
3 Any adjustment can be carried out by releasing the locknut on the operating rod and rotating the rod.

3 Master cylinder - removal, overhaul and refitting

1 Disconnect the fluid outlet pipe from the master cylinder.
2 Remove the four setscrews which secure the clutch pedal box to the engine compartment rear bulkhead. These screws are accessible from within the car (Fig. 5.2).
3 Remove the pedal box and master cylinder as an assembly.

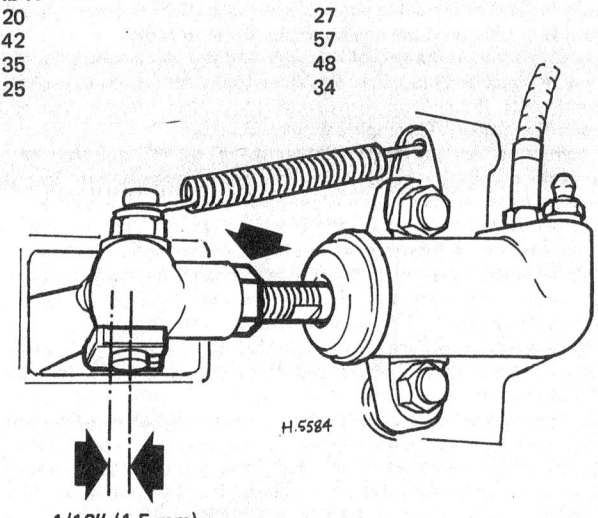

1/16" (1.5 mm)

Fig. 5.1. Clutch free movement diagram — early models, RHD (Sec. 2)

4 Extract the lockscrew and withdraw the pedal pivot pin. Pull the pedal back so that the split pin can be withdrawn.
5 Extract the split pin and clevis pin from the pushrod fork end.
6 Remove the two setscrews and detach the master cylinder from the pedal box.
7 Clean external dirt from the master cylinder and pull off the rubber boot from the master cylinder body rim.
8 Depress the pushrod slightly and extract the circlip (10). The pushrod (9), piston (7) and the other internal components will now be ejected from the cylinder body (Fig. 5.3).
9 At this stage wash all components in clean hydraulic fluid or methylated spirit (nothing else) and examine the surfaces of piston and cylinder for scoring or 'bright' wear areas. If these are evident then the master cylinder should be renewed complete.
10 If the components are found to be in good condition, discard the

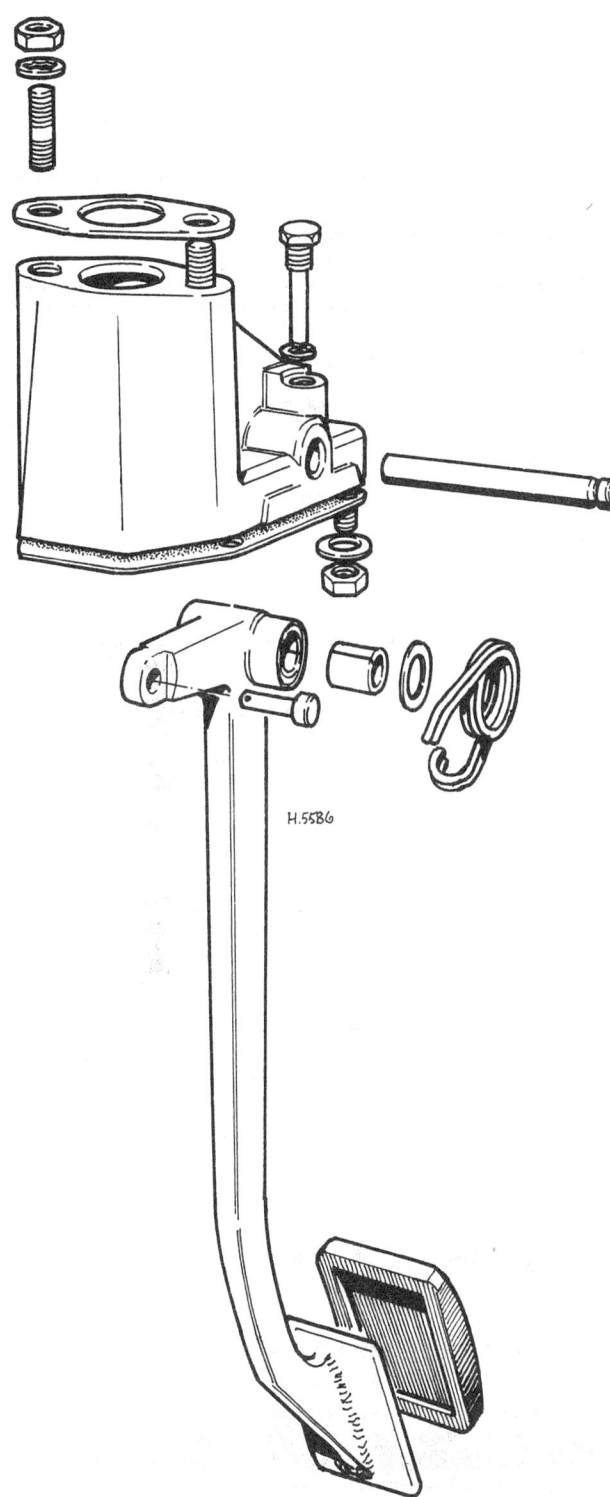

Fig. 5.2. Clutch pedal and master cylinder mounting box (Sec. 3)

rubber seals and obtain a repair kit which will contain all the necessary new seals and other items.
11 Fit the seals using the fingers only to manipulate them into position and making sure that the lips are correctly positioned.
12 Dip the internal components in clean hydraulic fluid before

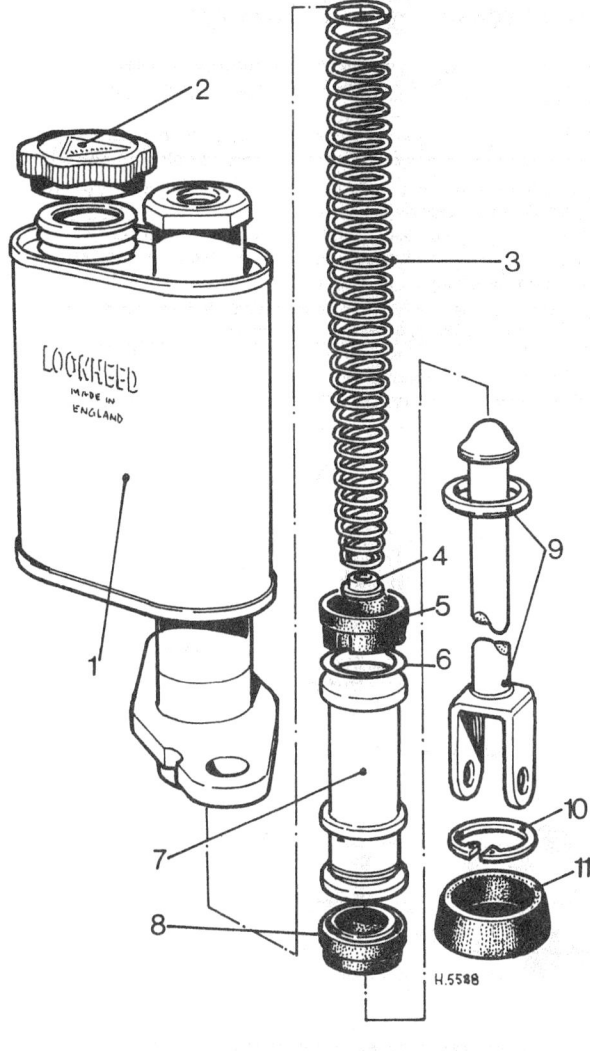

Fig. 5.3. Exploded view of the clutch master cylinder (Sec. 3)

1	Cylinder/reservoir	7 Piston
2	Filler/vent cap	8 Secondary cup seal
3	Piston return spring	9 Push-rod
4	Spring retainer	10 Circlip
5	Cup seal	11 Rubber boot
6	Washer	

installing them in the master cylinder body.
13 When reassembly is complete, refit the master cylinder by reversing the removal process and fill it with clean fluid.
14 Bleed the clutch hydraulic system (Section 5) and check the free-movement (Section 2).

4 Clutch slave cylinder - removal, overhaul and refitting

1   Unbolt and remove the slave cylinder cover.
2   On LHD models, disconnect the fluid pipe and plug the broken connections to prevent dirt ingress.
3   On RHD models, slacken the fluid pipe union, but do not attempt to remove the flexible hose.
4   Slide the rubber boot off the slave cylinder and along the pushrod. On early models, disconnect the return spring. (Later models are not fitted with a return spring.) Unbolt the cylinder and withdraw it off the pushrod which remains attached to the release lever.

5   On RHD models, unscrew the cylinder from the hose union and plug the broken connections to prevent dirt ingress.

6   The pushrod can be disconnected from the release lever on early models by withdrawing the pivot bolt, or on later models by unclipping it.

7   Clean external dirt from the cylinder and then extract the circlip.

8   Apply air pressure from a tyre foot pump to the fluid inlet hole and expel the internal components.

9   Wash the internal parts in clean hydraulic fluid or methylated spirit (nothing else) and examine the surfaces of piston and cylinder bore for scoring or 'bright' wear areas. If these are evident, renew the slave cylinder complete.

10 Where the components are in good order, discard the seals and obtain a repair kit which will contain all the necessary new seals and other renewable items.

11 Fit the new seals using the fingers only to manipulate them into position ensuring the lips face the correct way.

12 Dip the internal components in clean hydraulic fluid and insert them into the slave cylinder taking care not to trap the seal lips.

13 Fit the circlip and the rubber boot.

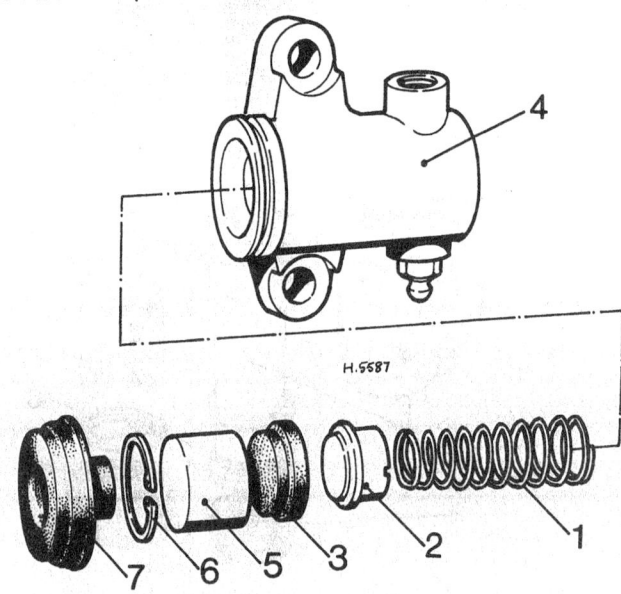

Fig. 5.4. Exploded view of the clutch slave cylinder (Sec. 4)

1   Piston return spring   5   Piston
2   Cup seal former   6   Circlip
3   Cup seal   7   Rubber boot
4   Body

14 Refit the slave cylinder on RHD models by first screwing it onto the end of the flexible hose.

15 On all models, enter the pushrod into the cylinder and bolt the cylinder to the bellhousing.

16 Reconnect the fluid pipe (LHD) or tighten the hose end fitting (RHD). Refit the cover. Reconnect the return spring and check the free movement on early models.

17 Fill the clutch master cylinder reservoir and then bleed the clutch hydraulic system as described in the next Section.

5   Clutch hydraulic system - bleeding

1   Bleeding the clutch hydraulic system (expelling air) is not a routine maintenance operation and should only be necessary when some portion of the hydraulic system has been disconnected or where, due to a leak, the level of fluid in the hydraulic reservoir has been allowed to drop too low. The presence of air in the system will result in poor clutch operation as, unlike fluid, the bubbles of air can be compressed.

2   Thoroughly clean the top of the clutch fluid reservoir and fill the reservoir with hydraulic fluid.

3   The bleed nipple for the system is located on the slave cylinder on the right-hand side of the clutch housing. Thoroughly clean the exterior of the nipple.

4   Attach a length of rubber tube to the nipple and allow it to hang in a clean glass jar, partly filled with hydraulic fluid. The open end of the tube must be submerged.

5   Unscrew the screw nipple one complete turn.

6   Have an assistant in the car to depress the clutch pedal slowly to the full extent of its travel. Tighten the screw nipple whilst the clutch pedal is held depressed.

7   Release pressure on the clutch pedal and repeat operations 5 and 6 until the fluid issuing from the tube is entirely free of air. Take care to replenish the reservoir frequently during these operations because if the fluid level is allowed to drop more than halfway, air will enter the system.

8   When you are satisfied that the system is clear of air, top up the master cylinder reservoir to the 'fluid level' mark.

9   Do not use the fluid which has been bled through the system as this will be aerated. Always use fresh fluid straight from a sealed container which has remained unshaken for the preceding 24 hours.

6   Clutch - removal

1   Access to the clutch is obtained by removing the engine/gearbox, as described in Chapter 1, and then unbolting the gearbox and withdrawing it from the engine.

2   Unscrew and remove the bolts which secure the clutch assembly to

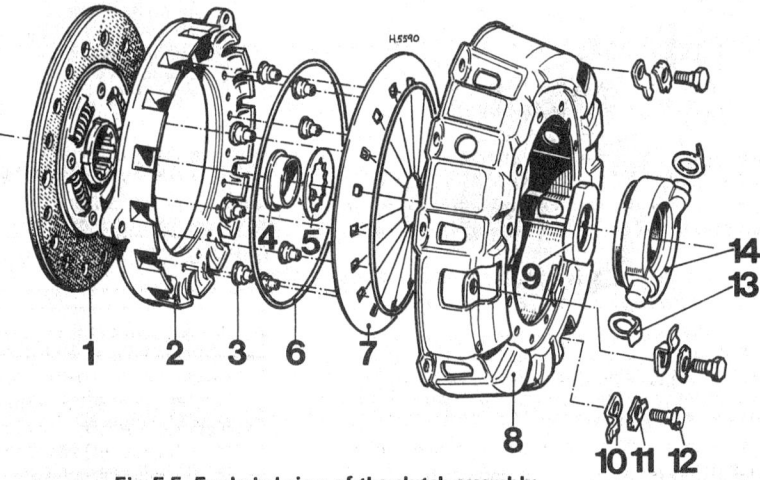

Fig. 5.5. Exploded view of the clutch assembly

1   Driven plate   5   Belleville washer   9   Release plate   13   Retainer
2   Pressure plate   6   Fulcrum ring   10   Retainer   14   Release bearing
3   Rivet   7   Diaphragm spring   11   Tab washer
4   Centre sleeve   8   Cover pressing   12   Setscrew

the flywheel. The position of any balance weights fitted must be noted and the weights retained for refitting in their original positions.
3 Withdraw the clutch assembly taking care to catch the driven plate as it falls from the face of the flywheel.

7 Clutch - inspection and renovation

1 Examine the friction facings. They will probably be highly polished, through which the grain of the material can be clearly seen, and mid-brown in colour. The facings are satisfactory if in this condition but if there are dark, highly glazed, patches which hide the grain or if there is a resinous deposit on the facings or if they have a black soaked appearance the indication is that they are contaminated with oil and the driven plate assembly should be renewed.
2 Examine the rivets of the driven plate. They should be well below the surface of the friction material and should be secure. Renew the driven plate if the facings are worn or if any rivets are loose.
3 Check the driven plate springs for fracture and security. Check the condition of the splines in the centre hub; excessive wear, which results from faulty alignment will mean renewing the plate.
4 Inspect the diaphragm spring for cracks or distortion.
5 The face of the pressure plate should not be ridged or pitted and this also applies to the face of the flywheel in the bearing area of the driven plate.
6 Check that the flange of the cover is not distorted.
7 If any of the faults just described are evident, renew the pressure plate assembly or the driven plate on a factory reconditioned exchange basis - do not waste your time trying to repair, overhaul or re-line them.
8 Before fitting new components always rectify oil leaks. These are probably due to a faulty crankshaft rear oil seal or a gearbox front oil seal.

8 Clutch release bearing and withdrawal mechanism - overhaul

1 With the gearbox separated from the engine, take the opportunity to inspect the withdrawal lever and release fork within the clutch bellhousing. Any wear in the pivot will necessitate renewal of the pin and bushes in the bellhousing and if wear has taken place in the fork as well then a new fork will be required.
2 If the clutch release bearing has been in use for 20,000 miles (32,000 km) or more it should be renewed as a matter of routine. The bearing is of graphite type.
3 To remove the bearing, disconnect the small coil spring clip at each side of the release fork and lift the bearing from the fork. Use new spring clips when installing.

9 Clutch - installation

1 With fingers free from grease, hold the driven plate against the flywheel so that the greater projecting side of the hub is towards the gearbox.
2 Place the pressure plate assembly on the flywheel so that the 'B' stamped close to one of the dowel holes coincides with the 'B' stamped on the flywheel.
3 Insert the clutch retaining bolts finger-tight.
4 Now centralise the driven plate by pushing a suitable guide tool through the splined hub of the driven plate to engage in the pilot bush of the flywheel. This tool may be an old gearbox primary shaft or a suitably stepped mandrel.
5 When the tool is a smooth sliding fit (having centralised the driven plate) then tighten the clutch securing bolts evenly to specified torque in diametrically opposite sequence.
6 Withdraw the guide tool.
7 Install the gearbox to the engine, supporting the weight of the gearbox so that it does not hang upon the primary shaft while the latter is engaged in the splined hub of the driven plate.
8 Insert the bolts which secure the clutch bellhousing to the engine and tighten them to specified torque.

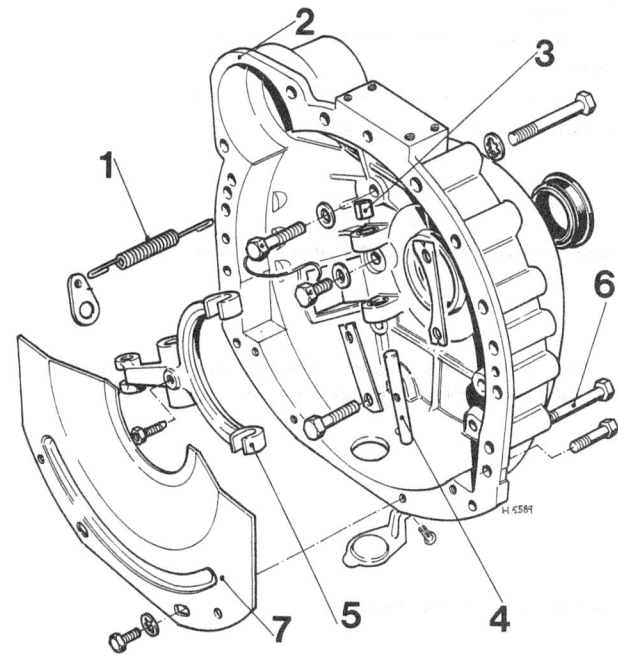

Fig. 5.6. Clutch bellhousing and release fork (Sec. 8)

1 *Pushrod return spring*	5 *Release fork*
2 *Bellhousing*	6 *Clutch bellhousing to*
3 *Release fork pivot bushes*	*engine bolts*
4 *Release fork pivot pin*	7 *Bellhousing lower cover plate*

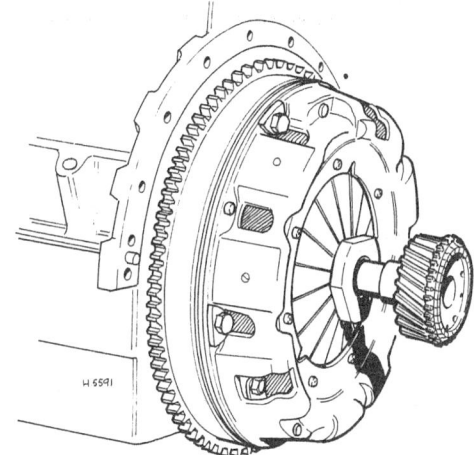

Fig. 5.7. Centralising the clutch driven plate (Sec. 9)

10 Clutch pedal - removal and refitting

1 Remove the pedal box as described in Section 3.
2 Disconnect the pedal return spring.
3 Disconnect the master cylinder pushrod from the pedal.
4 Remove the locating pin, then tap the clutch pedal pivot shaft from the pedal box casting.
5 Refit by reversing the removal operations, but smear grease on the pivot shaft before assembling it.

11 Fault diagnosis - clutch

Symptom	Reason/s
Judder when taking up drive (snatch)	Loose engine or gearbox mountings. Badly worn friction surfaces or contaminated with oil. Worn splines on gearbox input shaft or driven plate hub. Worn input shaft spigot bush in flywheel.
* Clutch spin (failure to disengage) so that gears cannot be meshed	Incorrect release bearing to diaphragm spring finger clearance. Driven plate sticking on input shaft splines due to rust. May occur after vehicle standing idle for long period. Damaged or misaligned pressure plate assembly.
Clutch slip (increase in engine speed does not result in increase in vehicle road speed - particularly on gradients)	Incorrect release bearing to diaphragm spring finger clearance. Friction surfaces worn out or oil contaminated.
Noise evident on depressing clutch pedal	Cracked, worn or damaged release bearing. Insufficient pedal free travel. Weak or broken pedal return spring. Weak or broken clutch release lever return spring. Excessive play between driven plate hub splines and input shaft splines.
Noise evident as clutch pedal released	Distorted driven plate. Broken or weak driven plate cushion coil springs. Insufficient pedal free travel. Weak or broken clutch pedal return spring. Weak or broken release lever return spring. Distorted or worn input shaft. Graphite bearing loose in retainer.

*This condition may also be due to the driven plate being rusted to the flywheel or pressure plate. It is possible to free it by applying the handbrake, engaging top gear, depressing the clutch pedal, and operating the starter motor. If really badly corroded, then the engine will not turn over, but in the majority of cases the driven plate will free. Once the engine starts, rev it up and slip the clutch several times to clear the rust deposits.

Chapter 6 Part I: Manual gearbox

For modifications, and information applicable to later models, see Supplement at end of manual

Contents

Specifications

Type ... ... Four forward and one reverse speed. Synchromesh on all forward gears

Ratios

1st gear	2.933 : 1 (early), 3.238 : 1 (later)
2nd gear	1.905 : 1
3rd gear	1.389 : 1
4th gear	1.00 : 1
Reverse gear	3.378 : 1 (early), 3.428 : 1 (later)

Endfloat tolerances

1st gear on mainshaft	0.005 to 0.007 in (0.13 to 0.18 mm)
2nd gear on mainshaft	0.005 to 0.008 in (0.13 to 0.20 mm)
3rd gear on mainshaft	0.005 to 0.008 in (0.13 to 0.20 mm)
Countergear endfloat	0.004 to 0.006 in (0.10 to 0.15 mm)

Oil type/specification ... ... Hypoid gear oil, viscosity SAE 90EP (Duckhams Hypoid 90)

Oil capacity

Gearbox without overdrive (early cars)	2½ Imp. pints (1.5 litres/3 US pints)
Gearbox with overdrive (early cars)	4 Imp. pints (2.25 litres/4¾ US pints)
Gearbox without overdrive (later cars)	3 Imp. pints (1.6 litres/3¼ US pints)
Gearbox with overdrive (later cars)	4½ Imp. pints (2.4 litres/5 US pints)

Overdrive

Type	Laycock de Normanville, ratio 0.778 : 1
Clutch movement from direct to overdrive	0.080 to 0.120 in (2.0 to 3.0 mm)
Hydraulic pressure:	
2.8 litre cars	400/420 lb/sq in (28.1 to 20.5 kg/sq cm)
4.2 litre cars	490/510 lb/sq in (34.5 to 35.8 kg/sq cm)

Torque wrench settings
Manual gearbox and overdrive

	lb ft	Nm
Clutch bellhousing to engine bolts	35	48
Gearbox output coupling flange nut	100	136
Overdrive unit output coupling flange nut	100	136
Gearbox mainshaft front nut	120	163
Top cover bolts	14	19
Rear cover bolts	14	19
Clutch bellhousing to gearbox bolts	42	57
Oil filler plug	25	34
Oil drain plug	25	34
Propeller shaft flange nuts	34	46
Reverse lever setscrew	25	34

1 General description

The gearbox is of four forward speed and one reverse type. Synchromesh is fitted to all forward speeds. Except for reverse gear, the detents for the gears are incorporated in the synchromesh assemblies.

The reverse gear detent is conventional with a spring-loaded ball engaging in a groove in the selector rod.

Two interlock balls and a pin prevent the engagement of more than one gear at a time.

An oil pump, driven from the rear end of the mainshaft, pressure feeds the gears on standard gearboxes. Where an overdrive unit is

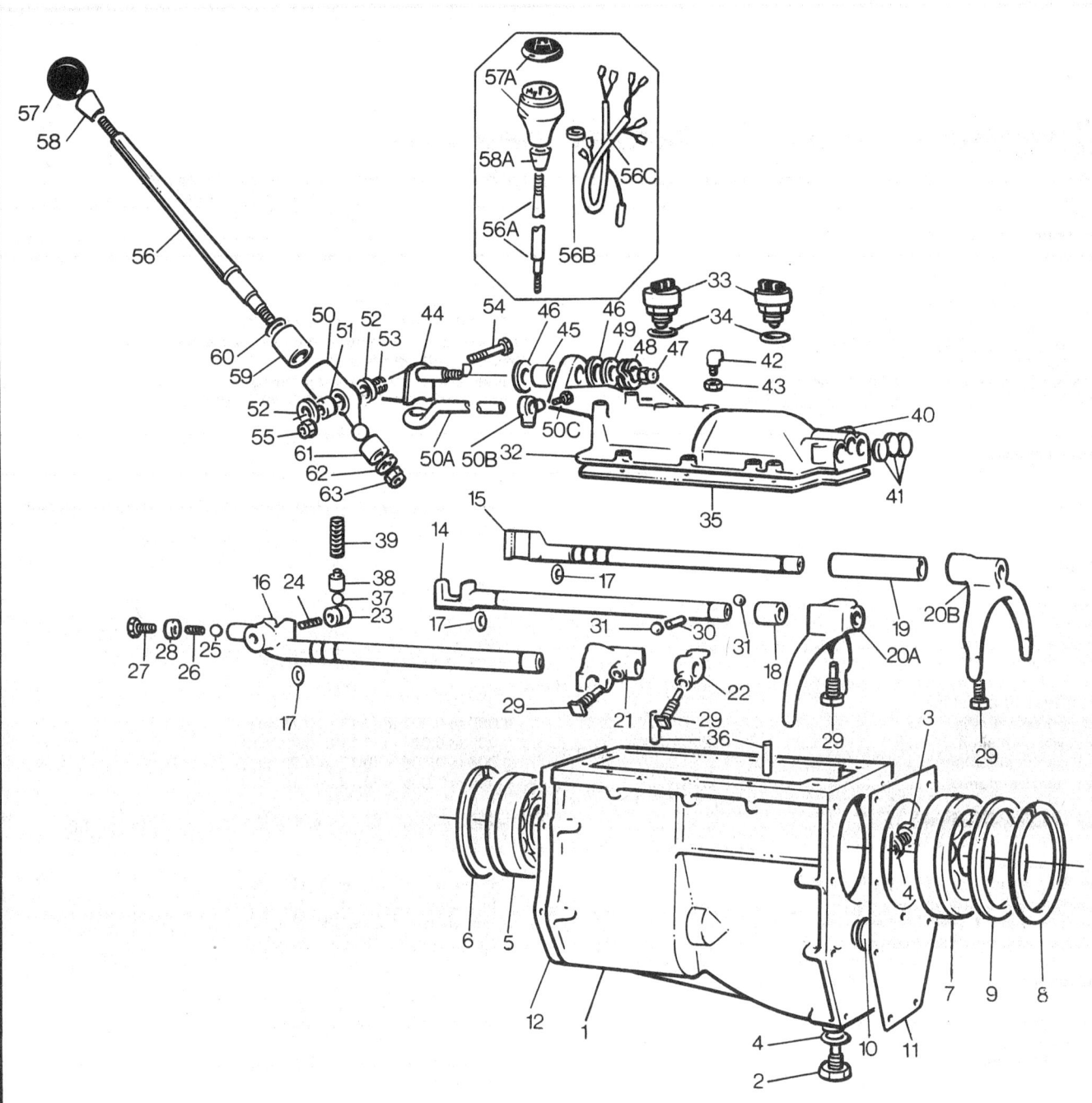

Fig. 6.1. Gear casing and top cover detail

1	Casing	20b	3rd/4th shift fork	38	Plunger	54 Pivot pin
2	Drain plug	21	Reverse shift fork	39	Spring	55 Nut
3	Filler/level plug	22	Locating arm	40	Welch plug	56 Gearshift lever (not with
4	Fibre washer	23	Plunger	41	Welch plug	overdrive)
5	Rear bearing	24	Spring	42	Breather	56a Gearshift lever (with
6	Circlip	25	Ball	43	Locknut	overdrive)
7	Front bearing	26	Spring	44	Pivot	56b Locknut
8	Circlip	27	Screw	45	Bush	56c Overdrive switch lead
9	Collar	28	Nut	46	Washer	57 Knob
10	Fibre blanking disc	29	Dowel bolt	47	Nut	57a Overdrive switch and knob
11	Gasket	30	Interlock pin	48	Spring washer	58 Locking cone (not with
12	Gasket	31	Interlock balls	49	'D' washer	overdrive)
14	1st/2nd selector rod	32	Top cover	50	Selector lever	58a Locking cone (with
15	3rd/4th selector rod	33	Switches for reversing lamps	50a	Remote control rod	overdrive)
16	Reverse selector rod		and overdrive isolation	50b	Remote control finger	59 Upper bush
17	'O' ring	34	Gasket	50c	Screw	60 Washer
18	Stop	35	Gasket	51	Bush	61 Lower bush
19	Stop	36	Dowel	52	Washer	62 Washer
20a	1st/2nd shift fork	37	Ball	53	Spring washer	63 Nut

installed, the overdrive oil pump provides the pressurised lubrication for the gearbox as well.

2 Lubrication and maintenance

1 At the intervals specified in 'Routine maintenance' at the beginning of this manual, place the car on level ground and remove the combined level/filler plug from the left-hand side of the gearbox (early cars) or the right-hand side (later cars). The oil should be at the bottom of the hole.

2 Where overdrive is fitted, the same oil from the gearbox feeds the overdrive therefore checking the gearbox oil level automatically checks the overdrive oil level as well.

3 The gearbox and (where fitted) the overdrive should be drained and refilled at the intervals specified in 'Routine maintenance'. Although the two units use common oil, they must be drained separately.

4 The drain plugs are located at the bases of the gearbox and the overdrive unit and whenever the overdrive is drained, also remove the filter plug from the side of the overdrive casing and thoroughly clean the filter and magnetic washers before refitting them.

5 Always observe strict cleanliness when refilling the overdrive unit or gearbox, or topping-up.

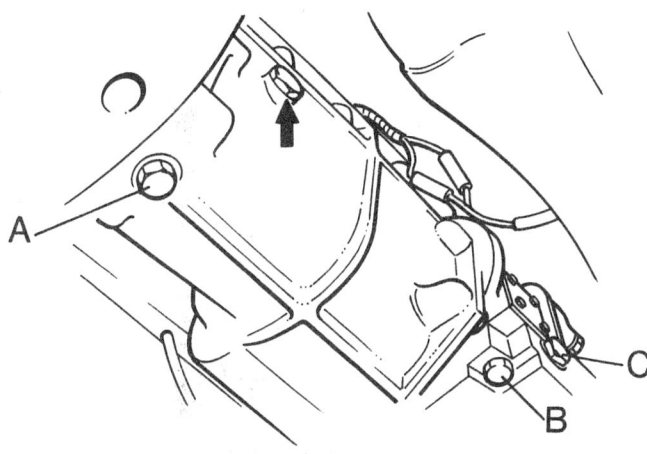

Fig. 6.2. Gearbox drain plug (A) overdrive drain plug (B) and overdrive filter plug (C). Gearbox combined filler/level plug (early cars) arrowed. Later cars have filler/level plug on opposite side of casing (Sec. 2)

3 Gearbox - removal and installation (Series I)

1 Remove the engine, gearbox and overdrive (where fitted) as a combined unit and as described in Chapter 1, Section 5.

2 Separate the engine and gearbox as described in Chapter 1, Section 7.

3 Installation is a reversal of removal again as described in Chapter 1, Sections 52 and 53, but after installation in the car, run the car on the road in top gear as soon as possible in order that the mainshaft speed will be high enough to prime the oil pump.

4 To remove the gearbox on Series 2 and 3 cars, refer to Chapter 13, Supplement. The operations described apply equally to 4 and 5-speed gearboxes.

4 Gearbox - dismantling into major assemblies

1 If an overdrive is fitted, remove it as described in Section 11. Remove the clutch release bearing and fork (Chapter 5, Section 8) and unbolt and remove the clutch bellhousing from the gear casing.

2 Place the gear lever in neutral, unscrew and remove the eight setscrews and two nuts and lift off the top cover (early cars). On later cars, ten setscrews are used to retain the top cover. These setscrews are of varying lengths and must be refitted in their original positions. A good way of ensuring this is to make a template of the top cover with holes punched in it corresponding to the bolt holes in the top cover and then place the bolts in their respective holes in the template as each one is withdrawn.

3 **To remove the rear extension (gearbox without overdrive),** flatten the locking tab on the output coupling flange nut. Engage 1st and reverse gears together to lock the mainshaft.

4 Unscrew and remove the flange nut and withdraw the flange complete with thrust washer and four coupling flange bolts.

5 Unscrew and remove the speedometer pinion lockbolt and then withdraw the pinion and bush from the rear extension.

6 Unscrew and remove the setscrews which retain the rear extension to the main gearbox casing and withdraw the extension at the same time collecting the distance piece, the oil pump driving pin and oil filter from the output shaft.

7 Working within the rear extension, relieve the staking of the three countersunk screws which secure the oil pump gear housing. Withdraw the housing by screwing in two of the retaining screws into the tapped holes provided in the housing. It is important that the oil pump gears are marked with spirit pen or masking tape to ensure that they are meshed the same way up on reassembly. Renew the rear extension housing oil seal and the bearing if the latter is worn or noisy when turned.

8 *To remove the countershaft* from the main gear casing, extract the fibre plug from the front of the shaft.

9 Drive out the countershaft so that it emerges from the front of the casing. Make sure that the countershaft rear thrust washer drops down as shown in the illustration otherwise it may be trapped by reverse gear when removing the mainshaft (Fig. 6.4).

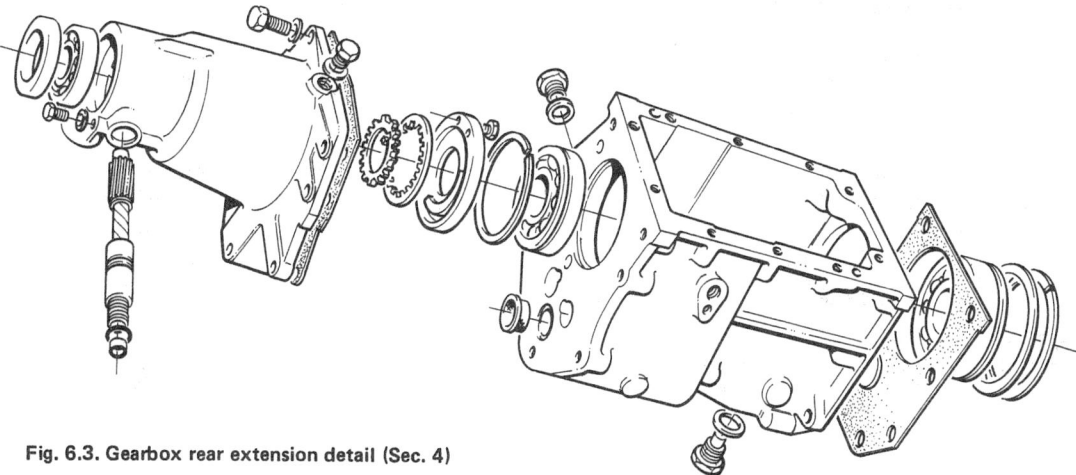

Fig. 6.3. Gearbox rear extension detail (Sec. 4)

10 *To remove the constant pinion shaft,* rotate the shaft until the cut-away parts of the driving gear are facing the top and bottom of the casing. Ease the constant pinion shaft and front bearing from the gear casing using two screwdrivers as levers.

11 *To remove the mainshaft,* rotate it until one of the cut-away parts in the 3rd/4th synchro. hub is aligned in such a way to prevent the hub fouling the constant gear of the countershaft gear cluster which is still lying in the gear casing.

12 Using a soft faced hammer, drive the mainshaft through the rear bearing making sure that reverse gear is held tight against 1st gear in the process.

13 Remove the mainshaft rear bearing from the gearbox casing.

14 Slacken reverse lever bolt so that the lever can be moved easily backwards and forwards.

15 Lift the mainshaft assembly upwards and out of the gearbox making sure that reverse gear does not slide off the end of the mainshaft. Fitting a small worm-drive clip to the shaft will prevent this happening.

16 The countershaft cluster gear assembly, needle rollers and retaining rings and thrust washers can now be extracted from the bottom of the gearbox.

17 Withdraw reverse idler shaft and lift out the gear noting the Woodruff key on the shaft.

---

5 Mainshaft - dismantling and reassembly

---

1 Before dismantling the mainshaft, note that the needle rollers must be kept in their individual gear sets as they are size graded for their individual locations and must not be mixed up.

2 Withdraw reverse gear from the mainshaft.

3 Withdraw 1st gear, retaining the 120 needle rollers, spacers and sleeve.

4 Withdraw 1st/2nd synchro. unit, retaining the two loose synchro.

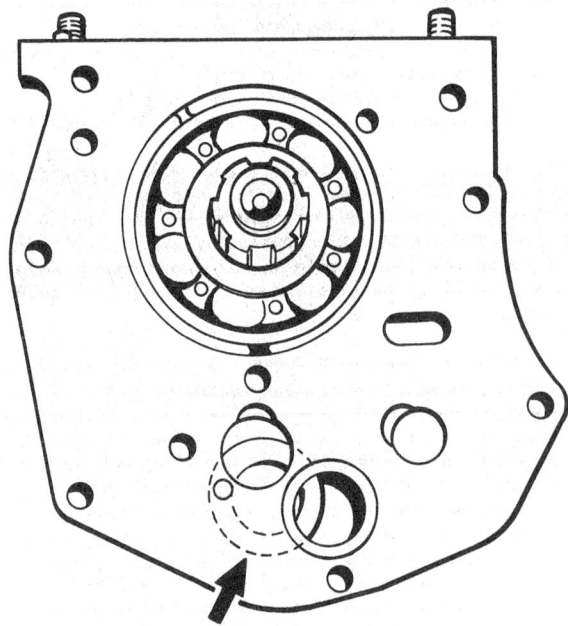

Fig. 6.4. Position of countergear thrust washer after withdrawal of countershaft (Sec. 4)

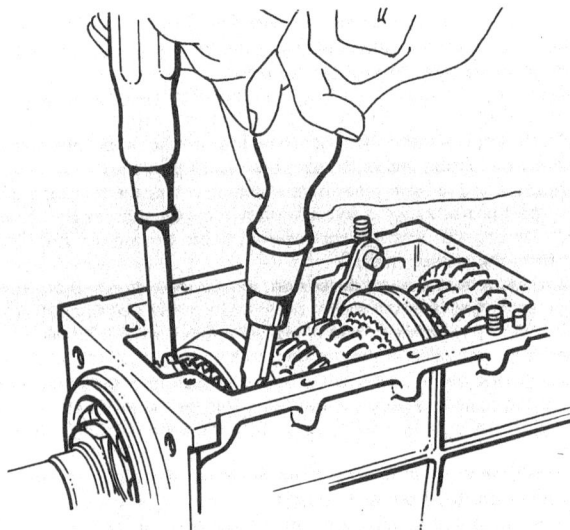

Fig. 6.5. Removing constant pinion shaft (Sec. 4)

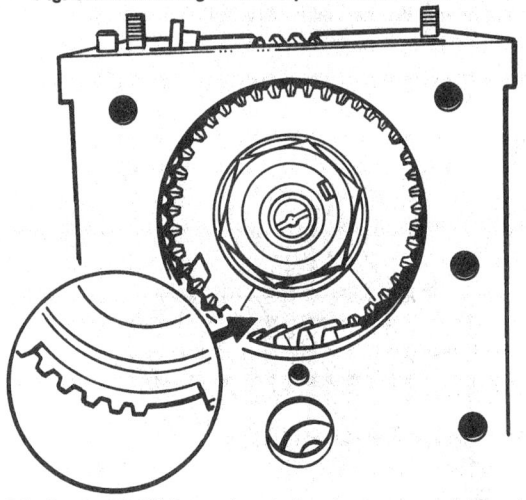

Fig. 6.6. Setting 3rd/4th synchro. hub prior to removal of mainshaft (Sec. 4)

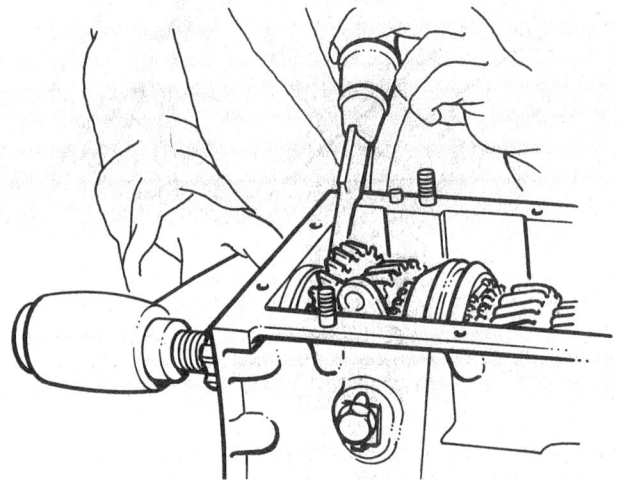

Fig. 6.7. Driving mainshaft from rear bearing (Sec. 4)

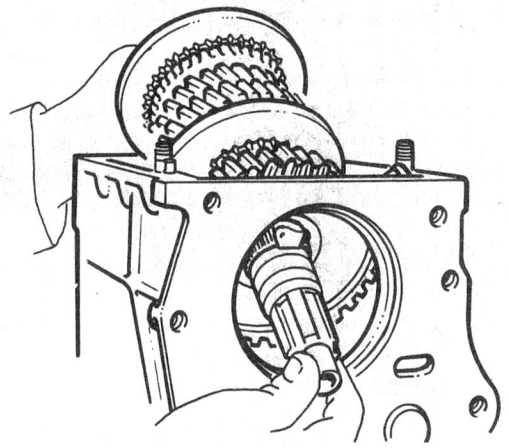

Fig. 6.8. Removing mainshaft assembly (Sec. 4)

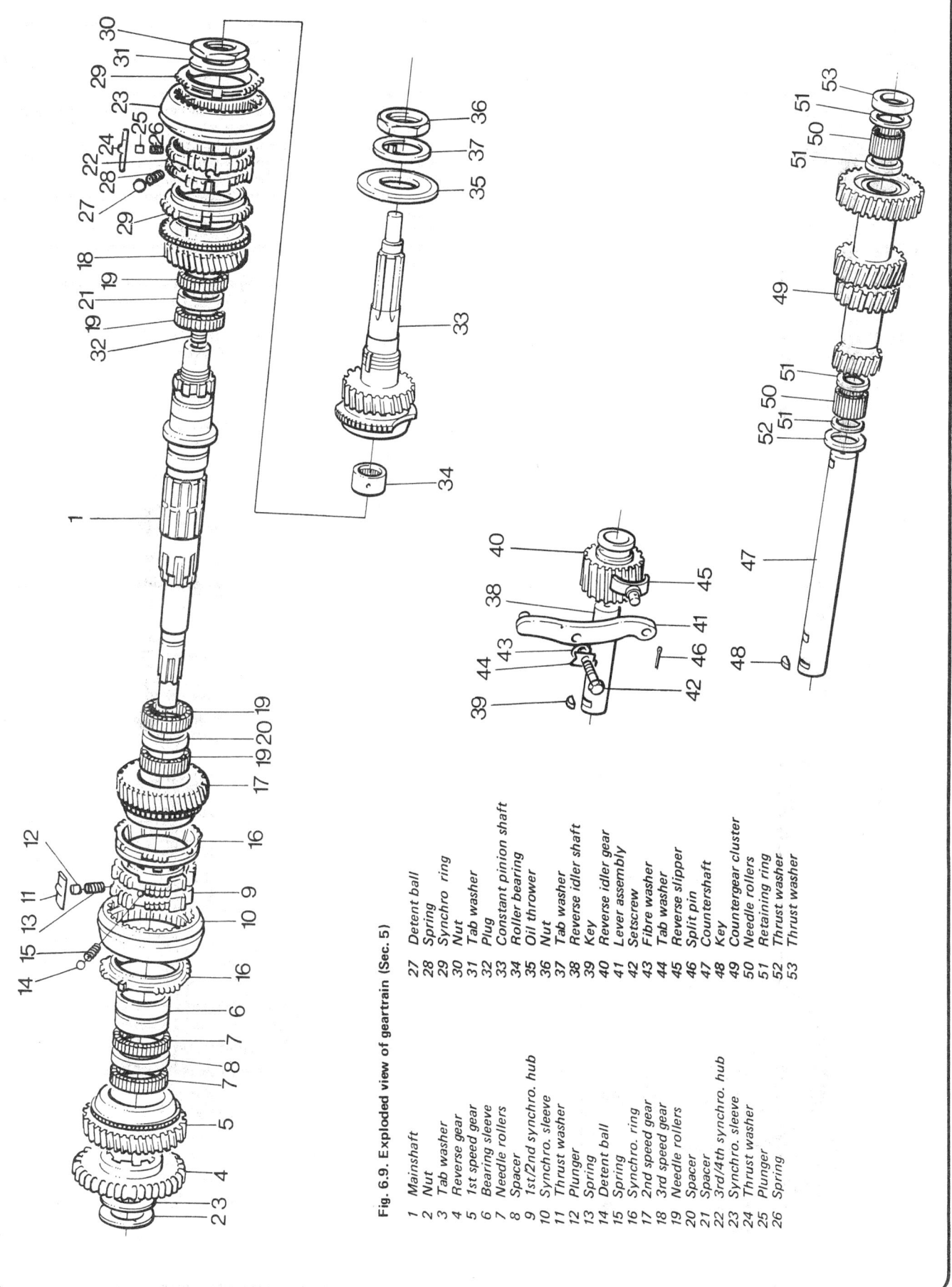

Fig. 6.9. Exploded view of geartrain (Sec. 5)

1 Mainshaft
2 Nut
3 Tab washer
4 Reverse gear
5 1st speed gear
6 Bearing sleeve
7 Needle rollers
8 Spacer
9 1st/2nd synchro. hub
10 Synchro. sleeve
11 Thrust washer
12 Plunger
13 Spring
14 Detent ball
15 Spring
16 Synchro. ring
17 2nd speed gear
18 3rd speed gear
19 Needle rollers
20 Spacer
21 Spacer
22 3rd/4th synchro. hub
23 Synchro. sleeve
24 Thrust washer
25 Plunger
26 Spring
27 Detent ball
28 Spring
29 Synchro ring
30 Nut
31 Tab washer
32 Plug
33 Constant pinion shaft
34 Roller bearing
35 Oil thrower
36 Nut
37 Tab washer
38 Reverse idler shaft
39 Key
40 Reverse idler gear
41 Lever assembly
42 Setscrew
43 Fibre washer
44 Tab washer
45 Reverse slipper
46 Split pin
47 Countershaft
48 Key
49 Countergear cluster
50 Needle rollers
51 Retaining ring
52 Thrust washer
53 Thrust washer

rings. Withdraw 2nd speed gear, needles and spacer.

5   Grip the mainshaft securely in a vice fitted with jaw protectors, flatten the lock tab and unscrew the nut from the front end of the mainshaft. Draw off 3rd/4th synchro. unit and 3rd speed gear with 106 needles and spacer.

6   Examine all components for wear and gear endfloat detailed in 'Specifications' and renew as necessary.

7   Reassembly is a reversal of dismantling but make sure that needle rollers of one grading only are used for each gear. Finally retain the reverse gear on the shaft using a worm-drive clip or similar device pending installation in the gearbox of the complete mainshaft assembly. Tighten the mainshaft front nut to specified torque and use a lockwasher.

---

6   Synchromesh units - dismantling and reassembly

1   The synchromesh units are overhauled in the same way but their component parts, although similar in appearance are not interchangeable. The 3rd/top synchro. hub has a groove machined in it to identify it.

2   To dismantle a synchromesh unit, cover it with a stout piece of rag and push out the hub from the sleeve. Collect the balls, springs and other components.

3   Examine each part for wear particularly the contours of the teeth and grooves, renewing as necessary.

4   Commence reassembly by fitting the synchro. sleeve to the hub so that the deeper boss of the hub is on the same side as the narrow

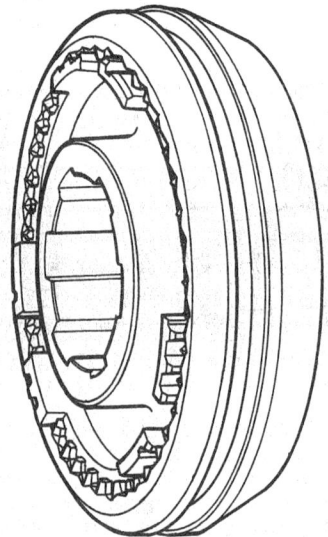

Fig. 6.10. Synchro. hub to sleeve relationship (Sec. 6)

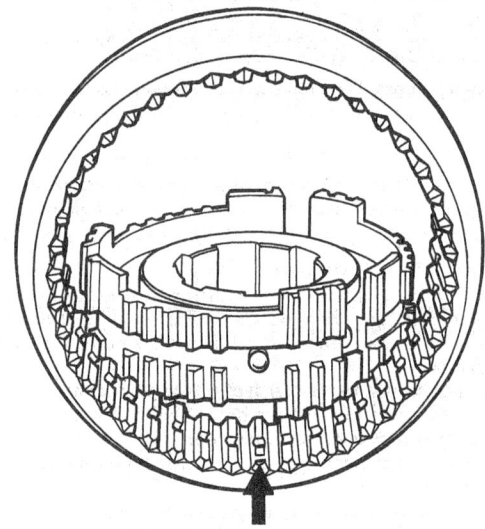

Fig. 6.11. Synchro. sleeve tooth with three grooves (Sec. 6)

chamfer of the sleeve.

5   Locate the three balls and springs in line with the teeth which have the three detent grooves on them.

6   Set the synchro. hub so that the holes for the balls and springs are exactly flush with the top of the sleeve (wider chamfer uppermost). Place a packing piece under the hub to set its height.

7   Install the three springs, plungers and their thrust members holding them in position with thick grease and depressing the thrust members as far as possible. Compress the springs using a worm-drive clip or piston ring clamp and then lift the synchro. assembly from the temporary packing piece. Depress the hub and at the same time push down the thrust members with a screwdriver until they engage in the groove in the sleeve (Figs. 6.14 and 6.15).

8   Using a soft-faced hammer, tap the synchro hub downwards until the balls can be heard and felt to engage in the neutral groove of the sleeve (Fig. 6.16).

---

7   Constant pinion shaft - dismantling and reassembly

1   Extract the roller bearing from inside the shaft.

2   Tap back the tab washer and remove the large nut, the tab washer and the oil thrower.

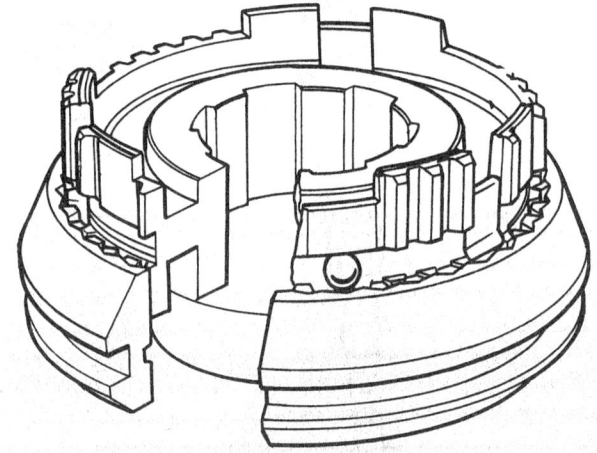

Fig. 6.12. Setting synchro. hub on sleeve ready for insertion of balls and springs (Sec. 6)

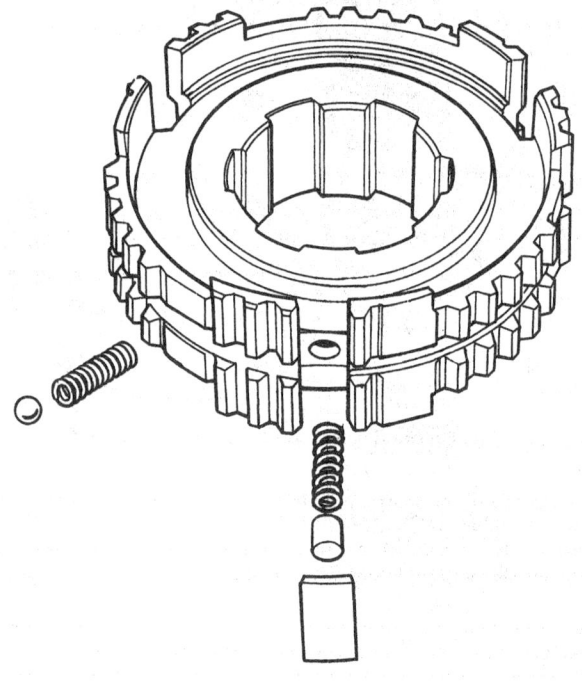

Fig. 6.13. Synchro. hub showing relative positions of ball, plunger and thrust member (Sec. 6)

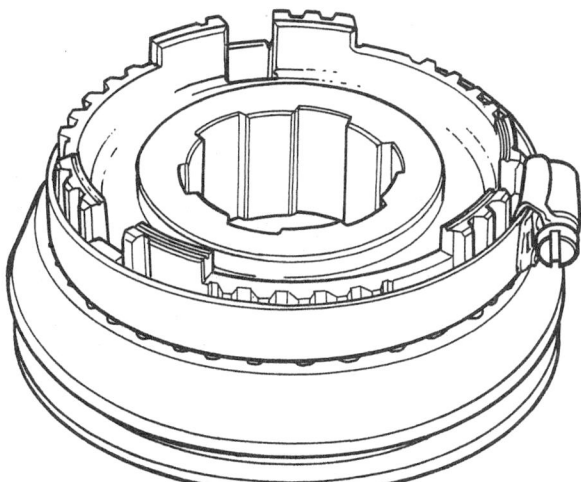

Fig. 6.14. Using a clip to compress the synchro. spring (Sec. 6)

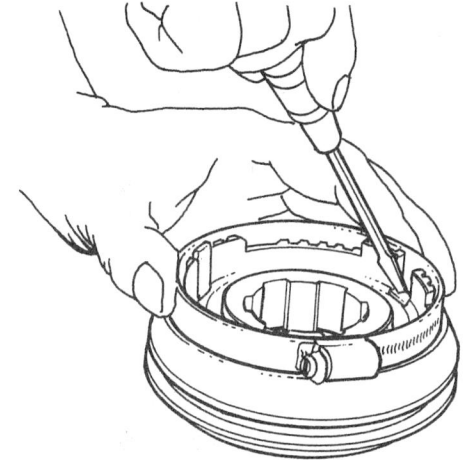

Fig. 6.15. Pushing down the synchro. thrust members (Sec. 6)

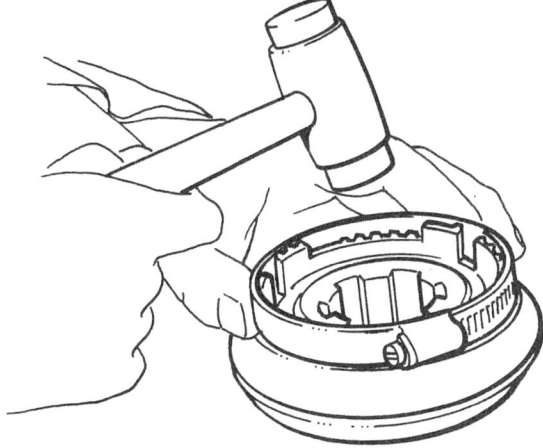

Fig. 6.16. Tapping the synchro hub fully into engagement (Sec. 6)

3   Tap the end of the shaft on the bench or strike it with a soft-faced hammer to dislodge the shaft bearing.
4   Reassembly is a reversal of dismantling but make sure that the shaft bearing is square and fully seated on the shaft.

8   Gearbox top cover - dismantling and reassembly

1   Unscrew the self-locking nut and remove the double coil spring, washers and fibre washer which secure the gearshift lever to the top

cover.
2   Withdraw the gearlever.
3   Cut the locking wire and unscrew the selector rod retaining screws.
4   Withdraw 3rd/4th selector rod and extract the shift fork, spacer tube and interlock balls. Note the loose interlock pin at the front of the 1st/2nd selector rod.
5   Withdraw reverse selector rod and extract reverse fork, stop spring and detent plunger.
6   Withdraw 1st/2nd selector rod and extract the shift fork and the short spacer tube.
7   Reassembly is a reversal of dismantling but make sure that the interlock ball and pin are installed correctly when assembling the selector rods. Always renew the 'O' rings on the selector rods.
8   Install the reverse plunger and spring. Fit the ball and spring and start the screw and locknut on their threads. Press in the plunger as far as it will go and then tighten the screw to hold the plunger in its fully depressed state.
9   Release the screw until the plunger comes out far enough for the ball to engage in its circular groove. Hold the screw in this position and tighten the locknut.

9   Gearbox - reassembly

1   Fit one retaining ring to the front end of the counter gear. Using grease, locate 29 needle rollers in position and fit the inner thrust washer, making sure that the peg on the washer engages in the groove which is machined on the front face of the countergear.
2   Fit the second retaining ring and the 29 needle rollers to the rear end of the countershaft gear again using grease to retain the components.
3   Install the reverse idler gear, lever and idler shaft.
4   Using a dab of thick grease, stick the countergear rear thrust washer to the inside of the gearbox casing.
5   Stick the second thrust washer to the front of the countergear and then carefully lower the gear into position in the gear casing.
6   Using a rod which is slightly smaller in diameter than the countershaft, insert it through the gear casing so that it passes through the countergear without displacing the needle rollers or thrust washers.
7   Using feeler blades, check the clearance (endfloat) between the rear thrust washer and the end face of the countergear. This should be between 0.004 and 0.006 in (0.10 and 0.15 mm). Any adjustment which may be needed is carried out by changing the thrust washers. These are available in five thicknesses: 0.152 in (3.86 mm), 0.156 in (3.96 mm), 0.159 in (4.04 mm), 0.162 in (4.11 mm) and 0.164 in (4.17 mm).
8   Withdraw the rod from the countergear and lower the countergear to the bottom of the gear casing.
9   Install a new gasket to the front face of the gear casing.
10 Insert the reassembled mainshaft through the top of the gear casing and pass the rear of the mainshaft through the rear bearing aperture.
11 Insert the constant pinion shaft/bearing assembly through the bearing aperture at the front of the gear casing, making sure that the cut-away parts of the driving gear are at the top and bottom and that the internal roller bearing is in position.
12 Tap the constant pinion shaft into engagement with the front end of the mainshaft.
13 Hold the constant pinion shaft securely in position and then install the mainshaft rear bearing using a piece of tubing applied to its inner race to drive it home.
14 Carefully raise the countergear until its gears mesh with those of the mainshaft. Insert the countershaft from the rear of the gear casing, taking care not to displace the thrust washers or needle rollers. Fit the Woodruff key which locates the countershaft in the gear casing.

Gearbox without overdrive

15 If the oil pump gears were removed, refit them to the oil pump in their original attitude as marked before removal. Coat the gears and interior of the pump body with oil. Insert the pump housing screws and stake them.
16 Fit a new gasket to the rear face of the gear casing.
17 Install the distance piece and driving pin to the oil pump in the rear extension. Fit the output shaft oil filter.
18 Locate the rear extension onto the gear casing and secure it with the setscrews.
19 Install the speedometer drive gear to the end of the mainshaft, fit the speedometer driven gear and bush so that the hole in the bush is in

line with the hole in the rear extension. Insert the speedometer pinion lock bolt.

20 Install the flange to the rear end of the mainshaft making sure that the coupling bolts are in position in the flange bolt holes before fitting the flange.

21 Fit a new tab washer and screw on the mainshaft nut. Lock two gears to prevent the mainshaft turning and then tighten to specified torque and bend over the locking tab.

Gearbox with overdrive

22 Refit the overdrive as described in Section 11.

All gearboxes

23 To install the top cover, first fit a new gasket. Check that the gears and top cover selectors are in the neutral position. Check that reverse idler gear is not in mesh by pushing reverse lever fully to the rear.

24 Lower the top cover onto the gear casing until the shift forks engage with the grooves in the synchromesh units.

25 Install and tighten the top cover bolts and nuts making sure that they are returned to their original positions.

26 Refit the clutch bellhousing complete with new constant pinion shaft oil seal (lip towards gearbox). Note that the two clutch bellhousing bolts adjacent to the clutch fork trunnions are locked with wire. The other bolts are locked with tab washers.

27 Refit the clutch release lever and bearing.

10 Overdrive unit - description, maintenance and adjustment

1 The overdrive unit consists of a hydraulically controlled epicyclic gear housed in a casing at the rear of the gearbox. When engaged, the overdrive unit reduces the engine speed in relation to the road speed so reducing engine wear and giving improved fuel economy.

2 The overdrive is operated by an electric solenoid which is actuated by a switch mounted on the gearshift knob and it can only be engaged when top gear has been selected due to the provision of an isolator switch.

3 Topping-up and changing the oil have been covered in conjunction with the gearbox in Section 2 of this Chapter.

4 Adjustment of the solenoid should not be regarded as routine but in the event of faulty operation of the overdrive unit, the adjustment should be checked.

5 The solenoid box is located on the left-hand side of the overdrive unit and is accessible from underneath the car.

6 Remove the solenoid cover plate (four screws) and expose the solenoid lever.

7 Move the lever to the right until a rod 3/16 in (4.76 mm) in diameter when pushed through the hole in the lever, will register with the hole in the overdrive casing. Now turn the plunger nut until the point is reached where the plunger is pushed right home in the solenoid and the nut just makes contact with the fork of the lever. Remove the rod.

8 Energise the solenoid by applying current to it from the car battery and recheck the alignment of the holes. If they are in correct alignment, refit the solenoid cover plate. Adjustment can be verified by connecting a 0 to 30 amp ammeter in series with the solenoid supply cable and when the solenoid is energised, the current consumption should be 1 amp.

9 The overdrive isolator switch should not normally require adjustment but if it becomes faulty then it must be renewed and adjustment of the new switch will almost certainly be required.

10 To renew the switch, disconnect the battery and remove the cover from the transmission tunnel.

11 Support the rear end of the engine using a hoist or a crossbar and threaded lifting eye supported on the top surfaces of the front wing valances.

12 Remove the four screws from the engine rear mounting bracket and then lower the rear of the engine by no more than 1 to 2 in (25.4 to 50.8 mm).

13 Disconnect the leads from the isolator switch which is located on the left-hand side of the gearbox. Unscrew the switch and retain the washers.

14 Install the new switch using the original washers and then connect a continuity meter between the switch terminals. Place the gearlever in neutral when the meter should indicate a very high resistance (open circuit). Now press the gearlever towards top gear when the meter

Fig. 6.17. Exploded view of the overdrive unit (Sec. 12)

1	Adaptor plate	19	Plug	37	Cam
2	Gasket	20	Washer	38	Operating piston
3	Stud	21	Oil pump plunger assembly	39	'O' ring
4	Stud	22	Oil pump body	40	Bridge piece
5	Front casing	23	Spring	41	Nut
6	Shaft	24	Screw	42	Tab washer
7	Cam	25	Fibre washer	43	Accumulator piston
8	Lever	26	'O' ring	44	Ring
9	Tension pin	27	Non-return valve	45	Spring
10	'O' ring	28	Ball	46	Support rod
11	Welch plug	29	Spring	47	Packing washer
12	Stop	30	Support rod	48	Plug
13	Breather	31	Plug	49	Washer
14	Stud	32	Copper washer	50	Solenoid
15	Main operating valve	33	Oil filter	51	Gasket
16	Ball	34	Magnetic ring	52	Nut
17	Plunger	35	Plug	53	Gasket
18	Spring	36	Washer	54	Thrust ring

55	Retaining plate	73	Roller
56	Spring	74	Spring
57	Clutch sliding member	75	Clutch inner member
58	Ball bearing	76	Thrust washer
59	Circlip	77	Rear casing assembly
60	Corrugated washer	78	Stud
61	Circlip	79	Oil seal
62	Brake ring	80	Oil seal
63	Sun wheel	81	Speedometer driving gear
64	Planetary carrier assembly	82	Speedometer driven gear
65	Annulus assembly	83	Bearing assembly
66	Oil thrower	84	'O' ring
67	Spring ring	85	Screw
68	Spring ring	86	Copper washer
69	Ball bearing	87	Connecting flange
70	Circlip	88	Bolt
71	Ball bearing	89	Nut
72	Uni-directional clutch cage	90	Washer
		91	Split pin

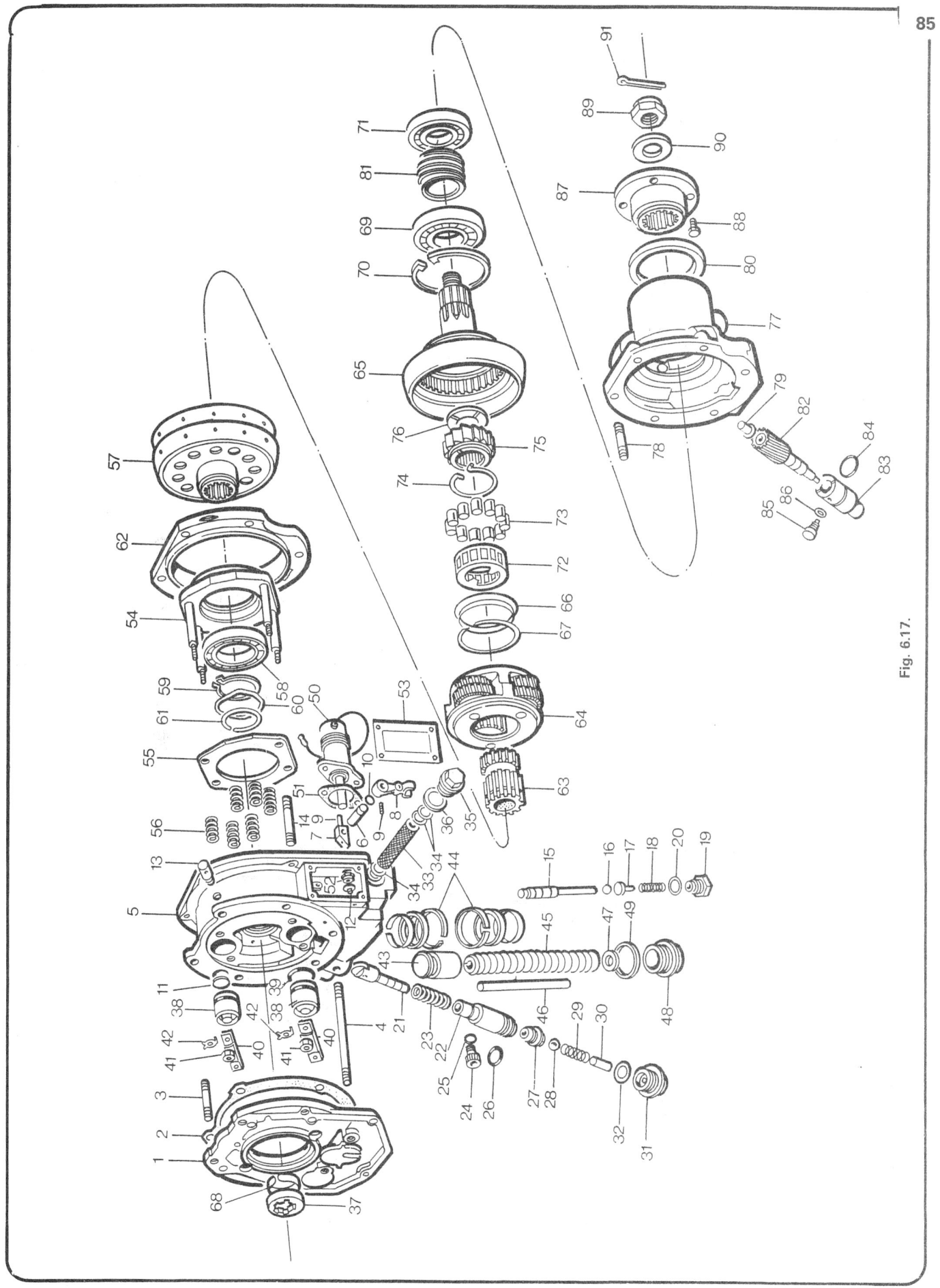

Fig. 6.17.

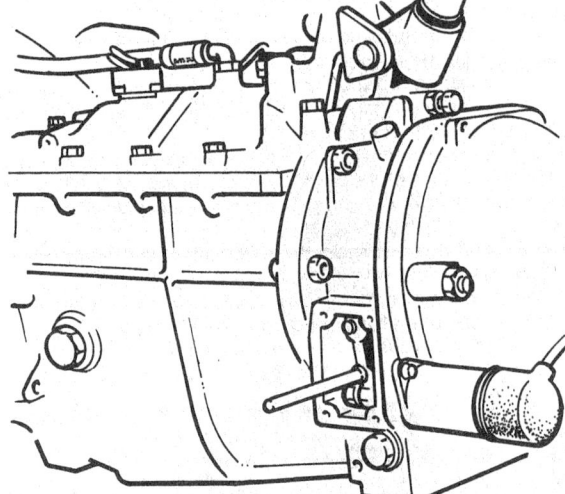

Fig. 6.18. Adjusting the overdrive unit solenoid (Sec. 10)

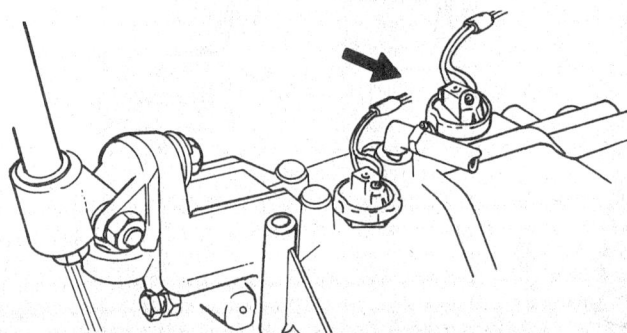

Fig. 6.19. Overdrive isolator switch (arrowed) (Sec. 10)

should indicate a short circuit immediately the gearlever moves. Add or remove washers from the switch as necessary to achieve this situation.

15 Reverse the removal operations to complete the fitting.

11 Overdrive unit - removal and refitting

1 On Series 1 cars, the overdrive can only be removed after the complete engine/transmission has been withdrawn as described in Chapter 1. On Series 2 and 3 cars, the overdrive can be removed independently as described in Chapter 13, Supplement, at the end of this manual.

2 Remove the gearbox from the engine also as described in Chapter 1.

3 Remove the nuts from the four short studs which retain the overdrive unit to the adaptor plate on the rear face of the gear casing. Also remove the two nuts from the long studs at the base of the overdrive unit.

4 Withdraw the overdrive unit from the mainshaft leaving the adaptor plate in positon.

5 The adaptor plate is held in position by seven nuts which can be removed if required.

6 To refit the overdrive unit to the gearbox, secure the unit upside-down in a vice.

7 With the internal splines correctly aligned (see Section 12), do not turn the output flange until the unit has been fitted to the gearbox.

8 Check that the cam is not worn and that the flat spring ring on the gearbox mainshaft is not distorted nor protrudes above the splines.

9 Turn the gearbox mainshaft so that the cam has its highest point uppermost. The lowest point will now align with the overdrive pump roller. Engage bottom gear and do not turn the mainshaft again until the overdrive unit has been fitted to the gearbox.

10 Locate a new gasket to the front face of the overdrive unit. Mate the gearbox carefully to the overdrive unit making sure that the pump roller rides up the chamfer of the cam and that the overdrive pushes fully up to the adaptor plate using hand pressure only. If the overdrive stands away from the adaptor plate by about 5/8 in (15.88 mm) then

this indicates that the internal splines have become misaligned. In this case, remove the overdrive unit and re-align the splines by turning the inner member of the uni-directional clutch in an anticlockwise direction. This can be done using a long screwdriver.

11 When the overdrive unit has been correctly fitted to the gearbox, tighten the four nuts (short studs) and the two nuts (long studs) at the base of the unit.

12 Connect the engine and gearbox and install in the car, as described in Chapter 1.

13 Top-up the gearbox (which will fill the overdrive unit) with the correct grade and quantity of oil.

12 Overdrive unit - overhaul

1 Absolute cleanliness must be observed in the following operations even to the extent of preventing particles from cleaning cloths remaining inside the unit. The operations described in paragraphs 9, 11, 12, 13, and 14 can all be carried out without removing the overdrive unit from the car provided the overdrive accumulator is first exhausted by switching on the ignition, engaging top gear and operating the overdrive switch between ten and twelve times.

2 With the unit removed from the car, clean away all external dirt.

3 Secure the unit in a vice fitted with jaw protectors so that the front casing is uppermost.

4 Flatten the tab washers which lock the four nuts which hold the operating piston bridge pieces. Remove the nuts, washers and bridge pieces.

5 Release the two solenoid retaining screws so that the front casing of the overdrive unit can be removed.

6 Remove the four nuts which secure the front and rear casings and then separate the casings. The brake ring is spigotted into the casings and will normally remain attached to the front casing but it may be extracted if necessary by applying a few taps with a soft-faced hammer.

7 Lift out the clutch sliding member complete with thrust-ring, bearing and sun wheel.

8 Lift out the planet carrier and gear train.

9 *To dismantle the operating valve,* remove the plug from the bottom of the unit (same side as the solenoid). Extract the spring, plunger and ball. Extract the operating valve by drawing it down with a piece of wire.

10 Remove the operating pistons by gripping their centre bosses with a pair of pliers and exerting a rotary pull.

11 *To remove the solenoid,* withdraw the cover plate (four screws), extract the two securing screws and ease the plunger out of the yoke of the valve operating lever.

12 *Access to the accumulator* is gained by removing the large plug from the bottom of the unit on the right-hand side. Once the plug is unscrewed to its full length, all spring compression is released and the spring, support pin and washer can all be withdrawn with the plug. The accumulator piston can be withdrawn by engaging a piece of wire in the groove in its bore.

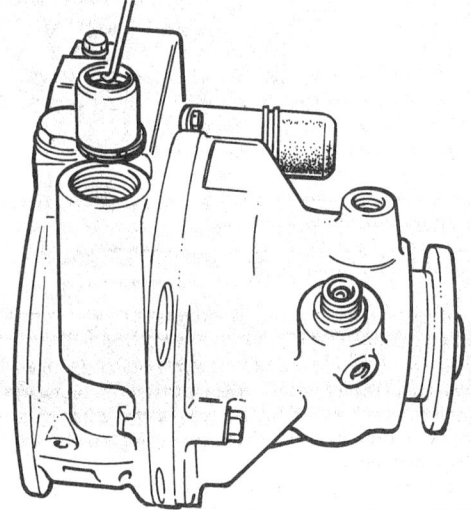

Fig. 6.20. Extracting the accumulator piston from the overdrive unit (Sec. 12)

13 *To remove the pump non-return valve,* unscrew and remove the plug which is centrally located in the bottom of the unit. The valve body can only be extracted by using a special key (Tool no. L213). Extract the spring and ball.

14 *To remove the pump,* first withdraw the non-return valve as just described and then withdraw the pump body. A bolt can be screwed into the body and using a nut and distance piece, it can be extracted from its recess. The pump plunger and spring will come out at the same time.

15 *The oil filter* is accessible after removing the plug immediately below the solenoid cover plate. Extract the gauze filter. Four magnetic rings are located in the filter assembly - two in the plug recess and two in the casing recess.

16 *The clutch sliding member and sun wheel* are removable after withdrawing the circlip from the sun wheel and prising off the corrugated washer and sliding member.

17 *The planet carrier assembly* should be inspected for wear on the gear teeth and excessive clearance in the bearings. Any fault can only be rectified by renewing the carrier assembly complete as individual components are not supplied.

18 To dismantle *the rear casing and annulus,* refer to Fig. 6.17. Extract the spring ring (67) and oil thrower (66).

19 Remove the assembly ring from the uni-directional clutch and allow the rollers to come out. The hub will then be easily removable from the cage and leave the spring exposed. Extract the bronze thrust washer which is located between the hub of the clutch and the annulus.

20 To remove the annulus, remove the speedometer dowel screw (85), withdraw the speedometer drive bush (83) and the pinion (82).

21 Remove the coupling flange (87) and extract the oil seal. Press the annulus forward out of the rear casing. The front and rear bearings will remain in the rear casing with the speedometer drive gear sandwiched between them.

22 Extract the circlip (70) and drive out the speedometer gear and rear bearing. Finally drive out the front bearing.

23 With the overdrive dismantled, thoroughly clean each component and carry out a very detailed inspection for wear or damage paying particular attention to the following components:

24 Front casing and brake ring.
Operating cylinder bores and accumulator (scoring or leaks).
Sealing discs and plugged oil passages (leaks).
Worn centre bush.
Operating pistons (38) and sealing ring (39).
Pump roller and bronze bush.
Pump plunger (wear or scoring).
Pump body, valve seat and ball (wear or scoring).
Pump spring (distortion).
Accumulator piston (scoring or broken rings).
Accumulator spring (distortion or collapse).
Operating valve (distortion).
Restrictor jet (clear).
Filter and magnetic rings (clean in petrol).
Brake ring (62) (scoring or cracks).

25 Clutch sliding member.
Friction lining (charring or wear). If worn, renew sliding member complete.
Thrust ring bridge piece pins (tight or bent).
Ball race (noisy or worn).
Clutch springs (distortion or collapse).

26 Planet carrier and gear train
Sun-wheel teeth (chipping or wear).
Sun-wheel bush (wear). If worn renew sun-wheel complete.

27 Rear casing and annulus.
Uni-directional clutch rollers (chipping or wear).
Cage (ears distorted or bent).
Bronze washers.
Annulus gear teeth (damage or chipping).
Speedometer pinion (wear or chipped teeth).
Always renew the rear oil seal (80) at time of major overhaul.

28 Commence reassembly by inserting the pump plunger, spring and body in the central holes in the bottom of the front casing. Make sure that the flat on the plunger locates against the thrust button below the centre bush.

29 Tap the pump body home until its groove is in alignment with the screw hole in the front casing. Install the screw and its fibre washer.

30 Reseat the non-return valve ball using a copper drift and then screw in the non-return valve body. Fit the ball spring, pin, copper washer and plug.

31 Insert the piston into the accumulator casing followed by the spring, pin, fibre washer and plug.

32 When installing the operating pistons, ease the rubber seals into the cylinder bores and make sure that the centre bosses of the pistons face towards the front of the unit.

33 Install the operating valve so that the rounded end engages with the flat of the small cam of the operating shaft. Insert the 5/16 in (7.93 mm) diameter ball, plunger and spring and screw in the plug with copper washer.

34 Refit the oil filter with two magnetic rings in the casing recess and two in the plug recess.

35 The front casing is now complete except for the solenoid and can be placed to one side ready for fitting to the unit later.

36 Press the front bearing into the rear casing and fit its circlip.

37 Support the inner track of the bearing and press in the annulus until the bearing abuts on the shoulder.

38 Fit the speedometer drive gear and then press the rear bearing onto the tailshaft and into the rear casing simultaneously. Install a new oil seal.

39 Fit the bolts to the coupling flange and press on the coupling flange. Fit the washer and castellated nut. Tighten the nut to specified torque and insert a new split pin.

40 Insert the speedometer pinion gear and bush making sure that the 'O' ring seal is in good condition.

41 Turn the annulus to engage the gear so aligning the holes in the casing and bush. Fit the locating screw and its copper washer.

42 Fit the spring into the roller cage of the uni-directional clutch and then insert the inner member into the cage and engage it with the other end of the spring. Engage the slots of the inner member with the roller cage tongues checking that the spring rotates the cage so that when the rollers are installed they will be pushed up the inclined faces of the inner member. The cage is spring-loaded in an anticlockwise direction when viewed from the front.

43 Position the assembly front face downwards and install the rollers at the same time turning the clutch clockwise. A narrow band or clip can be used to facilitate this operation.

44 Refit the uni-directional clutch, entering the rollers into the outer member of the annulus. Fit the oil thrower and retaining clip.

45 Assemble the planet carrier to the annulus and sun-wheel. To do this, turn each gear until the dot on one tooth of the large gear is located radially outwards.

46 Install the sun-wheel to mesh with the planet gears (without moving the position of the dots) and then insert the assembly to mesh with the internal gear in the annulus. Align the splines of the planet carrier

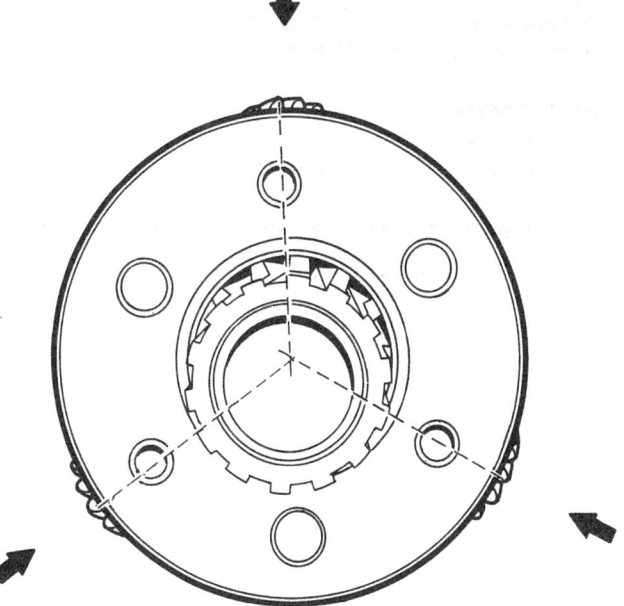

Fig. 6.21. Assembly position for planet carrier, annulus and sun-wheel. Note dots (arrowed) on one tooth of each gear (Sec. 12)

and the uni-directional clutch.

47 Press the thrust bearing into the thrust ring and then press this assembly onto the hub of the clutch sliding member. Secure the assembly with the circlip.

48 Slide the assembly onto the sun-wheel splines until the inner lining is in contact with the annulus and then fit the corrugated washer and circlip.

49 Fit the retaining plate over the bolts of the thrust ring bearing assembly. Apply jointing compound to both faces of the brake ring flange and tap the brake ring home into the front casing.

50 Install the clutch return springs into the front casing.

51 Offer the front casing/brake ring assembly to the rear casing making

sure that the thrust ring bolts pass through the holes in the casing without jamming. The pressure of the clutch springs will tend to keep the two casings apart but the four securing nuts should be tightened progressively and in diagonally opposite sequence to overcome this.

52 Fit the two bridge pieces and new tab washers.

53 Engage the solenoid plunger in the fork of the operating lever and after fitting a gasket to the solenoid flange, fix the solenoid to the casing with its two screws.

54 Adjust the solenoid, as described in Section 10.

55 Install the solenoid cover plate and gasket (four screws).

56 The overdrive unit is now ready for installation to the gearbox, as described in Section 11.

---

13 Fault diagnosis - manual gearbox

Symptom	Reason/s
Ineffective synchromesh	Worn baulk rings or synchro hubs.
Jumps out of one or more gears (on drive or over-run)	Weak detent springs or worn selector forks or worn gears.
Noisy, rough, whining and vibration	Worn bearings and/or thrust washers (initially) resulting in extended wear generally due to play and backlash.
Noisy and difficult engagement of gears	Clutch fault (See Chapter 5).

Note: It is sometimes difficult to decide whether it is worthwhile removing and dismantling the gearbox for a fault which may be nothing more than a minor irritant. Gearboxes which howl, or where the synchromesh can be 'beaten' by a quick gearchange, may continue to perform for a long time in this state. A worn gearbox usually needs a complete rebuild to eliminate noise because the various gears, if re-aligned on new bearings will continue to howl when different wearing surfaces are presented to each other.

The decision to overhaul therefore, must be considered with regard to time and money available, relative to the degree of noise or malfunction that the driver has to suffer.

---

14 Fault diagnosis - overdrive unit

Symptom	Reason/s
Lack of engagement	Insufficient oil. Break in electrical circuit. Solenoid lever out of adjustment. Dirt on pump non-return valve seat. Worn accumulator. Choked filter.
Will not disengage *	Solenoid sticking. Blocked restrictor jet in operating valve. Solenoid lever out of adjustment. Clutch sticking (in overdrive unit).

* If these conditions occur on no account reverse the car as extensive damage will be caused.

Clutch slip when overdrive selected	Insufficient oil. Solenoid lever out of adjustment. Dirt on pump non-return valve seat. Worn accumulator. Operating valve incorrectly seated. Worn or glazed clutch linings (in overdrive unit).

Chapter 6 Part II: Automatic transmission

For modifications, and information applicable to later models, see Supplement at end of manual

Contents

Specifications

Type	Borg-Warner three element hydrokinetic torque converter with hydraulically operated planetary gear set to provide 3 forward and 1 reverse ratio

Application
Model 8	3.4 and 4.2 litre engined cars
Model 12	4.2 litre (Series 2) early models
Model 35F	2.8 litre engined cars
Model 65	3.4 and 4.2 litre engined cars (Series 2 and 3)

Model 8
Ratios:
1st	2.40 : 1
2nd	1.46 : 1
3rd	1.00 : 1
Reverse	2.00 : 1
Maximum ratio of torque converter	2.00 : 1 (infinitely variable)

Shift speeds:

Selector	Throttle position	Upshift 1–2	2–3	3–2	Downshift 3–1	2–1
D1	Minimum	6-7 mph (10-11 kph)	10-12 mph (16-19 kph)	6-12 mph (10-19 kph)	— —	3-6 mph (5-10 kph)
	Kickdown	42-46 mph (68-74 kph)	66-73 mph (106-117 kph)	59-67 mph (95-108 kph)	16-20 mph (26-32 kph)	16-20 mph (26-32 kph)
D2	Minimum	—	10-12 mph (16-19 kph)	6-12 mph (10-19 kph)	—	—
	Kickdown	—	66-73 mph (106-117 kph)	59-67 mph (95-108 kph)	—	
	Zero	—	Any speed	—	9-17 mph (14-27 kph)	

Fluid type	ATF to M2C 33G (Duckhams Q-Matic)
Fluid capacity, including torque converter *	16.5 Imp. pints (9.4 litres/19.8 US pints)

* This cannot be completely drained at subsequent oil changes

Model 12
Ratios as model 8

Shift speeds (with 3.31 : 1 and 3.54 : 1 axle ratio):

Throttle position	Upshifts 1–2	2–3	Downshifts 3–2	2–1
Minimum	6-10 mph (9-16 kph)	14-18 mph (22-29 kph)	—	—
Full	39-45 mph (62-72 kph)	73-82 mph (117-132 kph)	—	—

Throttle position	Upshifts			Downshifts	
	1–2	2–3	3–2	2–1	
Kick-down	–	–	63-73 mph (101-117 kph)	13-17 mph (21-27 kph)	
Zero	–	–	–	7-17 mph (11-27 kph)	
Part	–	–	20-26 mph (32-42 kph)	–	

Shift speed (with 3.07 : 1 axle ratio)

Throttle position	Upshifts		Downshifts	
	1–2	2–3	3–2	2–1
Minimum	7-11 mph (11-18 kph)	16-20 mph (25-32 kph)	–	–
Full	45-51 mph (72–82 kph)	85-94 mph (136-151 kph)	–	–
Kick-down	–	–	73-83 mph (117-133 kph)	15-19 mph (24-30 kph)
Zero	–	–	–	9-19 mph (14-30 kph)
Part	–	–	23-29 mph (37-47 kph)	–

Fluid type as model 8
Fluid capacity as model 8

Model 35F

Ratios:
1st	2.40 : 1
2nd	1.46 : 1
3rd	1 : 1
Reverse	2.09 : 1
Torque converter ratio	2 : 1 to 1 : 1 (infinitely variable)

Shift speeds:

Selector	Throttle Position	Upshifts		Downshifts	
		1–2	2–3	3–2	2–1
D	Light	9-14 mph (14-22 kph)	14-20 mph (22-32 kph)	–	–
D	Full with kick-down	31-40 mph (49-64 kph)	60-65 mph (96-104 kph)	52-60 mph (83-96 kph)	19-26 mph (37-48 kph)
2	Zero	–	–	–	7-9 mph (11-14 kph)

Fluid type as model 8
Fluid capacity as model 8

Models 65 and 66

Ratios:
1st	2.39 : 1
2nd	1.45 : 1
3rd	1 : 1
Reverse	2.09 : 1
Torque converter ratio	1.91 : 1 to 1 : 1 (infinitely variable)
Fluid type as model 8	
Fluid capacity	14.5 Imp. pints (8.2 litres/17.4 US pints)

Torque wrench settings

All transmissions except Types 65 and 66	lb f ft	Nm
Torque converter to driveplate bolts	30	41
Torque converter housing to engine bolts	35	48
Oil pan securing bolts	13	18
Output coupling flange nut	50	68
Oil cooler pipe unions	21	29
Filler tube union nut	25	34
Transmission case to torque converter housing	60	83
Selector lever to transmission casing nut	35	48

Type 65 and 66 transmissions		
Transmission case to torque converter housing:		
Small bolts	25	34
Large bolts	40	54
Oil pan bolts	5	7
Oil pan drain plug	10	14
Output coupling flange bolt	80	109

15 General description

1   The automatic transmission unit used in all models is of Borg-Warner manufacture but different versions of this unit are fitted, according to the car engine capacity and date of production.

2   Application details are given in 'Specifications' Section but the main difference between the transmission units is that only cars equipped with the model 8 unit can be started by towing or running down an incline, due to the fact that they have an extra rear oil pump. This pump provides hydraulic fluid pressure at speeds over 20 mph (32 kph). The other model transmission units have a front pump only, and hydraulic fluid pressure is not generated unless the engine is running.

3   In the event of a breakdown, refer to *Jacking and towing* (at the back of the book) before attempting to tow a car fitted with automatic transmission.

4   There are certain minor differences between the different transmission units, mostly concerned with the speed selection arrangement but all units incorporate a fluid torque converter coupled to a hydraulically-operated planetary gearbox to provide three forward ratios and reverse.

5   All forward ratios are automatically engaged in accordance with accelerator position and car speed. Overriding control is still maintained by manual selection and a kick-down facility is provided for rapid change down.

6   Servicing and overhaul operations should be restricted to those described. Due to the complexity of the transmission unit and the need for special tools it is not recommended that major overhauls are undertaken.

7   In the event of a fault developing, always diagnose the problem **before** removing the unit from the car. This fault finding can be carried out either by referring to the 'Fault diagnosis' Sections in this Chapter or by consulting your Jaguar/Daimler dealer.

8   Factory reconditioned units are normally available through your dealer on an exchange basis, and in the case of a major fault developing in the original unit, this method of rectification can usually show a marked swing against overhaul charges.

16 Model 8 transmission - maintenance

1   The most important maintenance task is the regular checking of the fluid level.

2   At the intervals specified in 'Routine Maintenance', operate the car on the road for at least 5 miles (8 km) and then place it on a level surface and with the engine still running, move the speed selector lever through all positions finally placing the lever in 'P'.

3   Switch off the engine, withdraw the dipstick and wipe it clean on a piece of non-fluffy cloth. Re-insert it and then withdraw it for the second time and read off the fluid level. The operations described in this paragraph should be completed within one minute.

4   If necessary, add specified fluid to the combined dipstick/oil filler tube to bring the level up to the 'FULL' mark. The difference between the 'LOW' and 'FULL' marks is equivalent to 1½ Imp. pints (0.75 litres).

5   The only other maintenance items are to keep the exterior of the transmission casing clean to prevent the unit overheating and if an oil cooler is fitted, to periodically check the condition and security of the fluid flow and return pipes to the cooler which is located in the base of the cooling system radiator.

6   Operating experience with this type of transmission has now brought a recommendation from the manufacturers that the fluid should be renewed at 30 000 mile (48 000 km) intervals. In the absence of a drain plug, remove the oil pan to do this. Take care not to be scalded by the hot oil and always clean the filter while the oil pan is removed. Use a new gasket when refitting.

7   As the transmission cannot be completely drained, refill with approximately ¾ of the quantity of clean fluid compared with the 'from dry' capacity shown in the Specifications.

8   Refer to Chapter 13, Supplement, for details of BW Type 66 transmission on Series 3 cars.

17 Model 8 transmission - adjustments

Speed selector linkage adjustment

1   In the event of faulty speed selection occurring or failure of the parking pawl to hold the car when 'P' is selected, first check the adjustment of the speed selector linkage.

2   Disconnect the selector rod from the actuating lever on the side of the transmission unit.

3   Pull the selector hand control into 'P', and then push the lever on the side of the transmission casing fully forward towards the front of the car.

4   Attempt to reconnect the selector rod to the actuating lever. When

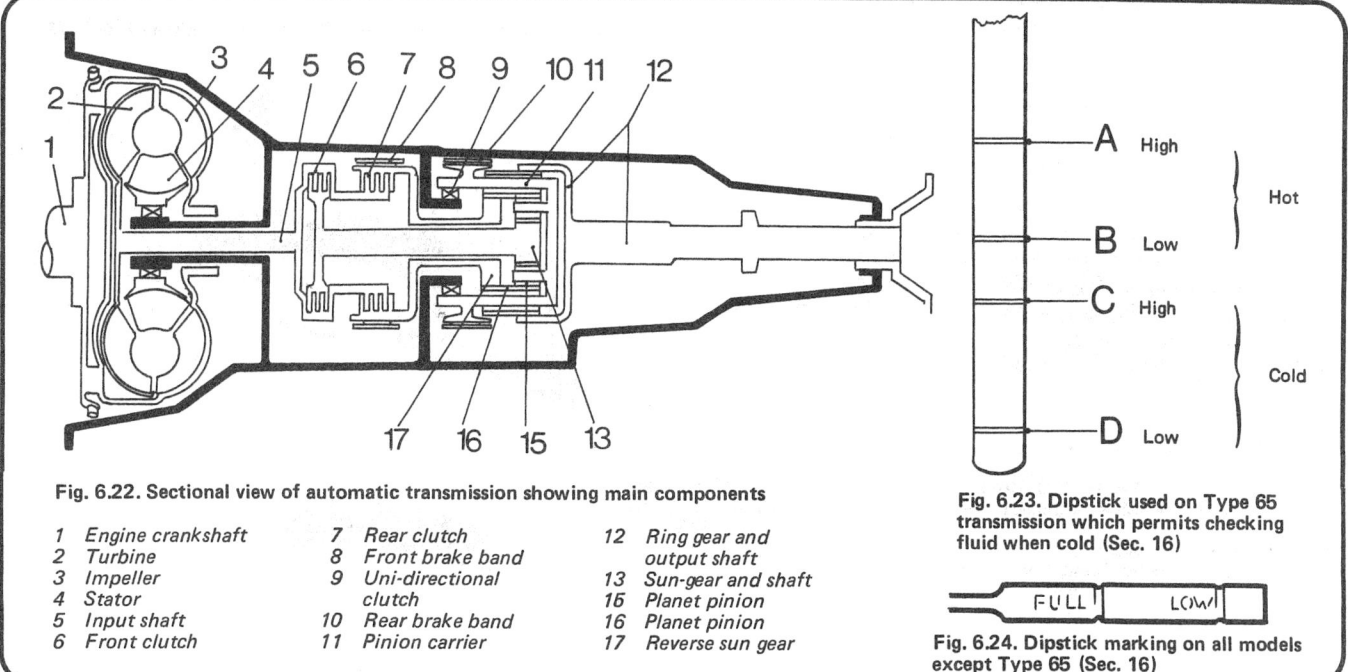

Fig. 6.22. Sectional view of automatic transmission showing main components

1 Engine crankshaft	7 Rear clutch	12 Ring gear and
2 Turbine	8 Front brake band	output shaft
3 Impeller	9 Uni-directional	13 Sun-gear and shaft
4 Stator	clutch	15 Planet pinion
5 Input shaft	10 Rear brake band	16 Planet pinion
6 Front clutch	11 Pinion carrier	17 Reverse sun gear

Fig. 6.23. Dipstick used on Type 65 transmission which permits checking fluid when cold (Sec. 16)

Fig. 6.24. Dipstick marking on all models except Type 65 (Sec. 16)

it is in perfect alignment, release the locknuts on the linkage tube and adjust the effective length of the linkage until the selector rod will connect with the actuating lever without having to deflect either component.

5   Refit the connecting nut, tighten the locknuts and then check the speed selection in all positions.

Kick-down cable adjustment

6   An oil pressure gauge will ideally be needed for this operation, although adjustment can be carried out on a trial-and-error basis as follows:

7   Place the speed selector lever in 'D1' or 'D2' and using minimum accelerator pressure to cause the car to increase speed, check that the 2 to 3 upshift occurs at between 1100 and 1200 rev/min.

8   A momentary increase in engine speed between 200 and 400 rev/min during upshift indicates low fluid pressure.

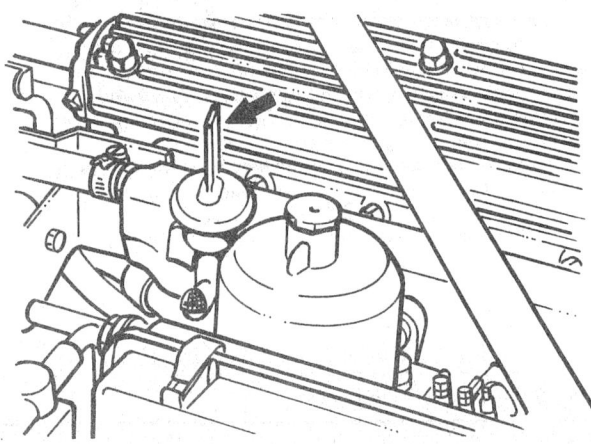

Fig. 6.25. Location of automatic transmission dipstick on 2.8 litre models (Sec. 16)

9   A jerky upshift (or 2 to 1 downshift) indicates high fluid pressure.

10 To lower the pressure, release the locknut on the kick-down rod and turn it to reduce its length.

11 To increase the pressure, unscrew the rod to effectively lengthen it.

12 If a pressure gauge is available, connect it to the take-off point on the transmission casing. With the fluid at normal operating temperature, and 'D1' or 'D2' selected, apply the handbrake and increase the idling speed to 1250 rev/min. The pressure gauge should indicate between 70 and 75 lb/sq in (4.92 and 5.27 kg/sq cm). Adjust if necessary, as previously described.

Front band adjustment

13 This operation should be carried out after the first 1000 miles (1600 km) running of a new car or after a new transmission unit has been installed. It may also be necessary if indicated after reference to 'Fault diagnosis'.

14 Remove the drain plug from the oil pan and drain the oil into a clean container (Fig. 6.29). If the car has just come in off the road, be very careful as the oil can be extremely hot! If a drain plug is not fitted, remove the oil pan, keep it level and tip the fluid from it.

15 Unscrew the oil pan bolts and lift the oil pan from the transmission casing.

16 Release the locknut on the front servo adjusting screw, unscrew the screw and then slide a block (¼ in - 6.3 mm) thick between the servo piston pin and the end of the adjusting screw. Tighten the adjusting screw to a torque of 10 in/lb. If a torque wrench is not available, use a spring balance connected to a socket wrench (Fig. 6.30).

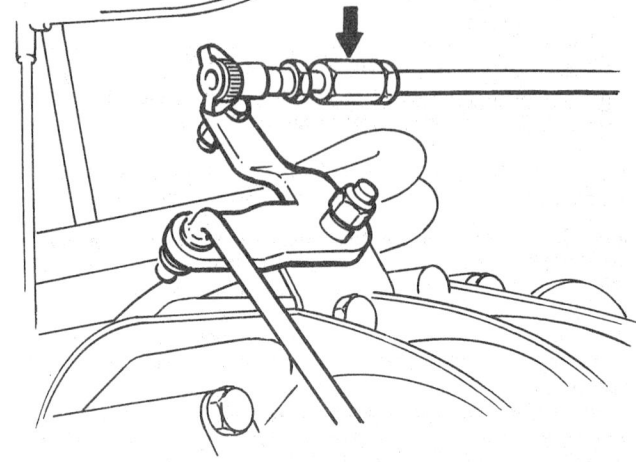

Fig. 6.27. Kickdown rod adjuster (Model 8 transmission) (Sec. 17)

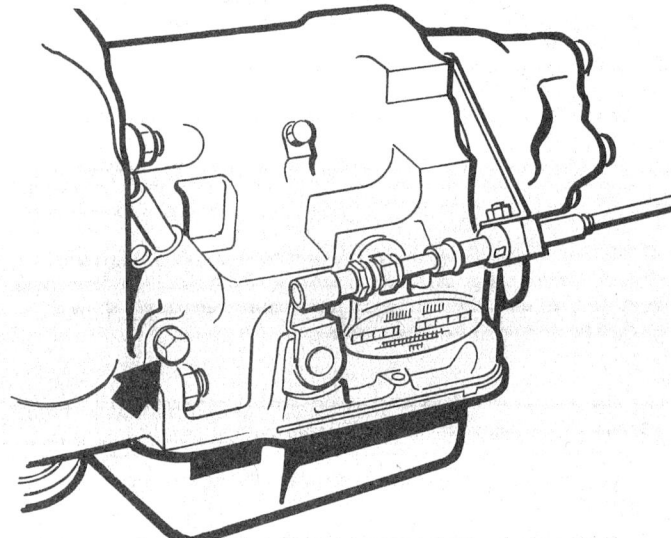

Fig. 6.28. Pressure take off point (Model 8 transmission) (Sec. 17)

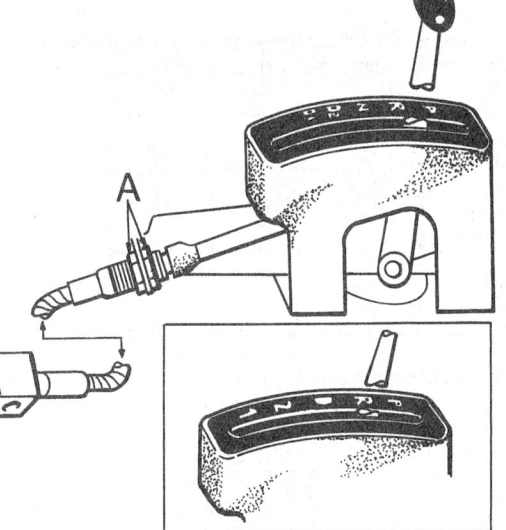

Fig. 6.26. Speed selector linkage (Model 8 transmission) A = locknuts (Sec. 17)

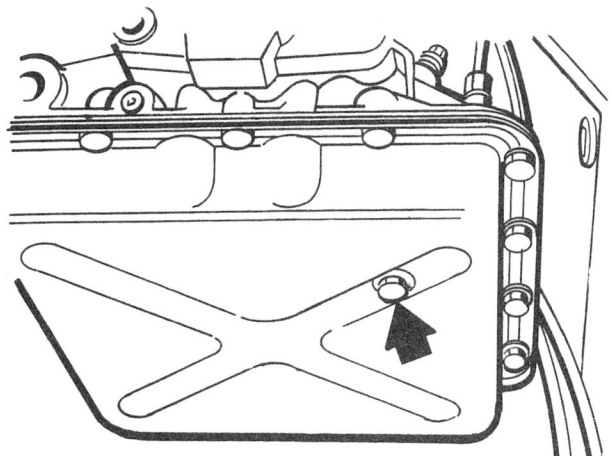

Fig. 6.29. Transmission drain plug (Model 8 transmission) (Sec. 17)

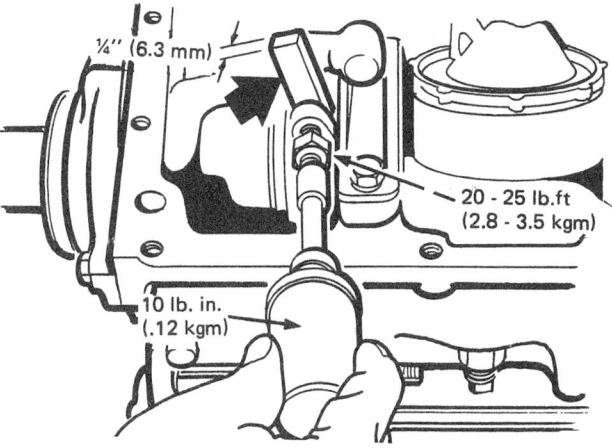

¼" (6.3 mm)

20 - 25 lb.ft
(2.8 - 3.5 kgm)

10 lb. in.
(.12 kgm)

Fig. 6.30. Adjusting front brake band (Model 8 transmission) (Sec. 17)

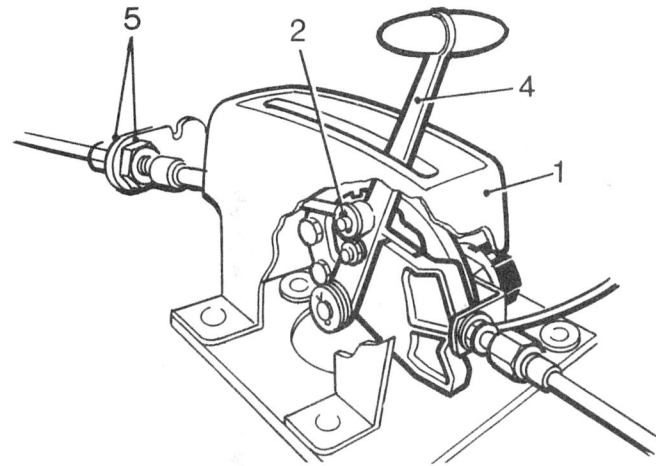

Fig. 6.31. Speed selector lever (Model 12 transmission) (Sec. 18)

1 Cover
2 Cable clevis pin
4 Selector lever
5 Locknuts

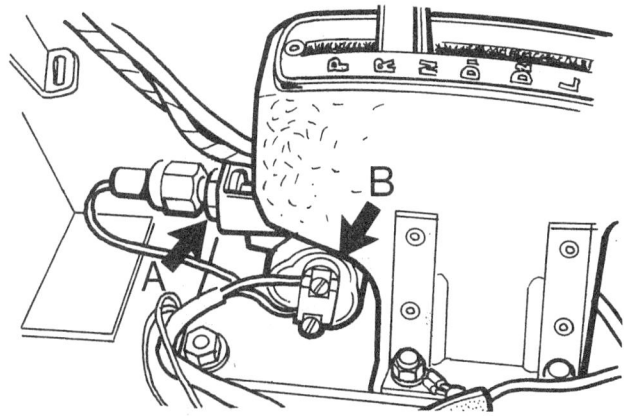

**Fig. 6.32. Starter inhibitor switch and reversing lamp switch
(Model 12 transmission) (Sec. 18)**

A Starter inhibitor switch   B Reversing lamp switch

17 Back off the adjusting screw 1½ turns exactly and tighten the adjusting screw locknut to between 20 and 25 lb/ft (28 and 35 Nm). Remove the spacer block.

Rear band adjustment
18 This will normally only be required if indicated after reference to 'Fault diagnosis' Section.
19 The rear brake band adjusting screw is located on the right-hand side of the transmission casing and access is provided through a hole in the transmission tunnel.
20 Release the adjuster screw locknut and unscrew it three or four turns.
21 Check that the adjuster screw turns freely and then screw it in using a torque wrench to a torque of 10 lb/ft (14 Nm).
22 Unscrew the adjusting screw exactly 1½ turns and tighten the locknut to a torque of between 35 and 40 lb/ft (48 and 55 Nm).

18 Model 12 transmission - adjustments and tests

Speed selector linkage adjustment
1 Working within the car, release the selector cover screws, raise the cover, turn it through 90° and lift it over the control lever.
2 Disconnect the selector cable from the control lever.
3 Move the lever on the side of the transmission casing fully to the rear (P) and then push it forward one notch to (R).
4 Move the hand control to position (R).
5 Release the locknuts on the selector cable and adjust its length until its connecting eye slips onto the pin on the hand control without any

need to move either component to ensure perfect engagement.
6 Tighten the locknuts, fit a new cable split pin and refit the selector cover.

Starter inhibitor switch adjustment (early models)
7 Check that the speed selector linkage adjustment is correct and then remove the cover from the speed selector lever.
8 Place the selector control in 'N' or 'P' and disconnect the lead from the inhibitor switch.
9 Connect a test-lamp and a small battery in series with the single terminal on the inhibitor switch.
10 Release the plunger switch locknut (A) (Fig. 6.32) and rotate the switch until the lamp just illuminates. Turn the plunger switch inwards (clockwise) for exactly ½ turn and retighten the locknut.
11 Disconnect the lamp and battery, remake the original connections, switch on the ignition and make sure that the starter motor will only operate in 'N' or 'P'.

Starter inhibitor switch adjustment (later models)
12 Later models have a different switch assembly. Connect a test-lamp and battery in series, as previously described in this Section.
13 Release the switch locknuts and with the selector lever in 'N' move the position of the switch until the test lamp lights up.
14 Tighten the switch locknuts and then recheck the switch operation with the test bulb and battery. The lamp should remain on in 'N' or 'P' and remain out in all other selector positions.
15 Remove the test rig and reconnect the electrical feed lead to the switch terminal.

Vacuum control unit adjustment
16 Speed selection is controlled partly by the car's roadspeed and partly by engine manifold depression acting on a vacuum control unit.
17 It can be suspected that the vacuum control unit diaphragm is ruptured if one of the following conditions is observed:

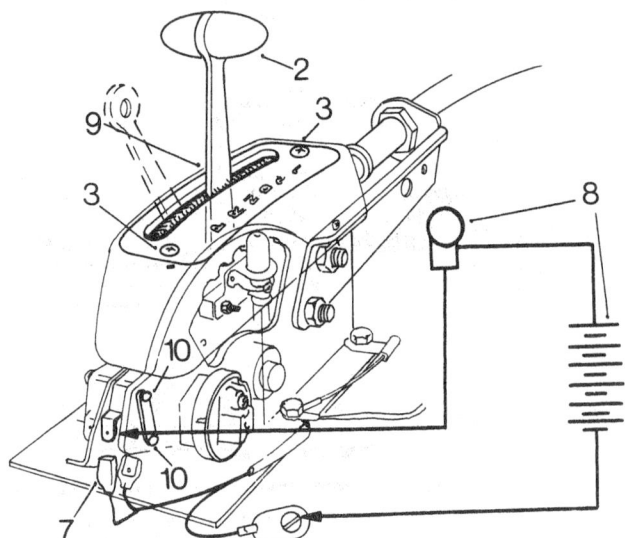

Fig. 6.33. Later type starter inhibitor switch arrangement (Model 12)
(Sec. 18)

2 Selector lever knob	8 Test circuit
3 Cover screws	9 Selector lever
7 Switch feed cable	10 Switch securing locknuts

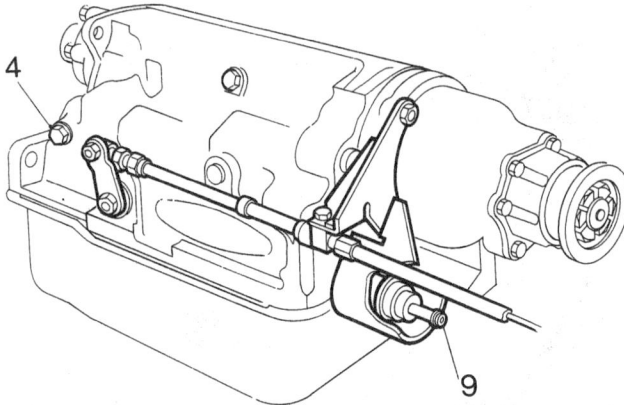

Fig. 6.34. Pressure take off point (4) vacuum control unit (9) on
Model 12 automatic transmission (Sec. 18)

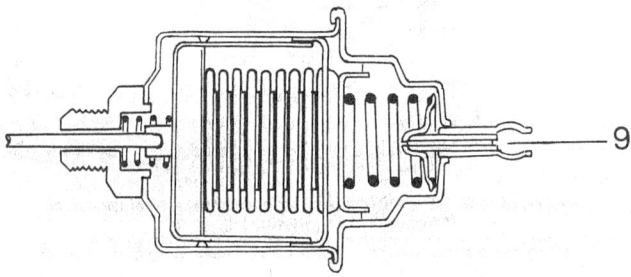

Fig. 6.35. Sectional view of vacuum control unit on Model 12
transmission showing adjuster screw (9) (Sec. 18)

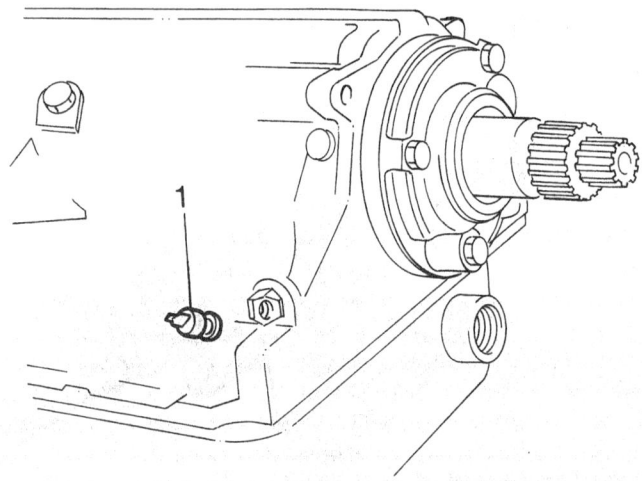

Fig. 6.36. Kickdown solenoid terminal (1) on Model 12
transmission (Sec. 18)

(i)   Smoky exhaust due to oil being drawn from transmission through ruptured diaphragm into inlet manifold.
(ii)   Fluid level consistently falling at regular checks.
(iii)   Rough or jerky upshifts or downshifts.

18 The vacuum control unit under these circumstances must be renewed as a complete assembly.
19 To check and adjust the vacuum control unit, vacuum and pressure gauges will be required.
20 Ensure that all engine adjustments are correct, also the ignition settings. Have the engine and transmission at normal running temperature (operate on road for minimum 5 miles/8 km).
21 Connect the vacuum gauge to the heater control take off point at the forward end of the inlet manifold.
22 Remove the hexagonal plug (4) from the front left-hand side of the transmission casing and connect the pressure gauge (Fig. 6.34).
23 Start the engine, select '1' or 'R' and apply the hand and foot brakes firmly. Increase the engine speed until vacuum gauge reads 9 to 10 in Hg (23 to 25 cm) at 1200 rev/min. The fluid pressure gauge should read between 70 and 90 lb/sq in (4.92 and 6.32 kg/sq cm).
24 If the pressure reading is outside that specified, remove the vacuum hose from the control unit and insert a screwdriver. Turn the internal screw clockwise to increase pressure or anticlockwise to decrease it. One full turn of the screw will vary the pressure by about 5 lb/sq in (0.35 kg/sq cm) (Fig. 6.35).

Kick-down switch and solenoid adjustment
25 Disconnect the lead from the kick-down switch output terminal and insert a test bulb between the terminal and a good earth.

26 Switch on the ignition and depress the accelerator pedal to the kick-down position.
27 If the circuit is satisfactory, the test-lamp will illuminate. If it does not, release the locknut on the kick-down switch and turn the switch until the lamp does light up. Tighten the lock nut (Fig. 6.37).
28 To test the kick-down solenoid, disconnect the lead from the solenoid lead through connector terminal. Connect a jumper lead momentarily between the battery positive terminal and the solenoid lead through connector terminal (Fig.6.36). A distinct click should be heard if the solenoid is operating satisfactorily. Renewal of the solenoid will necessitate removal of the oil pan. Remove the solenoid by turning it through 180° in an anti-clockwise direction.

Rear brake band adjustment
29 This operation should be carried out after the first 1000 miles (1600 km) running on a new car or when a new transmission has been installed and at 24000 miles (38600 km) intervals thereafter.
30 The adjuster screw is located on the right-hand side of the transmission casing. Release the locknut and unscrew it two turns. (Fig. 6.38).
31 Lubricate the adjuster screw and check that it turns freely. Tighten the screw to a torque of 10 lb/ft (14 Nm) and then loosen it exactly 1¼ turns. Retighten the locknut to a torque of 35 lb/ft (48 Nm).
32 The front brake band on this type of transmission is self-adjusting.

19 Model 35F transmission - adjustments

Speed selector linkage adjustment
1   The adjustment procedure is very similar to that described in

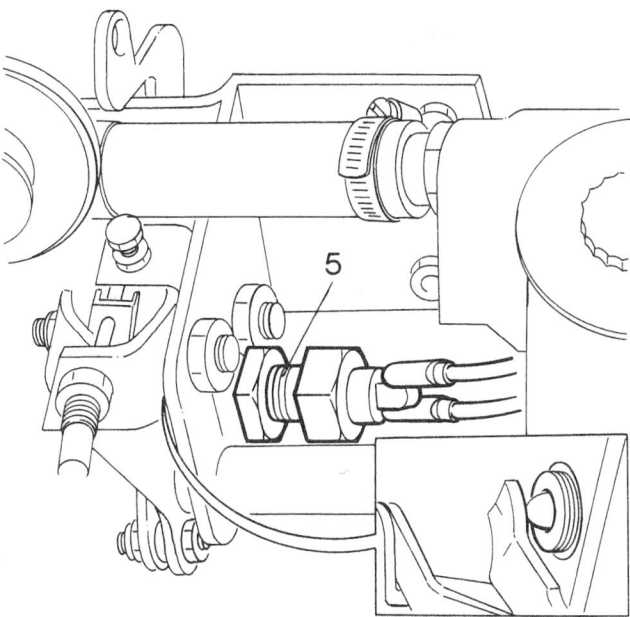

Fig. 6.37. Kickdown switch (5) and locknut on Model 12 transmission (Sec. 18)

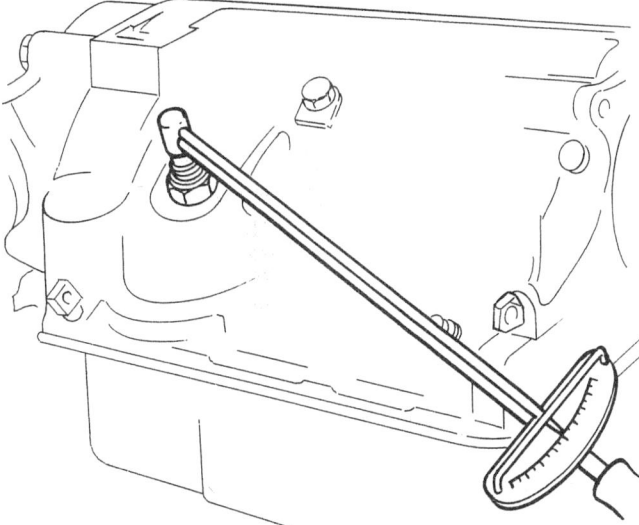

Fig. 6.38. Adjusting rear brake band (Model 12 transmission) (Sec. 18)

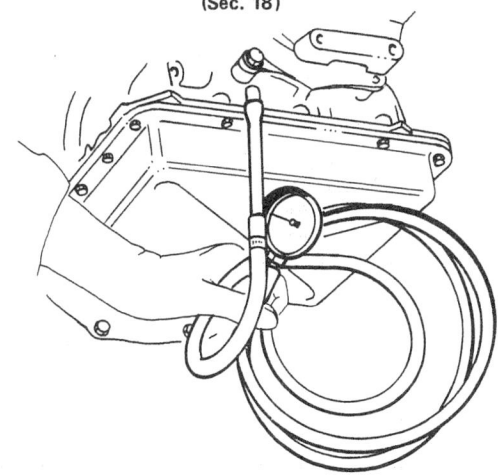

Fig. 6.40. Pressure take off point (Model 35F transmission) (Sec. 19)

Section 17, for the model 8 transmission, except that the connection of the selector rod to the lever should be carried out while both components are in the 'R' position.

Downshift (kick-down) cable adjustment

2 The downshift cable is preset in production by a stop which is crimped to it at the carburettor end. All that is necessary is to maintain a clearance of about 0.015 in (0.38 mm) between the crimped stop and the end face of the threaded cable adjuster. To do this, release the locknut and turn the cable adjuster in, or out, as necessary.

3 In the event of the crimped stop moving or a new cable being fitted (supplied with loose stop), then the cable must be adjusted by one of the following methods:

4 *Method 1:* Run the car on the road for a minimum of five miles (8 km) until the transmission attains normal operating temperature. Connect a pressure gauge to the take-off point on the rear of the transmission casing.

5 Select 'D' or '2' and increase the engine speed to 1000 rev/min. The pressure gauge should read between 95 and 100 lb/sq in (6.68 and 7.03 kg/sq cm). If the pressure indicated is lower than specified, increase the effective length of the downshift outer cable by turning the cable adjuster. If the pressure is higher, decrease the length of the cable by again turning the adjuster.

6 *Method 2:* Where a pressure gauge is not available, the oil pan can be removed (this must be done in any event if the cable is being renewed) and the cable adjusted to provide downshift valve cam settings as shown in the diagrams (Fig. 6.41).

7 Whichever method is used, when the cable adjustment is correct, crimp the cable stop so that it provides a clearance, as described in paragraph 2.

Starter inhibitor switch adjustment

8 This is carried out in a similar manner to that described in Section 18.

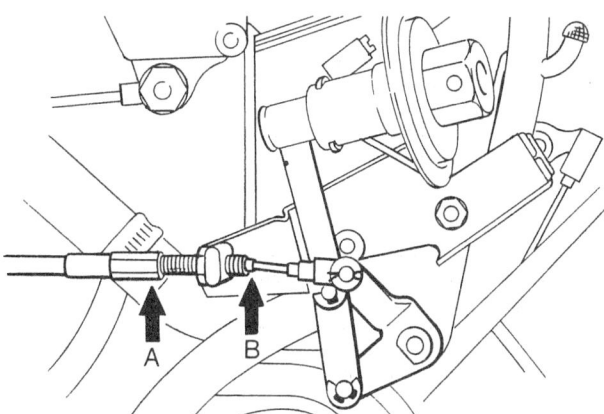

Fig. 6.39. Downshift cable adjustment (Model 35F transmission) (Sec. 19)

A *Adjuster* B *Crimped stop*

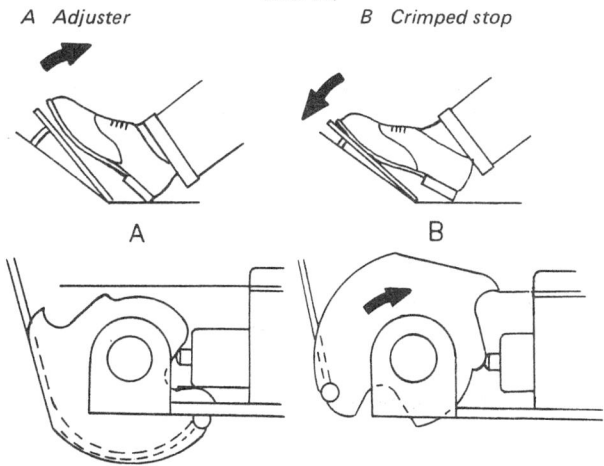

Fig. 6.41. Downshift valve cam settings (Model 35F transmission) (Sec. 19)

A *Pedal fully released* B *Pedal fully depressed*

Front brake band adjustment

9   Drain the transmission and carry out the adjustment, as described in Section 17, for the model 8 transmission.

Rear brake band adjustment

10   The operations are similar to those described for the model 12 transmission in Section 18, paragraphs 29 to 31 except that the adjuster screw should be released by only ¾ of a turn before locking it with the locknut.

---

20 Model 65 transmission - adjustments

Speed selector rod adjustment

1   Remove speed selector lever cover and release selector cable locknuts.
2   Disconnect cable from selector arm on the transmission and then set both components in '1'.
3   Adjust the effective length of the cable using the locknuts until the cable can be connected to the arm with the clevis pin eyes in both components in perfect alignment.

Downshift cable adjustment

4   Refer to Section 19, paragraphs 2 to 7.

Front brake band adjustment

5   Remove the transmission cover, carpet and remove the access plate.
6   Slacken the locknut on the adjustment screw then torque tighten the screw to 5 lb ft (7 Nm).
7   Back the screw off ¾ of a turn then hold it stationary in this position whilst tightening the locknut.
8   Fit the access plate and replace the carpet.

Rear brake band adjustment

9   Drive the car onto a ramp or raise it on jacks. Apply the handbrake.
10   Select 'P', raise the ramp and slacken the adjuster locknut.
11   Torque tighten the screw to 5 lb ft (7 Nm) then back it off ¾ of a turn.
12   Hold the screw stationary in this position and tighten the locknut.
13   Lower the car to the ground.

---

21 Stall speed test

1   Should the performance of the automatic transmission not appear to be up to standard, the following stall test can be carried out and the necessary conclusions drawn from the test results.
2   The stall speed is the maximum speed at which the engine can drive the torque converter impeller while the turbine is being held stationary.
3   Run the car on the road for at least 5 miles (8 km) until both the engine and the transmission are at normal operating temperature.
4   Apply the handbrake fully and chock the roadwheels.
5   Select '1' or 'R' and depress the accelerator fully. Note and record the maximum reading on the tachometer.
6   Do not extend the stall test beyond 10 seconds or repeat it at less than half hourly intervals as overheating of the transmission may occur.
7   Use the following table to compare the tachometer readings obtained.

Model 8, 12 or 35F

Rev/min obtained	Condition indicated
Under 1000	Stator free wheel slipping
1350 to 1550	Engine not developing full power
1600 to 1700	Conditions normal
Over 2100	Clutch slip or brake band fault

Model 65

Rev/min obtained	Condition indicated
Under 1400	Stator free wheel slipping
1600 (approx)	Engine not developing full power
2200	Conditions normal
Over 2400	Clutch slip or brake band fault

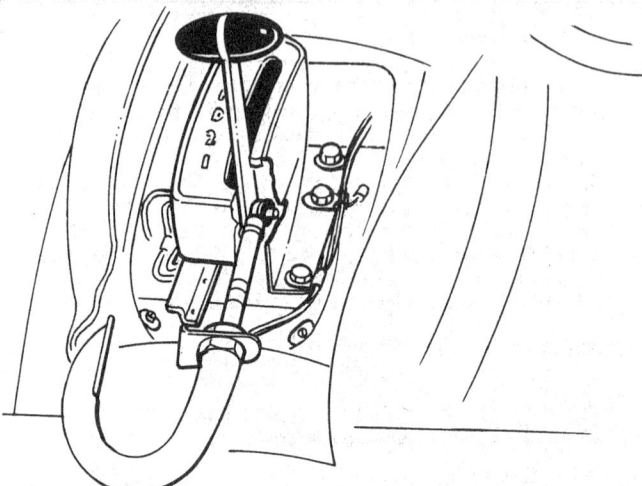

Fig. 6.42. Speed selector cable and adjuster nuts on Model 65 transmission (Sec. 20)

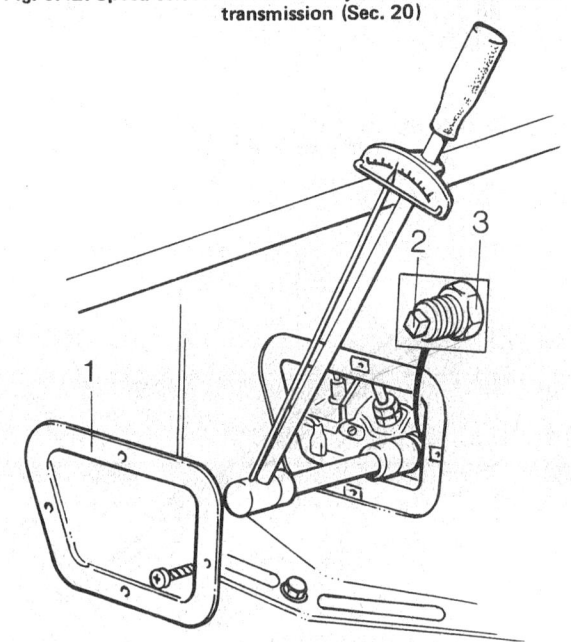

Fig. 6.43. Adjusting front brake band (Model 65 transmission) (Sec. 20)

1   Cover plate   3   Locknut
2   Adjuster screw

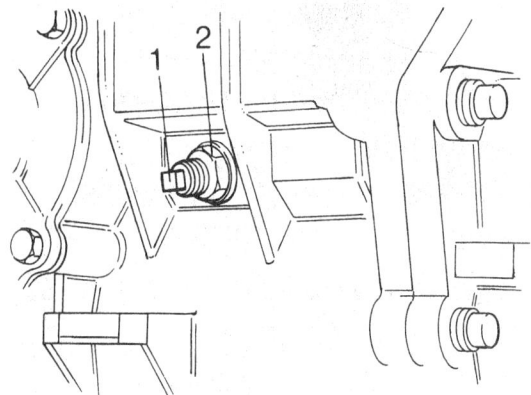

Fig. 6.44. Rear brake band adjuster (Model 65 transmission) (Sec. 20)

1   Adjuster screw   2   Locknut

22 Rear oil seal - renewal

1   Leakage of fluid from the rear end of the transmission extension housing will almost certainly be from a worn output shaft oil seal.
2   Disconnect the front end of the propeller shaft (see Chapter 7) and place the shaft to one side.
3   Unscrew and remove the output shaft coupling flange nut. The nut may be secured by a split pin or a tab washer. The coupling flange will have to be held quite still while the nut is unscrewed. Make up a lever for this which can be bolted to the coupling flange using the original bolts which will still be in position in the flange.
4   Withdraw the coupling flange and washer.
5   Prise out the oil seal and then tap in a new one using a piece of tubing as a drift.
6   Apply grease to the coupling flange surfaces which will be in contact with the lips of the oil seal, install the coupling, tighten the nut to specified torque and fit a new split pin or bend over the tab washer.
7   Reconnect the propeller shaft and then check and top-up the fluid level in the automatic transmission unit.

23 Automatic transmission - removal and installation

1   The recommended method of removing the automatic transmission is to remove the engine and transmission as a combined unit and then separate them.
2   The necessary operations are described in Chapter 1, Sections 6 and 8.
3   Reconnection of the transmission to the engine and installation are described in Chapter 1, Sections 52 and 53.

24 Fault diagnosis - automatic transmission

Symptom	Reason/s
Engine will not start in 'N or 'P'	Faulty starter or ignition circuit. Incorrect speed selector linkage adjustment. Incorrectly adjusted inhibitor switch.
Engine starts in selector positions other than 'N' or 'P'	Incorrect speed selector linkage adjustment. Incorrectly adjusted inhibitor switch.
Severe bump when selecting	Idling speed too high.
'D' or 'R' or excessive creep when handbrake released	Downshift cable incorrectly adjusted. Vacuum circuit fault (Type 12). Solenoid fault (Type 12).
Poor acceleration and low maximum speed	Incorrect fluid level. Incorrect linkage adjustment. Incorrect downshift cable adjustment.
No movement when 'R' selected	Incorrect rear band adjustment.
Poor upshift quality	Front band requires adjustment.
No movement in 'D'	Front brake band requires adjustment. Fault in one-way clutch.

Chapter 7 Propeller shaft

For modifications, and information on later models, see Supplement at end of manual

Contents

Specifications

Type	Two section open with needle roller universal joints and flexible mounted centre bearing. Sliding joint incorporated in front section

Shaft diameter

Early cars:	
Automatic or manual gearbox	2 in (50.8 mm)
Later cars:	
Automatic transmission	2 in (50.8 mm)
Manual gearbox	Front 3 in (76.2 mm), Rear 2 in (50.8 mm)

Torque wrench settings

	lb f ft	Nm
Propeller shaft flange nuts	34	46
Centre bearing baseplate bolts	18	25

1 General description

1 An open propeller shaft is fitted which is divided in the centre. The forward end of the rear section is supported on a rubber-mounted ball race and a universal joint is fitted at its rear end.
2 The front section has a universal joint at each end and incorporates a sliding spline within a flexible gaiter.
3 No lubrication or maintenance is required as all joints and bearings are prepacked with grease during production.

2 Propeller shaft (front section) - removal and refitting

Early cars

1 Unscrew and remove the four self-locking nuts from the front and rear flanges of the propeller shaft.
2 Compress the shaft at the sliding splines section and withdraw the propeller shaft towards the rear of the car.
3 Refitting is a reversal of removal but make sure that the mating faces of the flanges are clean and free from particles of grit.

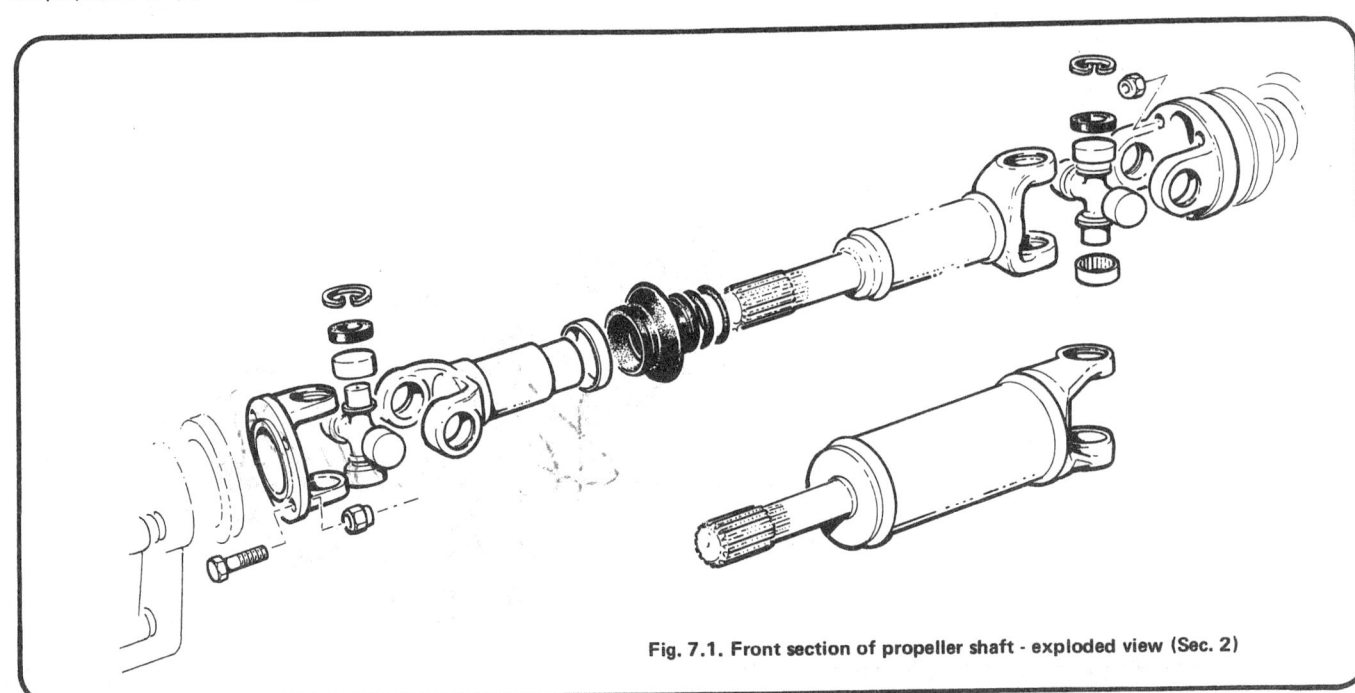

Fig. 7.1. Front section of propeller shaft - exploded view (Sec. 2)

Series 2 models

4   Removal of the propeller shaft from these models will necessitate supporting the weight of the rear of the engine on a suitable hoist or a cross bar and threaded lifting eye.

5   With the engine weight supported, remove the exhaust intermediate pipe.

6   Remove the rear and intermediate heat shields.

7   Disconnect the engine rear mounting plate by withdrawing the setscrews, spacers and washers.

8   Place a jack under the gearbox (suitably insulated from damage with a block of wood) and release the self-locking nut which secures the engine rear mounting. If the car is equipped with automatic transmission, do not position the jack under the oil pan but place it with a block of wood under the cast section of the transmission casing.

9   Remove the bracket and engine mounting plate from the gear casing.

10 Disconnect the gearbox/propeller shaft coupling flange and the flanges just forward of the centre bearing and lift the front section of the propeller shaft from the car.

11 Refitting is a reversal of removal.

---

3   Propeller shaft (rear section) - removal and refitting

---

1   On Series 2 models, remove the exhaust intermediate pipe and the rear heat shield.

2   Unscrew and remove the four self-locking nuts from the front and rear flanges of the rear section of the propeller shaft. Mark the relative position of the centre bearing support bracket to the underside of the body.

3   Remove the four setscrews which secure the support bracket.- Retain any shims which are located between the bracket and body, noting carefully their position.

4   Withdraw the propeller shaft towards the rear of the car.

5   Refitting is a reversal of removal but make sure that the connecting flange faces are clean and return any centre bearing support bracket shims to their original positions.

6   Check the alignment of the propeller shaft, as described in Section 5.

---

4   Centre bearing - removal, overhaul and refitting

---

1   Remove the rear section of the propeller shaft complete with centre bearing as described in the preceding Section.

Fig. 7.2. Method of supporting weight of engine while engine mountings are dismantled (Sec. 2)

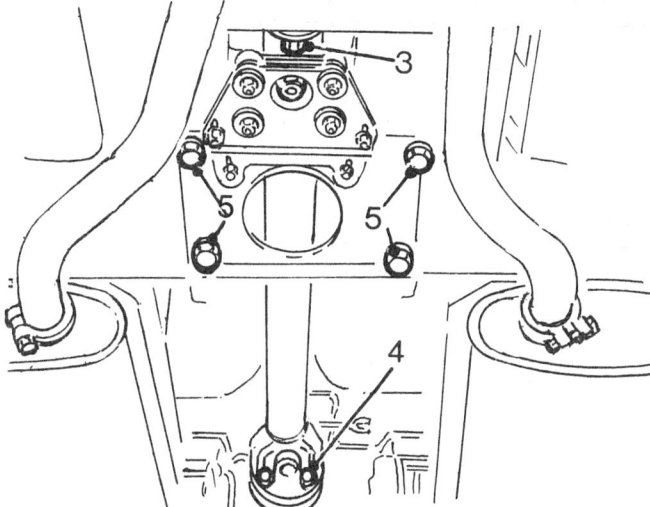

Fig. 7.3. Propeller shaft centre bearing support plate (Sec. 3)

3   *Coupling flanges of front and   5   *Support plate*
    rear sections of propeller shaft   *bolts*
4   *Propeller shaft to final drive*
    pinion drive flange

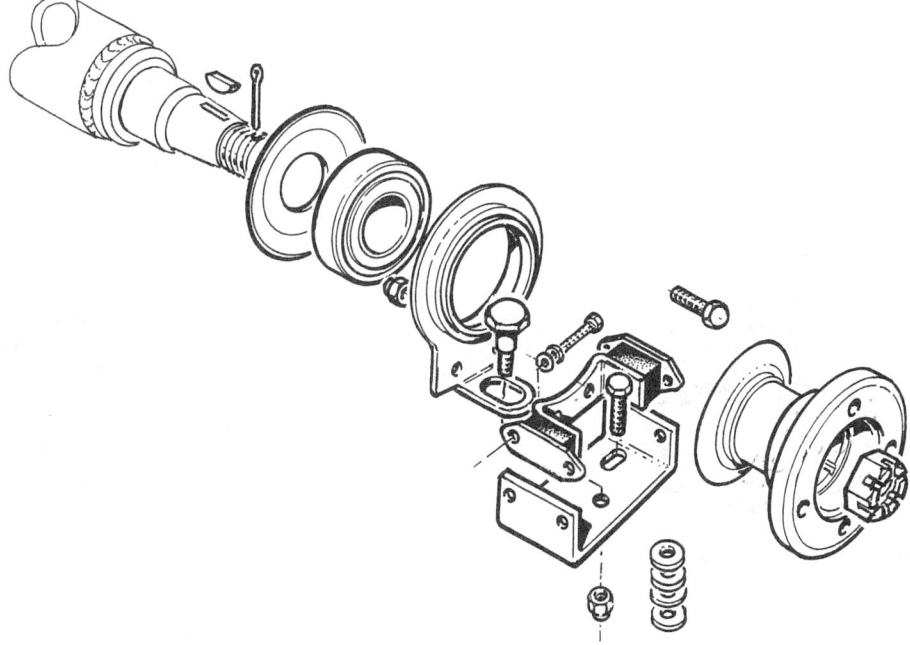

Fig. 7.4. Exploded view of the propeller shaft centre bearing (Sec. 4)

2   The flange coupling is secured to the rear propeller shaft by two Woodruff keys and a castellated nut (early cars) or by splines (later cars). Withdraw the nut and pull off the coupling.

3   Extract the Woodruff keys (early cars) and outer dust cover.

4   Using a soft-faced mallet, drive the shaft through the bearing and its housing and then press the bearing from the housing.

5   Remove the two self-locking nuts and bolts which secure the body mounting bracket to the centre bearing plate.

6   Remove the four bolts and lockwashers which secure the mounting rubbers to the body mounting bracket.

7   Renew any worn components and reassemble and refit by reversing the removal and dismantling process.

8   Check the alignment of the propeller shaft as described in Section 5.

---

5   Propeller shaft - alignment (except Series 2 and 3)

1   Whenever the propeller shaft has been removed or the centre bearing disturbed, its alignment must be checked in the following way. It is advisable to check the alignment also if the engine/transmission has been removed and refitted. Incorrect alignment of the propeller shaft can cause judder when taking off from a standing start.

2   Make up an alignment jig in accordance with the dimensions given in the diagram (Fig. 7.5).

3   First check the *horizontal alignment* by holding up the jig to the shaft. The sides of all three legs should contact the propeller shaft simultaneously, two legs on the rear section of the shaft and one leg on the front section.

4   Any adjustment needed to make sure that all three legs contact simultaneously, should be carried out by releasing the setscrews which secure the centre bearing bracket to the propeller shaft tunnel and moving the bracket sideways.

5   To check the vertical alignment, again use the jig and hold it against the bottom face of the shafts. The ends of all three legs should make contact with the shaft simultaneously. If they do not, add or extract shims between the centre bearing bracket and the propeller shaft tunnel.

6   On later cars equipped with a manual gearbox which have a 3 in (76.2 mm) diameter front propeller shaft section the vertical alignment (with shims) should be checked and adjusted as just described, but the horizontal alignment differs from earlier cars. The jig previously described should be modified so that its centre leg is increased in width by 1/8 in (3.175 mm). Also modify the front leg of the jig to accommodate the greater diameter of the front section of the shaft.

7   Use the jig as previously described so that the wider centre leg will give an offset of the centre bearing to the left-hand side of the car. Movement of the centre bearing can be carried out by releasing the setscrews and pushing the bearing within the travel permitted by the elongated bolt holes of its support bracket.

8   On completion, tighten the centre bearing setscrews.

9   This offset alignment of the propeller shaft in the horizontal plane also applies to cars with automatic transmission built from 1973 onwards even though with this type of transmission, the diameter of both sections of the propeller shaft is still 2 in (50.8 mm).

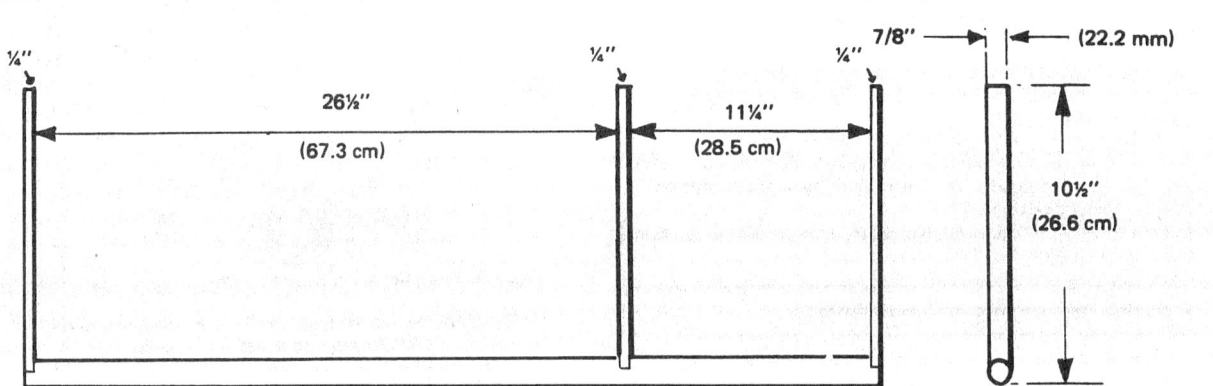

Fig. 7.5. Propeller shaft alignment jig (Sec. 5)

¼"   26½" (67.3 cm)   ¼"   11¼" (28.5 cm)   ¼"   7/8" (22.2 mm)   10½" (26.6 cm)

Fig. 7.6. Checking propeller shaft horizontal alignment (Sec. 5)

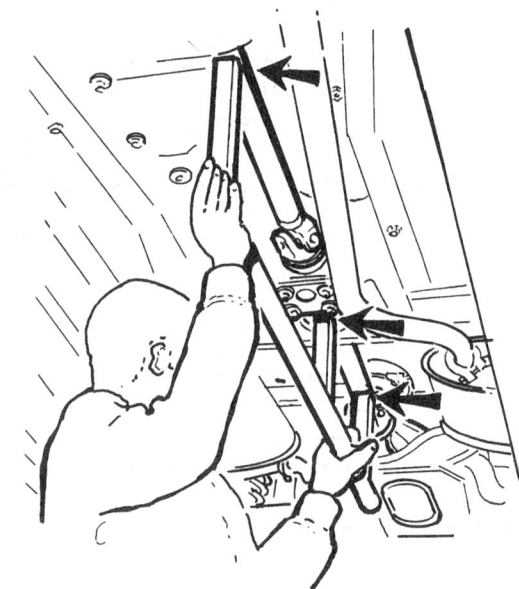

Fig. 7.7. Checking propeller shaft vertical alignment (Sec. 5)

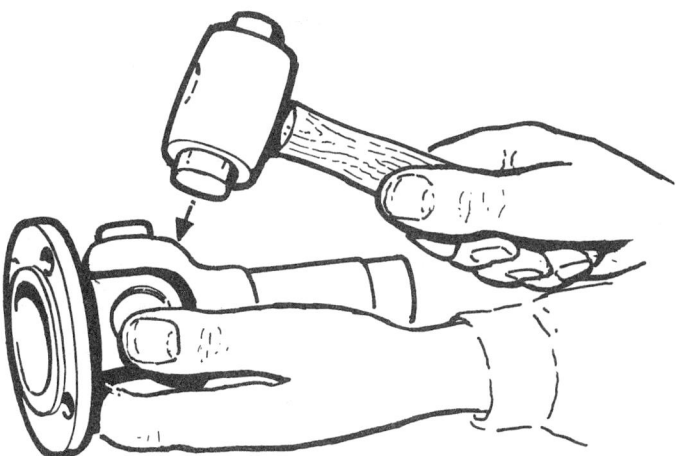

Fig. 7.8. Ejecting a universal joint bearing cup (Sec. 6)

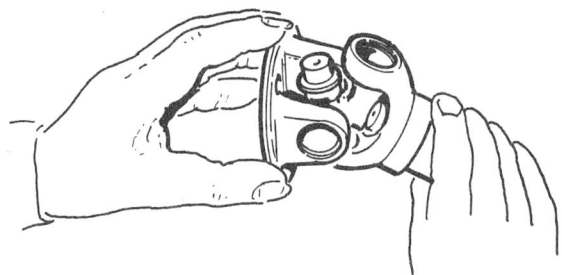

Fig. 7.10. Separating universal joint yoke from spider (Sec. 6)

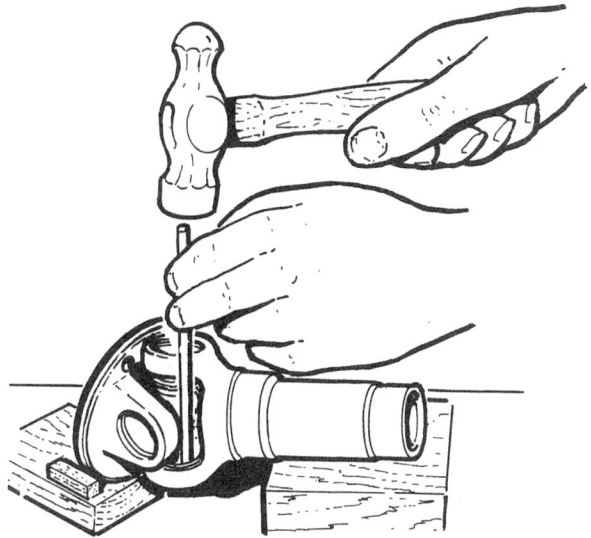

Fig. 7.9. Alternative method of removing a universal joint bearing cup (Sec. 6)

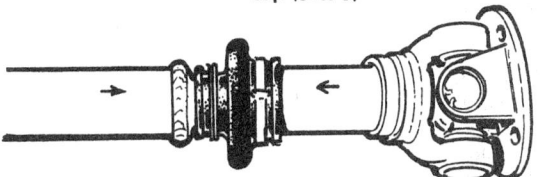

Fig. 7.11. Propeller shaft sliding joint alignment marks (Sec. 6)

6 Universal joints - overhaul

1 Wear in the needle roller bearings is characterised by judder and vibration in the transmission on over-run, 'clonks' on taking up the drive, and in extreme cases of lack of lubrication, metallic squeaking and ultimately grating and shrieking sounds as the bearings break up.

2 It is easy to check if the needle roller bearings are worn; with the propeller shaft in position, try to turn the shaft with one hand and with the other hand hold the rear axle flange and repeat this procedure for the other joints. Any movement between the shaft and the front, centre or rear couplings is indicative of bearing failure and/or wear in the spider. The old bearings will have to be discarded and replaced by a new universal joint assembly.

3 Remove the propeller shaft, in the manner described in Sections 2 and 3.

4 Thoroughly clean all dirt from the snap rings and the top of the bearing surfaces.

5 Remove all the snap rings by pinching with a pair of pliers and at the same time prising out with a screwdriver. If a ring proves difficult to remove it may be because it is jammed by the end of the bearing race so lightly tap the end of the race to relieve the pressure.

6 Hold the joint in the hand and with a hide faced or other type of soft hammer, tap the yoke lug as shown in Fig. 7.8. This will cause the top bearing to work outwards until it can finally be removed with the fingers. If the top bearing proves obstinate it can be tapped out from inside with a small diameter punch or piece of bar but be careful not to damage the bearing if this is not being renewed.

7 Repeat the above procedure for the opposite bearing.

8 The splined sleeve yoke to flange can now be separated from the shaft yoke as depicted.

9 Rest the two trunnions which are now exposed, on wood blocks and tap the yoke with a soft nosed hammer to remove the two remaining races.

10 It is now advisable to look carefully at the yoke cross holes. It is a very rare event but these holes have been known to wear to a certain degree of ovality. If this has occurred the defective item will have to be renewed.

11 On early model cars it is advisable to fit new cork gaskets and gasket retainers on the spider using a tubular drift.

12 Smear the wall of the race with grease to keep the rollers in position in the housing for assembly.

13 Insert the spider in the yoke holes, place the bearings in position and then lightly tap it home using a soft flat faced drift slightly smaller than the yoke hole in diameter.

14 Repeat the above for the opposite bearing in the yoke.

15 Fit new snap rings to the bearings and ensure they correctly located in the grooves.

16 Now place the mating yoke in position on the spider and fit the bearings and snap rings in the same manner as described above. It is essential that the sliding joint is refitted with its fixed yoke in line with the fixed yoke at the end of the propeller shaft; arrows are stamped on the two items to facilitate alignment. Apply grease to the mating surfaces of the sliding section of the shaft.

17 Make sure that the joint moves freely in all directions, if it appears to bind tap lighly with a wooden mallet to relieve any pressure of the bearings on the end of the spider.

18 Refit the propeller shaft to the car as described in Sections 2 and 3.

7 Fault diagnosis - propeller shaft

Symptom	Reason/s
Judder on take-off	Shaft out of alignment.
Vibration when vehicle running on road	Out of balance or distorted propeller shaft. Backlash in splined shaft. Loose flange securing bolts. Worn universal joint bearings.

Chapter 8 Final drive

For modifications, and information on later models, refer to Supplement at end of manual

Contents

Specifications

Type	Independently mounted with open universally-jointed halfshafts

Axle ratios (early models)

	2.8 litre	4.2 litre
Standard - 4 speed manual	4.27 : 1	3.54 : 1
Overdrive	4.55 : 1	3.77 : 1
Automatic transmission	4.27 : 1	3.54 : 1

Axle ratios (later models)

	2.8 litres	3.4 litres	4.2 litres
Standard - 4 speed manual	4.09 : 1	3.54 : 1	3.31 : 1
Automatic transmission	4.09 : 1	3.54 : 1	3.058 : 1
N. America (standard) - 4 speed manual	—	—	3.54 : 1
N. America (auto-transmission):			
Pre-1982	—	—	3.07 : 1
1982-on	—	—	2.88 : 1

Differential tolerances

Output shaft endfloat	0.001 to 0.003 in (0.02 to 0.07 mm)
Backlash (as etched on pinion gear):	
Pinion bearing preload (early)	8 to 12 lb in (0.09 to 0.14 kg m)
Pinion bearing preload (later)	25 to 30 lb in (0.3 to 0.35 kg m)
Oil capacity	2¾ Imp. pints (1.5 litres/3¼ US pints)

Lubricant type/specification

Standard differential	Hypoid gear oil, viscosity SAE 90EP (Duckhams Hypoid 90S)
Limited slip differential (drain and refill)	Powr-Lok approved gear oil, viscosity SAE 90 (Duckhams Hypoid 90DL)
Limited slip differential (top-up only)	Hypoid gear oil, viscosity SAE 90EP (Duckhams Hypoid 90S)

Torque wrench settings

	lb f ft	Nm
Driveshaft castellated nut	100	136
Caliper mounting bracket bolts (later cars)	70	95
Pinion nut (early cars)	120 to 130	163 to 177
Pinion nut (later cars) initial setting	100	136
Crownwheel bolts	80	109
Differential bearing cap bolts	60	82
Differential carrier bolts	75	102

1 General description

1 The final drive unit is mounted independently from the hubs. Short driveshafts having a universal joint at each end transmit power from the final drive output shafts to the roadwheels.

2 The output shafts of the final drive unit are carried on double row, angular contact ball bearings. The inner, or splined, ends of the shafts engage with mating splines in the side gears of the differential assembly.

3 Later cars have final drive units which may differ from earlier models in the following respects:

    (i)   Pinion shaft bearings preloaded by a collapsible spacer instead of shims.

    (ii) Driveshaft oil seals integral with caliper mounting bracket.

    (iii) Modified crownwheel and pinion design.

    (iv) Optional limited slip differential unit available.

4 In view of the special tools required it is not recommended that servicing operations extend beyond those described in this Chapter. In the event of complete overhaul to the final drive unit being required,

it is better to renew the unit on a factory exchange basis rather than 'mix' new and old components even assuming that final drive components can be obtained without undue delay. Where this recommendation is followed, it should be noted that reconditioned units are supplied without driveshafts, hubs or brake components and these items should therefore be retained from the original unit. When carrying out operations to the drive train on cars equipped with a limited slip differential unit (Powr-Lok), never jack-up one rear wheel and turn the wheel while the opposite one is still on the ground. Always jack-up both rear wheels otherwise damage to the unit may be caused.

2 Rear hub - removal, overhaul and refitting

Note: *New oil seals for the rear hub carrier must be soaked in clean engine oil for at least 12 hours prior to fitting.*

1 Jack-up the rear end of the car and support it securely under the bodyframe on axle stands. Remove the roadwheel.

2 Remove the suspension outer pivot grease nipple, withdraw the split

pin and unscrew and remove the castellated nut and washer from the end of the axle halfshaft.

3   Using a suitable extractor, push the splined end of the driveshaft out of the hub assembly. Note the location of the inner oil seal track and the endfloat spacer.

4   Unscrew and remove the nut from the end of the lower wishbone outer pivot shaft (arrowed Fig. 8.1) and drive out the pivot shaft. Remove the hub and hub carrier.

5   Turn the hub carrier upside-down so that the hub inner bearing is at the top and then press out the hub. Discard the outer oil seal.

6   Remove the three setscrews and withdraw the water deflector. Prise out the inner oil seal and remove the inner track from the inner bearing.

7   Drive out the inner and outer bearings if these are to be renewed. Use a suitable extractor to withdraw the inner track of the outer bearing.

8   If new hub bearings are fitted, press the new outer tracks of the inner and outer bearings into the hub carrier. Apply wheel bearing grease to the bearing components.

9   Hold the hub carrier so that the outer bearing is at the top. Locate the inner race of the outer bearing and then press a new outer oil seal into its recess.

10   Fit the water deflector and press the hub complete with outer seal track into the inner track of the outer bearing until the hub is fully home.

11   Hold the hub and hub carrier vertically so that the inner end of the hub is uppermost.

12   Locate the inner track of the inner bearing on the hub followed by the special collar of the official tool no. J.15. Press the track onto the hub until its inner face is flush with the special collar.

13   Mount a dial gauge as shown Tap the hub carrier downwards, zero the dial gauge and then use two levers inserted between the hub and hub carrier to move the carrier upwards. Record the maximum reading on the dial gauge.

14   Remove the Special Collar and then fit a spacer (if necessary) to give endfloat of between 0.002 and 0.006 in (0.051 to 0.152 mm). Spacers are supplied in thicknesses of 0.109 to 0.151 in (2.77 to 3.87 mm) in steps of 0.003 in (0.076 mm) and are lettered 'A' (smallest) to 'R' (largest) omitting letters 'I', 'N' and 'O' as given in the following table:

Letter	Thickness in.	mm
A	0.109	2.77
B	0.112	2.85
C	0.115	2.92
D	0.118	3.00
E	0.121	3.07
F	0.124	3.15
G	0.127	3.23
H	0.130	3.30
J	0.133	3.38
K	0.136	3.45
L	0.139	3.53
M	0.142	3.61
P	0.145	3.68
Q	0.148	3.75
R	0.151	3.87

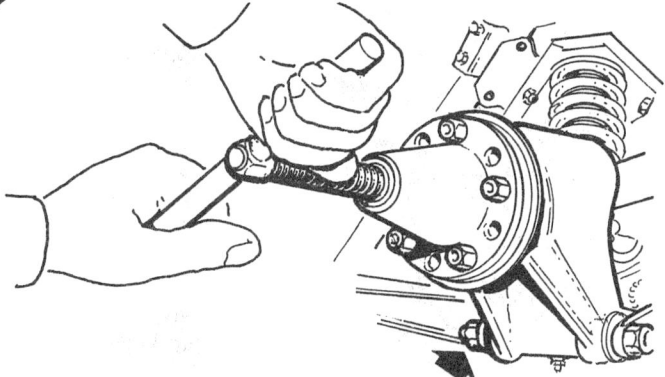

Fig. 8.1. Rear hub showing hub extractor and lower wishbone outer pivot shaft (arrowed) (Sec. 2)

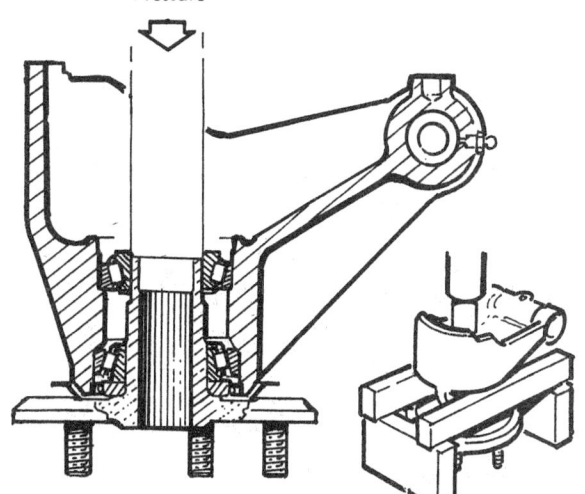

Fig. 8.2. Pressing rear hub from carrier (Sec. 2)

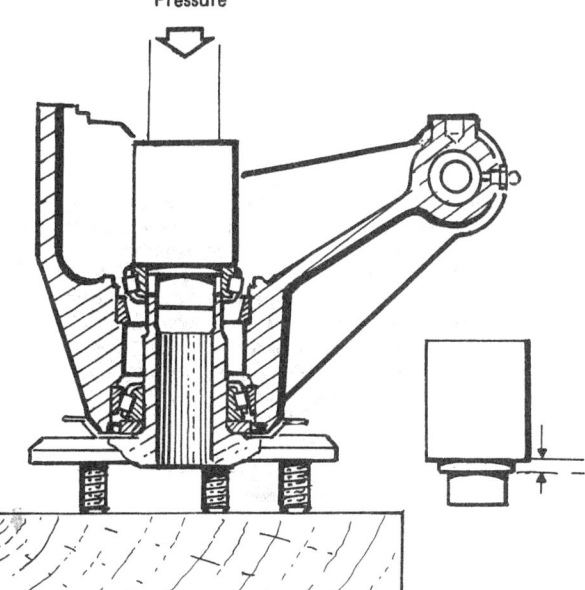

Fig. 8.3. Pressing in rear hub inner track of inner bearing using special collar of official tool (Sec. 2)

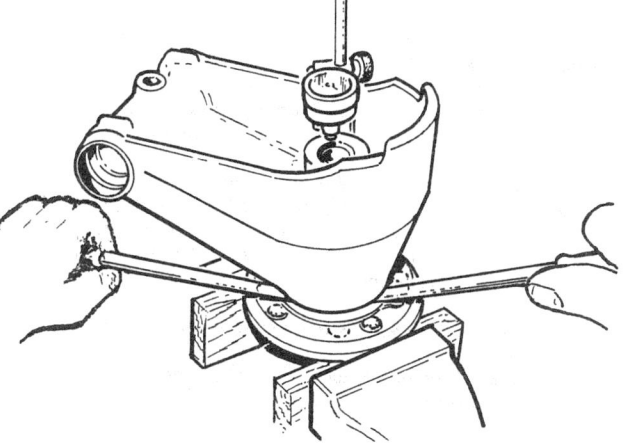

Fig. 8.4. Checking rear hub bearing-endfloat (Sec. 2)

15 For example, assume that the endfloat measured with the collar in position is 0.25 in (0.64mm). Take the mean permissible endfloat as 0.004 in (0.10 mm) and subtract this from the measured endfloat, giving 0.021 in (0.53 mm). The Special Collar is 0.150 in (3.81 mm) thick so the thickness of the spacer to be fitted will be 0.150 - 0.021 in ie; 0.129 in (3.28 mm). The nearest spacer in thickness to this is 0.130 in (3.30 mm) so fit a letter 'H' spacer in place of the Special Collar.

16 Fit the inner oil seal and its seating ring.

17 Locate the hub assembly between the jaws of the suspension wishbone, install the pivot shaft and nuts.

18 Clean the splines of the hub and halfshaft with a suitable solvent and then apply a thin coating of thread locking compound to the splines.

19 Engage the hub with the halfshaft splines, fit the washer and castellated nut and tighten to specified torque.

20 Install a new split pin to the castellated nut and refit the outer pivot grease nipple.

21 It is worth rechecking the hub bearing endfloat again at this stage by attaching the dial gauge as shown and levering the hub outwards. (Fig. 8.5).

22 Where possible, do not drive the car for a period of between 4 and 12 hours in order to allow the thread locking compound to harden.

23 Remove the hub bearing grease cap and inject wheel bearing grease until no more will go in. Do not pressurise the grease, or it will be forced past the oil seals. Refit the cap.

24 Refit the roadwheel and lower the car to the ground.

3 Axle driveshaft - removal and refitting (Series I)

1 Remove the rear suspension assembly, as described in Chapter 11, Section 19 and then remove the hub assembly as described in the preceding Section.

2 Remove the rear shock absorber which is nearest the front of the car. To do this, remove the upper and lower mounting pivot nuts and drive out the pivot pin until the shock absorber mounting is released.

3 Unscrew and remove the four self-locking nuts which secure the halfshaft inner universal joint to the output flange of the final drive unit.

4 Withdraw the halfshaft but extract and note the exact location of any shims which are used for camber purposes.

5 Refitting is a reversal of removal but make sure that the camber shims are returned to their original locations.

4 Driveshaft universal joints - overhaul

1 The procedure is very similar to that described in Chapter 7 for the overhaul of propeller shaft universal joints to which reference should be made.

5 Output shaft oil seal and bearing (Series I) - renewal

1 Remove the driveshaft as described in Section 3.

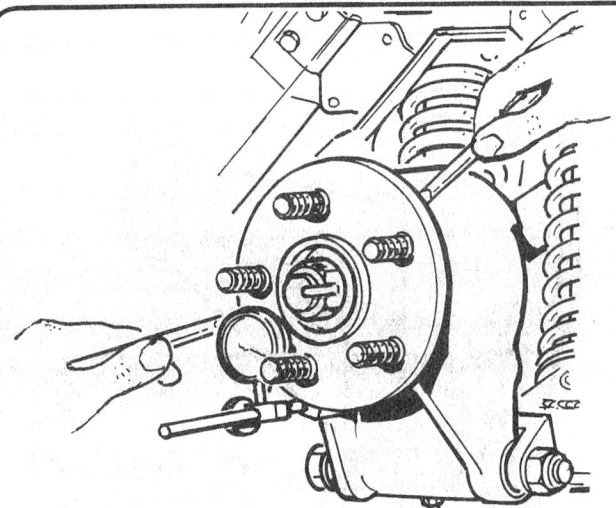

Fig. 8.5. Re-checking bearing endfloat with hub installed to car (Sec. 2)

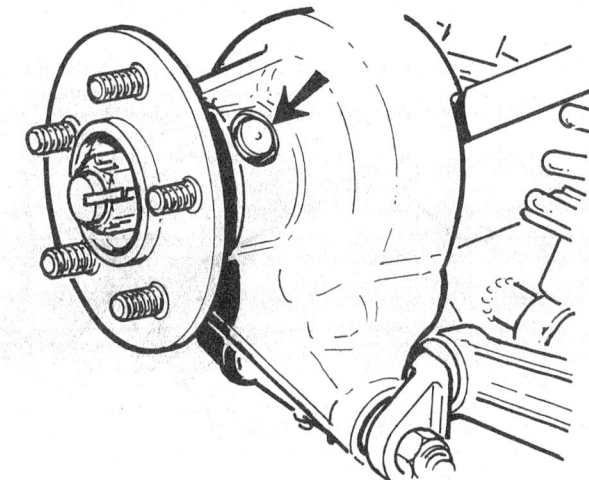

Fig. 8.6. Rear hub grease cap (Sec. 2)

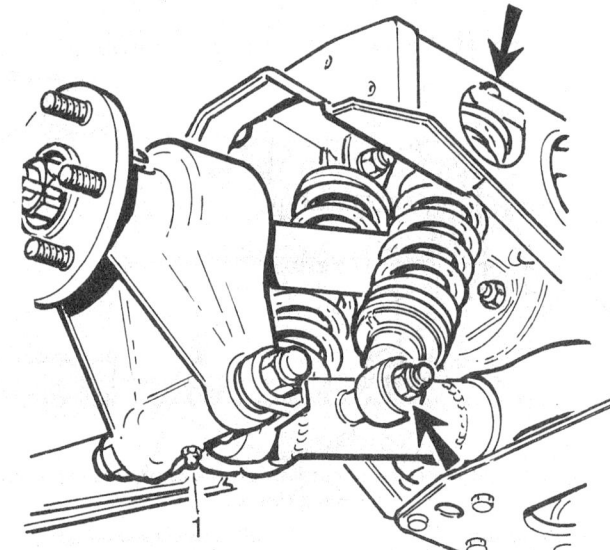

Fig. 8.7. Rear shock absorber mountings. Outer pivot grease nipple (1) (Sec. 3)

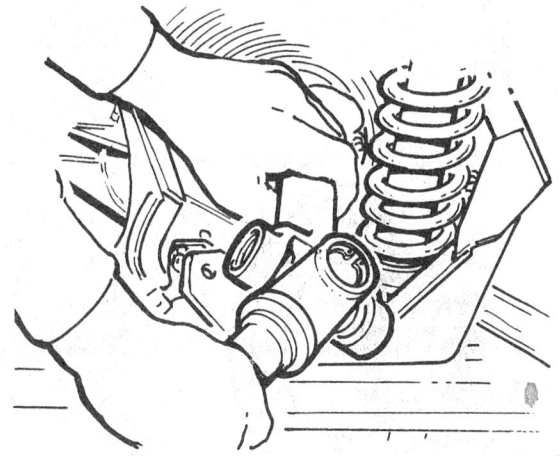

Fig. 8.8. Withdrawing a driveshaft (Sec. 3)

2   Cut the locking wire and remove the two bolts which secure the brake caliper to the final drive unit.

3   Remove the brake discs, noting carefully the number of shims located between the disc and the driveshaft flange.

4   *On earlier cars,* a locking ring is used to retain the output shaft. With this design, extract the two bolts and the locking plate which retain the locking ring to the caliper mounting bracket. **On no account remove the other three adjacent bolts** which secure the caliper mounting bracket which must not be disturbed.

5   Release the locking ring by tapping it with a hammer and brass or copper drift engaged in the slots in the ring.

6   When the ring is completely free, withdraw the shaft assembly through the caliper mounting bracket and do not disturb the setting of the mounting as the operation is carried out.

7   Bend down the lock tab and unscrew the bearing nut, extract the bearing from the shaft.

8   The oil seal on this type of earlier assembly is fitted inside the locking ring and renewal should be carried out by renewing the seal and ring as an assembly.

9   Refitting is a reversal of the removal and dismantling operations.

6   Output shaft oil seal and bearing (early Series 2) - renewal

1   Repeat the operations described in paragraphs 1, 2 and 3, of the preceding Section.

2   Cut the locking wire and remove the five bolts which secure the caliper mounting bracket. Support the caliper.

3   Withdraw the output shaft together with the caliper mounting bracket shims, ball bearing and the square section oil seal from the ball bearing housing.

4   Flatten the tab on the locking plate and unscrew the nut from the output shaft.

5   Withdraw the ball bearing and caliper mounting bracket from the output shaft. The oil seal is integral with the caliper mounting bracket and the assembly must be renewed complete.

6   Smear the square section new oil seal with oil and press it squarely into its seat in the bearing housing.

7   Apply hypoid gear oil to the caliper bracket seal, fit the four special flange bolts and position the caliper mounting bracket and oil seal assembly over the output shaft. Slide the ball bearing onto the shaft, a new tab washer and the nut. Tighten nut to torque and bend up the tab of the lockwasher.

8   Oil the splines of the output shaft and fit it into the differential housing.

9   Insert and tighten (finger-tight) the five bolts which retain the caliper mounting bracket.

10 It should be noted that the oil seal is slightly oversize so that it will be compressed when all bolts are fully tightened.

11 Using feeler blades, measure between the inner face of the caliper mounting bracket and the differential housing (A).

12 Shims are available in the following thicknesses:

0.003 in (0.076 mm), 0.005 in (0.127 mm), 0.010 in (0.254 mm), 0.030 in (0.762 mm)

Select those which are of a thickness which when subtracted from the measurement (A) will leave a gap of 0.003 in (0.076 mm). When the bolts are tightened, this is the required 'nip' for bearing and oil seal.

13 Remove the output shaft, apply a thin coat of jointing compound to the shims (which have just been selected) and to the mating faces of the flanges. Insert the output shaft with coated shims, insert bolts and tighten to specified torque in diagonally opposite sequence.

14 Wire the five bolts to lock them.

15 Install the brake discs to the output shaft flanges, refitting any shims to their original locations.

16 Install the caliper to the mounting bracket. Check that the brake disc is central in the jaws of the caliper. This can be done using feeler blades. Any adjustment which may be required should be carried out by altering the shim pack which is located between the drive flange and the disc.

17 Lock the caliper bolts with wire.

18 Refit the driveshaft as described in Section 3.

7   Pinion oil seal (early models with bearings preloaded with shims) - renewal

1   Disconnect the propeller shaft rear flange from the final drive unit pinion companion flange.

2   Make up a suitable lever, 3 or 4 ft (0.9 or 1.2 m) in length and drilled so that by bolting it to the companion flange, the flange can be held still while the flange nut is unscrewed.

3   Remove the nut, washer and flange and then prise out the defective oil seal.

4   Fit the new oil seal gasket into the seal recess, fit the oil seal so that its lip is towards the final drive unit and its dust-excluding face is visible when installed.

5   Fit the companion flange, washer and nut and holding the flange quite still, tighten the nut to a torque of between 120 and 130 lb ft (166 and 179 Nm).

6   Reconnect the propeller shaft.

7   Top-up the final drive unit.

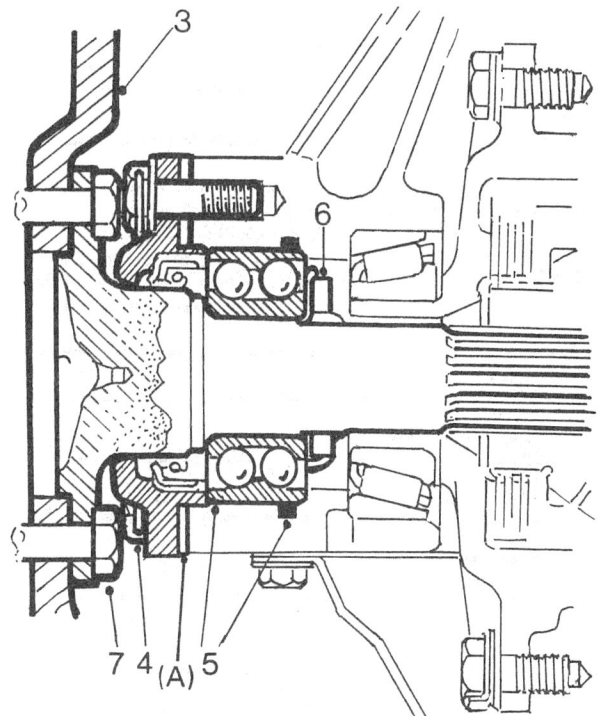

Fig. 8.11. Sectional view of output shaft flange and bearing — early Series 2 (Sec. 6)

3   Brake disc
4   Caliper mounting bracket bolt
5   Bearing and oil seal
6   Output shaft nut
7   Special flange bolt
A   Shim

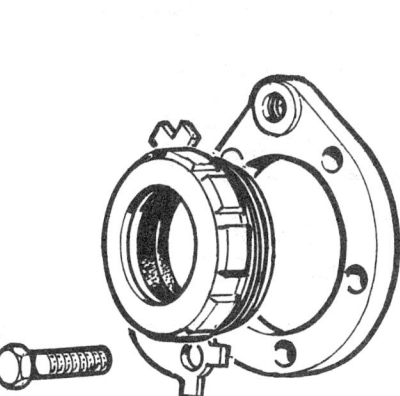

Fig. 8.9. Output shaft locking ring (Series I cars) (Sec. 5)

Fig. 8.10. Output shaft (caliper mounting) bracket on early Series 2 cars (Sec. 6)

8 Pinion oil seal (later models with bearing collapsible spacer) renewal

1 Disconnect the propeller shaft from the final drive pinion companion flange. Disconnect the driveshaft from the output flanges of the final drive unit.

2 Wind a cord round the companion flange of the pinion and attach it to a spring balance. Check and record the force required to start the flange moving. Take the average of several recordings.

3 Hold the companion flange still by fitting a tool similar to the one described in the preceding Section.

4 Unscrew and remove the pinion nut and washer and withdraw the companion flange.

5 Prise out the faulty oil seal and install the new one.

6 Refit the companion flange (complete with propeller shaft flange bolts) the washer and screw on the pinion nut.

7 Tighten the nut to 100 lb/ft (138 Nm) holding the flange still with the tool to prevent it turning.

8 Check the rotating force required to turn the flange using the cord and spring balance. Tighten the pinion nut, *only a fraction of a turn at a time,* until the force recorded on the spring balance matches that recorded before dismantling.

9 If the nut is overtightened, the collapsible type spacer which is located between the pinion bearings will be overcompressed and a new spacer will have to be fitted. It is no good attempting to reduce the preload by backing off the nut. A new spacer can only be fitted after almost complete dismantling of the final drive unit.

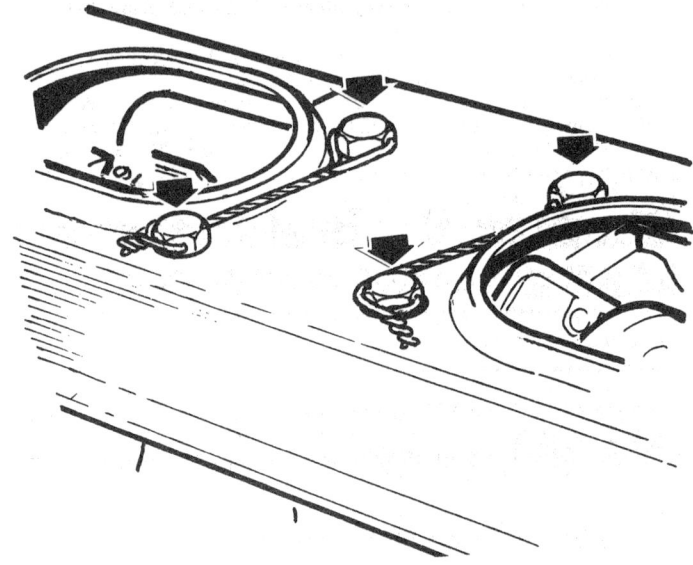

Fig. 8.12. Final drive unit mounting bolts (Sec. 9)

9 Final drive unit - removal and installation

1 Remove the rear suspension as described in Chapter 11, Section 19. Drain the oil from the final drive unit.

2 Invert the suspension assembly on the bench and remove the 14 bolts which secure the tie plate.

3 Disconnect the four shock absorber/roadspring assemblies but do not dismantle them.

4 Remove the four self-locking nuts which secure the driveshaft inner universal joint flange to the brake disc and final drive output flanges.

5 Withdraw the driveshafts noting the number and location of the camber shims.

6 Remove a nut from one end of the suspension inner wishbone pivot shafts and drive out the shafts.

7 Withdraw the hubs, driveshafts and radius arm assemblies.

8 Disconnect handbrake levers from the compensator.

9 Disconnect the brake lines from the caliper units.

10 Turn the final drive assembly over and cut the locking wire from the differential carrier bolts. Unscrew the bolts and remove the crossbeam from the carrier by tilting the crossbeam forward over the nose of the pinion.

11 Installation is a reversal of removal but observe the following points:

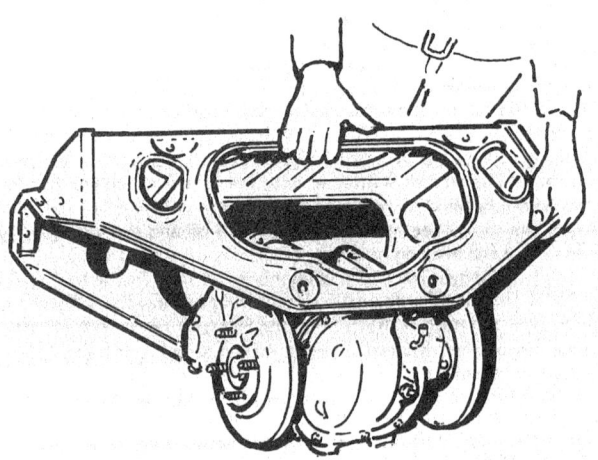

Fig. 8.13. Separating crossbeam from final drive unit (Sec. 9)

Tighten the differential carrier bolts to the specified torque and lock the bolts with new wire.

Never substitute nylon type self-locking nuts for the all metal type used on the output shaft flange studs.

10 Fault diagnosis - final drive

Symptom	Reason/s
Noise on drive or overrun	Low oil level. Loose crownwheel bolts. Loose bearing cap bolts. General wear in bearings or gearteeth.
Noise on turn	Seized, broken or damaged pinion or side gear or thrust washers.
Knock during gearshift or when taking up drive	Excessive crownwheel to pinion backlash. Worn gears. Worn driveshaft or output shaft splines. Drive pinion nut loose. Loose crownwheel bolts or bearing cap bolts. Worn side gear splines. Wear in driveshaft universal joints.

Chapter 9 Braking system

For modifications, and information on later models, see Supplement at end of manual

Contents

Specifications

Type	4 wheel disc, hydraulic. Dual circuit with vacuum servo assistance. Handbrake mechanical to rear wheels
Caliper type	Girling
Disc diameter	
Front	11.18 in (28.4 cm)
Rear	10.375 in (26.3 cm)
Disc thickness	
Front (Series 1)	0.5 in (12.7 mm)
Front (Series 2 and 3)	0.95 in (24.13 mm)
Rear (all models)	0.5 in (12.7 mm)
Master cylinder bore diameter	0.875 in (22.23 mm)
Servo unit	Girling Type 100
Brake fluid type/specification	Hydraulic fluid to SAE J1703D (Duckhams Universal Brake and Clutch Fluid)

Torque wrench settings	lb ft	Nm
Disc retaining bolts	35	48
Caliper retaining bolts:		
Front	55	75
Rear	50	68
Brake pedal pivot bolt	18	25
Master cylinder banjo bolt	23	31
Master cylinder tipping valve nut	40	54

1 General description

1 The braking system is of four wheel disc type. The hydraulic system is of dual circuit type with a tandem master cylinder. Servo assistance is provided.
2 The rear calipers and discs are mounted inboard on the differential housing and output flanges.
3 The handbrake operates through mechanical linkage to the rear calipers which incorporate automatically adjustable handbrake mechanism.

2 Disc pads - inspection and renewal

1 At the intervals specified in 'Routine maintenance', examine the thickness of the friction material on the disc pads.
2 In the case of the front brakes, remove the roadwheels.
3 The pads are clearly visible through the aperture in the caliper units and if the friction material has worn down to 1/8 in (3.2 mm) or less then they must be renewed (photos).
4 Always renew the pads in axle sets.
5 Withdraw the spring clips and pull out the pad retaining pins. On

later models, anti-chatter springs are fitted to the pads.

6   Withdraw the pads from the caliper, gripping their edges with a pair of pliers if they are hard to remove (photo).

7   Brush out any dust from the interior of the caliper and then depress the caliper pistons squarely into their bores in order to accommodate the new, thicker pads. Depressing the pistons will cause the fluid level to rise in the master cylinder reservoir and eventually overflow, so it is advisable to draw off some of the hydraulic fluid from the reservoir before commencing operations. A poultry baster or an old hydrometer is useful for drawing off some fluid. Do not spill any hydraulic fluid on the paintwork as it acts as a paint stripper!

8   Install the new pads making sure that the friction lining is against the disc, insert the retaining pins and spring clips.

9   Apply the footbrake several times to bring the pads into contact with the discs and then top-up the fluid reservoir to the indicated level.

10 For renewal of handbrake friction pads, see Section 15.

3   Front caliper - removal, overhaul and refitting

1   Jack-up the front of the car and remove the roadwheel.

2   Disconnect the hydraulic hose at the junction with the rigid brake pipe (see Section 6). Plug the pipes.

3   Cut the locking wire, remove the caliper mounting bolts and withdraw the caliper. Withdraw the disc pads.

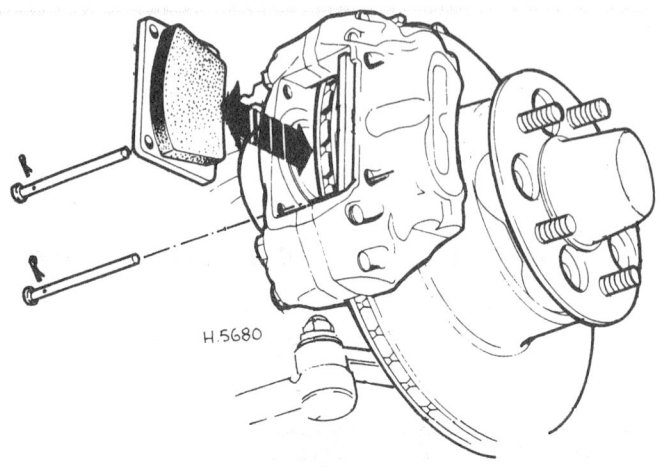

Fig. 9.1. Removing disc pads (Sec. 2)

2.3A Front disc caliper (3-piston type)

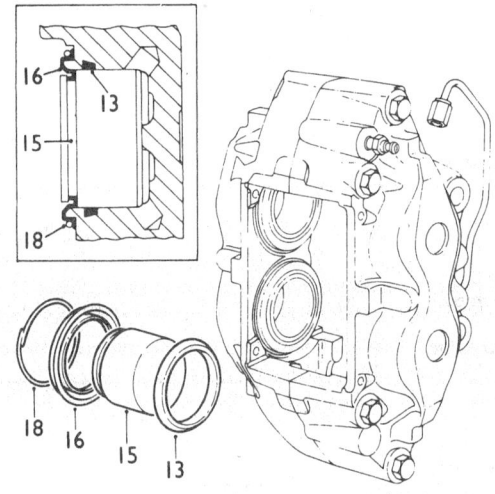

Fig. 9.1A. Later type 4-piston front caliper (Sec. 2)

13	Piston seal	16	Dust-excluding boot
15	Piston	18	Dust-excluding boot retaining clip

2.3B Rear disc caliper

2.6 Removing a disc pad

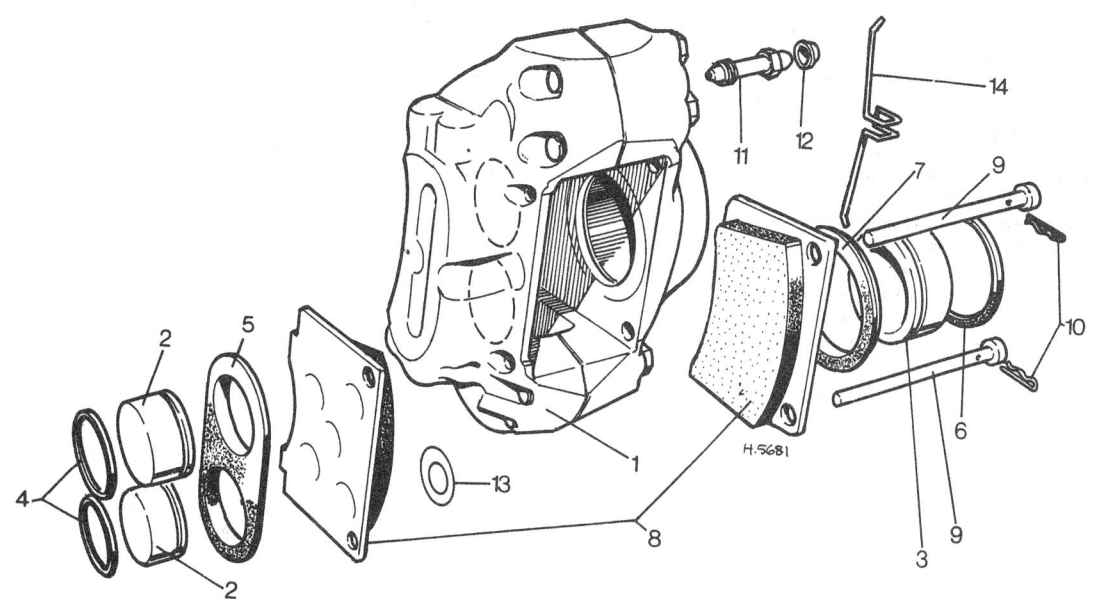

Fig. 9.2. Exploded view of a front disc caliper (earlier three piston type) (Sec. 3)

1	Caliper body	6	Piston seal	11	Bleed nipple
2	Outer pistons	7	Dust excluder	12	Dust cap
3	Inner piston	8	Friction pad	13	Mounting shim
4	Piston seals	9	Pad retaining pin	14	Anti-chatter spring
5	Dust excluder	10	Clip		(later models)

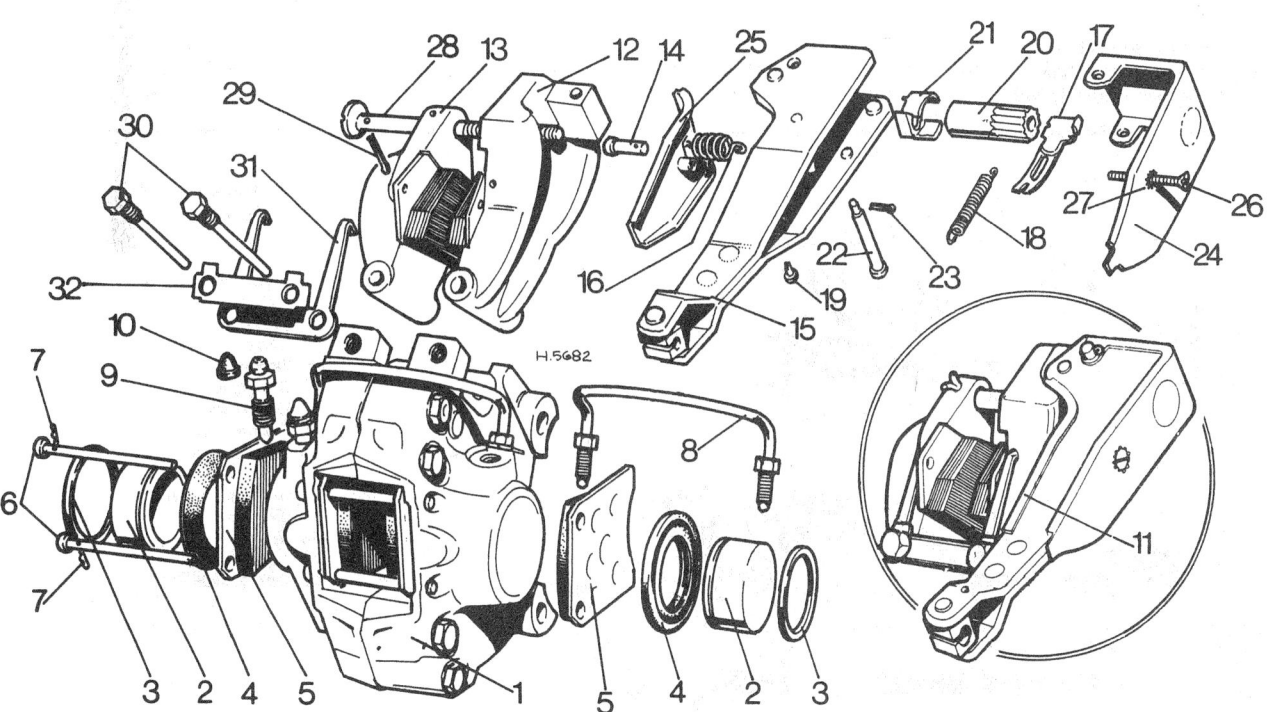

Fig. 9.3. Exploded view of a rear disc caliper (Sec. 4)

1	Caliper body	11	Handbrake mechanism	22	Hinge pin
2	Piston	12	Pad carrier assembly	23	Split pin
3	Piston seal	13	Pad carrier assembly	24	Protection cover
4	Dust excluder	14	Anchor pin	25	Protection cover
5	Friction pad	15	Operating lever	26	Bolt
6	Pad retaining pin	16	Return spring	27	Washer
7	Clip	17	Pawl assembly	28	Bolt
8	Bridge pipe	18	Tension spring	29	Split pin
9	Bleed nipple	19	Anchor pin	30	Bolt
10	Dust cap	20	Adjuster	31	Retraction plate
		21	Friction spring	32	Tab washer

4   Clean away all external dirt. **On no account unscrew the bolts which secure the two halves of the caliper body together.**

5   Detach the rubber dust excluders from the locating grooves.

6   Place a pad of rag between the piston end faces and apply air from a tyre pump to the fluid union on the caliper body. This will eject the pistons far enough so that they can be extracted with the fingers. There are two outer and one inner piston, on calipers fitted to early cars, later cars are fitted with four piston calipers.

7   Examine the surfaces of the pistons and the cylinders for scoring or 'bright' wear areas. If these are evident, renew the caliper complete.

8   Where the components are in good condition, extract and discard the seals which are located in the cylinder grooves.

9   Obtain a repair kit which will contain the new seals and other renewable items. Manipulate the new seals into their cylinder grooves using the fingers only.

10 Dip each piston in clean hydraulic fluid and enter it squarely into its cylinder.

11 Refit the dust excluders and engage their lips in the cylinder grooves. Depress the pistons fully into their cylinders.

12 Refit the caliper to the stub axle carrier and tighten the bolts to the specified torque wrench setting. Lock the bolts with new wire.

13 Refit the disc pads.

14 Reconnect the hydraulic hose and bleed the front circuit, as described in Section 13.

15 Refit the roadwheel and lower the car to the ground.

---

4   Rear caliper - removal, overhaul and refitting

Early cars

1   Remove the rear suspension assembly as described in Chapter 11, Section 19. Support the suspension on blocks placed centrally under it.

2   Extract the split pin and clevis pin and disconnect the handbrake cable from the compensator linkage. Disconnect the pull-off springs.

3   Lift the lock tabs and withdraw the pivot bolts together with the retraction plate.

4   Remove the handbrake friction pad carriers from the caliper bridges by moving them to the rear round the discs and then withdrawing them from the rear of the suspension assembly (refer to Section 15 of this Chapter).

5   Disconnect the hydraulic hose from the caliper body and plug the hole.

6   Remove the disc pads, as described in Section 2.

7   Cut the locking wire and remove the two bolts which secure caliper to the final drive unit.

8   Withdraw the caliper through the aperture in the front of the crossmember.

Series 2 cars

9   Remove the handbrake caliper in the following way. Remove the nuts and bolts which secure the tie plate to the rear suspension unit and withdraw the tie-plate.

10 Fully release the handbrake and remove the split pin and clevis pin which secure the handbrake cable to the caliper operating lever on one side of the car and then disconnect the cable from the opposite caliper.

11 Disconnect the return spring from the handbrake operating lever.

12 Flatten the caliper mounting bolt lock tabs, unscrew and remove the bolts, the tab washer and the retraction lever. **On no account unscrew the bolts which secure the two halves of the caliper body together.**

13 Slide the caliper around the brake disc and withdraw it through the gap exposed by the removal of the tie-plate.

14 Disconnect the hydraulic line from the caliper and plug the open ends to prevent loss of fluid and entry of dirt.

15 Withdraw the disc pads from the caliper and then cut the locking wire from the caliper mounting bolts and unscrew and remove the bolts.

16 Slide the caliper around the brake disc and withdraw it through the gap exposed by removal of the tie-plate.

17 Overhaul of the caliper is similar to that described for the front caliper in Section 3, except that only two pistons are employed in the rear unit. Refer also to Sections 15 and 16 of this Chapter.

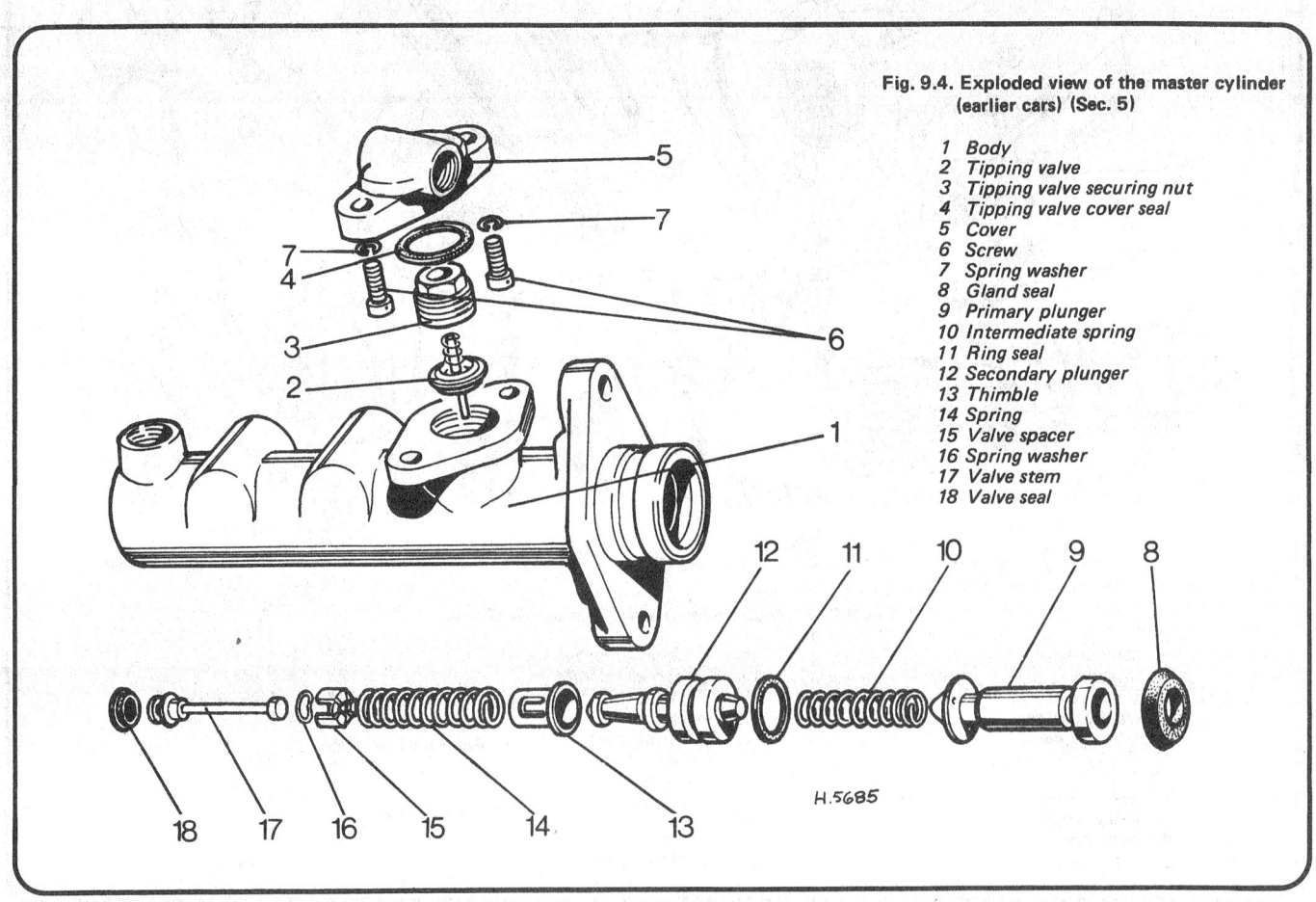

Fig. 9.4. Exploded view of the master cylinder (earlier cars) (Sec. 5)

1   Body
2   Tipping valve
3   Tipping valve securing nut
4   Tipping valve cover seal
5   Cover
6   Screw
7   Spring washer
8   Gland seal
9   Primary plunger
10 Intermediate spring
11 Ring seal
12 Secondary plunger
13 Thimble
14 Spring
15 Valve spacer
16 Spring washer
17 Valve stem
18 Valve seal

H.5685

18 To refit the caliper, locate it in position and secure it with two mounting bolts. Lock the bolts with new wire. Check that the brake disc is central within the caliper opening. If necessary, adjustment can be carried out by adding or removing brake disc shims.

19 Reverse the rest of the removal operations and when installation is complete, bleed the rear brake circuit as described in Section 13.

5 Master cylinder (early cars) - removal, overhaul and refitting

1 Remove the cap from the master cylinder reservoir and draw off as much fluid as possible by syphoning or using a poultry baster or old hydrometer.

2 Disconnect the brake lines from the master cylinder body.

3 Unscrew and remove the two flange nuts and withdraw the master cylinder from the front face of the vacuum servo unit.

4 Clean away all external dirt.

5 Extract the two screws and their washers and withdraw the tipping valve cover and seal.

6 Remove the tipping valve securing nut, depress the primary plunger and withdraw the tipping valve.

7 Eject the remainder of the internal components, either by carefully shaking them out or by applying air pressure from a tyre pump at one fluid inlet union while holding a finger over the second inlet.

8 Examine the surfaces of the plungers and the cylinder bore for scoring or 'bright' wear areas. If these are evident, renew the master cylinder complete.

9 If these components are in good condition then separate the plungers and intermediate spring. Lift the leaf of the spring retainer and withdraw the spring and valve sub-assembly from the secondary plunger.

10 Extract the spring, valve spacer and spring washer from the valve stem, also the seal from the valve head.

11 Discard all rubber seals and obtain a repair kit which will contain all the renewable items.

12 Install the new seals using the fingers only to manipulate them into position on the primary and secondary plungers.

13 Fit the valve seal (smallest diameter first) onto the valve head. Position the spring washer on the valve stem so that it flows away from the valve stem shoulder.

14 Fit the valve spacer, legs first, then attach the spring retainer to the valve stem so that the key hole end is first.

15 Slide the secondary spring over the retainer and then position the sub-assembly on the secondary plunger. The spring must be compressed whilst the leaf of the retainer is depressed behind the head of the plunger. This operation will be made easier if the sub-assembly is carefully secured in a vice and the vice jaws closed to compress the spring until it is nearly coil bound. Use a small screwdriver to press the spring retainer back against the secondary plunger. Depress the leaf of the retainer behind the head of the plunger.

16 Fit the intermediate spring between the primary and secondary plungers. Dip the plungers in clean hydraulic fluid and insert them into the cylinder bore (valve end leading).

17 Depress the primary plunger from the bore and install the tipping valve assembly. Fit the seal and screw in the tipping valve securing nut to a torque of 40 lb/ft (54 Nm). Install the tipping valve cover and a new seal.

18 Fit the master cylinder to the vacuum servo unit.

19 Reconnect the brake lines and bleed the complete hydraulic system (both circuits), as described in Section 13.

6 Master cylinder (later cars) - removal, overhaul and refitting

1 Slacken the clips which secure the reservoir hoses to the master cylinder adaptors, disconnect the hoses and plug them.

2 Disconnect the rigid brake lines from the master cylinder body and plug the lines.

3 Unbolt the master cylinder from the servo unit (photo).

4 Clean away all external dirt.

5 Prise the reservoir hose adaptors from their sealing grommets on the master cylinder body. Prise out the grommets.

6 Depress the primary piston into the bore of the master cylinder and extract the secondary piston stop pin from the grommet housing nearest the front of the master cylinder.

7 Extract the circlip from the end of the master cylinder and tap the

6.3 Brake booster and master cylinder

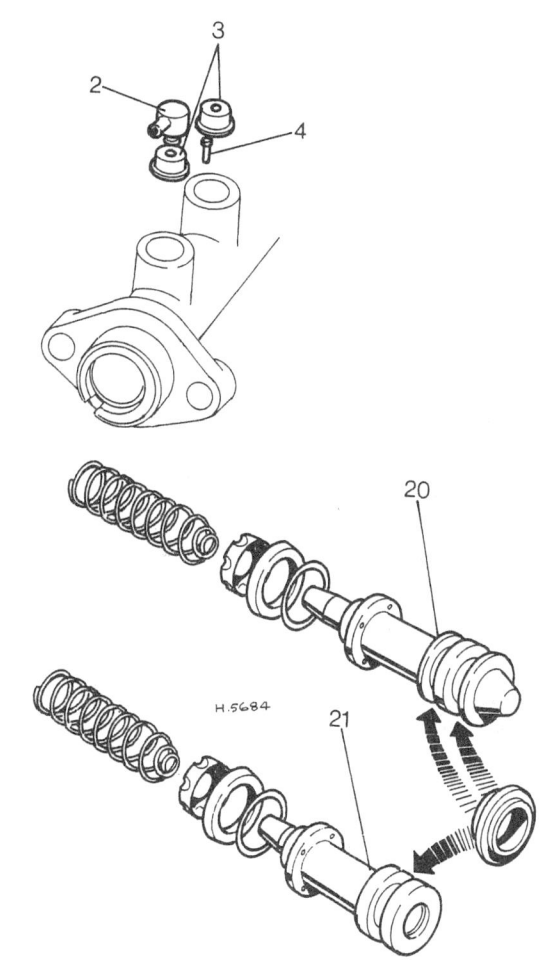

Fig. 9.5. Later type master cylinder (Sec. 6)

2 Fluid pipe adaptor
3 Grommets
4 Lock pin
20 Secondary piston
21 Primary piston

flange end on a block of wood to eject the primary piston and spring and the secondary piston and spring. If these components are difficult to remove, apply air from a tyre pump at the fluid outlet port.

8   Keep the piston assemblies separate noting that the secondary piston spring is thicker and longer than the primary spring.

9   Examine the surfaces of the pistons and cylinder bore for scoring or 'bright' wear areas. If these are evident, renew the master cylinder complete.

10 If these components are in good condition, remove the spring, spring seat, recuperating seal and washer from the secondary piston. Also prise the seals from the rear of the secondary piston.

11 Dismantle the primary piston in a similar way.

12 Discard all the seals and obtain a repair kit.

13 Use only the fingers to manipulate the seals into position and commence reassembly by fitting the secondary piston inner seal into its groove so that its lip faces the front of the master cylinder.

14 Install the second seal to the secondary piston with its lip in the reverse direction to the first one fitted.

15 Fit the washer, recuperating seal, spring seat and the spring over the front end of the secondary piston.

16 Install primary piston rear seal (lip away from circlip) and then fit the washer, recuperating seal, spring seat and spring over the front end of the piston.

17 Apply hydraulic fluid to the piston assemblies and insert the secondary piston and spring into the master cylinder followed by the primary piston. Depress the piston and fit the circlip.

18 Depress the primary piston and fit the secondary piston stop pin.

19 Refit the grommet and adaptors and install the master cylinder to the servo by reversing the removal operations. Bleed the system.

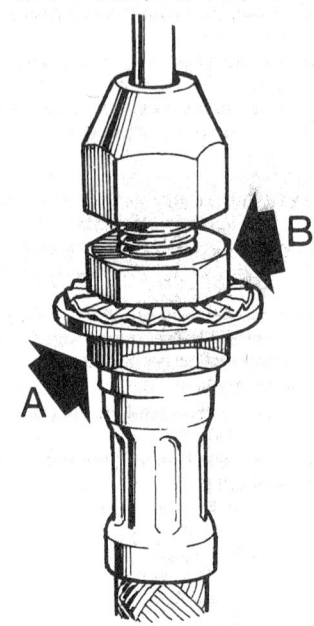

Fig. 9.6. Flexible to rigid hydraulic hose connection (Sec. 7)

A   Flexible hose and fitting   B   Locknut

---

7   Flexible hydraulic hoses, inspection, removal and refitting

1   Periodically, inspect the condition of the flexible brake hoses. If they appear swollen, chafed or when bent double with the fingers tiny cracks are visible, then they must be renewed.

2   Always uncouple the rigid pipe from the flexible hose first, then release the end of the flexible hose from the support bracket. Now unscrew the flexible hose from the caliper or connector. If this method is followed, no kinking of the hoses will occur.

3   When installing the hose, always use a new copper sealing washer.

4   When installation is complete, check that the flexible hose does not rub against the tyre or other adjacent components. Its attitude may be altered to overcome this by releasing its bracket support locknut and twisting the hose in the required direction by not more than one quarter turn.

5   Bleed the hydraulic system (Section 13).

---

8   Rigid brake lines - inspection, removal and refitting

1   At regular intervals wipe the steel brake pipes clean and examine them for signs of rust or denting caused by flying stones.

2   Examine the fit of the pipes in their insulated securing clips and bend the tongues of the clips if necessary to ensure a positive fit.

3   Check that the pipes are not touching any adjacent components or rubbing against any part of the vehicle. Where this is observed, bend the pipe gently away to clear.

4   Any section of pipe which is rusty or chafed should be renewed. Brake pipes are available to the correct length and fitted with end unions from most Jaguar/Daimler dealers and can be made to pattern by many accessory suppliers. When installing the new pipes use the old pipes as a guide to bending and do not make any bends sharper than is necessary.

5   The system will of course have to be bled when the circuit has been reconnected.

---

9   Front brake disc - inspection, removal and refitting

1   Jack-up the front of the car and remove the roadwheels.

2   Withdraw the disc pads.

3   Examine the discs for deep grooves or scoring or cracks. If these are evident, renew the disc. Light scoring is normal.

4   Check the disc for 'run-out'. A dial gauge should be used for this although feeler blades placed between the face of the disc and a fixed

point are a satisfactory substitute.

5   Turn the disc and check that the 'run-out' or out of true does not exceed 0.004 in (0.10 mm). If it does the disc must be renewed.

6   It is most important that for optimum brake efficiency the hub endfloat is as specified in Chapter 11.

Cars with 3-piston type calipers

7   To remove the disc, first unbolt the hub from the disc. The bolts can be reached using a socket inserted through the aperture in the disc shield.

8   Tap off the hub grease cap, extract the split-pin, remove the nut and thrust washer and withdraw the hub with the hand.

9   The brake disc can now be slid out of the caliper jaws, over the end of the stub axle and removed. There is no need to remove the caliper or to disconnect the hydraulic brake hose for this operation.

Cars with 4-piston type calipers

10 To remove the disc, first withdraw the hub as described in paragraphs 7 and 8.

11 Cut the locking wire and unbolt the caliper. Mark the location of shims fitted between the steering arm and the caliper.

12 Slacken the bolt which secures the steering arm to the hub carrier.

13 Ease the caliper to one side (without disconnecting the hydraulic brake hose) and withdraw the disc.

All models

14 Refitting is a reversal of removal. Tighten all bolts to the specified torque.

---

10 Rear brake disc (except Series 2) - inspection, removal and refitting

1   Repeat the operations described in the preceding Section, paragraphs 2 and 5.

2   Remove the rear suspension assembly, as described in Chapter 11, Section 19, if the brake disc must be renewed.

3   Remove the brake caliper, as described in Section 4, of this Chapter.

4   Turn the suspension assembly upside-down and remove the hydraulic shock absorber/spring units, also as described in Chapter 11.

5   Release the clip and slide back the halfshaft inner universal joint shield.

6   Remove the four self-locking nuts which secure the inner universal joint and brake disc to the output shaft flange.

7 Withdraw the halfshaft noting the camber shims between the universal joint and brake disc.

8 Tap the bolts which secure the halfshaft universal joints and brake disc back as far as possible.

9 Lift the suspension lower wishbone, hub carrier and halfshaft assembly upwards until there is enough clearance to withdraw the brake disc from its mounting bolts.

10 For optimum brake performance it is most important that the endfloat of the rear hubs is as specified in Section 2, of Chapter 8.

11 Refitting is a reversal of removal but make sure that the rear brake hydraulic circuit is bled as described in Section 13.

11 Rear brake disc (Series 2) - inspection, removal and refitting

1 Refer to paragraphs 3, 4 and 5 of Section 9. If the brake disc must be renewed, jack-up the car and remove the roadwheel from the side of the car concerned.

2 Support the bodyframe securely on stands.

3 Remove the brake caliper, as previously described.

4 Drive out the shock absorber lower mounting pin and then cut the locking wire from the radius arm locking bolt and remove the bolt.

5 Unscrew and remove the grease nipple from the hub pivot shaft and then support the hub on wooden blocks.

6 Lever the radius arm from the spigot anchor point.

7 Release the clip which secures the halfshaft inner universal joint cover and slide the cover clear of the joint.

8 Disconnect the inner universal joint from the brake disc, by unscrewing the securing nuts, tapping the bolts towards the final drive unit and carefully retaining the camber shims.

9 Lift out the brake disc. It may be necessary to jack up the car a little higher to facilitate removal of the disc.

10 Refitting is a reversal of removal but the disc must run central in the caliper aperture. If this is not the case, add or remove shims located between the disc and the final drive output flange. Compensate for this by adding or subtracting a shim of similar thickness from the camber angle shim pack (between the disc and the driveshaft) so that the total thickness of shims remains the same. For example, if a shim 0.04 in (1 mm) thick was **added** between the disc and output flange, the same thickness shim must be **removed** from between the disc and driveshaft.

12 Pressure differential warning actuator

1 The purpose of this device which is fitted to certain models is to monitor the pressures in the front and rear brake hydraulic circuits and to give a visual warning when a drop in pressure occurs in either circuit. Such a drop in pressure may be due to a leak in the hydraulic pipes or hoses, a failed seal in the caliper or master cylinder and the cause should be sought and rectified immediately.

2 The device is essentially a piston which is kept in balance by the equal pressures of the two circuits of the hydraulic system. When pressure in one circuit falls, the piston is displaced and completes an electrical circuit to illuminate a warning lamp.

3 Early types of pressure differential warning actuator need resetting after being displaced but later models have an integral automatic reset.

Early type

4 To reset the early type actuator, check that the master cylinder reservoir is full.

5 Switch on the ignition and run the engine at idling speed.

6 Attach a bleed tube to the front right-hand caliper bleed nipple, placing the open end of the tube in a suitable container.

7 Apply gentle pressure to the brake pedal and have an assistant slowly open the bleed nipple as pressure on the pedal is increased. When the actuator warning lamp goes off, the device is reset and depressing the brake pedal must cease. Hold the pedal in its partly depressed state and tighten the bleed nipple.

8 If you were slow in stopping the pressure increase on the brake pedal and the actuator piston was displaced in the opposite direction and the warning lamp comes on again, repeat the operations previously described on the left-hand rear caliper.

9 Remove the bleed tube, switch off the engine and top-up the reservoir.

10 Any fault in a pressure differential warning actuator should only be rectified by renewing the unit, no overhaul is possible.

13 Hydraulic circuit - bleeding

1 Removal of air from the hydraulic system is essential to the correct operation of the brakes. Whenever either of the hydraulic circuits has been 'broken' or a component removed and replaced, the system must be bled.

2 If only one circuit of the dual line hydraulic system has been disconnected then only that circuit need to be bled. If the master cylinder has been removed and refitted then both circuits will of course require bleeding.

3 An indication of air in the system is a 'spongy' pedal or when the pedal travel is reduced by repeated applications of the brakes. In the latter case, the trouble may be due to a worn or faulty master cylinder and this should be rectified immediately.

4 If there is any possibility of incorrect fluid having been put into the system, drain all the fluid out and flush through with methylated spirit. Renew all piston seals and cups since these will be affected and could possibly fail under pressure.

5 Gather together a clean glass jar, a length of tubing which fits tightly over the bleed nipples and a tin of the correct brake fluid.

6 To bleed the system on cars not equipped with a pressure differential warning actuator, clean the areas around the bleed nipples and then attach a bleed tube to the nipple on the left-hand rear caliper.

7 Place the end of the tube in a clean glass jar containing sufficient fluid to keep the end of the tube submerged during the operation.

8 Open the bleed valve with a spanner and quickly press down the brake pedal. After slowly releasing the pedal, pause for a moment to allow the fluid to recoup in the master cylinder and then depress again. This will force air from the system. Continue until no more air bubbles can be seen coming from the tube. At intervals make certain that the reservoir is kept topped up, otherwise air will enter at this point again. Tighten the bleed valve when the pedal is fully depressed.

9 Repeat the operations on the right-hand rear caliper and then follow with the front caliper.

10 On cars which are fitted with an early type pressure differential warning actuator (not with automatic reset), bleeding must be carried out so that the following conditions apply:

   a) *Use only light pressure on the footbrake.*
   b) *Do not depress the brake pedal fully to the floor.*
   c) *Never check the 'feel' of the brake pedal until the hydraulic system has been completely bled.*

11 On cars which are fitted with the later automatic reset type actuator, the foregoing precautions need not be observed.

Always discard fluid which has been bled from the system and top-up the system with fluid which has been stored in an airtight container and has remained unshaken for the preceding 24 hours.

14 Handbrake cable - adjustment

1 Under normal circumstances, the self-adjusting characteristic of the disc brake caliper units is applied to the handbrake mechanism and no further adjustment is required. However, due to cable stretch, some supplementary adjustment may be needed after high mileages when the handbrake control has excessive travel when applying the brake fully. Fully release the handbrake control.

2 Working under the car, slacken the locknut at the forked end of the cable threaded adjuster.

3 Extract the split pin, clevis pin and washer and disconnect the fork from the handbrake lever.

4 Check that the handbrake actuating arms at the rear calipers are fully released by pressing them in towards the calipers.

5 Unscrew the clevis fork on the end of the handbrake cable until it can be reconnected to the handbrake lever and the clevis pin inserted without any tendency for the cable to pull on the caliper actuating levers.

6 Refit the washer and split pin to the clevis pin.

15 Handbrake friction pads - renewal

1 The friction pads for the handbrake are quite separate from the disc pads which are actuated by the hydraulic system. Under normal

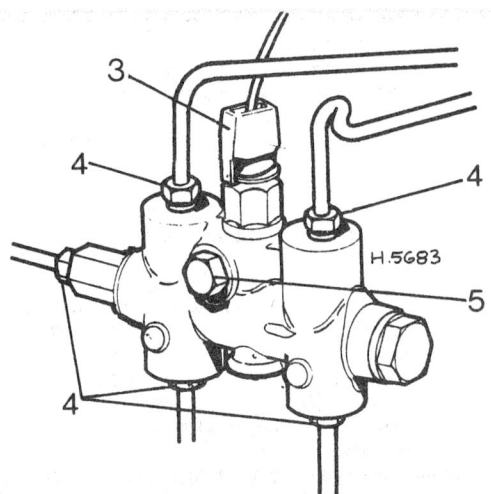

Fig. 9.7. Pressure differential warning actuator (Sec. 12)

3 *Electrical connector*   5 *Actuator mounting*
4 *Fluid pipe unions*   *bolt*

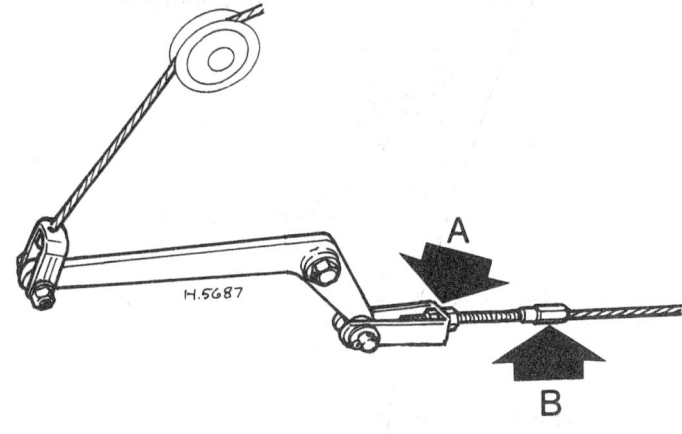

Fig. 9.8. Handbrake cable adjustment (Sec. 14)

A *Locknut*   B *Cable end fitting*

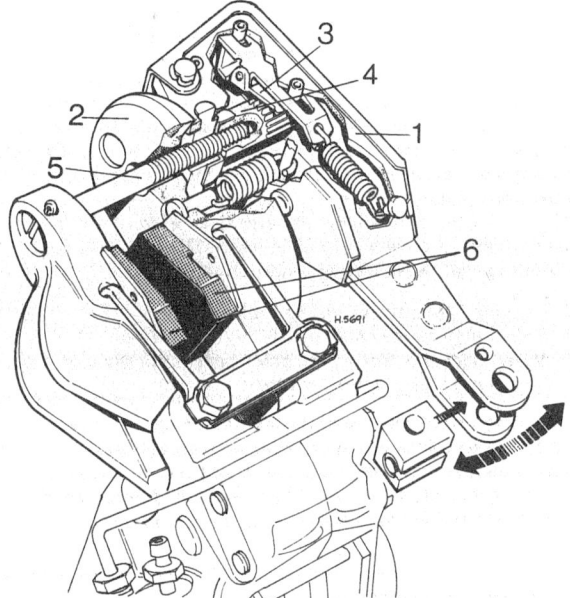

**Fig. 9.9. Cutaway view of the handbrake mechanism attached to the
rear caliper (Sec. 15) (Refer also to Fig. 9.3)**

1 *Operating lever*   4 *Adjuster nut*
2 *Pad carrier assembly*   5 *Adjuster bolt*
3 *Pawl assembly*   6 *Friction pad*

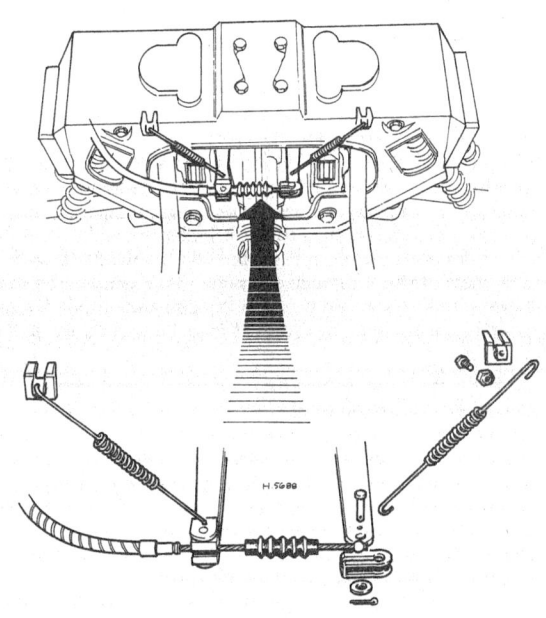

**Fig. 9.10. Handbrake cable attachment to rear caliper operating lever
(Sec. 15)**

conditions, the handbrake pads will last indefinitely. Where they are
in need of renewal proceed as follows:

2 Disconnect the handbrake cables by removing the split pin and
clevis pin and detaching the fork end on one lever so that the outer
cable can be withdrawn from the trunnion on the other lever.

3 Raise the locktabs and withdraw the pivot bolts and retraction
plate.

4 Remove the friction pad carriers by withdrawing them to the rear
around the brake disc and out at the rear of the suspension assembly.
On Series 2 cars, it is easier to remove the tie-plate from the rear
suspension and remove the carriers through the gap provided (see
Section 4).

5 Repeat for the second caliper.

6 With the friction pad carriers removed, extract the worn pads by
slackening the nuts on the outer face of each carrier and inserting a
suitably hooked tool in the hole in each pad securing plate.

7 Install the new pads so that the exposed part of the pad backplate

is uppermost.

8 Fit new retraction fingers and assemble the carrier to the main
caliper body. Leave the pivot bolts slack (refer to paragraphs 4 to 9,
of Section 16).

9 Pull and release the handbrake control several times until the
ratchet ceases to operate which will indicate that the mechanism is
now fully adjusted.

10 Apply the handbrake fairly hard and then tighten the pivot bolts and
lock the tab washers.

11 Reconnect the handbrake linkage to the operating levers and check
the handbrake adjustment, as described in Section 14.

16 Handbrake friction pad carrier - dismantling and reassembly

1 With the carrier removed as described in the preceding Section,
remove the cover securing screw, discard the split pin and withdraw
the pivot clevis pin and detach the dust cover.

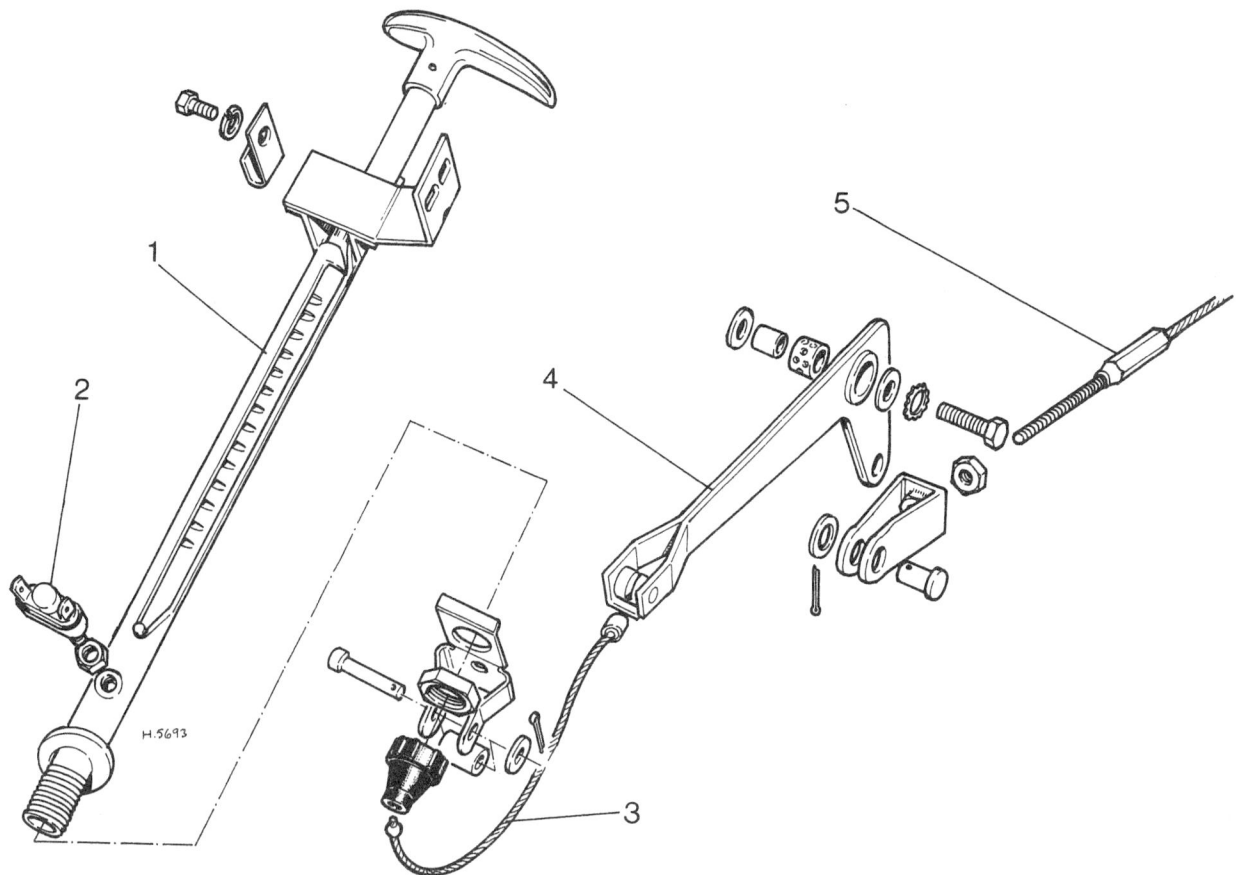

Fig. 9.11. Handbrake control (1) showing warning switch (2) primary cable (3) intermediate lever (4) and secondary cable (5). Earlier versions had a pulley into which primary cable was engaged (Sec. 17)

2   Remove the split pin from the screwdriver slot and unscrew the adjuster bolt from the ratchet nut. Withdraw the nut and bolt.
3   Detach the pawl return spring and remove the pawl over the locating dowel. Detach the operating lever return spring and remove the operating lever and lower cover plate.
4   Reassembly is a reversal of dismantling but if new components have been fitted, refit the friction pad carrier in the following way.
5   Ensure that the handbrake pivot bolts are slack.
6   Set the adjuster bolt until there is ¼ in (6.35 mm) free-movement between the head of the bolt and the outer pad carrier.
7   Pull the inner and outer pad carriers away from the disc and then bend the brass retraction fingers until there is 1/16 in (1.6 mm) clearance between each pad and the disc.
8   Take up the free-movement of the adjuster bolt until the head of the bolt is just in contact with the seating of the outer pad carrier.
9   Fit a new split pin to lock the adjuster bolt.
10 Repeat the operations described in paragraphs 9, 10 and 11 of Section 15.

17 Handbrake cable and control - removal and refitting

1   To renew the handbrake cable assembly, work underneath the car and disconnect the cable from the operating levers of the rear calipers.
2   Disconnect the clevis fork at the forward end of the cable from the intermediate lever.
3   Remove the cable clips from the body and withdraw the cable.
4   If the handcontrol must be removed, disconnect the primary cable from the intermediate lever.
5   Slip the primary cable nipple out of the clevis fork.
6   Working within the car, pull back the carpet to gain access to the handbrake control support bracket. Remove the two bracket setscrews.

7   Working within the engine compartment, remove the plastic grommet from the lower end of the handbrake control.
8   Disconnect the two leads from the handbrake warning lamp switch and then withdraw the control into the car interior.
9   Refitting is a reversal of removal but adjust the handbrake on completion, as described in Section 14.

18 Combined brake warning lamp - description

1   A warning lamp is located on the instrument panel which is connected to three switches, the handbrake 'OFF' switch and the two fluid level switches one of which is fitted in each of the master cylinder reservoirs.
2   When the ignition is switched on, the lamp will light up if the handbrake is applied. Once the handbrake is released, if the lamp fails to go out, then either the brake hydraulic fluid is at a low level and must be immediately replenished or the handbrake 'ON' switch is in need of adjustment.

19 Handbrake 'ON' switch - adjustment

1   The switch is screwed into the lower end of the handbrake control outer tube, see Fig. 9.11.
2   When the handbrake is fully released, the switch plunger is depressed to break the warning lamp circuit.
3   If the lamp remains on, remove the handbrake control and primary cable as described in Section 14. Disconnect the switch terminals.
4   Release the locknut and unscrew the switch.
5   Check that the handbrake control is in the fully released position and then screw the switch right in. Unscrew the switch exactly ½ a turn, temporarily connect the switch leads and check the operation of the

switch with the ignition on.

6 If the operation is satisfactory, tighten the switch locknut and refit the handbrake control and the primary cable.

20 Vacuum servo unit - description

1 A vacuum servo unit is fitted into the brake hydraulic circuit in series with the master cylinder, to provide assistance to the driver when the brake pedal is depressed. This reduces the effort required by the driver to operate the brakes under all braking conditions.

2 The unit operates by vacuum obtained from the induction manifold and comprises basically a booster diaphragm and non-return valve. The servo unit and hydraulic master cylinder are connected together so that the servo unit piston rod acts as the master cylinder pushrod. The driver's braking effort is transmitted through another pushrod to the servo unit piston and its built in control system. The servo unit piston does not fit tightly into the cylinder, but has a strong diaphragm to keep its edges in constant contact with the cylinder wall, so assuring an air tight seal between the two parts. The forward chamber is held under vacuum conditions created in the inlet manifold of the engine and, during periods when the brake pedal is not in use, the controls open a passage to the rear chamber so placing it under vacuum conditions as well. When the brake pedal is depressed, the vacuum passage to the rear chamber is cut off and the chamber opened to atmospheric pressure. The consequent rush of air pushes the servo piston forward in the vacuum chamber and operates the main pushrod to the master cylinder.

3 The controls are designed so that assistance is given under all conditions and, when the brakes are not required, vacuum in the rear chamber is established when the brake pedal is released. All air from the atmosphere entering the rear chamber is passed through a small air filter.

4 Under normal operation conditions the vacuum servo unit is very reliable but should a fault develop then the complete assembly must be renewed as repair kits or internal components are no longer supplied. Operations must therefore be restricted to the maintenance tasks described in the next Section.

5 It must be emphasised that failure of a servo unit will not affect the safety of the braking system, merely cause higher pedal pressures than are normally required.

21 Vacuum servo unit - maintenance

1 Occasionally check the security and condition of the vacuum hose to the inlet manifold.

2 At specified intervals (see 'Routine Maintenance') or when the foot

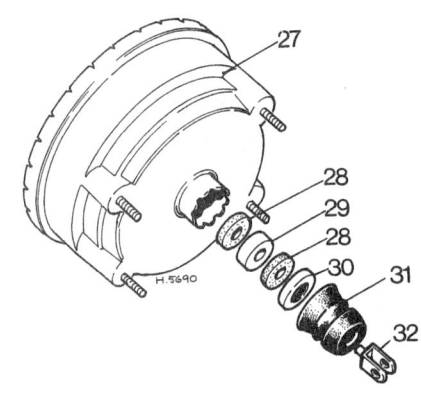

Fig. 9.12. Brake vacuum servo air filter components (Sec. 21)

27 Rear shell
28 Filter felts
29 Air filter

30 Filter retainer
31 Dust cover
32 Clevis fork

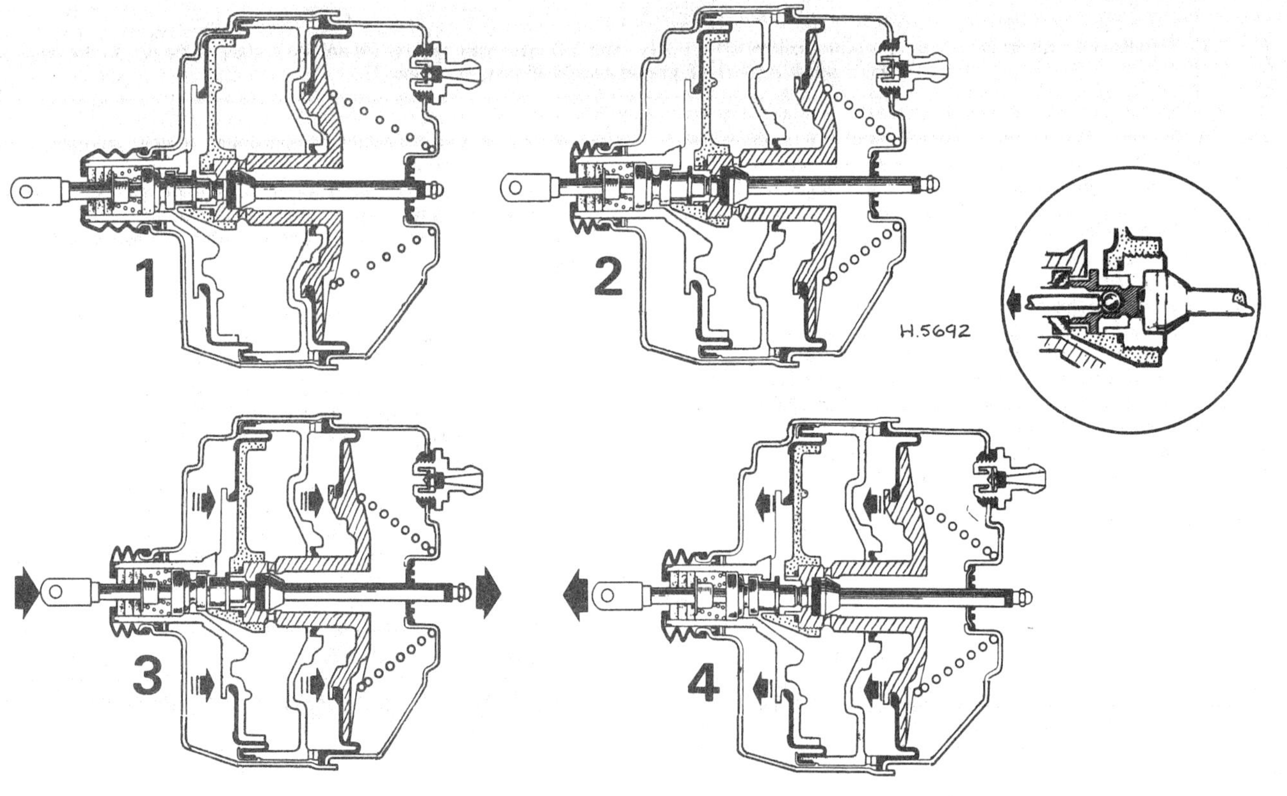

Fig. 9.13. Sectional view of brake vacuum servo unit showing various modes of operation (Sec. 20)

1 Brake pedal released   2 Brake pedal applied   3 Brake held applied   4 Brake being released

brake pedal seems to be sluggish in operation, renew the air filter.

3   Remove the brake vacuum servo unit, as described in Section 22 of this Chapter.

4   Remove the dust cover, detach the end cap and withdraw the filter and filter felt rings. Cut the filter rings to permit them to press over the clevis fork.

5   Fit the new filter felts by cutting them cleanly again so that they will pass over the clevis fork. Ensure that the cuts in the various filter rings are not in line but stagger their position.

6   Refit the end cap and dust cover.

7   Refit the brake vacuum servo unit, as described in Section 22.

8   Deterioration of the non-return valve grommet on the front face of the vacuum servo unit may cause a vacuum leak and consequent loss of servo assistance. Should this happen, prise out the non-return valve by inserting a screwdriver between the valve and the grommet.

9   Pull out the grommet gripping it with pliers.

10   Apply rubber grease to the internal bore of the new grommet and push the non-return valve into it. Push the grommet complete with non-return valve into the front face of the servo unit.

Following this method there is reduced risk of the grommet being

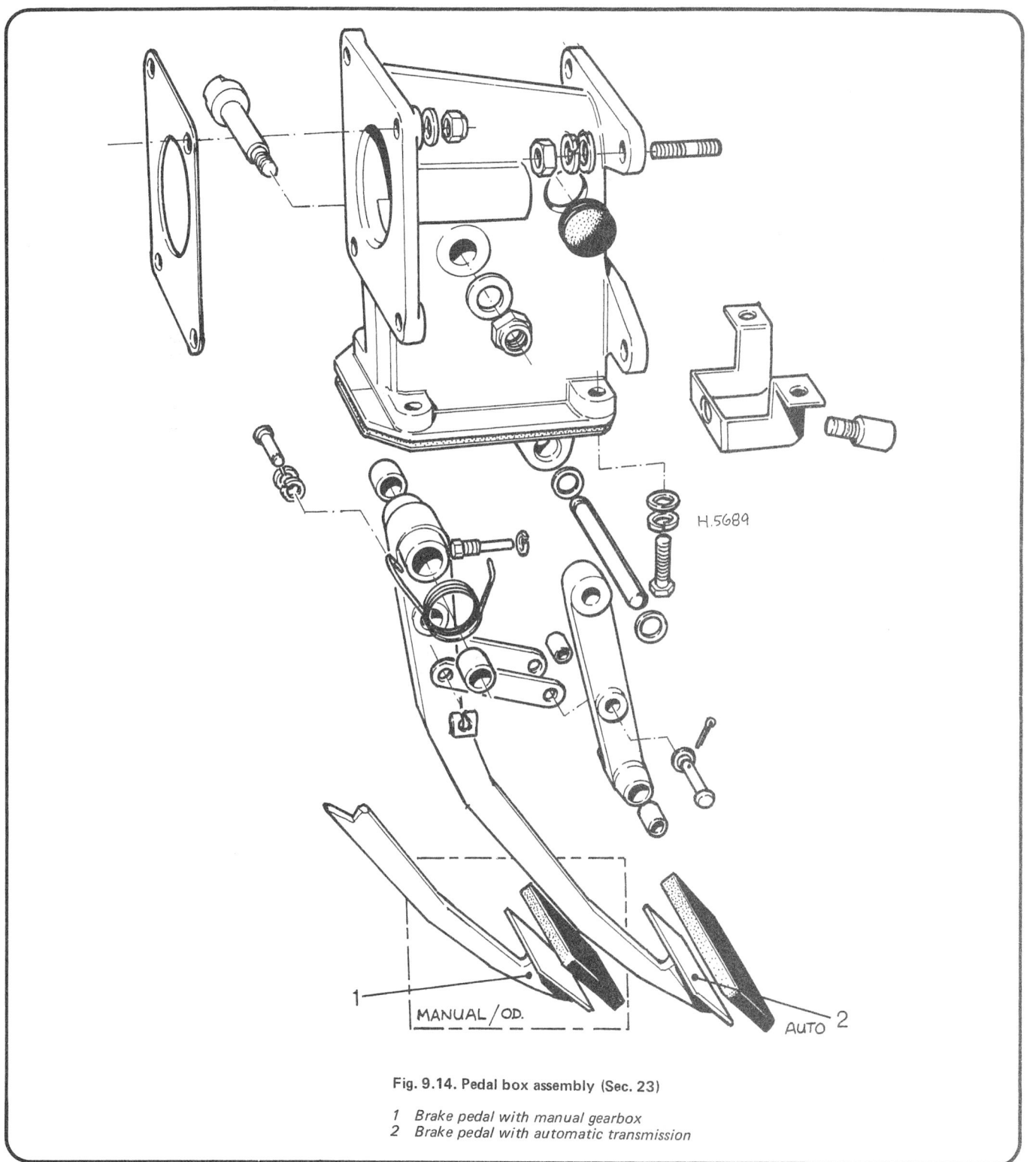

H.5689

Fig. 9.14. Pedal box assembly (Sec. 23)

1   Brake pedal with manual gearbox
2   Brake pedal with automatic transmission

pushed into the interior of the servo unit which would probably require complete dismantling of the unit to retrieve it.

22 Vacuum servo unit - removal and refitting

1   The vacuum servo unit is removed in conjunction with the pedal box and hydraulic master cylinder.
2   Disconnect the brake lines from the master cylinder and plug the lines.
3   Disconnect the vacuum pipe from the servo unit.
4   Working inside the car above the brake pedal arm, remove the four setscrews and lockwashers from the bottom mounting of the pedal box.
5   Remove the four self-locking nuts and washers which secure the pedal box to the vertical face of the engine compartment rear bulkhead.
6   Withdraw the pedal box as an assembly complete with vacuum servo unit, master cylinder and reservoir.
7   Refitting is a reversal of removal but bleed the hydraulic system on completion, as described in Section 13.

23 Brake pedal - dismantling and reassembly

1   Remove the pedal box, vacuum servo and master cylinder assembly as described in the preceding Section.
2   Remove the two rubber sealing plugs from the sides of the pedal box.
3   Disconnect the vacuum servo pushrod from the pedal lever by removing the split pin and the clevis pin.
4   Remove the vacuum servo unit from the pedal box (four self-locking nuts).
5   Remove the self-locking nut and washer from the pedal pivot bolt and drive out the bolt. Retain the fibre washers which are located on the pedal pivot bolt.
6   Withdraw the pedal lever shaft locking pin and spring washer and extract the lever shaft.
7   Withdraw the pedal and lever assembly from the pedal box.
8   Extract the two split pins, clevis pins and links and disconnect the pedal from the pedal lever.
9   Reassembly is a reversal of dismantling.

24 Fault diagnosis - braking system

Symptom	Reason/s
Pedal travels almost to floor before brakes operate	Brake fluid level too low. Caliper leaking. Master cylinder leaking (bubbles in master cylinder fluid). Brake flexible hose leaking. Brake line fractured. Brake system unions loose. Pad linings over 75% worn.
Brake pedal feels springy	New pads not yet bedded-in. Brake discs badly worn or cracked. Master cylinder securing nuts loose.
Brake pedal feels 'spongy' and 'soggy'	Caliper leaking. Master cylinder leaking (bubbles in master cylinder reservoir). Brake pipe line or flexible hose leaking. Unions in brake system loose.
Excessive effort required to brake car	Pad linings badly worn. New pads recently fitted — not yet bedded-in. Harder pads fitted than standard causing increase in pedal pressure. Pads or discs contaminated with oil, grease or hydraulic fluid. Servo unit inoperative or faulty.
Brakes uneven and pulling to one side	Pads or discs contaminated with oil, grease or hydraulic fluid. Tyre pressures unequal. Radial ply tyres fitted at one end of the car only. Brake caliper loose. Brake pads fitted incorrectly. Different type of pads fitted at each wheel. Anchorages for front suspension or rear suspension loose. Brake discs badly worn, cracked or distorted.
Brakes tend to bind, drag or lock-on	Air in hydraulic system. Caliper pistons seized. Handbrake cables too tight.

Chapter 10 Electrical system

For modifications, and information on later models, refer to Supplement at end of manual

Contents

Specifications

System	12 volt, negative earth with battery and alternator

Wiper blades ... ...   Champion C38-01

Battery
Early models ... ...   12 volt, 60 Ah (20 hr rate)
Series 2 ... ...   12 volt, 66 Ah (20 hr rate)

Alternator (without air-conditioning)
Type:
    Early models ... ...   Lucas 11AC
    Series 2 ... ...   Lucas 18ACR
Voltage   12
Output:
    11AC ... ...   43 amps
    18ACR ... ...   45 amps
Stator phases   3
Phase connection ... ...   Star
Resistance/phase at 68°F (20°C) ± 5% ... ...   0.107 ohms
Resistance of rotor winding in ohms at 68°F (20°C) ... ...   3.8 ± 5%
Control unit (11AC only) ... ...   Lucas 4TR
Warning lamp control unit (11AC only) ... ...   Lucas 3AW

Alternator (early air-conditioning systems)
Type ... ...   Butec
Nominal voltage   12
Maximum output ... ...   60 amps
Maximum operating speed ... ...   4500 rev/min (engine speed)
Resistance of rotor coil ... ...   3.6 to 4 ohms
Regulator ... ...   Butec R2

Alternator (later air-conditioning systems)

Type	Lucas 20ACR
Voltage	12
Output	66 amps
Rotor winding resistance	3.6 ohms
Integral control unit	Lucas 11TR

Starter motor (2.8 litre early models)

Type	Lucas M45G inertia drive

Starter motor (3.4 and 4.2 litre, early models)

Type	Lucas M45G pre-engaged

Starter motor (later 2.8 litre and Series 2 models)

Type	Lucas 3M100 pre-engaged or inward or outward inertia type

Fuses (all models except Series 2)

No.	Circuit protected	Capacity (amps)
1	Screen washer, instruments, horn relay, tachometer	35
2	Map reading lamp, interior lamp, air-conditioning relay	35
3	Windscreen wiper, flasher, heater motor, stop lamps	35
4	Horns	50
5	Left-hand side and tail lamps	10
6	Outer headlamp	35
7	Inner headlamps (main beam)	35
8	Outer headlamp (LH dip)	35
9	Outer headlamp (RH dip)	35
10	Right-hand side and tail lamps	10
11 Separate ⎫	Hazard warning circuit	35
12 in-line ⎬	Heated rear window	15
13 fuses ⎭	Overdrive solenoid/reversing lamp	8

Fuses (Series 2)

No.	Circuit protected	Capacity (amps)
1	Fog lamps	25
2	Hazard warning	35
3	Map, interior lamps, cigar lighter, electrically operated aerial	35
4	Instruments, choke warning lamp	10
5	Stop lamps, flashers, battery cooling, horn relay, kick-down switch (automatic transmission)	35
6	Reversing lamps	10
7	Panel lamps	10
8	Left-hand side/tail	10
9	Right-hand side/tail	10
10	Air-conditioning/heater motors	35
11	Air-conditioning relay, windscreen wipers, windscreen washer	35
12 ⎫	Heated rear window	25
In-line ⎪	Headlamp main beam	25
type ⎬	Headlamp dipped beam	10
fuses ⎭	Horn relay	17

Bulbs

Description of lamp	Wattage
Outer headlamp UK	60/45
(sealed beam unit) N. America	37.5/50
Inner headlamps UK	50
(main beam sealed beam units) N. America	37.5
Front parking/flasher	6/21
Front parking (N. America)	6
Front rear indicators (N. America)	21
Sidemarker	6
Stop/tail	6/21
Rear number plate	6
Reversing	21
Interior and door pillar	10
Map reading	6
Luggage compartment	6
Instrument illumination	2.2
Warning lamps	1.5
Switch indicator strips	2
Automatic transmission indicator	2
Opticell light unit (Series 2)	6
Centre console (Series 2)	2.2
Cigar lighter	2.2
Choke warning lamp ⎱ Emission control	2.2
Choke handle lamp ⎰ cars only	2.0

1 General description

All models have a 12 volt negative earth electrical system.

The major components comprise a battery which is located under the bonnet against the rear bulkhead, an alternator and output control unit which may be integral or externally mounted according to alternator type, and an inertia or pre-engaged type starter motor.

On cars equipped with an air-conditioning system, a heavy duty alternator is fitted.

The battery supplies a steady current for the ignition, lighting and other electrical circuits and provides a reserve of electricity when the current consumed by the electrical equipment exceeds that being produced by the charging system.

Although full instructions for the periodic overhaul and minor servicing of the various electrical components are given in this Chapter it must be appreciated that rectification of major faults will require specialised knowledge and equipment and therefore, where such faults arise, the defective item should be removed and replaced with a serviceable item which can usually be obtained on an exchange basis.

Wiring diagrams covering the various models will be found at the end of the Chapter.

2 Battery - maintenance and inspection

1 Keep the top of the battery clean by wiping away dirt and moisture.
2 Remove the plugs or lid from the cells and check that the electrolyte level is just above the separator plates. If the level has fallen, add only distilled water until the electrolyte level is just above the separator plates.
3 As well as keeping the terminals clean and covered with petroleum jelly, the top of the battery, and especially the top of the cells, should be kept clean and dry. This helps prevent corrosion and ensures that the battery does not become partially discharged by leakage through dampness and dirt.
4 Once every three months, remove the battery and inspect the battery securing bolts, the battery clamp plate, tray and battery leads for corrosion (white fluffy deposits on the metal which are brittle to touch). If any corrosion is found, clean off the deposits with ammonia and paint over the clean metal with an anti-rust/anti-acid paint.
5 At the same time inspect the battery case for cracks. If a crack is found, clean and plug it with one of the proprietary compounds marketed for this purpose. If leakage through the crack has been excessive then it will be necessary to refill the appropriate cell with fresh electrolyte as detailed later. Cracks are frequently caused to the top of battery cases by pouring in distilled water in the middle of

winter *after* instead of *before* a run. This gives the water no chance to mix with the electrolyte and so the former freezes and splits the battery case.
6 If topping up the battery becomes excessive and the case has been inspected for cracks that could cause leakage, but none are found, the battery is being over-charged and the voltage regulator will have to be checked.
7 With the battery on the bench at the three monthly interval check, measure its specific gravity with a hydrometer to determine the state of charge and condition of the electrolyte. There should be very little variation between the different cells and if a variation in excess of 0.25 is present it will be due to either:

a) Loss of electrolyte from the battery at some time caused by spillage or a leak, resulting in a drop in the specific gravity of electrolyte when the deficiency was replaced with distilled water instead of fresh electrolyte.
b) An internal short circuit caused by buckling of the plates or a similar malady pointing to the likelihood of total battery failure in the near future.

8 The specific gravity of the electrolyte for fully charged conditions at the electrolyte temperature indicated, is listed in Table A. The specific gravity of a fully discharged battery at different temperatures of the electrolyte is given in Table B.

Table A

Specific Gravity - Battery Fully Charged

1.268 at 100°F or 38°C electrolyte temperature
1.272 at 90°F or 32°C electrolyte temperature
1.276 at 80°F or 27°C electrolyte temperature
1.280 at 70°F or 21°C electrolyte temperature
1.284 at 60°F or 16°C electrolyte temperature
1.288 at 50°F or 10°C electrolyte temperature
1.292 at 40°F or 4°C electrolyte temperature
1.296 at 30°F or-1.5°C electrolyte temperature

Table B

Specific Gravity - Battery Fully Discharged

1.098 at 100°F or 38°C electrolyte temperature
1.102 at 90°F or 32°C electrolyte temperature
1.106 at 80°F or 27°C electrolyte temperature
1.110 at 70°F or 21°C electrolyte temperature
1.114 at 60°F or 16°C electrolyte temperature
1.118 at 50°F or 10°C electrolyte temperature
1.122 at 40°F or 4°C electrolyte temperature
1.126 at 30°F or-1.5°C electrolyte temperature

3 Battery - removal and refitting

Cars excluding Series 2

1 The battery is located within the engine compartment. It may be on the left or right-hand side according to which side the steering is positioned.
2 Disconnect the negative terminal first whenever servicing the battery.
3 Then remove the positive terminal, and remove the battery frame holding-down screws and lift the frame away.
4 Lift out the battery carefully to avoid spilling electrolyte on the paintwork.
5 Replacement is a reversal of removal procedure but when reconnecting the terminals, clean off any white deposits present and smear with petroleum jelly.

Series 2 cars

6 The battery incorporates a cooling fan on these cars; remove the battery in the following way:
7 Peel back the flexible covers from the battery terminals, release the pinch bolts and disconnect the leads from the battery terminals.
8 Disconnect the leads to the battery cooling fan by detaching them

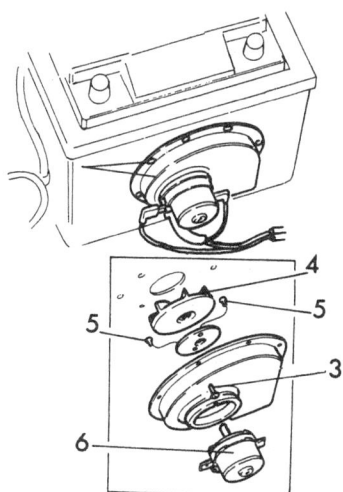

Fig. 10.1. Battery with cooling fan (Sec. 3)

3 Fan securing screw
4 Impeller
5 Keeper plate and screws
6 Electric motor

at the snap connectors.

9   Slacken the battery holding down bolts.

10 Prise the flexible outlet pipe from the cooling jacket grommet.

11 Detach the battery positive lead from the clip on the cooling jacket.

12 Ease the battery and its cooling jacket forward until the jacket can be withdrawn from the battery.

13 Lift the battery from the car.

14 The cooling fan can be removed from the cooling jacket after withdrawing the seven securing screws. The nylon impeller can be levered from the motor shaft.

15 Reassembly and refitting are reversals of removal and dismantling.

4   Electrolyte replenishment

1   If the battery is in a fully charged state and one of the cells maintains a specific gravity reading which is 0.25 or more lower than the others, and a check of each cell has been made with a voltage meter to check for short circuits (a four to seven second test should give a steady reading of between 1.2 to 1.8 volts), then it is likely that electrolyte has been lost from the cell with the low reading at some time.

2   Top up the cell with a solution of 1 part sulphuric acid to 2.5 parts of water. If the cell is already fully topped up draw some electrolyte out of it with a hydrometer.

3   When mixing the sulphuric acid and water **never add water to sulphuric acid** - always pour the acid slowly onto the water in a glass container. **If water is added to sulphuric acid it will explode.**

4   Continue to top up the cell with the freshly made electrolyte and then recharge the battery and check the hydrometer readings.

5   Battery charging

1   In winter time when heavy demand is placed upon the battery, such as when starting from cold, and much electrical equipment is continually in use, it is a good idea to occasionally have the battery fully charged from an external source at the rate of 3.5 or 4 amps (see Section 7).

2   Continue to charge the battery at this rate until no further rise in specific gravity is noted over a four hour period.

3   Alternatively, a trickle charger at the rate of 1.5 amps can be safely used overnight.

4   Specially rapid 'boost' charges which are claimed to restore the power of the battery in 1 to 2 hours are most dangerous as they can cause serious damage to the battery plates.

6   Alternator - general description and maintenance

1   Briefly the alternator comprises a rotor and stator. Current is generated in the coils of the stator as soon as the rotor revolves. This current is three-phase alternating which is then rectified by positive and negative silicon diodes and the level of voltage required to maintain the battery charge is controlled by a regulator unit.

2   Maintenance consists of occasionally wiping away any oil or dirt

which may have accumulated on the outside of the unit.

3   No lubrication is required as the bearings are grease sealed for life.

4   Check the drivebelt tension periodically to ensure that its specified deflection is correctly maintained. The correct tension of the belt is indicated when the mid point of the top run of the belt can be depressed ½ in (12.7 mm). Adjustment is carried out by releasing the alternator pivot mounting bolts and the adjustment link bolts and moving the alternator away from or towards the engine. Retighten the bolts on completion.

5   On cars which are equipped with power steering or/and air-conditioning the drivebelt arrangement is complex and although all the belts should be tensioned as just described, renewal of an inner belt will necessitate removal of the outer belts first.

7   Alternator - special precautions

Take extreme care when making circuit connections to a vehicle fitted with an alternator and observe the following. When making connections to the alternator from a battery always match correct polarity. Before using electric-arc welding equipment to repair any part of the vehicle, disconnect the connector from the alternator and disconnect the positive battery terminal. Never start the car with a battery charger connected. Always disconnect both battery leads before using a main charger. If boosting from another battery, always connect in parallel using heavy cable.

8   Alternator (Lucas 11AC type) - testing in-situ

1   Disconnect the lead from the negative terminal of the battery.

2   Disconnect the lead from the main output terminal of the alternator and connect a moving coil DC ammeter (range up to 75 amps) between the main output terminal and the end of the lead which was originally connected to it.

3   Detach the terminal connector block from the base of the control unit and then connect the black and the brown/green cables together by a short jump lead.

4   Reconnect the lead to the battery negative terminal, switch on the ignition and start the engine. Slowly increase the engine speed until the engine speed is about 2000 rev/min indicated on the tachometer. Check the ammeter which should record approximately 40 amps.

5   A low current reading will mean a faulty alternator or poor circuit connections. If the circuit connections are checked and found to be in order, measure the resistance of the rotor coil by means of an ohmmeter connected between the field terminal blades, having first disconnected the external wiring. The indicated resistance must be approximately 3.77 ohms. Where an ohmmeter is not available, connect a 12 volt supply with an ammeter in series between the field terminals, when the indicated reading should be 3.2 amps (Fig. 10.5). If a zero reading is shown on the ammeter or infinity on the ohmmeter, an open circuit is indicated in the field system which includes the brush gear, slip-rings or windings. If the meters record readings much above or below the valves specified, there may be a short circuit in the rotor winding which will necessitate a new rotor/slip ring assembly.

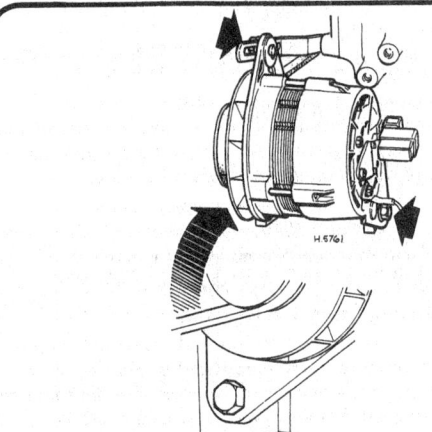

Fig. 10.2. Alternator mounting and adjustment link bolts (Sec. 6)

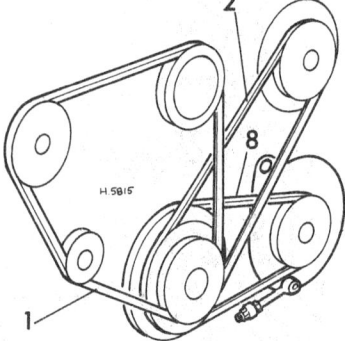

Fig. 10.3. Drivebelt arrangement on cars equipped with optional systems (Sec. 6)

1 Water pump/power steering pump drivebelt	2 Air compressor drivebelt (air conditioning system)
	8 Alternator drivebelt

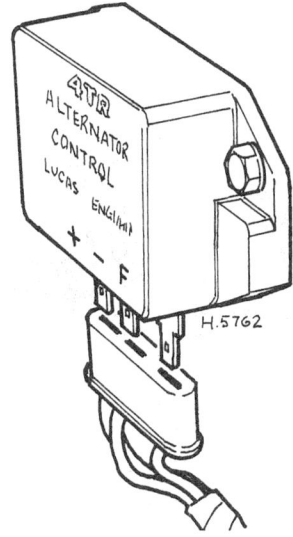

Fig. 10.4. Lucas 4TR alternator control unit (Sec. 8)

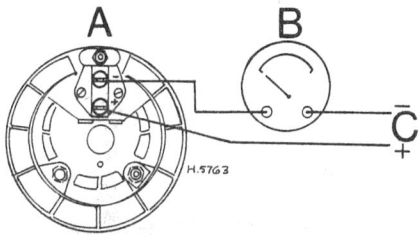

Fig. 10.5. Circuit for testing 11AC type alternator with ammeter (Sec. 8)

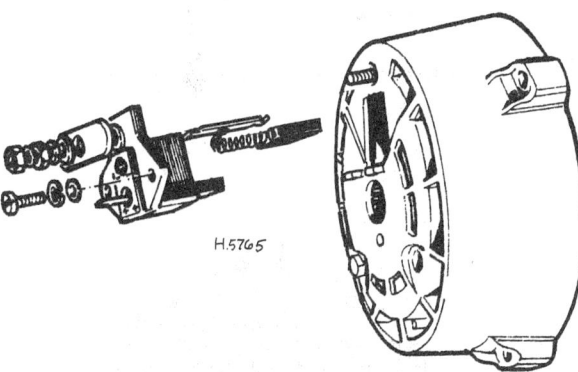

Fig. 10.6. Brushgear (early type 11AC alternator) (Sec. 10)

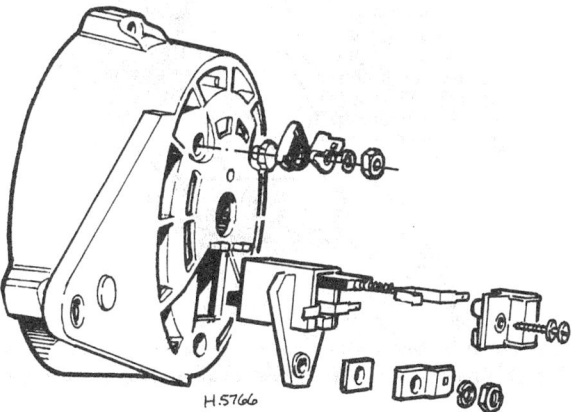

Fig. 10.7. Brushgear (later type 11AC alternator) (Sec. 10)

9 Alternator - removal and installation

1   Disconnect the battery.
2   On cars with a remotely sited cooling system expansion tank, drain the coolant and remove the tank as described in Chapter 2.
3   Disconnect the leads from the slip ring end cover, making sure to mark the cables for exact refitting.
4   Slacken the alternator mounting bolts and adjuster link bolts, push the unit in towards the engine, slip the drivebelt off the pulleys and then remove the mounting bolts and lift the alternator away.
5   *On cars equipped with an air-conditioning system*, the air compressor and its mounting bracket will have to be disconnected in order to gain access to the alternator. *On no account disconnect any of the air-conditioning system hoses* but release the compressor mountings and bracket and support the compressor without moving it any more than is absolutely necessary.
6   Installation is the reversal of removal but adjust the alternator drivebelt as described in Section 6 of this Chapter, also the air compressor belt as described in Chapter 12, Section 29.

10 Alternator (Lucas 11AC type) - overhaul

1   Remove the alternator from the car as described in Section 9.
2   An exploded view of the slip ring end cover is given in Fig. 10.10 but where figures are quoted in the following paragraphs the reference is to Fig. 10.8.
3   Take off the shaft nut (1) and its spring washer (21).
4   Withdraw the fan (20).
5   Break the staking of the nuts to the bolts (3) and then unscrew the bolts. Examine the threads of the bolts and if they are damaged discard the bolts.
6   Mark the drive end bracket (4).
7   Withdraw the drive end bracket (4) and the rotor (16) from the stator (8).
8   It is advisable not to separate the rotor from the drive end bracket unless the bearing is suspect or the rotor is to be replaced. In this event, first remove the shaft key (5) and the collar (2). Now use a hand press to remove the rotor from the drive end bracket.
9   Remove the terminal nuts and their washers and insulating pieces, the brush box screws and the hegagon headed setscrew from the slip ring end cover and the stator and diode heat sink assemblies can now be withdrawn.
10 Close up the retaining tongue at the root of each field terminal blade and withdraw the brush spring together with the terminal assemblies from the brushbox.
11 There are detail differences between the brush gear on earlier and later type alternators which should be noted.
12 *On earlier type brush gear,* check the length of the brushes which should not be below 5/32 in (3.97 mm). Discard them if they are at, or are approaching that dimension. New brushes are supplied complete with spring and terminal blade and have merely to be pushed in until the tongue registers; but, to be sure that the terminal is properly retained, carefully lever up the retaining tongue so that it makes an angle of 30° with the terminal blade.
    See that the brushes are in good condition, that they are not chipped or showing any obvious defect.
    Check that the brushes move freely in the holders. If they appear sluggish, clean the bearing sides with a cloth moistened with petrol and if this does not effect a cure, polish the sides with a smooth file but make sure that all trace of dust is removed before refitting to the holders.
    If you have suitable equipment available, it is a good idea to check the brush spring pressures. With the brush spring compressed to 25/32 in (19.84 mm) the brush spring pressure when fitted to the holder should be 4 - 5 ozs (113 - 114 grms), and 7½ - 8½ ozs (212 - 242 grms) with the spring compressed to 13/32 in (10.31 mm).
13 *On later type brush gear,* check that the brushes protrude beyond the brush box moulding (when in the free position) by not less than 0.2 in (5.0 mm). If they do not, renew them. New brushes are supplied complete with brush spring and terminal blade and each brush is secured in position by a plate and screw.
14 Examine the slip rings. The surfaces should be smooth and free

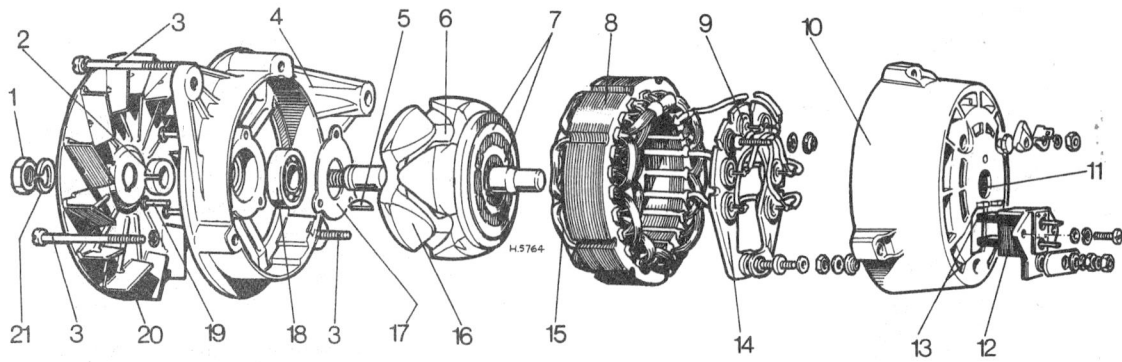

Fig. 10.8. Exploded view of Lucas 11AC alternator (Sec. 10)

1   Pulley nut
2   Collar
3   Tie bolts
4   Drive end bracket
5   Key
6   Field winding (rotor)
7   Slip rings
8   Stator
9   Silicon diodes
10 Slip ring end bracket
11 Needle roller bearing
12 Brush box
13 Brushes
14 Diode heat sink
15 Stator windings
16 Rotor
17 Bearing retaining plate
18 Ball bearing
19 Rivets
20 Fan
21 Spring washer

from oil or other foreign matter. They can be cleaned with a cloth moistened in petrol but if there is any evidence of burning it is permissible to use fine glass paper. **Do not** use emery cloth or similar abrasive.

15 It is unlikely that the slip rings will be scored or pitted but discard them if they are in this condition. Do not try to rectify them by machining as any resultant eccentricity could adversely affect the high speed performance of the alternator.

16 Check the rotor windings by connecting an ohmmeter or 12 volt DC supply between the slip rings in the manner described in Section 8 paragraph 5, where this test was then made with the brush gear in circuit. Reading should be the same as given in those paragraphs.

17 Test for defective insulation between each of the slip rings and one of the rotor poles using a mains low wattage test lamp for the purpose. If the lamp lights it indicates that the coil is earthing and the rotor/slip ring assembly must be replaced.

18 Unsolder the three stator cables from the heat sink assembly but take care not to overheat the diodes.

19 Identify the three cables as 'A', 'B', and 'C' and this gives three pairs of cables 'AB', 'AC' and 'BC' for testing the stator windings.

20 Measure the voltage drop across each of these pairs of cables in turn whilst passing a 20 amp current between the cable ends. The voltage drop should be about 4.3 volts in each of the three measurements. If any reading is outside of that value, the stator must be renewed.

21 Using a mains test lamp, check for defects in the insulation between the stator coils and lamination pack, by connecting the lamp between any of the three cable ends and the lamination pack. If the lamp lights, the stator coils are earthing and a replacement stator must be fitted.

22 Check the diodes before you re-solder the cables to the heat sink assembly.

23 Check each diode by connecting it in series with a 1.5 watt test bulb across a 12 volt DC supply and then reverse the connections. The lamp should light and current should flow in one direction only. If the lamp lights when current is flowing in either direction or it does not light at all, the diode is defective.

24 Diodes are not individually replaceable but are supplied already pressed into the appropriate heat sink portion which, as already described, consists of two mutually insulated assemblies, one of positive and the other of negative polarity. The positive assembly carries three cathode base diodes marked in black.

25 When soldering the interconnections, use 'M' grade 45/55 tin/lead solder. Be careful not to overheat the diodes or bend their pins. It is advisable to lightly grip the diode pins with a pair of long nosed pliers when soldering so that the pliers will absorb excess heat.

26 After soldering, the connections must be neatly arranged around the heat sinks as shown and tacked down with 'MMM' EC 1022 adhesive where shown in the figure in order to ensure adequate clearance for the rotor (Fig. 10.10).

27 The stator connections must pass through the appropriate notches at the edge of the heat sink.

28 When reassembling the alternator, take care that a clearance of

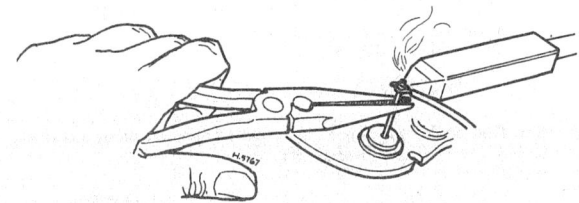

Fig. 10.9. Soldering alternator diodes using pliers as a heat sink (Sec. 10)

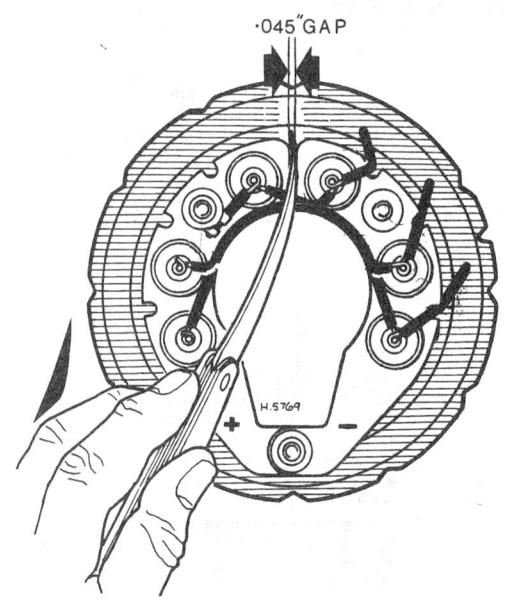

·045"GAP

Fig. 10.10. Slip ring end cover layout (11AC alternator) (Sec. 10)

0.045 in (1.143 mm) is maintained between the positive and negative heat sinks as shown in Fig. 10.10.

29 Renew any bearings which are so worn that they permit excessive side movement of the rotor shaft.

30 The needle roller bearing in the slip ring end cover is supplied complete with end cover.

31 If the drive end bearing requires renewal, file flat the heads of the three retainer plate rivets and punch out the rivets. Press the bearing from the bracket.

32 Pack the new bearing with high melting point grease, press it into position and fit the retaining plate using the new rivets supplied.

33 When reassembling, remember not to overtighten the brushbox screws, make sure that the drive end bracket, slip ring end bracket and

lamination pack alignment marks are correctly located and re-stake the tie bolts after having tightened the nuts.

11 Alternator (Butec type) - testing in-situ

1   The following tests will indicate a faulty alternator but before carrying them out, remove the sensing diode block.

2   Check the stator phase for earthing to the alternator frame. Connect 110 or 230 volt supply and test lamp as shown in Fig. 10.12. The circuit should not be completed, if it is and the bulb lights up, then the stator is of delta connected type, all phases will indicate earthing.

3   Now carry out a stator winding continuity test. Using an ohmmeter or test lamp, check the continuity of each phase as shown in Fig. 10.13. Each phase should indicate a similar reaction.

4   To carry out an alternator phase test, run the engine at an idling speed of 460 rev/min. Connect an AC voltmeter or a 12 volt test lamp between two of the three AC terminals in turn. Voltage or lamp brilliance should be nearly the same across phases 1—2, 2—3 and 1—3. Any pronounced difference indicates earthed or shorted stator terminals.

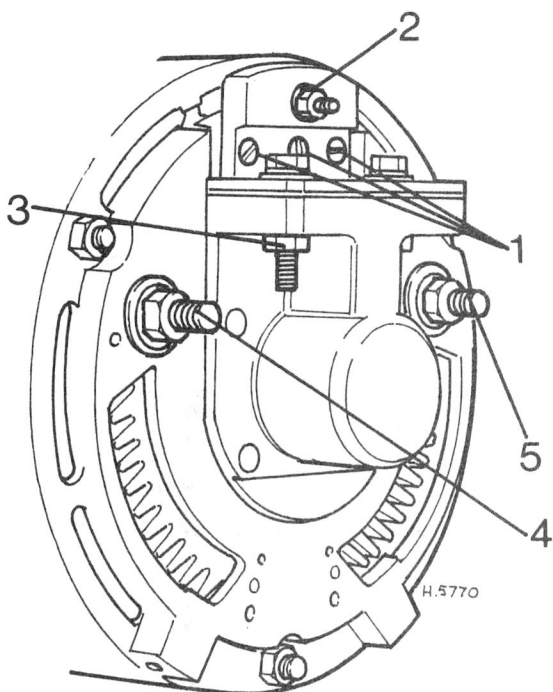

Fig. 10.11. Terminal identification (Butec alternator) (Sec. 11)

1   *AC output tappings*
2   *Sensing diode terminal*
3   *Field terminal*
4   *Negative DC terminal*
5   *Positive DC terminal*

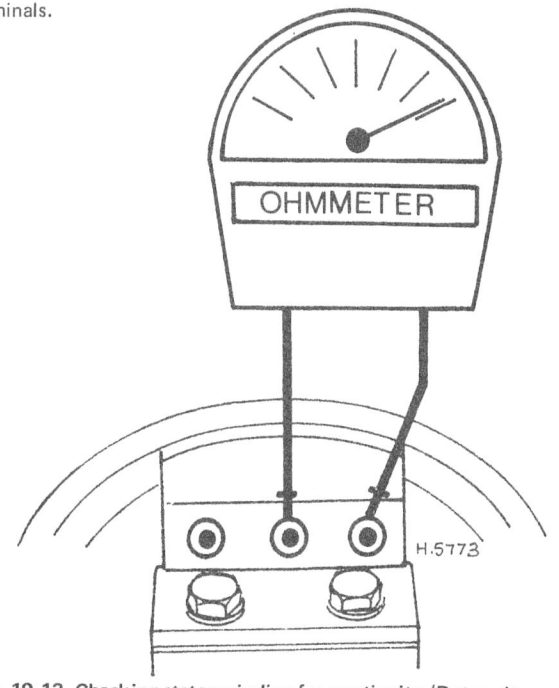

Fig. 10.13. Checking stator winding for continuity (Butec alternator) (Sec. 11)

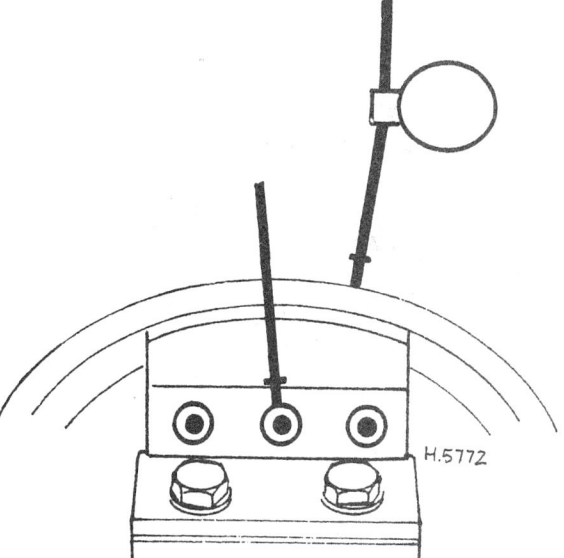

Fig. 10.12. Checking stator phase for earthing (Butec alternator) (Sec. 11)

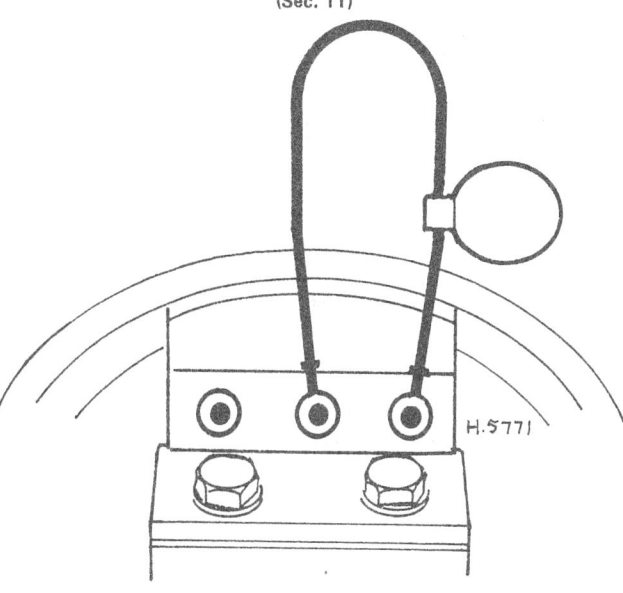

Fig. 10.14. Carrying out alternator phase test (Butec type) (Sec. 11)

12 Alternator (Butec type) - overhaul

1   Unscrew and remove the nut and washer and then with a suitable extractor, withdraw the fan/pulley assembly and extract the Woodruff key.

2   Remove the brushes, washer, insulating cover, gasket and jumper leads having first removed the two field terminal nuts.

3   Unscrew the four brush holder screws and remove the brush holder from the slip ring end housing.

4   Unscrew and remove the three self-locking nuts and the tie bolts which hold the alternator together.

5   Using a hammer and a brass drift held against the end of the rotor shaft, remove the slip ring end housing and the stator.

6   To disconnect the stator from the slip ring end housing, remove the three AC terminal nuts and stator connections and separate the stator from the housing with a soft-faced mallet.

7   With a suitable extractor, remove the rotor from the drive end housing.

8   With the alternator dismantled, the following tests can be carried out if suitable meters or test bulb circuits are available.

9   To test the rotor coil resistance, place the probes from an ohmmeter, one on each of the slip rings. The coil resistance should be between 3.6 and 4 ohms. No resistance indicates an open circuit in the rotor coil. Shorted turns in the coil can be suspected if on inspection the brush springs are found to have collapsed.

10 It is not recommended that any of the diodes are tested as special equipment is needed and there is also a great risk of damaging servicable components. If a diode fault is suspected, have them checked out by your dealer.

11 Clean the stator with a fuel soaked cloth and then check each AC terminal to each of the other two terminals using a test lamp rig to see that a complete circuit is made in each case. Also test for insulation breakdown between each terminal and the stator case (Figs. 10.17 and 10.18).

12 The drive end housing bearing can be renewed by removing the four screws from the bearing retainer plate and tapping out the bearing.

Press in the new bearing but apply pressure to the outer track only.

13 Rotor slip rings and bearing can be renewed by extracting them with a two or three-legged puller. When fitting the new slip ring assembly warm it slightly before pressing it onto the rotor shaft. Make sure that the slots in the slip rings align with the slot in the shaft which carries the cables from the rotor coil. The slip ring coil leads will require unsoldering and resoldering for this operation.

14 Commence reassembly by assembling the rotor and drive end housing.

15 Install the stator over the rotor and line up the tie bolt holes.

16 Secure the three stator connections to the insulator block in the slip ring end housing.

17 Place the housing assembly into position using the tie bolts to align the housing with the stator.

18 Tighten the tie bolts to the specified torque wrench setting.

19 Refit the brush holder assembly and renew the 'O' ring seal.

20 Insert the brushes. If they are less than 0.19 in (4.76 mm) in length, renew them. Let the brushes rest on the slip rings, place the tab jumpers over the terminal screws and brush springs (compressed). Fit a new gasket, insulating cover, washers and nuts.

21 Refit the Woodruff key, fan and pulley, washer and nut.

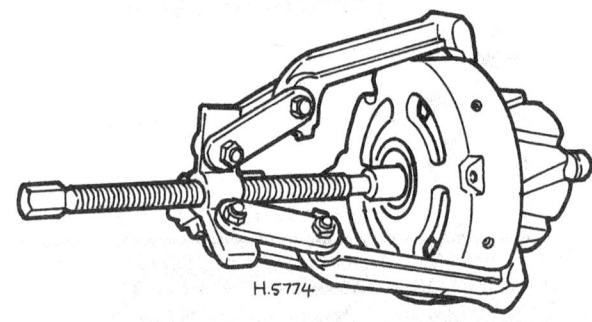

Fig. 10.15. Separating rotor and drive end housing (Butec alternator) (Sec. 12)

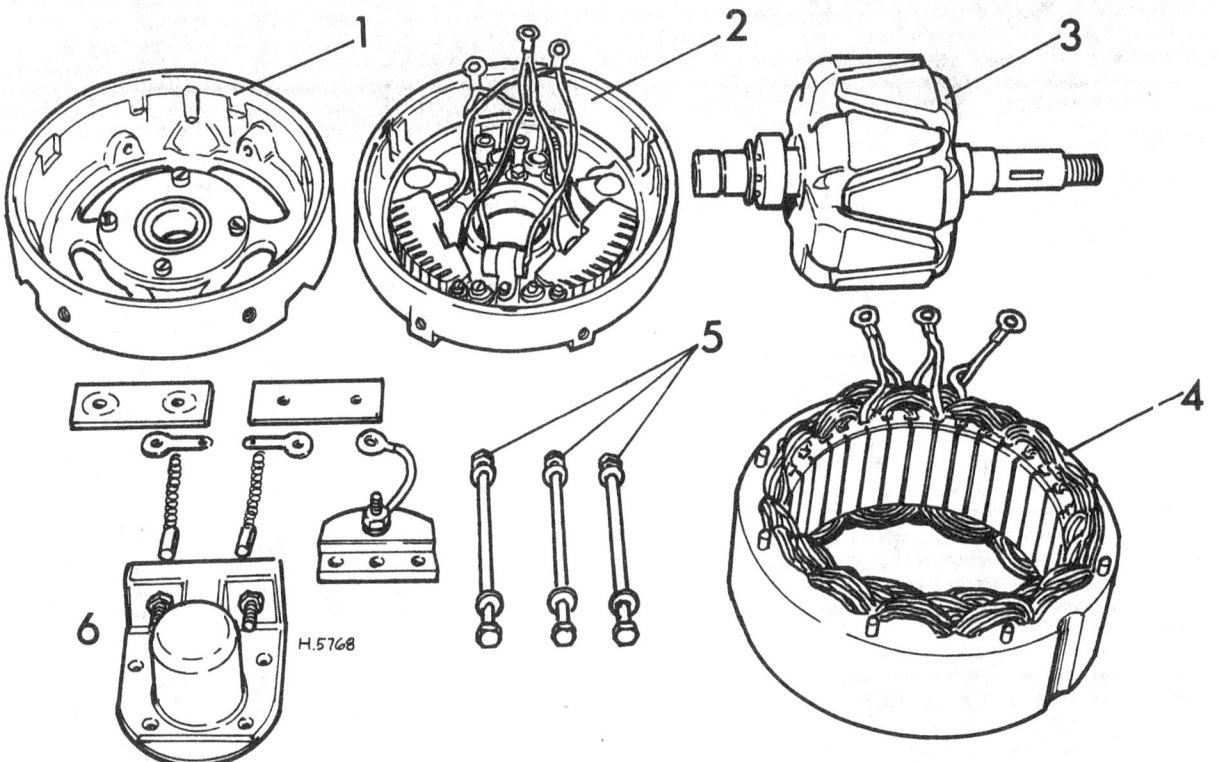

Fig. 10.16. Exploded view of Butec type alternator (Sec. 12)

| 1 Drive end bracket | 3 Rotor | 5 Tie bolts |
| 2 Slip ring end bracket | 4 Stator | 6 Brush assembly |

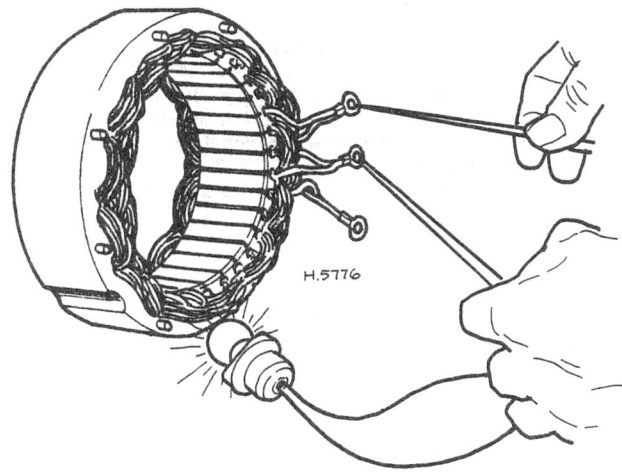

Fig. 10.17. Checking stator windings for continuity (Butec alternator) (Sec. 12)

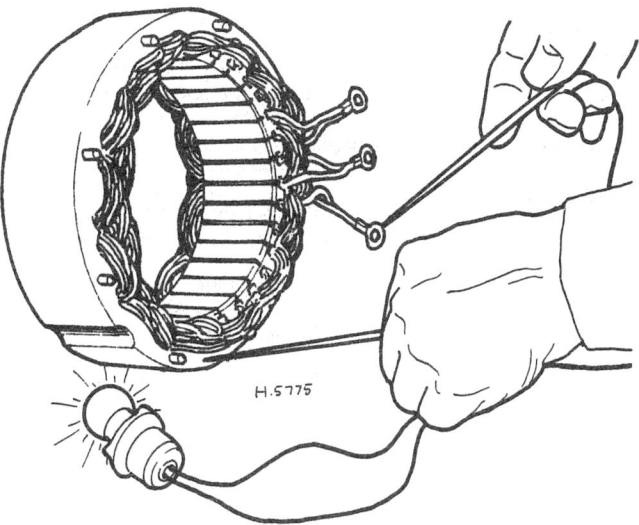

Fig. 10.18. Checking stator windings for insulation breakdown (Butec alternator) (Sec. 13)

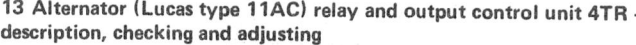

13 Alternator (Lucas type 11AC) relay and output control unit 4TR - description, checking and adjusting

1 In the interest of safety and as a protection to the alternator, a relay is incorporated in the ignition switch/steering column lock circuit to isolate the field windings.

2 The relay is located just below the 4TR control unit within the engine compartment.

3 The 4TR output control unit is an electronic type unit in which switching is achieved by transistors, not mechanical contacts.

4 Check and adjustment of the control unit can only be carried out satisfactorily if the alternator and associated circuits are correct and a well charged battery is in use.

5 Leave the existing connections to the alternator and the control unit undisturbed but move the tags sufficiently on the control unit to allow connection of a high quality voltmeter between the positive and negative terminals. It is advisable to use a voltmeter of the suppressed zero type capable of reading to 12 - 15 volts.

6 Run the alternator, whether testing in-situ or on the bench, at charging speed for eight minutes.

7 Switch on an electrical load of approximately 2 amps (side and tail lights will give this loading).

8 Now run the engine at 1500 rpm when the voltmeter should show a reading of 13.9 to 14.3 volts with an ambient temperature of 20 to 26° C (68 to 78° F).

9 If the reading is outside the above limits, but has risen to some degree above battery terminal voltage before finally reaching a steady value, the unit can be adjusted to bring it within limits.

10 If the voltmeter reading remains steady at battery terminal voltage or if, on the other hand, it increases in an uncontrolled manner, the control unit is faulty and as it cannot be serviced it must be replaced.

11 To adjust the control unit, first stop the engine and then take out the control unit mounting screws, leave the voltmeter connected.

12 Lift the control unit away from the bulkhead and if you look at the rear you will find a blob of sealing compound which conceals a potentiometer adjuster. Carefully chip away the sealing compound.

13 Check that the voltmeter is still firmly connected between positive and negative terminals of the control unit.

14 Start the engine and again run it at 1500 rpm. Turn the potentiometer by means of the slot, in a clockwise direction to increase, and in an anticlockwise direction, to decrease the setting. The potentiometer should be turned only a small amount at a time as you will find that a small movement will make a considerable difference to the voltage reading.

15 When the voltage reading is within limits (see paragraph 8), stop the engine. Now check the setting by restarting the engine and again checking at 1500 rpm with a load of 2 amps.

16 If the readings are correct, remove the voltmeter and then refit the control unit after sealing the potentiometer.

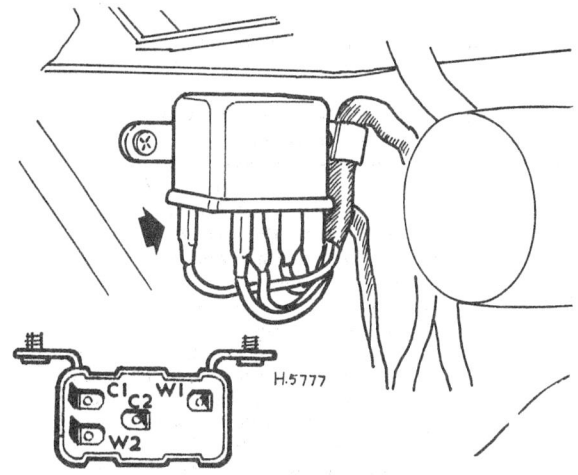

Fig. 10.19. Location of relay fitted in conjunction with Lucas 11AC alternator) (Sec. 13)

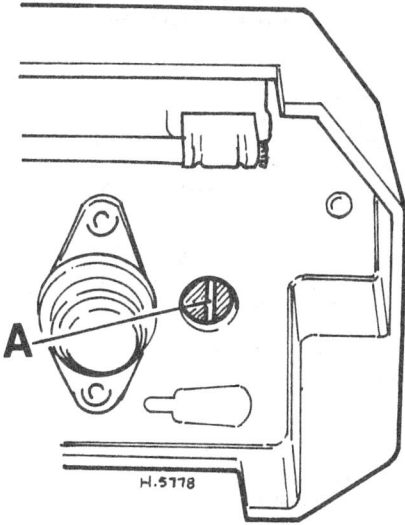

Fig. 10.20. 4TR control unit fitted in conjunction with Lucas 11AC alternator) (Sec. 13)

A = Adjuster

14 Alternator (Lucas 11AC) warning lamp control unit 3AW - description and testing

1   This device is connected to one of the pairs of diodes in the alternator and operates in conjunction with the ignition warning lamp to verify that the alternator is charging.
2   The device is mounted adjacent to the output control unit within the engine compartment.
3   A lamp control unit can often be damaged by excessive voltages resulting from a faulty diode or open circuit in the alternator or an open circuit in the alternator to battery circuit.
4   Before renewing a lamp control unit, use a moving coil voltmeter to check the voltage between the alternator 'AL' terminal and earth. This should be between 6 and 7.5 volts with the engine running at 1500 rev/min.
5   If a higher voltage is recorded, check that all circuit connections are clean and tight.
6   The warning lamp control unit is a sealed unit rather similar in appearance to a flasher unit and it can only be renewed as a sealed component.

15 Alternator (Butec) regulator R2 - description and testing

1   This type of regulator is fully transistorised without any moving parts.
2   Output voltage adjustment can be carried out by turning a screw which is accessible after extracting a socket screw from the front of the unit.
3   **Never disconnect the battery leads while the engine is running or the alternator and the regulator will be damaged.**
4   If low voltage output is suspected because of a discharged battery, remove the plug from the base of the regulator and bridge the 'Negative' and 'Field' contacts on the plug itself. This action will permit the alternator to run full field and if the low voltage condition persists, it must indicate a faulty alternator, not the regulator.
5   If the low voltage condition continues, check the regulator adjustment. To do this, check that (engine running at 1500 rev/min) at least 12 volts exists between the positive (+) and negative (—) terminals on the regulator. If necessary remove the socket screw and adjust the screw located behind it to give 14 volts on normal engine load. Note the setting of the adjuster screw then rotate it fully clockwise and measure the voltage between the field and the negative terminals which should be less than 1.5 volts. If it is as specified, return the adjuster screw to its original position. If the voltage is not as specified, remove the regulator and have your dealer bench test the internal diodes and transistors and printed circuit.
6   Individual faulty components can be removed and renewed but it is recommended that this work is left to your dealer.

16 Alternator (Lucas 18ACR and 20ACR) - testing in-situ

1   This heavier duty type alternator is substituted for the Butec model previously used on cars with an air-conditioning system. It differs from earlier Lucas types by having an integral regulator unit.
2   A moving coil ammeter and a moving coil voltmeter will be required to carry out these tests.
3   Start the cold engine and run it at 3000 rev/min for 3 or 4 minutes.
4   Disconnect the lead from the battery negative terminal.
5   Connect the ammeter in series with the alternator main output cable and starter solenoid.
6   Remove connectors from the alternator, detach the moulded end cover and then re-make the connections.
7   Connect a jump lead to short out the 'F' and '—' terminals of the control unit.
8   Reconnect the lead to the battery negative terminal.
9   Switch on all the car lights with the headlamps on main beam. Switch on the ignition and check that the warning lamp is on.
10 Start the engine, slowly increase its speed to 3000 rev/min. The reading on the ammeter should be equivalent to the alternator maximum rated output which is 45 amps (18ACR type) or 66 amps (20ACR type). If it is not, the alternator requires overhaul and reconditioning.
11 Having completed the output test, now check for voltage drop.

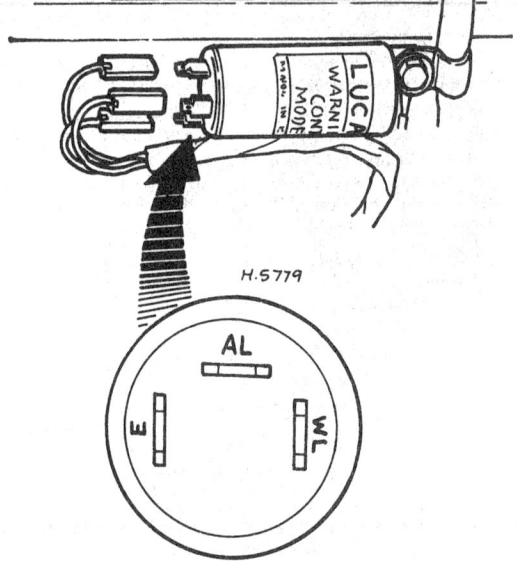

Fig. 10.21. Lucas 3AW warning lamp control unit fitted in conjunction with Lucas 11AC alternator (Sec. 14)

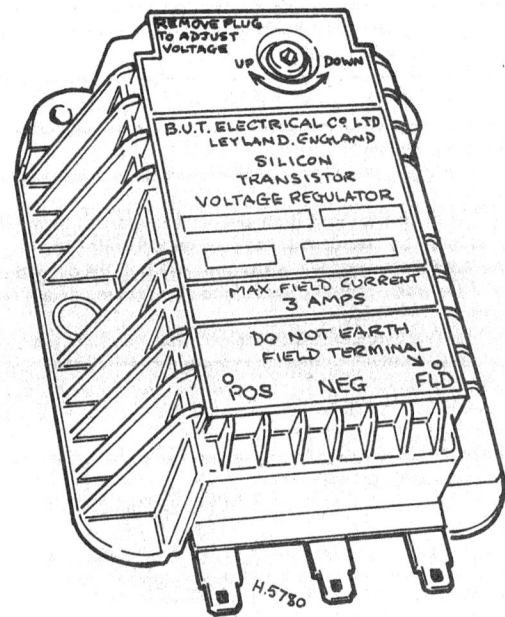

Fig. 10.22. Butec type voltage regulator (Sec. 15)

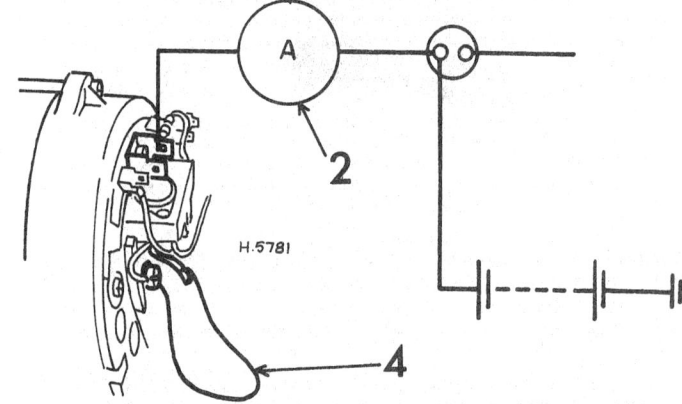

Fig. 10.23. Alternator output test (Lucas type 20 ACR) (Sec. 16)

2   Ammeter   4   Jump lead

12 Connect a voltmeter between the battery positive terminal and the alternator main output terminal.
13 Switch on all the car lights including the headlamps on main beam. Start the engine and run at 3000 rev/min. Record the voltmeter reading and then switch off the engine.
14 Transfer the voltmeter connections to the battery negative terminal and the alternator negative terminal.
15 Repeat the operations described in paragraph 13, and again note the reading on the voltmeter. The readings recorded should not exceed 0.5 volts for the positive side. Higher readings indicate high resistance in the circuit.

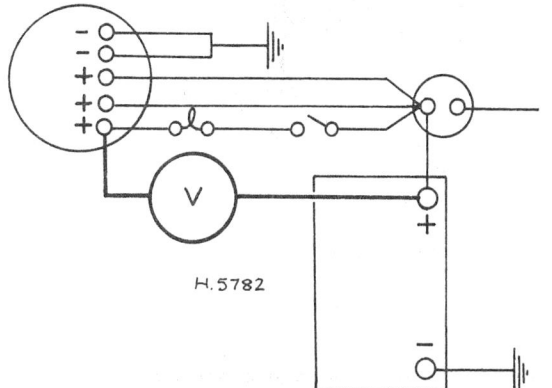

Fig. 10.24. Voltage drop test (Lucas type 20 ACR) between positive terminals (Sec. 16)

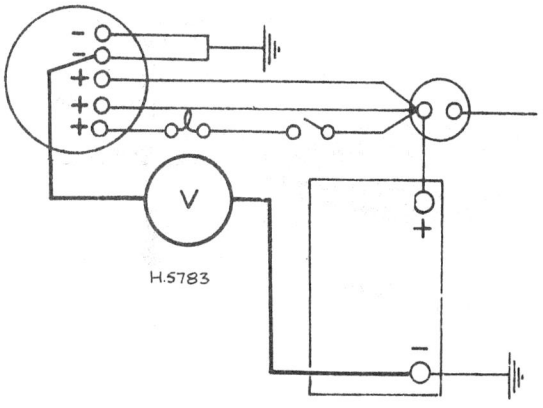

Fig. 10.25. Voltage drop test (Lucas type 20 ACR) between negative terminals (Sec. 16)

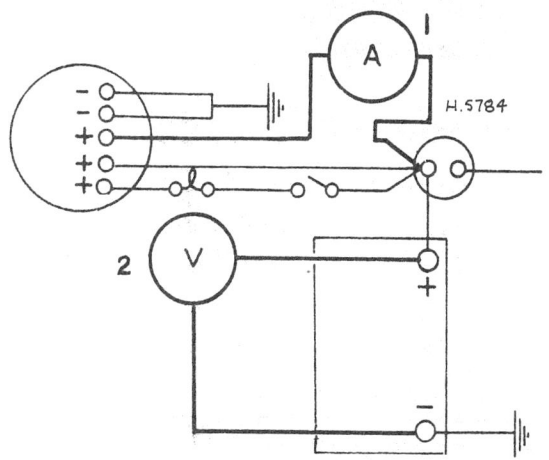

Fig. 10.26. Control unit test (Lucas type 20 ACR alternator) (Sec. 16)

1   Ammeter   *2   Voltmeter*

16 To test the control unit, first make sure that all connections are clean and secure and the battery in a fully charged condition (charge from an outside source if necessary).
17 Connect an ammeter in series with the starter solenoid and the alternator main output cable.
18 Connect the voltmeter between the battery terminals.
19 Start the engine and run it at 3000 rev/min until the ammeter reads less than 10 amps. The voltmeter reading should be between 13.6 and 14.4 volts. If the reading fluctuates or is outside the range specified, then the control unit is faulty.

17 Alternator (Lucas 18ACR and 20ACR) - overhaul

1   The main difference between the two alternators lies in the control unit. The following description relates to the model 20ACR but applies equally to the 18ACR provided reference is made to the appropriate illustration.
2   With the alternator removed from the car, remove the pulley retaining nut and washer and draw off the pulley. Remove the fan, spacer and Woodruff key.
3   Remove the moulded cover plate.
4   Unscrew the brush holder screws noting they also secure the radio interference suppression capacitor and black earth cable.
5   Disconnect the red leads from the 'IND' and '+' terminals of the alternator.
6   Withdraw the brush moulding complete with control box.
7   Disconnect the three stator windings from their respective heatsinks.
8   Remove the four screws which secure the heatsink/terminal block assembly and the small screw which connects the earth strap to the alternator frame.
9   Unscrew and remove the three tie bolts from the alternator frame.
10 Separate the slip ring end bracket and stator from the rotor and drive end bracket. To do this, insert a lever and prise them apart.
11 With the alternator dismantled, check the brushes for wear. The brushes must protrude beyond the holder by at least 0.32 in (8 mm) otherwise renew them noting the location of the leaf spring at the side of the inner brush.
12 The slip rings should normally only require cleaning with a fuel soaked cloth but if essential, they can be burnished with finest grade glasspaper (not emery).
13 To test the servicability of the rotor, connect an ohmmeter between the slip rings. Resistance should be 3.6 ohms at 20°C (68°F). Alternatively, where an ohmmeter is not available, connect an ammeter and 12 volt supply between the slip rings, the ammeter should indicate about 3 amps.
14 To test for defective insulation between the slip rings and the rotor

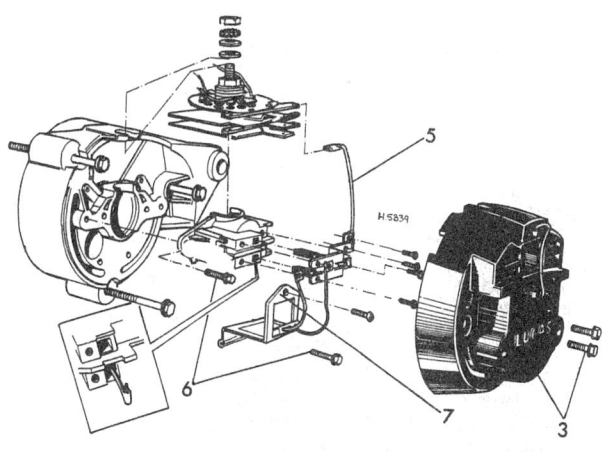

Fig. 10.27. Control unit on Lucas 18 ACR alternator (Sec. 17)

3   End cover screws   *6   Regulator securing screws*
5   Rectifier plate cables   *7   Brushgear/regulator assembly*

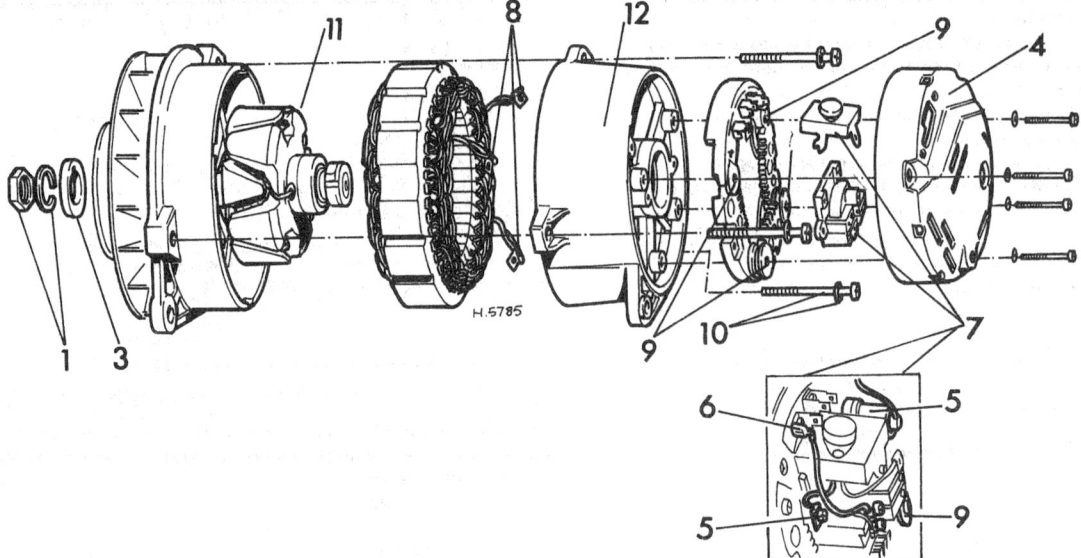

Fig. 10.28. Exploded view of Lucas 20 ACR alternator (Sec. 17)

1	Pulley nut and washer	5	Brush fixing screws	7	Brush moulding and control box
3	Spacer	6	Leads to 'Ind' and '+'	8	Stator winding terminals
4	Cover		terminals	9	Heatsink/terminal block and earth strap screws

7   Brush moulding and control box   10   Tie bolts
8   Stator winding terminals   11   Rotor/drive end bracket
9   Heatsink/terminal block and earth strap screws   12   Slip ring end bracket

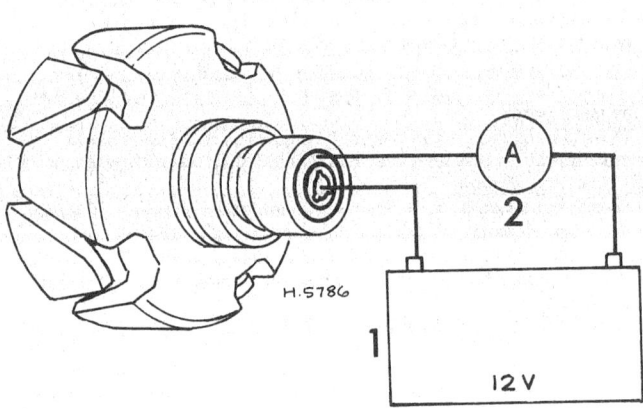

Fig. 10.29. Checking slip ring resistance (Lucas 20 ACR) (Sec. 17)

1   Battery   2   Ammeter

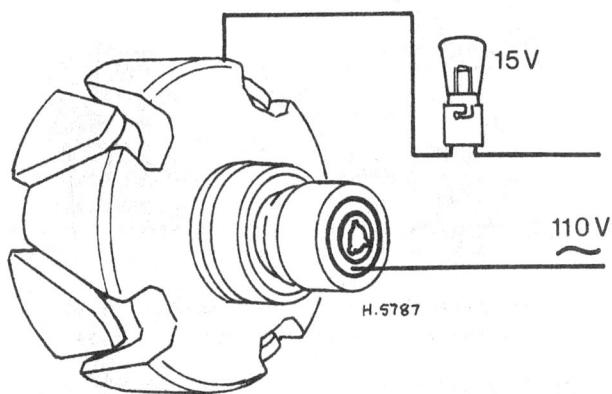

Fig. 10.30. Checking insulation of slip rings and rotor (Lucas 20 ACR) (Sec. 17)

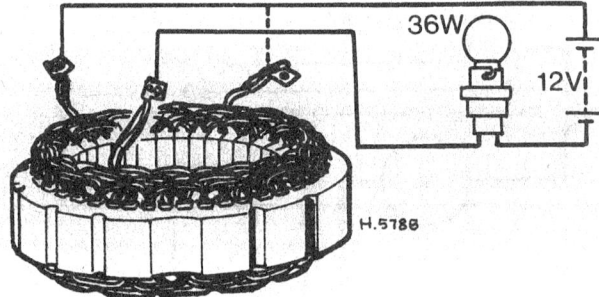

Fig. 10.31. Checking stator continuity (Lucas 20 ACR) (Sec. 17)

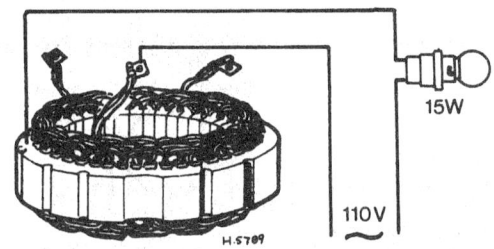

Fig. 10.32. Checking insulation of stator (Lucas 20 ACR) (Sec. 17)

poles, a 110 volt supply should be connected with a 15 watt test lamp between the slip rings and rotor poles in turn. If the lamp lights then the coil is earthed to the rotor core. In this event a new rotor/slip ring assembly will be required.

15 The stator can be tested for continuity by connecting any two of the three stator cables in series with a 12 volt battery supply and a 36 watt test lamp. The lamp should light up.

16 Repeat the test by moving the test lamp circuit to the third stator cable. Failure of the lamp to light on either of these tests indicates an open circuit and the stator must be renewed.

17 The insulation of the stator can be checked with a 110 volt test lamp rig. Connect the leads to the laminated yoke and to any one of the three stator cables. If the lamp lights up, the stator coils are earthed and the stator must be renewed.

18 To test the diodes, connect one battery terminal to the heatsink under test. Connect the other battery terminal in series with the test lamp (1.5W) and each diode pin in turn. Reverse the connections between the heatsinks and the diode pins in turn. The lamp should light in one direction only. If he lamp lights in both directions or does not light up at all, a new rectifier heatsink is needed.

19 When soldering the diode assemblies, carry out the operations, as described in Section 10, of this Chapter, paragraphs 25 and 26.

20 Reassembly is a reversal of dismantling but the following points must be observed.

21 If the rotor and drive end bracket have been separated, support the inner track of the drive end bearing using the distance collar. Do not use the drive end bracket as a support while fitting the rotor to it or it may crack.

22 Tighten the tie bolts evenly and make sure that the brushes are correctly located before refitting the brush moulding.

23 It is very important that the aluminium casing of the control unit does not touch the alternator body when it is installed in its final position. This would cause the field circuit to be fully switched on and the alternator would then supply maximum output irrespective of battery charge conditions.

18 Starter motors - general description

1 The starter motor used may be of inertia drive or pre-engaged type depending upon the car model, engine capacity, type of transmission used and the date of production of the vehicle.

2 The pre-engaged type of starter motor incorporates a solenoid mounted on top of the starter motor body. When the ignition switch is operated, the solenoid moves the starter drive pinion, through the medium of the shift lever, into engagement with the flywheel or driveplate starter ring gear. As the solenoid reaches the end of its stroke and with the pinion by now fully engaged with the flywheel ring gear, the main fixed and moving contacts close and engage the starter motor to rotate the engine.

   This fractional pre-engagement of the starter drive does much to reduce the wear on the flywheel ring gear associated with inertia type starter motors.

19 Starter motor - testing in position in the car

   The following tests cover both types of starter motor:

1 Switch on the lights and the ignition. Ensure that the selector lever of automatic models is in the 'P' or 'N' position.

2 Operate the starter control, if the lights go dim but the motor is not heard to operate, it shows that current is flowing through the motor windings but that, for some reason, the armature is not rotating. It may be that the pinion has not disengaged from the starter ring on the flywheel in which case the motor will have to be removed from the car for examination.

3 If, when the starter is operated, the lamps retain their full brilliance and the motor does not operate, check the circuit for continuity starting with the battery connections (especially the earth connection), then look carefully at the engine earth connection followed by the connections to the motor and the starter switch. If it is established that voltage is getting to the motor when the switch is operated, an internal fault in the motor is indicated.

4 Sluggish or a slow action of the motor is usually caused by a loose connection resulting in high resistance in the circuit, check as described in paragraph 3.

5 If the motor is heard to operate but it does not turn the engine, a fault in the drive is indicated which will involve removal of the motor for rectification.

20 Starter motor (inertia type) - removal and refitting

1 Disconnect the lead from the battery negative terminal.

2 Withdraw the three union connections from the lower face of the inlet manifold, release the hose clips at the centre junction and remove the inlet manifold rear starting pipe.

3 Remove the overflow pipe from the rear carburettor.

4 Remove the two nuts which secure the starter motor to the crankcase and withdraw the linked bolts.

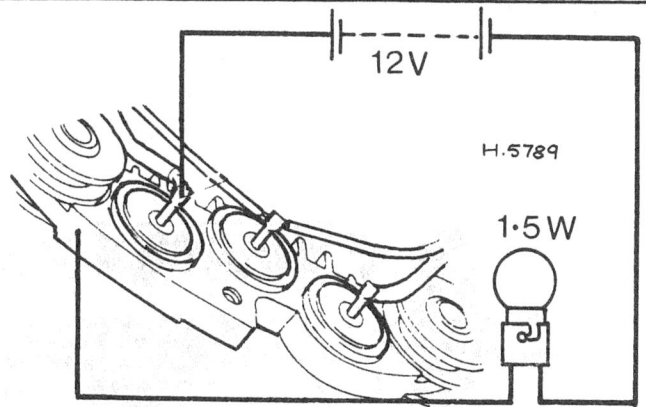

Fig. 10.33. Testing diodes (Lucas 20 ACR) (Sec. 17)

5 On cars equipped with automatic transmission, the dipstick must be withdrawn from the transmission unit, also the dipstick/filler tube.

6 Withdraw the starter motor forward and then remove it rearwards through the chassis frame.

7 Refitting is a reversal of removal.

21 Starter motor (pre-engaged type) - removal and refitting

1 Disconnect the lead from the battery negative terminal.

2 Disconnect the lead from the oil pressure switch and then remove the switch from the oil filter body (not late Series II and all Series III).

3 Disconnect the solenoid electrical leads, also those from the starter motor terminals. Remove the air cleaner.

4 Remove the two setscrews which secure the starter motor to the crankcase.

5 Withdraw the starter motor forwards to clear the starter drive and then remove it to the rear and upwards between the manifold and the wing valance. Retrieve the spigot plate.

6 Refitting is a reversal of removal but ensure that the spigot plate is correctly located on its positioning pins.

22 Starter motor (inertia type) - overhaul

1 Before completely dismantling the motor to check for a fault, first make sure that the brushes are not the cause of the trouble. This can be done by slackening the nut and bolt securing the 'window' cover band, slide the band clear of the 'windows' and the brushes can now be lifted out for examination. It is also possible to check the weight of the brush spring (correct tension 30-40 ozs) using a spring balance through the window.

2 Leave the brushes out of their holders if they are satisfactory and further dismantling is necessary.

3 Remove the nuts from the terminal post at the commutator end bracket.

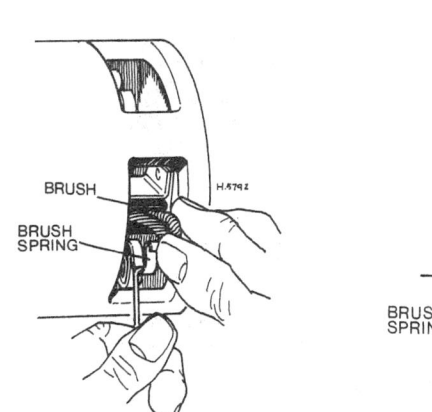

Fig. 10.34. Checking brush gear (inertia type starter) (Sec. 22)

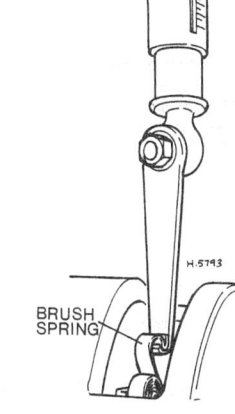

Fig. 10.35. Checking brush spring tension (inertia type starter) (Sec. 22)

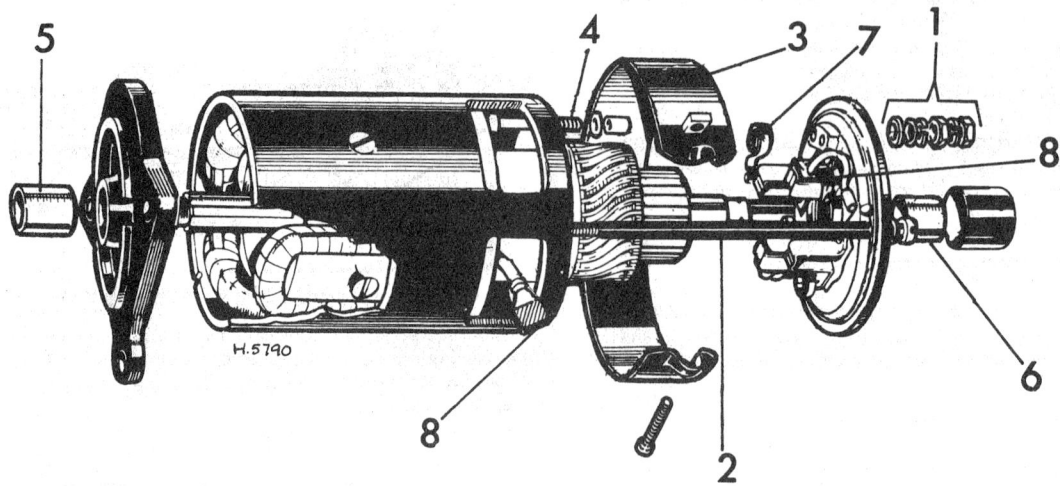

Fig. 10.36. Inertia drive type starter motor (Sec. 18)

1	Terminal nuts and washers	3	Cover band	5	Bush	7	Brush spring
2	Tie bolts	4	Terminal post	6	Bush	8	Brushes

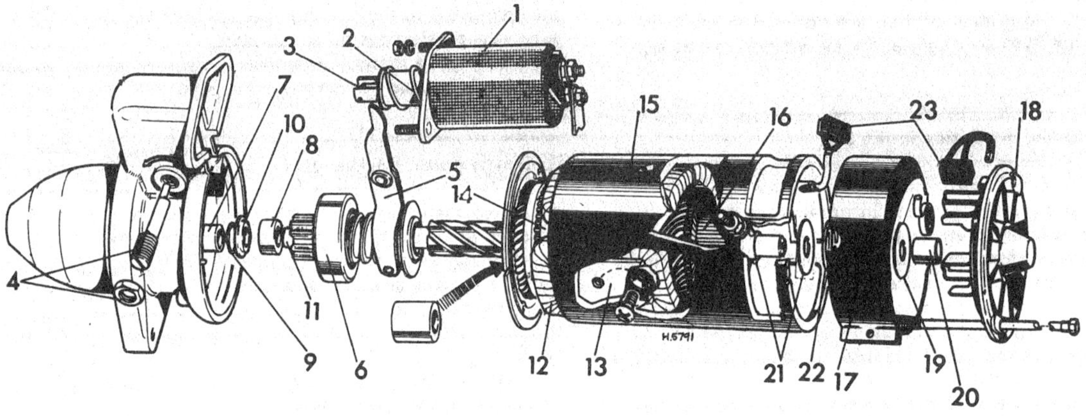

Fig. 10.37. Pre-engaged type starter motor (Sec. 18)

1	Solenoid	7	Bronze bush	13	Pole shoes	19	Thrust washer
2	Return spring	8	Thrust collar	14	Armature	20	Bronze bush
3	Clevis pin	9	Jump ring	15	Yoke	21	Brake shoes and cross peg
4	Pivot pin	10	Thrust ring	16	Commutator	22	Brake ring
5	Engagement lever	11	Armature shaft extension	17	Cover band	23	Brushes
6	Roller clutch	12	Field ring	18	Commutator end bracket		

4   Unscrew the two through bolts, and making sure that the brushes do not foul the yoke, remove the commutator end bracket from the yoke.

5   Relate the brushes, if they are serviceable, to their respective holders and then undo the lead securing screws and remove the brushes. (Fig. 10.38).

6   Withdraw the driving end bracket, complete with the armature and drive, from the yoke.

7   Now refer to Fig. 10.39 for dismantling of the drive.

8   Take out the split pin from the shaft nut (B), hold the squared end of the shaft with a spanner and then unscrew the nut. Some models have a jump ring instead of a split pin. Use a compressor to compress the spring.

9   Take off the main spring (C) followed by the remainder of the

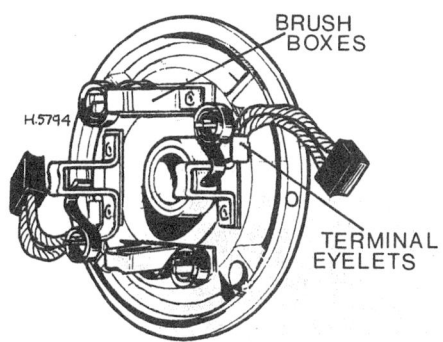

Fig. 10.38. Brush connections (inertia type starter) (Sec. 22)

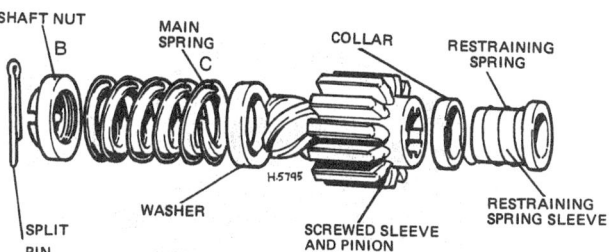

Fig. 10.39. Inertia type starter motor drive (Sec. 22)

components.

10 Renew any worn components, noting particularly the following:

The minimum permissible length of the brushes is 5/16 in (7.9 mm). The insulators between the commutator segments must not be undercut.
No attempt should be made to machine the armature core or to true a distorted armature shaft.
If either the screwed sleeve or the pinion of the drive are worn or damaged, they must be replaced as a pair, not separately.

11 Reassembly is a reversal of dismantling.

23 Starter motor (pre-engaged type) - overhaul

Type M45G

1 Before completely dismantling the motor to check for a fault, first make sure that the brushes are not the cause of the trouble. This can be done by slackening the nut and bolt securing the window cover band and then sliding the band clear of the windows. The brushes can now be lifted out for examination. They should be free in their holders, undamaged, a minimum length of 5/16 in (7.94 mm) and the spring tension, on a new brush, should be 52 ozs (1.47 kg).
2 Disconnect the copper link between the lower solenoid terminal and the yoke of the motor.
3 Take off the two solenoid unit securing nuts, detach the extension cables and withdraw the solenoid from the drive end bracket. Be careful when disengaging the solenoid plunger from the starter drive engagement lever.
4 If you have not already done so, slacken the nut and bolt securing the cover band, slide the band clear of the windows, lift off the brush springs and then remove the brushes from the holders.
5 Unscrew and remove the two through bolts from the commutator end bracket.
6 The commutator end bracket and yoke can now be removed from the intermediate and drive end bracket.
7 Remove the rubber seal from the drive end bracket.
8 Slacken the nut on the starter drive engagement lever eccentric pivot pin and then unscrew and remove the pin.
9 Separate the drive end bracket from the armature and intermediate bracket assembly.
10 Using a mild steel tube of suitable bore, remove the thrust washer from the end of the armature shaft extension.
11 Prise the jump ring out of its groove and then slide the drive assembly and the intermediate bracket from the shaft.
12 Prise out the jump ring and separate the operating bush and engagement spring.
13 The commutator should appear in a burnished condition, free from pitting or burning. It may be cleaned with a fuel soaked cloth or polished with fine glass paper if absolutely necessary. Do not undercut the insulators between the segments.
14 The porous bronze bearings in the commutator and drive end brackets should be renewed if they are worn. They are best removed by tapping a thread into them and then screwing in a bolt to extract them.
15 Soak the new bearings in clean engine oil for 24 hours before

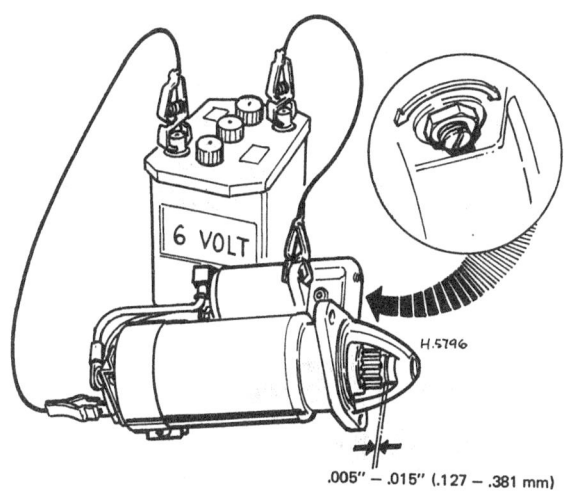

.005" – .015" (.127 – .381 mm)

Fig. 10.40. Setting starter motor pinion (pre-engaged starter) (Sec. 23)

installing them. No reaming is required.
16 Reassembly is the reverse of the above sequence but when refitting the commutator end bracket, ensure that the moulded brake shoes seat squarely and then turn them so that the ends of the cross peg in the armature shaft engage correctly with the slots in the shoes.
17 After final assembly it will be necessary to check for correct movement of the pinion, and for opening and closing of the starter switch contacts.
18 To check pinion movement, refer to Fig. 10.40 and connect the solenoid Lucar terminal to a **6 volt** battery as shown (do not use a 12 volt supply otherwise the armature will turn).
19 Measure the distance between the pinion and the thrust washer on the extension of the armature shaft when the pinion is lightly pressed towards the armature. This dimension should be 0.005 in to 0.015 in (0.13 to 0.38 mm).
20 If the setting is outside of those limits, disconnect the battery.
21 Now adjust the setting by first slackening the nut on the eccentric pivot pin (inset at Fig. 10.40) and then turn the pin clockwise to decrease and anticlockwise to increase the gap. The head of the arrow stamped on the end of the pin should be set only between the limits of the arrows cast in the drive end bracket.
22 Tighten the pin securing nut and then reconnect the battery and recheck the setting.
23 Having correctly set the pinion travel, the next task is to check the opening and closing of the starter switch contacts.
24 Refer to Fig. 10.41, remove the copper link connecting the solenoid 'STA' with the starter motor terminal.
25 Connect a switched 10 volts DC supply between the solenoid Lucar terminal and the large terminal 'STA'. **Do not** close the switch at this stage.
26 Connect a separately energised test lamp across the solenoid main

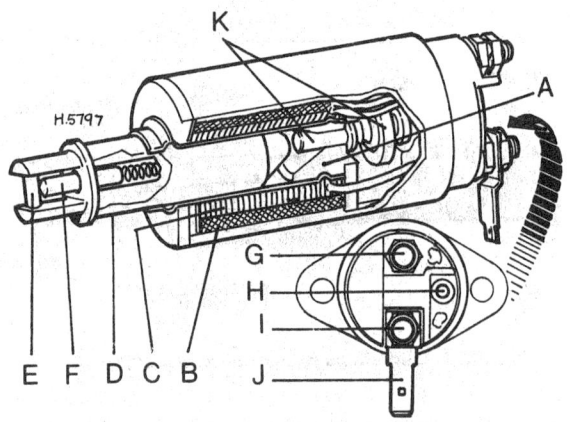

Fig. 10.41. Pre-engaged type starter solenoid switch (Sec. 23)

A Core
B Shunt winding
C Series winding
D Plunger
E Clevis pin
F 'Lost motion' device

G Starter terminal
H Solenoid terminal
I Battery terminal
J Accessories terminal
K Spindle and moving
   contact assembly

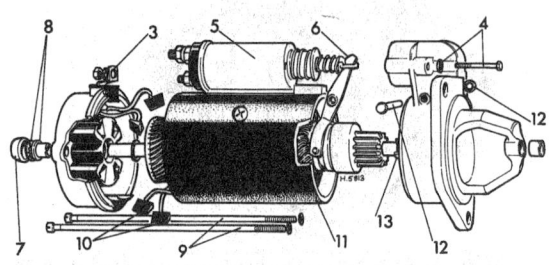

Fig. 10.43. Components of the Lucas 3M100 starter motor (Sec. 23)

3 Electrical link
5 Solenoid
6 Piston/engagement lever
   connection
7 End cap seal
8 Spire ring and bush

9 Tie bolts
10 Brushes
11 Yoke/field coil
12 Pivot pin and spire
   ring
13 Armature shaft

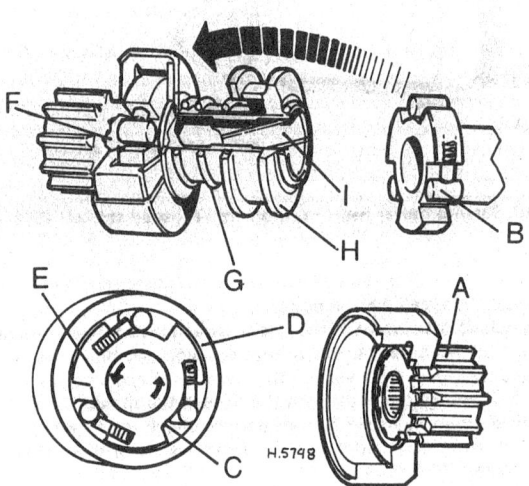

Fig. 10.42. Roller clutch drive components (pre-engaged starter) (Sec. 23)

A Alternative construction (pinion
   pressed and snap-ringed into
   driven member)
B Spring loaded rollers
C Cam tracks
D Driven member (with pinion)

E Driving member
F Bush
G Engagement spring
H Operating bush
I Driving sleeve

terminals.
27 Use a tool, an open ended spanner is ideal with its jaws passing over
the armature shaft extension, to act as a stop and so restrict the pinion
travel to its out of mesh clearance which is normally 1/8 in (3.17 mm).
28 Now energise the shunt winding using a 10 volt DC supply and then
close the switch in the series winding circuit. The solenoid contacts
should close fully and remain closed, a steady beam from the test lamp
will indicate that this is so.
29 Switch off and remove the stop.
30 Switch on again and hold the pinion assembly in the fully engaged

position.
31 Switch off and observe the test lamp. The solenoid contacts should
open as indicated by the test lamp extinguishing.
32 Examine the roller clutch drive assembly. If it is in good condition
it should take up the drive instantaneously in one direction and should
rotate easily and smoothly in the other. There should be no roughness
or tendency to bind in movement around or along the shaft splines.
Similarly, the operating bush must be free to slide smoothly along the
driving sleeve when the engagement spring is compressed. Make sure
that the trunnion blocks pivot freely on the pegs of the engaging lever.
33 Finally, lubricate all moving parts of the roller clutch drive with
general purpose grease.

Type 3M100

34 The operations described in the foregoing paragraphs generally apply
to the later type of starter motor but the following differences must
be noted.
35 There is no brush cover band on this type of starter.
36 The spire retaining rings must be renewed on reassembly.
37 The commutator end cover is removed after withdrawing it enough
to be able to disengage the two field coil brushes from the brush box.
38 The minimum length of the brushes before renewal is 0.375 in
(9.5 mm). When renewing the brushes, note which field coil conductor
is fitted with the long or short brush flexible connector. Unsolder the
old brushes and use resin cored solder to attach the new ones.
39 Drive the spire ring onto the armature shaft so that there is a
clearance between the retaining ring and the bearing bush shoulder of
no more than 0.010 in (0.25 mm).

24 Fuses

1   The fuse units are located behind the instrument sub panel.
2   Access to the fuses is obtained by removing the screws from the top
left and top right-hand corners of the instrument sub panel. The panel
then hinges downward.
3   The fuses and the circuits which they protect are listed in
'Specifications' at the beginning of this Chapter.
4   Always renew a blown fuse with one of similar rating and if it blows
for a second time, trace the cause before renewing it again.
5   Where a heated rear window and an air-conditioning system are
installed, separate fuses in independent fuse holders are located also
behind the instrument panel.
6   On cars equipped with an overdrive, a separate in-line fuse is located
just above the steering column.

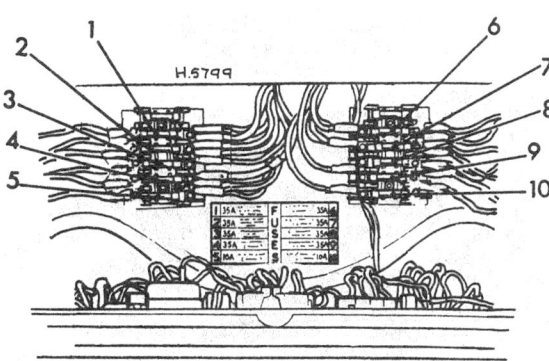

Fig. 10.44. Fuse arrangement (for 'Key' see Specifications Section) (Sec. 24)

25 Flasher (direction indicator) unit - checking and renewal

1   The flasher unit which controls the direction indicators is located behind and to the right of the steering column.

2   Any fault in the system should first be checked out by testing the bulbs in the indicator lamps and the security of the wiring.

3   If these are in order, remove the old unit and then connect together the leads which have been removed from terminals 'B' and 'L' of the flasher unit. Turn on the ignition switch and turn the direction indicator switch first to the left and then to the right. Check that the appropriate bulbs light up. If they do then the bulbs and wiring are in good order.

4   Any difference in the speed of flashing between one side of the car and the other may be due to a gradual internal collapse of the unit. Exceptionally fast flashing of an indicator bulb usually means that a bulb is failing.

26 Hazard warning flasher unit

1   The system operates in conjunction with the four direction indicator lamps.

2   The hazard warning system actuates all four flasher lamps simultaneously.

3   The flasher unit is located close to the direction indicator flasher unit.

4   The system indicator lamp is accessible for renewal after removing the warning lamp cluster which is located between the speedometer and the revolution counter.

5   If one bulb in the system fails, the remaining three bulbs in the system will still function.

27 Bulbs - renewal

The design of the lamps illustrated in this Section may vary

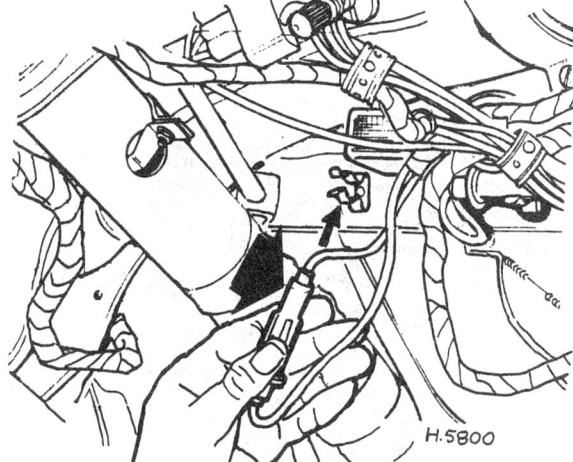

Fig. 10.45. Location of overdrive unit fuse (Sec. 24)

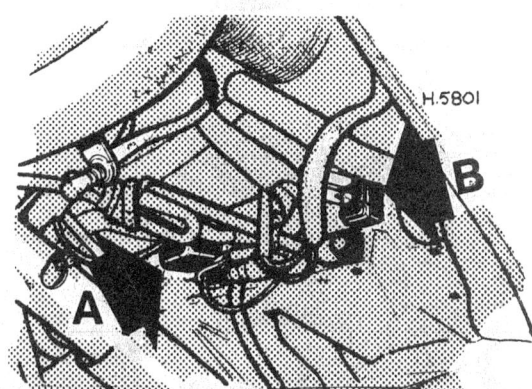

Fig. 10.46. Location of hazard warning (A) and direction indicator flasher unit (B) (Sec. 25)

according to the model and date of production but the bulb renewal operations apply to all versions.

Headlamps

1   The headlamps are of sealed beam type. To renew an outer lamp unit, remove the upper retainer screw and withdraw the headlamp embellisher noting the two retaining lugs at the lower edge. On Series 2 cars, the embellisher incorporates a mesh filter covering a fresh air intake (photo).

2   Unscrew the three retaining screws and the headlamp retaining rim (photo).

3   Withdraw the headlamp sealed beam unit and detach the socket from the rear of the headlamp (photo).

4   Refitting is a reversal of removal but on no account alter the setting of the headlamp adjusting screws.

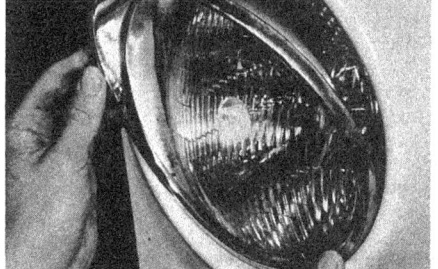

27.1 Removing headlamp embellisher

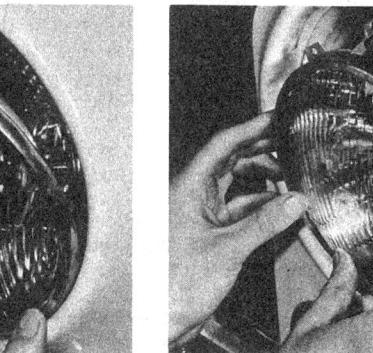

27.2 Removing headlamp sealed beam unit

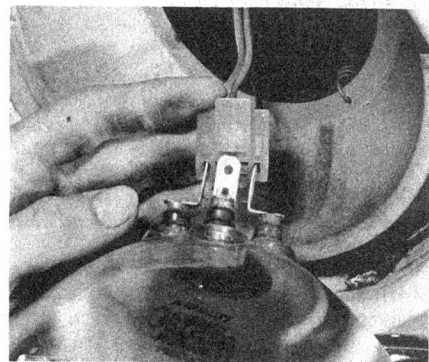

27.3 Disconnecting headlamp unit

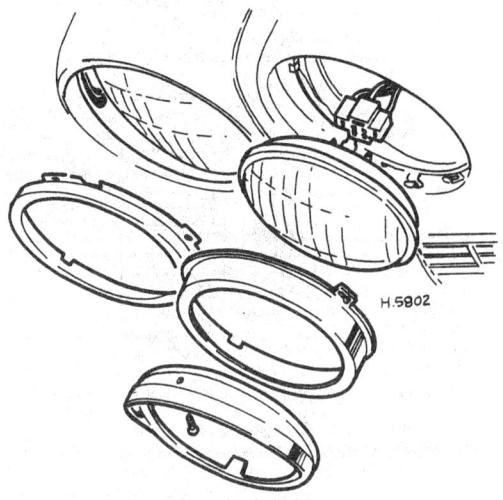

Fig. 10.47. Headlamp components (Sec. 27)

27.5 Removing front parking flasher lamp lens (typical)

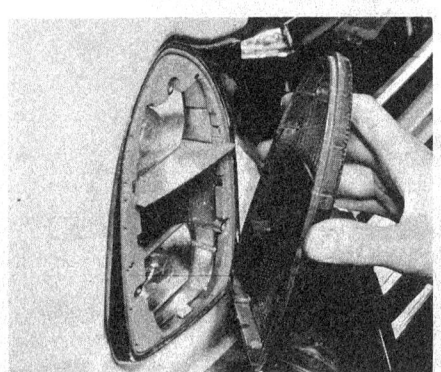

27.7 Removing rear lamp lens

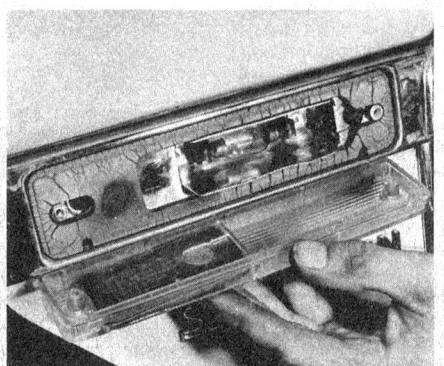

27.8 Removing reversing lamp lens

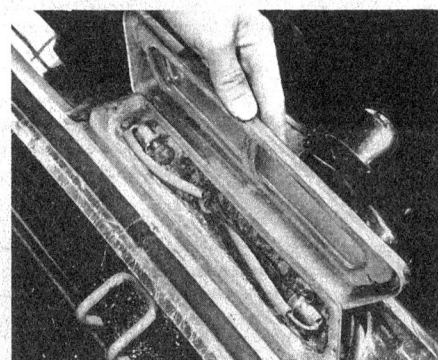

27.9 Removing rear number plate lens

Front parking, direction indicator, side marker, flasher repeater lamps

5   Access to all these bulbs is obtained by removing the lamp lens securing screws and withdrawing the lens. Not all these lamps are fitted to all cars. The specification depends upon operating territory (photo).

Rear lamp and direction indicator lamp

6   Remove the three lens securing screws and withdraw the lens.
7   When refitting the tail/stop lamp bulb which is of twin filament type, note the offset pins (photo).

Reversing lamp

8   Remove the two lens securing screws and withdraw the lens and the festoon type bulb (photo).

Rear number plate lamp

9   Remove the two screws which are located in the centre section of the rear bumper and withdraw the lens (photo).

Interior lamp

10 Remove the lens cover by inserting a screwdriver under the bright plated part.
11 The bulb is of festoon type.
12 Replace the lens by inserting the top edge into the base and then snapping the bottom edge into place.

Map reading lamp

13 Press in the side clips of the bulb holder which is located under the centre of the screen rail above the instrument panel. Withdraw the holder downwards (Fig. 10.49).
14 The bulb is accessible through a hole in the base of the lamp.

Fig. 10.48. Interior lamp bulb (Sec. 27)

Warning lamps

15 The bulbs for these lamps are housed in a cluster which is located between the speedometer and the revolution counter. Prise the cover plate off and remove the capless type bulbs.

Indicator strip lamps

16 These bulbs are removable simply by pulling them out of their sockets along the bottom rear edge of the instrument panel.

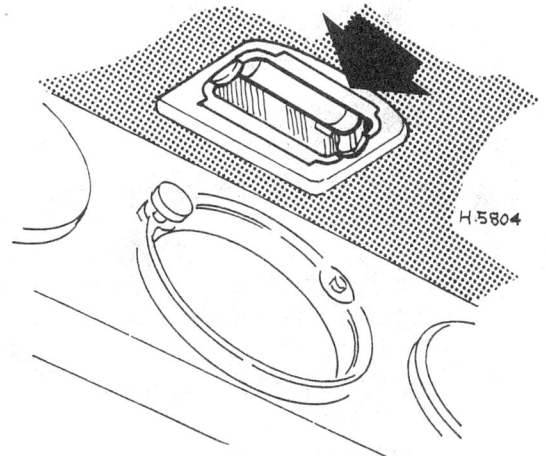

Fig. 10.49. Map reading lamp bulb (Sec. 27)

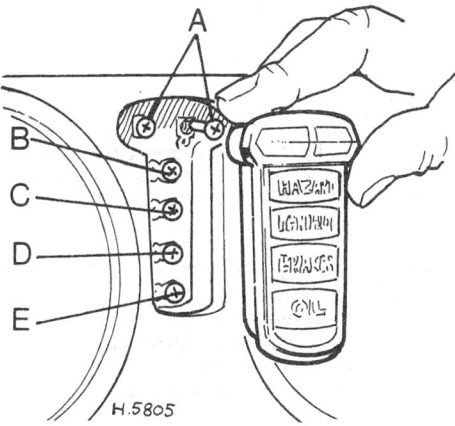

Fig. 10.50. Warning lamps (Sec. 27)

A   Direction indicators   D   Brake warning
B   Hazard warning   E   Oil pressure warning
C   Ignition warning

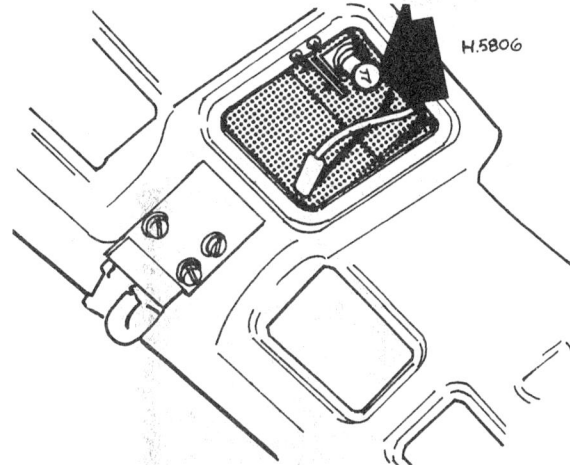

Fig. 10.51. Luggage compartment lamp bulb (Sec. 27)

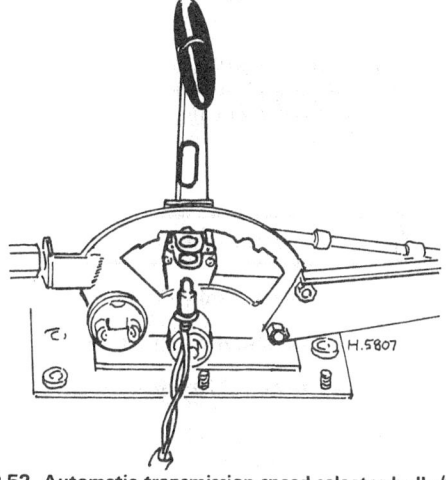

Fig. 10.52. Automatic transmission speed selector bulb (Sec. 27)

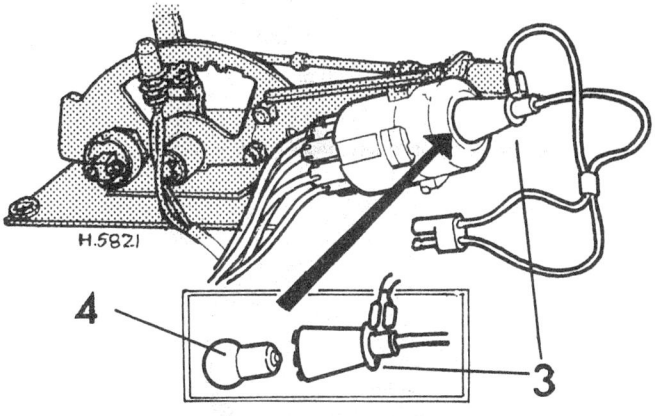

Fig. 10.53. Opticell assembly (Sec. 27)

3   Bulb holder   4   Bulb

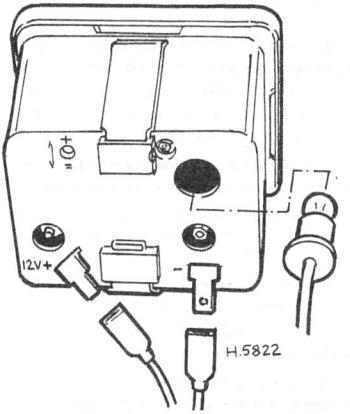

Fig. 10.54. Rear view of Series 2 clock (Sec. 27)

Luggage compartment lamp
17 Open the luggage compartment lid and remove the bulb by reaching through the aperture in the luggage compartment lid inner panel.

Automatic transmission indicator bulb
18 Remove the securing screws which retain the cover on the speed selector control. On Series 2 cars, prise out the window lift switch panel.
19 Remove the control lever knob by unscrewing the two halves in opposing directions.
20 Withdraw the two screws and remove the speed position indicator cover.
21 Remove the bulb cover and the bulb.

Door pillar lamp
22 These lamps are fitted to the top of the door pillars on Series 2 cars.
23 The lens is squeezed slightly and pulled from the lamp base to gain access to the festoon type bulb.

Fibre optic (Opticell) illumination system (Series 2 cars)
24 This system provides illumination to the ignition, lighting and heater/air-conditioning control switches from a central light source through fibre elements and diffuser lenses.
25 To renew the bulb, disconnect the battery, remove the centre console escutcheon and the window control switch panel. Pull the bulb holder from the opticell reflector and extract the bayonet type bulb.

Speedometer and tachometer bulbs

26 The bulbs can be withdrawn from the rear of these instruments
after the instruments have been partially withdrawn as described in
Section 38 or 39.

Clock illumination bulb (Series 2 cars)

27 A separate clock illuminating bulb is used on Series 2 cars and this is
accessible only after first disconnecting the battery and dropping the
centre oddments tray. Pull the bulb holder from the back of the clock
case.

28 Headlamp beam alignment

1   It is recommended that the headlamps are aligned on modern
optical beam setting equipment at a service station.
2   However, where these facilities are not available or in an emergency,
proceed in the following way.
3   Place the car on a level surface (during the hours of darkness) 25
ft (7.6 m) from and square to a wall or screen.
4   Switch the headlamps to full beam and observe the light patterns
from the four headlamps on the wall. These patterns should have their
centres at the same height on the wall as their lens centre points are
from the ground and at the same horizontal distances from each other
as the headlamp lens centres are from each other on the car.
5   If adjustment is required, remove the headlamp surround by
removing the retaining screw and springing the surround from the
bottom clips. Turn the appropriate adjuster screws as required.
6   Holts Amber Lamp is useful for temporarily changing the
headlight colour to conform with the normal usage on Continental
Europe.

29 Steering column ignition/starter switch and lock

1   The ignition/starter switch has five positions:

   1 Lock; 2 Park; 3 Accessories; 4 Ignition; 5 Start

2   In the 'Lock' position, the key can be removed but the steering
wheel cannot be turned.
3   In the 'Park' position the key can be removed and the car can be
pushed and steered for repair purposes.
4   In the 'Accessories' position, the radio and electrically-operated
windows (where fitted) can be operated.
5   In the 'On' position, the ignition is switched on.
6   In the 'Start' position, the starter motor is actuated. On releasing
the key it returns to the 'On' position. This arrangement gives enough
time for the engine and starter motor drive to stop should a second
attempt have to be made to start the engine, otherwise damage could be
caused to the starter drive and flywheel ring gear.
7   The ignition section of the lock assembly can be removed by
disconnecting the connector plug and removing the contact plate (two
screws). It should be noted that two relays are incorporated in the
circuits which are controlled by the ignition switch to prevent over-
loading of the switch contacts. The relays are located under the fascia
panel on the fuse box mounting bracket. Always check these components
if a fault develops in the ignition/starter circuit.
8   The steering lock is secured to the upper end of the steering column
by two shear-headed bolts. If the lock must be removed for any reason,
the original bolts must be drilled out.
9   When refitting the new lock, check the operation of the lock tongue
in the column cut-out before finally tightening and shearing the new
securing bolts.

30 Direction indicator switch - removal and refitting

1   Disconnect the lead from the battery negative terminal.
2   Remove the steering wheel as described in Chapter 11.
3   Remove the three screws which secure the direction indicator switch
and cowl to the steering outer column.
4   Disconnect the cables which run to the switch by separating the plug
connectors.
5   Refitting is a reversal of removal.

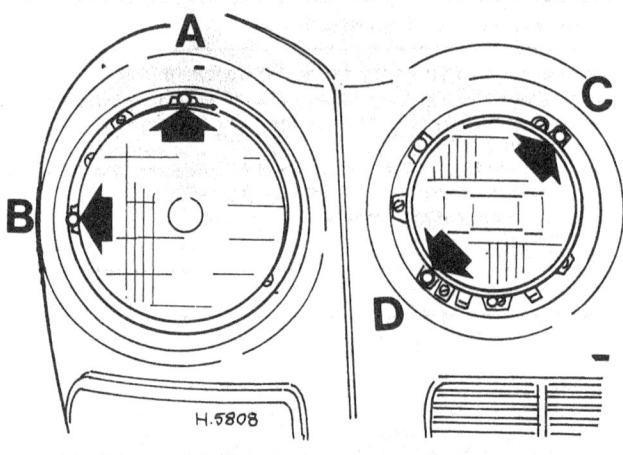

Fig. 10.55. Headlamp adjusting screws (Sec. 28)

A   *Outer vertical*   C   *Inner vertical*
B   *Outer horizontal*   D   *Inner horizontal*

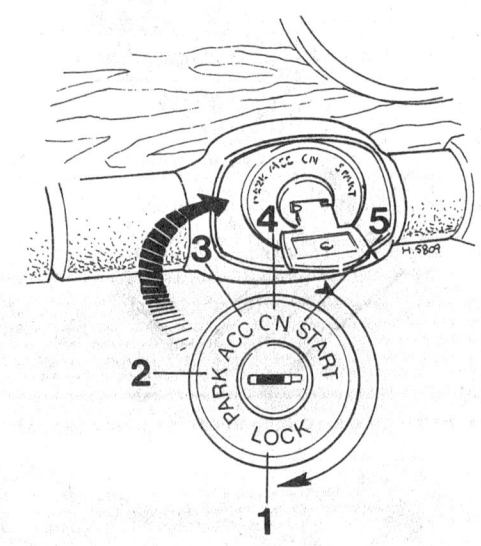

Fig. 10.56. Ignition key positions (Sec. 29)

1   Lock   *3   Accessories*
2   Park   *4   Run*
                                     5   Start

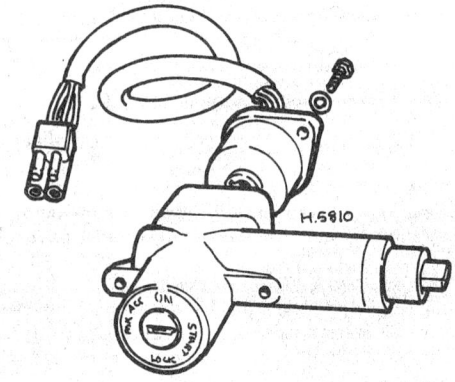

Fig. 10.57. Steering column lock and ignition switch (Sec. 29)

31 Overdrive switch - removal and refitting

1   Disconnect the lead from the battery negative terminal.
2   Insert a thin knife blade or similar tool between the switch cover and the gear lever knob. Gently prise away the cover (with switch attached) from the snap ring retainer.
3   Disconnect the two cables from the switch connectors and separate the switch from the cover by removing the two securing screws.
4   Refitting is a reversal of removal.

32 Horns and relay

1   The twin horns are mounted just below and to each side of the radiator.
2   The horn circuit incorporates a relay and actuation is by means of the steering wheel horn ring or centre button.
3   The horns only sound when the ignition is switched on.
4   If the horns fail to work, first check the fuse and then the wiring and connections. If these are in order and the battery is fully charged, then the relay is probably the cause and it should be renewed. The relay is located within the engine compartment on the right-hand side towards the front.

33 Windscreen wiper blades and arms - removal and refitting

1   To remove a wiper blade, release the small tag which secures it to the wiper arm and pull the blade from the arm (photo).
2   The wiper arms can be removed from the splined driving spindles after first pulling the arms away from the windscreen until they lock.

3   When refitting the wiper arms, make sure that the wiper motor is in the parked position, having been switched off by the wiper control switch (not the ignition key) and set the arms complete with blades, parallel with the lower edge of the windscreen before pressing the arm fully onto its spindle.

34 Windscreen wiper motor and linkage - removal and refitting

1   Remove the wiper arms from their driving spindles.
2   Disconnect and remove the battery.
3   Unscrew the large nut which connects the driving cable conduit to the wiper motor (photo).
4   Withdraw the electrical plug connector from the socket in the motor.
5   Remove the two setscrews, washers and clamp strap and then withdraw the motor and driving cable by drawing the cable through its conduit (photo).
6   If the driving spindle assemblies are worn they can only be removed after first withdrawing the screen rail fascia. To do this, insert a thin blade under the edge of the loudspeaker grille and lever up the fascia. The grille is retained by plastic pegs. Remove the two screws now exposed also the two other screws from the underside of the screen fascia roll (just above the fresh air outlets).
7   Unscrew and remove the two nuts which secure the wheelbox backplate and withdraw the cable drive conduit.
8   Unscrew the nuts which secure the wheelbox to the scuttle and withdraw the wheelbox, spacer and seals.
9   Refitting the wheelboxes is a reversal of removal except that the flared ends of the conduit tube must register with the narrow slots in the cover plate.
10 After refitting the wiper motor, the wiper arms must be installed in

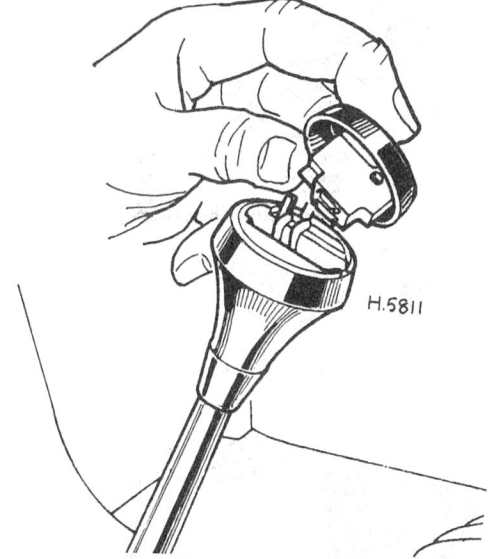

Fig. 10.58. Removing the overdrive switch (Sec. 31)

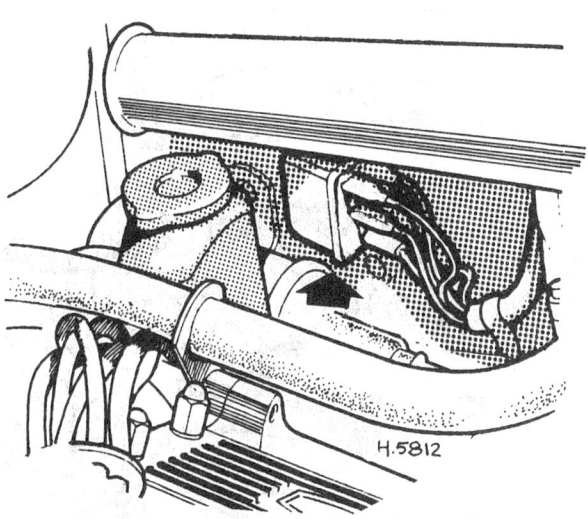

Fig. 10.59. Location of horn relay (Sec. 32)

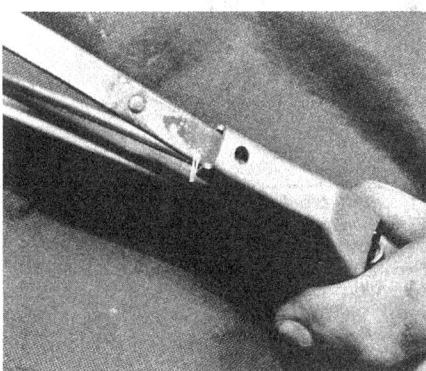

33.1 Disconnecting wiper blade from arm

34.3 Windscreen wiper driving cable conduit unit

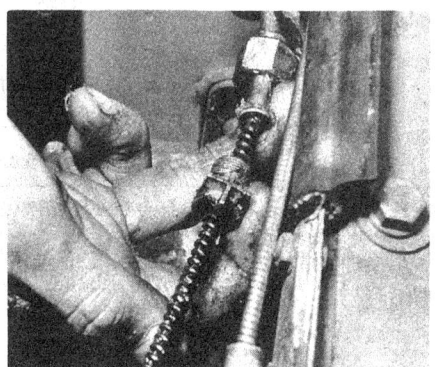

34.5 Withdrawing wiper driving cable

the following way:

11 Switch on the ignition and then switch on the wiper switch to slow speed. Switch off the wiper switch so that the driving spindles will stop in the 'Parked' position. Install the wiper arms so that they lie parallel with the lower edge of the windscreen.

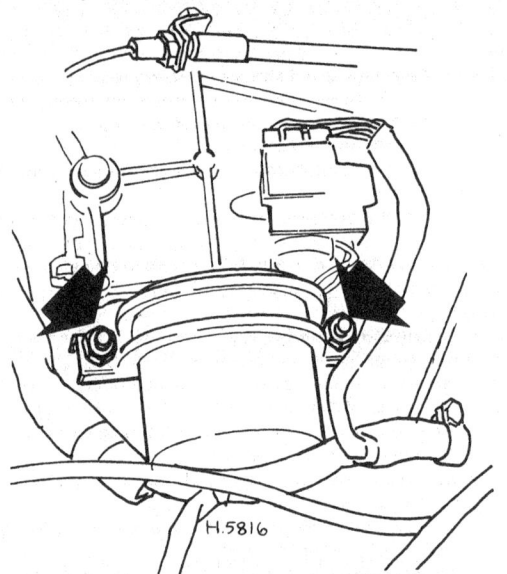

Fig. 10.60. Wiper motor mounting bolts (Sec. 34)

35 Windscreen wiper motor - overhaul

1 With the motor removed from the car as described in Section 34, withdraw the gearbox cover screws and remove the cover.
2 Prise the circlip from the groove in the gearwheel crankpin and extract the flat washer, conical spring, friction plate, connecting rod assembly and its flat washer.
3 Remove the circlip and washer which secure the shaft to the gearbox.
4 Draw the gear from the shaft, collecting the dished washer from the underside of the gearwheel.
5 Note the gearbox to yoke alignment marks and then withdraw the two fixing bolts and detach the yoke assembly and the armature from the gearbox. Take care that once removed, the yoke does not come near any swarf or iron filings which might be attracted to its pole pieces.
6 Mark the location of the moulded slider block in relation to the terminal assembly as this controls the wiper parking position.

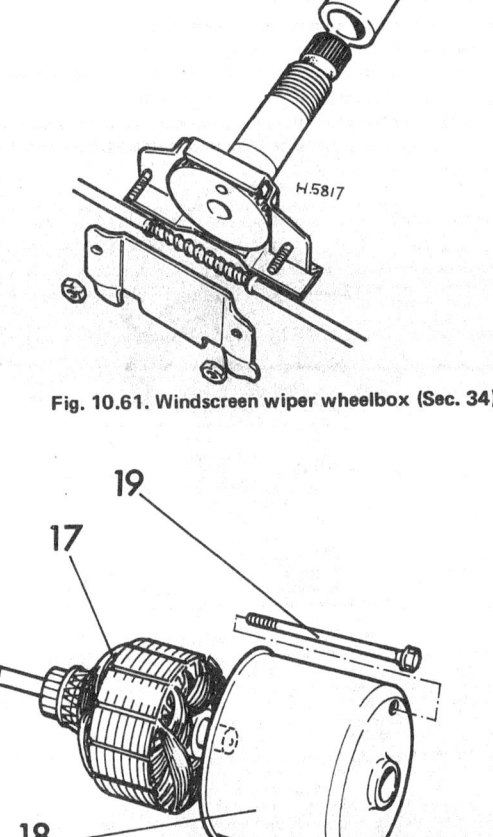

Fig. 10.61. Windscreen wiper wheelbox (Sec. 34)

Fig. 10.62. Exploded view of the windscreen wiper motor (Sec. 35)

1	Gearbox cover	11	Slider block
2	Screw	12	Gearbox
3	Circlip	13	Limit switch
4	Washer	14	Screws
5	Spring	15	Bush
6	Friction plate	16	Brush gear
7	Crankarm	17	Armature
8	Gear	18	Yoke
9	Dished washer	19	Tie bolts
10	Cable rack		

7 Remove the screws which secure the brushgear and the terminal and limit switch assembly and withdraw the assemblies.

8 Inspect the brushes for wear. The main (diametrically opposite) brushes should be renewed if they are worn to 3/16 in (4.8 mm) or less. If the narrow section of the third brush is worn to the full width of the brush, it must be renewed. Check that the brushes move freely in their holders.

9 Clean the commutator of the armature with a fuel soaked rag or polish it with very fine glasspaper.

10 Renew any gearbox components which are worn.

11 Reassembly is a reversal of dismantling but check the following points.

12 Before refitting the armature to the yoke, check that the thrust disc and felt lubricating disc are in position in the yoke bearing. The thrust disc should be located flat against the endface of the bearing, followed by the felt washer which has a hole in its centre to allow the ball in the end of the armature shaft to contact the thrust disc. Prior to fitting the components, apply oil to the felt washer.

13 Apply grease liberally to all gearbox components.

14 If new parts have been fitted, check the armature endfloat which must be between 0.002 and 0.008 in (0.05 and 0.2 mm). With the wiper motor completely assembled and the thrust screw released and in the uppermost position, tighten the screw until it just makes contact and then unscrew it one quarter of a turn and tighten the locknut.

36 Windscreen washer - description and jet adjustment

1 The washer assembly comprises a plastic fluid container, an independently mounted motor, twin jets and an operating switch.

2 It is recommended that a reliable brand of washer solvent is mixed with water in the container instead of using plain water.

3 The motor/pump unit is mounted on the engine compartment rear bulkhead, the reservoir is at the front of the engine compartment.

4 The jets can be removed for cleaning, if required, by unscrewing them from the jet holder.

5 Adjustment is carried out by moving the jets with a thin screwdriver blade (photo).

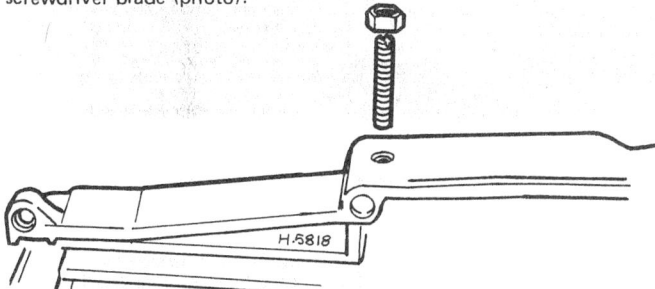

Fig. 10.63. Wiper motor armature endfloat adjuster screw and locknut (Sec. 35)

36.5 Adjusting windscreen washer jet

37 Speedometer cable - renewal

1 Reach up behind the instrument panel and unscrew the knurled ring from the back of the speedometer. Withdraw the cable and ring.

2 Disconnect the opposite end of the speedometer cable from the gearbox or automatic transmission and then detach the cable from its securing clips.

3 Withdraw the inner cable from the outer conduit.

4 Before installing the new inner cable, smear the lower two thirds of its length with a thin coating of multi-purpose grease.

5 Connect the cable assembly to the transmission and then position the cable in its original contour without moving the position of the securing clips.

6 Rotate the inner cable with the fingers to ensure that it is correctly engaged at the transmission end and then check that the inner cable projects by 3/8 in (9.5 mm) from the end of the outer conduit at the speedometer head end.

7 Engage the cable assembly with the back of the speedometer and tighten the knurled ring with the fingers.

38 Speedometer - removal and refitting

1 Disconnect the lead from the battery negative terminal.

2 Disconnect the speedometer cable from the rear of the speedometer, as described in the preceding Section.

3 Disconnect the trip control cable by unscrewing the knurled ring.

4 Apply hand pressure against the speedometer bezel, turn it in an anticlockwise direction until it stops and then withdraw it.

5 Disconnect the headlamp main beam warning lamp and the two instrument illumination lamps.

6 Refitting is a reversal of removal.

39 Tachometer - removal and refitting

1 The tachometer is of impulse type and is wired in circuit with the S/W terminal on the ignition coil and the ignition switch.

2 The instrument can be removed by applying hand pressure against the bezel and turning it in an anticlockwise direction.

3 Withdraw the instrument far enough to be able to pinch the prongs of the socket retainer clip together and to withdraw the plug and

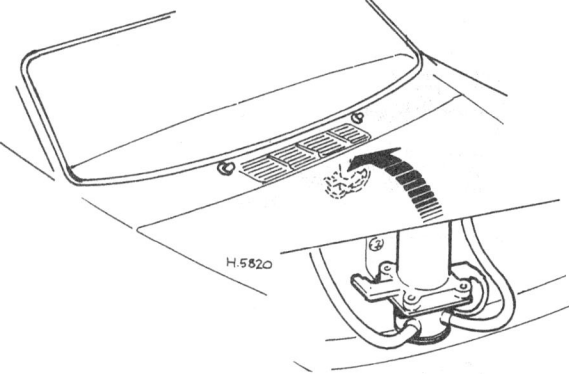

Fig. 10.64. Windscreen washer pump location (Sec. 36)

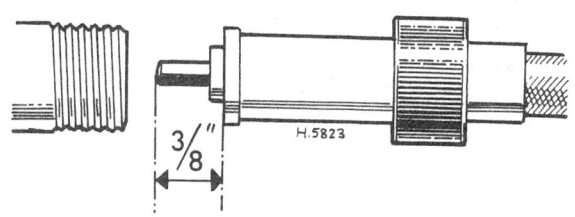

Fig. 10.65. Speedometer inner cable projection at speedometer head end (Sec. 37)

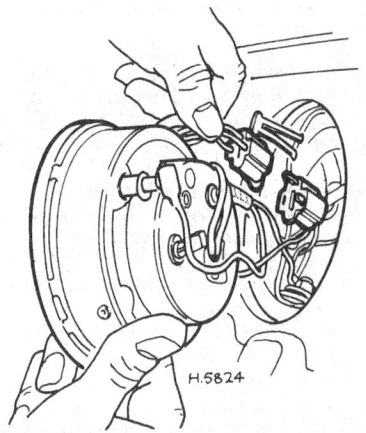

Fig. 10.66. Removing tachometer (Sec. 39)

socket assembly.

4   Refitting is the reverse of removal.

40 Instrument sub-panel - removal and refitting

1   Disconnect the lead from the battery negative terminal.

2   Remove the two screws from the top of the main instrument panel and hinge it downwards (photos).

3   Withdraw the electrical harness plug.

4   Remove the four setscrews and withdraw the sub-panel complete with instruments.

5   If the individual instruments are to be removed, first withdraw the instrument voltage stabiliser.

6   Unscrew and remove the six cross-headed screws, disconnect the two electrical leads from the clock and then remove the base panel complete with the instruments mounted on it.

7   Individual instruments can be removed after extracting their securing screws but take great care not to damage the printed circuit.

8   Refitting is a reversal of removal.

40.2A Removing instrument sub-panel screw

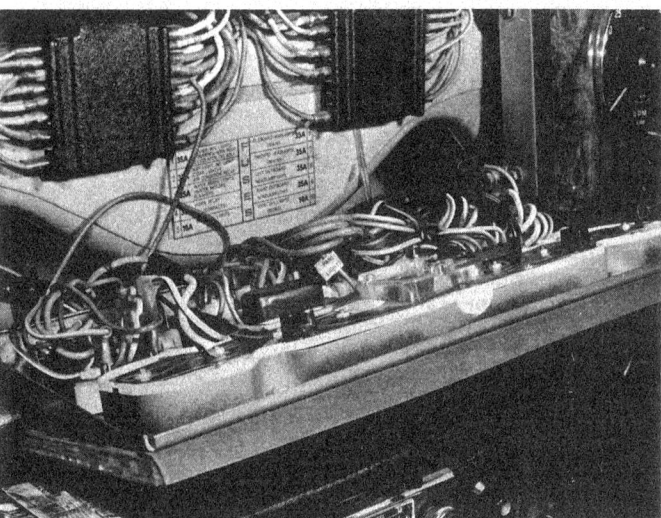

40.2B Instrument sub-panel hinged downward to expose fuses

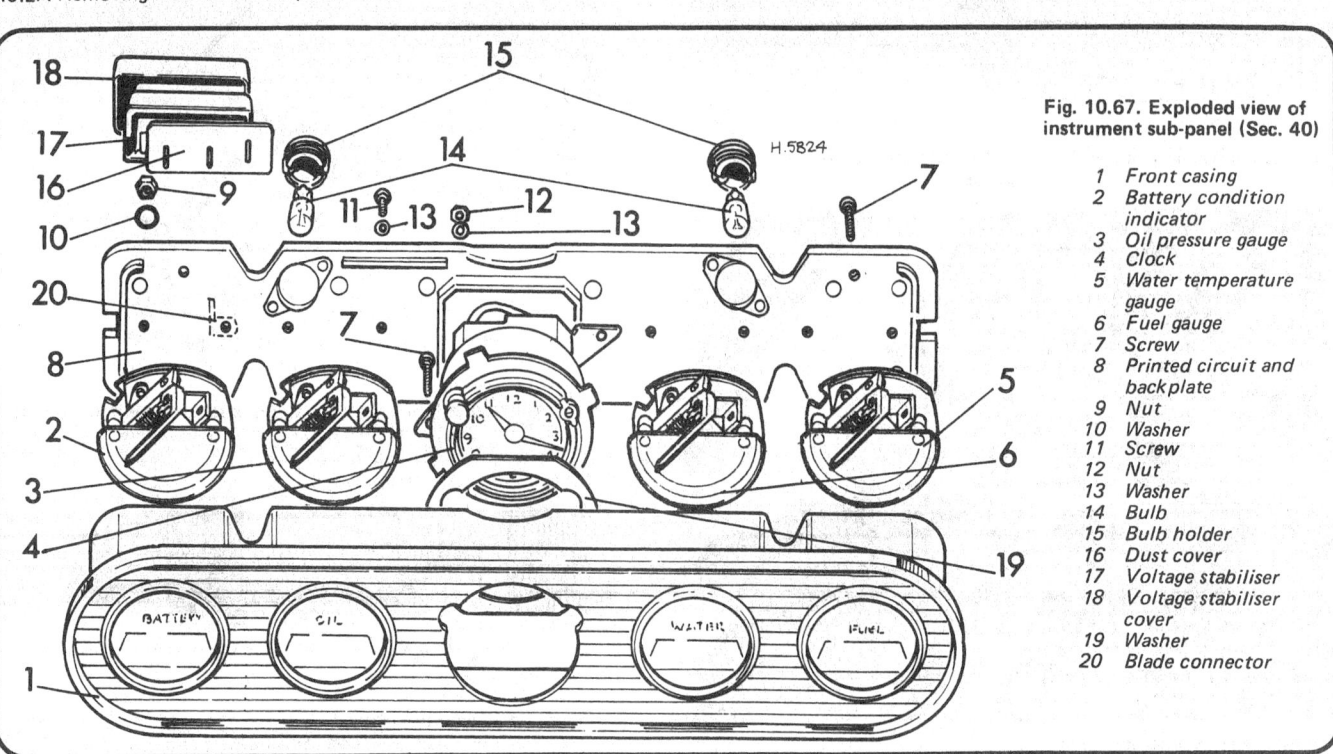

Fig. 10.67. Exploded view of instrument sub-panel (Sec. 40)

1   Front casing
2   Battery condition indicator
3   Oil pressure gauge
4   Clock
5   Water temperature gauge
6   Fuel gauge
7   Screw
8   Printed circuit and backplate
9   Nut
10 Washer
11 Screw
12 Nut
13 Washer
14 Bulb
15 Bulb holder
16 Dust cover
17 Voltage stabiliser
18 Voltage stabiliser cover
19 Washer
20 Blade connector

41 Switch sub-panel - removal and refitting

1 Disconnect the lead from the battery negative terminal.
2 Remove the two screws from the top of the main instrument panel and hinge it downwards. On later cars, the panel can be levered out.
3 Disconnect the leads from the switches marking any that need it to ensure exact reconnection later.
4 Unscrew the four screws and detach the sub-panel.
5 The switches are secured in the sub-panel by plastic locking tabs which should be depressed to release the switches.

42 Electric clock - removal and refitting

1 The clock can be removed after carrying out the operations described in Section 40, paragraphs 1 to 6.
2 Refitting is a reversal of these operations.

43 Heated rear window

1 The heating element on all but the earliest cars is applied to the inside surface of the glass. Great care must be taken not to damage the element with sharp objects or, when cleaning the glass, with rings on the fingers.
2 Use only water to clean the glass and never stick labels onto the inside of the rear window if they are likely to cover any of the fine wires of the element.

44 Seatbelt warning system

1 This system is installed in cars destined for operation in North America.
2 Audible and visual alarm signals are given if the front seats are occupied but the belts not fastened and with the engine started, a gear is engaged or speed position (automatic transmission) selected.
3 Any fault in the system should be checked out by testing the circuit fuse and the wiring and connections.
4 On Series 2 cars, the system is modified so that the engine will not start unless the following operations have been carried out (front seat/s occupied).

Handbrake fully applied.
Selector lever in 'N' or 'P' (automatic transmission) or neutral (manual gearbox).
Seatbelt fastened.

5 If the front seat passenger leaves the car while the engine is running, the warning devices will operate for seven seconds and then cease.
6 If the driver leaves his seat while the engine is running no warning signals will be given when he returns and selects a gear without refastening his seatbelt.
7 The engine can be started for purposes of maintenance or tuning by reaching inside the car and turning the starter switch so that no weight is applied to either front seat. Under these conditions, no warning or starter cut-out will be operative.
8 The seatbelt warning system buzzer/control unit is located under the fascia panel on the passenger side. The unit is mounted on the heater blower casing and on Series 2 cars, the fascia side panel and the glove compartment liner must both be removed first.

45 Electrically operated windows

1 These devices are supplied as optional equipment but are factory installed at time of production.

Driver's control switches

2 To remove the driver's control switches, first disconnect the lead from the battery negative terminal.
3 Lift the centre armrest lid and remove the screws which secure it to the console. Withdraw the nylon catch and withdraw the pocket from the console.
4 Remove the switch escutcheon panel by pressing it out from the

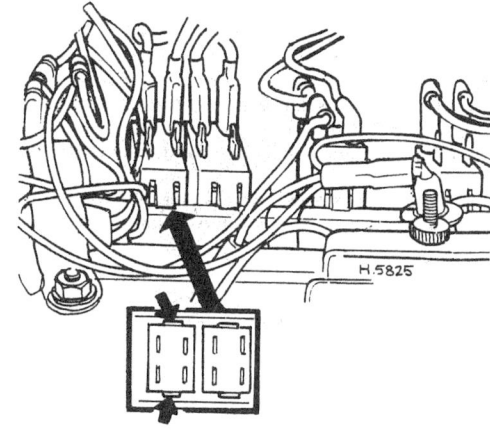

Fig. 10.68. Instrument panel rocker switches showing locking tabs (Sec. 41)

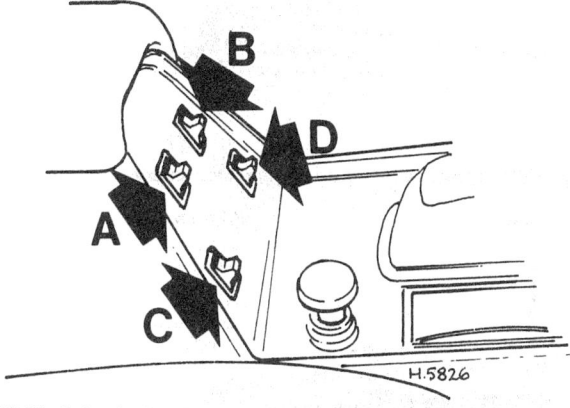

Fig. 10.69. Driver's electrically-operated window control panel (Sec. 45)

A Right-hand rear
B Left-hand rear
C Front right-hand (and master switch)
D Front left-hand

rear. On Series 2 cars, the switch panel can simply be levered from its location in the centre console.
5 If one switch is to be renewed, remove the control button from it and then extract the three screws which secure the console panel to the console.
6 Remove the four screws which secure the switch carrier plate to the console panel and move the panel to one side.
7 Extract the two screws and washers which secure the switch to the carrier plate, disconnect the leads and remove the switch.
8 Refitting a new switch is a reversal of the removal operations but make sure that the leads are correctly connected to the switch terminals.

Rear passenger's control switches

9 Remove the armrest from the door interior panel.
10 Disconnect the leads from the switch, identifying them so that they can be correctly refitted.
11 Remove the switch escutcheon plate and detach the switch from the armrest. On Series 2 cars, the switch panel is located below the heater air outlet. Prise the switch from its location.
12 Refitting is a reversal of removal.

Front window motors

13 To remove a front window motor, first disconnect the lead from the battery negative terminal.
14 Remove the door interior panel and the armrest as described in Chapter 12.
15 Disconnect the leads from the motor by separating the plug and socket connection.
16 Extract the two setscrews and remove the gearbox which controls the swivelling quarterlight ventilator.
17 Remove the upper bolt which secures the glass channel to the door

inner panel.

18 Remove the four setscrews and remove the window regulator mechanism from the door panel. Slide the mechanism towards the hinged edge of the door in order to clear the regulator arm roller from the channel. Now lift the regulator arm so that it passes on the outer side of the glass channel.

19 Withdraw the assembly through the aperture in the door interior panel.

20 The motor can be separated from the regulator after removing the three securing screws but on Series 2 cars do not let the spring

disengage suddenly as this could cause damage or injury.

21 Refitting is a reversal of removal.

Rear window motors

22 Remove the door interior panel and the armrest, as described in Chapter 12.

23 Disconnect the lead from the battery negative terminal.

24 Disconnect the leads from the window motor by separating the plug and socket.

25 Remove the four setscrews and detach the regulator mechanism from the door panel.

26 Adjust the position of the window glass until the regulator arm can be removed from the channel. Withdraw the regulator through the aperture in the door. It may be necessary to remove the door glass in some cases to facilitate withdrawal of the regulator, in this case refer to Chapter 12.

27 Separate the motor from the regulator by unscrewing the three setscrews.

28 Refitting is a reversal of removal.

Relay control box

29 The relay control box is located behind the left-hand front kick panel on early cars or on later cars (including Series 2) under the centre console.

30 To remove the relay, first disconnect the lead from the battery negative terminal and then remove the kick panel or console according to type.

31 The relay is held onto its mounting by two screws. Always identify the connecting cables before removing them from the control box terminals so that they can be reconnected correctly.

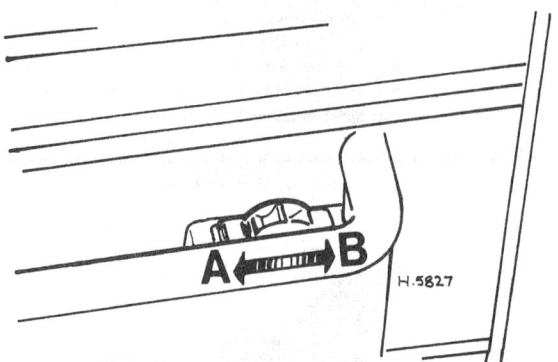

Fig. 10.70. Passenger's electrically-operated window control (Sec. 45)

A Lower   B Raise

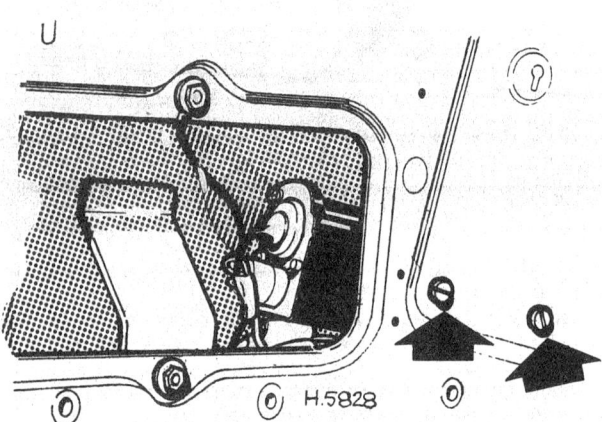

Fig. 10.71. A front window operating motor (Sec. 45)

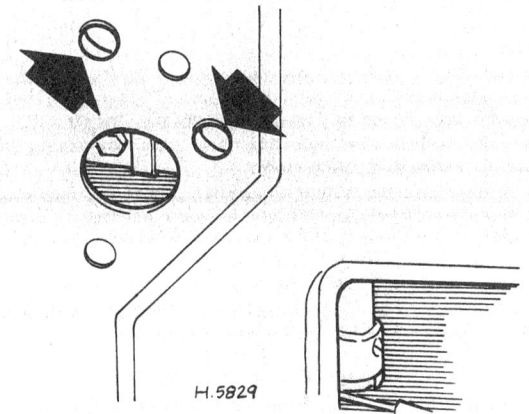

Fig. 10.72. A rear window operating motor (Sec. 45)

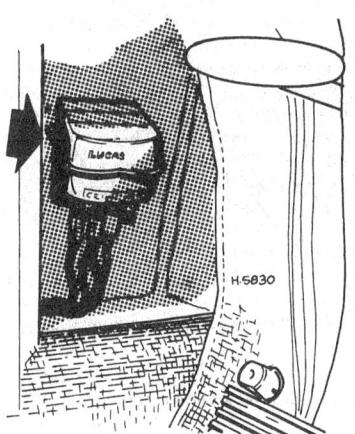

Fig. 10.73. Window lift relay (early cars) (Sec. 45)

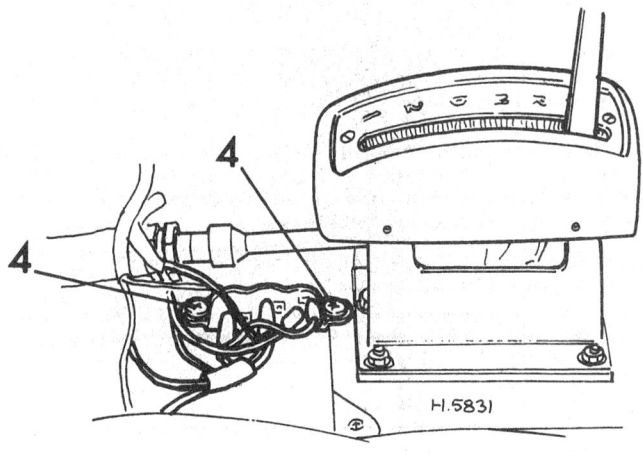

Fig. 10.74. Window lift relay (Series 2) (Sec. 45)

4 Relay securing screws

46 Solenoid-operated door locking system

1   Series 2 models are equipped with this system, the control switch for which is mounted on the centre console below the window lift switches.
2   Access to the switch can be gained after prising out the window lift switch panel and removing the console escutcheon (3 screws).
3   A door lock solenoid can be removed if the window is fully closed, the battery disconnected and the door interior trim withdrawn.
4   The solenoid is secured by two setscrews and its operating piston is hooked to the door lock pushrod.
5   The system circuit breakers are located above the fuse block on the driver's side of the car. For access, remove the fascia crash roll and driver's side under scuttle casing (Chapter 12, Section 51).
6   The door lock solenoid relays are accessible after carrying out the following operations.
7   Disconnect the battery and then push the left-hand front seat fully forward. Remove the rear seat cushion.
8   Prise the carpet and insulating material away from the rear of the transmission tunnel and the front of the box section which supports the rear seat cushion (4 in Fig. 10.78).
9   Support the relays (1 and 2) with the hand through the hole in the front crossmember while the relay securing screws are removed (6). Withdraw the relays through the hole (7) in the crossmember and disconnect the leads (8) as necessary.
10   Refitting of all components is a reversal of removal.

47 Instrument panel lighting switch (Series 2 cars) - removal and refitting

1   To remove this switch, disconnect the battery and then remove the two screws which secure the panel to which the switch is mounted.
2   Depress the spring loaded plunger and pull off the control knob.
3   Unscrew the switch retaining ring, remove the heat shield from under the locknut.
4   Disconnect the leads from the switch terminals and withdraw the switch.
5   Refitting is a reversal of removal.

48 Master lighting switch (Series 2 cars) - removal and refitting

1   Disconnect the battery.
2   Remove the fascia side panel from the driver's side.
3   Depress the spring loaded plunger and pull the control knob from the switch.
4   Unscrew the switch retaining bezel and then remove the switch shroud.
5   Push the switch through the mounting plate and disconnect the plug from the rear of the switch.
6   Refitting is a reversal of removal.

Fig. 10.75. Location of door locking switch on Series 2 cars (Sec. 46)

2   *Window lift switch panel*   5   *Door locking switch*
3   *Console escutcheon*

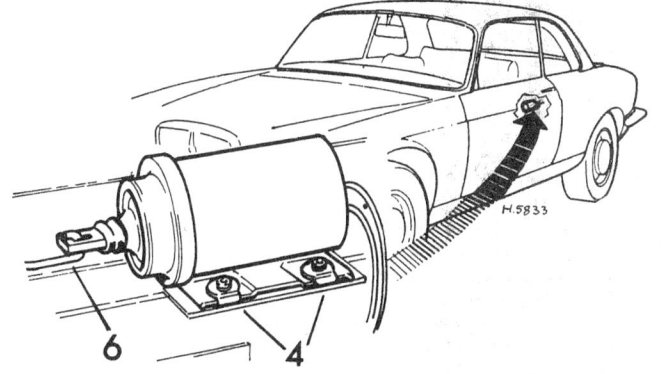

Fig. 10.76. Location of door lock solenoid (Sec. 46)

4   *Securing screws*   6   *Door lock push-rod connecting hook*

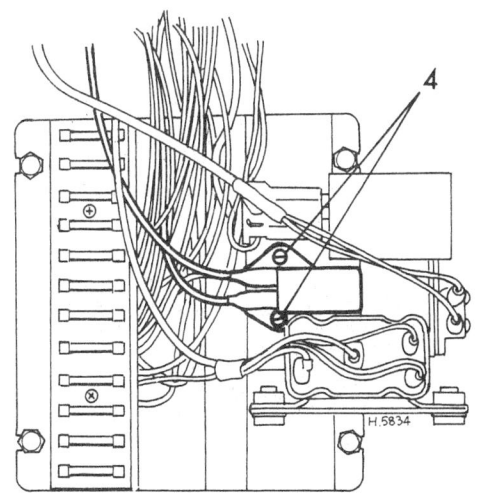

Fig. 10.77. Location of circuit breakers on Series 2 cars (Sec. 46)

4   *Breaker securing screws*

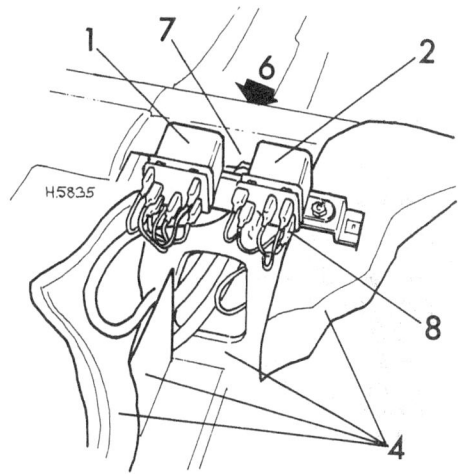

Fig. 10.78. Door lock solenoid relays (Sec. 46)

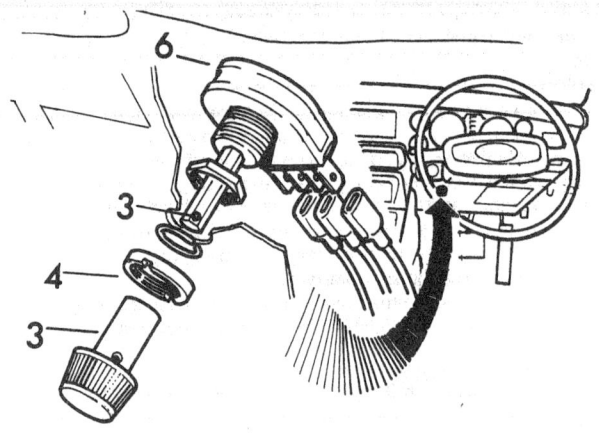

Fig. 10.79. Instrument panel lighting rheostat (Sec. 47)

3   Knob and spring-loaded plunger   4   Ring
                                      6   Rheostat casing

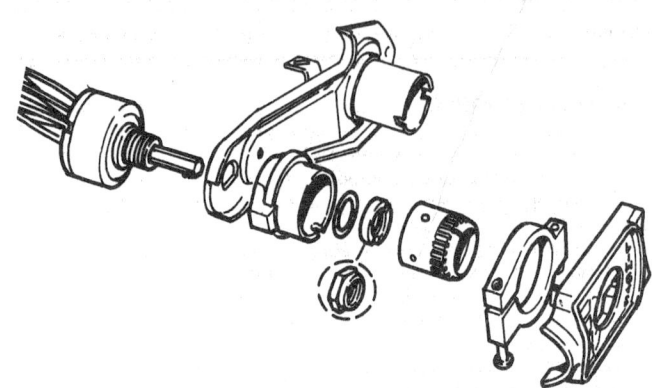

Fig. 10.80. Exploded view of master lighting switch (Sec. 48)

49 Door pillar switch - removal and refitting

1   Disconnect the battery.
2   Lever the switch from the door pillar using a sharp screwdriver.
3   Disconnect the electrical lead from the back of the switch and tape it to prevent it falling into the cavity of the door pillar.
4   Corrosion is often a problem with these switches and it is a good idea to smear the switch plunger with petroleum jelly before installing it.
5   Refitting is a reversal of removal.

50 Cigar lighter - removal and refitting

1   Disconnect the battery.
2   Lever out the electric window control switch panel.
3   Withdraw the console trim panel.
4   Press together the sides of the cigar lighter bulb assembly and then remove from the bezel.
5   Disconnect the lead from the cigar lighter.
6   Unscrew the bezel and withdraw the cigar lighter from the console escutcheon.
7   Refitting is a reversal of removal.

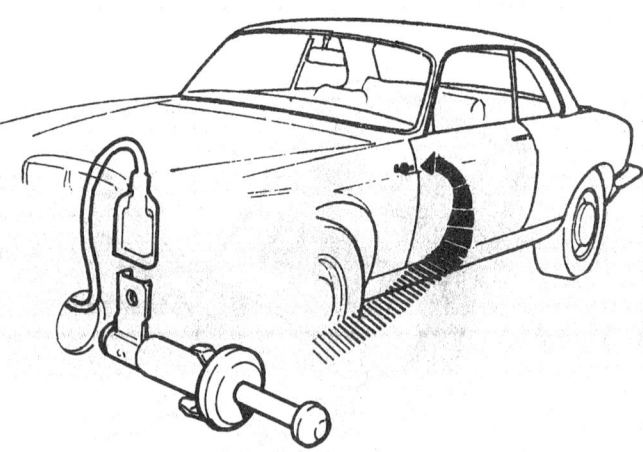

Fig. 10.81. Door pillar switch (Sec. 49)

51 Fault diagnosis – electrical system

Symptom	Reason/s
Starter fails to turn engine	Battery discharged. Battery defective internally. Battery terminal leads loose or earth lead not securely attached to body. Loose or broken connections in starter motor circuit. Starter motor switch or solenoid faulty. Starter motor pinion jammed in mesh with flywheel gear ring. Starter brushes badly worn, sticking, or brush wires loose. Commutator dirty, worn or burnt. Starter motor armature faulty. Field coils earthed.
Starter turns engine very slowly	Battery in discharged condition. Starter brushes badly worn, sticking or brush wires loose. Loose wires in starter motor circuit.
Starter spins but does not turn engine	Starter motor pinion sticking on the screwed sleeve. Pinion or flywheel gear teeth broken or worn. Battery discharged.
Starter motor noisy or excessively rough engagement	Pinion or flywheel gear teeth broken or worn. Starter motor retaining bolts loose.
Battery will not hold charge for more than a few days	Battery defective internally. Electrolyte level too low or electrolyte too weak due to leakage. Plate separators no longer fully effective. Battery plates severely sulphated. Fan belt slipping. Battery terminal connections loose or corroded. Alternator not charging. Short in lighting circuit causing continual battery drain. Regulator unit not working correctly.
Ignition light fails to go out, battery runs flat in a few days	Fan belt loose and slipping or broken. Alternator brushes worn, sticking, broken or dirty. Alternator brush springs weak or broken. Internal fault in alternator. Regulator incorrectly set. Open circuit in wiring of regulator unit.

Failure of individual electrical equipment to function correctly is dealt with alphabetically, item-by-item, under the headings listed below

Electrically-operated windows

Complete system failure	Faulty control box. Blown fuse.
Driver's window normal, remainder inoperative	Sticking switch. Circuit earthed.
Failure of one window only	Faulty switch. Poor electrical connection. Stiff mechanism or sticking window.

Horn

Horn operates all the time	Horn push either earthed or stuck down. Horn cable to horn push earthed.
Horn fails to operate	Blown fuse or faulty relay. Cable or cable connection loose, broken or disconnected. Horn has an internal fault.
Horn emits intermittent or unsatisfactory noise	Cable connections loose. Horn incorrectly adjusted.

Symptom	Reason/s
Lights	
Lights do not come on	Blown fuse.
	Faulty relay.
	If engine not running, battery discharged.
	Wire connections loose, disconnected or broken.
	Light switch shorting or otherwise faulty.
Lights come on but fade out	If engine not running battery discharged.
	Light bulb filament burnt out or bulbs or sealed beam units broken.
	Wire connections loose, disconnected or broken.
	Light switch shorting or otherwise faulty.
Lights give very poor illumination	Lamp glasses dirty.
	Lamps badly out of adjustment.
Lights work erratically - flashing on and off, especially over bumps	Battery terminals or earth connection loose.
	Lights not earthing properly.
	Contacts in light switch faulty.
Wipers	
Wiper motor fails to work	Blown fuse.
	Faulty relay.
	Wire connections loose, disconnected or broken.
	Brushes badly worn.
	Armature worn or faulty.
	Field coils faulty.
Wiper motor works very slowly and takes excessive current	Commutator dirty, greasy or burnt.
	Armature bearings dirty or unaligned.
	Armature badly worn or faulty.
Wiper motor works slowly and takes little current	Brushes badly worn.
	Commutator dirty, greasy or burnt.
	Armature badly worn or faulty.
Wiper motor works but wiper blades remain static	Wiper motor gearbox parts badly worn.
	Stripped splines on wheelbox spindles.

Wiring diagrams commence overleaf

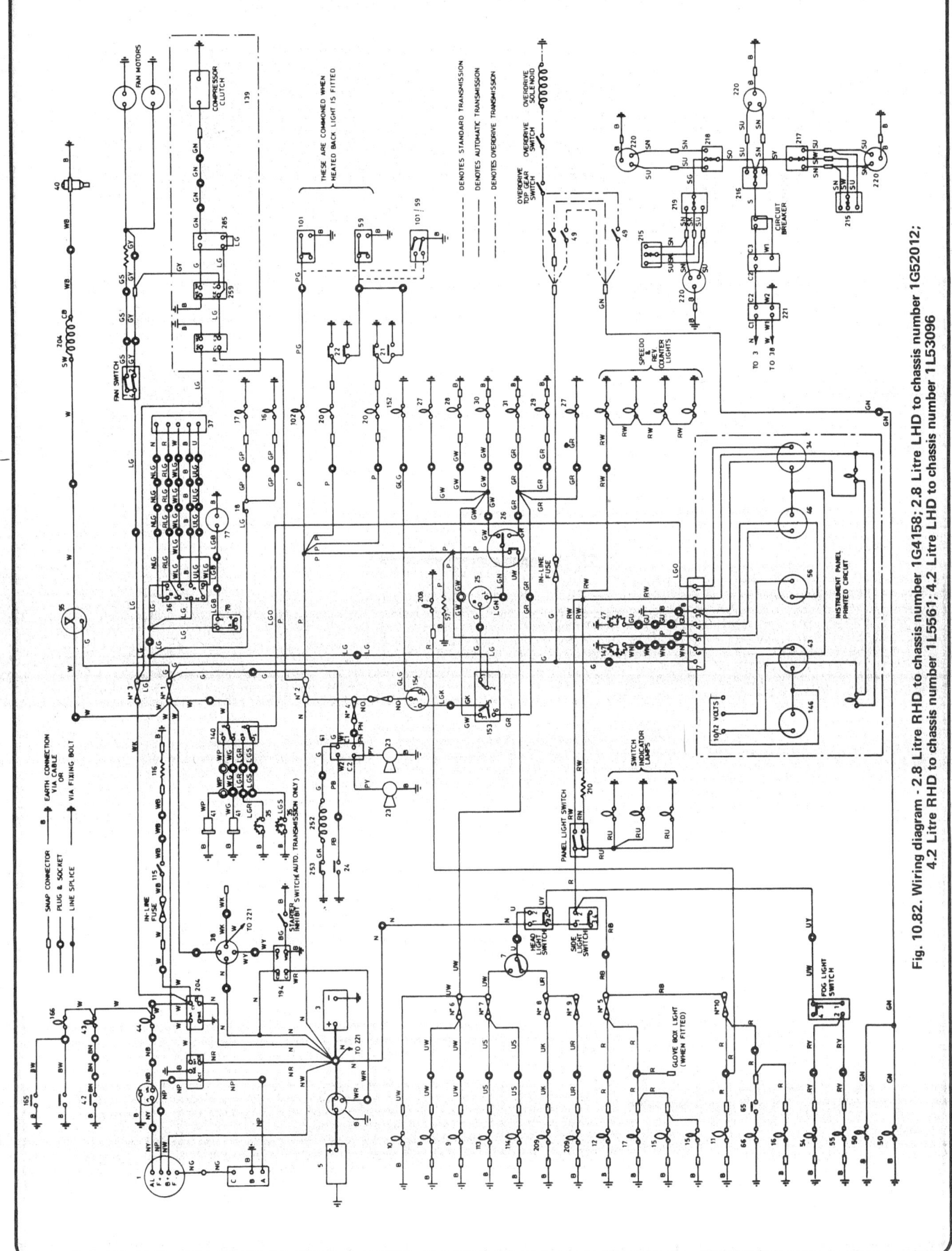

Fig. 10.82. Wiring diagram - 2.8 Litre RHD to chassis number 1G4158; 2.8 Litre LHD to chassis number 1G52012; 4.2 Litre RHD to chassis number 1L5561; 4.2 Litre LHD to chassis number 1L53096

Fig. 10.82. Wiring diagram - 2.8 Litre RHD to chassis number 1G4158; 2.8 Litre LHD to chassis number 1G52012; 4.2 Litre RHD to chassis number 1L5561; 4.2 Litre LHD to chassis number 1L53096

1   Alternator
3   Battery
4   Starter solenoid
5   Starter motor
6   Lighting switch
7   Headlamp dip switch
8   Headlamp outer, RH
9   Headlamp outer, LH
10 Main beam warning lamp
11 Side lamp RH
12 Side lamp LH
14 Panel lamps
15 Number plate lamps
16 Stop and tail lamp RH
17 Stop and tail lamp LH
18 Stop lamp switch
20 Interior lights
21 Door switch RH
22 Door switch LH
23 Horns
24 Horn push
25 Flash unit
26 Direction indicator switch
27 Direction indicator warning lamps
28 Flasher lamp, front, RH
29 Flasher lamp, front, LH
30 Flasher lamp, rear, RH
31 Flasher lamp, rear, LH
34 Fuel gauge
35 Fuel gauge tank unit
36 Windscreen wiper switch
37 Windscreen wiper motor
38 Ignition switch
39 Ignition coil
40 Distributor
41 Fuel pump
42 Oil pressure switch
43 Oil pressure warning lamp or gauge
44 Ignition warning lamp
46 Water temperature gauge
47 Water temperature transmitter

49 Reverse lamp switch
50 Reverse lamps
54 Foglamp RH
55 Foglamp LH
56 Clock
57 Cigar lighter
59 Interior lights switch
60 Radio
61 Horn relay
64 Bi-metal instrument voltage stabiliser
65 Boot light - switch
66 Boot light
67 Line fuse
75 Automatic gearbox safety
77 Electric windscreen washer
78 Electric windscreen washer switch
95 Revolution counter
101 Map light switch
102 Map light
113 Headlamp inner, RH
114 Headlamp inner, LH
115 Rear window demist switch
116 Rear window demist unit
139 Air conditioning/heater circuit (to)
140 Fuel tank changeover switch
146 Battery condition indicator
147 Oil pressure transmitter
150 Rear window demist warning light
152 Hazard warning light
153 Hazard warning switch
154 Hazard warning flasher unit
159 Split brake test switch and warning lamp
160 Split brake differential switch
165 Ballast resistor
166 Handbrake switch
178 Handbrake warning lamp
179 Radiator cooling fan thermostat
180 Radiator cooling fan motor
181 Automatic gearbox kickdown switch
182 Automatic gearbox kickdown solenoid
182 Brake fluid level switch

183 Ignition amplifier OPUS
185 Aerial motor
186 Aerial motor relay
187 Air conditioning relay
194 Starter solenoid/Ballast coil relay
198 Seat belt switch - driver
199 Seat belt switch - passenger
200 Seat switch - passenger
201 Seat belt warning gearbox switch
202 Seat belt warning lamp
204 Ignition protection relay
205 Fuel pump solenoid
206 Battery cooling fan motor
207 Battery cooling fan thermostat
208 Cigar lighter illumination
209 Left and right-hand dipped beam lamps
210 Panel lamps rheostat
212 Choke warning light switch
213 Choke warning light
215 Window lift master switch
216 Window lift switch, front, RH
217 Window lift switch, rear, RH
218 Window lift switch, front, LH
219 Window lift switch, rear, LH
220 Window lift motor
221 Window lift safety relay
231 Headlamp relay
244 Seat switch - driver
245 Sequential seat belt control unit
250 Inertia switch
251 Windscreen wiper relay
252 Emission control valve solenoid
253 Emission control valve switch
254 Unidirectional parking light switch
255 Fibre optics illumination lamp
256 Blocking diode - brake warning
257 Door lock solenoid
258 Door lock solenoid relay
259 Thermal circuit breaker
260 Door lock switch
285 Thermal override switch

Cable colour code

B = Black
D = Dark
G = Green
K = Pink
L = Light

M = Medium
N = Brown
O = Orange
P = Purple
R = Red

S = Slate
U = Blue
W = White
Y = Yellow

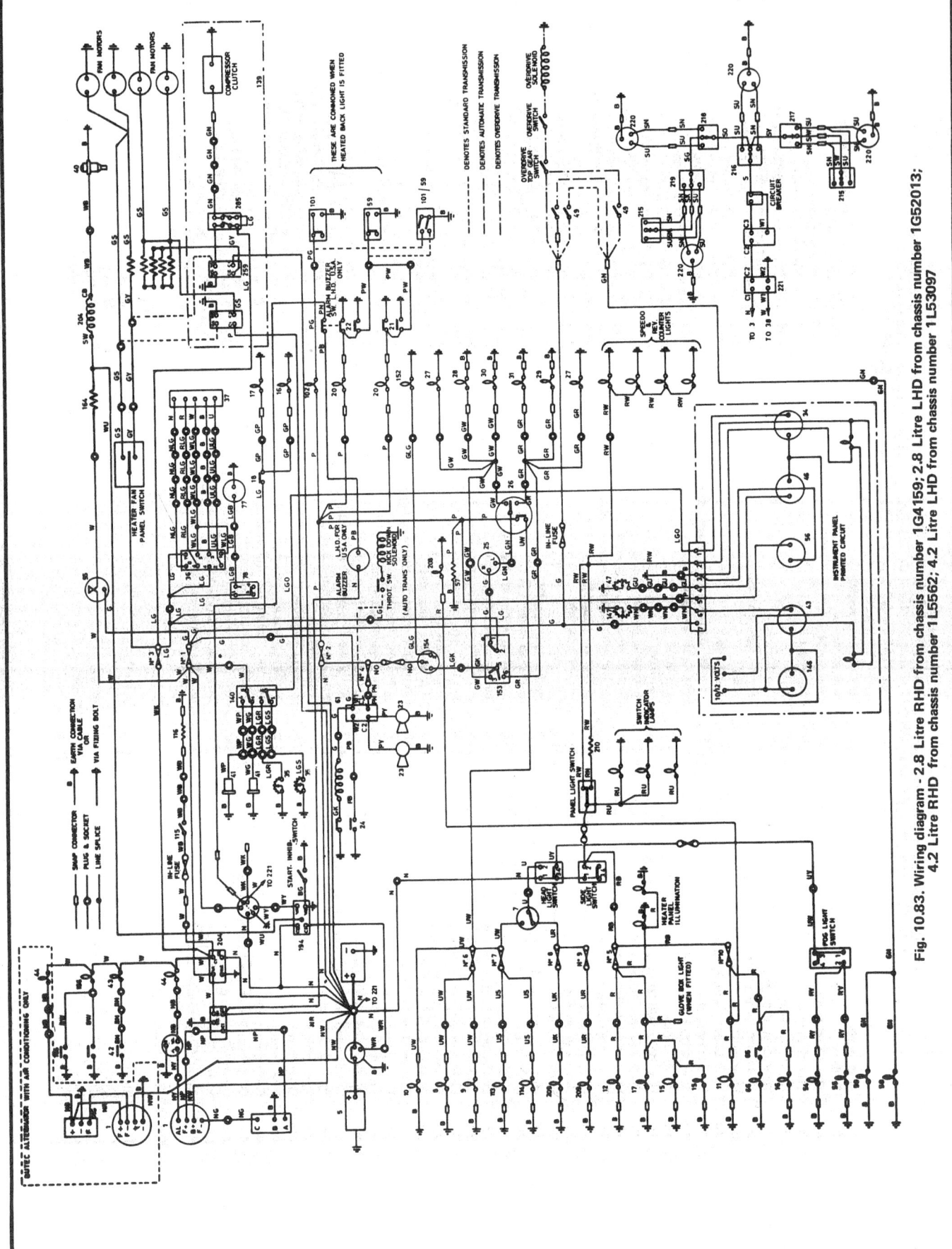

Fig. 10.83. Wiring diagram - 2.8 Litre RHD from chassis number 1G4159; 2.8 Litre LHD from chassis number 1G52013; 4.2 Litre RHD from chassis number 1L5562; 4.2 Litre LHD from chassis number 1L53097

Fig. 10.83. Wiring diagram - 2.8 Litre RHD from chassis number 1G4159; 2.8 Litre LHD from chassis number 1G52013; 4.2 Litre RHD from chassis number 1L5562; 4.2 Litre LHD from chassis number 1L53097

1 Alternator
3 Battery
4 Starter solenoid
5 Starter motor
6 Lighting switch
7 Headlamp dip switch
8 Headlamp outer, RH
9 Headlamp outer, LH
10 Main beam warning lamp
11 Side lamp RH
12 Side lamp LH
14 Panel lamps
15 Number plate lamps
16 Stop and tail lamp RH
17 Stop and tail lamp LH
18 Stop lamp switch
20 Interior lights
21 Door switch RH
22 Door switch LH
23 Horns
24 Horn push
25 Flash unit
26 Direction indicator switch
27 Direction indicator warning lamps
28 Flasher lamp, front, RH
29 Flasher lamp, front, LH
30 Flasher lamp, rear, RH
31 Flasher lamp, rear, LH
34 Fuel gauge
35 Fuel gauge tank unit
36 Windscreen wiper switch
37 Windscreen wiper motor
38 Ignition switch
39 Ignition coil
40 Distributor
41 Fuel pump
42 Oil pressure switch
43 Oil pressure warning lamp or gauge
44 Ignition warning lamp
46 Water temperature gauge
47 Water temperature transmitter

49 Reverse lamp switch
50 Reverse lamps
54 Foglamp RH
55 Foglamp LH
56 Clock
57 Cigar lighter
59 Interior lights switch
60 Radio
61 Horn relay
64 Bi-metal instrument voltage stabiliser
65 Boot light - switch
66 Boot light
67 Line fuse
75 Automatic gearbox safety
77 Electric windscreen washer
78 Electric windscreen washer switch
95 Revolution counter
101 Map light switch
102 Map light
113 Headlamp inner, RH
114 Headlamp inner, LH
115 Rear window demist switch
116 Rear window demist unit
139 Air conditioning/heater circuit (to)
140 Fuel tank changeover switch
146 Battery condition indicator
147 Oil pressure transmitter
150 Rear window demist warning light
152 Hazard warning light
153 Hazard warning switch
154 Hazard warning flasher unit
159 Split brake test switch and warning lamp
160 Split brake differential switch
164 Ballast resistor
165 Handbrake switch
166 Handbrake warning lamp
178 Radiator cooling fan thermostat
179 Radiator cooling fan motor
180 Automatic gearbox kickdown switch
181 Automatic gearbox kickdown solenoid
182 Brake fluid level switch

183 Ignition amplifier OPUS
185 Aerial motor
186 Aerial motor relay
187 Air conditioning relay
194 Starter solenoid/Ballast coil relay
198 Seat belt switch - driver
199 Seat belt switch - passenger
200 Seat switch - passenger
201 Seat belt warning gearbox switch
202 Seat belt warning lamp
204 Ignition protection relay
205 Fuel pump solenoid
206 Battery cooling fan motor
207 Battery cooling fan thermostat
208 Cigar lighter illumination
209 Left and right-hand dipped beam lamps
210 Panel lamps rheostat
212 Choke warning light switch
213 Choke warning light
215 Window lift master switch
216 Window lift switch, front, RH
217 Window lift switch, rear, RH
218 Window lift switch, front, LH
219 Window lift switch, rear, LH
220 Window lift motor
221 Window lift safety relay
231 Headlamp relay
244 Seat switch - driver
245 Sequential seat belt control unit
250 Inertia switch
251 Windscreen wiper relay
252 Emission control valve solenoid
253 Emission control valve switch
254 Unidirectional parking light switch
255 Fibre optics illumination lamp
256 Blocking diode - brake warning
257 Door lock solenoid
258 Door lock solenoid relay
259 Thermal circuit breaker
260 Door lock switch
285 Thermal override switch

Cable colour code

B = Black
D = Dark
G = Green
K = Pink
L = Light

M = Medium
N = Brown
O = Orange
P = Purple
R = Red

S = Slate
U = Blue
W = White
Y = Yellow

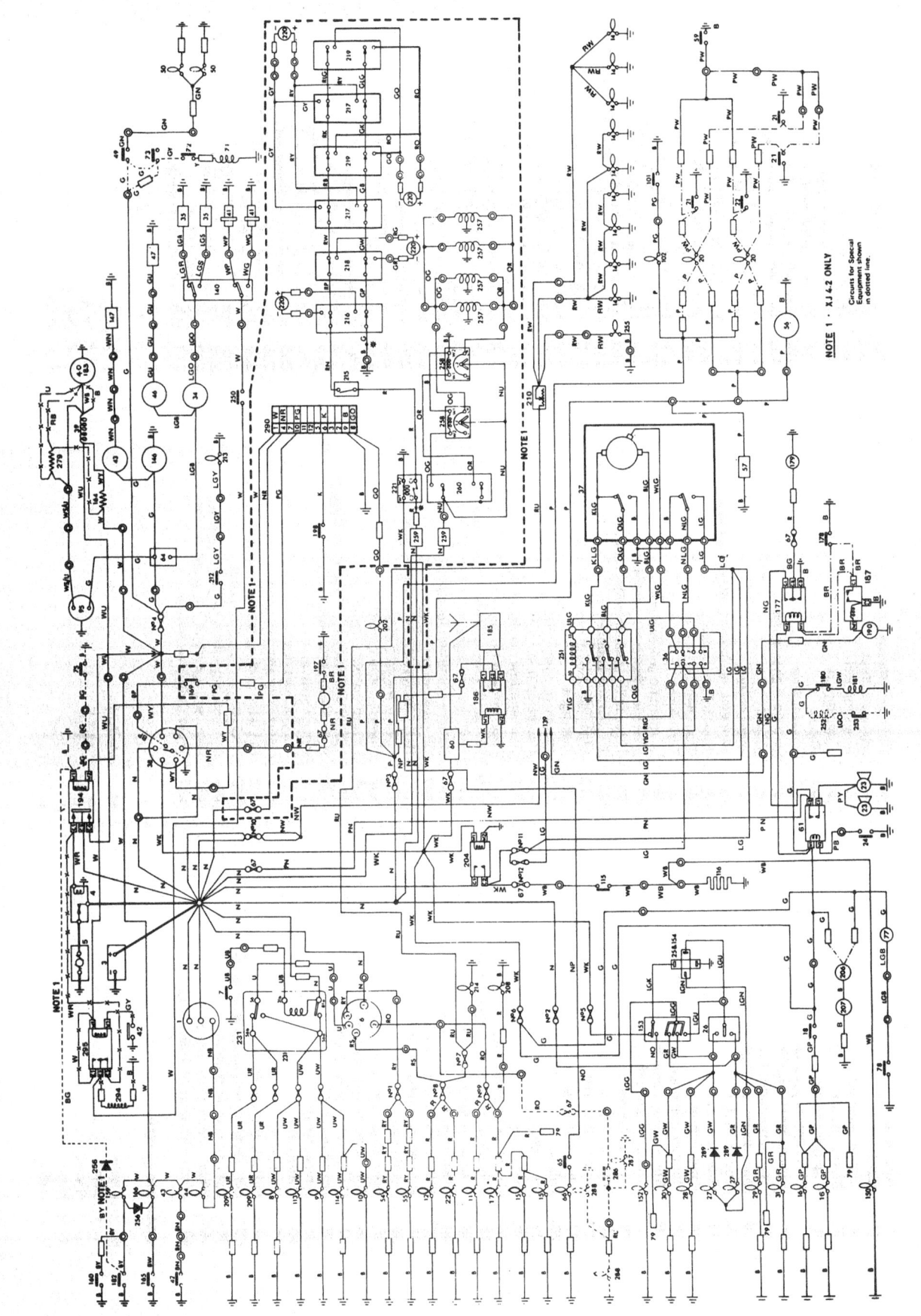

Fig. 10.84. Wiring diagram - Series II models

NOTE 1 - XJ 4.2 ONLY

Circuits for Special Equipment shown in dotted line.

Fig. 10.84. Wiring diagram - Series II models

1	Alternator
3	Battery
4	Starter solenoid
5	Starter motor
6	Lighting switch
7	Headlamp dip switch
8	Headlamp outer, RH
9	Headlamp outer, LH
10	Main beam warning lamp
11	Side lamp RH
12	Side lamp LH
14	Panel lamps
15	Number plate lamps
16	Stop and tail lamp RH
17	Stop and tail lamp LH
18	Stop lamp switch
20	Interior lights
21	Door switch RH
22	Door switch LH
23	Horns
24	Horn push
25	Flash unit
26	Direction indicator switch
27	Direction indicator warning lamps
28	Flasher lamp, front, RH
29	Flasher lamp, front, LH
30	Flasher lamp, rear, RH
31	Flasher lamp, rear, LH
34	Fuel gauge
35	Fuel gauge tank unit
36	Windscreen wiper switch
37	Windscreen wiper motor
38	Ignition switch
39	Ignition coil
40	Distributor
41	Fuel pump
42	Oil pressure switch
43	Oil pressure warning lamp or gauge
44	Ignition warning lamp
46	Water temperature gauge
47	Water temperature transmitter

49	Reverse lamp switch
50	Reverse lamps
54	Foglamp RH
55	Foglamp LH
56	Clock
57	Cigar lighter
59	Interior lights switch
60	Radio
61	Horn relay
64	Bi-metal instrument voltage stabiliser
65	Boot light - switch
66	Boot light
67	Line fuse
75	Automatic gearbox safety
77	Electric windscreen washer
78	Electric windscreen washer switch
95	Revolution counter
101	Map light switch
102	Map light
113	Headlamp inner, RH
114	Headlamp inner, LH
115	Rear window demist switch
116	Rear window demist unit
139	Air conditioning/heater circuit (to)
140	Fuel tank changeover switch
146	Battery condition indicator
147	Oil pressure transmitter
150	Rear window demist warning light
152	Hazard warning light
153	Hazard warning switch
154	Hazard warning flasher unit
159	Split brake test switch and warning lamp
160	Split brake differential switch
164	Ballast resistor
165	Handbrake switch
166	Handbrake warning lamp
178	Radiator cooling fan thermostat
179	Radiator cooling fan motor
180	Automatic gearbox kickdown switch
181	Automatic gearbox kickdown solenoid
182	Brake fluid level switch

183	Ignition amplifier OPUS
185	Aerial motor
186	Aerial motor relay
187	Air conditioning relay
194	Starter solenoid/Ballast coil relay
198	Seat belt switch - driver
199	Seat belt switch - passenger
200	Seat switch - passenger
201	Seat belt warning gearbox switch
202	Seat belt warning lamp
204	Ignition protection relay
205	Fuel pump solenoid
206	Battery cooling fan motor
207	Battery cooling fan thermostat
208	Cigar lighter illumination
209	Left and right-hand dipped beam lamps
210	Panel lamps rheostat
212	Choke warning light switch
213	Choke warning light
215	Window lift master switch
216	Window lift switch, front, RH
217	Window lift switch, rear, RH
218	Window lift switch, front, LH
219	Window lift switch, rear, LH
220	Window lift motor
221	Window lift safety relay
231	Headlamp relay
244	Seat switch - driver
245	Sequential seat belt control unit
250	Inertia switch
251	Windscreen wiper relay
252	Emission control valve solenoid
253	Emission control valve switch
254	Unidirectional parking light switch
255	Fibre optics illumination lamp
256	Blocking diode - brake warning
257	Door lock solenoid
258	Door lock solenoid relay
259	Thermal circuit breaker
260	Door lock switch
285	Thermal override switch

Cable colour code

B	=	Black	M	=	Medium	S	=	Slate
D	=	Dark	N	=	Brown	U	=	Blue
G	=	Green	O	=	Orange	W	=	White
K	=	Pink	P	=	Purple	Y	=	Yellow
L	=	Light	R	=	Red			

Chapter 11 Suspension and steering

For modifications, and information applicable to later models, see Supplement at end of manual

Contents

Specifications

Front suspension

Type	Independent with wishbones, coil springs and telescopic shock absorbers and anti-roll bar
Castor angle	2¼⁰ ± ¼⁰ positive
Camber angle	½⁰ ± ¼⁰ positive
Front wheel toe-in	1/16 to 1/8 in (1.6 to 3.2 mm)
Steering axis inclination	1½⁰

Rear suspension

Type	Independent with wishbone, radius arm and dual coil springs with telescopic shock absorbers
Coil spring free-length	10.59 in (26.9 cm)
Identification colour	Blue/red
Camber angle	¾⁰ ± ¼⁰ negative
Wheel alignment	Parallel ± 1/32 in (0.08 mm)

Steering

Type	Power assisted (except 2.8 litre standard) rack and pinion with collapsible type column
Number of turns lock-to-lock:	
Early models	3.33
Later models	2.87
Turning circle:	
Standard wheelbase:	
Series 1 and 2 models	36 ft (11 m)
Series 3 models	42 ft (12.85 m)
Long wheelbase	38 ft (11.6 m)
Power steering fluid type	ATF to M2C 33G (Duckhams Q-matic)

Wheels and tyres

Roadwheels	Ventilated pressed steel 15 in diameter
Tyres	Radial ply E70VR15SP sport

Pressures (2.8 litre)*:

	Front	Rear
Driver and two passengers, speeds up to 100 mph (160 kph)	24 lb/sq in (1.68 kg/sq cm)	26 lb/sq in (1.8 kg/sq cm)
Full load plus luggage, speeds up to 100 mph (160 kph)	24 lb/sq in (1.68 kg/sq cm)	30 lb/sq in (2.1 kg/sq cm)

Pressures (3.4 and 4.2 litre)*:

Driver and two passengers, speeds up to 100 mph (160 kph)	27 lb/sq in (1.9 kg/sq cm)	26 lb/sq in (1.8 kg/sq cm)
Full load plus luggage, speeds up to 100 mph (160 kph)	27 lb/sq in (1.9 kg/sq cm)	30 lb/sq in (2.1 kg/sq cm)

* Where sustained speeds of 100 mph (160 kph) are maintained, increase the above pressures by (2.8 litres) 4 lb/sq in (0.28 kg/sq cm) and (3.4 and 4.2 litres) by 6 lb/sq in (0.42 kg/sq cm).

Torque wrench settings

	lb ft	Nm
Front suspension		
Stub axle to stub axle carrier	85	115
Steering arm to stub axle carrier	50	68
Disc to hub	35	48
Caliper to stub axle carrier	55	75
Upper swivel balljoint to stub axle carrier	50	68
Lower swivel balljoint to lower wishbone	55	75
Upper wishbone pivot shaft nuts	50	68
Lower wishbone pivot shaft nuts	45	61
Upper swivel balljoint to wishbone	30	41
Upper pivot shaft to crossmember	50	68
Spring pan bolts	30	41
Shock absorber mounting bracket	30	41
Shock absorber upper mounting	30	41
Shock absorber lower mounting	45	61
Buffers to spring pan	18	25
Upper wishbone rebound rubbers	18	25
Anti-roll bar bracket to body	30	41
Anti-roll bar to link and link to wishbone	18	25
Suspension crossmember clamp bolt	30	41
Suspension crossmember front mounting bolt	100	136
Rear mounting to body	25	34
Rear mounting to crossmember	16	22
Rear suspension		
Tie-plate to crossbeam bolts	18	25
Inner pivot bracket to final drive unit	60	82
Final drive to crossbeam	75	102
Caliper mounting bolts	50	68
Wishbone inner pivot shaft nuts	50	68
Wishbone outer pivot shaft nuts	95	129
Driveshaft inner flange bolts	55	75
Driveshaft to hub carrier	55	75
Radius rods to wishbone	65	88
Radius rods to body	40	54
Radius rod safety strap bolts	40	54
Radius rod safety strap to floor panel	30	41
Shock absorber upper mounting	35	48
Shock absorber lower mounting	35	48
Vee mounting to body	30	41
Vee mounting to cross beam	18	25
Bump stop rubber to body	18	25
Steering		
Pinion housing cover plate	18	25
Rack balljoints	50	68
Trackrod-end locknuts	140	190
Trackrod-end balljoint to steering arm	45	61
Steering gear mounting bolts	18	25
Universal joint pinch bolts	18	25
Steering wheel to shaft	28	38
Steering column to lower bracket	18	25
Lower column to body	7	10
Column to upper bracket	18	25
Fluid pipe adaptor on rack housing	50	68
Wheels		
Roadwheel nuts	45	61

1 General description

The front suspension assembly comprises a pressed steel crossmember to which is attached the steering mechanism and the upper and lower suspension wishbones.

The front suspension incorporates coil springs, hydraulic telescopic shock absorbers and an anti-roll bar fitted between the two lower wishbones. Series 2 cars have gas-pressurised hydraulic shock absorbers.

The rear suspension assembly also comprises a pressed steel crossmember, rubber mounted to the body and located by radius arms. The open driveshafts are located in the transverse plane by two links. The suspension incorporates four coil springs which enclose hydraulic telescopic shock absorbers. Series 2 cars have gas-filled shock absorbers.

The steering gear is of rack and pinion type with power assistance on all models except earlier Standard Jaguar 2.8 versions on which power steering was optionally available only. The steering column is of collapsible type incorporating shear plugs and universal joints.

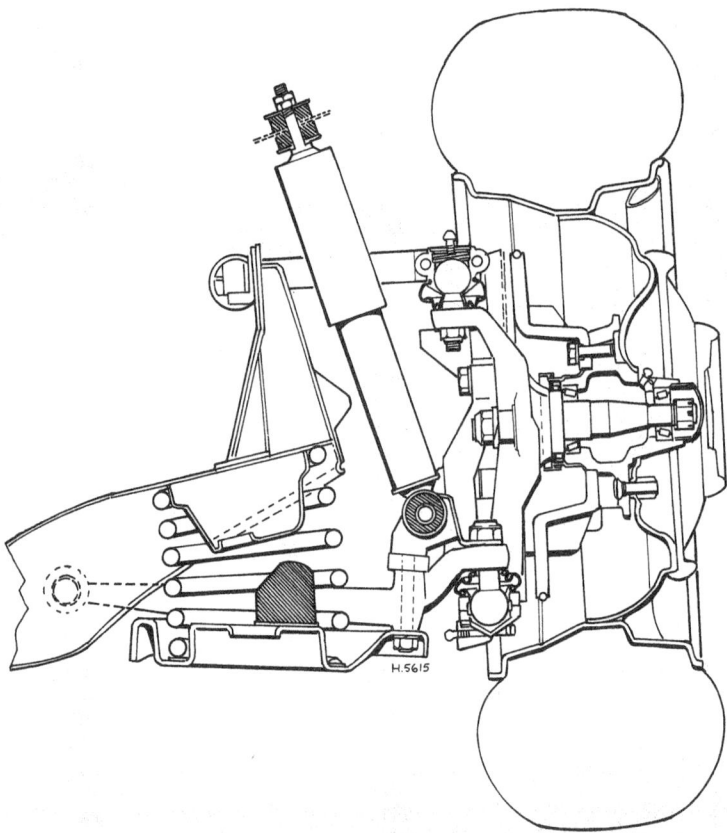

Fig. 11.1. Sectional view of one side of the front suspension

2 Maintenance and inspection

1 At the intervals specified in 'Routine Maintenance' at the beginning of this manual, apply grease to the four top and bottom swivel balljoints of the front suspension. When sufficient grease has been injected, a small nylon plug on the top of the balljoint will lift (photos).
2 Remove the hub caps from the front roadwheels and apply the grease gun to the exposed nipple. A bleed hole is provided to indicate when sufficient grease has been injected (photo).
3 Check and adjust the front hub bearings (Section 5) and the front wheel alignment (Section 31).
4 Grease the inner and outer pivot bearings of the rear suspension. Remove the rear hub grease plug and fill (but do not pressurise) with grease (photos).
5 Check the reservoir oil level in the steering pump and lubricate sparingly the rack and pinion assembly using the nipple provided (photos).
6 Give four or five strokes of the grease gun to the trackrod-end grease nipple (photo).
7 Check the security of all suspension and steering nuts and bolts, examine rubber dust excluders and gaiters for splits or cuts and renew as necessary. Check steering linkage and balljoints for wear and adjust or renew as described in this Chapter.

3 Front shock absorbers - removal, testing and refitting

1 The shock absorbers should be removed and tested whenever (i) the cornering or roadholding characteristics of the car appear to have deteriorated, (ii) there is evidence of oil on the shock absorber casing or at 30,000 mile (48,000 km) intervals.
2 To remove a shock absorber, disconnect the upper mounting nuts and cushions which are accessible within the engine compartment.

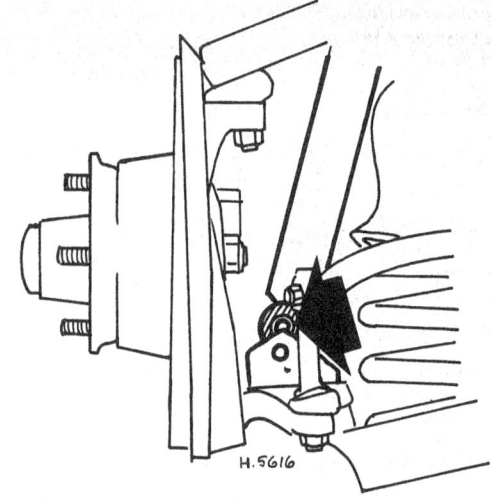

Fig. 11.2. Front shock absorber lower mounting disconnected (Sec. 3)

3 Unscrew and remove, the self-locking nut from the lower mounting and withdraw the bolt.
4 Compress the shock absorber and remove it from the car.
5 Grip the shock absorber lower mounting in the jaws of a vice so that the shock absorber is held vertically. Now fully extend and contract the unit ten or twelve times. If there is any lack of resistance in either direction or seizure, then the unit (which is sealed) must be renewed. Never attempt to dismantle a shock absorber, particularly the gas-pressurised type used on Series 2 cars.
6 Refitting the shock absorber is a reversal of removal but if the original unit is being installed, check the rubber bushes and cushions for deterioration and renew, if necessary.

2.1A Front suspension upper balljoint grease nipple

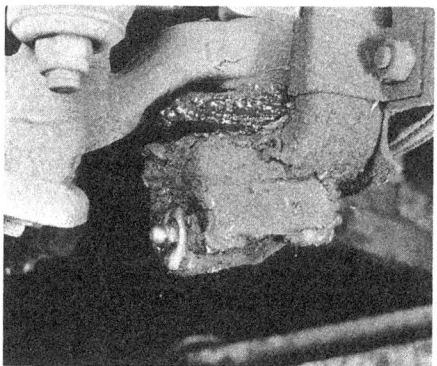

2.1B Front suspension lower balljoint grease nipple

2.2 Front hub grease nipple

2.4A Rear suspension inner pivot grease nipple

2.4B Rear suspension outer pivot grease nipple

2.4C Rear hub grease plug hole

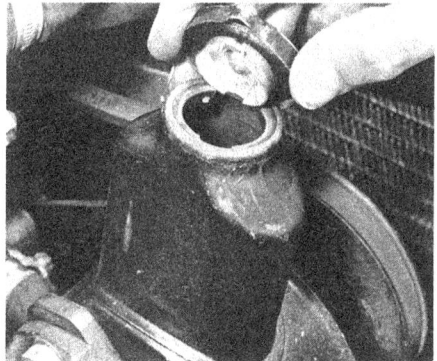

2.5A Power steering reservoir

2.5B Steering rack grease nipple

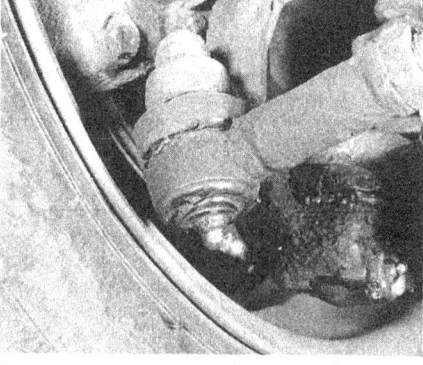

2.6 Track rod end grease nipple

4 Anti-roll bar - removal and refitting

1   Place the car over a pit or raise and support it securely on stands placed under its front end.

2   Remove the two self-locking nuts which secure the anti-roll bar link to the bracket on the front suspension lower wishbone.

3   Remove the four setscrews which secure the keeper plates to the front crossmember. Lift the anti-roll bar away. On some models it will be necessary to disconnect one tie-rod balljoint.

4   The link arm bush can be renewed by pressing it out of the link arm eye. The rubber support bushes are split to enable them to be removed easily. Their splits should face the rear of the car.

5   Refitting is a reversal of removal but do not fully tighten the nuts and setscrews until the weight of the car has been lowered onto the roadwheels.

5 Front hub - overhaul and adjustment

Note: *New oil seals for the front hub must be soaked in clean engine oil for at least 12 hours prior to fitting.*

1   Apply the handbrake fully, jack-up the front of the car and remove the front roadwheel.

2   Remove the front disc caliper (see Chapter 9).

3   Prise off the dust cap from the end of the hub and extract the split pin from the castellated nut.

4   Unscrew and remove the castellated nut and thrust washer and pull the hub assembly from the stub axle.

5   Prise out the oil seal and withdraw the inner races of the tapered roller bearings. The outer tracks can be drifted from the hub if new bearings are to be fitted.

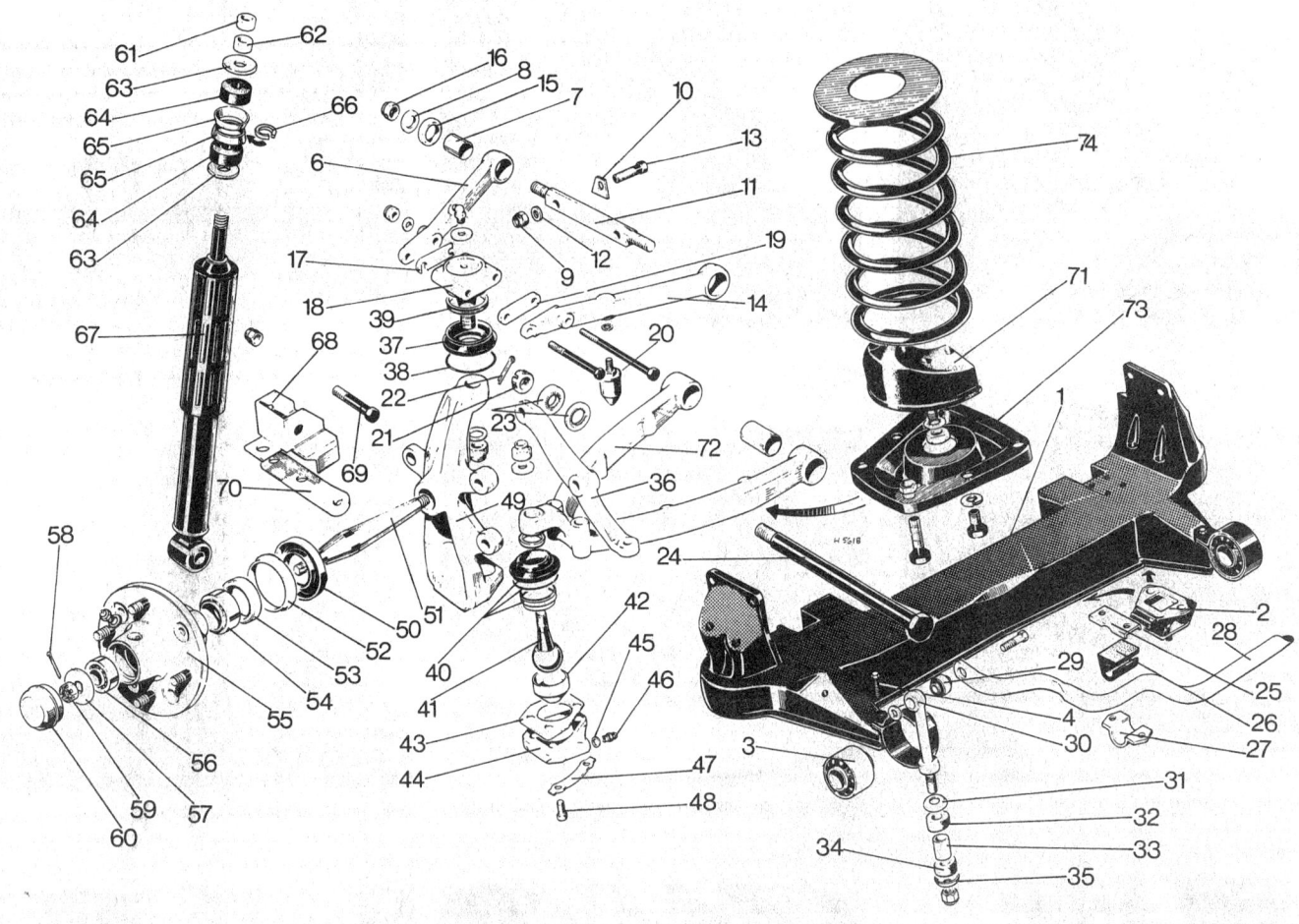

Fig. 11.3. Exploded view of the front suspension

1 Crossmember	20 Buffer	39 Insert	58 Split pin
2 Flexible mounting	21 Castellated nut	40 Spigot	59 Castellated nut
3 Flexible bush	22 Split pin	41 Ballpin	60 End cap
4 Setscrew	23 Washer	42 Ball socket	61 Locknut
6 Upper wishbone arm	24 Pivot shaft	43 Shims	62 Nut
7 Bush	25 Keeper plate	44 Cap	63 Washer
8 Washer	26 Flexible bush	45 Washer	64 Cushion
9 Self-locking nut	27 Clamp	46 Nipple	65 Cup washers
10 Shim (camber adjusting)	28 Anti-roll bar	47 Lockplate	66 Spacer
11 Pivot shaft	29 Flexible bush	48 Bolt	67 Shock absorber
12 Washer	30 Link	49 Stub axle carrier	68 Bracket
13 Bolt	31 Washer	50 Water deflector	69 Bolt
14 Upper wishbone arm	32 Cushion	51 Stub axle	70 Bracket
15 Washer	33 Distance piece	52 Oil seal	71 Bump stop
16 Self-locking nut	34 Cushion	53 Water deflector	72 Lower wishbone
17 Shim (castor adjusting)	35 Washer	54 Inner bearing	73 Spring pan
18 Upper balljoint	36 Steering arm	55 Front hub	74 Spring
19 Distance piece	37 Dust excluder	56 Outer bearing	
	38 Retaining ring	57 'D' washer	

6 If the original bearings are being refitted, clean the races and dry
them.

7 Apply grease to the bearing racks and races, install them to the hub
and fit a new oil seal.

8 Refit the hub to the stub axle and screw on the castellated nut with
its thrust washer finger-tight.

9 Tighten the nut until while turning the hub at the same time, its
rotation is felt to be slightly restricted. Unscrew the nut between
one and two flats and insert a new split pin.

10 The correct endfloat of a front hub bearing is between 0.002 and
0.006 in (0.05 and 0.15 mm) which should ideally be checked on a
dial gauge.

11 Apply grease to the hub grease nipple, as described in Section 2,
refit the dust cap, install the caliper and bleed the front hydraulic

circuit.

12 Refit the roadwheel and lower the car to the ground.

13 Later models have tapered roller bearings and oil seals without water
deflectors.

6 Front coil spring - removal and refitting

1 A coil spring compressor will be needed for this operation. A
suitable tool can be made up from a length of rod suitably threaded
using nuts and large washers or crosspieces.

2 With the coil spring compressed, remove the six setscrews and
lockwashers which secure the seat pan to the lower wishbone.

3 Slowly release the spring compressor until the tension of the coil

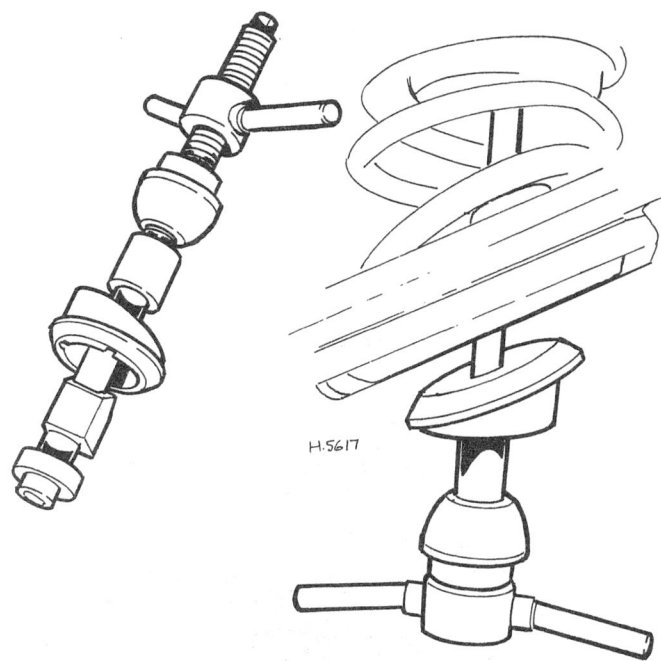

Fig. 11.4. Typical coil spring compressor (Sec. 6)

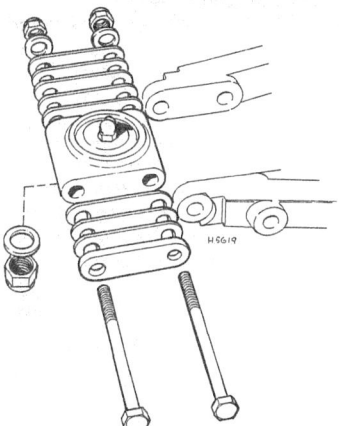

Fig. 11.5. Front suspension upper swivel balljoint and castor control shims (Sec. 8)

spring is relieved. Remove the compressor, spring and seat pan. On some models, packing pieces may be found on top of the spring or in the spring pan. These are used to adjust side-to-side riding height. To check the riding height, measure between the centres of the outer headlamps and the ground. The two dimensions should be equal at 24.5/8 in (611 mm). If necessary vary the packing pieces. The addition or removal of a packing piece will vary the riding height by 5/16 in (7.93 mm).
4   Refitting is a reversal of removal but align the seat pan holes with the tapped holes in the lower wishbone by using pilot studs. Withdraw these once the spring is installed.

7   Stub axle carrier - removal and refitting

1   Raise the front of the car by placing a jack under the lower wishbone. Remove the roadwheel.
2   Remove the brake caliper (Chapter 9).
3   Remove the hub/disc assembly (Section 5).
4   Remove the self-locking nut which secures the upper balljoint to the stub axle carrier.
5   Remove the nut which secures the lower balljoint to the lower wishbone.
6   Using a suitable extractor, separate the upper and lower balljoints and withdraw the stub axle carrier.

7   The stub axle can be driven out of the carrier after removing the securing nut and washer.
8   Refitting is a reversal of removal.

8   Front suspension upper swivel balljoint - removal and refitting

1   The front suspension upper wishbone balljoint is a sealed unit and if worn must be renewed as a unit.
2   To remove the balljoint, jack-up the car under the lower wishbone and remove the roadwheel.
3   Remove the bolts which secure the balljoint to the upper wishbone. Take great care to retain the packing pieces and shims and to record their locations precisely as they control the castor angle.
4   Remove the self-locking nut which secures the balljoint to the stub axle carrier. Use a suitable balljoint separator to disconnect the balljoint from the stub axle carrier.
5   During the foregoing operation, restrict the movement of the stub axle carrier by tying it with a piece of wire to prevent strain on the brake flexible hose.
6   Refitting is a reversal of removal but make sure that the shims are returned to their original positions and that the balljoint securing bolts have their heads nearer the front of the car.

9   Front suspension lower swivel balljoint - overhaul and adjustment

1   Remove the stub axle carrier complete with balljoint as described in Section 7.
2   Remove the retaining ring and withdraw the flexible gaiter from the balljoint.
3   Extract the insert from around the taper pin.
4   Flatten the tab washers and remove the four setscrews which secure the ball pin cap to the stub axle carrier.
5   Remove the cap, shims, ball pin socket and the ball pin.
6   Renew any worn components and reassemble and re-shim in the following way.
7   The vertical clearance of the ball pin in its socket (before lubrication) should be between 0.004 and 0.006 in (0.10 and 0.15 mm). Select shims as necessary to achieve this. Lightly grease the ball pin and socket when the correct shims have been determined. Check that with grease added and the ball cap fully tightened, the torque required to move the ball pin does not exceed 9 lbf in (10 kgf cm).
8   Refit the stub axle carrier complete with the balljoint, as described in Section 7, and then grease the joint as described in Section 2.

10 Front suspension lower wishbone - removal and refitting

1   Remove the coil spring, as described in Section 6.
2   Remove the stub axle carrier, as described in Section 7.
3   Extract the split pin, castellated nut and washer from one end of the lower wishbone pivot shaft. Drift out the shaft.
4   The flexible bushes can be pressed out of the wishbone eyes and new ones installed if they are worn. Use soapy water or a spot of hydraulic fluid to lubricate the bushes when installing them. Check that the bushes project equally on each side of the eye.
5   Reassembly is a reversal of dismantling but do not fully tighten the pivot nut until the weight of the car has been lowered onto the roadwheels

11 Front suspension upper wishbone - removal, dismantling and refitting

1   Raise the car by placing a jack under the lower wishbone and remove the front roadwheel.
2   Remove the self-locking nut and separate the balljoint separator.
3   Tie the stub axle carrier to the suspension crossmember to prevent strain on the flexible brake hose.
4   Remove the two bolts which secure the upper wishbone pivot shaft to the crossmember. Take great care to retain and identify the locations of the shims as these control the camber angle and they must be returned to their original positions.
5   Withdraw the upper wishbone assembly.
6   Remove the self-locking nuts and their plain washers and withdraw the wishbone arms from the pivot shaft.
7   Release the locknuts and unscrew the rebound buffers from the wishbone.
8   The flexible bushes can be renewed after pressing them from the

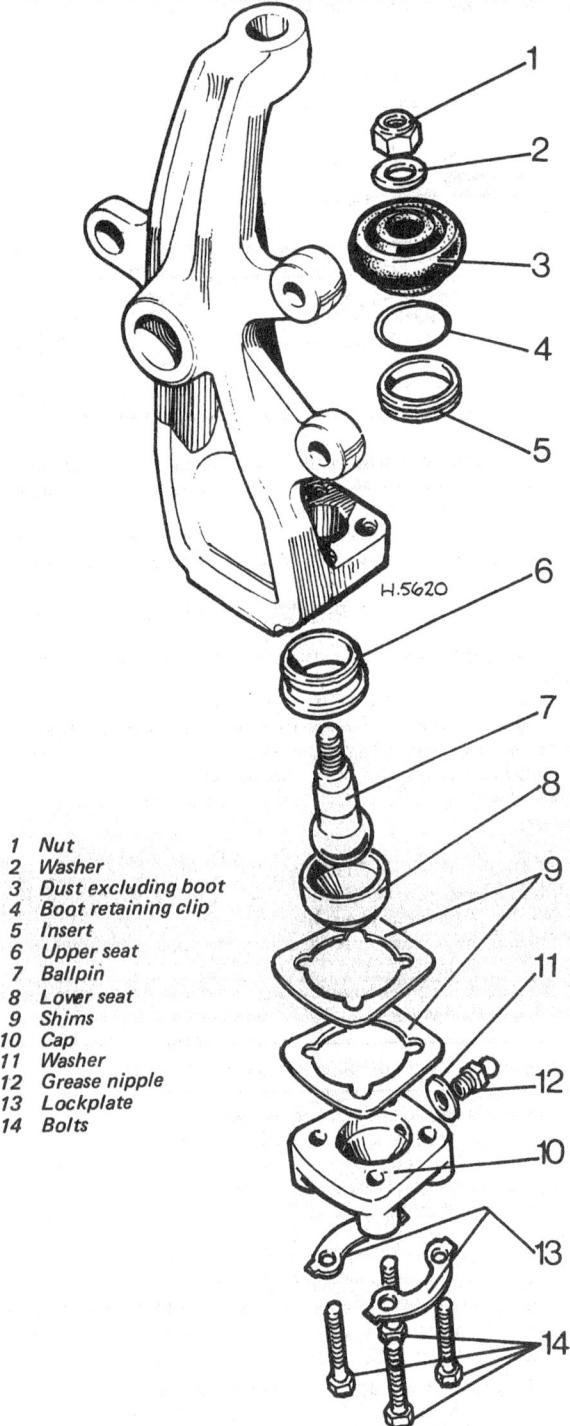

1 Nut
2 Washer
3 Dust excluding boot
4 Boot retaining clip
5 Insert
6 Upper seat
7 Ballpin
8 Lower seat
9 Shims
10 Cap
11 Washer
12 Grease nipple
13 Lockplate
14 Bolts

Fig. 11.6. Exploded view of front suspension lower swivel balljoint (Sec. 9)

wishbone eyes. Use soapy water or a smear of hydraulic brake fluid to facilitate pressing in the new ones.
9 Reassembly and refitting are reversal of removal and dismantling but do not tighten the castellated nuts which hold the wishbone arms to the pivot shaft until the weight of the car has once again been lowered onto the roadwheels.

12 Front suspension assembly - removal and installation

1 If major operations are to be carried out to the front suspension, it may be advantageous to remove the suspension assembly complete.

2 Disconnect the battery.
3 Jack-up the car under the suspension crossmember and remove both front roadwheels.
4 Support the car bodyframe on blocks or axle stands placed adjacent to the front jacking points. Make sure that there is at least 16 in (40 cm) clearance under the front of the car in order to be able to withdraw the suspension assembly. Do not remove the jack from under the front crossmember.
5 With a suitable hoist, take the weight of the engine without distorting the engine flexible mountings.
6 Disconnect the brake pipes at the unions on the wing valances within the engine compartment. Release the locknuts on the brake flexible pipe end fittings and pull the flexible pipes through the holes in the valances so that the pipes are under the wings. Plug all open brake pipes.
7 Disconnect the power steering flexible pipes from the steering unit. Seal the openings.
8 Detach the anti-roll bar mountings from the bodyframe.
9 Disconnect the shock absorber top mountings.
10 Remove the pinch bolt which secures the steering column lower universal joint to the steering pinion shaft. Alternatively, the steering rack may be unbolted and suspended on wires. Retain all mounting components.
11 Disconnect the leads from the horns.
12 Remove the nuts which secure the suspension assembly to the rear mounting rubbers. Note that the bolts are bonded to the rubbers and cannot be separated.
13 Remove the two nuts which secure the engine front mounting brackets to the support rubbers.
14 Remove the two self-locking nuts from the suspension assembly front mountings and drive out the bolts.
15 Lower the jack under the suspension crossmember and withdraw it forward from the car.
   Take great care when separating the steering column lower universal joint. Never strike it to release it from the pinion splines or the steering column shear plugs may be damaged. Prise the universal joint clamp open with a screwdriver to ease its removal.
16 Installation is a reversal of removal but the column and rack pinion will require alignment, as described in Section 26, also bleed the power steering and hydraulic brake circuits. If the suspension assembly mounting bushes are worn they can be renewed without removing the assembly. Always renew bushes in pairs, never one side only.

13 Rear spring and shock absorber - removal and refitting

1 Remove the self-locking nut from the end of the shock absorber lower mounting pivot pin.
2 Support the suspension wishbone with a jack and drive out the pivot pin.
3 Remove the spacer from the front shock absorber.
4 Disconnect the shock absorber upper mounting from the rear crossmember and withdraw the shock absorber/coil spring.
5 The coil spring must now be compressed so that the lower split type retainer can be removed and the spring removed in a downward direction.
6 Test the shock absorber as described in Section 3, paragraph 5.
7 Renew the mounting bushes if the original ones are worn.
8 Refitting is a reversal of removal.

14 Rear hubs - removal, overhaul and refitting

1 The operations are described in Chapter 8, Section 2 in conjunction with the axleshafts.

15 Rear suspension radius arm - removal and refitting

1 Jack-up and support the centre of the rear suspension unit.
2 Cut the locking wire from the radius arm safety strap and bolt.
3 Unscrew the two bolts which secure the safety strap to the body floor.
4 Unscrew the radius arm securing bolt and remove the safety strap.

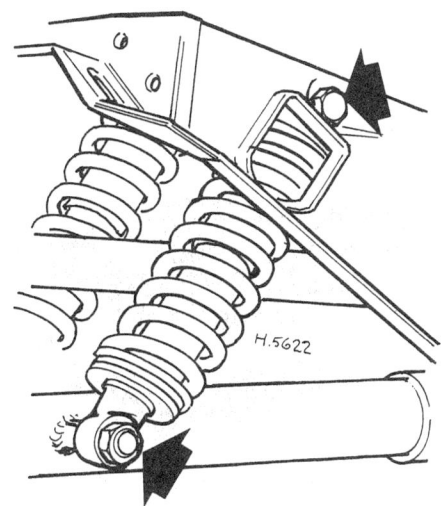

Fig. 11.7. Rear shock absorber mountings (Sec. 13)

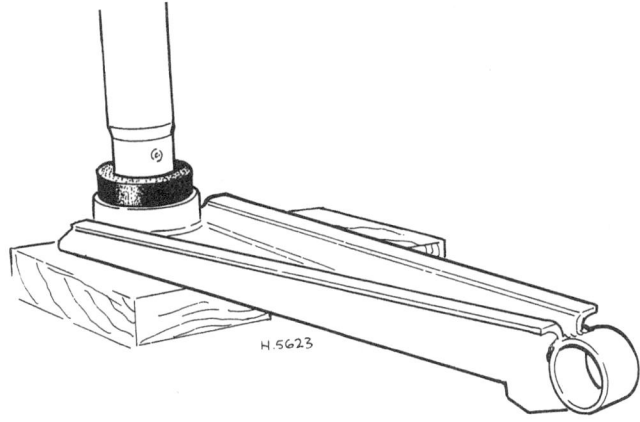

Fig. 11.8. Removing a rear suspension radius arm bush (Sec. 15)

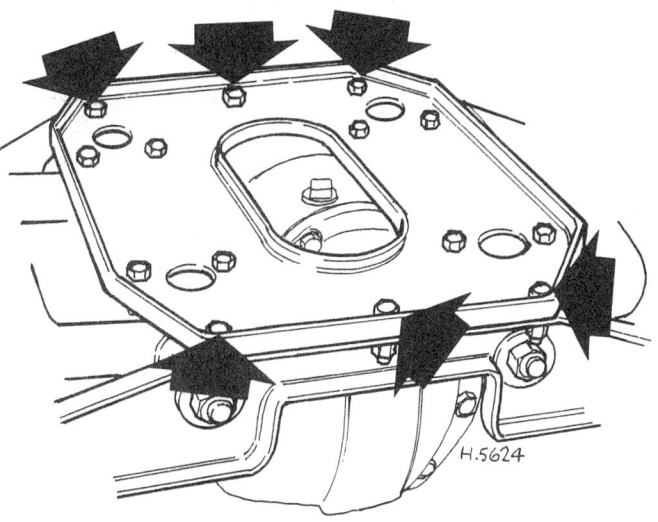

Fig. 11.9. Tie plate to cross beam securing bolts (Sec. 16)

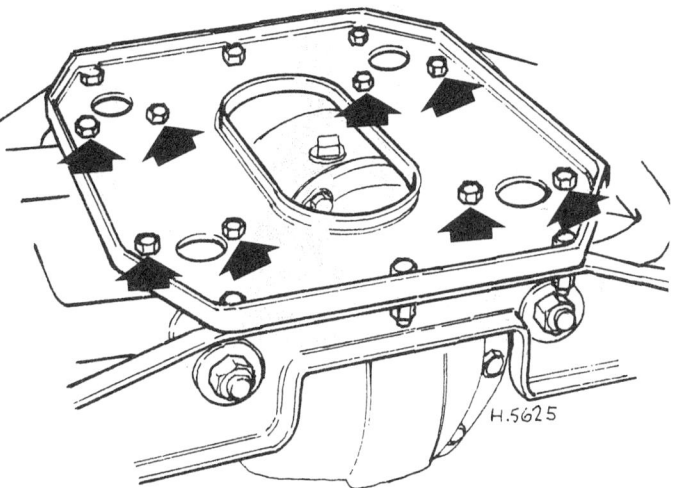

Fig. 11.10. Tie plate to inner pivot mounting bracket bolts (Sec. 16)

5   Withdraw the radius arm from the mounting post on the body.
6   Unscrew the self-locking nut which is nearest the front of the
shock absorber lower pivot pin. Drive the pin far enough to clear the
forward shock absorber and spacer. Extract the spacer, bend back the
tabs of the lockwasher and remove the bolt which secures the radius
arm to the lower wishbone mounting.
7   Remove the radius arm and examine the flexible bushes for
deterioration.
8   If inspection has proved the need for renewal of the flexible bushes
make sure that the larger bush is fitted so that the two holes in it are in
longitudinal alignment with the arm. When installing the smaller bush,
make sure that the metal centre sleeve projects equally on each side
of the bush.
9   It is recommended that a press is used to remove and install the
flexible bushes.
10 Refitting is a reversal of removal but make sure that the radius arm
securing bolts are tightened to the specified torque wrench settings.
Use new locking wire inserted through the hole in the bolt head and
secured round the safety strap.

---

16 Rear suspension wishbone - removal and installation

1   Drain the oil from the final drive unit, remove the rear suspension

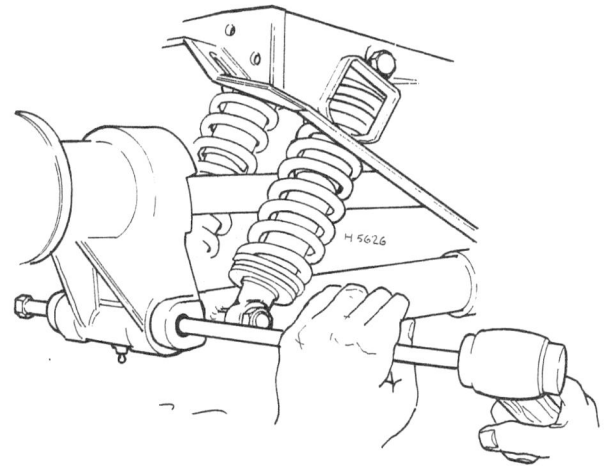

Fig. 11.11. Driving out rear suspension wishbone outer pivot shaft
(Sec. 16)

assembly (Section 19) and then invert it on a bench.
2   Remove the six self-locking nuts and bolts which secure the tie-plate
to the crossbeam.
3   Now remove the eight self-locking nuts and bolts which secure the
tie-plate to the wishbone inner pivot mounting brackets. Remove the
tie-plate.
4   Remove one of the self-locking nuts which secure the hub bearing
assembly pivot shaft to the wishbone and drive out the pivot shaft.

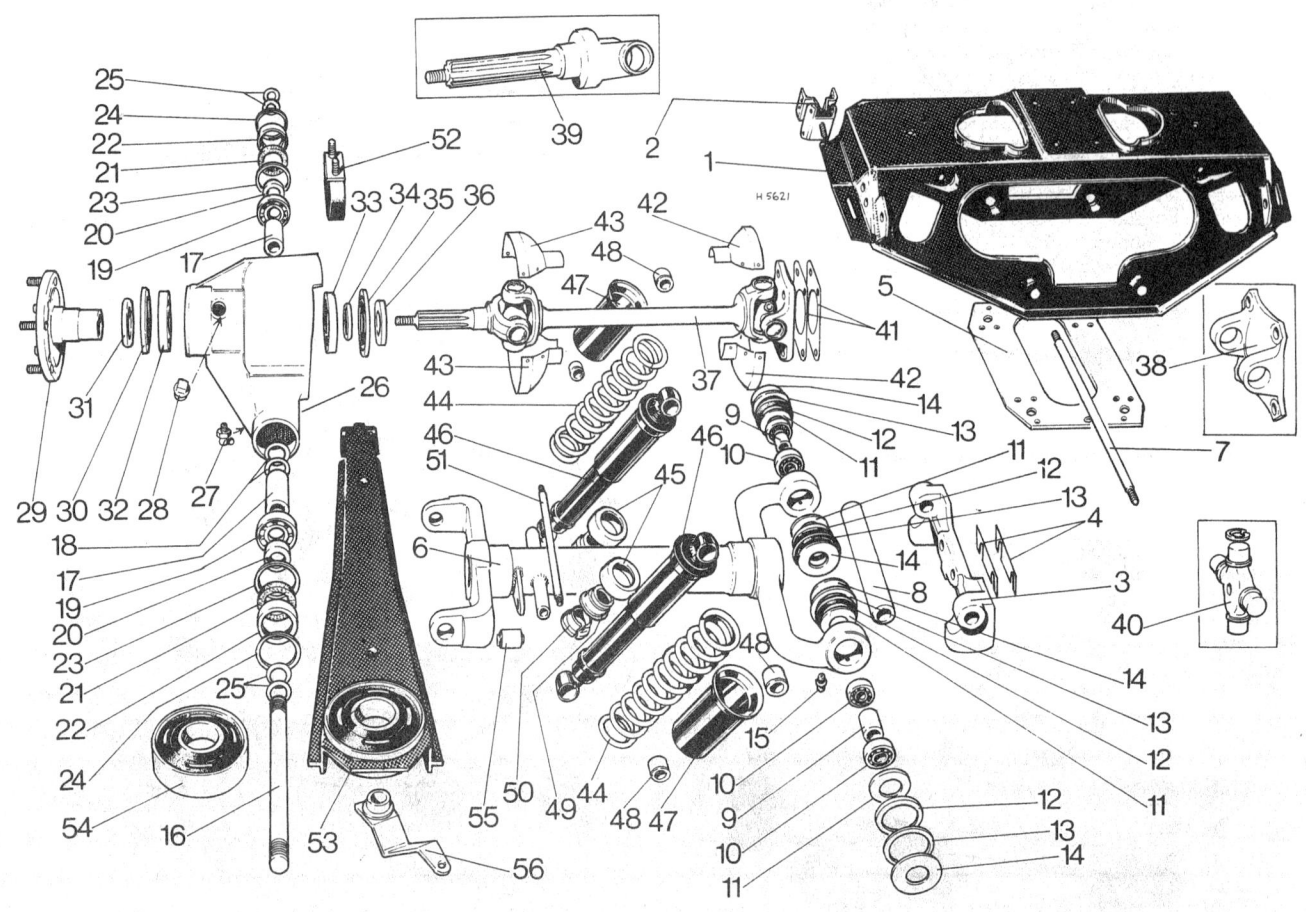

Fig. 11.12. Exploded view of the rear suspension

1 Crossmember	15 Grease nipple	29 Hub	43 Joint cover (outer)
2 Flexible mounting	16 Outer pivot shaft	30 Outer oil seal	44 Coil spring
3 Inner pivot mounting	17 Sleeve	31 Ring	45 Packing ring
4 Shims	18 Shim	32 Outer bearing	46 Shock absorber
5 Bracing plate	19 Bearing	33 Inner bearing	47 Dust shield
6 Wishbone	20 Ring	34 Spacer	48 Flexible bush
7 Inner pivot shaft	21 Oil seal	35 Oil seal	49 Seat
8 Spacer tube	22 Oil seal retainer	36 Ring	50 Retainer
9 Spacer tube	23 Spacer	37 Driveshaft	51 Shock absorber lower
10 Needle bearing	24 Washer	38 Driveshaft flange	mounting shaft
11 Thrust washer	25 Shim	39 Splined yoke	52 Bump stop
12 Seal	26 Hub carrier	40 Universal joint	53 Radius arm
13 Retainer	27 Grease nipple	41 Shim (camber control)	54 Flexible bush
14 Thrust washer	28 Grease retaining cap	42 Joint cover (inner)	55 Flexible bush
			56 Safety strap

5   Separate the hub carrier from the wishbone, noting any shims and their location so that they will be returned to their original positions.

6   The use of a rod as a dummy pivot shaft will keep the shims together. Place a piece of masking tape over each of the oil seals to prevent them being displaced.

7   Remove the self-locking nut, nearest the front of the car, from the pivot shaft which connects the roadsprings and shock absorbers to the wishbone. Tap the pivot shaft to the rear until it clears the front shock absorber and spacer. Retrieve the spacer and then move the shock absorber towards the centre of the suspension assembly.

8   Turn down the locking tab and remove the special bolt which holds the radius arm to the wishbone. Remove the radius arm.

9   Remove the pivot shaft which secures the lower ends of the roadspring/shock absorber assemblies.

10 Drive the inner pivot shaft out of the wishbone and inner pivot mounting bracket.

11 Withdraw the wishbone assembly and collect the four outer thrust washers, inner thrust washers, oil seals and their retainers. Renew the oil seals if they have deteriorated.

12 Remove the two bearing tubes. There is no need to remove the spacer which is located between the inner pivot mounting bracket unless the mounting bracket is being renewed. If it must be removed, tap it out. The needle rollers can be extracted by tapping the cages out of the wishbone and then extracting the needle roller spacer.

13 If the needle rollers have been removed from the larger fork of

the wishbone, press one of the roller cages into position so that the numbers on the cage face outwards. Press in the second cage. Repeat the operations on the opposite side of the wishbone.

14 Insert the bearing tubes, apply grease to the four outer thrust washers, oil seals, retainers and locate them on the wishbone.

15 Offer up the wishbone to the inner pivot mounting bracket so that the radius arm mounting bracket is towards the front of the car. Align the holes and spacers. Insert a rod as a dummy shaft through each side of the crossbeam and wishbone. These rods locate the wishbone, thrust washers, crossbeam and inner pivot mounting bracket and so facilitate installation of the pivot shaft proper. The dummy shaft should be fractionally smaller in diameter than the pivot shaft itself.

16 Tap the pivot shaft into position, having smeared it with grease. As it passes through the crossbeam, the wishbone and the inner pivot mounting bracket, the temporary rods will be displaced from the opposite end. Keep the rods and shaft in contract at all times otherwise a spacer or thrust washer may drop out of position.

17 With the wishbone inner pivot shaft installed, tighten the two self-locking nuts to a torque of 55 lb/ft (75 Nm).

18 Install the eight bolts which secure the tie plate to the inner pivot mounting bracket then refit the six bolts which secure the tie plate to the crossbeam.

19 Refit the radius arm to the wishbone as described in Section 15.

20 Remove the tap which was used to hold the oil seal tracks in position and offer up the wishbone/hub assembly.

21 Again using a rod as a dummy shaft, align the wishbone hub assembly oil seal tracks and spacers. Apply grease to the wishbone outer pivot shaft and gently tap it into position so displacing the dummy shaft.

22 Slide the pivot shaft through the wishbone and hub carrier. Using feeler blades, check the clearance between the hub carrier and the wishbone. Where necessary, install shims between the hub carrier and the wishbone to centralise the hub carrier. Tighten the nuts on the pivot shaft to a torque of 55 lb/ft (75 Nm).

23 Refit the rear suspension assembly.

24 The rear suspension camber angle should be checked after a major overhaul (see Section 32).

25 Refill the final drive unit with specified oil.

26 Lubricate the wishbone grease nipples.

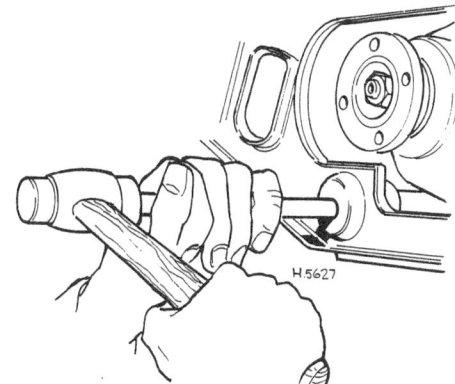

Fig. 11.13. Installing rear suspension wishbone inner pivot shaft (propeller shaft removed for clarity) (Sec. 16)

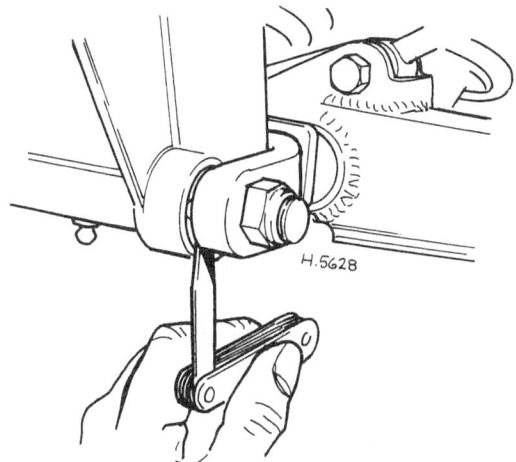

Fig. 11.14. Checking clearance between hub carrier oil seal retainer and wishbone of rear suspension (Sec. 17)

---

17 Rear suspension wishbone outer pivot - dismantling, reassembly and bearing adjustment

1 Support the hub carrier and wishbone securely.

2 Remove one of the self-locking nuts which secure the outer pivot shaft.

3 Drive out the pivot shaft and retain any shims which may be located between the hub carrier and the wishbone.

4 Separate the hub carrier and the wishbone.

5 Remove the oil seal retainer and prise out the oil seals.

6 Remove the inner races of the tapered roller bearings by tapping them out with a drift.

7 Remove the spacers and shims.

8 If new tapered roller bearings have been fitted, it will be necessary to adjust them in the following way.

9 Disconnect the hub from the rear axle halfshaft as described in Chapter 8, Section 2.

10 Refit the inner races for the outer pivot tapered roller bearings. Fit the spacers and a shim pack of known thickness followed by the tapered roller bearings and oil seals.

11 The bearing adjustment is controlled by shims which are located between the two pivot shaft spacer tubes.

12 To calculate the shims required to provide the specified preload of the outer pivot tapered roller bearings, drill a hole in a piece of steel plate and secure the plate in the jaws of a vice. Bolt the pivot shaft to the plate.

13 Slide an oil seal retainer onto the shaft and then install the outer pivot assembly to the shaft but without any oil seals and including an excess of shims between the spacer tubes.

14 Place an inner wishbone fork outer thrust washer onto the fulcrum shaft so that it abuts the oil seal retainer. Fill the remaining space on the shaft with washers and screw on a nut to a torque of 95 lb/ft (132 Nm).

15 Press the hub carrier assembly towards the steel support plate using a rotating motion in order to settle the tapered roller bearings. Maintain a steady hand pressure against the hub carrier and using a

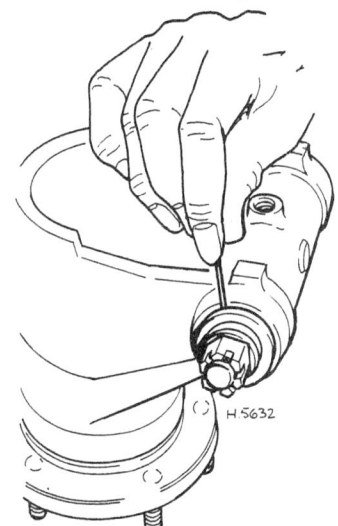

Fig. 11.15. Checking rear suspension wishbone outer pivot tapered bearing endfloat (Sec. 17)

feeler blade, measure the clearance between the large diameter washer and the machined face of the hub carrier.

16 Subtract this measurement from the thickness of the shim pack which was included between the spacer tubes, or subtract the thickness of the shim pack from the clearance measured or the other way round, whichever is the greater.

The result indicates the bearing preload. The specified preload should be between 0.000 to 0.002 in (0.00 to 0.05 mm) and the shim pack should be adjusted as necessary to bring the actual preload into line with that specified.

17 Refit the hub carrier to the axleshaft, install new oil seals (lips inwards) and then fit the pivot shaft into position in the hub carrier.
18 Offer up the hub carrier to the wishbone. Ease the dummy shaft through the wishbone in conjunction with the pivot shaft. Using feeler blades, measure the gap between the oil seal retainer and the wishbone.
19 Install shims as necessary to centralise the hub carrier in the wishbone fork and to prevent the ends of the fork from closing as the pivot shaft nuts are tightened to their specified torque wrench settings.
20 It will be found easier to install the wishbone if a dummy shaft is passed through the hub carrier before offering the wishbone to the carrier.
21 Refitting is otherwise a reversal of removal. Apply grease to the lubrication nipples on completion.

18 Rear suspension wishbone inner pivot mounting bracket - removal and refitting

1   Drain the oil from the final drive unit and remove the rear suspension unit as described in Section 19. Remove the tie-plate as described in Section 16, paragraphs 2 and 3.
2   Remove the self-locking nut from one end of the wishbone inner pivot shaft, drive out the shaft.
3   Withdraw the wishbone forks from between the crossbeam and pivot mounting bracket. Collect the oil seal retainers, oil seals, inner and outer thrust washers and tubes.
4   Cut the lockwire from the two setscrews which secure the inner pivot bracket to the differential unit.
5   Remove the spacer from the mounting bracket.
6   Remove the two setscrews, noting the shims located between the bracket and the differential unit.
7   Remove the wishbone inner pivot mounting bracket.
8   Refitting is a reversal of removal but make sure that the original shims are refitted between the mounting bracket and the differential. If new components have been fitted check the clearance with feeler blades and insert shims as necessary to eliminate this clearance after having passed the pivot shaft through the crossmember and the inner pivot mounting bracket.
9   Tighten the pivot bolt nut to specified torque.
10 Refill the final drive unit.

19 Rear suspension assembly - removal and installation

1   If major operations are to be carried out to the rear suspension, it may be advantageous to remove the suspension assembly complete.
2   Remove the self-tapping screws which secure the exhaust tail pipes to the rear silencers and withdraw the pipes.
3   Release the clamps which secure the rear silencers to the intermediate pipes. Remove the rear exhaust silencers.
4   Release the clamps which secure the intermediate pipes to the front silencers. Withdraw the pipes from the suspension assembly.
5   Remove the locking wire from the radius arm safety straps and securing bolts. Remove the bolts which secure the safety strap to the body floor.

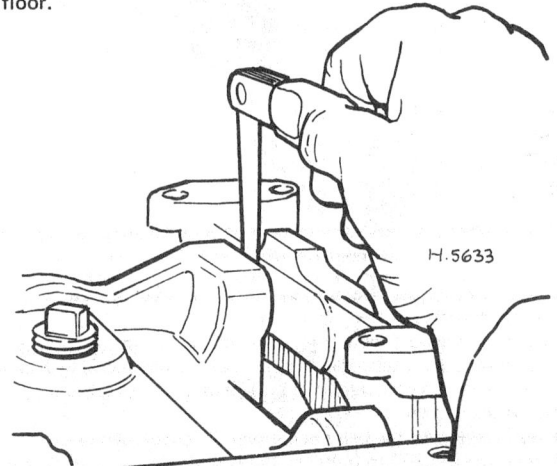

H.5633

Fig. 11.16. Checking gap between rear suspension inner pivot bracket and differential casing (Sec. 18)

6   Remove the radius arm securing bolts and withdraw the safety straps.
7   Withdraw the radius arms from their mounting posts on the body.
8   Place a wooden block (9 x 9 x 1 in/22.8 x 22.8 x 2.54 cm thick) between the rear suspension tie plate and a jack, preferably of trolley type.
9   Now jack-up the rear of the car and position two chassis stands under the bodyframe members just forward of the radius arm mounting posts. Place blocks of wood between the chassis stands and the bodyframe to avoid damage.
10 Remove the rear roadwheels.
11 Disconnect the flexible brake pipe at the support bracket on the body.
12 Disconnect the handbrake cable from the caliper actuating lever which is mounted on the suspension crossbeam. Withdraw the outer cable from the trunnion on the opposite lever.
13 Remove the four bolts which secure the mounting rubbers at the front of the crossbeam to the bodyframe.
14 Remove the nuts and bolts which secure the rear mounting rubbers to the crossbeam.
15 Disconnect the propeller shaft from the differential pinion flange.
16 Lower the rear suspension assembly on the jack and withdraw it from under the car.
17 Installation is a reversal of removal but note the following points:
   Renew any mounting rubbers which have deteriorated.
   Tighten the radius arm to wishbone bolts after the weight of the car has been lowered onto the roadwheels.
   Bleed the brake hydraulic circuit.

20 Trackrod-ends and rack bellows - renewal

1   If wear is found in the trackrod-end balljoints then they must be renewed as sealed assemblies.
2   Unscrew and remove the taper pin nut and separate the balljoint from the steering arm using a suitable extractor or forked wedges.
3   Hold the trackrod-end quite still with an open-ended spanner applied to its flats and unscrew the locknut one quarter of a turn. Hold the trackrod quite still and unscrew the trackrod-end from it. If the bellows are perforated, release their clips and withdraw them.
4   Screw on the new trackrod-end until it almost touches the locknut and then tighten the locknut making sure that the trackrod-end is again supported in an open-ended spanner.
5   Reconnect the trackrod-end to the steering arm.
6   The front wheel alignment must be checked and adjusted, as described in Section 31.
7   It is important that the lengths of the trackrods are equal. If for any reason they have become unequal, set the trackrod-ends on the rods so that the distance between the centre of the trackrod-end balljoint and the face of the inner balljoint is 11½ in (292.1 mm). Release the outer clip on the flexible bellows to measure and it is emphasised that this is an initial front wheel setting and precise alignment must be carried out, as described in Section 31, as soon as possible.
8   Ball pin knock which may be heard when turning right or left may be due to wear in the trackrod inner balljoints. No adjustment can be carried out and new trackrod/ball pin assemblies must be fitted. This work can be carried out without removing the rack from the car as described in the next Section.
9   If the rack bellows are split and leaking grease, they must be renewed immediately.
10 Remove the track rod as previously described, release the bellows clip and withdraw the bellows.
11 Wipe away old lubricant and smear the inboard balljoint with 2 oz (57 g) of fresh grease.
12 Fit the new bellows and clip and then check the front wheel alignment.

21 Trackrod inner ball pin assembly - renewal

1   Disconnect the trackrod outer balljoint from the steering arm.
2   Remove the bellows retaining clip from the rack housing.
3   Peel the bellows back until the inner balljoint is exposed and then flatten the tabs of the lockwasher which secures the balljoint assembly to the rack.
4   Remove the inner balljoint and trackrod and extract the spring.

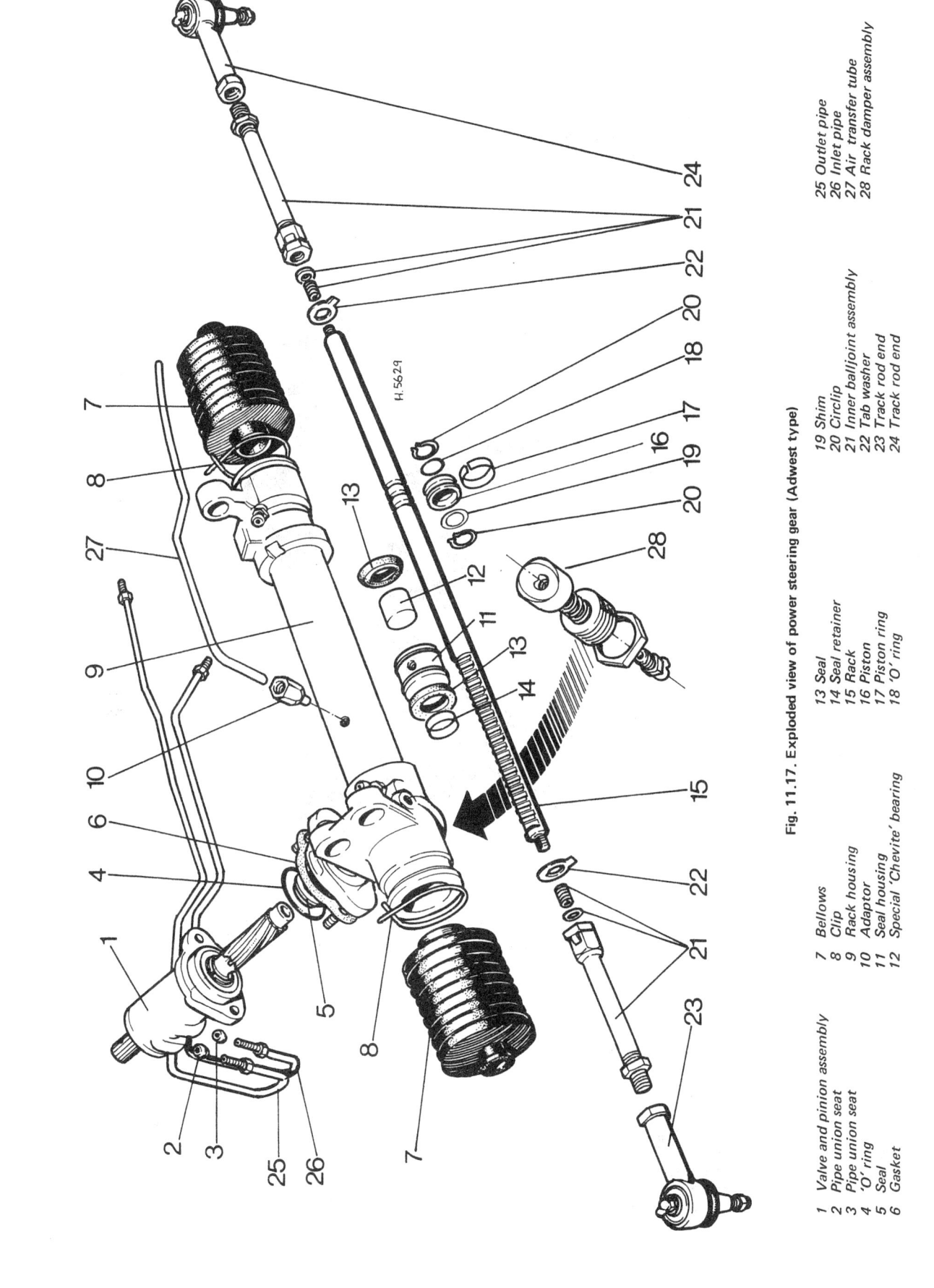

H.5629

Fig. 11.17. Exploded view of power steering gear (Adwest type)

1 Valve and pinion assembly	7 Bellows	13 Seal	19 Shim	25 Outlet pipe
2 Pipe union seat	8 Clip	14 Seal retainer	20 Circlip	26 Inlet pipe
3 Pipe union seat	9 Rack housing	15 Rack	21 Inner balljoint assembly	27 Air transfer tube
4 'O' ring	10 Adaptor	16 Piston	22 Tab washer	28 Rack damper assembly
5 Seal	11 Seal housing	17 Piston ring	23 Track rod end	
6 Gasket	12 Special 'Chevite' bearing	18 'O' ring	24 Track rod end	

Fig. 11.18. Exploded view of the steering upper column (Sec. 23)

1 Column
2 Steering column
3 Cowl support bracket
4 Cowl
5 Upper shaft
6 Cone
7 Grub screw
8 Split collets *
9 Horn contact
10 Striker plate
11 Direction indicator switch
12 Switch cover
13 Locknut
14 Washer
15 Nut
16 Lockwasher
17 Steering wheel
18 Screw
19 Circlip

* Series 1 shown.
  Split collets are
  reversed for
  Series 2

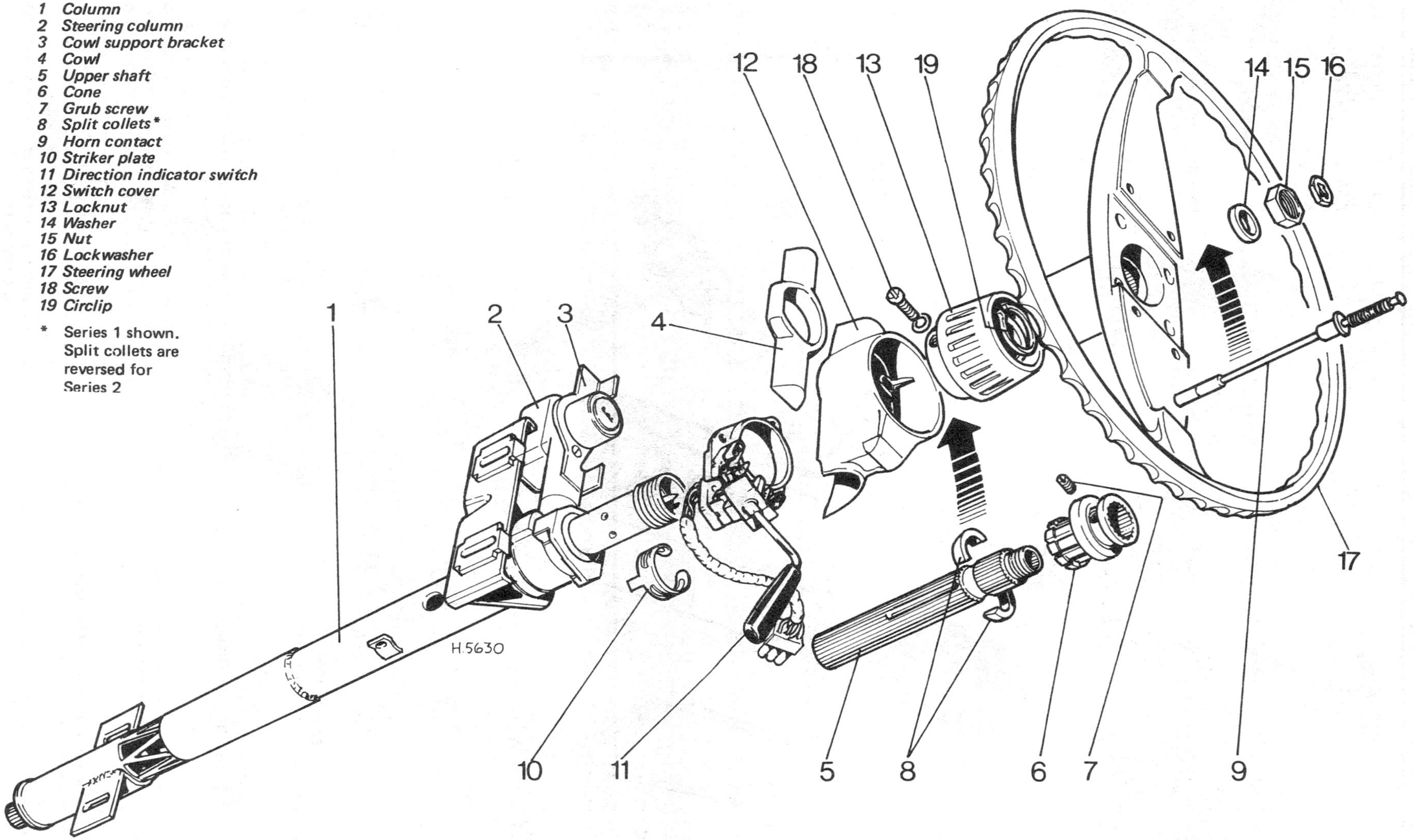

H 5630

23.3 Removing steering wheel crash pad

23.4A Removing horn ring

23.4B Horn contact plunger and spring

5   Remove the trackrod-end and then discard the worn inner balljoint and trackrod.
6   Install the trackrod-end to the new rod/inner balljoint assembly (supplied complete), setting the components, as described in the preceding Section, paragraph 7.
7   Refit the inner balljoint to the rack, using a new lockwasher.
8   Refit the bellows, reconnect the trackrod-end to the steering arm and check the front wheel alignment (Section 31).

22 Steering gear - adjustment in-situ

1   Should rack rattle occur when travelling over rough surfaces, the rack pad requires adjustment.
2   Release the locknut which secures the rack pad adjusting screw.
3   Screw the rack adjusting screw inwards until a stiff resistance is encountered and then release the screw one flat. Tighten the locknut.

23 Steering wheel - removal and refitting

1   Unscrew the large circular locknut (13) (Fig. 11.18) until the shank at the bottom of the nut is clear of the steering column surround. The safety screw (18) which is now exposed can be extracted.
2   Withdraw the steering wheel complete with the short section of the steering shaft (5).
3   Extract the self-tapping screws from the underside of the steering wheel hub to release the spoke crash pad (photo).
4   Remove the self-tapping screws which secure the horn ring or pad to the steering wheel and detach the horn ring (photo). Extract the horn contact plunger and spring (photo).
5   Unscrew the lockwasher (16) and the nut (15), withdraw the steering wheel from the shaft and extract the two halves of the split collet (8).
6   Remove the circlip (19) from the split cone (6) and withdraw the steering shaft.
7   Refitting is a reversal of removal but observe the following points.
    Check that the front roadwheels are in the 'straight-ahead' position and that the spokes of the steering wheel are horixontal before inserting the steering shaft into the upper end of the steering column assembly.
    Refit the safety screw (18) before tightening the locknut (13).
8   The steering wheel attachment components differ slightly on later cars as shown in Fig. 11.19, and removal is described in Chapter 13, Section 21.

24 Steering upper column - removal and refitting

1   Disconnect the battery.
2   Remove the steering wheel, as described in the preceding Section.
3   Remove the three screws which secure the direction indicator switch and cowl to the outer column.
4   Disconnect the direction indicator switch leads by separating the plug and socket.
5   Remove the speedometer and the tachometer from the instrument panel, as described in Chapter 10.
6   Disconnect the horn switch lead from the contact on the steering

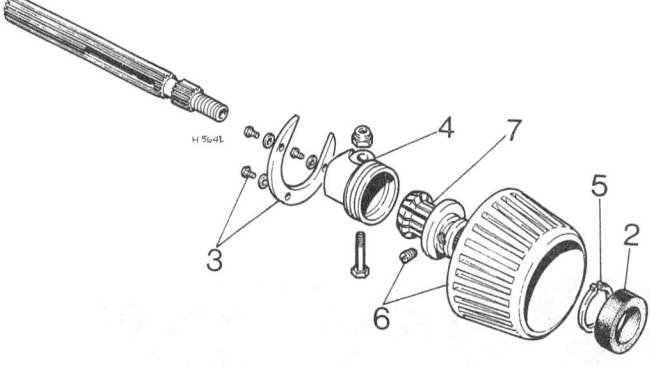

Fig. 11.19. Attachment components of Series 2 steering wheel (Sec. 23)

2   Cushion rubber
3   Retaining plate and screws
4   Collet adaptor
5   Circlip
6   Hand locknut and grub screw
7   Split collet

column.
7   Disconnect the ignition switch leads at the plug and socket connector.
8   Remove the pinch bolt which secures the upper universal joint to the steering column.
9   Remove the two nuts which secure the upper column mounting bracket to the support bracket on the body. Note the location of any packing washers under the bracket, and support the column as the bracket is released. Work through the instrument holes to reach these nuts.
10 Remove the two nuts or setscrews which secure the lower mounting bracket to the bulkhead and again note any packing washers which may be located under this bracket.
11 Withdraw the upper column from the universal joint splines. Take great care not to use force on the column or it may collapse due to shearing of the safety plastic plugs. A new column will then be required as no repair is possible.
12 Refitting is a reversal of removal but set the front roadwheels in the straight-ahead position and connect the upper column to the universal joint splines so that the pinch bolt holes are in alignment with the column groove. Tighten the pinch bolt to the specified torque.

25 Steering lower column - removal and refitting

1   Turn the steering wheel until the pinch bolt on the lower universal joint is accessible and then remove it (photo). On later cars, detach the pinion shaft heat shield.
2   Reset the front roadwheels in the 'straight-ahead' position.
3   Remove the upper column, as described in the preceding Section.
4   Withdraw the lower column.

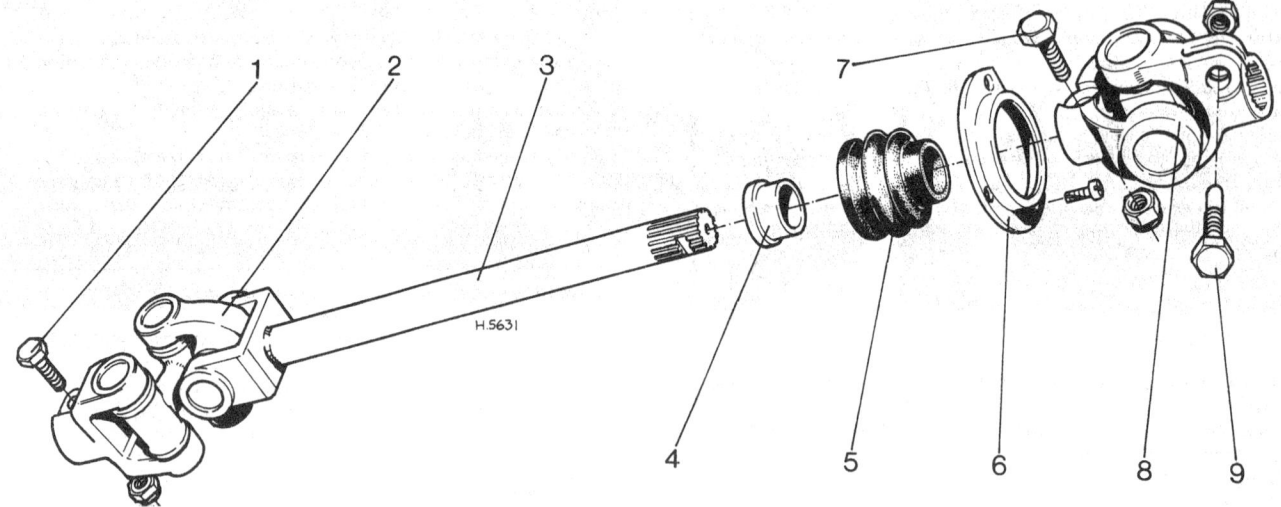

Fig. 11.20. Steering lower column components (Sec. 25)

1 Pinch bolt   4 Bush   7 Pinch bolt
2 Bottom universal joint   5 Gaiter   8 Top universal joint
3 Lower column   6 Retaining plate   9 Pinch bolt

25.1 Steering column balljoint arrangement

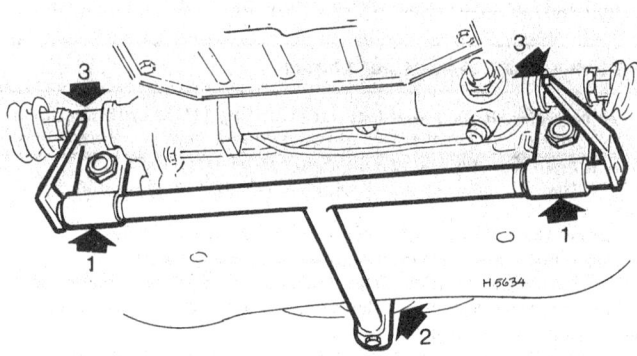

Fig. 11.21. Special tool being used to align steering gear (Sec. 26)

1 Attachment brackets   3 Checking levers
2 Sliding section

5 Refitting is a reversal of removal.

26 Steering gear - removal and installation

1 Raise the front of the car and support it securely or place the car over a pit.
2 Remove the upper and lower steering columns as described in Sections 24 and 25.
3 Disconnect the fluid pipes from the steering housing and allow the fluid to drain into a clean container. Plug the openings.
4 Disconnect the trackrod-ends from the steering arms, as described in Section 20.
5 Remove the three bolts which secure the steering gear to the

bodyframe. Note the position of the two rubber-faced thrust washers and the four plain washers for refitting.
6 Withdraw the steering gear assembly from under the car and collect the two stiffeners which are located inside the support brackets.
7 Installation of the steering gear will require the use of a special alignment tool (JD 36) and if this cannot be borrowed, then the steering gear should be refitted and the car driven to your dealer's to have it aligned at the earliest opportunity.
8 Attach the steering housing to the front suspension assembly but leave the bolts finger-tight.
9 Pull both bellows from the rack housing having first cut the securing wire.
10 The two attachment brackets of the special alignment tool must now be located on the large hexagonal heads of the lower wishbone

pivot shafts (Fig. 11.21).
11 Release the locking screw and move the sliding section of the tool
(2) until the slot registers with the weld flange at the front of the
suspension member. Lock the tool in this position.
12 Lift the two checking levers (3) until contact is made with one or
both rack shafts. Move the position of the steering gear if necessary
until both levers make contact. Tighten the three securing bolts
fully and remove the tool.
13 Reconnect the flexible bellows and fit new locking wire.
14 Reconnect the fluid lines to the steering housing, refit the upper
and lower steering columns.
15 Refill the steering pump reservoir to the 'FULL' mark with clean
automatic transmission fluid. Bleed the system, as described in
Section 29.
16 Reconnect the trackrod-ends and check the front wheel alignment,
as described in Section 31.

27 Steering gear (Adwest type) - overhaul

1 The following operations are in respect of power steering gear. On
cars with manual steering assemblies, ignore any reference to the
hydraulic components.
2 With the steering gear removed from the car, clean away all
external dirt.
3 Remove the fluid pipes (25 and 26) (Fig. 11.17).
4 Cut the locking wire and peel back the bellows to expose the inner
balljoints.
5 Flatten the tab washer and unscrew and remove the inner ball pin and
trackrod as a unit. Do not dismantle th ball pin assembly. Collect the
spring and spacer.
6 Remove the rack adjuster pad components.
7 Mark the relative position of the pinion housing to the rack housing
also the groove in the pinion to the pinion housing. Note the position
of the rack. Remove the three locknuts, remove the valve body and
discard the gasket.
8 Any wear or faults occurring in the valve and pinion housing
assembly can only be rectified with a new assembly. Where this action
is taken then new top and backing seals will be required, also a joint
gasket.
9 Similarly if wear or faults are evident in the rack assembly then a
replacement rack housing should be obtained which will contain end
cap seals, 'Clevite' bearing and needle bearings.
10 Commence reassembly by placing a new sealing joint gasket over the

three studs in the rack housing.
11 Refit the pinion housing making sure that the marks made before
removal are in alignment with the rack in the original relative
position.
12 Refit the inner balljoints using new lockplates. Screw on the
trackrod-ends and set the trackrod lengths, as described in Section 20.
13 Refit and adjust the rack pad assembly.
14 Reconnect the fluid pipes and then apply grease to the rack ball
housings, fit the bellows and their clips.
15 Apply a grease gun to the nipple on the housing and inject 1 oz
(28.35g) of grease. Do not inject excessive amounts of grease which
would distend the flexible bellows or block the fluid transfer tube.

28 Power steering pump - removal and refitting

1 Disconnect the hose from the outlet at the rear of the pump
reservoir. Allow the fluid to drain into a suitable container and then
plug the openings. On later cars, remove the air cleaner cover.
2 Disconnect the second (high pressure) hose from the reservoir.
3 Disconnect the pump adjusting link from the water pump. Press
the pump inwards, lift the jockey pulley against spring pressure and
slip the drivebelt from the pump pulley.
4 Pull the pump outwards and disconnect the bottom pivot mounting
bolt. Lift the pump and its mounting bracket from the engine
compartment.
5 Refit the pump by reversing the removal operations. The pump
drivebelt is automatically tensioned by the spring-loaded jockey pulley
but when installing the belt, pull the pump fully away from the engine
and then tighten the adjuster link bolt.
6 Reconnect the fluid hoses, and fill the reservoir to the full mark on
the dipstick with Automatic Transmission fluid. Turn the pump pulley
anticlockwise a few revolutions to expel any air which may be trapped
in the pump.
7 Bleed the complete system, as described in the next Section.

29 Power steering system - bleeding

1 Check that the pump reservoir is full. Jack-up the front of the car.
2 With the engine idling, turn the steering wheel from lock-to-lock.
Do this slowly until any lumpiness in the steering action has disappeared.
3 Top-up the pump reservoir with specified fluid.

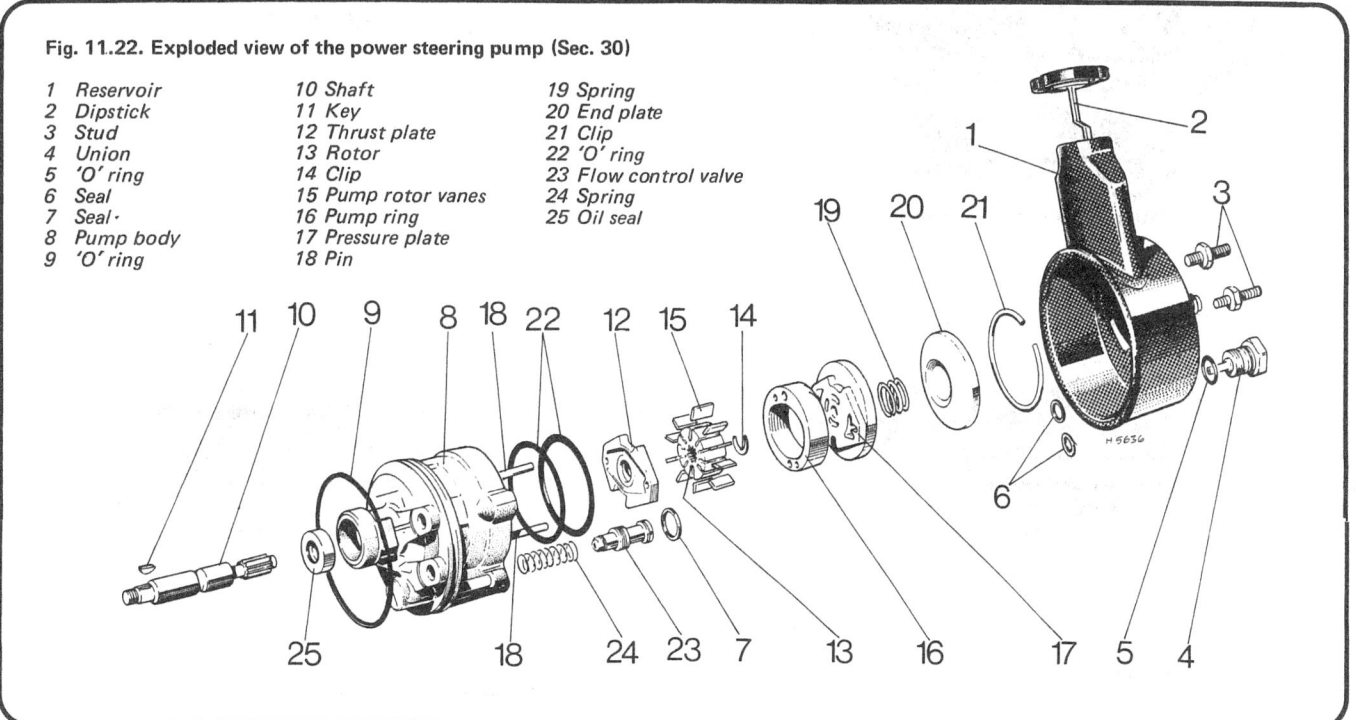

Fig. 11.22. Exploded view of the power steering pump (Sec. 30)

1 Reservoir
2 Dipstick
3 Stud
4 Union
5 'O' ring
6 Seal
7 Seal
8 Pump body
9 'O' ring
10 Shaft
11 Key
12 Thrust plate
13 Rotor
14 Clip
15 Pump rotor vanes
16 Pump ring
17 Pressure plate
18 Pin
19 Spring
20 End plate
21 Clip
22 'O' ring
23 Flow control valve
24 Spring
25 Oil seal

30 Power steering pump - overhaul

1   In the event of a fault occurring or wear taking place, it is recommended that a replacement pump is obtained but where it is preferred to overhaul the original unit, proceed as follows making sure first that spare parts are available.

2   Drain the fluid from the pump and clean off all external dirt.

3   Remove the nut and withdraw the pulley. (Later models have a detachable pulley (3 setscrews) mounted on a hub which is pressed onto the pump shaft).

4   Secure the pump carefully in the jaws of a vice and then remove the outlet union (4) (Fig. 11.22). Extract the 'O' ring from the recess.

5   Remove the two mounting studs (3) and detach the reservoir from the pump body.

6   Extract the three 'O' rings from the recesses in the pump body.

7   Remove the endplate retaining ring by inserting a pin through the hole in the pump body and then prising out the ring with a screwdriver.

8   Remove the endplate (20) and spring (19) and 'O' ring (22).

9   Remove the flow control valve (23) and spring (24).

10 Remove the Woodruff key (11) and gently tap the end of the shaft until the pressure plate, pump ring, rotor and thrust plate can be withdrawn as an assembly. Remove the pressure plate 'O' ring (22) from the pump body.

11 Separate the components taking care not to damage the pump rotor vanes.

12 Remove the clip (14), withdraw the rotor (13) and thrust plate (12). Extract the shaft oil seal (25).

13 Discard and renew all oil seals and examine components for scoring or grooves. The pump shaft and bush are supplied as a complete assembly. Check that the flow control valve slides freely in its bore, if not, renew it.

14 Commence reassembly, by smearing a new shaft seal with petroleum jelly. Install the seal to the pump body using a piece of tubing. Install the pump shaft, splined end first, from the hub end of the pump body.

15 Install the dowel pins to the pump body and then fit the thrust plate over the pins so that the face with the recesses is uppermost.

16 Fit the rotor to the splined shaft so that the countersunk side is downwards towards the thrust plate. Check that the rotor is free on the splines.

17 Fit the retaining clip to the shaft groove and then fit the pump ring to the dowel pins so that the directional arrow is uppermost.

18 Insert the vanes in the rotor slots so that the rounded end of the vane is facing outwards.

19 Apply petroleum jelly to the pressure plate 'O' ring and fit it into the lowest groove in the pump body. Smear the outside edge of the pressure plate with petroleum jelly and fit it to the dowel pin so that the spring circular recess is uppermost. Push the plate downwards using a piece of tubing applied to its outer edge. Do not tap the plate into position.

20 Install the end plate 'O' ring into its groove in the pump body, first having applied petroleum jelly to it.

21 Fit the spring (19) into the circular groove in the pressure plate.

22 Smear the edge of the endplate with petroleum jelly and place it in position so that the retaining ring is on top. Check that the gap in the clip is not opposite the hole used for removal. Apply pressure until the retaining clip can be sprung into the groove in the body.

23 Insert the valve, spring leading, into the bore in the pump. Locate new 'O' ring seals in position for the reservoir retaining bolts and the outlet union.

24 Smear the large reservoir 'O' ring seal with petroleum jelly and insert it into its groove in the pump body.

25 Fit the reservoir retaining studs, the outlet union and 'O' rings.

26 Refit the Woodruff key, pulley, lockwasher and nut.

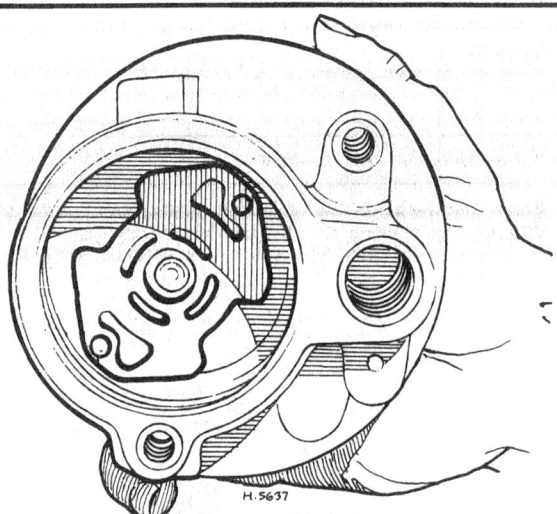

Fig. 11.23. Fitting thrust plate to steering pump (Sec. 30)

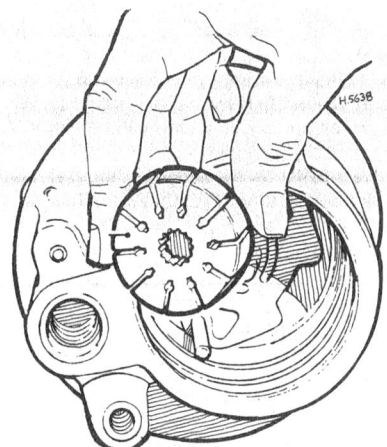

Fig. 11.24. Fitting rotor to steering pump (Sec. 30)

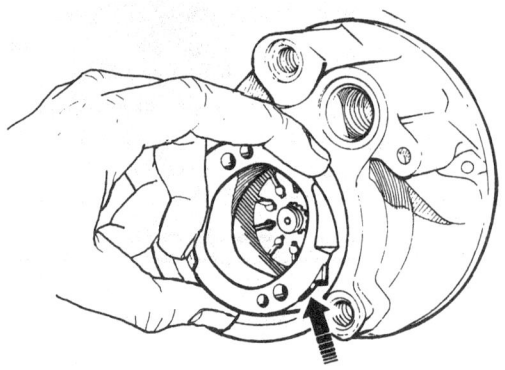

Fig. 11.25. Installing pump ring (Sec. 30)

Fig. 11.26. Installing vanes to steering pump rotor plate (Sec. 30)

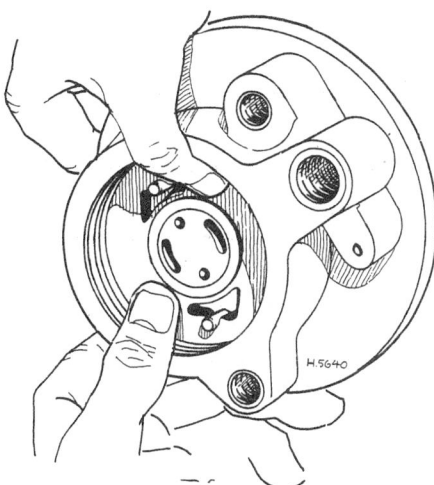

Fig. 11.27. Installing pressure plate to steering pump (Sec. 30)

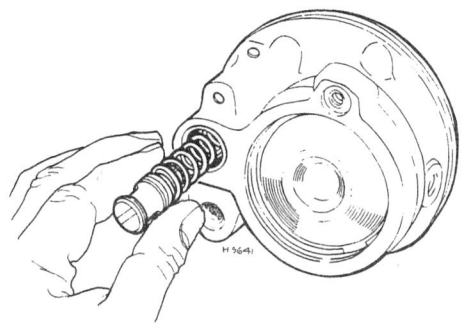

Fig. 11.28. Installing flow control valve to steering pump (Sec. 30)

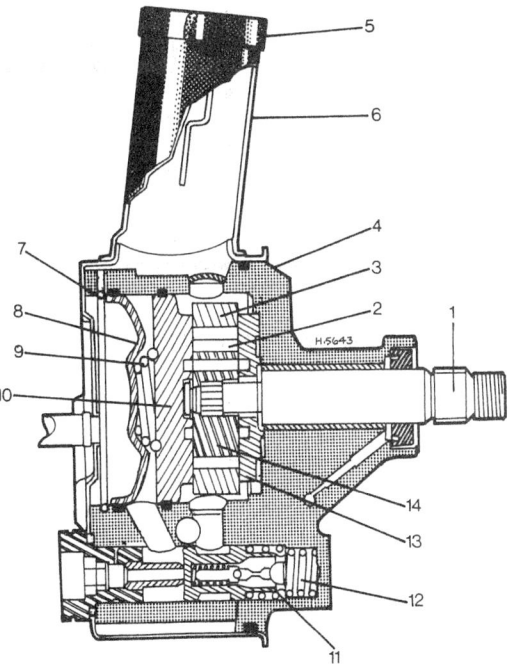

Fig. 11.29. Sectional view of power steering pump (Sec. 30)

1 Driving shaft	8 End plate
2 Pump vane	9 Spring
3 Pump ring	10 Pressure plate
4 Body	11 Flow control valve
5 Filler cap	12 Spring
6 Reservoir	13 Thrust plate
7 Oil seal	14 Rotor

31 Steering angles and front wheel alignment

1   Accurate front wheel alignment is essential for good steering and slow tyre wear. Before considering the steering angle, check that the tyres are correctly inflated, that the front wheels are not buckled, the hub bearings are not worn or incorrectly adjusted and that the steering linkage is in good order, without slackness or wear at the joints.

2   Wheel alignment consists of four factors:

Camber, is the angle at which the front wheels are set from the vertical when viewed from the front of the car. Positive camber is the amount (in degrees) that the wheels are tilted outwards at the top from the vertical.

Castor is the angle between the steering axis and a vertical line when viewed from each side of the car. Positive castor is when the steering axis is inclined rearwards.

Steering axis inclination is the angle, when viewed from the front of the car, between the vertical and an imaginary line drawn between the upper and lower suspension swivels.

Toe-in is the amount by which the distance between the front inside edges of the roadwheels (measured at hub height) is less than the diametrically opposite distance measured between the rear inside edges of the front roadwheels.

3   Due to the need for very accurate measuring equipment it is not within the scope of the home mechanic to check steering angles but the method of adjusting them is described in the following paragraphs for reasons of interest.

4   Camber angle is altered by adding or removing shims at the joint of the upper wishbone pivot and the crossmember.

5   Castor angle is altered by transposing shims from one side to the other of the upper wishbone balljoint. Whenever the castor angle is

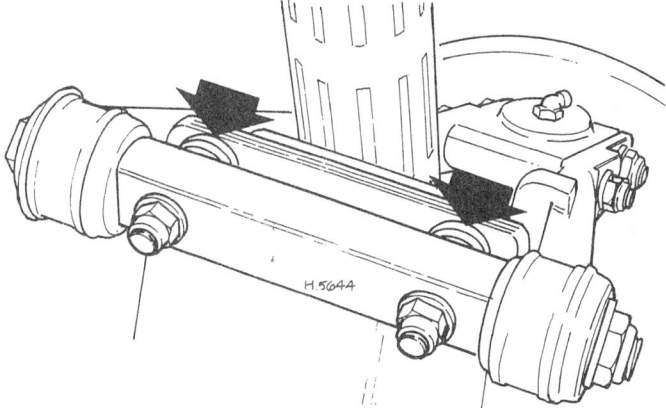

Fig. 11.30. Location of camber angle shims on front suspension upper wishbone (Sec. 31)

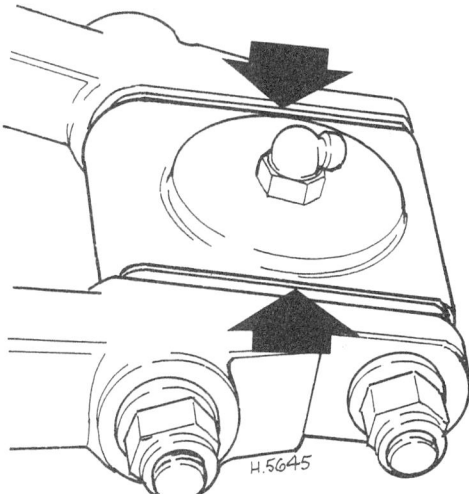

Fig. 11.31. Location of castor angle shims on front suspension upper balljoint (Sec. 31)

altered, the front wheel alignment (toe) will need adjusting.

6   Front wheel tracking (toe) checks are best carried out with modern setting equipment but a reasonably accurate alternative and adjustment procedure may be carried out as follows:

7   Place the car on level ground with the wheels in the straight-ahead position.

8   Obtain or make a toe-in gauge. One may be easily made from tubing cranked to clear the sump and bellhousing, having an adjustable nut and setscrew at one end.

9   Using the gauge, measure the distance between the two inner wheel rims at hub height at the rear of the wheels.

10 Rotate the wheels (by pushing the car forwards) through 180° (half a turn) and again using the gauge, measure the distance of hub height between the two inner wheel rims at the front of the wheels. This measurement should be from 1/16 to 1/8 in (1.6 to 3.2 mm) less than that previously taken at the rear of the wheel and represents the correct toe-in.

11 Where the toe-in is found to be incorrect, slacken the locknuts on each outer trackrod and rotate each trackrod an equal amount until the correct toe-in is obtained. Tighten the locknuts ensuring that the balljoints are held in the centre of their arc of travel during tightening.

12 It cannot be over emphasised that both during initial setting and subsequent adjustment, the effective lengths of the two trackrods must be exactly equal (see also Section 20).

32 Rear wheel alignment

1   The rear wheels are adjustable for camber but again due to the need for precise measuring equipment and setting links (tool no. JD21) this work should be left to your Jaguar/Daimler dealer.

2   The camber angle is altered by varying the thickness of the shims which are fitted between the driveshaft inner joint flange and the brake disc.

33 Roadwheels and tyres

1   Whenever the roadwheels are removed it is a good idea to clean the insides of the wheels to remove accumulation of mud and in the case of the front ones, disc pad dust.

2   Check the condition of the wheel for rust and repaint if necessary.

3   Examine the wheel stud holes. If these are tending to become elongated or the dished recesses in which the nuts seat have worn or become overcompressed, then the wheel will have to be renewed.

4   With a roadwheel removed, pick out any embedded flints from the tread and check for splits in the sidewalls or damage to the tyre carcass generally.

5   Where the depth of tread pattern is 1 mm or less, the tyre must be renewed.

6   Rotation of the roadwheels to even out tyre wear is no longer recommended. Each tyre develops a characteristic wear pattern according to its position; subsequent disturbance may upset handling and accelerate the rate of wear.

7   If the wheels have been balanced on the car, the relationship of the wheel and hub should not be altered if the wheel is removed. Marking one wheel stud and the corresponding hole in the roadwheel with a dab of paint will enable the original fitted position to be regained.

8   It is recommended that wheels are re-balanced halfway through the life of the tyres to compensate for the loss of tread rubber due to wear.

9   Finally, always keep the tyres (including the spare) inflated to the recommended pressures and always replace the dust caps on the tyre valves. Tyre pressures are best checked first thing in the morning when the tyres are cold.

34 Fault diagnosis - suspension and steering

Symptom	Reason/s
Steering feels vague, car wanders and floats at speed	Tyre pressures uneven. Shock absorbers worn. Spring broken. Steering gear balljoints badly worn. Suspension geometry incorrect. Steering mechanism free play excessive. Front suspension and rear axle pick-up points out of alignment.
Stiff and heavy steering	Tyre pressures too low. No grease in swivel joints. No grease in steering and suspension balljoints. Front wheel toe-in incorrect. Suspension geometry incorrect. Steering gear incorrectly adjusted too tightly. Steering column badly misaligned. Loose steering pump belt.
Wheel wobble and vibration	Wheel nuts loose. Front wheels and tyres out of balance. Steering balljoints badly worn. Hub bearings badly worn. Steering gear free play excessive. Front springs weak or broken.
Rattle on rough roads	Worn inner balljoints on ends of rack. Incorrect rack pad adjustment. Worn rack housing bushes.

Chapter 12 Bodywork and fittings

For modifications, and information applicable to later models, see Supplement at end of manual

Contents

1 General description

1 The bodywork is of all steel, welded construction in either two or four door body styles. Long wheelbase versions were introduced in 1972 under the Jaguar and Daimler insignia.

2 A full air-conditioning system may be optionally specified on all models.

2 Maintenance – bodywork and underframe

The general condition of a vehicle's bodywork is the one thing that significantly affects its value. Maintenance is easy but needs to be regular. Neglect, particularly after minor damage, can lead quickly to further deterioration and costly repair bills. It is important also to keep watch on those parts of the vehicle not immediately visible, for instance the underside, inside all the wheel arches and the lower part of the engine compartment.

The basic maintenance routine for the bodywork is washing – preferably with a lot of water, from a hose. This will remove all the loose solids which may have stuck to the vehicle. It is important to flush these off in such a way as to prevent grit from scratching the finish. The wheel arches and underframe need washing in the same way to remove any accumulated mud which will retain moisture and tend to encourage rust. Paradoxically enough, the best time to clean the underframe and wheel arches is in wet weather when the mud is thoroughly wet and soft. In very wet weather the underframe is usually cleaned of large accumulations automatically and this is a good time for inspection.

Periodically, except on vehicles with a wax-based underbody protective coating, it is a good idea to have the whole of the underframe of the vehicle steam cleaned, engine compartment included, so that a thorough inspection can be carried out to see what minor repairs and renovations are necessary. Steam cleaning is available at many garages and is necessary for removal of the accumulation of oily grime which sometimes is allowed to become thick in certain areas. If steam cleaning facilities are not available, there are one or two excellent grease solvents available such as Holts Engine Cleaner or Holts Foambrite which can be brush applied. The dirt can then be simply hosed off. Note that these methods should not be used on vehicles with wax-based underbody protective coating or the coating will be removed. Such vehicles should be inspected annually, preferably just prior to winter, when the underbody should be washed down and any damage to the wax coating repaired using Holts Undershield. Ideally, a completely fresh coat should be applied. It would also be worth considering the use of such wax-based protection for injection into door panels, sills, box sections, etc, as an additional safeguard against rust damage where such protection is not provided by the vehicle manufacturer.

After washing paintwork, wipe off with a chamois leather to give an unspotted clear finish. A coat of clear protective wax polish, like the many excellent Turtle Wax polishes, will give added protection against chemical pollutants in the air. If the paintwork sheen has dulled or oxidised, use a cleaner/polisher combination such as Turtle Extra to restore the brilliance of the shine. This requires a little effort, but such dulling is usually caused because regular washing has been neglected. Care needs to be taken with metallic paintwork, as special non-abrasive cleaner/polisher is required to avoid damage to the finish. Always check that the door and ventilator opening drain holes and pipes are completely clear so that water can be drained out. Bright work should be treated in the same way as paint work. Windscreens and windows can be kept clear of the smeary film which often appears, by the use of a proprietary glass cleaner like Holts Mixra. Never use any form of wax or other body or chromium polish on glass.

3 Maintenance – upholstery and carpets

Mats and carpets should be brushed or vacuum cleaned regularly to keep them free of grit. If they are badly stained remove them from the vehicle for scrubbing or sponging and make quite sure they are dry before refitting. Seats and interior trim panels can be kept clean by wiping with a damp cloth and Turtle Wax Carisma. If they do become stained (which can be more apparent on light coloured upholstery) use a little liquid detergent and a soft nail brush to scour the grime out of the grain of the material. Do not forget to keep the headlining clean in the same way as the upholstery. When using liquid cleaners inside the vehicle do not over-wet the surfaces being cleaned. Excessive damp could get into the seams and padded interior causing stains, offensive odours or even rot. If the inside of the vehicle gets wet accidentally it is worthwhile taking some trouble to dry it out properly, particularly where carpets are involved. *Do not leave oil or electric heaters inside the vehicle for this purpose.*

4 Minor body damage – repair

Note: *For more detailed information about bodywork repair, the Haynes Publishing Group publish a book by Lindsay Porter called The Car Bodywork Repair Manual. This incorporates information on such aspects as rust treatment, painting and glass fibre repairs, as well as details on more ambitious repairs involving welding and panel beating.*

Repair of minor scratches in bodywork

If the scratch is very superficial, and does not penetrate to the metal of the bodywork, repair is very simple. Lightly rub the area of the scratch with a paintwork renovator like Turtle Wax New Color Back, or a very fine cutting paste like Holts Body + Plus Rubbing Compound, to remove loose paint from the scratch and to clear the surrounding bodywork of wax polish. Rinse the area with clean water.

Apply touch-up paint, such as Holts Dupli-Color Color Touch or a paint film like Holts Autofilm, to the scratch using a fine paint brush; continue to apply fine layers of paint until the surface of the paint in the scratch is level with the surrounding paintwork. Allow the new paint at least two weeks to harden: then blend it into the surrounding paintwork by rubbing the scratch area with a paintwork renovator or a very fine cutting paste, such as Holts Body + Plus Rubbing Compound or Turtle Wax New Color Back. Finally, apply wax polish from one of the Turtle Wax range of wax polishes.

Where the scratch has penetrated right through to the metal of the bodywork, causing the metal to rust, a different repair technique is required. Remove any loose rust from the bottom of the scratch with a penknife, then apply rust inhibiting paint, such as Turtle Wax Rust Master, to prevent the formation of rust in the future. Using a rubber or nylon applicator fill the scratch with bodystopper paste like Holts Body + Plus Knifing Putty. If required, this paste can be mixed with cellulose thinners, such as Holts Body + Plus Cellulose Thinners, to provide a very thin paste which is ideal for filling narrow scratches. Before the stopper-paste in the scratch hardens, wrap a piece of smooth cotton rag around the top of a finger. Dip the finger in cellulose thinners, such as Holts Body + Plus Cellulose Thinners, and then quickly sweep it across the surface of the stopper-paste in the scratch; this will ensure that the surface of the stopper-paste is slightly hollowed. The scratch can now be painted over as described earlier in this Section.

Repair of dents in bodywork

When deep denting of the vehicle's bodywork has taken place, the first task is to pull the dent out, until the affected bodywork almost attains its original shape. There is little point in trying to restore the original shape completely, as the metal in the damaged area will have stretched on impact and cannot be reshaped fully to its original contour. It is better to bring the level of the dent up to a point which is about ⅛ in (3 mm) below the level of the surrounding bodywork. In cases where the dent is very shallow anyway, it is not worth trying to pull it out at all. If the underside of the dent is accessible, it can be hammered out gently from behind, using a mallet with a wooden or plastic head. Whilst doing this, hold a suitable block of wood firmly against the outside of the panel to absorb the impact from the hammer blows and thus prevent a large area of the bodywork from being 'belled-out'.

Should the dent be in a section of the bodywork which has a double skin or some other factor making it inaccessible from behind, a different technique is called for. Drill several small holes through the metal inside the area – particularly in the deeper section. Then screw long self-tapping screws into the holes just sufficiently for them to gain a good purchase in the metal. Now the dent can be pulled out by pulling on the protruding heads of the screws with a pair of pliers.

The next stage of the repair is the removal of the paint from the damaged area, and from an inch or so of the surrounding 'sound' bodywork. This is accomplished most easily by using a wire brush or abrasive pad on a power drill, although it can be done just as effectively by hand using sheets of abrasive paper. To complete the preparation for filling, score the surface of the bare metal with a screwdriver or the tang of a file, or alternatively, drill small holes in the affected area. This will provide a really good 'key' for the filler paste.

To complete the repair see the Section on filling and re-spraying.

Repair of rust holes or gashes in bodywork

Remove all paint from the affected area and from an inch or so of the surrounding 'sound' bodywork, using an abrasive pad or a wire brush on a power drill. If these are not available a few sheets of abrasive paper will do the job just as effectively. With the paint removed you will be able to gauge the severity of the corrosion and therefore decide whether to renew the whole panel (if this is possible) or to repair the affected area. New body panels are not as expensive as most people think and it is often quicker and more satisfactory to fit a new panel than to attempt to repair large areas of corrosion.

Remove all fittings from the affected area except those which will act as a guide to the original shape of the damaged bodywork (eg headlamp shells etc). Then, using tin snips or a hacksaw blade, remove all loose metal and any other metal badly affected by corrosion. Hammer the edges of the hole inwards in order to create a slight depression for the filler paste.

Wire brush the affected area to remove the powdery rust from the surface of the remaining metal. Paint the affected area with rust inhibiting paint like Turtle Wax Rust Master; if the back of the rusted area is accessible treat this also.

Before filling can take place it will be necessary to block the hole in some way. This can be achieved by the use of aluminium or plastic mesh, or aluminium tape.

Aluminium or plastic mesh or glass fibre matting, such as the Holts Body + Plus Glass Fibre Matting, is probably the best material to use for a large hole. Cut a piece to the approximate size and shape of the hole to be filled, then position it in the hole so that its edges are below the level of the surrounding bodywork. It can be retained in position by several blobs of filler paste around its periphery.

Aluminium tape should be used for small or very narrow holes. Pull a piece off the roll and trim it to the approximate size and shape required, then pull off the backing paper (if used) and stick the tape over the hole; it can be overlapped if the thickness of one piece is insufficient. Burnish down the edges of the tape with the handle of a screwdriver or similar, to ensure that the tape is securely attached to the metal underneath.

Bodywork repairs – filling and re-spraying

Before using this Section, see the Sections on dent, deep scratch, rust holes and gash repairs.

Many types of bodyfiller are available, but generally speaking those proprietary kits which contain a tin of filler paste and a tube of resin hardener are best for this type of repair, like Holts Body + Plus or Holts No Mix which can be used directly from the tube. A wide, flexible plastic or nylon applicator will be found invaluable for imparting a smooth and well contoured finish to the surface of the filler.

Mix up a little filler on a clean piece of card or board – measure the hardener carefully (follow the maker's instructions on the pack) otherwise the filler will set too rapidly or too slowly. Alternatively, Holts No Mix can be used straight from the tube without mixing, but daylight is required to cure it. Using the applicator apply the filler paste to the prepared area; draw the applicator across the surface of the filler to achieve the correct contour and to level the filler surface. As soon as a contour that approximates to the correct one is achieved, stop working the paste – if you carry on too long the paste will become sticky and begin to 'pick up' on the applicator. Continue to add thin layers of filler paste at twenty-minute intervals until the level of the filler is just proud of the surrounding bodywork.

Once the filler has hardened, excess can be removed using a metal plane or file. From then on, progressively finer grades of abrasive paper should be used, starting with a 40 grade production paper and finishing with 400 grade wet-and-dry paper. Always wrap the abrasive paper around a flat rubber, cork, or wooden block – otherwise the surface of the filler will not be completely flat. During the smoothing of the filler surface the wet-and-dry paper should be periodically rinsed in water. This will ensure that a very smooth finish is imparted to the filler at the final stage.

At this stage the 'dent' should be surrounded by a ring of bare metal, which in turn should be encircled by the finely 'feathered' edge of the good paintwork. Rinse the repair area with clean water, until all of the dust produced by the rubbing-down operation has gone.

Spray the whole repair area with a light coat of primer, either Holts Body + Plus Grey or Red Oxide Primer – this will show up any imperfections in the surface of the filler. Repair these imperfections with fresh filler paste or bodystopper, and once more smooth the surface with abrasive paper. If bodystopper is used, it can be mixed with cellulose thinners to form a really thin paste which is ideal for filling small holes. Repeat this spray and repair procedure until you are satisfied that the surface of the filler, and the feathered edge of the paintwork are perfect. Clean the repair area with clean water and allow to dry fully.

The repair area is now ready for final spraying. Paint spraying must be carried out in a warm, dry, windless and dust free atmosphere. This condition can be created artificially if you have access to a large indoor working area, but if you are forced to work in the open, you will have to pick your day very carefully. If you are working indoors, dousing the floor in the work area with water will help to settle the dust which would otherwise be in the atmosphere. If the repair area is confined to one body panel, mask off the surrounding panels; this will help to minimise the effects of a slight mis-match in paint colours. Bodywork fittings (eg chrome strips, door handles etc) will also need to be masked off. Use genuine masking tape and several thicknesses of newspaper for the masking operations.

Before commencing to spray, agitate the aerosol can thoroughly, then spray a test area (an old tin, or similar) until the technique is mastered. Cover the repair area with a thick coat of primer; the thickness should be built up using several thin layers of paint rather than one thick one. Using 400 grade wet-and-dry paper, rub down the surface of the primer until it is really smooth. While doing this, the work area should be thoroughly doused with water, and the wet-and-dry paper periodically rinsed in water. Allow to dry before spraying on more paint.

Spray the top coat using Holts Dupli-Color Autospray, again building up the thickness by using several thin layers of paint. Start spraying in the centre of the repair area and then work outwards, with a side-to-side motion, until the whole repair area and about 2 inches of the surrounding original paintwork is covered. Remove all masking material 10 to 15 minutes after spraying on the final coat of paint.

Allow the new paint at least two weeks to harden, then, using a paintwork renovator or a very fine cutting paste such as Turtle Wax New Color Back or Holts Body + Plus Rubbing Compound, blend the edges of the paint into the existing paintwork. Finally, apply wax polish.

5   Major body damage - repair

Where serious damage has occurred or large areas need renewal due to neglect, it means certainly that completely new sections or panels will need welding in and this is best left to professionals. If the damage is due to impact it will also be necessary to completely check the alignment of the body shell structure. Due to the principle of construction the strength and shape of the whole can be affected by damage to a part. In such instances the services of a Jaguar/Daimler agent with specialist checking jigs are essential. If a body is left misaligned it is first of all dangerous as the car will not handle properly and secondly uneven stresses will be imposed on the steering, engine and transmission, causing abnormal wear or complete failure. Tyre wear may also be excessive.

6   Maintenance - hinges and locks

1   Oil the hinges of the bonnet, boot and doors with a drop or two of light oil periodically. A good time is after the car has been washed.
2   Oil the bonnet, release the catch pivot pin and the safety catch pivot pin periodically.
3   Do not over lubricate door latches and strikers. Normally a little oil on the rotary cam spindle alone is sufficient.

7   Doors - tracing rattles and their rectification

1   Check first that the door is not loose at the hinges and that the latch is holding the door firmly in position. Check also that the door lines up with the aperture in the body.
2   If the hinges are loose or the door is out of alignment it will be necessary to reset the hinge positions, as described in Sections 26 or 27.
3   If the latch is holding the door properly it should hold the door tightly when fully latched and the door should line up with the body. If it is out of alignment it needs adjustment. If loose, some part of the lock mechanism must be worn out and requires renewal.
4   Other rattles from the door would be caused by wear or looseness in the window winder, the glass channels and sill strips, or the door buttons and interior latch release mechanism.

8   Bonnet - removal and refitting

1   Disconnect the battery earth lead and place an old blanket or similar item on the front bumper to protect it.
2   Open the bonnet as far as it will go and mark its position relative to the hinges.

3   Disconnect the headlight wiring connectors.
4   Unbolt the bonnet check strap. Do not allow the bonnet to remain unsupported with the check strap disconnected.
5   With one or two assistants supporting the bonnet, remove the bolts and washers which secure it to the hinges. Lift away the bonnet and store it in a safe place.
6   Refit in the reverse order to removal. Use the marks made at the hinges to achieve roughly correct alignment; check for fit and adjust if necessary before finally tightening all the bolts.

9 Bonnet lock - removal, adjustment and refitting

1   Slacken the locknut at the base of the dovetail bolt. Insert a screwdriver blade in the slot in the end of the dovetail bolt and unscrew the bolt complete with locknut, washers and spring.
2   To remove the lock section, slacken the nut which secures the cable and disconnect the cable from the release lever.
3   Remove the two setscrews which secure the striker and remove the striker, catch, baseplate and spacers.
4   Refitting is a reversal of removal but adjustment of the effective length of the dovetail bolt will almost certainly be required. To do this, adjust the dovetail bolt with a screwdriver until the bonnet will close smoothly and easily but without any tendency to rattle when closed. When this situation is reached, tighten the dovetail bolt locknut.

10 Bonnet hinges - removal and refitting

1   The hinge assemblies are contained in boxes located in the front subframe.
2   Remove the bonnet as previously described.
3   Unhook the bonnet counterbalance springs from their upper attachments.
4   *On all cars except Series 2,* remove the front bumper.

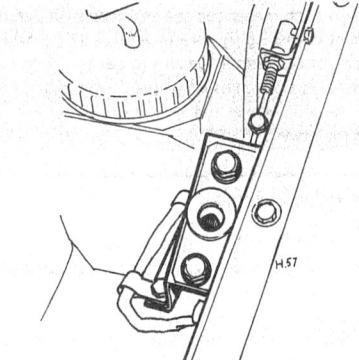

Fig. 12.1. Bonnet lock striker plate (Sec. 9)

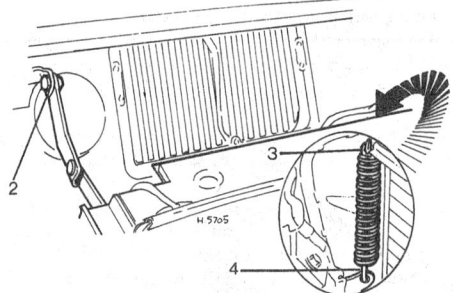

Fig. 12.2. Bonnet counterbalance springs (Sec. 10)

2   *Stay bolt*   4   *Attachments*
3   *Attachments*

5   *On Series 2 cars,* remove the radiator lower grille (Section 11), then extract the four bolts from inside the wheel arch which secure the sides of the front apron panel to the body. Remove the three screws which secure the underside of the apron panel and withdraw the panel. Remove the radiator (Chapter 2).
6   The hinge assembly can now be unbolted and withdrawn.
7   Refitting is a reversal of removal.

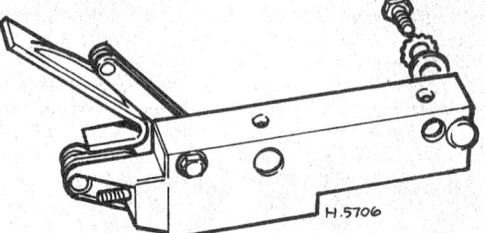

Fig. 12.3. Bonnet hinge assembly (Series 2 cars) (Sec. 10)

11 Radiator grille - removal and refitting

All cars except Series 2
1   Raise the bonnet to its fully open position.
2   Remove the six nuts and remove the grille.

Series 2 cars
3   On these models, remove the two nuts and crosshead screws which secure the grille to the bonnet. Remove the grille by withdrawing it evenly.
4   The centre bar can be removed in two sections after unscrewing the retaining nuts.
5   The lower grille is secured by two screws located behind the spotlamps. To remove the grille, withdraw the screws and lift the grille upwards to disengage its locating pegs at the lower edge.
6   Refitting in all cases is a reversal of removal but do not tighten the grille securing screws fully until the grille has been aligned squarely in the body aperture.

12 Luggage compartment lid - removal and refitting

1   Raise the lid to its fullest extent.
2   Disconnect the reversing lamp cables.
3   Mark the position of the hinge plates in relation to the underside of the lid.
4   Remove the securing setscrews and with the help of an assistant lift the lid from the car.
5   Refitting is a reversal of removal.

13 Luggage compartment lid lock - removal and refitting

1   Open the lid to its fullest extent.
2   Remove the clip which secures the link to the lock control and disconnect the link.
3   Remove the three securing screws and withdraw the lock.
4   The lock control can be removed from the lid if the retaining plate is first slid to one side.
5   Refitting is a reversal of removal, any adjustment can be made by slackening the two striker screws and moving the striker within the limits of the elongated screw holes.

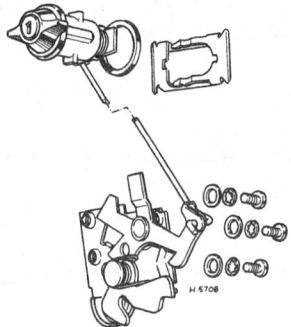

Fig. 12.4. Luggage compartment lid lock (Sec. 13)

14 Front door lock - removal and refitting

Early cars
1   Remove the four countersunk screws which secure the wood capping

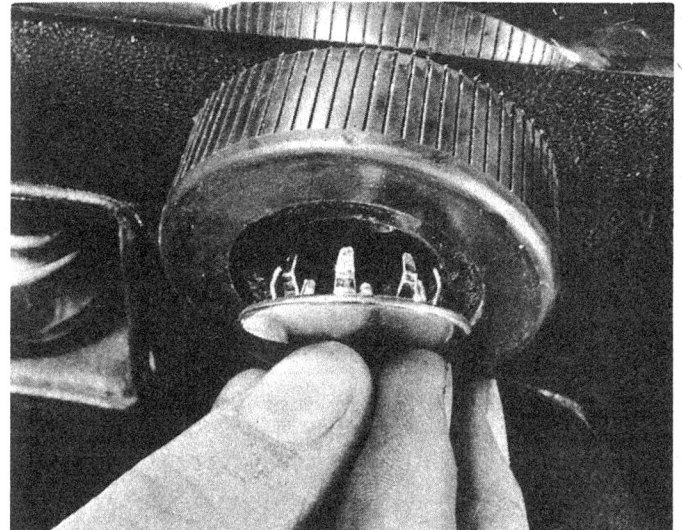

14.3A Removing blanking plate from ventilator control knob

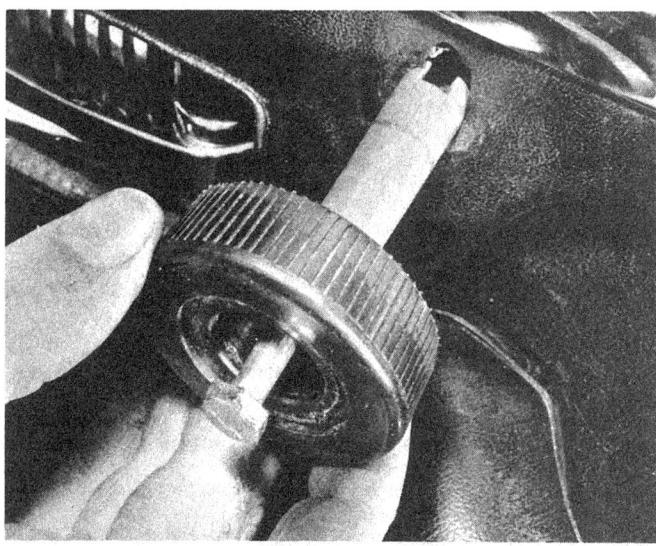

14.3B Withdrawing ventilator control knob

14.5 Removing door armrest

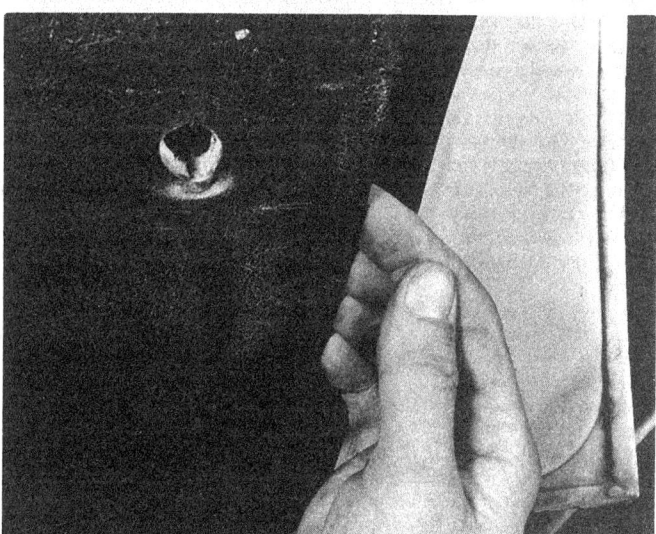

14.7 Removing door interior panel

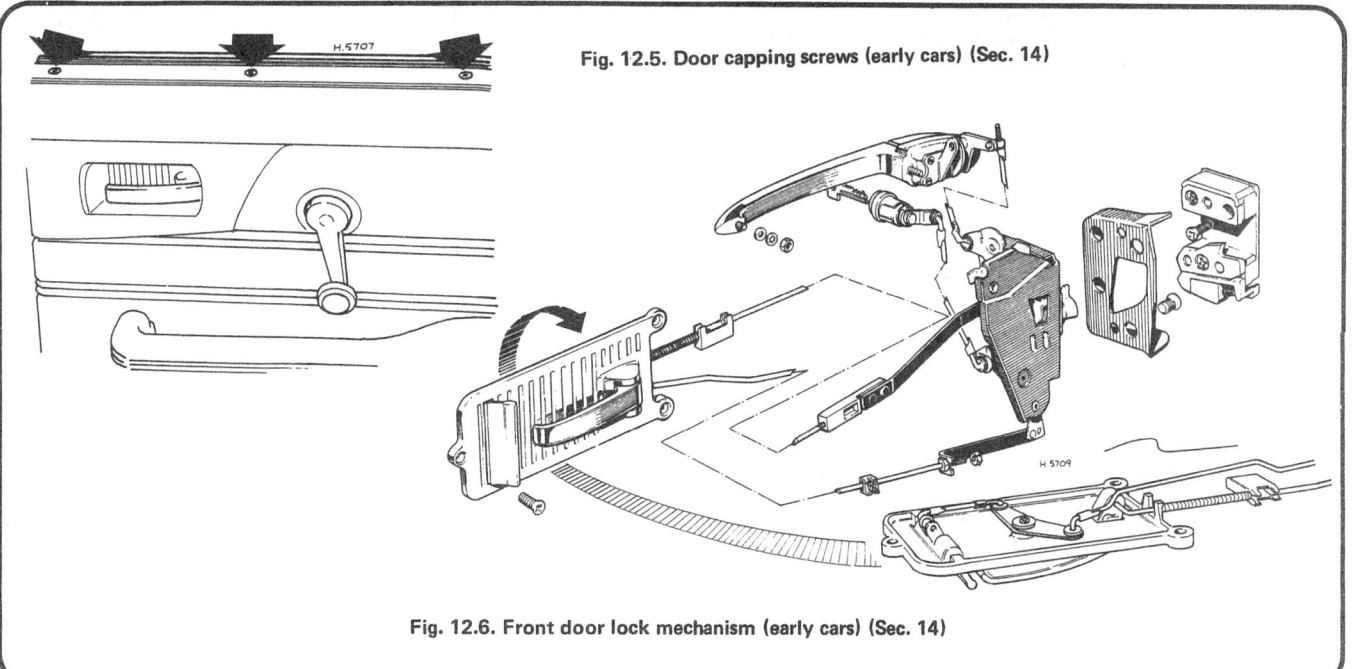

Fig. 12.5. Door capping screws (early cars) (Sec. 14)

Fig. 12.6. Front door lock mechanism (early cars) (Sec. 14)

to the door interior waist rail.

2 Four more screws will be exposed once the wood capping is removed and these should be unscrewed and the padded waist rail removed.

3 Prise out the centre plate (using a thin blade) from the swivelling ventilator control knob. The screw now exposed should be removed and the knob withdrawn (photos).

4 Remove the centre screw from the window regulator handle and pull off the handle (cars without electric windows).

5 Remove the two securing screws from its lower edge and withdraw the armrest (photo).

6 Carefully peel away the interior trim panel covering, where it is stuck to the edge of the window glass aperture.

7 Insert a wide blade or rule between the trim panel and the door and prise off the panel which is secured by spring clips. Work the fingers round the edge of the trim panel until all the spring clips are released (photo).

8 Temporarily refit the window regulator handle and wind the window up to its fullest extent.

9 Lift the insert from the bottom of the glass rear channel and remove the screw now exposed.

10 Remove the lower section of this channel by drawing it downward.

11 Release the two link rods which connect the exterior handle pushbutton and the key-operated lock by detaching the spring clips and prising the rods from the nylon bushes in the levers.

12 Remove the link rod which connects the remote control handle to the latch from its nylon coupling block and withdraw the nylon bearing from the door panel.

13 Disconnect the link rod which connects the inside safety locking lever to the latch lever after first releasing the locknuts and withdrawing the rod through the slot in the lever.

14 Remove the three screws which secure the latch and dovetail plate to the door and withdraw the latch through the aperture in the door panel.

15 The exterior handle can be removed after withdrawing the two securing screws.

16 The remote control unit can be removed after withdrawing its three securing screws.

17 The private lock is held in position by a spring clip which is accessible from inside the door cavity.

18 Refitting is a reversal of removal but observe the following points.

19 Check that the operating lever on the key-operated lock is towards the rear of the car when installed.

20 Adjust the outside handle pushbutton lever link rod by turning the trunnion so that there is a slight free-movement of the pushbutton when the link rod is connected to the latch. It is important that the screw in the pushbutton (which is located behind the pivoted lever) should be screwed in to its fullest extent.

21 Reconnect the link rod to the locking lever on the latch but do not tighten the adjuster nuts (Fig. 12.8) until they have been set to provide a slight free-movement in the lock lever before corresponding

movement in the latch locking lever takes place. The link rod lever should be connected to the rear hole in the latch lever.

22 Check the operation of the latch lever in the remote control unit. Slight free-movement must be provided by screwing the link rod in or out of the nylon adjuster block (A) which is attached to the handle.

23 The door should close smoothly and positively without rattle or any tendency for the striker plate to force the door upwards or downwards as it is closed. Adjust the position of the striker plate (by releasing its securing screws) until this situation is achieved.

Later cars

24 On later cars, disc type door locks are fitted which differ from earlier assemblies by the fact that the locks can only be locked by the use of the key.

25 Access to the lock mechanism is as described for the earlier type lock but the attachment details are as shown in Fig. 12.9.

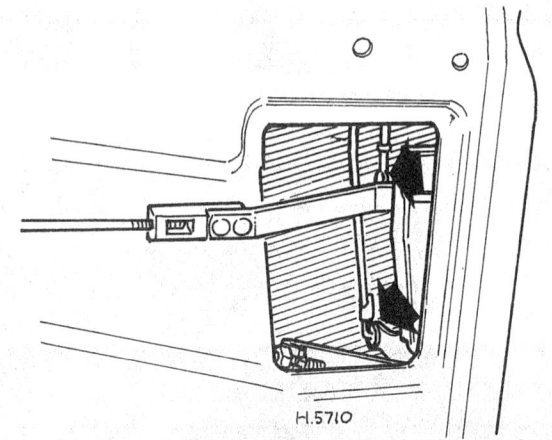

Fig. 12.7. Front door lock push-button and latch adjustment points (early cars) (Sec. 14)

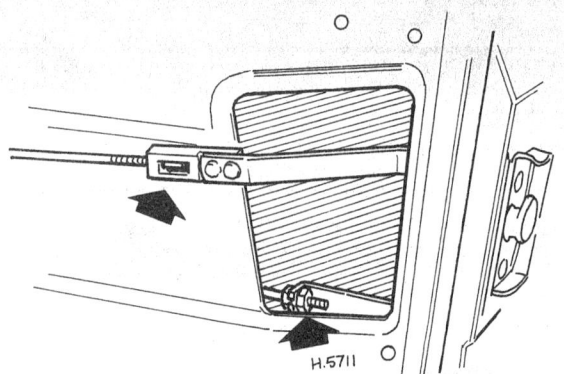

Fig. 12.8. Front door lock remote control adjustment points (early cars) (Sec. 14)

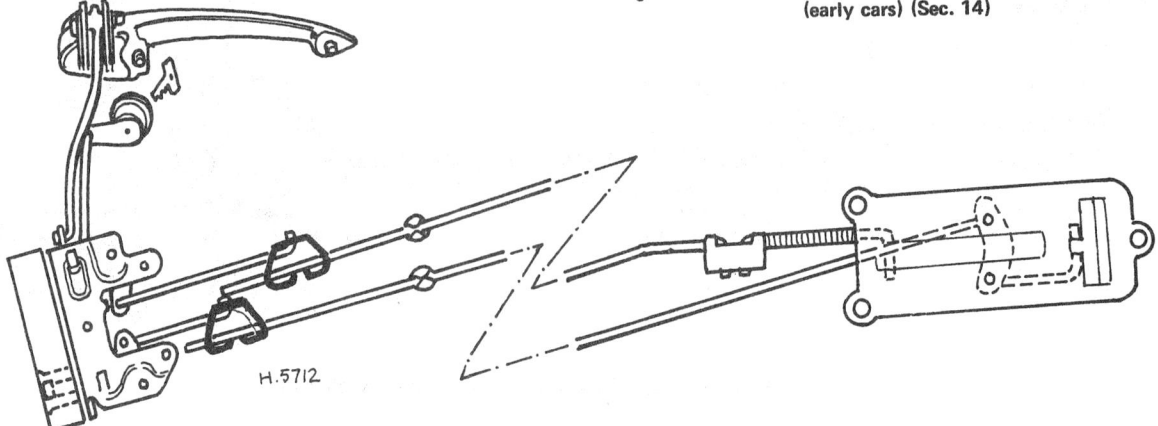

Fig. 12.9. Front door lock and latch (later cars) (Sec. 14)

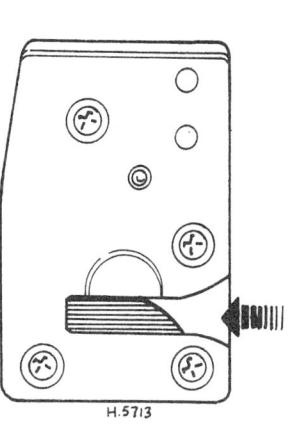

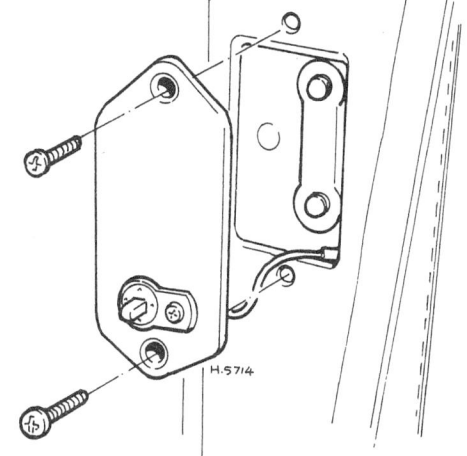

14.29 Front door trim panel removed showing
loudspeaker leads and power operated window
connections

Fig. 12.10. Door latch outer unit
disc in open position (Sec. 14)

Fig. 12.11. Rear door courtesy lamp switch plate removed
(Sec. 14)

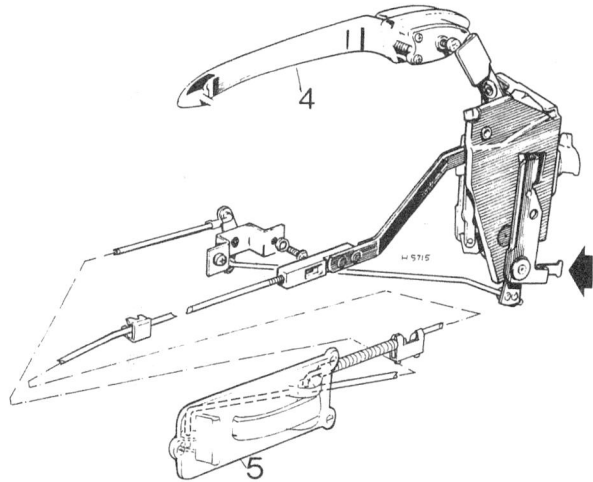

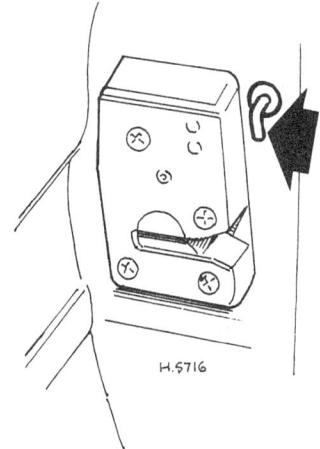

Fig. 12.12. Rear door lock mechanism (early cars)(Sec. 15)

4 Lock (arrow indicates child safety latch)

5 Remote control (rear view)

Fig. 12.13. Rear door latch on later cars
(child safety catch arrowed) (Sec. 15)

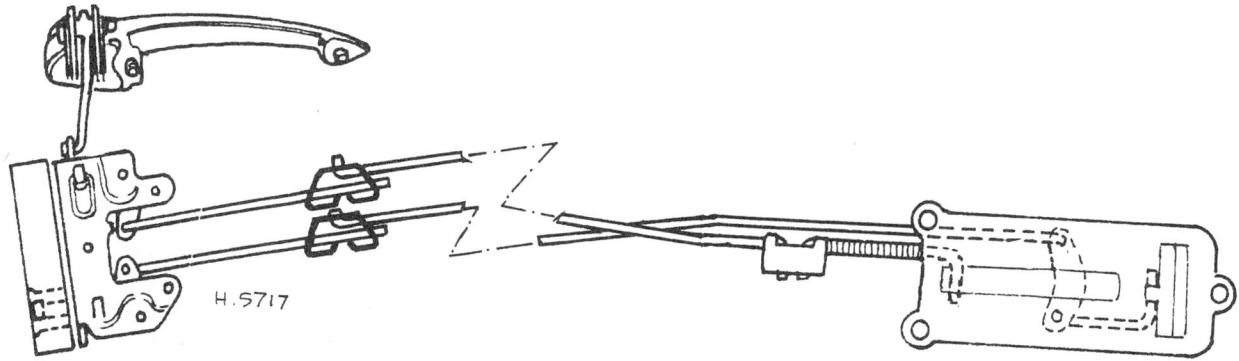

Fig. 12.14. Rear door lock mechanism (later cars) (Sec. 15)

26 When refitting this type of lock, make sure that the remote control lock lever is forward and the latch outer unit disc is in the open position.

27 Offer the latch outer unit to the latch mechanism so that the mounting holes are in alignment and then set the mechanism so that the pawl pin is beside the pawl operating lever. This is most important as the lock will be damaged if the latch outer unit and the latch mechanism plate is secured while the components are in opposing positions.

28 The striker plate on later model cars can only be removed from inside the door pillar. Access is obtained by disconnecting the battery and removing the rear door courtesy lamp switch plate. Adjustment of the striker plate can be carried out simply by releasing the two securing screws.

Series 2 cars

29 Access to the door locks on these cars is similar to the procedure described earlier in this Section except that radio speakers may be built into the armrests. In this case withdraw the screws from the lower edge of the armrest and withdraw it far enough to be able to disconnect the speaker leads (photo).

30 Disconnection of the remotely controlled exterior mirror is described in Section 53, and the crash roll which is fitted to the door interior panel is held in position by four screws and locating pegs.

Fig. 12.15. Method of access to rear door striker plate (later cars) (Sec. 15)

---

15 Rear door lock - removal and refitting

Early cars

1 The operations are similar to those described in the preceding Section, paragraphs 1 to 23, except for the following differences.

2 There is no ventilator control or armrest to be removed from the interior trim panel.

3 The screw located in the pushbutton operates the contactor directly on the lock latch and no link rod is fitted.

Later cars

4 On later cars, disc type door locks are fitted which incorporate a child safety locking device.

5 To remove this type of lock, wind the window up to its fullest extent and remove the link rods which connect the remote control unit to the latch mechanism (at the latch end).

6 Remove the exterior handle link rod from the handle.

7 Prise the safety lever from the latch mechanism lever.

8 Extract the four screws which secure the latch to the door edge and withdraw the latch from the door cavity.

9 Refitting is similar to the procedure described in Section 14, paragraphs 26 and 27 for the front door locks, except it is not necessary to set the latch plate mechanism although the latch outer unit disc must be in the open position as shown in Fig. 12.10.

10 The rear door lock striker plate can only be removed after withdrawing the panel edging trim and peeling away the adhesive tape which covers the access hole. Adjustment of the striker plate can be carried out simply by releasing (but not removing) the securing screws.

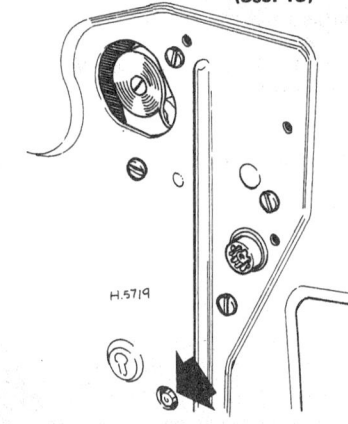

Fig. 12.16. Swivelling ventilator frame setscrew (early cars) (Sec. 16)

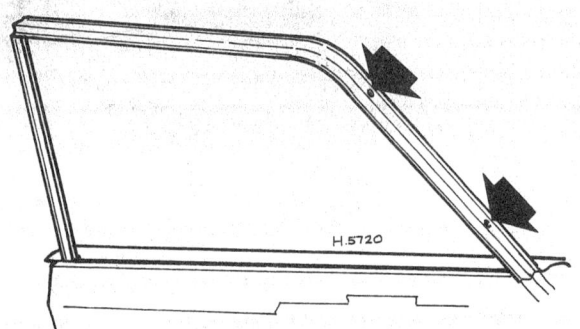

Fig. 12.17. Swivelling ventilator frame securing screws (early cars) (Sec. 16)

---

16 Front door swivelling ventilator - removal and refitting

1 Remove the door interior trim panel as described in Section 14.

2 Remove the two screws and withdraw the ventilator gearbox.

3 Remove the two setscrews and detach the buffer and bracket from the bottom of the door panel.

4 Remove the single setscrew and the two screws from the glass frame front channel.

5 Wind the window fully down and withdraw the ventilator from the door frame.

6 Refitting is a reversal of removal.

---

17 Front door glass (4 door cars) - removal and refitting

1 Remove the door interior panel (Section 14) and the swivelling ventilator (Section 16).

2 Prise out the weatherstrip from the doorframe.

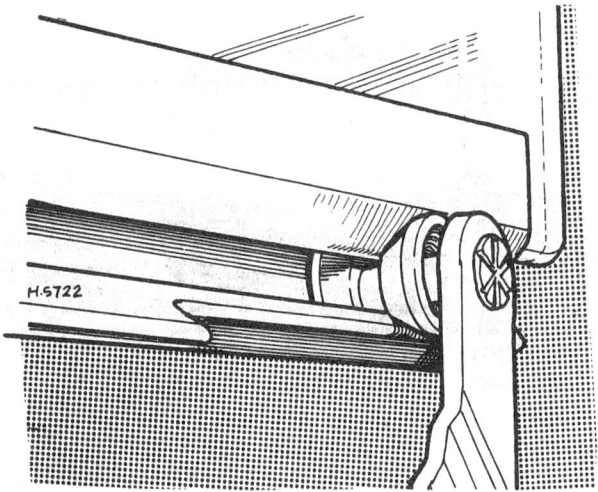

Fig. 12.18. Window regulator connection to glass channel (early cars) (Sec. 17)

3 Wind the glass up to the halfway position, slide it forward to clear the regulator arm and remove it from the door.
4 Refitting is a reversal of removal.

18 Rear door glass (4 door cars) - removal and refitting

1 Remove the door interior trim panel, as described in Section 14.
2 Remove the four screws and nuts and withdraw the detachable top section of the glass frame channel.
3 Wind the window fully up and then slide it forward to disengage the regulator arm and channel and then withdraw the glass upwards from the door cavity.

19 Rear door fixed quarter light (4 door cars) - removal and refitting

1 Remove the door interior trim panel, as previously described.
2 Remove the three screws which secure the bottom of the quarter light frame to the door panel.
3 Remove the two screws which secure the top of the frame to the window channel and then withdraw the quarterlight glass and frame.
4 Refitting is a reversal of removal.

20 Door glass and carrier (Series 2, two door cars) - removal and refitting

1 Remove the crashroll from the door interior panel. The crashroll is secured by four screws.
2 Remove the door interior trim panel (Section 14).
3 Remove the three screws which secure the glass bezel guide to the front of the door.
4 Remove the five screws which secure the crashroll retaining plate.
5 Prise away the anti-rattle pads which are located between the door frame and the glass.
6 Carefully remove the waterproof sheet clear of the window lift mechanism.
7 Lower the window sufficiently to be able to extract the four screws which secure the window mounting plate.
8 Slacken the two nuts which secure the window lift quadrant guide channel to the glass mounting.
9 Raise the window to its fullest extent then extract the two screws which secure the glass to the mounting plate.
10 Remove the rubber weatherstrip from the glass edge (closing face).
11 Ease the glass from the mounting plate and lift it from the door.
12 To remove the glass carrier assembly, extract the chrome beading and weatherstrip from the door and then raise the carrier to its fullest extent. Disengage the spring from the glass carrier plate.
13 Lower the carrier plate enough to permit access to the guide channel which locates the lift motor quadrant.
14 Remove the two nuts which secure the guide channel to the glass carrier, slide the channel from the lift motor quadrant and lift the guide from the door.
15 Disengage the spring assembly from the spigot mounting and lift the spring assembly from the door.
16 Remove the nylon pads from the top corners of the pulley mechanism frame.
17 Move the glass to give access to the four setscrews which secure the carrier plates, remove the setscrews and separate the outer plate from the inner one and withdraw the plates from the door.
18 Remove the four setscrews which secure the pulley mechanism to the door, retain the washers and then remove the carrier/pulley assembly from the door.
19 Refitting is a reversal of removal but observe the following points.
20 Make sure that the longer setscrews are located in the outer ends of the glass carrier plates.
21 Do not fully tighten screws on the carrier/pulley assembly until the glass is installed and the window fully raised.
22 When fitting the glass, close the door and adjust the glass to give a 9/32 in (7 mm) clearance between the drip rail and the edge of the glass.

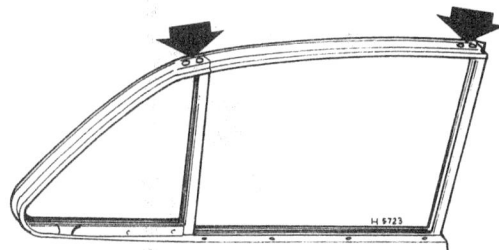

Fig. 12.19. Rear door glass frame channel screws (Sec. 18)

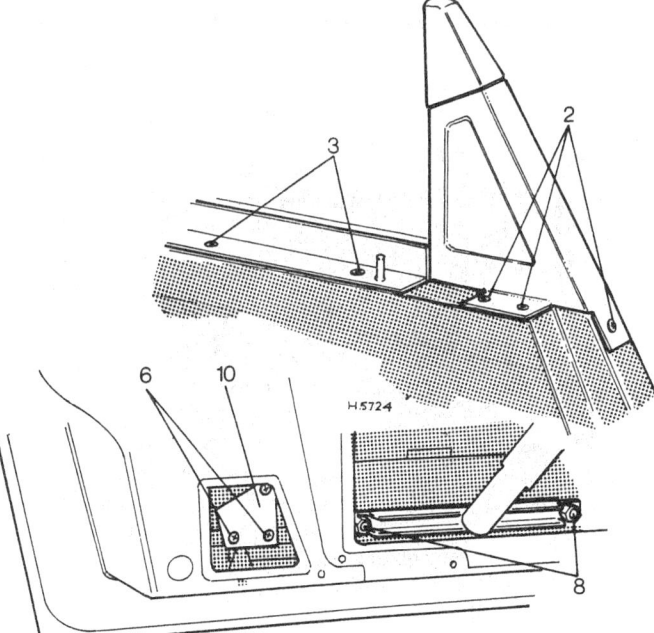

Fig. 12.20. Glass securing details (Series 2, two door cars) (Sec. 20)

2 Glass bezel guide screws	8 Window light quadrant guide unit
3 Crash roll plate screws	10 Glass to mounting plate securing screws
6 Window mounting plate screws	

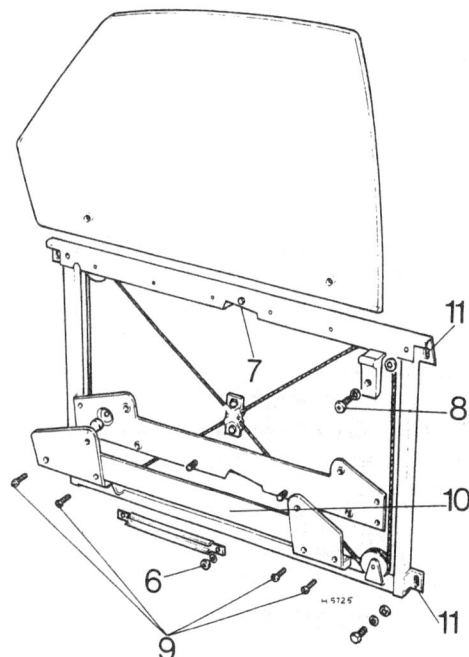

Fig. 12.21. Door glass carrier details (Series 2, two door cars)

6 Guide channel nuts	9 Carrier plate screws
7 Spring assembly	10 Carrier plate
8 Nylon anti-rattle pad screw	11 Pulley frame brackets

21 Rear quarter glass and carrier (Series 2 - two door cars) - removal and refitting

1 Remove the rear quarter trim panel, as described in Section 25.

2 Remove the rear quarter crashroll (two screws) and its mounting (five screws).

3 Peel away the waterproof sheet from the door and remove the two bolts which secure the glass buffer to the quarter panel, withdraw the buffer.

4 Lower the glass to its halfway position and support it at its lower edge.

5 Remove the four setscrews which secure the window lift motor to the quarter panel. Move the motor to the rear while disengaging the quadrant arm from the glass guide channel.

6 Withdraw the motor from the door aperture.

7 Pull the glass into the fully closed position and disengage the glass guide rollers from the carrier plate. Withdraw the glass completely.

8 To remove the glass carrier, extract the two bolts which secure the carrier to the lower mounting bracket, also the single bolt which secures it to the side mounting bracket.

9 Remove the two crosshead screws which secure the upper section of the glass carrier to the quarter panel.

10 Lower the glass carrier and disengage the upper section from the chrome beading. The carrier can now be withdrawn.

11 Refitting of the carrier and the glass is a reversal of removal but apply grease to the guide channels.

22 Electrically-operated windows

1 Refer to Chapter 10, Section 45, for details of this system

23 Solenoid-operated door locks

1 Refer to Chapter 10, Section 46, for details of this system fitted to Series 2 cars.

24 Window regulator (early cars) - removal and refitting

1 Remove the door interior trim panel as previously described.

2 Remove the four screws which secure the regulator mechanism to the door and then disengage the regulator arm and withdraw the mechanism from the door cavity.

3 Refitting is a reversal of removal.

25 Rear quarter trim panel (Series 2 - two door) - removal and refitting

1 Push both front seats fully forward and remove the screw from each side of the transmission tunnel. These screws secure the rear seat cushion to the seat pan crossmember.

2 Draw the seat cushion forward and remove it from the car.

3 Remove the two screws which secure the lower edge of the rear seat squab to the seat pan. Push the squab upwards and disengage it from its upper securing clips. Remove the squab.

4 Release the screws and remove the door sill tread plate.

5 Pull away the edging strip from the front edge of the quarter trim panel.

6 Remove the bolt which secures the seat belt lower anchor plate noting carefully the sequence of washers and spacers.

7 Prise off the plastic cover plate from the upper anchor plate and unbolt the seat belt.

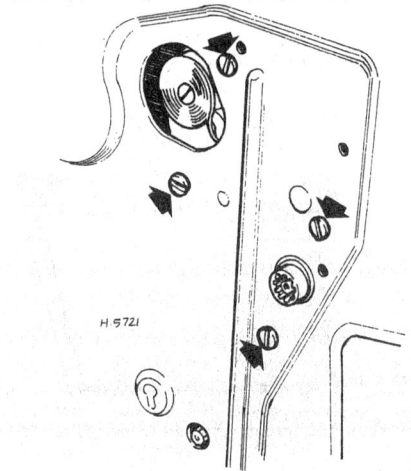

Fig. 12.23. Window regulator securing screws (early cars) (Sec. 24)

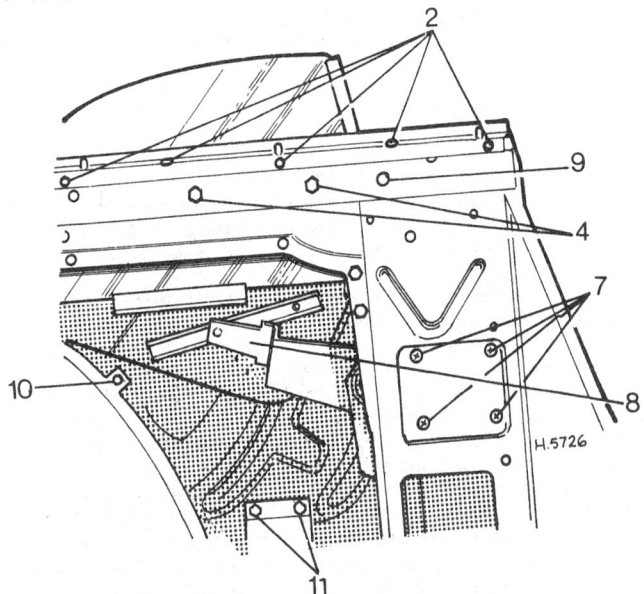

Fig. 12.22. Rear quarter glass details (Series 2, two door cars) (Sec. 21)

2	Crash roll screws	9	Glass carrier to panel screws
4	Glass buffer bolts	10	Glass carrier to side mounting
7	Window lift motor setscrews		bracket screws
8	Window lift quadrant arm	11	Glass carrier to lower mounting bracket screws

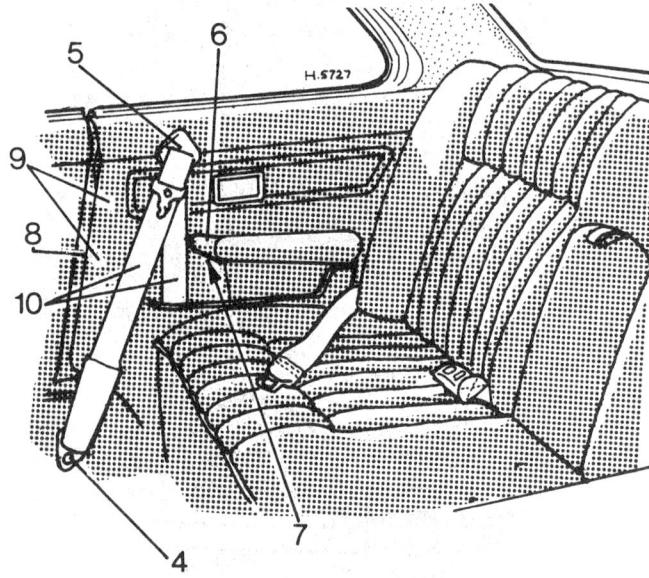

Fig. 12.24. Rear quarter trim panel details (Series 2 two door cars) (Sec. 25)

4	Seat belt lower anchorage	8	Edging trim
5	Seat belt upper anchorage	9	Quarter trim panel
6	Armrest bezel	10	Seat belt
7	Armrest screw		

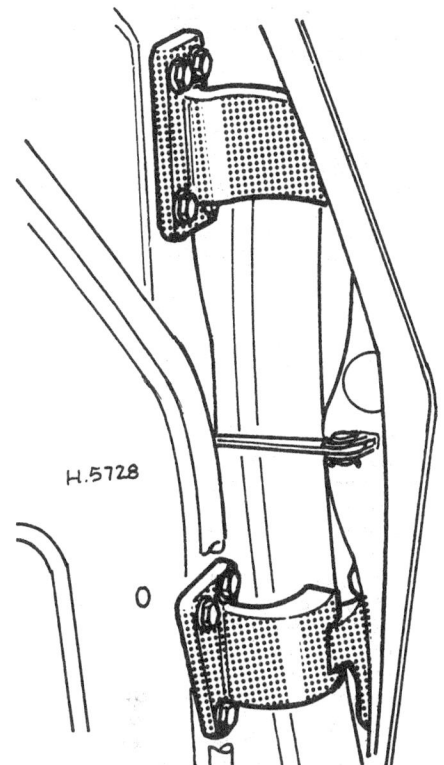

Fig. 12.25. Front door hinge locations (early cars) (Sec. 26)

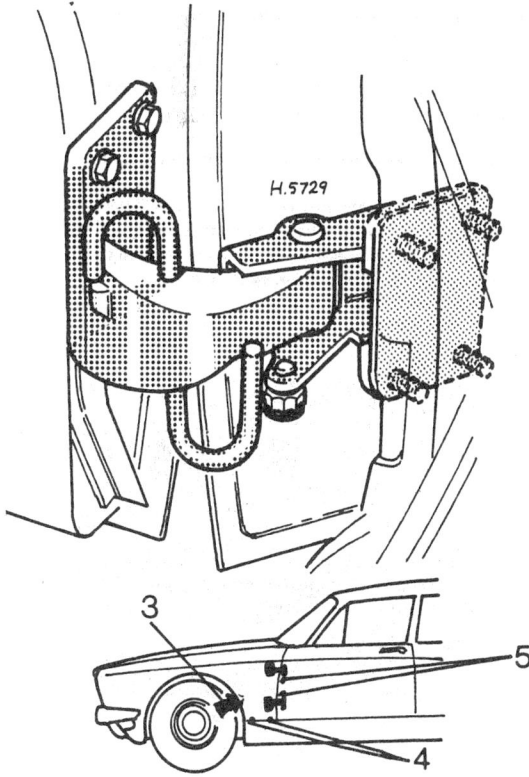

Fig. 12.26. Door hinge (Series 2 cars) (Sec. 27)

3 Under wing access panel   5 Wing to body pillar bolts
4 Wing to sill bolts

8 Remove the chrome bezel from the front of the armrest by extracting the screw and sliding the bezel forward. Remove the screw exposed by the removal of the bezel.
9 Peel the trim from the lip of the door aperture and prise the quarter trim panel from the car body.
10 Feed the seat belt through the hole in the panel and lift the panel from the car.
11 Refitting is a reversal of removal.

26 Front door (except Series 2 cars) - removal and refitting

1 Extract the split pin and the clevis pin from the door check strap bracket.
2 Mark the outline of the hinges on the door.
3 Open the door to its widest and support it under its lower edge on blocks covered with pads of rag.
4 Unscrew and remove the six bolts which secure the hinge plates to the door edge. Lift the door away.
5 If the hinges must be removed from the body pillar, mark the outline of the hinge plates before removing them. The wing will have to be separated from the lower sill and the valance before the hinge plate bolt heads can be unscrewed; see the next Section, paragraph 2.
6 Refitting is a reversal of removal and if the hinge plates are aligned with the marks made before removal, there should be no need for adjustment. However, where new components have been installed, do not tighten the hinge bolts until the door has been correctly aligned within the frame to give equal gaps all round. In extreme cases of mis-alignment shims may be required to be inserted under the hinge plates.
7 Finally, adjust the door lock striker plate to provide smooth positive closure.

27 Front door (Series 2) - removal and refitting

1 The procedure is similar to that described in the preceding Section except that spring type door checks are used instead of straps.
2 Access to the hinge bolts is obtained by removing the under wing panel and extracting the bolts which secure the lower edge of the wing to the sill and the rear of the wing to the body pillar. Prise the wing from the body pillar by driving in two wedges so that sufficient space is provided to engage a spanner on the hinge bolt heads.

28 Rear door - removal and refitting

1 The operations are similar to those described in the previous Sections 26 or 27, except that the hinges are secured to the door by two bolts and a special screw.

29 Windscreen - removal and refitting

This is a job best left to profressionals but where it is decided to carry out the work yourself, proceed in the following way with the help of an assistant.
1 Where a windscreen is to be renewed then if it is due to shattering, the fascia air vents should be covered before attempting removal. Adhesive sheeting is useful to stick to the outside of the glass to enable large areas of crystallised glass to be removed.
2 Where the screen is to be removed intact then an assistant will be required. First release the rubber surround from the bodywork by running a blunt, small screwdriver around and under the rubber weatherstrip both inside and outside the car. This operation will break the adhesive of the sealer originally used. Take care not to damage the paintwork or cut the rubber surround with the screwdriver. Remove the windscreen wiper arms and interior mirror and place a protective cover on the bonnet. Remove the bright trim from the rubber surround.
3 Have your assistant push the inner lip of the rubber surround off the flange of the windscreen body aperture. Once the rubber surround starts to peel off the flange, the screen may be forced gently outwards by careful hand pressure. The second person should support and remove the screen complete with rubber weatherseal.
4 Before fitting a windscreen, ensure that the rubber surround is completely free from old sealant, glass fragments and has not hardened

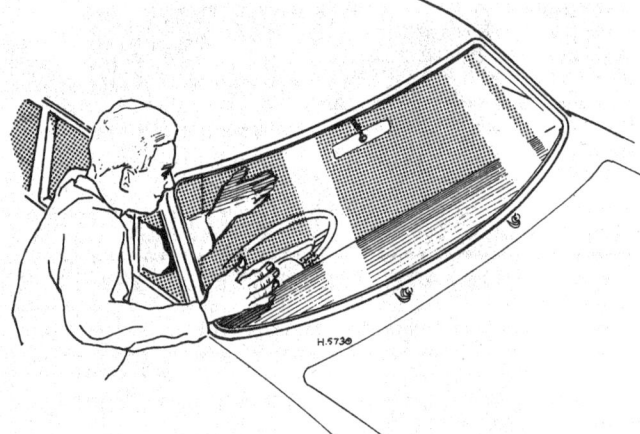

Fig. 12.27. Windscreen removal (Sec. 29)

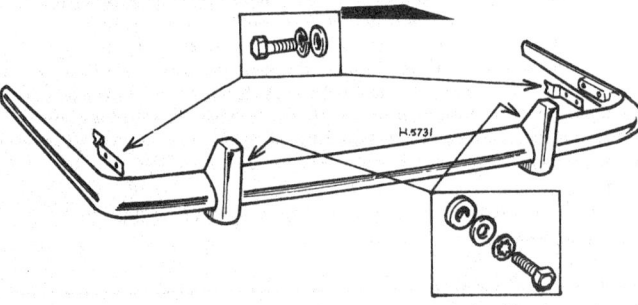

Fig. 12.28. Metal section rear bumper and fittings (Sec. 30)

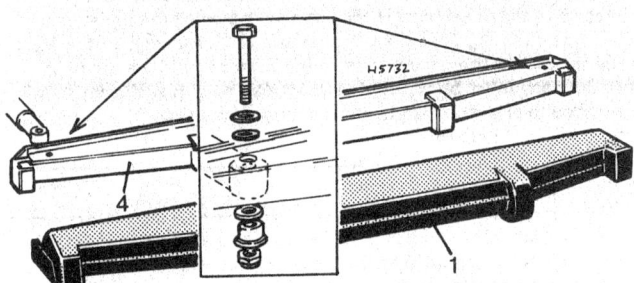

Fig. 12.29. Impact absorbing type bumper (Sec. 30)

1   *Impact absorbing cover*   4   *Bumper bar*

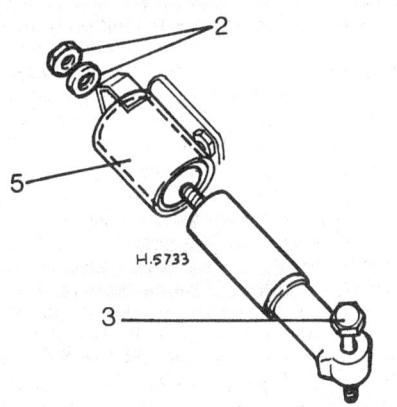

Fig. 12.30. Energy absorbing strut used with impact absorbing type bumper (Sec. 30)

2   *Strut to mounting tube nut*   5   *Rubber insulating sleeve*
3   *Strut to bumper bolt*

or cracked. Fit the rubber surround to the glass and apply a bead of suitable sealant between the glass outer edge and the rubber.
5   Cut a piece of strong cord greater in length than the periphery of the glass and insert it into the body flange locating channel of the rubber surround.
6   Apply a thin bead of sealant to the face of the rubber channel which will eventually mate with the body.
7   Offer the windscreen to the body aperture and pass the ends of the cord, previously fitted and located at bottom centre into the vehicle interior.
8   Press the windscreen into place, at the same time have an assistant pulling the cords to engage the lip of the rubber channel over the body flange.
9   Remove any excess sealant with a paraffin soaked rag.
10 Removal and installation of the rear window glass is carried out in an identical manner but (if fitted) disconnect the leads to the heating element in the glass.

30 Bumpers - removal and refitting

1   Removal and dismantling standard type metal section bumpers is simply a matter of removing the securing bolts and lifting the bumper assembly from the car.
2   Impact-absorbing type bumpers installed on later cars supplied to North America must be renewed if deformed and great care must be taken to set their height and alignment correctly.
3   This type of bumper is dismantled by first unbolting and then peeling the absorbent cover from the bumper bar.
4   Unbolt and remove the bumper bar and then withdraw the telescopic strut assemblies. To do this, unscrew the nut which retains the strut in its mounting tube and then place a bolt in the strut front eye and use this as the point of impact to drive the strut from its tube. If the struts are damaged or offer little or no resistance when compressed then they must be renewed as units.

31 Heating and ventilation system - description

1   The heating system comprises the necessary intake and ducting to direct air to the windscreen, front interior and rear passenger compartment by passing the air over a matrix which is heated from the engine cooling system.
2   The necessary controls are provided to regulate the air temperature and the volume and direction of flow of the air. On earlier cars, the controls are operated by vacuum from the engine. On Series 2 cars, the controls are of vacuum and mechanically actuated type. A vacuum tank provides a reserve to enable six operations of the controls to be carried out after the engine has been switched off.

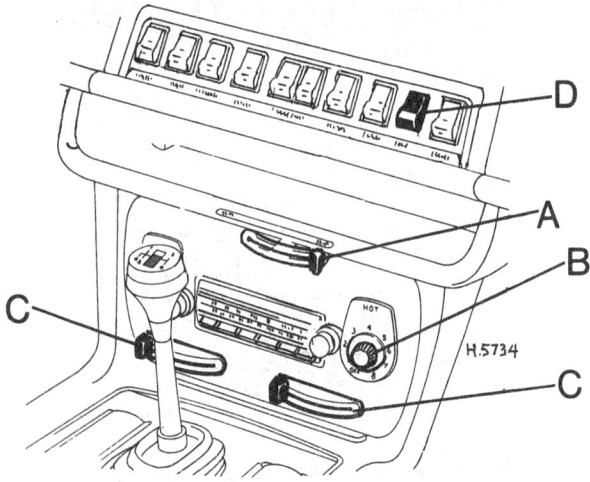

Fig. 12.31. Heater controls (Sec. 31)

A   *Fresh air*   C   *Air distribution*
B   *Heat*   D   *Fan*

3   A two-speed booster fan is provided for use in conditions when the car is not moving forward fast enough to provide the normal ram effect.

4   An independent fresh air supply is provided from outlets on the fascia panel and on later cars a further fresh air outlet at lower level is positioned for both front seat occupants.

32 Heater vacuum servo system components (except Series 2 cars) - removal and refitting

1   Failure of any one of the components of the vacuum control system will normally require renewal of the unit. Before taking this action however, always check the connecting hoses for security of joints and for perforation.

Flap actuator

2   This flap allows fresh air to be drawn into the heating system.

3   To remove it, prise off the air intake grille from the scuttle by inserting two small screwdrivers at opposite sides of the grille (photo).

4   Raise the bonnet and detach the vacuum pipe from the actuator unit.

5   Remove the two nuts which are accessible from within the plenum chamber and withdraw the actuator securing bolts.

6   Disconnect the coupling rod from the flap and then remove the actuator unit.

32.3 Air intake grille removed

7   Refitting is a reversal of removal but make sure that no preload is placed on the diaphragm when connecting the coupling rod to the flap. The rod length can be adjusted to avoid this situation by screwing the rod in or out.

Fig. 12.32. Heater vacuum servo system (early cars) (Sec. 32)

1   Air flap modulator
2   Actuator
3   Heat control modulator
4   Heater sensing unit
5   Water valve
6   Vacuum tank
7   Non-return valve
A   To manifold
B   Water inlet
C   Water outlet

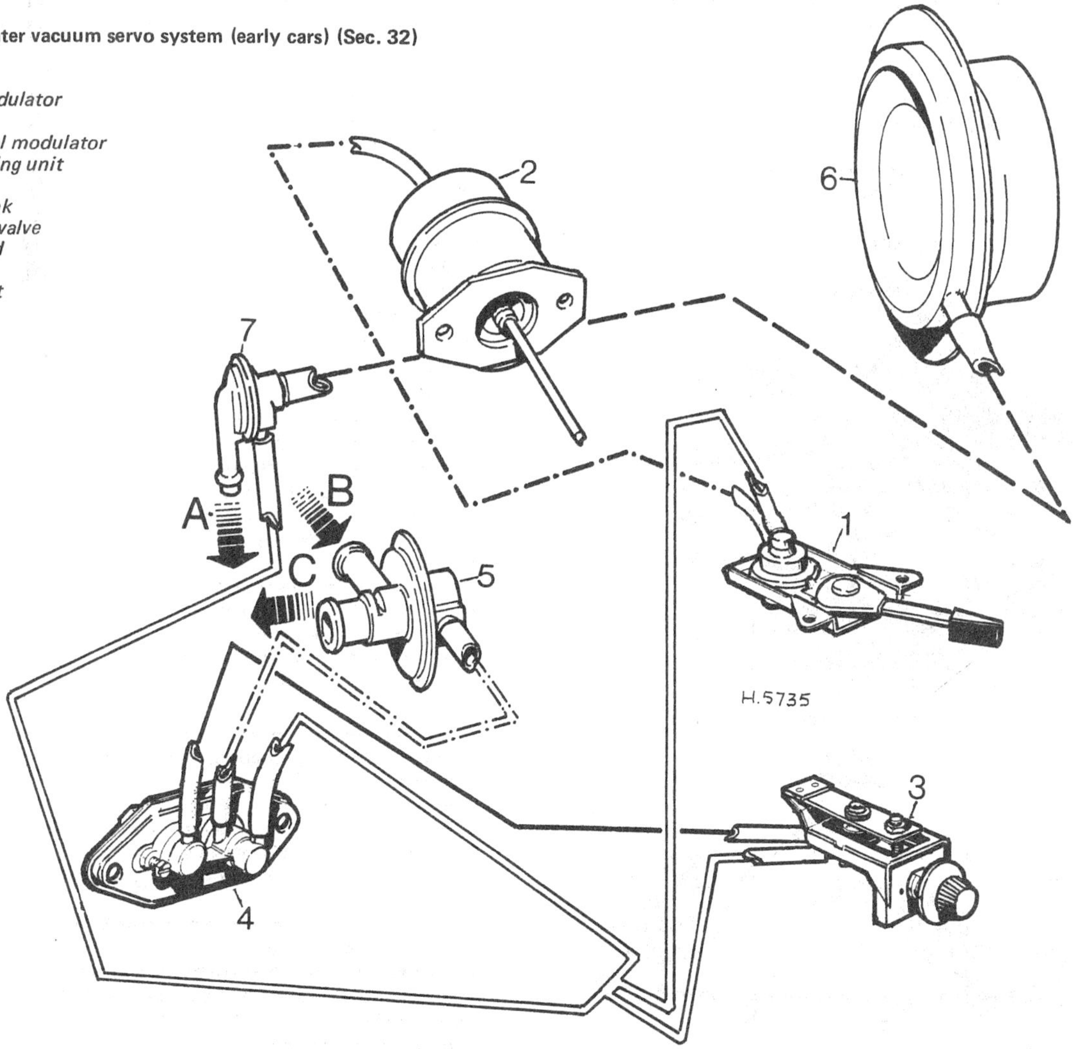

H.5735

Flap control quadrant modulator

8 This is mounted centrally in the panel above the radio aperture and is a conical valve which controls the degree of vacuum which exists between the vacuum tank and the flap actuator.

9 To remove the modulator, withdraw the knobs from the three heater control levers, also the knobs from the heat control rotary modulator and the radio.

10 Insert a small screwdriver behind the lever escutcheons and lever them from the nylon bush retainers. Remove the control panel fascia.

11 Extract the four screws and withdraw the heater control panel to the rear in order to gain access to the modulator securing screws.

12 Disconnect the vacuum pipes, remove the two securing screws and lift out the modulator.

13 Refitting is a reversal of removal.

Water valve servo unit

14 This is a diaphragm valve which, controlled by a combination of the vacuum tank, heat control rotary modulator and heat sensing unit, regulates the flow of water through the heater matrix.

15 To remove the unit, drain the cooling system, as described in Chapter 2.

16 Disconnect the hoses from the unit and remove it.

17 Refitting is a reversal of removal.

Heat control rotary modulator

18 This device is very similar to the flap control modulator except that it has a rotary type control knob. Refer to paragraphs 8 to 13, of this Section for removal and refitting operations.

Heat sensing unit

19 This unit is located in the air ducts below the instrument panel and is basically a valve which automatically controls the coolant flow through the water valve irrespective of the engine water pump speed.

20 Access to this component is obtained in the same way as described for the flap control modulator (paragraphs 8 to 11).

21 Disconnect the three vacuum pipes from the unit, remove the two securing screws and lift the unit away.

22 Refitting is a reversal of removal but install a new joint between the sensing unit and the duct if necessary.

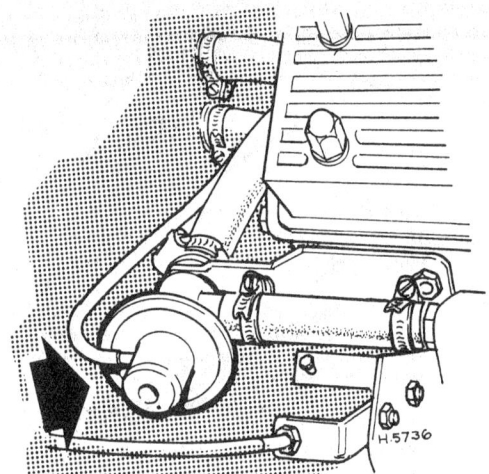

Fig. 12.33. Location of heater water valve servo unit (Sec. 32)

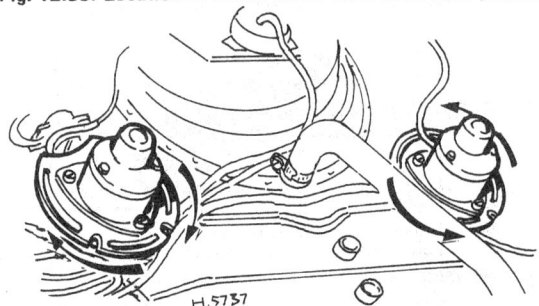

Fig. 12.34. Heater fans (early cars) showing direction of rotation (Sec. 33)

33 Heater fans (except Series 2 cars) - removal and refitting

1 The twin heater booster fans are speed controlled by resistance units wired in series. In the event of wear or a fault occurring in the fan motors, they must be renewed as units.

2 To remove a fan/motor assembly, disconnect the leads from the resistance units on the engine compartment rear bulkhead.

3 Remove the motor mounting plate screws, lift the motor/fan assembly from the bulkhead, detaching the electrical leads from their clips as it is withdrawn.

4 Remove the mounting plate and impeller for fitting to the new motor. It must be noted that the units are handed for left and right-hand rotation; do not interchange them and check that the correct type has been obtained as a replacement.

5 Refitting is a reversal of removal but renew the motor mounting plate sealing gasket, if necessary, to provide a tight joint.

34 Heater matrix (except Series 2 cars) - removal and refitting

1 The heater matrix is located on the engine compartment rear bulkhead and it is retained in position by the compression of foam rubber pads which takes place when the heater/air duct assembly is installed.

2 Drain the cooling system (Chapter 2).

3 Disconnect the battery.

4 Disconnect the coolant hoses from the matrix.

5 Remove the radio/heater control panel as described in Section 26 paragraphs 9, 10 and 11.

6 Disconnect the radio and the heater control vacuum pipes having first marked them so that they can be correctly reconnected.

7 Remove the side fascia panels as described in Section 47.

8 Remove the instrument panel as described in Chapter 10.

9 Remove the centre console as described in Section 45.

10 Remove the four nuts and detach the two struts which support the fascia assembly.

11 Remove the left and right-hand air ducts (four screws).

12 Remove the plenum chamber from the bulkhead (eight screws).

13 Withdraw the heater matrix. If the matrix is leaking have it professionally repaired or renew it. If the matrix is blocked, try reverse flushing it or use proprietary cleansing compound strictly in accordance with the manufacturer's instructions.

14 Refitting is a reversal of removal but renew the foam pads instead of refitting the original deformed ones.

35 Heater controls (Series 2 cars) - removal and refitting

1 Disconnect the battery and remove the centre console (Section 46).

2 Remove the two bolts which secure the control panel mounting plate to the heater (Fig. 12.35).

3 Remove the three screws which secure the vacuum switches to the mounting plate. Identify the vacuum pipes and disconnect them from the switches.

4 Extract the circlip from the shaft of the temperature control switch.

5 Remove the mounting plate from its studs.

6 The micro or vacuum switches can be removed from the mounting plate after extracting the securing screws.

7 Refitting is a reversal of removal.

36 Heater temperature control cable assembly (Series 2 cars) - removal and refitting

1 Disconnect the battery and remove the centre console (Section 46).

2 Remove the under scuttle casing.

3 Remove the radio/heater control mounting panel from the left-hand side of the heater.

4 Remove the four self-tapping screws which secure the air outlet duct in the right-hand footwell.

5 Remove the three self-tapping screws which secure the duct assembly in the right-hand footwell and at the rear outlet. One of these screws is located behind the control mounting panel and needs the use of a right-angled crosshead screwdriver.

6 Set the temperature control knob in the vent position, loosen the

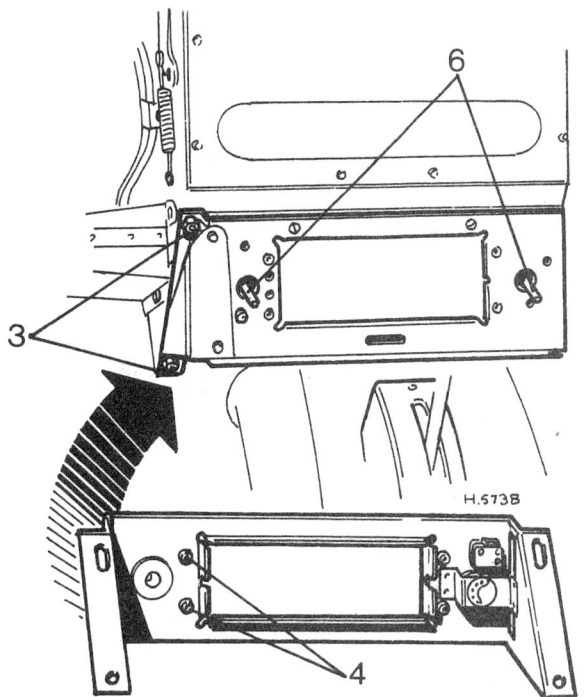

Fig. 12.35. Heater control mounting plate (Series 2) (Sec. 35)

3 *Mounting plate to heater nuts*
4 *Vacuum switch screws*
6 *Airflow and temperature control switch shafts*

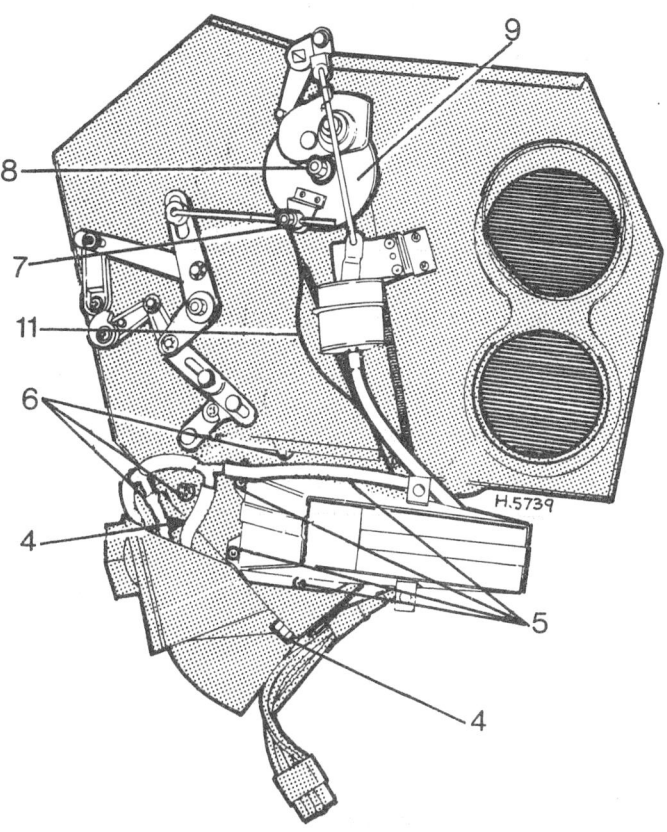

Fig. 12.36. Heater temperature control cable assembly (Series 2 cars)
(Sec. 36)

4 *Control panel to heater securing unit*
5 *Footwell air outlet duct screws*
6 *Rear air outlet screws*
7 *Flap link rod nut*
8 *Drive wheel pivot nut*
9 *Main drive wheel*
11 *Temperature control cable*

flap link operating rod locknut on the main drive wheel. Remove the
nut and washer from the pivot of the main drive wheel.
7 Lift the jockey pulleys against the tension of the springs and
withdraw the main drive wheel from its pivot.
8 Ease the radio/heater control panel and the right-hand footwell
outlet assembly away from the heater.
9 Disconnect the control cable.
10 When refitting the cable, wind it round the main drive wheel 3½
times. Make sure that the cable can be locked to the bollard on the
wheel by the washer under the locking screw but do not tighten it at
this stage.
11 Set the temperature control at the 10 o'clock position and locate
the cable round the jockey pulleys in such a way that the upper strand
of the cable leaves the bollard and passes round the forward pulley.
Pull the ends of the cable as far as possible horizontally and then adjust
the cable until the nipples are level with each other.
12 Tighten the bollard locking screw and fit the cable end nipples into
the main driving wheel making sure that the ends of the cable do not
cross.
13 Refit the radio/heater control panel and the footwell outlet assembly.
14 Keeping the cable taut, refit the main driving wheel to the pivot and
screw on the nut and washer.
15 The flap linkage should be adjusted as described in the next Section.
16 Complete the refitting by reversing the rest of the removal operations.

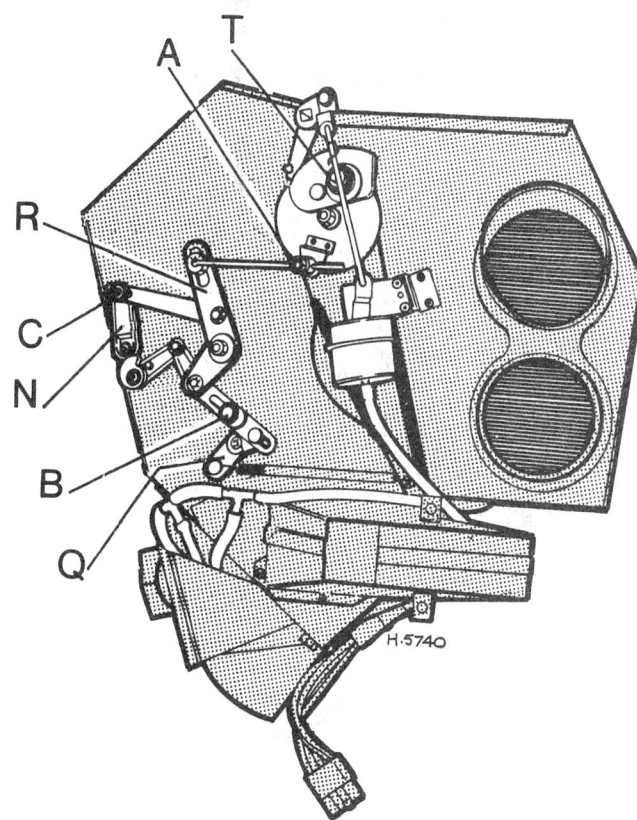

Fig. 12.37. Heater flap linkage (Series 2 cars) (Sec. 37)

A *Locking screw*
B *Locking screw*
C *Locking screw*
N *Lever operating flap*
Q *Lever operating flap*
R *Lever*
T *Eccentric pivot*

37 Heater flap linkage (Series 2) - adjustment

1 Turn the temperature control knob to vent.
2 Refer to Fig. 12.37 and slacken the locking screws 'A', 'B' and 'C'.
3 Turn the lever 'R' to a fully clockwise position and hold in this
position using firm finger-pressure. Tighten locking screw 'A'.

4 Press flap 'N' to a fully clockwise position and tightening locking screw 'C'.

5 Turn the temperature control knob to defrost. Using a screwdriver engaged in the slotted end of the adjusting link, push the operating flap 'Q' fully clockwise and tighten lockscrew 'B'.

6 The eccentric pivot 'T' on the upper flap actuating cam is adjustable through 180° to vary the level of face level air temperature.

38 Heater air intake and outlet grilles (Series 2) - removal and refitting

Demister duct outlets

1 These can be removed by levering them from their surround.

2 Refit by pressing firmly into place.

Demister flap and actuator

3 Remove the crash roll from the fascia (Section 51).

4 Remove the two nuts which secure the flap assembly to the screen rail.

5 Disconnect the plastic ducting and the vacuum tube and lift the flap/actuator assembly from the screen rail.

6 Refitting is a reversal of removal.

Ventilator fascia outlets

7 Disconnect the battery.

8 Remove the fascia (Section 51).

9 Unclip the side outlets at the rear of the fascia or remove the four securing screws from the centre outlet.

10 Refitting is a reversal of removal.

Rear ventilator

11 Raise the console glovebox lid and extract the two screws which secure the lid retaining bar.

12 Withdraw the three screws which secure the hinge plate to the glovebox.

13 Extract the three screws which secure the glovebox liner.

14 Pass the hand under the glovebox liner and grip the bayonet type locking ring of the air vent assembly. Press in and rotate the vent anticlockwise until the locking ring releases. Withdraw the air vent assembly.

15 Refitting is a reversal of removal.

Fig. 12.38. Demister duct (Series 2 cars) (Sec. 38)

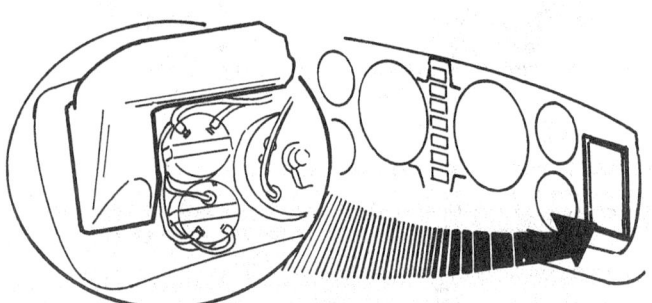

Fig. 12.40. Ventilator fascia outlet (Series 2 cars) (Sec. 38)

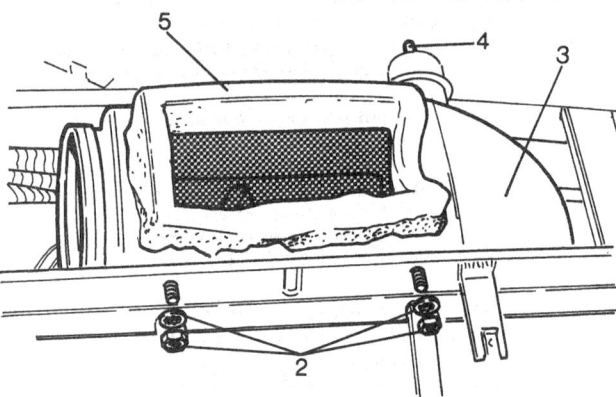

Fig. 12.39. Demister flap and actuator (Series 2 cars) (Sec. 38)

2 Securing nuts	4 Vacuum tube connection on actuator
3 Plastic ducting	5 Flap assembly

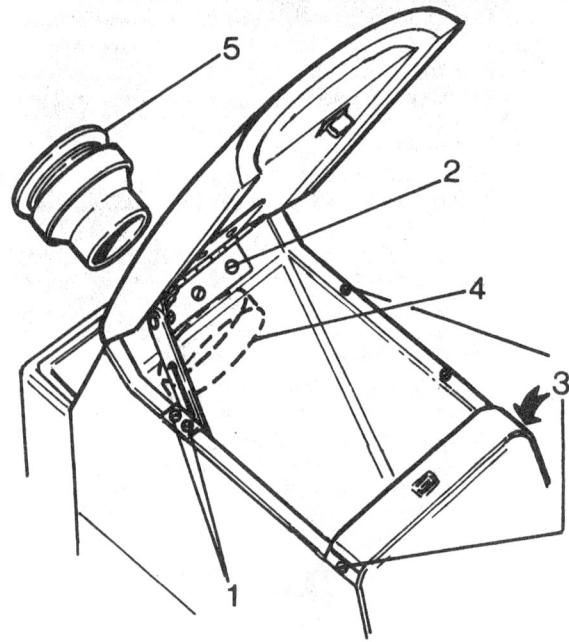

Fig. 12.41. Rear ventilator (Series 2 cars) (Sec. 38)

1 Lid retaining bar screws	4 Air vent locking ring
2 Hinge plate screws	5 Air vent assembly
3 Liner screws	

Fresh air intakes

16 To remove the grille from the scuttle just in front of the windscreen, prise it out with a sharp screwdriver.
17 Disconnect the washer tube from the washer jet.
18 To remove the intake grille located above the outer headlamp lens, withdraw the screw and lift the embellisher upwards to clear the lower retaining tags.

39 Heater motor/fan units (Series 2) - removal and refitting

1 Disconnect the battery.
2 Remove the under scuttle casing from the right-hand side if access to the right-hand motor is required or from the left-hand side if the left-hand motor is to be removed.
3 Remove the fusebox and move it to one side or alternatively remove the glovebox liner dependent upon whether the car is LHD or RHD and to which motor access is required. Inspection will enable the correct procedure to be adopted.
4 Pull the pliable air duct from the outlets at the side of the heater unit.
5 Remove the side fascia panels.
6 Extract the two screws which secure the fresh air outlet control bracket.
7 Unscrew and remove the two motor mounting nuts, disconnect the vacuum tube from the actuator, disconnect the electrical leads and withdraw the motor/fan assembly.
8 Reassembly is a reversal of removal but the top air flap should be closed so that it can enter into its aperture and seal. To close the flap apply vacuum to the actuator by connecting a length of tubing between the open end of the original tubing and the actuator.

40 Heater motor resistance unit (Series 2 cars) - removal and refitting

Left-hand drive cars

1 Disconnect the battery and remove the fascia under scuttle casing from the driver's side.
2 Remove the side panel from the centre console.
3 Mark the cables and disconnect them from the resistance unit.
4 Remove the three securing screws and withdraw the resistance unit from the heater casing.

Right-hand drive cars

5 Disconnect the battery.
6 Remove the glove compartment liner.
7 Repeat operations described in paragraphs 3 and 4.
8 Refitting is a reversal of removal.

41 Heater motor relays (Series 2 cars) - removal and refitting

1 Disconnect the battery.
2 Remove the left-hand side casing from the centre console.
3 Remove the left-hand air outlet duct (four screws) from the footwell.
4 Mark the electrical leads and disconnect them.
5 Remove the securing nuts and withdraw the relay unit.
6 Refitting is a reversal of removal but make sure that the earth lead is secured under one of the relay securing nuts.

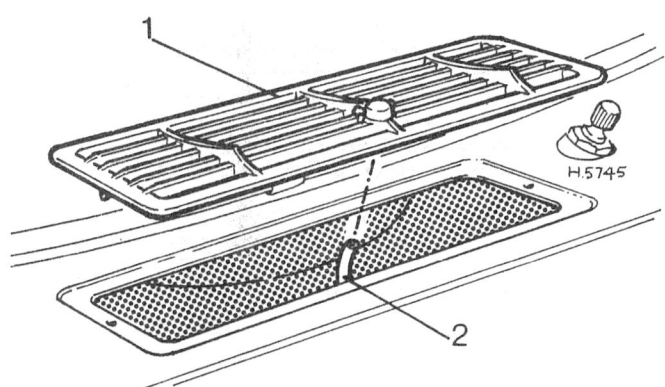

Fig. 12.42. Fresh air intake grille (Series 2 cars) (Sec. 30)

1 Grille   2 Washer tube

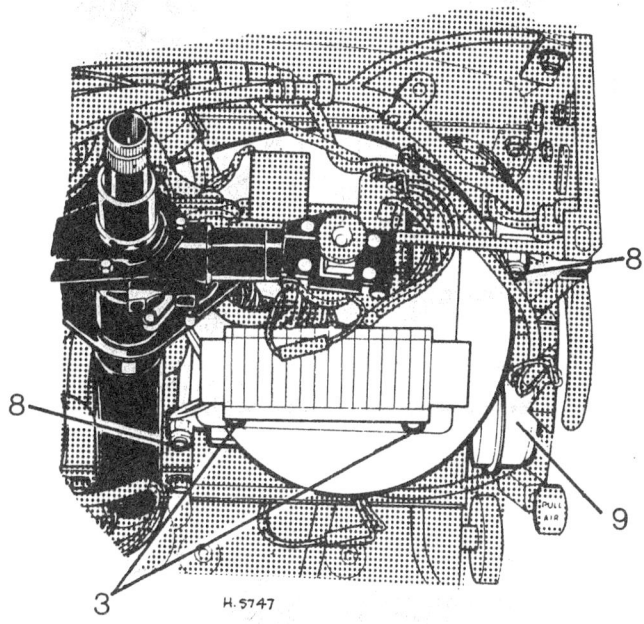

Fig. 12.44. Heater motor mounting (Series 2 cars) (Sec. 39)

3 Fuse block mounting nuts
8 Heater motor assembly mounting nuts
9 Vacuum actuator

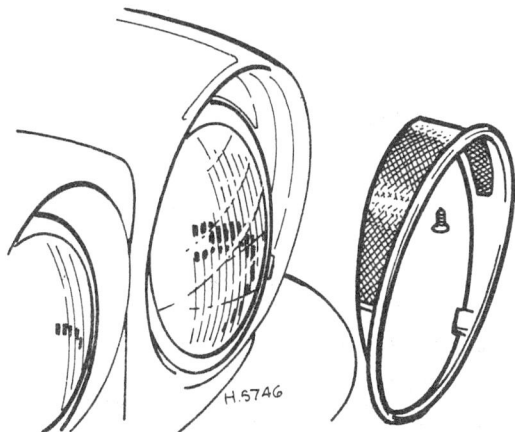

Fig. 12.43. Headlamp fresh air intake (later cars) (Sec. 38)

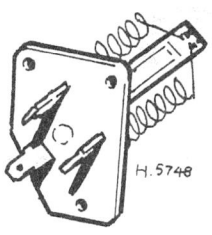

Fig. 12.45. Heater motor resistance unit (Series 2 cars) (Sec. 40)

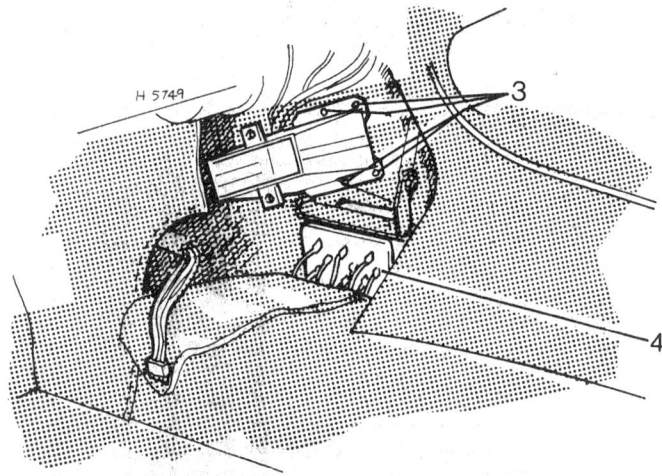

Fig. 12.46. Location of heater motor relays (Series 2 cars) (Sec. 41)

3   Footwell air outlet duct   4   Heater relay

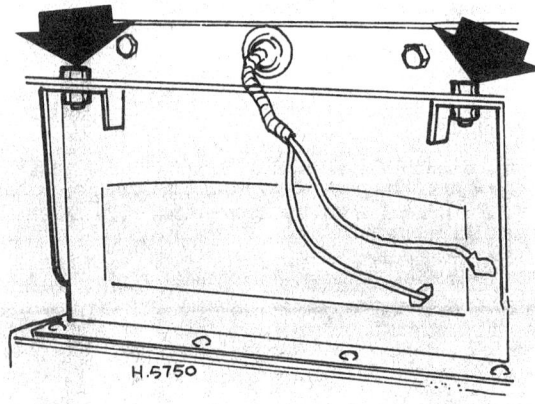

Fig. 12.47. Heater securing nuts on bulk head (Series 2 cars) (Sec. 42)

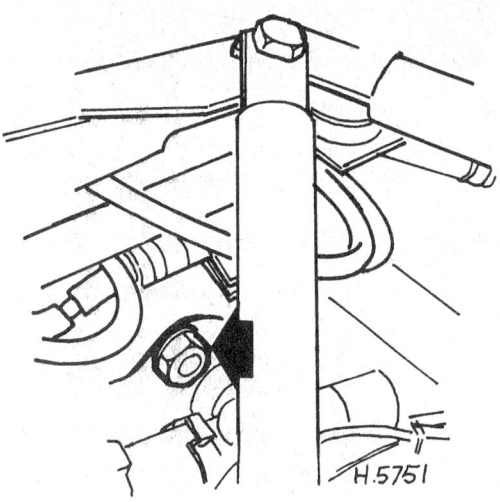

Fig. 12.48. Heater securing nuts on top rail (Series 2 cars) (Sec. 42)

42 Heater unit (Series 2 cars) - removal and refitting

1   Disconnect the battery and drain the cooling system.
2   Carry out the following operations described in other Sections of this Chapter:

   Remove the fascia crash roll.
   Remove the fascia side panel from the driver's side.
   Remove the fascia side panel from the passenger's side.
   Remove the glove compartment liner.
   Remove the centre parcels shelf.
   Remove the centre console.
   Remove the fascia panel.

3   Disconnect the heater hoses from the nozzles on the engine compartment rear bulkhead.
4   Remove the two large nuts from the centre of the bulkhead within the engine compartment.
5   Remove the two retaining nuts from the centre of the top rail.
6   Remove the bayonet fixing type stub pipes from the sides of the heater unit.
7   Disconnect the vacuum control tubes but first mark them clearly for reconnection.
8   Disconnect the multi-pin connectors at each side of the heater unit.
9   Ease the heater unit out and lift it from the car. Take care to protect the carpet against coolant which may be spilled during removal. The gearlever on manual gearbox cars should be in 2nd, 4th or reverse and on automatic transmission cars in '1' to prevent obstruction during removal of the heater.
10 Refitting is a reversal of the removal operations.

43 Heater matrix (Series 2 cars) - removal and refitting

1   Remove the heater unit, as described in the preceding Section.
2   Using a quick drying paint, mark the relative positions of all the heater control rods, knobs and cams.
3   Disconnect the tensioning springs from the heater matrix control flap operating arms.
4   Disconnect the operating rods.
5   Disconnect the inlet and outlet pipes from the heater casing.
6   Remove the heater matrix cover plate (six screws).
7   Remove the single screw which secures the cam and the operating arm to the footwell outlet flap shaft and remove the arm.
8   Withdraw the heater matrix from the side of the heater casing using a steady pull.
9   If the matrix has been leaking, do not waste your time trying to solder it as the heat must be localised otherwise more damage will be caused. It is better to renew the matrix on an exchange basis. If the matrix is blocked, try reverse flushing with a cold water hose. In extreme cases use a proprietary descaler and cleanser. If this fails, renew the matrix.
10 Refitting is a reversal of removal but make sure that the shock absorbing pads are correctly positioned and that the control rods are connected with their paint marks in alignment.

44 Air-conditioning system

1   This is a factory-fitted option and operations must be restricted to those described in this Section. On no account disconnect any part of the system as the gases and chemicals contained in the circuit can cause injury if released. If it is essential to remove one of the system components in order to gain access to other parts or assemblies always have the air-conditioning system discharged and later re-charged by your Jaguar/Daimler dealer or a professional refrigeration engineer.
2   At the intervals specified in 'Routine Maintenance' check the compressor drivebelt tension. This should be ½ in (12.7 mm) total deflection at the centre of the belt.
3   Any adjustment should be carried out on the threaded adjuster rod which is accessible from under the car.
4   During the Winter when the air-conditioner is not normally in use, it is recommended that the system is operated for about ten minutes per week in order to maintain the components in good order.
5   If bubbles or foam appear in the sight glass (which is located

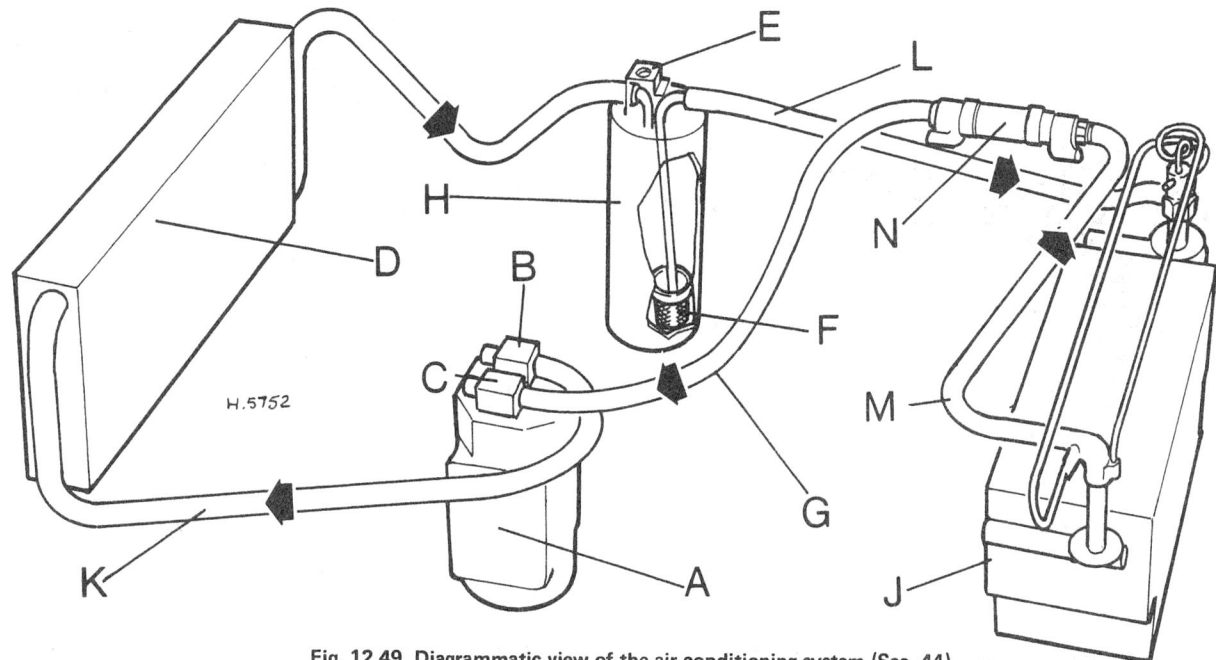

Fig. 12.49. Diagrammatic view of the air conditioning system (Sec. 44)

A	Compressor	E	Sight glass
B	Discharge valve	F	Bobbin
C	Suction valve	G	Dessicant
D	Condensor		

H	Receiver/drier	L	Liquid
J	Evaporator	M	Cold vapour line
K	Hot vapour line	N	Heat exchanger (fuel cooler)

adjacent to the compressor) when the system is operating, the system requires servicing by your dealer.

6 Every 12 months or before the Summer have the oil level in the compressor checked by your dealer. This is a job requiring special equipment.

7 Water condensate is discharged from the air-conditioning system evaporator casing soon after the car stops and the blowers are switched off. This is a normal characteristic and a pool of water observed under cars fitted with these systems need cause no alarm.

45 Centre console (except Series 2) - removal and refitting

1 Disconnect the battery.

2 Disconnect and remove the overdrive switch from the control lever (see Section 10).

3 Remove the gearlever knob.

4 Remove the two screws from the front of the top finisher plate, remove the plate and disconnect the cigar lighter lead.

5 Remove the heater/radio control panel, as described in Section 32, paragraphs 8 to 11.

6 Remove the rear ashtray support panel (two screws).

7 If electrically-operated windows are fitted, remove the switch control panel and disconnect the leads from the switches. The control panel is secured by pegs located in nylon bushes and it should be prised away from them.

8 Remove the two screws which secure the rear of the console to the support brackets, also the two screws located in the top outer corners of the parcel tray.

9 Withdraw the console and detach the two rear heater duct pipes

10 Refitting is a reversal of removal.

46 Centre console (Series 2) - removal and refitting

1 Disconnect the battery.

2 Remove the console side trim. These are retained by two screws on the ventilation louvres.

3 Pull off the heater and ventilation control knobs and withdraw the panel far enough to be able to unscrew the four screws which secure the centre shelf to the console and fascia. Take care not to damage the opticell fibre elements.

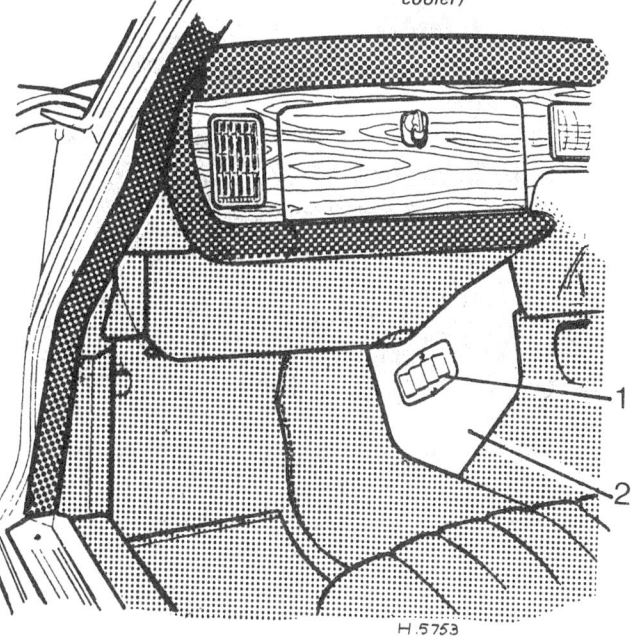

Fig. 12.50. Centre console side trim panel (Series 2 cars) (Sec. 46)

1   Ventilator louvre screws   2   Panel

4 Detach the temperature air sensor pipe from the centre shelf and move the tray clear of the console.

5 Prise the window lift control panel clear of the top finisher.

6 Remove the three screws which secure the top finisher to the console, raise the top finisher and detach the leads from the cigar lighter and the door lock switch.

7 Feed the window lift switch panel and switches through the aperture in the top finisher. Lift the finisher from the console.

8 Remove the front seat cushions. To do this, extract the securing screws from the brackets at the front edge of the cushions. Raise the front of the cushion and pull forward. If a seatbelt warning system is fitted, disconnect the leads from the switch.

9 Push the front seats fully forward and extract the screws which

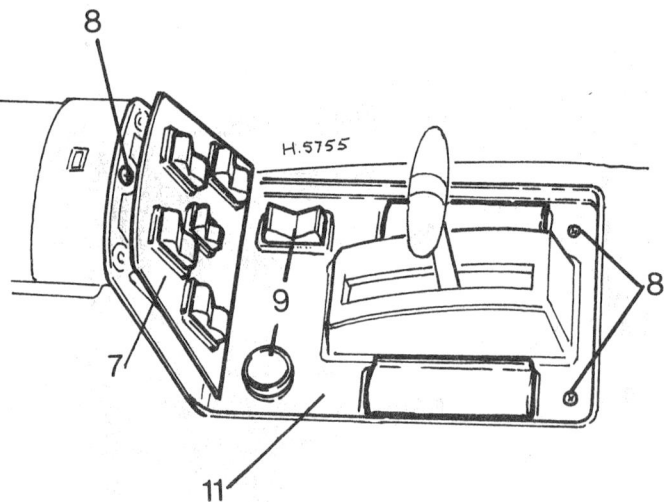

Fig. 12.51. Centre console top finisher (Series 2 cars) (Sec. 46)

7 *Window lift switch panel*	9 *Cigar lighter and door lock*
8 *Securing screws*	*switch*
	11 *Finisher panel*

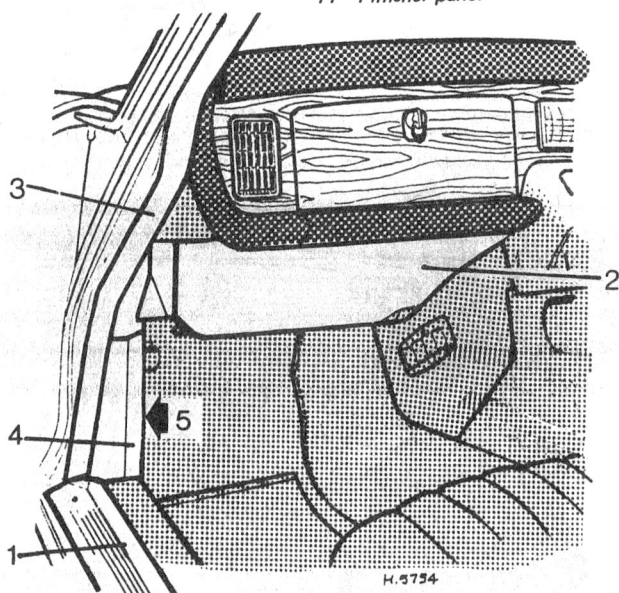

Fig. 12.52. Side fascia panel details (Series 2 cars) (Sec. 48)

1 *Sill tread plate*	4 *Trim*
2 *Underscuttle casing*	5 *Side fascia panel*
3 *Weatherseal*	

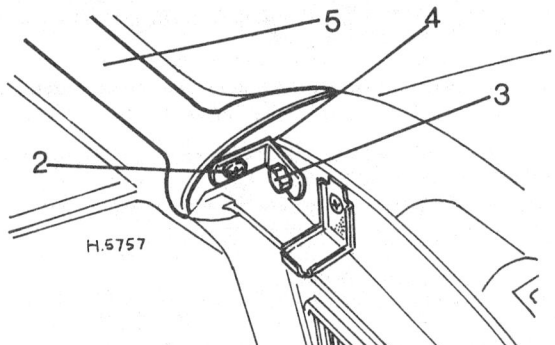

Fig. 12.53. Windscreen pillar trim details (Sec. 48)

2 *Mounting screw* 4 *Angle bracket* 5 *Trim*
3 *Mounting screw*

secure the rear window lift switch pedestal. Raise the pedestal and disconnect the electrical leads.

10 Extract the two screws which secure the rear of the centre console to the transmission tunnel.

11 Disconnect the multi-pin connector which is exposed by withdrawal of the pedestal. Raise the rear of the console and extract the two screws which secure the wiring harness to the air duct.

12 Slide the console towards the rear, detach the wiring harness from the clips and then feed the radio and ventilation panel through the aperture in the front of the console. Slide the console away from the fascia, disengaging the heater air duct pipes from the outlets.

13 Lift the centre console over the gear control lever and remove it.

14 Refitting is a reversal of removal.

47 Side fascia panel (except Series 2) - removal and refitting

1 Disconnect the battery.

2 Remove the speedometer and tachometer, as described in Chapter 10.

3 Remove the fresh air outlet from the side fascia panel.

4 Remove the steering wheel and upper shaft, as described in Chapter 11.

5 Remove the direction indicator switch and cowl, as described in Chapter 10.

6 Detach the ignition switch escutcheon (two screws).

7 Remove the cover from the warning lamp cluster.

8 Hinge the instrument panel downward having first removed the knurled thumb screws.

9 Remove the two hexagon headed setscrews which are now visible, also the single nut which is accessible through the air vent aperture. The side fascia panel can now be withdrawn.

48 Side fascia panel (Series 2) - removal and refitting

1 Remove the tread plate from the door sill.

2 Remove the under scuttle casing (see Section 51, paragraph 4).

3 Pull off the weatherseal from the edge of the door opening.

4 Extract the two screws from the base of the panel in the footwell.

5 Disengage the side panel from the air vent regulator control and lift the panel from the car.

6 The windscreen pillar trim can be removed if required by first withdrawing the crash roll from the fascia (Section 51) and then extracting the right-angled bracket screws located at the base of the pillar and then prising the trim from its retaining clip.

7 Refitting is a reversal of removal.

49 Glovebox panel (except Series 2) - removal and refitting

1 Disconnect the battery.

2 Remove the fresh air outlet from the panel.

3 Hinge the instrument panel downward having first removed the two screws from the upper corners.

4 Remove the two hexagon headed setscrews now visible, also the single nut which is accessible through the air vent aperture. The glovebox panel can now be withdrawn.

50 Fascia panel (except Series 2) - removal and refitting

1 Disconnect the battery.

2 Lever up the loudspeaker grille using a thin screwdriver or blade.

3 With the grille removed, remove the two screws which are now visible.

4 Remove the two self-tapping screws from the underside of the fascia safety roll. These are located just above the fresh air outlets. The fascia panel may now be detached.

5 Refitting is a reversal of removal.

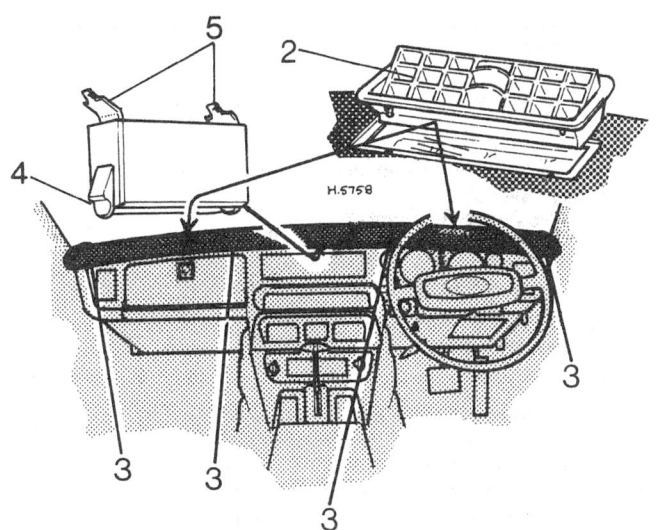

Fig. 12.54. Fascia panel (Series 2 car) (Sec. 51)

2   Demister vent
3   Crash roll screws

4   Map reading lamp
5   Lamp terminals

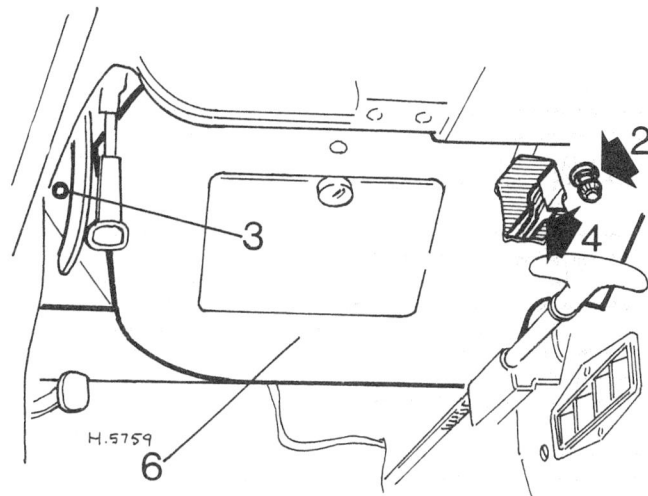

Fig. 12.55. Underscuttle details (Series 2 cars) (Sec. 51)

2   Speedometer trip control
3   Fascia support bracket

4   Rheostat leads
6   Underscuttle casing

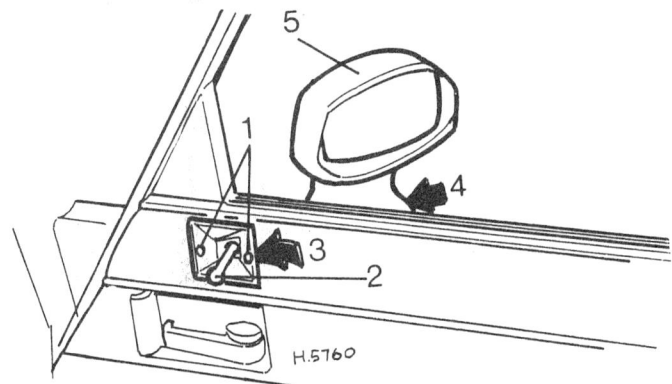

Fig. 12.56. Exterior rear view mirror (remote controlled - Series 2 cars) (Sec. 53)

1   Screws
2   Escutcheon plate
3   Grub screw

4   Mirror mounting screws
5   Mirror

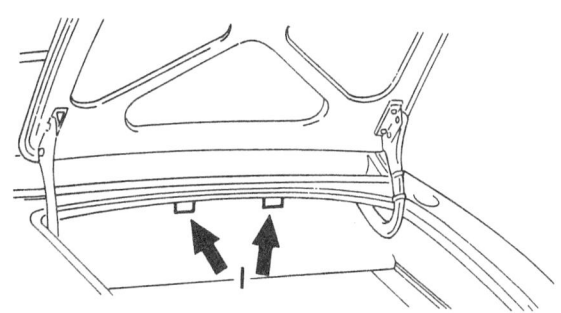

Fig. 12.57. Air extraction flap valves (1) (Sec. 54)

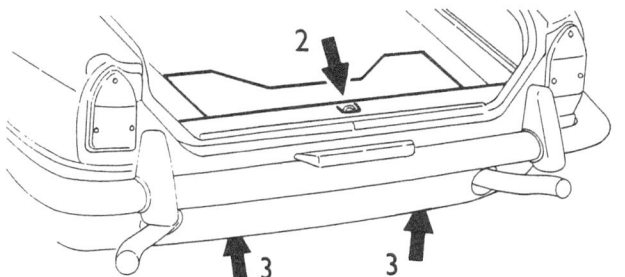

Fig. 12.58. Air extraction aperture (2) and ducts (3) (Sec. 54)

---

51 Fascia panel (Series 2) - removal and refitting

---

1   Disconnect the battery.
2   Prise the demister air vents from the crash roll and then unscrew the four screws which secure the crash roll.
3   Prise the map light from its housing in the crash roll and disconnect the leads. Remove the crash roll.
4   Remove the underscuttle casing from the driver's side. To do this, the speedometer trip control securing ring will have to be unscrewed, the casing securing screws removed and the rheostat switch leads disconnected.
5   Remove the four screws which secure the fascia to the screen rail.
6   Remove the two nuts which secure the outer ends of the fascia to the lower mounting brackets.
7   Pull off the heater and ventilation control knobs.
8   Withdraw the radio panel far enough forward to permit access to the screws which secure the centre tray.
9   Remove the four screws which secure the centre shelf to the console. Detach the temperature air sensor pipe from the centre tray and move the tray clear of the fascia.
10 Remove the two nuts which secure the fascia to the heater unit.
11 Slacken the clamp screws which secure the ignition and light switch shrouds. Withdraw the shrouds and clamps and detach the opticell unit.
12 Slacken the steering column upper mounting bolts but do not

completely remove them.

13 Remove the direction indicator switch shroud (three screws) and then ease the fascia panel forward and disconnect the multi-pin connectors which supply the instruments.

14 Disconnect the cable from the rear of the speedometer.

15 Remove the fascia panel complete with air ventilator ducting.

16 Refitting is a reversal of removal but it will be an easier job if the demister duct nuts are slackened.

52 Instrument panel - removal and refitting

1 Reference should be made to Chapter 10, Section 40, for a description of removal and refitting of the instrument sub-panel.

2 If the hinged instrument panel must be removed, extract the hinge pins and lift the panel away.

3 Refitting is a reversal of removal.

53 Exterior mirror (Series 2) - removal and refitting

1 The mirror on these cars is remotely controlled.

2 Remove the two screws which secure the control lever escutcheon plate to the inside of the door.

3 Partially withdraw the control lever and the plate from the door and slacken the grub screw which secures the escutcheon plate to the control lever.

4 Remove the two screws which secure the mirror to the door.

5 Withdraw the mirror and the mounting pad, pulling the control cable through the door.

6 Refitting is a reversal of removal.

54 Air extraction system

1 In addition to the heating and ventilation system, an air extraction system is incorporated in all later models.

2 Air is drawn from the car interior through flap valves into the luggage boot. This air is then extracted through an aperture in the luggage boot floor and ducts in the rear under panel.

3 Do not obstruct these flaps or ducts.

Chapter 13 Supplement:
Revisions and information on later models

Contents

---

1 Introduction

The purpose of this Supplement is to cover the changes which have been made to the Jaguar/Daimler 3.4 and 4.2 litre models as the result of the introduction of the Series 3 versions in March 1979.

Certain information, which was not available at the time of original publication of this manual, is also given in respect of late Series 2 models.

Where no modifications have been made, the original material given in the twelve main Chapters should be used. Owners of Series 3 cars should use Series 2 details unless Chapter 13 amendments are shown for their particular vehicles.

---

2 Specifications

These Specifications are supplementary to, or revisions of, the Specifications at the beginning of the preceding Chapters. Where no specific information to the contrary is given, Series 3 values are the same as Series 2.

Engine (Series 3)
Cylinder block
Bore diameter after honing – 3.4:
  Piston grade F .... 3.2673 to 3.2676 in (82.989 to 82.997 mm)
  Piston grade G .... 3.2677 to 3.2680 in (83.000 to 83.007 mm)
  Piston grade H .... 3.2681 to 3.2684 in (83.010 to 83.017 mm)

Series 3 model XJ6 4.2

Piston grade S	0.0007 to 0.0013 in (0.018 to 0.033 mm) greater than diameter of piston (measured at bottom of skirt, at 90° to gudgeon pin)
Bore diameter after honing – 4.2:	
Piston grade F	3.6250 to 3.6253 in (92.075 to 92.083 mm)
Piston grade G	3.6254 to 3.6257 in (92.085 to 92.093 mm)
Piston grade H	3.6258 to 3.6261 in (92.095 to 92.103 mm)
Piston grade S	As for 3.4 engine

Crankshaft

Main journal diameter – 3.4	2.7497 to 2.7502 in (69.842 to 69.855 mm)
Main bearing running clearance	0.0008 to 0.0025 in (0.0203 to 0.0635 mm)
Regrind undersizes:	
'Sursulf' hardened (see text)	None
Others	0.020 in (0.51 mm) only

Connecting rods

Big-end bearing running clearance	0.0010 to 0.0027 in (0.0254 to 0.0686 mm)

Piston rings (3.4 only)

Top compression ring width	0.0615 to 0.0625 in (1.562 to 1.588 mm)
Second compression ring width	0.0772 to 0.0782 in (1.961 to 1.986 mm)
Top compression ring end-gap	0.013 to 0.018 in (0.33 to 0.46 mm)
Second compression ring end-gap	0.009 to 0.014 in (0.23 to 0.36 mm)

Camshafts

Journal diameter	0.9990 to 0.9995 in (25.375 to 25.387 mm)
Bearing running clearance:	
3.4	0.0005 to 0.0022 in (0.013 to 0.056 mm)
4.2	0.0005 to 0.0020 in (0.013 to 0.051 mm)

Valves

Valve head diameter (4.2):
Inlet	1.870 to 1.880 in (47.50 to 47.75 mm)
Exhaust	1.620 to 1.630 in (41.15 to 41.40 mm)
Valve stem diameter	0.3100 to 0.3125 in (7.87 to 7.94 mm)

Valve springs

Free length, 3.4:
Outer	2.103 in (53.42 mm)
Inner	1.734 in (44.04 mm)

Free length, 4.2:
Outer	1.938 to 2.000 in (49.23 to 50.80 mm)
Inner	1.656 to 1.719 in (42.06 to 43.66 mm)

Oil filter (4.2 fuel injection)

Champion A101

Torque wrench settings

	lbf ft	Nm
Cam cover dome nuts:		
Up to engine Nos. 8L 137745, 8A 14209 and 7M 4666	5 to 6	7 to 8
Later models	7 to 8	10 to 11
Crankshaft pulley-to-damper bolts	12 to 15	16 to 20
Crankshaft nose bolt	125 to 150	170 to 203

Cooling system (Series 3)

Thermostat

Opening temperature:
Up to 1981 (UK) and all US models	190°F (88°C)
Later UK models	180°F (82°C)

Pressure cap

Blow-off pressure	15 lbf/in² (1.05 kgf/cm²)

Fuel system

Carburettors, US models (Series 2)

Make and type	Twin Zenith Stromberg CD 175

Needle specification:
1974, fixed orifice EGR	B1CG
1974, variable orifice EGR	B2AZ
1975 to 1977	B2BC
Spring colour	Natural

Carburettors, UK models (Series 2 and 3)

Make and type	Twin SU HIF 7 (from engine Nos 8A 5099 and 8L 26204)

Needle specification:
3.4 litre	BDW
4.2 litre	BDN (internal vent) or BDY (external vent)

Adjustment data (carburettors)

Idle speed	750 rpm
CO emission at idle	3.0% maximum (or as specified on vehicle decal)

Fuel injection system

Make and type	Lucas/Bosch 'L' Jetronic

Application:
US	4.2 litre, 1978 on
UK	4.2 litre, 1979 on

Adjustment data (fuel injection)

Idle speed	700 to 800 rpm (or as specified on vehicle decal)
CO emission at idle	0.5 to 1.5% (or as specified on vehicle decal)

Fuel octane requirement

UK models	97 octane (4-star)
US models	87 (minimum) octane, unleaded if catalyst and/or Lambda sensor fitted

Ignition system (Series 2 and 3)

Electronic (breakerless) system

Application	4.2 litre only

Distributor make and type:
Series 2, except California	Lucas 45DE6 (Opus system)
Series 2, California	Lucas 43DE6 (Opus system)
Series 3	Lucas 45DM6 (Constant Energy system)

Pick-up air gap:
43DE6 and 45DE6	0.014 to 0.016 in (0.36 to 0.41 mm)
45DM6	0.008 to 0.014 in (0.20 to 0.36 mm)

Ignition timing
Refer also to vehicle decal; follow decal if different from below

All 3.4 models (Series 2 and 3) – static or dynamic (vacuum
disconnected, engine idling) .... 8° BTDC
4.2 models – dynamic, using stroboscope:
    UK models (Series 3) .... 6° BTDC *
    North American models (Series 3):
        1979–80 .... 4° BTDC at 800 rpm
        1982 .... 14° BTDC *
        1983 .... 14° BTDC **
        1984 on .... 17° BTDC **

* *Vacuum disconnected at idle*
** *Vacuum disconnected at 700 rpm*

Spark plugs
Make and type (Series 3):
    3.4 litre .... Champion N12YCC or N12YC
    4.2 litre, UK .... Champion N9YCC or N9YC
    4.2 litre, US .... Champion 2404 or N12YC
Electrode gap (Series 3) .... 0.035 in (0.90 mm)

Clutch (Series 3)
Torque wrench settings

	lbf ft	Nm
Operating lever pivot bolt	30	41
Lower cover to bellhousing	7	10
Tie-plate to bellhousing	37	50
Bellhousing to gearbox	59	80
Bellhousing to engine	21	29
Bellhousing cover plate	15	20
Slave cylinder nuts	12	16
Master cylinder nuts	12	16
Pedal box nuts	12	16
Hydraulic unions	7	10

Manual gearbox (Series 3)
General
Number of speeds .... 5 forward (all synchro) and 1 reverse
Oil capacity .... 3.5 Imp pints (2.0 litres, 4.2 US pints) approx
Oil type/specification*:
    Drain and refill .... Hypoid gear oil, viscosity SAE 75 (Duckhams Hypoid 75)
    Top-up **only** .... Hypoid gear oil, viscosity SAE 80EP (Duckhams Hypoid 80)

*Note: If baulking problems are experienced with 5-speed gearboxes, it is permissible to drain the oil and refill with Dexron II type ATF (Duckhams D-Matic) – see Section 11

Gear ratios
1st 3.321:1
2nd 2.087:1
3rd 1.396:1
4th 1.000:1
5th 0.883:1
Reverse 3.428:1

Overhaul data
1st gear bush, 5th gear, layshaft and mainshaft/input shaft
endfloats .... 0.0002 to 0.0020 in (0.005 to 0.051 mm)

Torque wrench settings
See clutch Specifications for external attachments

	lbf ft	Nm
Front cover to gearcase	21	29
Rear cover to gearcase	21	29
Centre plate to gearcase	21	29
Output flange nut	150	203
5th gear selector fork pivot bracket to centre plate	21	29
Coupling pin to main selector rod	15	20
Oil drain and filler plugs	26	35
Oil pump screws	7	10
Reverse lever mounting pin	21	29
Remote control housing	15	20

Automatic transmission (Series 3)
General
Make and type .... Borg Warner type 66

Fluid capacity:
From dry .... 14.0 Imp pints (8.0 litres, 16.8 US pints) approx
Drain and refill .... 10.5 Imp pints (6.0 litres, 12.6 US pints) approx
'MIN' to 'MAX' on dipstick .... 1.5 Imp pints (0.9 litre, 1.8 US pints) approx
Fluid type .... ATF to M2C 33G (Duckhams Q-Matic)

Gear ratios
1st 2.39:1
2nd 1.45:1
3rd 1.00:1
Reverse 2.09:1
Torque converter .... 2.3:1 maximum

Test data
Control pressure .... 60 to 90 lbf/in² (4.2 to 6.3 kgf/cm²)
Stall speed (desired) .... 1950 to 2100 rpm

Final drive (Series 3)
Ratios
Standard 3.31:1
Alternative 3.07:1

Output shaft adjustment shims
Incremental value .... 0.002 in (0.051 mm)

Braking system (Series 2 and 3)
Brake discs — refinishing limits
Minimum thickness:
Front .... 0.90 in (22.86 mm)
Rear .... 0.45 in (11.43 mm)
Permissible thickness variation .... 0.0005 in (0.0127 mm) max
Surface flatness .... Within 0.0004 in (0.0102 mm)
Run-out .... 0.002 in (0.051 mm) max

Handbrake adjustment
Desired lever travel .... 5 clicks
Pull to achieve desired travel .... 88 lbf (40 kgf) max

Brake pads (front and rear)
Minimum thickness of friction material .... 0.16 in (4.0 mm)

Electrical system (Series 2 and 3)
Battery
Make and type (later models) .... AC Delco Maintenance Free
Capacity (typical) .... 55 Ah

Alternator
Alternative types .... Lucas 25 ACR or A133, Motorola 9AR 25 12P

Test data:	25 ACR	A133	9AR
Regulated voltage	13.5	13.6 to 14.4	14.0
Maximum output (amps)	66	65 or 75	70
Rotor resistance (ohms, at 68°F/20°C)	3.6	2.5	3.6
Brush length, new (in/mm)	0.8/20	0.8/20	0.35/9
Brush length, minimum (in/mm)	0.4/10	0.4/10	0.15/4

Alternator drivebelt
Desired tension .... 0.15 in (3.8 mm) deflection at midpoint of run under 3.2 lb (1.5 kg) pressure

Fuses — Series 2 with fuel injection
Main fuse box:

Fuse no	Circuits protected	Fuse rating (Amp)
1	Fog lamps	20
2	Hazard warning	15
3	Interior and map reading lamps, clock, boot lamps, cigar lighter	35
4	Instruments, fuel pumps, reverse lamps	15
5	Direction indicators	15
6	Stop lamps, horn relay, screen washer, battery cooler	35
7	Panel lamps	15
8	Left-hand side and tail lamps	15
9	Right-hand side and tail lamps and cigar lighter lamp	15
10	Air conditioning or heater motors	50

Fuse no	Circuits protected	Fuse rating (Amp)
11	Windscreen wipers	20
12	Air conditioner	15

Fuse box on radiator top rail:

–	Headlamp main beam (RH)	25
–	Headlamp dipped beam (RH)	10
–	Headlamp main beam (LH)	25
–	Headlamp dipped beam (LH)	10

In-line fuses (pre-1984 models):

Location	Circuits protected	Fuse rating (Amp)
RH bulkhead	Horn relay	35
Under main fuse box	Heated rear window	35
Centre console	Radio	1.5 to 5 dependent upon equipment
Under boot floor	Aerial motor relay	10
Centre console	Rear fog lamps	10

In-line fuses (1984-on models):

RHD – adjacent servo	Horn	15
LHD – adjacent battery	Horn	15
Behind RH front centre console side casing	Cigar lighter	20
Under carpet, LH side of centre console	Front seat motor	30
Behind LH centre console side facing	Air conditioner amplifier	3
Behind trim in luggage boot below parcels shelf	RH tail and number plate lamps (red/black)	3
	LH tail and number plate lamps (red/yellow)	3
	Side marker lamp (red)	
Rear of radio	Radio/cassette	2

Fuses – Series 3 (typical)
Main fuse box – RHD:

Fuse no	Circuits protected	Fuse rating (Amp)
1	Anti-run-on valve (3.4 litre)	10
2	Hazard warning	15
3	Air conditioner or heater motors	50
4	Panel instruments, reverse lamps, low coolant sensor and lamp	15
5	Heated rear window	35
6	Air conditioner relay and compressor clutch	15
7	Windscreen wipers	35
8	Panel illumination	15
9	Rear fog lamps	10
10	Direction indicators	15
11	Battery cooling fan, horn relay, radiator electric fan relay, screen washers, stop lamps	35
12	Cruise control	2

Main fuse box – LHD:

1	Fog lamps	20
2	Hazard warning Seat belt logic unit	15
3	Map and interior lamps, clock, aerial, cigar lighter	15
4	Panel instruments, reverse lamps, low coolant sensor and lamp	15
5	Heated rear window	35
6	Windscreen wipers	35
7	Spare	
8	Panel illumination	15
9	Spare	
10	Direction indicators	15
11	Battery cooling fan, horn relay, radiator electric fan relay, windscreen washers, stop lamps, service interval counter (N America)	35
12	Cruise control	2

Fuse no	Circuits protected	Fuse rating (Amp)
Auxiliary fuse box – RHD:		
13	Map and interior lamps, clock, aerial, cigar lighter	15
14	Door lock relay, electric door mirror, door lamps	5
15	Fog lamps	20
16	Spare	–
17	Front parking lamps	3
Auxiliary fuse box – LHD:		
13	Air conditioner relay and compressor clutch	15
14	Front parking lamps	3
15	Front parking lamps	10
16	Air conditioner or heater motors	50
17	Door lock relay, electric door mirrors, door lamps	3
Headlamp fuse box:		
1	Radiator electric cooling fan (see text)	12 continuous/25 blow
2	RH dip	10/20
3	RH main	17/35
4	LH dip	10/20
5	LH main	17/35

Bulbs– Series 3 (typical)

	Wattage
Headlamps – LHD:	
Tungsten type – outer	60/45
Tungsten type – inner	50
Halogen type – outer	60/55
Halogen type – inner	55
Headlamps – RHD:	
Halogen type – outer	60/55
Halogen type – inner	55
Headlamps – N America:	
Tungsten type – outer	37.5/60
Tungsten type – inner	50
Halogen type – outer	37.5/60
Halogen type – inner	50
Front parking	4
Front direction indicator	21
Front parking/direction indicator	5/21
Front fog	55
Direction indicator repeater	4
Front side marker	4
Rear side marker	4
Rear door guard	5
Stop lamp	21
Stop lamp – high level (N. America)	5
Tail lamp	5
Rear direction indicator	21
Reverse lamp	21
Rear number plate	4
Rear fog	21
Instrument illumination	2.2
Warning cluster	1.2
LH direction warning	3
Heated rear window warning	2.8
Bulb failure	2.2
RH direction warning	3
Map	6
Clock illumination	2.2
Switch panel illumination	1.2
Automatic transmission selector quadrant	2.2
Cigar lighter illumination	2
Fibre optic source	5
Interior	5
Reading	4
Luggage boot	5

Suspension and steering (Series 3)
Suspension geometry (from VIN 360 146)

Front wheel alignment (toe)	0 to 0.125 in (0 to 3.2 mm) toe-in
Front camber angle	0° 15′ to 0° 45′ negative*
Front castor angle	3° 15′ to 3° 45′ positive

* 0° 15′ maximum side to side difference

Tyres (normal use)

Tyre make and size (original equipment):	
UK models	Dunlop ER 70 VR 15 SP Sport Super or Pirelli P5 205 70 VR 15
US models	Pirelli P5 205/70 VR 15 or P5 215/70 VR 15

Tyre pressures .... See Chapter 11 Specifications, or refer to vehicle's tyre information sticker

Tyres (mud and snow)

Maker's recommendation (see text) .... Dunlop Weathermaster 185SR 15 SP M & S

Tyre pressures:

	Front	Rear
Up to 85 mph (136 km/h)	27 lbf/in^2 (1.86 bar)	26 lbf/in^2 (1.79 bar)
85 to 100 mph (136 to 160 km/h)	35 lbf/in^2 (2.41 bar)	34 lbf/in^2 (2.35 bar)

Torque wrench setting

	lbf ft	Nm
Wheel nuts (alloy roadwheels)	75 max	102 max

Bodywork and fittings (Series 3)

Torque wrench setting

	lbf ft	Nm
Wing-to-bulkhead crossbraces	30 to 35	41 to 48

General dimensions, weights and capacities (Series 3)

Dimensions

Overall length:
UK models .... 195.25 in (4.959 m)
US models .... 199.50 in (5.067 m)
Overall width .... 69.70 in (1.770 m)
Overall height .... 54.20 in (1.377 m)
Wheelbase .... 112.80 in (2.865 m)

Weights

Kerb weight (UK models):
3.4 litre .... 3902 lb (1766 kg) approx
4.2 litre .... 4044 lb (1830 kg) approx
Gross vehicle weight (UK models):
3.4 litre .... 4831 lb (2186 kg)
4.2 litre .... 4973 lb (2250 kg)
Gross vehicle weight (US models) .... 4979 lb (2258 kg)

Capacities (approximate)

Engine oil (drain and refill, including filter change) .... 14.5 Imp pints (8:25 litres, 17.5 US pints)
Cooling system .... 32 Imp pints (18.2 litres, 38.5 US pints)
Fuel tanks .... 10.5 Imp gallons (47.7 litres, 12.6 US gallons) per tank
Manual gearbox .... 3.5 Imp pints (2.0 litres, 4.2 US pints)
Automatic transmission:
From dry .... 14.0 Imp pints (8.0 litres, 16.8 US pints)
Drain and refill .... 10.5 Imp pints (6.0 litres, 12.6 US pints)
Final drive .... 2.75 Imp pints (1.6 litres, 3.25 US pints)

3 Routine maintenance

Maintenance intervals (all models)

1   The maintenance intervals recommended by the maker for Series 3 models have been extended to 7500 miles (12 000 km) instead of the 6000 mile (9600 km) intervals specified at the beginning of the manual. No equivalent to the 3000 mile (4800 km) maintenance schedule is specified; the items previously specified for 3000 miles should be carried out at 7500 miles.

2   On all models, the 6000/7500 mile maintenance items should be undertaken every 6 months if the stated mileage is not covered in that time. Similarly, the 12 000/15 000 mile items should be undertaken at least once a year, and so on.

3   Changing the oil in the manual gearbox is not specified as a routine maintenance operation for Series 3 models. The DIY mechanic may think it worth while to change the oil at 30 000 mile (48 000 km) intervals.

4   Also on Series 3 models, the interval specified for changing the final drive oil has been extended to 30 000 miles (48 000 km).

Additional maintenance tasks (all models)

5   Every 6000/7500 miles, lubricate those moving parts of the automatic transmission selector linkage which are exposed beneath the car. Use clean engine oil or light machine oil for this. Also lubricate the bonnet hinge pins.

6   Every 12 000/15 000 miles, carry out the following tasks:

(a)   Check the tightness of the propeller shaft flange bolts
(b)   Check the condition of the handbrake pads

(c)   Check the endfloat of the front hub bearings and adjust if necessary (Chapter 11, Section 5)

4 Engine (Series 2 and 3)

Engine/transmission — removal

1   The operations are basically similar to those described in Chapter 1, Section 5 or 6, except that the following additional work may be required on later models or those destined for operation in North America.

2   Remove the sump-to-transmission stiffener plate on models so equipped (photo).

3   On models with evaporative emission control equipment, disconnect the flexible hoses from the carbon canister pipes.

4   On fuel injection models, the following operations will be required instead of those operations associated with carburettors. Refer to Section 7 of this Chapter for details:

(a)   Depressurize the fuel system
(b)   Remove the air cleaner and the airflow meter
(c)   Disconnect and plug the fuel feed and return lines
(d)   On air conditioned cars, disconnect the fuel lines (not the refrigerant pipes) from the fuel cooler. Unbolt the fuel cooler from the air cleaner brackets and move it to one side
(e)   Disconnect all electrical leads and plugs from the valves, sensors and switches of the fuel injection system, but take care to identify the wires before disconnecting them

5   On cars equipped with air conditioning, if the condenser, the compressor or the fuel cooler cannot be moved sufficiently far due to

4.2 Sump-to-transmission stiffener plate

the limitations of their flexible connecting hoses, prior to engine
removal, then *the air conditioning system must be discharged by your
dealer or a competent refrigeration engineer*. The components which
are causing obstruction can then be removed from the engine
compartment.

Cylinder head – removal (engine in car)
6   The following operations are additional to those described in
Chapter 1, Section 11.
7   On carburettor models, disconnect the throttle cables from the
control lever and abutment brackets.
8   On fuel injection models, carry out the work described in
paragraph 4.
9   Release the heater hose from the water valve.
10   Remove the pipes from the radiator header tank or thermostat
housing and (if necessary) remove or reposition the expansion tank.
11   On BW 65 or 66 automatic transmission models, disconnect the
kickdown cable, and unbolt the dipstick tube from the inlet manifold.
12   On models with air conditioning and carburettors, disconnect and
plug the fuel hoses at the fuel cooler. **Do not** disconnect the refrigerant
hoses. Unbolt the fuel cooler and move it aside, taking care not to
strain the refrigerant hoses.
Vehicles with emission control equipment
13   Unscrew the union nut at the Y connection on the EGR system
(fixed orifice type). Extract the four screws and separate the cover from
the secondary throttle housing.
14   On variable orifice EGR systems, pull the vacuum pipe from the
valve.
15   Pull the vacuum pipe (anti-run-on system) from the tee piece at
the gulp valve.
16   Remove the two screws and detach the air duct.
17   Pull the float chamber and carburettor breather cross-over pipes
from their rubber connector pieces and plastic clips and place them to
one side of the engine compartment.
18   Slacken the pipe clip at the air injection rail non-return valve.
19   Unclip the air supply pipe and disconnect it from the air pump and
the air rail. Remove the air pump and bracket.
20   Disconnect the EGR supply pipe at the rear of the cylinder block.
21   Disconnect the EGR pipe from the exhaust manifold. Rest the pipe
across the transmission bellhousing and then unscrew the adaptor
from the manifold.
22   Remove the exhaust manifold heat shields.

Oil filter (cartridge type) – renewal
23   The oil filter on later models is of the screw-on disposable
cartridge type.
24   To renew the filter, first remove the air cleaner to improve access
and then unscrew and remove the filter. An oil filter wrench will
probably be required to remove it but if one is not available, drive a
large screwdriver through the filter casing and use it as a lever to
unscrew the filter. Be prepared for oil spillage.
25   Smear the rubber sealing ring of the new filter with engine oil and
screw on the filter hand-tight only.
26   When the engine is started, it will take a few seconds for the filter
to fill with oil and for the oil warning light to go out and the oil pressure
gauge to register.
27   The engine oil should be topped up to make up for the oil absorbed
by the new filter.
28   Check the filter for oil leaks.

Camshaft cover – prevention of oil leaks
29   Oil leaks from a camshaft cover gasket may be avoided by
renewing the gasket, regardless of its apparent condition, whenever
the cover has been removed. The gasket material swells on initial
contact with oil, so providing a good seal. Re-use of an old gasket will
not provide the same sealing effect.
30   The gasket faces of the camshaft cover and the cylinder head must
be clean and free from oil before the new gasket is fitted. Jointing
compound should not be used.
31   The D-shaped seal at the rear of the camshaft cover should be
coated with sealant before fitting.
32   Tighten the camshaft cover nuts evenly and progressively to the
specified torque.

Camshafts – removal and refitting
33   Disconnect the battery earth lead.
34   Remove the camshaft covers.
35   Remove the crankcase breather assembly from the front of the
cylinder head.
36   Slacken the nut which secures the idler sprocket shaft.
37   Knock down the locktabs from the camshaft sprocket bolts.
Remove two bolts from each sprocket, and slacken but do not remove
the other two. It will be necessary to turn the crankshaft during this
operation.
38   Turn the crankshaft to bring No 6 piston to TDC on the firing
stroke. The notches in the camshafts should be at 90° to the camshaft
cover surface. Refer to Chapter 1, Section 50, for further details.
39   Remove the two remaining bolts from each sprocket.
40   Slacken the camshaft chain, using the tool described in Chapter 1,
Section 50.
41   Mark the relationship of the sprockets to the camshafts for
reference when refitting, then slide the sprockets up the slots in the
support brackets.
42   Slacken the camshaft bearing cap nuts evenly and progressively,
starting in the middle and working towards each end.
43   Remove the camshaft bearing caps, noting their mating marks.
44   Lift out the camshafts and recover the bearing shells.
45   Refitting is basically a reversal of the removal procedure. Refer to
Chapter 1, Sections 48 and 50, for guidance. Remember that the
camshafts and crankshaft **must not** be rotated with the timing chain
disconnected.

Crankcase ventilation hose restrictor
46   A restrictor is fitted in the crankcase ventilation hose on 1982 and
later models. At the same time the 'thimble' filter is no longer fitted in
the breather.
47   If the restrictor becomes blocked, the crankcase ventilation system
will not function correctly; one possible consequence is pressurization
of the crankcase and subsequent oil leaks.
48   The restrictor and its hose are sold as an assembly and cannot be
renewed separately.

Crankshaft front oil seal – renewal (engine in car)
49   Remove the crankshaft pulley and damper as described in Chapter
1, Section 17.
50   If the damper cone has remained on the crankshaft nose, prise
open its slot and remove it.
51   Remove the Woodruff key from the crankshaft nose.
52   Remove the sump as described in Chapter 1, Section 14.
53   Remove the distance piece from the crankshaft nose.
54   Carefully prise the oil seal from its location in the timing cover.
Take great care not to damage the crankshaft surface or the seal
location.
55   Coat the lips of the new seal with engine oil and fit it over the

Series 3 model XJ6 under bonnet view

1	Automatic transmission fluid dipstick	4	Cooling system expansion tank	7	Fuse box	10	Thermostat housing
2	Battery	5	Alternator	8	Washer fluid reservoir	11	Air cleaner
3	Engine oil dipstick	6	Engine oil filler cap	9	Crankcase ventilation filter	12	Airflow meter
						13	Brake fluid reservoir
						14	Braking system servo

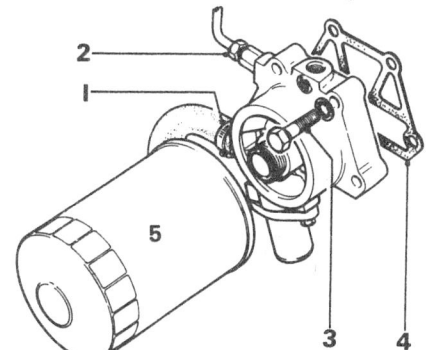

Fig. 13.1 Cartridge type oil filter and filter head (Sec 4)

1	Sump return pipe	4	Gasket
2	Camshaft oil feed	5	Filter cartridge
3	Bolt		

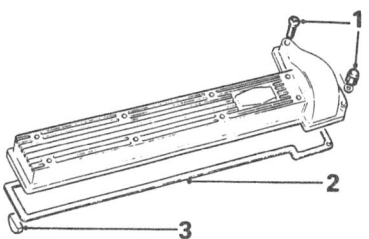

Fig. 13.2 Camshaft cover and gasket (Sec 4)

1	Nut and screw	3	D-shaped seal
2	Gasket		

crankshaft and into its recess. The open side of the seal faces inwards. Take care not to damage the seal lips on the crankshaft.

56 Refit the remaining components in the reverse order to removal.

Flywheel/driveplate locating dowels

57 Flywheel or driveplate locating dowels are not fitted to later Series 3 models.

Tappet guides – renewal

58 Tappet guide renewal must be entrusted to a Jaguar garage or other competent automotive engineer. Even in skilled hands there is a risk of damaging the cylinder head when the old guides are removed.

Cylinder block and head modifications (4.2 litre)

59 From engine No 8L 89109, waterways are incorporated between the bores in the cylinder block. Corresponding openings in the cylinder head and gasket provide improved coolant transfer between the block and the head.

60 The improved cylinder block can only be rebored to +0.020 in (0.508 mm).

61 The new pattern of cylinder head gasket can be fitted to new or old pattern blocks and heads. The old pattern gasket (without openings for the new waterways) **cannot** be fitted to a new pattern block.

62 A new pattern cylinder head can be fitted to an old pattern block. An old pattern cylinder head can only be fitted to a new pattern block after holes have been drilled in the head mating face to correspond with the new waterways in the block. This work should be carried out by a BL garage or other competent specialist.

Crankshaft regrinding (4.2 litre)

63 From engine Nos 8L 147650 and 7M 4796, the crankshafts on UK 4.2 litre models are hardened by a special process known as Sursulf hardening. These crankshafts can be recognised by their black surface finish.

64 No regrinding is permissible on Sursulf hardened crankshafts. If crankshaft wear has taken place to the extent that regrinding would normally be undertaken, the crankshaft must be renewed.

Piston ring identification

65 The top and second compression rings are not identical. Reference to Fig. 13.3 will enable one to be distinguished from the other.

---

5 Cooling system (Series 2 and 3)

General description

1 The principles of operation of the cooling system are still as described in Chapter 2, but various changes have been made to components and procedures.

2 Some models with air conditioning are equipped with one or two electric cooling fans mounted ahead of the condenser and radiator. The fans are thermostatically controlled, cutting in at a coolant temperature of 205°F (96°C), and will continue to operate *even after the engine is switched off* until a significantly lower temperature is obtained. Improvements in cooling system efficiency have eliminated the need for such fans on the latest models, except those destined for exceptionally hot territories.

3 On cars equipped with automatic transmission, a fluid cooler is incorporated in the centre section of the radiator bottom hose (photo).

4 Depending on operating territory and production date, coolant may be circulated to the inlet manifold, a secondary throttle housing and/or spacers between the carburettors and the manifold.

5 A plug is fitted on the right-hand side of the cylinder block; an electrically operated coolant heater can be installed instead of the plug where climatic conditions warrant it.

6 Commencing with 1982 model year vehicles, the header tank and associated filler cap are no longer fitted. A combined header/expansion tank is fitted on the left-hand inner wing. The expansion tank vents into an atmospheric recovery tank, except where headlamp wash/wipe components are fitted.

7 Most later models are equipped with a low coolant level sensor, mounted either in the radiator (pre-1982 models) or in the expansion tank.

Cooling system – draining

8 Drain plugs are fitted instead of drain taps on later models. The draining procedure is otherwise as described in Chapter 2.

Cooling system – flushing

9 For most effective flushing, regulate the inflow of flushing water so that the cooling system remains full, then run the engine at a fast tickover until the flushing water emerges from the drain holes free of contamination. Stop the engine before interrupting the flow of water.

10 Constant supervision is essential during this procedure, so that the

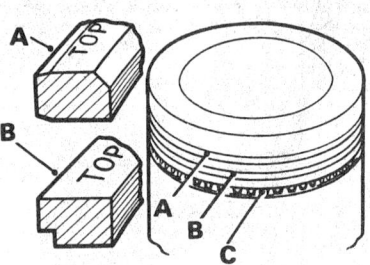

Fig. 13.3 Piston ring identification (Sec 4)

| A | Top compression | C | Oil control |
| B | Second compression | | |

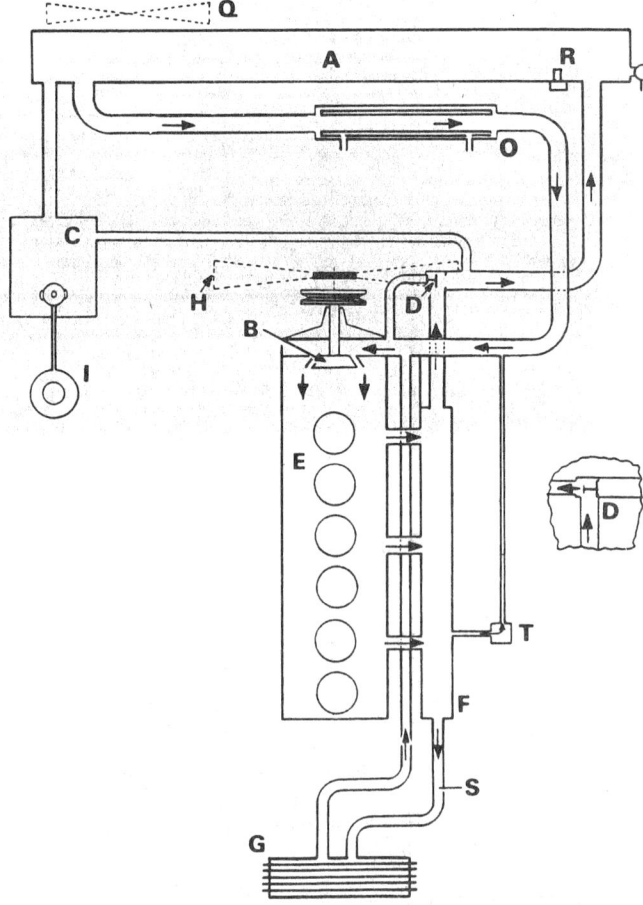

Fig. 13.4 Cooling system components – later models (Sec 5)

A	Radiator	H	Fan (engine-driven)
B	Water pump	I	Atmospheric recovery tank
C	Expansion tank	O	Transmission fluid cooler
D	Thermostat (closed in inset)	Q	Fan (electric)
E	Engine	R	Fan thermoswitch
F	Inlet manifold rail	S	Heater water valve location
G	Heater	T	Throttle housing

5.3 One end of the transmission fluid cooler

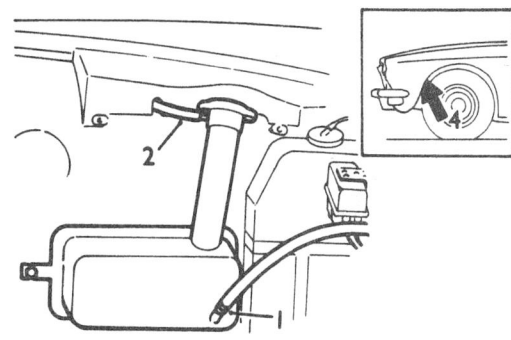

Fig. 13.5 Expansion tank location (Sec 5)

1   Connecting hose   4   Securing nuts under wheel
2   Vent pipe   arch

engine may be stopped immediately in the event of an interruption to the water supply.

Radiator – removal and refitting

11   Series 2 vehicles fitted with air conditioning **must** have the air conditioning system discharged before attempting radiator removal. On Series 3 vehicles it is not necessary to discharge the system provided that the condenser and receiver/drier can be moved sufficiently far out of the way without straining pipes and hoses. Refer to Chapter 12, Section 44, and to Section 21 of this Chapter, for precautions concerning the air conditioning system.
12   On all models, drain the coolant, disconnect the battery earth lead and remove the bonnet.
13   Release the hose clips and disconnect all hoses from the radiator. On Series 2 models, remove the screws from the bottom coolant pipe or oil cooler.
14   Unclip the wiring harness and (when so located) the headlamp relay from the radiator top rail.
15   Unbolt the fan cowl from the top rail, and the top rail from the body. Do not remove the fan cowl, but move it out of the way.
16   On Series 2 cars with air conditioning, remove the condenser and (if it is fitted to the top rail) the receiver/drier unit.
17   On Series 3 cars with air conditioning, unbolt the condenser from the top rail and retrieve the spacers. Similarly unbolt the receiver/drier unit.
18   On all models so equipped, remove or uncouple the air cleaner ram pipe.
19   Disconnect the wire(s) from the coolant level sensor and/or cooling fan thermoswitch, as applicable. Label the wires to avoid confusion on reassembly.
20   On Series 2 models, remove the self-locking nuts and the washers from the radiator locating studs.
21   Carefully lift the radiator from the car, moving aside the top tail, fan cowl and air conditioning components as necessary. Retrieve the foam padding.
22   Refitting is a reversal of removal. Fit all nuts and bolts loosely at first, then tighten them when all components are in position.
23   Refill the cooling system and (when applicable) have the air conditioning system recharged.

Expansion tank – removal and refitting

24   With the cooling system cold, remove the filler cap(s) to release any residual pressure.
25   Disconnect the vent pipe from the expansion tank filler neck, and (when fitted) unplug the low coolant level sensor.
26   On Series 3 models, remove the windscreen washer reservoir and the screw which secures the rear upper portion of its bracket.
27   On all models, have ready a container to catch escaping coolant, then disconnect the hose from the base of the expansion tank. Plug the hose or tie it up as high as possible.

28   Disconnect any remaining vent or bleed pipes from the tank.
29   Remove the nuts and bolts which secure the expansion tank. On Series 2 models, access to two of these nuts is via the wheel arch; these nuts also secure the fuel evaporative canister on North American models.
30   Remove the expansion tank, carefully moving the windscreen washer reservoir bracket aside on Series 3 models.
31   Refitting is a reversal of removal. Fill the tank with the correct coolant on completion, then refit the filler cap(s).

Thermostat – removal and refitting

32   Partially drain the cooling system saving the coolant for re-use.
33   Disconnect the battery earth lead.
34   Release the carburettor breather pipe from its clips and from the crankcase breather (when applicable).
35   Release all hose clips on the thermostat housing/header tank (photo). For ease of access, remove the radiator top hose completely.
36   Remove the securing bolts from the thermostat housing/header tank.
37   Carefully free the tank/housing from the engine, at the same time disconnecting the water pump hose.
38   Remove the thermostat and gasket.
39   Clean any sludge from inside the housing. Also clean the gasket mating surfaces.
40   Refit in the reverse order to removal, using a new gasket.
41   Refill the cooling system on completion.

Drivebelt tensioner/pulley (Series 2) – removal and refitting

42   Remove the power steering pump (see Chapter 11).
43   Remove the self-locking nut and the limiting stop arm.

5.35 Removing a hose from the thermostat housing

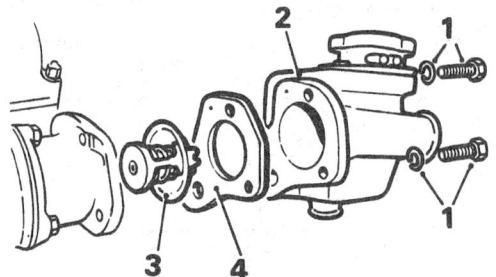

Fig. 13.6 Thermostat housing incorporating header tank (Sec 5)

1	Bolts and washers	3	Thermostat
2	Housing	4	Gasket

44 Withdraw the pulley/arm/spring assembly from the bracket.
45 If the spindle or bushes are worn, new components can be obtained. Press in new bushes so that their end faces are recessed $\frac{1}{16}$ in (1.59 mm).
46 Reassemble so that the right-angled crank on the coil spring arm engages in the hole in the bracket.
47 Smear the spindle with waterproof grease.
48 Fit the spindle into the bushes and then turn the arm anti-clockwise until the hooked end of the spring is engaged on the arm.
49 Locate the limiting stop arm onto the spindle and screw on a new self-locking nut a few threads.
50 Rotate the pulley arm anti-clockwise (viewed from the front of the steering pump) until the limiting stop arm engages on the flats of the spindle. Fully tighten the self-locking nut.
51 Refit, fill and bleed the steering pump.

Drivebelt (Series 3) – tensioning

52 Tensioning of the fan/water pump/steering pump drivebelt is not automatic on Series 3 cars. The drivebelt is correctly adjusted when a pressure of 6.4 lbf (2.9 kgf), applied in the middle of the longest run, produces a deflection of 0.17 in (4.3 mm).
53 To adjust the belt, first slacken the steering pump adjuster link trunnion bolt.
54 Slacken the adjuster link eye bolt and the steering pump pivot bolt.
55 Release the adjuster link locknut and move the adjuster nut up or down the link, so moving the steering pump on its pivot, until the correct tension is achieved (photo).
56 Tighten the adjuster link locknut, trunnion bolt and eye bolt, then tighten the steering pump pivot bolt.

Drivebelt (Series 3) – renewal

57 Release the adjuster link and steering pump pivot nuts and bolts as just described.
58 Slacken off the adjuster link until the old belt (if still present) can be slipped over the pulleys and between the fan blades. Remove the belt.
59 Feed the new belt between the fan blades and over the pulleys. Move the steering pump nearer to the engine if necessary.
60 Tension the belt as just described. Recheck the tension of a new belt after it has been in service for a short while.

Water pump – removal and refitting

61 Drain the cooling system and remove the fan cowl.
62 Remove the fan/water pump/steering pump drivebelt.
63 Remove the fan and viscous coupling (see Chapter 2).
64 Remove any remaining drivebelts (air pump, alternator, air conditioning compressor) and move their driven units out of the way. Take care not to disconnect or strain any air conditioning refrigerant lines.
65 On Series 2 cars, remove the support strap bolt from the water pump. Also remove the header tank.
66 Slacken all hose clips at the water pump and free the hoses.
67 Unscrew and remove the nuts and bolts which secure the water pump. Note carefully the locations of the long and short bolts.
68 Pull the water pump from the engine. If it is stuck, tap it carefully with a plastic or wooden mallet.

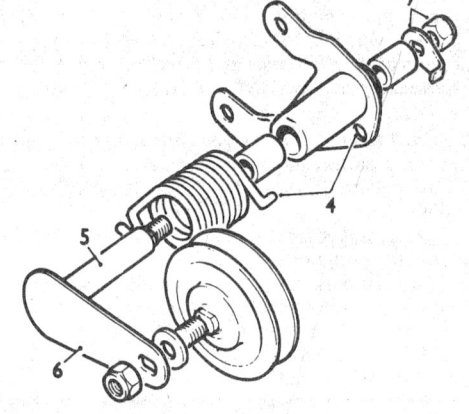

Fig. 13.7 Drivebelt tensioner – Series 2 (Sec 5)

4	Spring end and engagement hole	6	Arm
5	Spindle	7	Limiting stop arm

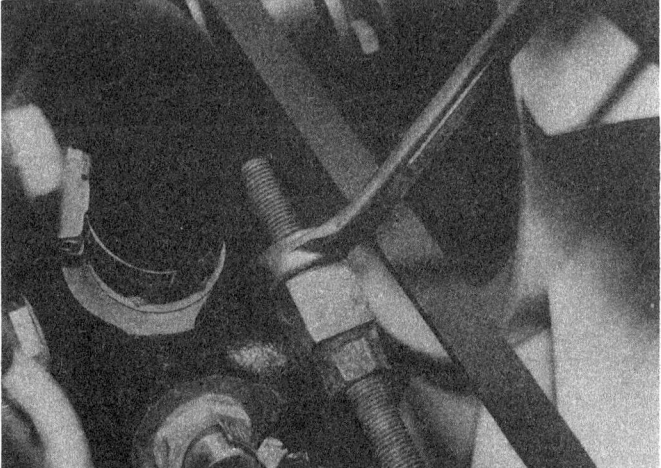

5.55 Steering pump adjuster trunnion

Fig. 13.8 Drivebelt tensioning arrangements – Series 3 (Sec 5)

1	Adjuster trunnion bolt	4	Adjuster nut
2	Adjuster eye-bolt	5	Adjuster locknut
3	Steering pump pivot bolt		

69 If the crankshaft pulley damper impedes removal of the water pump, this too must be removed.
70 Refitting is a reversal of removal. Use a new gasket and tighten the securing nuts and bolts evenly and progressively.
71 Refit and tension the drivebelt(s) and refill the cooling system.

Electric cooling fan(s) – removal and refitting

72 Disconnect the battery earth lead.
73 Remove the radiator lower grille and (on Series 2 cars only) remove the bonnet.
74 Disconnect the fan motor wiring connectors and (on Series 2 cars only) disconnect the horn positive leads.
75 Again on Series 2 cars, remove the bolt which holds the horn post steady bracket to the front flange of the lower cowl.
76 Remove the nuts and bolts which hold the fan mounting crossbeam to its end brackets.
77 On Series 3 models, remove the nuts and bolts which secure the fan mounting frame to the crossbeam, move the motor and retrieve the spacer washers.
78 Remove the crossbeam and fan(s) from the car.
79 The fan blades can be removed from the motor and the motor removed from the crossbeam if required. The motor must be renewed if defective.
80 Refitting is a reversal of removal. Check for correct operation on completion.

Fan motor relay – removal and refitting

81 Disconnect the battery earth lead.
82 Undo the screw which secures the relay cover to the wing valance and remove the cover.
83 Disconnect the wires from the relay, noting the correct connections for use when refitting. Remove the relay.
84 Refitting is a reversal of removal.

Fan thermoswitch – removal and refitting

85 Drain the cooling system.
86 Raise and support the front of the vehicle.
87 Working from below the car, note the wiring connections to the switch and disconnect them.
88 Unscrew and remove the thermoswitch from the radiator.
89 Refit in the reverse order to removal. Refill the cooling system on completion.

Thermostat rating (Series 3)

90 It will be noted from the Specifications that the thermostat opening temperature was lowered by some 10°F (6°C) on later UK models.
91 If overheating problems are experienced on cars fitted with a higher rated thermostat, the lower rated one recommended for later models should be fitted.

---

6 Fuel system – carburettor models (Series 2 and 3)

In-line fuel filter – renewal

1 Locate the fuel filter, which is situated in the engine compartment in the fuel supply line.
2 Disconnect the battery earth lead.
3 Slacken the hose clips on each side of the fuel filter. Disconnect and plug the hoses; be prepared for some fuel spillage. Remove the old filter and discard it.
4 Fit the new filter, making sure that a directional arrow (if present) points in the direction of fuel flow, ie towards the carburettors. Tighten the hose clips.
5 Mop up any fuel spilt, then reconnect the battery, run the engine and check for fuel leaks.

Fuel cooler (air conditioned models) – removal and refitting

6 For access to other components, the fuel lines may be disconnected from the fuel cooler, the cooler released and moved aside within the limits of the refrigerant flexible hoses. For complete removal, the air conditioning system **must** be discharged professionally beforehand. *Do not disconnect any refrigerant lines until this has been done.*

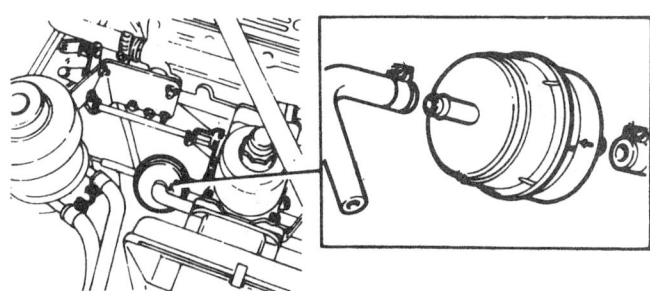

Fig. 13.9 In-line fuel filter – carburettor models (Sec 6)

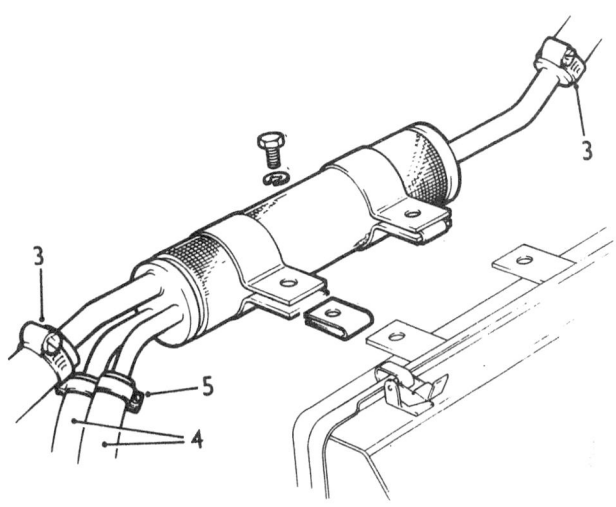

Fig. 13.10 Fuel cooler (typical) – air conditioned carburettor models (Sec 6)

3	*Refrigerant lines*	5 *Clip*
4	*Fuel lines*	

7 To remove the fuel cooler, have the air conditioning system discharged, then disconnect the battery earth lead.
8 Disconnect the refrigerant inlet and outlet hoses from the fuel cooler. Plug or cap the hoses immediately.
9 Disconnect and plug the fuel hoses. Be prepared for some fuel spillage.
10 Remove the two screws and washers which secure the fuel cooler. Remove the cooler and recover the mounting clips and the insulating sleeve.
11 Refitting is a reversal of removal. Have the air conditioning system recharged on completion.

Fuel pump (submerged type) – removal and refitting

12 The fuel pumps on later cars are fitted directly into the fuel tanks and are of AC Delco make.
13 Raise the rear of the car on stands and disconnect the battery.
14 Remove the roadwheel adjacent to the pump which is to be removed.
15 Drain the fuel tank into a suitable metal container. A drain plug is incorporated at the base of the tank.
16 Unbolt the cover plate from the vertical surface of the wheel arch. Withdraw the cover from the protective hose.
17 Disconnect the electrical leads from the pump and detach the fuel hose from the pump.
18 Turn the pump locking flange in an anti-clockwise direction and withdraw the pump together with sealing washers. Avoid damage to the pump filter as it is withdrawn.
19 Clean away old flange sealing gasket using a brass or copper scraper.
20 This type of pump cannot be overhauled and in the event of a fault developing, a new unit must be installed.

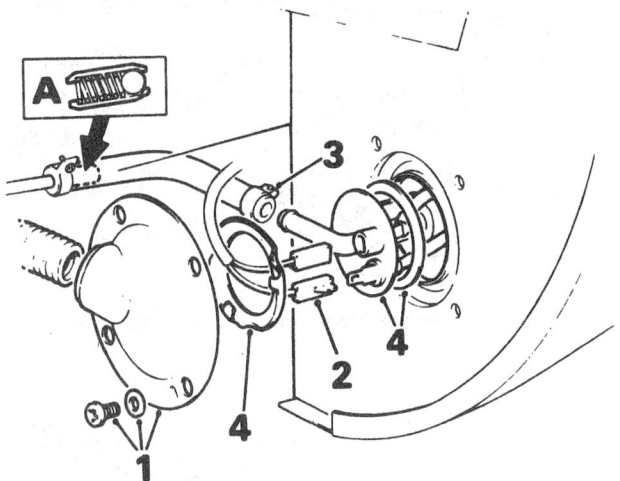

Fig. 13.11 Submerged type fuel pump (Sec 6)

A   Non-return valve   3   Fuel hose
1   Cover plate and fastening 4   Pump and sealing washers
2   Electrical connector

21 If the fuel hose is renewed, note the location of the non-return valve. The ball must be nearest the pump when the valve is installed.
22 Refitting is a reversal of removal. When the cover plate has been installed, seal it with a suitable underbody protective coating.

Fuel tank (1978 on) – removal and refitting

23 Drain the fuel from the tank to be removed into a suitable metal container. A drain plug is provided at the base of the tank.
24 Disconnect the battery.
25 Remove the side section of the rear bumper.
26 Extract the screws and lift away the rear quarter fuel tank cover.
27 Extract the self-tapping screw which holds the front edge of the luggage boot side casing. Remove the casing.
28 Remove the four screws which secure the mounting flange of the fuel filler cap. Prise the flange from the body. On North American cars, pull the vent pipe from the filler neck as it is withdrawn.
29 Remove the gasket and the O-ring seal.
30 Unscrew the bolt from the side panel within the luggage boot.
31 On vehicles equipped with submerged fuel pumps, reach up between the rear of the tank and the rear light unit and disconnect the leads from the fuel gauge sender unit. Disconnect the electrical leads and the fuel pipe from the pump before removing the tank.
32 On vehicles with internal fuel pumps, disconnect the pipe from the connector at the base of the fuel tank and push the pipe inwards until it is flush with the panel.
33 On all models, unscrew and remove the two bolts which are located in the exhaust silencer tunnel and recover the wedges.
34 Release the self-locking nut at the hanger bolt.
35 Gently lower the fuel tank until the electrical leads can be identified and disconnected. On North American versions, disconnect the other end of the vent pipe from the tank.
36 Refitting is a reversal of removal. Use new gaskets and check for leaks after a few gallons of petrol have been poured into the tank.

Carburettor adjustments (all models) – warning

37 The mixture on SU and Zenith carburettors is preset and should not normally need adjusting, unless carburettor overhaul has taken place.
38 On Zenith carburettors, a special tool is required if the mixture is to be adjusted. On SU carburettors, the mixture adjustment screw may be covered by a 'tamperproof' cap. In both cases, the object is to discourage adjustment by unqualified operators.
39 Satisfy yourself that you are not breaking any local, national or international anti-pollution laws before removing any tamperproof seals or plugs. Fit new tamperproof devices on completion of adjustment when this is required by law.
40 It is emphasized that haphazard 'adjustment' of twin carburettors is unlikely to prove successful. If the necessary tools and equipment

are not available, it is better to entrust the job to a competent specialist.

Zenith Stromberg carburettors (US models) – mixture adjustment

41 An exhaust gas analyser (CO meter) and carburettor adjusting tool S353 or equivalent will be required for this procedure.
42 Remove the air cleaner cover and filter element.
43 Disconnect the air injection system on the air pump side of the non-return valve. Plug the valve inlet. Start the engine and let it idle.
44 Insert the probe of an exhaust gas analyser into each tailpipe in turn and check the reading. The CO level should be within the limits given in the Specifications.
45 If adjustment is required, switch off the engine, withdraw the damper and then (having marked the relative position of the carburettor cover to the body) remove the cover screws. Lift off the cover, pull out the coil spring and withdraw the piston/diaphragm assembly.

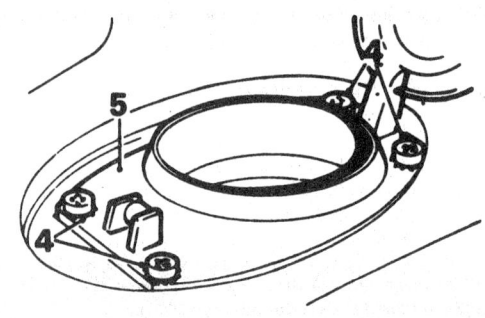

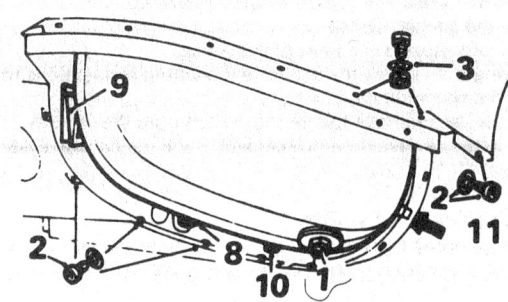

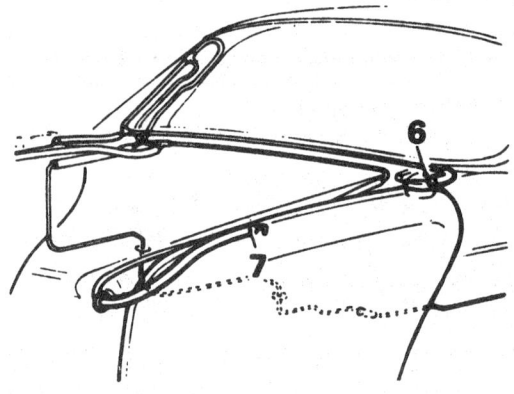

Fig. 13.12 Fuel tank attachment details – later models (Sec 6)

1   Drain plug   7   Vent pipe
2   Cover securing screws   8   Fuel pipe connector
3   Cover securing nuts and bolts 9   Rubber wedge
4   Filler neck securing screws 10 Hanger bolt
5   Filler neck   11 Gauge sender unit
6   Vent pipe

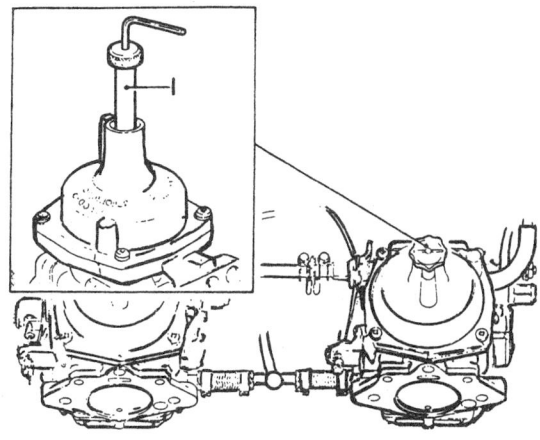

Fig. 13.13 Adjusting tool (1) required for Zenith Stromberg carbs (Sec 6)

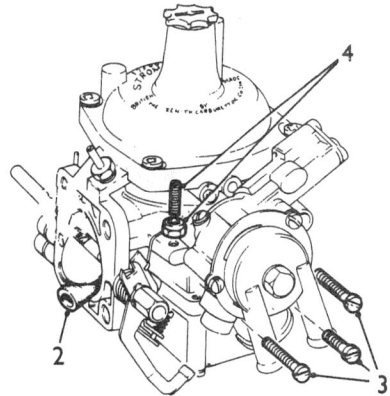

Fig. 13.14 Zenith Stromberg carburettor – removal of automatic choke (Sec 6)

2 Throttle plate wedge   4 Throttle stop screw and
3 Choke securing screws   locknut

46 Check that the surface of the Delrin disc on the needle is flush with the needle housing guide tube. If not, insert the special tool and turn the needle adjuster plug until the needle disc is flush. This is a basic needle setting.
47 Refit the piston/diaphragm, making sure that the 'pip' on the diaphragm locates correctly. Fit the cover.
48 Repeat the operations on the second carburettor.
49 Insert the adjusting tool so that the inner hexagon engages in the needle adjuster plug and the outer tool engages in the air valve.
50 Start the engine and with it idling, hold the tool outer component quite still to prevent the flexible diaphragm twisting and turn the inner component of the tool clockwise (to enrich) or anti-clockwise (to weaken). Do not turn the tool more than $\frac{3}{4}$ of a turn in either direction to achieve the specified CO level.
51 When the mixture has been adjusted on both carburettors, remove the tool, top-up the dashpots and fit the damper pistons.
52 Refit the air cleaners and reconnect the air injection system, having unplugged the non-return valve.

Zenith Stromberg automatic choke – removal, refitting and adjustment

53 The carburettors must be removed from the engine. Before this is done, the coolant hoses must be disconnected from the automatic choke. Provided that the expansion tank or header tank cap is first released and the choke coolant hoses are tied up as high as possible, there should be no loss of coolant.
54 Open the throttle of the removed carburettor and retain it in the open position with a piece of wood or flexible pipe.
55 Unscrew the automatic choke assembly from the carburettor body (three screws) and discard the gasket. Remove the throttle stop screw and locknut.
56 Unscrew and remove the centre bolt from the choke housing cover, then remove the clamp ring (three screws).
57 Carefully remove the aluminium heat sink, taking care not to damage the fins or the heat sensitive coil which is attached to it.
58 Remove the heat insulator.
59 Renew all damaged gaskets and seals. If the choke unit has been malfunctioning, renew it as an assembly.
60 To refit the choke unit, use a new gasket (without sealing compound) and tighten the three securing screws evenly.
61 Fit a new throttle stop screw and locknut.
62 Refer to Fig. 13.16. Open the throttle valve plate and remove the piece of wood, then allow the throttle to close. Adjust the idle speed screw until gap 'B' is 0.10 in (2.5 mm).
63 Lightly rotate the thermostat lever anti-clockwise to set the choke in the fully off position. Open and close the throttle, then measure gap 'A' (Fig. 13.16). The gap should be 0.045 to 0.055 in (1.14 to 1.40 mm). Turn the throttle stop screw as necessary to achieve this, then tighten the locknut without disturbing the position of the screw.
64 Refit the heat insulator so that the thermostat arm engages in the slot provided.
65 Refit the finned aluminium heat sink, engaging the arm of the

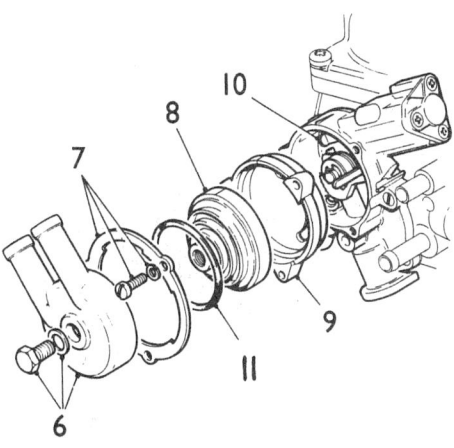

Fig. 13.15 Zenith Stromberg automatic choke components (Sec 6)

6 Cover and centre bolt   9   Insulator
7 Clamp ring and screws   10 Vacuum kick piston
8 Heat sink   11 Sealing ring

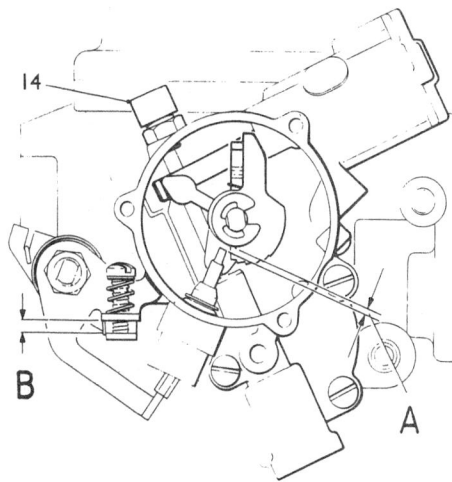

Fig. 13.16 Zenith Stromberg automatic choke adjustment (Sec 6)

A Fast idle pin-to-cam clearance   14 Throttle stop screw
B Idle speed screw lug clearance

thermostat with the rectangular loop of the temperature sensitive coil. To check this engagement, rotate the heat sink 30° to 40° in each direction and make sure that it returns to its central position unaided. Do not overdo this rotation or the coil may be damaged.

66 Refit the clamp ring but do not tighten the screws yet.
67 Turn the heat sink in an anti-clockwise direction until the index mark on its outer edge is aligned with the mark on the choke housing. Tighten the three clamp plate screws evenly.
68 Refit the sealing ring and choke housing cover. Connect the coolant hoses correctly.
69 Tighten the cover centre bolt to make a good seal, but do not overtighten.
70 Once the engine is started and reaches normal operating temperature, adjust the idle speed screw to give the specified idle speed.

SU HIF carburettors (UK models) – description
71 The HIF series carburettors fitted to later models are very similar in operation to the HS series described in Chapter 3. The main difference is that the float chamber is now immediately below the carburettor jet and is integral with the carburettor body – hence the designation HIF (Horizontal, Integral Float chamber).
72 As a consequence of the changed position of the float chamber, mixture adjustment is now carried out by means of a screw which causes the jet tube to move up or down relative to the jet needle.
73 A bimetallic strip, immersed in fuel in the float chamber, raises the jet slightly as fuel temperature increases and lowers it slightly when the temperature falls. In this way changes in mixture due to altered fuel temperature are minimised, as are exhaust emissions due to incorrect combustion.

SU HIF carburettors – removal and refitting
74 Refer to Chapter 3, Section 19. The procedure is essentially the same, making due allowance for the different throttle linkage.

SU HIF carburettor(s) – dismantling and reassembly
75 Clean the outside of the carburettor, then unscrew and remove the piston damper. If the damper retainer is stubborn, support the piston in the fully raised position and pull the damper firmly upwards.
76 Mark the position of the suction chamber relative to the carburettor body, then remove the three securing screws and lift off the chamber. Recover the identity tag.
77 Remove the piston spring and the piston complete with needle. Empty the oil out of the damper tube.
78 Note the relative alignment of the needle guide and the piston, then remove the grub screw and extract the needle guide and spring. Obtain a new grub screw for use on reassembly.
79 Remove the bottom cover plate, which is secured by four screws and washers. Recover the sealing ring.
80 Do not remove the jet adjusting screw unless there is some necessity to do so. Its sealing plug will have to be removed first. Note the O-ring in the groove in the adjusting screw head.
81 Remove the screw which secures the jet adjusting lever and recover its spring.
82 Remove the jet and the adjusting lever together, then separate them.
83 Unscrew and remove the float pivot pin, noting the washers

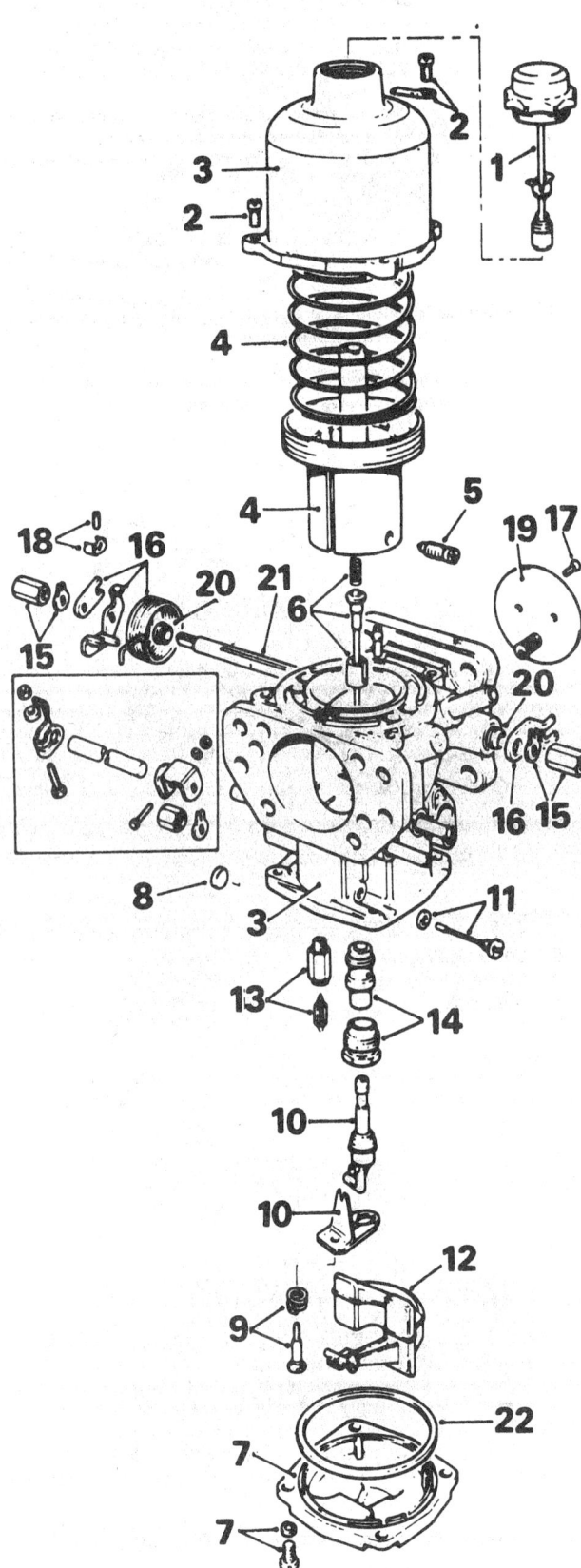

Fig. 13.17 Exploded view of the SU HIF series carburettor. Manual choke components (inset) are not fitted to XJ6 (Sec 6)

1	Piston damper	12 Float
2	Suction chamber screws	13 Needle valve and seat
3	Suction chamber	14 Jet bearing and locknut
4	Piston and spring	15 Throttle spindle nuts and
5	Needle retaining grub screw	lockwashers
6	Needle, spring and guide	16 Throttle levers and spring
7	Bottom cover and screw	17 Throttle disc screw
8	Sealing plug (jet	18 Idle speed adjustment screw
adjusting screw)		and clip
9	Jet adjusting lever screw	19 Throttle disc
and spring		20 Throttle spindle seals
10	Jet and adjusting lever	21 Throttle spindle
11	Float pivot pin	22 Sealing ring

underneath its head. Remove the float.

84 Extract the needle valve and unscrew its seat.

85 Release the jet bearing locknut and remove the jet bearing.

86 Relieve the lockwasher tabs and unscrew the nuts which secure the throttle levers and spring to the spindle. Note their relative positions, then remove the yoke, levers and spring.

87 Remove the screws which retain the throttle disc to the spindle. These screws may be very tight. Obtain new screws for use on reassembly.

88 Remove the idle speed adjustment screw and (if fitted) its tamperproofing components.

89 Close the throttle and mark the relationship of the throttle disc to the carburettor flange so that the disc can be refitted the right way up. Do not mark the disc close to the overrun valve.

90 Open the throttle and remove the throttle disc, being careful not to damage the overrun valve. Remove the throttle spindle and its seals, noting which way round it is fitted.

91 Clean all components and check for wear and damage. Obtain a repair or overhaul kit which will contain the necessary renewable items. Make sure that all the ball-bearings (6 per row) are present in the piston ball-race.

92 Reassembly is accomplished in the reverse order to dismantling. Use new gaskets, seals, lockwashers and throttle disc retaining screws. These screws have split ends, which should be spread apart to lock the screws in place when the throttle disc has been correctly fitted. The needle retaining screw must also be renewed.

93 Check the float level with the carburettor inverted (Fig. 13.18). Adjust if necessary by carefully bending the float arm.

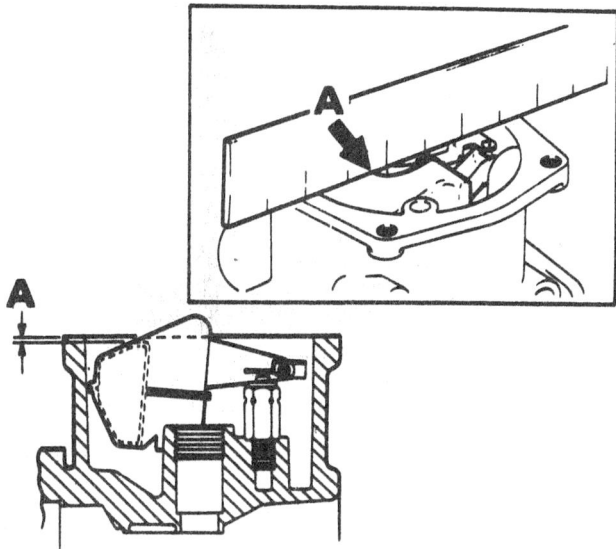

Fig. 13.18 Float level check – SU HIF carburettor (Sec 6)

$A = 0.04 \pm 0.02 \ in \ (1.0 \pm 0.5 \ mm)$

94 Set the jet initially so that it is flush with the bridge in the carburettor body, then turn the adjusting screw $3\frac{2}{3}$ turns clockwise to position the jet 0.118 in (3.0 mm) below the bridge. Final setting must be determined with the engine running.

95 Avoid twisting the suction chamber when refitting it over the piston and spring, as this can cause spring wind-up.

96 Refit the damper, making sure that its retainer enters the piston rod.

97 Refill the carburettor damper with clean engine oil, preferably of SAE 20 grade, then screw on the damper cap.

98 Do not seal any tamperproof devices until the carburettor has been adjusted on the vehicle.

SU HIF carburettors – idle speed and mixture adjustment

99 Make sure that ignition timing and all other engine adjustments are correct. The engine should be at normal operating temperature. An independent tachometer, a carburettor balancing device and a CO meter or other mixture analysing device will be required.

100 With the engine stopped, remove the air cleaner element.

101 Check the oil level in the carburettor dampers and top up if necessary.

102 If tamperproof caps are fitted to the idle speed adjusting screws, remove their lids. Remove the screws, discard the old tamperproof assemblies and fit new ones. Refit the screws so that they almost contact their respective throttle levers. **Do not** fit the lids of the tamperproof caps yet.

103 If the idle speed adjusting screws are not tamperproofed, simply unscrew them until they are just clear of the throttle levers.

104 Release the nuts which clamp the throttle spindle on each side of the rear carburettor (Fig. 13.19).

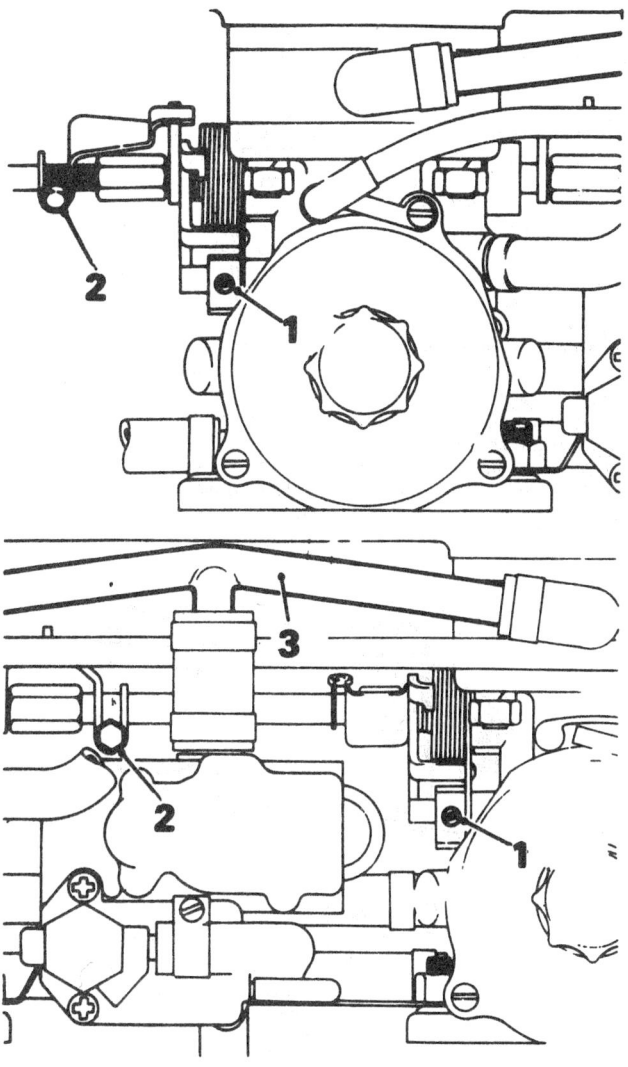

Fig. 13.19 Carburettor balance adjustment (Sec 6)

1   Idle speed adjustment screws   3   AED mixture tube
2   Throttle spindle clamp nuts

105 Raise each carburettor piston in turn with a finger and use a mirror to inspect the throttle discs. Both discs must be fully closed and the overrun valves must be properly seated.

106 Turn the idle speed adjusting screws clockwise until they just contact their throttle levers. From this position turn each screw clockwise by one further turn.

107 Start the engine and allow it to reach operating temperature. Check that the AED mixture tube is warm.

108 Connect the tachometer and the carburettor balancing device in accordance with their makers' instructions. With the engine running, turn the idle speed adjusting screws as necessary until the carburettors are in balance.

109 Read the tachometer and turn each idle speed adjusting screw equally, and in the same direction, to achieve the specified idle speed. Turning the screws clockwise increases the idle speed, and *vice versa*. When adjustment is correct, stop the engine and tighten the throttle clamp nuts.

110 If it is wished to adjust the idle mixture, remove the tamperproof caps from the mixture adjusting screws and connect the CO meter to the vehicle's exhaust system. Remove the balancing device.

111 Lift each carburettor piston in turn and turn the mixture adjusting screw clockwise to lower the jet, then anti-clockwise to raise the jet just flush with the bridge. (This is best judged by placing a thin steel rule across the bridge and feeling the jet make contact with the steel rule). From the flush position, turn the screw $3\frac{2}{3}$ turns clockwise. This will provide a datum position for each carburettor from which the subsequent adjustments can be made.

112 Start the engine and allow it to idle until normal operating temperature is reached, then run it at 2500 rpm (approx) for one minute. This 'clear out burst' must be repeated every 3 minutes until adjustment is complete.

113 Turn each mixture adjusting screw by the same amount, and in the same direction, until the fastest possible idle speed is obtained. From this position turn each screw equally anti-clockwise to weaken the mixture until the idle speed *just* begins to fall, then clockwise again until the maximum speed is *just* regained.

114 Readjust the idle speed if necessary to regain the specified value.

115 Read the CO meter and turn each mixture screw by the minimum amount necessary (clockwise to enrich, anti-clockwise to weaken) to bring the exhaust CO content within the limits specified. Again, readjust the idle speed if necessary.

116 Stop the engine and disconnect the test gear when adjustment is complete. Refit the air cleaner and (where so required) fit new tamperproof lids to the adjusting screws.

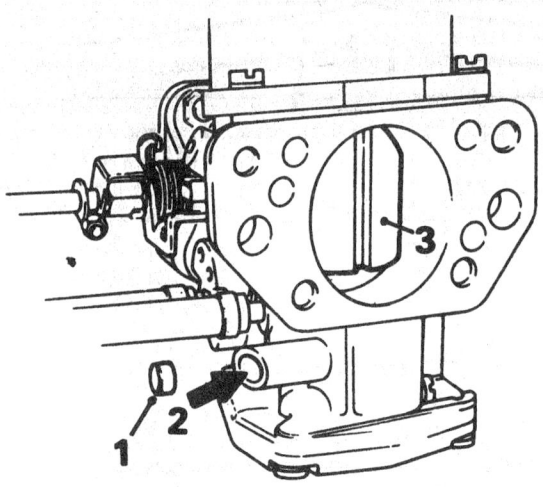

Fig. 13.20 Carburettor mixture adjustment (Sec 6)

1	Tamperproof plug	3	Piston
2	Adjustment screw		

SU HIF carburettors – throttle linkage adjustment

117 Inspect the throttle link yokes behind the rear carburettor and between the carburettors. On automatic transmission cars there should be no backlash at either yoke, ie both throttle butterflies should start to open simultaneously. On manual transmission models there should be a gap of up to 0.036 in (0.9 mm) between the tongue and the lower arm of the yoke between the carburettors, so that the rear butterfly may lead the front one by up to 3°. Adjust if necessary by releasing the clamp nuts on the throttle operating rods, moving the rods and tightening the hubs.

118 Adjust the throttle cable in its bracket so that with the pedal released, the operating lever is against the back stop, but there is no slack in the cable. Tighten the locknuts on the cable adjuster when adjustment is correct.

119 Slacken the locknut on the wide-open throttle stop screw and run the screw back a few turns. Move the operating lever to open the throttle butterflies fully, move the stop screw into contact with the operating lever and tighten the locknut.

120 Have an assistant operate the throttle pedal over its full travel and check that full movement of the throttle butterflies occurs. Adjust the pedal stop if necessary to achieve full travel without straining the cable. (The pedal stop should be reached at the same moment as the operating lever stop.)

121 On automatic transmission models, check the operation of the kickdown cable.

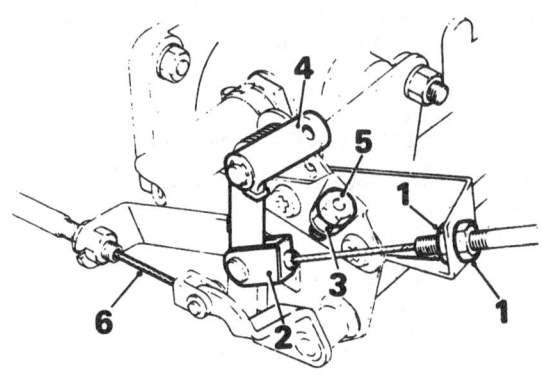

Fig. 13.21 Throttle linkage – SU HIF carburettors (Sec 6)

1	Adjuster locknuts	5	Wide-open throttle stop
2	Yoke		screw
3	Wide-open throttle stop	6	Kickdown cable (automatic
	screw locknut		transmission)
4	Operating lever		

Automatic enrichment device (AED) – fault diagnosis

122 The AED fitted with HS and HIF series carburettors differs somewhat from the unit described in Chapter 3. In particular, the later type AED has no electrical components and incorporates its own float chamber.

123 If malfunction of the AED is suspected, check first that all other engine systems are in good order and that there are no air leaks in the induction system (including the AED hot air pick-up system). Inspect the diaphragm (Fig. 13.22).

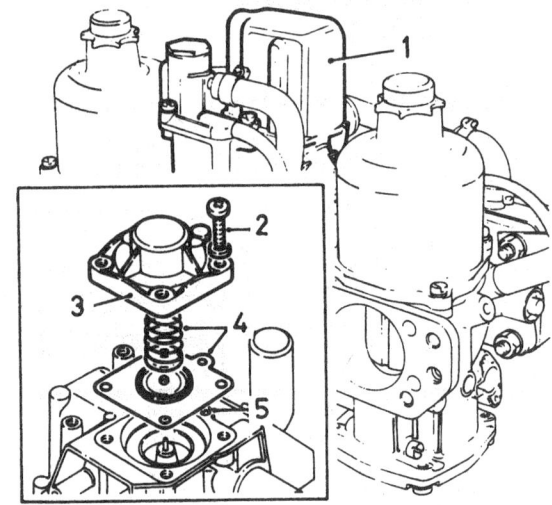

Fig. 13.22 Automatic enrichment device diaphragm (Sec 6)

1	AED	4	Diaphragm and spring
2	Screw	5	Locating dowel
3	Cover		

124 Check also that neither the AED nor the carburettors are flooding (evidenced by petrol dripping from an overflow pipe). The overflow pipes themselves must not be kinked, neither must they protrude more than 2 in (51 mm) below their bottom securing clip. A flooding AED may be corrected by removing the float chamber cover and cleaning or renewing the needle valve and seat. Use a new gasket on reassembly.

125 On models fitted with an anti-run-on valve, check that the pipe between the valve and the carburettor vents is not restricted or kinked.

126 If all the above points are in order, and regular service items such as fuel and air filter cleaning have been attended to, the jet needle lift screw (Fig. 13.24) may be adjusted one quarter turn clockwise in order to alleviate warm starting problems.

127 No other adjustment or repair to the AED is specified by the makers; a unit which is defective must therefore be renewed.

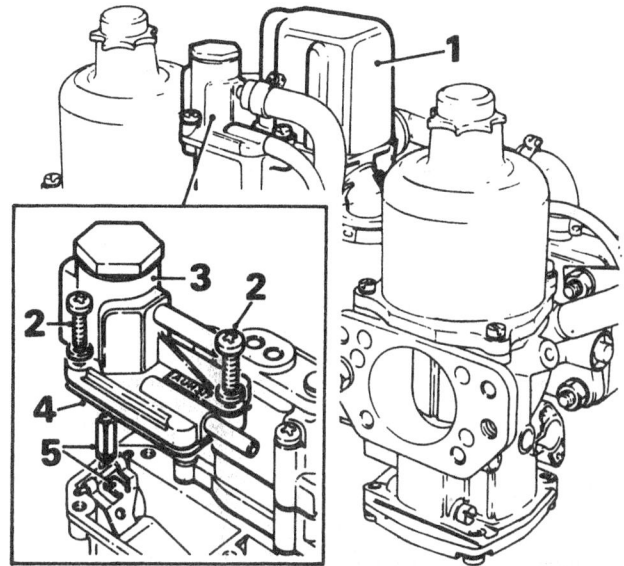

Fig. 13.23 Automatic enrichment device float chamber cover (Sec 6)

1	AED	4	Gasket
2	Screws	5	Needle valve
3	Cover		

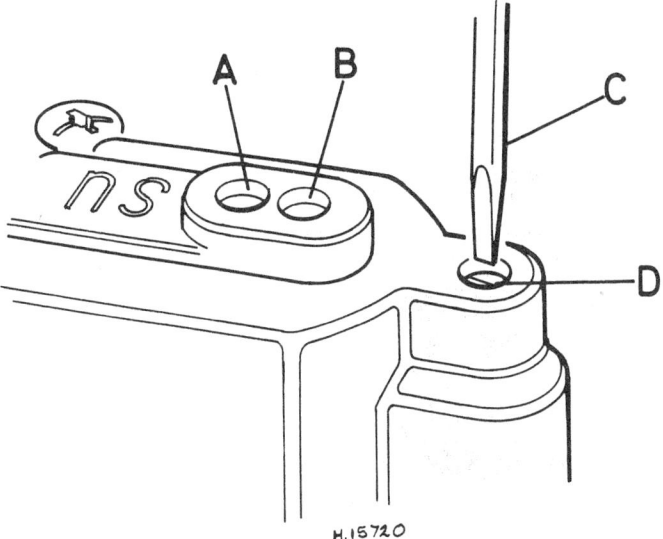

Fig. 13.24 Automatic enrichment device adjustment (Sec 6)

A	Main valve probe hole	C	Screwdriver
B	Main valve adjustment screw	D	Jet needle lift adjustment screw

7 Fuel system – electronic fuel injection

General description

1 The Lucas-Bosch electronic fuel injection system is fitted to 4.2 litre cars from 1978 (N America) or March 1979 (UK).

2 The systems can be divided into two sections: a constant pressure fuel supply, and an electronic sensing and control system which monitors engine operating conditions including load, speed, coolant and induction air temperatures and throttle opening. The information is then converted into electrical current pulses to open the injector valves to meter fuel for the combustion cycle in accordance with engine requirements.

3 Fuel is drawn from the tanks by an electric pump, passing through a changeover valve and a filter to a fuel rail and pressure regulator. Excess fuel is returned to the tank (after passing through a fuel cooler on air conditioned models).

4 The six fuel injectors are connected to the fuel rail and operated electro-mechanically.

5 Fuel is also supplied to a cold start injector.

6 Air is drawn through the air cleaner, an airflow meter and throttle assembly into the engine.

7 The electronic control unit (ECU), after having received information from the various engine sensors, computes the quantity of fuel required and triggers the injectors to open for the required period twice each engine cycle. Each time the injectors open, half the cylinder fuel requirement is supplied.

8 For cold starting, additional fuel is injected into the inlet manifold. The cold start injector is controlled by a cold start relay and thermotime switch.

9 The following additional features are built into the fuel injection system:

Flooding protection. Prevents the fuel pump operating when the ignition is switched on unless the engine is running or actually being cranked.

Auxiliary air valve. Acts as an aid to cold starting by diverting air past the throttle to regulate the idle speed according to engine temperature. This by-pass air is progressively reduced as the engine warms up by means of a bi-metal element within the auxiliary air valve.

Cranking enrichment. Provided by the electronic control unit at initial engine starting.

Throttle switch. Provides fuel enrichment to ensure maximum power at full throttle. On later European models, two throttle switches provide signals relating both to throttle position and to manifold vacuum; this enables fuel injection to be cut off completely in the overrun condition, subject to an adequate engine speed being maintained.

Oxygen sensor (North America only). Measures the free oxygen concentration in the exhaust gases. Excessive amounts of free oxygen indicate a weak mixture and when this fact is relayed to the ECU, additional fuel is supplied by increasing the injector opening periods.

10 Fuel return valves are located in both rear wheel arches. The valves are 'handed' ie left-hand and right-hand valves are not interchangeable.

11 An inertia switch, located on the passenger's side of the car near the front door pillar, disables the fuel pump in the event of severe impact. The switch can be reset after removing its cover.

Maintenance and adjustment

12 Regularly inspect the security of the system electrical connections, pipelines and hoses.

13 At the intervals specified in Routine Maintenance, renew the air cleaner element and the fuel filter.

Air cleaner element renewal

14 To renew the air cleaner element, slacken the clips on the inlet and outlet hoses and slide the air cleaner forwards until it is clear of its mounting spigots. Release the spring clips which secure the front cover, remove the self-locking nut which secures the endplate and withdraw the endplate and the filter element (photo).

15 Wipe clean the inside of the air cleaner casing. Fit a new element and refit the unit by reversing the removal operations.

Fuel filter renewal

16 On Series 2 and early Series 3 cars, the fuel filter is located in the engine compartment and is accessible after removing the air cleaner. On later models the filter is under the luggage compartment floor

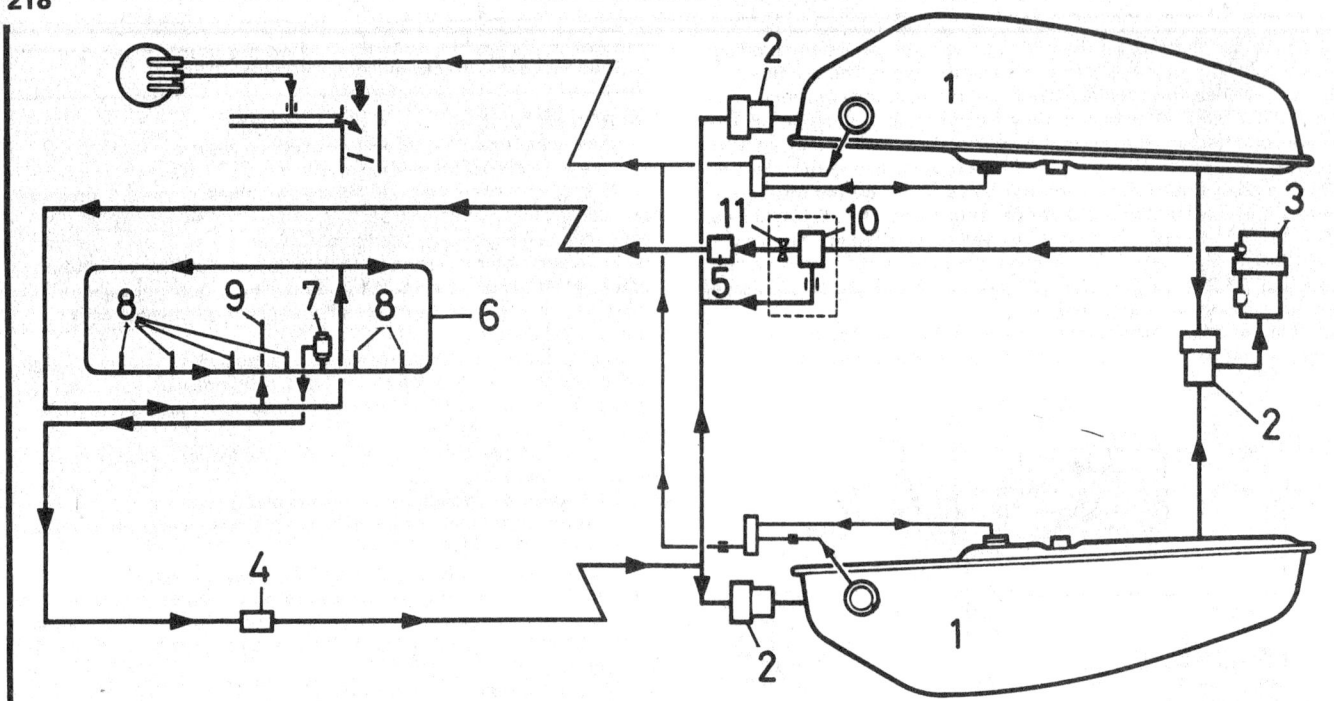

Fig. 13.25 Fuel injection system – scheme of operation (Sec 7)

1	Fuel tanks	4	Fuel cooler (air conditioned cars only)	6	Fuel rail	9	Cold start injector
2	Tank changeover valves	5	Fuel filter	7	Fuel pressure regulator	10	Air bleed valve
3	Fuel pump			8	Fuel injectors	11	Non-return valve

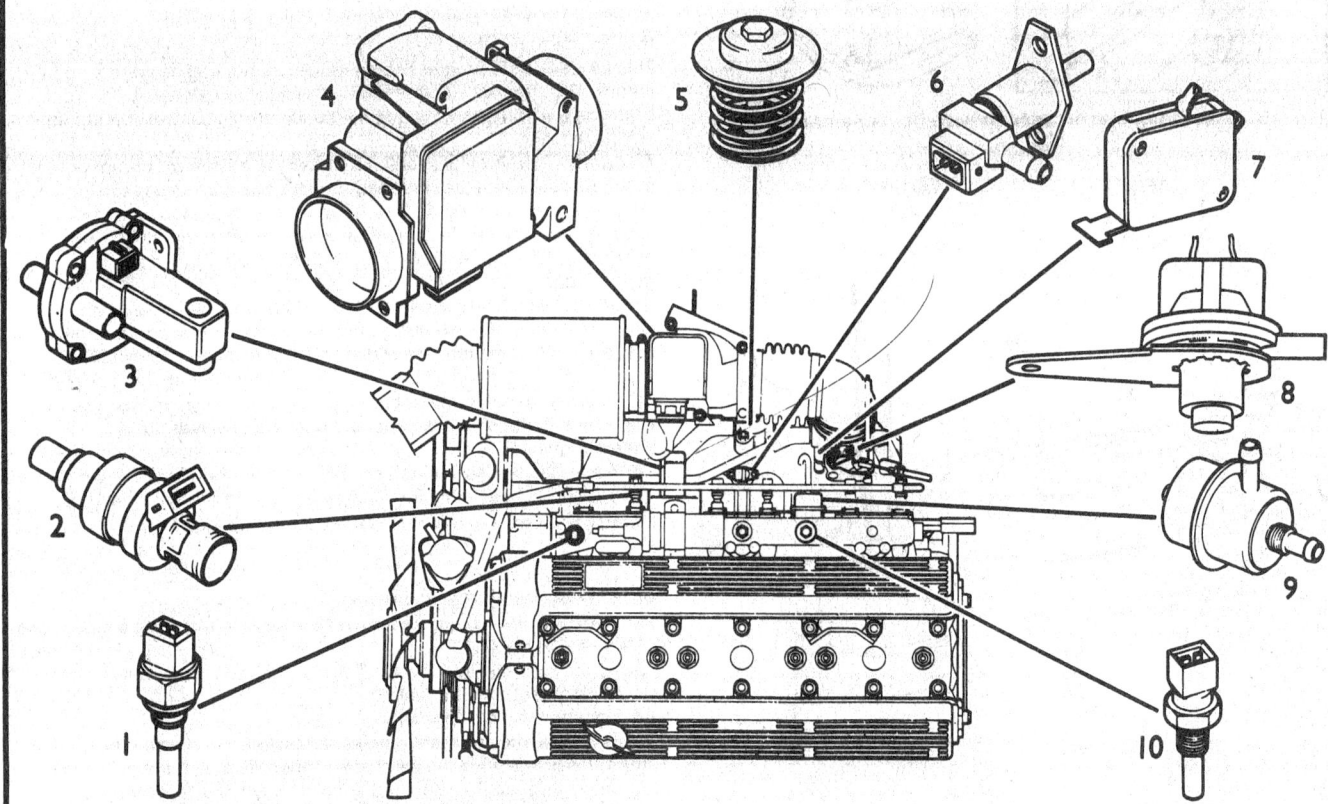

Fig. 13.26 Fuel injection system – location of engine components
(Sec 7)

1	Thermotime switch	4	Airflow meter	7	Throttle switch	9	Fuel pressure regulator
2	Fuel injectors	5	Overrun valve	8	Full load vacuum switch	10	Water temperature sensor
3	Auxiliary air valve	6	Cold start injector				

7.14 Air cleaner element renewal

7.16 Fuel filter located under luggage compartment floor

(photo). Gain access to the filter, depressurize the fuel system and proceed as follows.

17 Disconnect the battery earth lead.

18 Release the filter from its mounting bracket.

19 Clamp the hoses on either side of the filter, then release the hose clips and remove the filter. Be prepared for some fuel spillage.

20 Discard the old filter and fit the new one, observing any directional arrows which should point in the direction of fuel flow.

21 Secure the filter, remove the hose clamps and reconnect the battery earth lead. Mop up any spilt fuel, then run the engine and check the filter for leaks.

Idle speed adjustment

22 The only adjustment which should normally be undertaken by the home mechanic is to vary the engine idle speed.

23 The location of the idle speed adjusting screw is not immediately obvious. The owner who wishes to discover the screw should stand on the right-hand side of the car and look into the engine compartment. Observe the two hoses which run forwards from the throttle valve housing (on the rear of the block) towards the auxiliary air valve. One of these hoses is connected to an alloy casting, known as the air distribution block; the idle speed adjusting screw is located in a drilled and tapped hole in this block. Because of the orientation of the block, the screw is only properly visible with the aid of a mirror, but it is easy enough to insert an Allen key into the hole and turn the screw (photo).

24 If the idle speed adjustment screw is covered by a tamperproof

plug, make sure that you are not breaking any local, national or international anti-pollution laws before removing the plug. Fit a new plug on completion where this is required by law.

25 If the specified idle speed cannot be achieved, this may be due to an air leak on the induction side, to a faulty auxiliary air valve or to a maladjusted throttle linkage.

Idle mixture adjustment

26 The mixture is preset during manufacture and should **not** be tampered with unless the fuel injection system or the engine generally have been the subject of major overhaul, or new components have been fitted.

27 An accurate exhaust gas analyser will be required for this work. Adjust with the engine at normal operating temperature; on North American models, have the oxygen sensor disconnected. Bring the CO level within that specified.

28 The mixture adjusting screw is located under a tamperproof plug on the airflow meter (photo). Read paragraph 24 before removing the plug.

29 If necessary, readjust the idle speed after adjusting the mixture.

Depressurizing

30 Before disconnecting any fuel system components, the system **must** be depressurized as follows.

31 On early vehicles (with a combined fuel pump/injection system

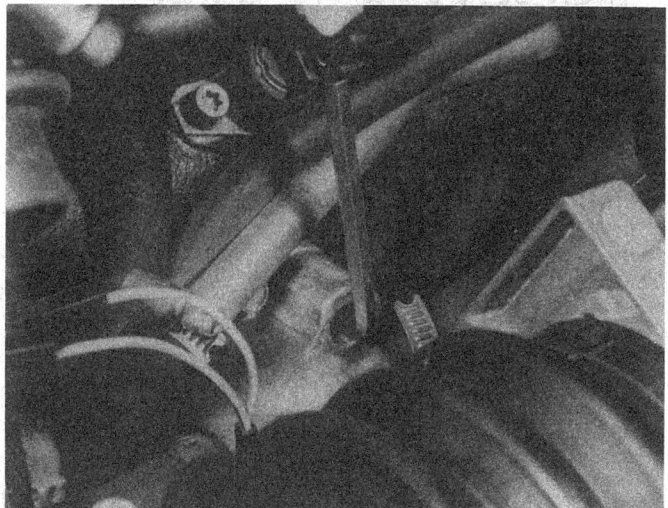

7.23 Allen key in idle speed adjustment hole

7.28 Screwdriver in the idle mixture adjustment hole

relay), remove the spare wheel and disconnect the fuel pump earth lead. On later models with a separate fuel pump relay, unplug the fuel pump relay.

32 Crank the engine on the starter motor for a few seconds.

33 Switch off the ignition and reconnect the fuel pump or relay. The system is now depressurized and will remain so until another attempt is made to start the engine.

34 Even with the system depressurized, fuel spillage will still occur when fuel lines are disconnected. It is the mechanic's responsibility to take adequate precautions against fire, explosion and vapour intoxication.

Fuel tank – removal and refitting

35 Refer to Section 6 of this Chapter and proceed as described for carburettor models. Depressurize the system first.

Fuel injection system components – removal and refitting

36 Needless tampering with components of the system is not recommended, neither is dismantling of the various assemblies. However, where it is established that an individual component is faulty or malfunctioning (confirmed by your dealer or after reference to the Fault Diagnosis Chart at the end of this Section), there is no reason why renewal of the component cannot be undertaken.

Cold start injector

37 This is mounted on the inlet manifold. Depressurize the system and disconnect the battery.

38 Clamp the fuel supply pipe to the injector to prevent fuel loss and then disconnect the pipe.

39 Unbolt the injector and remove it.

40 Refit by reversing the removal operations, but use a new gasket if necessary.

Fuel rail and injectors

41 Depressurize the system and disconnect the battery.

42 Pull the manifold pressure pipe from the inlet manifold.

43 Clamp the fuel supply pipe to prevent loss of fuel. Disconnect all hoses from the rail.

44 Disconnect all leads from the injectors (including cold start).

45 Remove the six nuts which hold the injector clamps to the induction ram pipe. Lift the fuel rail complete with injectors from the ram pipes. Mop up spilled fuel.

46 Tape over the injector holes in the ram pipes to prevent entry of dirt.

47 The injectors can be withdrawn from the fuel rail stubs after slackening the securing clips.

48 Refitting is a reversal of removal, but use a complete set of new O-rings on the injectors and check for fuel leakage on completion.

Fuel pressure regulator

49 This is mounted on the inlet manifold and is connected to the fuel rail and to inlet manifold depression.

50 Depressurize the system and disconnect the battery.

51 Unbolt the regulator bracket, but do not remove the regulator/bracket assembly until its orientation with respect to the manifold has been noted.

52 Clamp the regulator inlet and outlet hoses and then disconnect them.

53 Unbolt the regulator from its mounting bracket.

54 Refitting is a reversal of removal.

Fuel pump

55 The fuel pump is located below the luggage compartment floor and is electrically operated.

56 Disconnect the battery and remove the spare wheel.

57 Clamp the inlet and outlet pump hoses to prevent loss of fuel.

58 Disconnect the hoses and electrical leads from the pump.

59 Unbolt the pump/bracket assembly and remove it. The pump can be withdrawn from the clamp once the clamp-to-bracket nuts are unscrewed.

60 Refitting is a reversal of removal, but make sure that the earth wire makes a good metal-to-metal contact under one of the mounting screws.

Fuel cooler (air conditioned models only)

61 This is mounted adjacent to the air cleaner (Series 2) or compressor (Series 3).

62 The fuel pipes can be disconnected from the cooler provided that the fuel system has been depressurized first and the fuel pipes identified correctly. *On no account mistake the refrigerant pipes for fuel lines.*

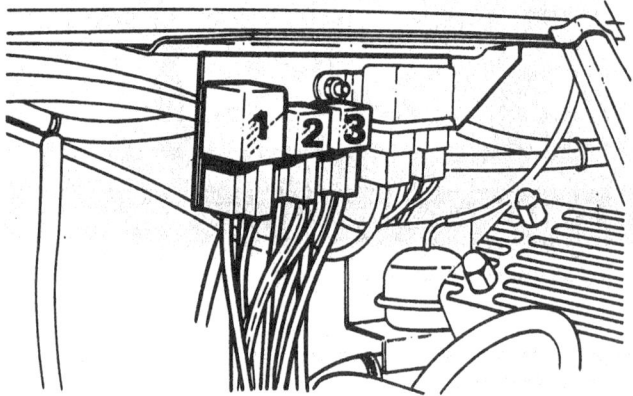

Fig. 13.27 Fuel injection system relays – later models (Sec 7)

1	*Diode unit*	*3* *Fuel pump relay*
2	*Cold start relay*	

Fig. 13.28 Fuel pressure regulator (1) is mounted on inlet manifold (Sec 7)

63 If the cooler is to be removed, have the air conditioning system discharged by your dealer before any work is carried out.

64 Refitting is a reversal of removal. Have the air conditioning system recharged by your dealer.

Fuel tank changeover valve

65 This is located adjacent to the fuel pump below the luggage compartment floor. When energized by the changeover switch, the valve opens the outlet pipe from the right-hand fuel tank. When de-

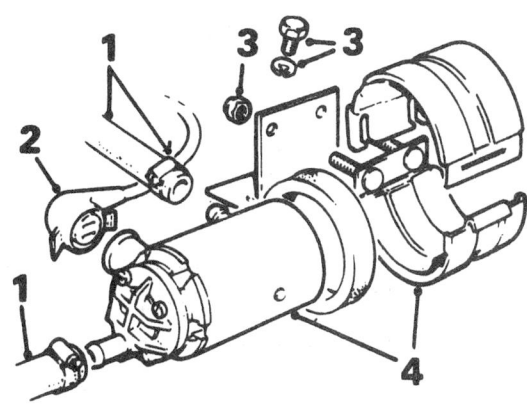

Fig. 13.29 Fuel pump connections and mountings (Sec 7)

1	Fuel hoses	3	Mounting nut and bolt
2	Electrical connector	4	Pump and bracket

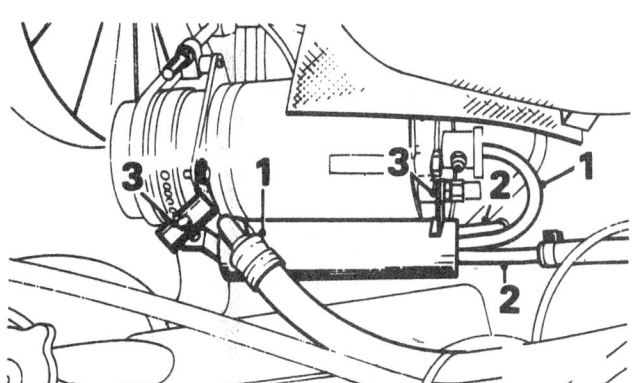

Fig. 13.30 Fuel cooler adjacent to air conditioning compressor (Sec 7)

1	Refrigerant lines	3	Mountings
2	Fuel lines		

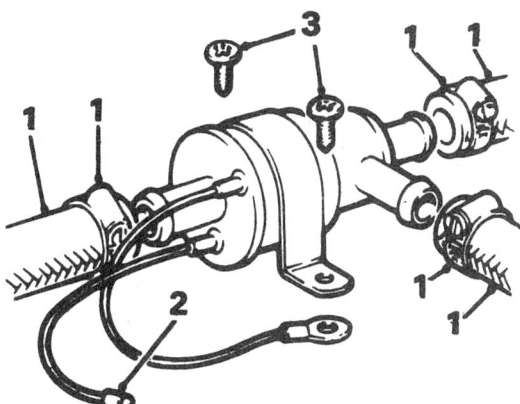

Fig. 13.31 Fuel tank changeover valve (Sec 7)

1	Fuel lines and clips	3	Fixing screws
2	Electrical connector		

energized, the valve opens the outlet pipe from the left-hand fuel tank.
66 Depressurize the fuel system, disconnect the battery and remove the spare wheel.
67 Clamp the valve hoses to prevent loss of fuel.
68 Disconnect the valve hoses and the electrical leads. Unbolt the valve mounting clamp and remove the valve.
69 Refitting is a reversal of removal. Make sure that the earth lead is making a good metal-to-metal contact under one of the mounting screws.

Fuel return valve(s)

70 Raise and support the rear of the vehicle and remove the rear wheel on the side concerned.
71 Depressurize the fuel system and disconnect the battery.
72 Remove the valve cover, which is secured by two screws.
73 Remove the two screws which secure the valve to the body (photo).
74 Clamp the hoses on both sides of the valve and release the hose clips.
75 Disconnect the electrical leads from the valve and free it from the hoses. Access to the connectors is through a cover plate (photo).
76 Refitting is a reversal of the removal procedure. Note that the valves are 'handed', ie left-hand and right-hand valves are not interchangeable. The left-hand valve has a bracket welded to it so that were it to be fitted on the right-hand side, it would foul the wheel. An

7.73 Fuel return valve (left-hand side)

7.75 Fuel return valve connectors behind cover plate

arrow on the valve shows the direction of fuel flow (rearwards).

Relay assembly

77 Early models have a single large relay, mounted on the bulkhead next to the battery, which controls the fuel pump and all other electrical functions of the fuel injection system. Later models have two relays and a diode unit, in the same location, which perform between them the same functions.

78 Disconnect the battery before removing a relay.

79 Identify the electrical connectors and then separate the relay from them.

80 When so secured, undo the screw and remove the relay from its bracket.

81 Refitting is a reversal of removal.

Ballast resistors

82 The ballast resistors are mounted as a composite unit on the right-hand engine compartment valance at the front, under the air cleaner. Their purpose is to protect the ECU from injector current faults; they are wired in series with each injector.

83 The ballast resistor unit is secured by two screws. Undo the screws and unplug the unit to remove it; reverse the procedure to refit.

Throttle switch

84 Two types of throttle switch are in use. Both types are mounted on the throttle valve housing. The first type of switch is operated by the end of the throttle spindle; the second type of switch is operated by contact with one of the throttle levers.

85 To remove either type of switch, first disconnect the battery. Disconnect the multi-plug or spade connectors from the switch, remove the securing screws and withdraw the switch.

86 Refit in the reverse order to removal, but do not fully tighten the

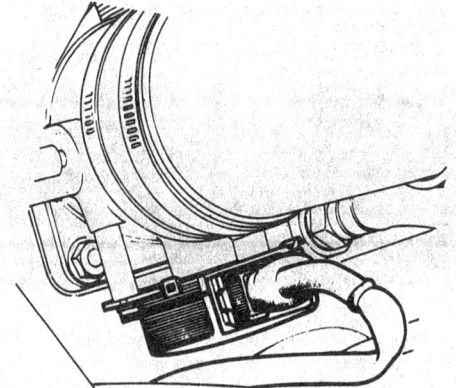

Fig. 13.32 Throttle switch operated directly by spindle (Sec 7)

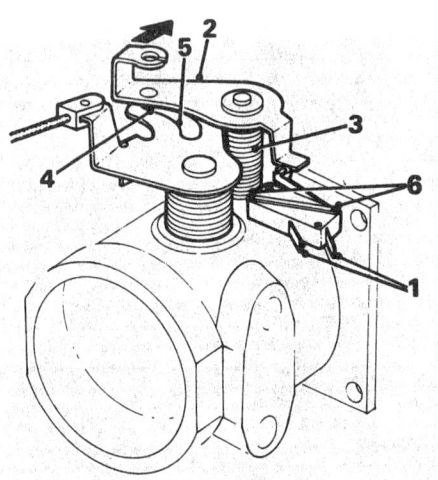

Fig. 13.33 Throttle switch operated by lever (Sec 7)

1 Terminals	4 Spigot
2 Throttle lever	5 Slot
3 Spring	6 Switch securing screws

securing screws or reconnect the switch until it has been adjusted as follows.

87 Check the throttle butterfly adjustment as described later in this Section.

88 Connect a continuity tester (eg torch bulb and battery) between terminals 3 and 18 of the spindle-operated switch, or between the only two terminals of the lever-operated switch.

89 Open and close the throttle. The spindle-operated switch should be 'on' (ie the bulb should light) as full throttle is approached. The lever-operated switch works in the opposite way, ie it should be 'on' only at idle (throttle released). In either case, if adjustment cannot be achieved by moving the switch within the limits allowed by its slotted mounting holes, the switch must be renewed.

Full load vacuum switch

90 The full load vacuum switch (also known as the vacuum throttle switch) is only found on later European cars. Its function is to command enrichment of the fuel mixture under conditions of wide throttle and low manifold vacuum, ie high load.

91 The switch is removed by disconnecting its electrical and vacuum lines and unbolting its mounting bracket (photo).

92 Refitting is a reversal of removal.

Electronic control unit (ECU)

93 This is mounted within the luggage compartment against the front bulkhead.

94 Disconnect the battery.

95 Remove the cover from the ECU then remove the retainer band, cable clamp clip and the end cover (photo).

96 Withdraw the wiring harness plug (photo). **Do not** move the idle fuel potentiometer during these operations.

97 Refitting is a reversal of removal. If a new ECU is being fitted, the idle speed and mixture should be checked and adjusted if necessary.

Airflow meter and air temperature sensor

98 The airflow meter is located between the air cleaner and the throttle valve housing.

99 Disconnect the battery.

100 Slacken the hose clips on each side of the airflow meter and then pull off the electrical connector (photo).

101 Unbolt the airflow meter and withdraw it, at the same time pulling off the air intake hoses.

102 The air temperature sensor is an integral part of the airflow meter.

103 Refitting is a reversal of removal. If a new airflow meter is being fitted, the idle speed and mixture should be checked and adjusted if necessary.

Thermotime switch

104 This is located at the front of the coolant rail on the right-hand side of the engine.

105 The switch must only be removed from a cold engine.

106 Disconnect the battery and pull the electrical connector from the switch (photo).

107 Remove the pressure cap from the cooling system expansion tank to release any pressure and then refit the cap securely.

108 Remove the switch.

109 On refitting, use a new sealing washer and smear the switch threads with gasket cement. Top-up the expansion tank if necessary.

Coolant temperature sensor

110 This is located at the rear of the coolant rail on the right-hand side of the engine.

111 The sensor must only be removed from a cold engine.

112 Removal and refitting are as for the thermotime switch.

Oxygen sensor (North America only)

113 This is screwed into the upper end of the exhaust downpipe just below the manifold.

114 Pull off the electrical connector and unscrew and remove the sensor.

115 Refitting is a reversal of removal, but coat the threads with lead-free anti-seize compound. Have a Jaguar dealer reset the service interval counter if a new sensor has been fitted.

Fuel cut-off switch (inertia type)

116 This is designed to cut off the fuel supply to the engine in the event of a collision. It is mounted under a cover under the passenger's side of the facia, near the door pillar (photo).

117 Remove the switch by pulling it from its clips and disconnecting the electrical leads.

118 When fitting a new switch, the lead polarity to the terminals does not matter. Depress the plunger on top of the switch on completion of installation.

7.91 Full load vacuum switch

7.95 Releasing the ECU retainer band

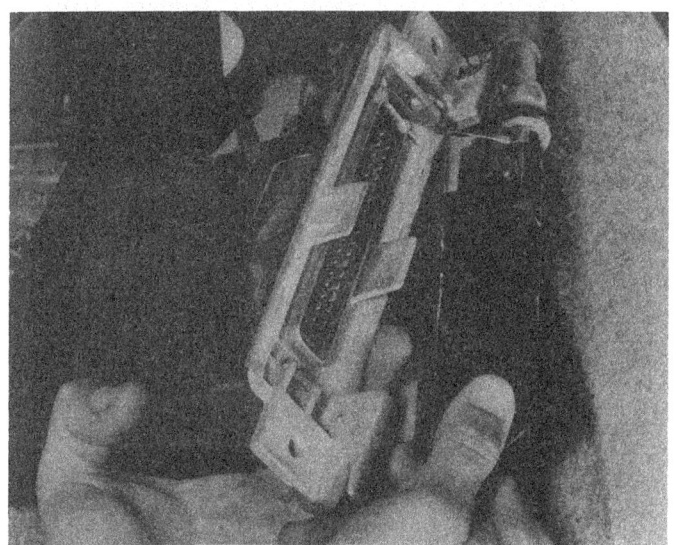

7.96 Disconnecting the multi-plug from the ECU

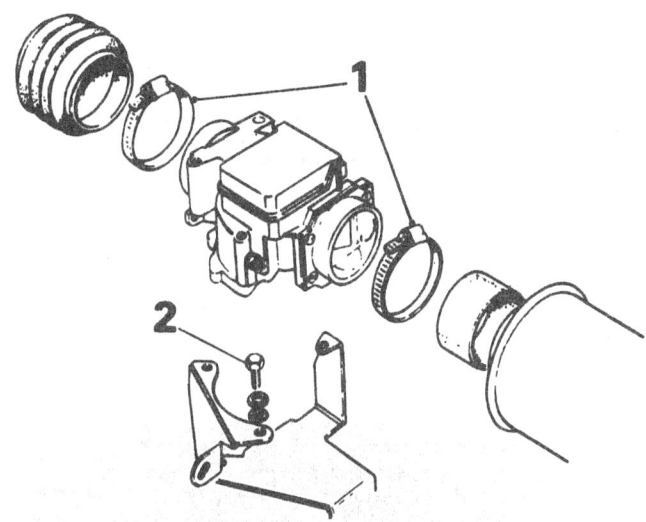

Fig. 13.34 Airflow meter hose clips (1) and securing bolt (2)
(Sec 7)

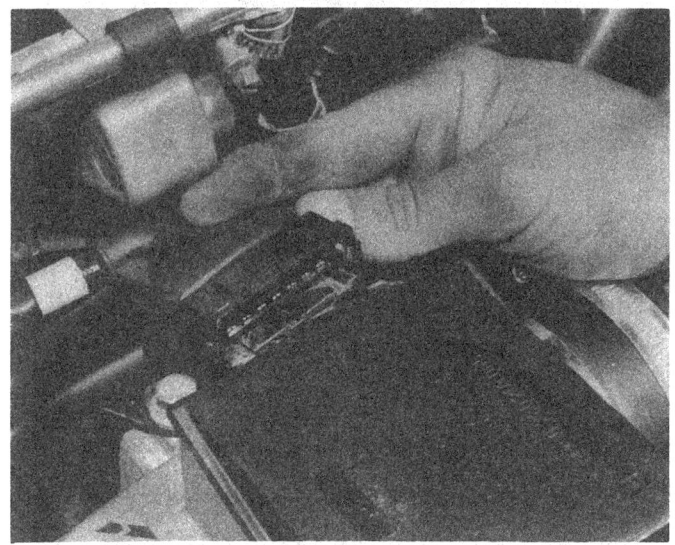

7.100 Airflow meter electrical connector

7.106 Thermotime switch connector

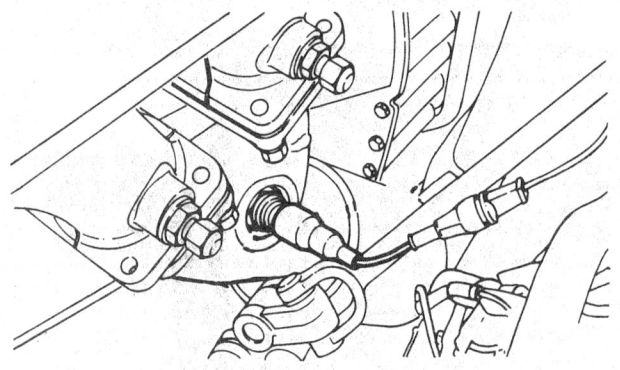

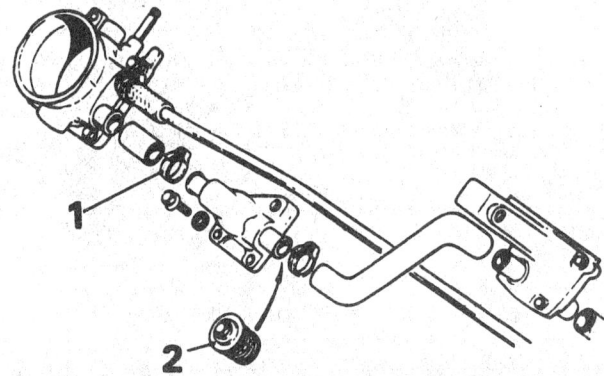

Fig. 13.36 Overrun valve (2) is located below air distributor block (Sec 7)

1 Hose clip

124 Withdraw the overrun valve
125 Refitting is a reversal of removal.
Auxiliary air valve
126 This is mounted on the coolant outlet rail. It must only be removed from a cold engine.
127 Disconnect the battery.
128 Remove the pressure cap from the cooling system expansion tank to release any residual pressure, then refit the cap tightly.
129 Disconnect the air hoses from the valve, then unbolt and remove the valve. Clean away the old gasket.
130 Smear both sides of the new gasket with non-setting gasket cement before refitting.
131 Top-up the expansion tank if necessary.

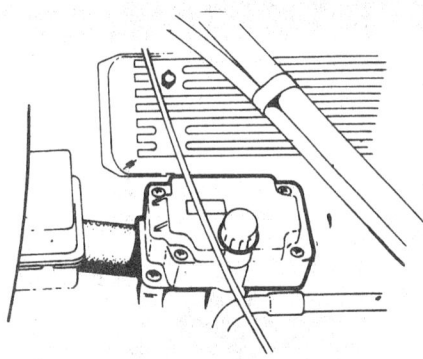

Fig. 13.35 Oxygen sensor (above) and early type service interval counter (below) (Sec 7)

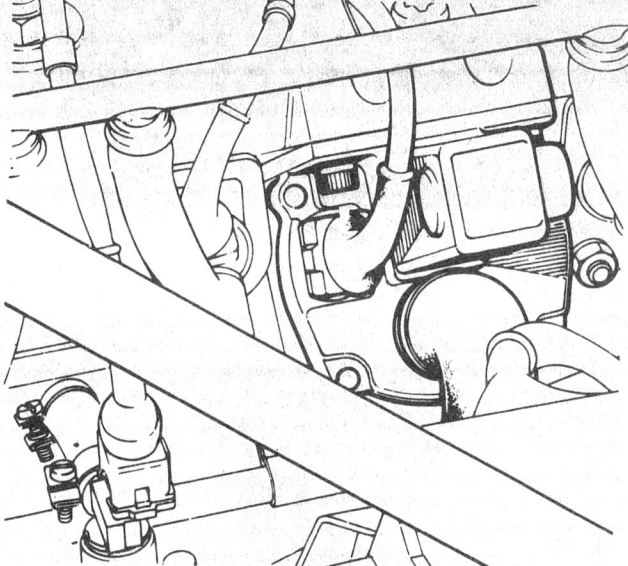

Fig. 13.37 Auxiliary air valve mounted on coolant rail (Sec 7)

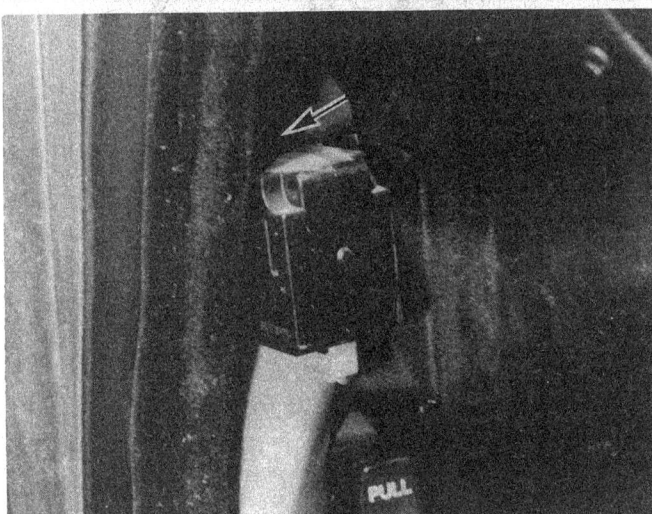

7.116 Fuel cut-off inertia switch. Reset button (arrowed) is on top

Overrun valve (when fitted)
119 This is located under the air distributor block. It limits manifold depression under conditions of closed throttle overrun to ensure that a supply of air is available to maintain a combustible fuel/air mixture.
120 Disconnect the battery.
121 Remove the airflow meter as previously described.
122 Remove the auxiliary air hose from the air distribution block.
123 Unbolt the air distribution block from the inlet manifold, lift it up and disconnect the throttle butterfly hose.

Throttle linkage – removal, refitting and adjustment
Throttle pedal
132 This can be removed by unscrewing the bottom mounting plate nuts, pulling the pedal away from the mounting plate and unclipping the spring at the rear.
133 Refitting is a reversal of removal.
Throttle cable
134 Disengage the throttle return spring at the operating lever. Slacken the outer cable locknuts and slip the cable assembly from its bracket in the engine compartment.

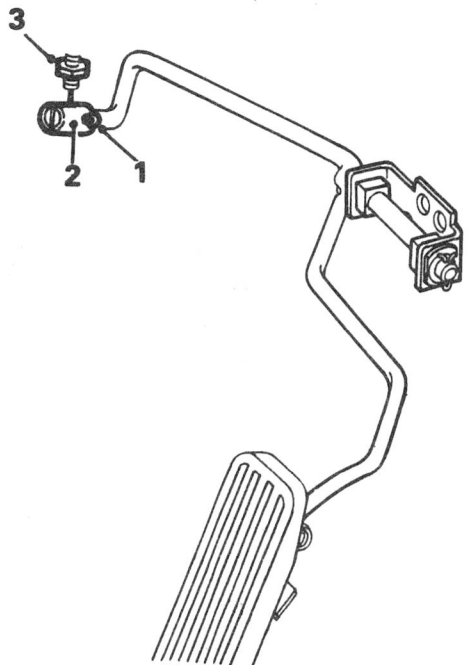

Fig. 13.38 Throttle cable fixings at pedal end (Sec 7)

1	Split pin	3	Locknut
2	Sleeve		

135 Remove the C-clip which retains the cable yoke clevis pin and detach the inner cable from the operating lever.
136 Slacken the cable locknut at the bulkhead above the footwell. Remove the casing above the footwell which covers the accelerator pedal rod.
137 Withdraw the split pin from the top of the operating rod above the pedal.
138 Disengage the throttle cable and nipple from the operating rod.
139 Remove the locknut from the end of the cable inside the car. Withdraw the cable assembly into the engine compartment.
140 Refitting is a reversal of removal. Make good the sealing of the cable entry at the bulkhead and renew any faulty grommets. On completion, adjust in the following way.
Adjustment
141 Release the cable locknuts at the bracket within the engine compartment. Now adjust the locknuts so that all slack is removed from the inner cable, but without moving the throttle operating lever. Tighten the locknuts.

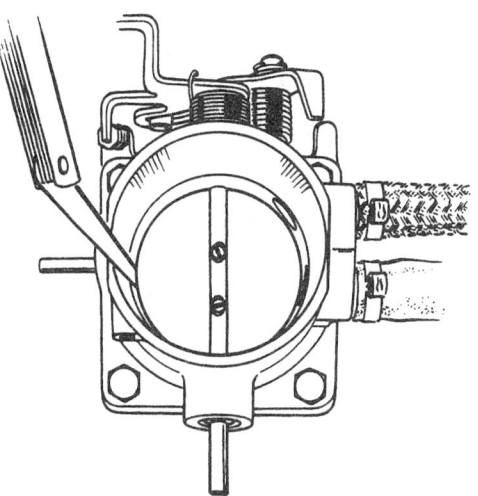

Fig. 13.39 Throttle butterfly valve adjustment (Sec 7)

Throttle butterfly valve – adjustment
142 Remove the elbow and the convolute hose to expose the fuel injection system throttle body.
143 Slacken the throttle stop screw locknut and back off the screw.
144 Check that the throttle butterfly valve is fully closed.
145 Using a feeler gauge 0.002 in (0.05 mm) thick, insert it between the upper edge of the valve plate and the throttle housing to keep the valve open.
146 Turn the throttle stop screw until it just contacts the stop arm and then tighten the locknut.
147 Remove the feeler gauge and check the adjustment of the throttle switch as described earlier in this Section.

Thermal vacuum switch – description and function
148 During 1983 a modification was made to the fuel pressure regulation system, whereby at high fuel rail temperatures the regulator vacuum circuit is temporarily opened. This results in maximum fuel pressure being obtained, so purging the fuel rail of any vapour locks. In this way, hot starting difficulties are avoided.
149 The device which regulates this function is known as a thermal vacuum switch. The switch is clamped to the top rung of the fuel rail and receives vacuum hose connections from the inlet manifold and the fuel pressure regulator.
150 Earlier cars which suffer from hot start difficulties, particularly when left to stand for half an hour or so after a high speed run, may benefit from having a thermal vacuum switch fitted. The parts required should be available from an authorised Jaguar/Daimler dealer.

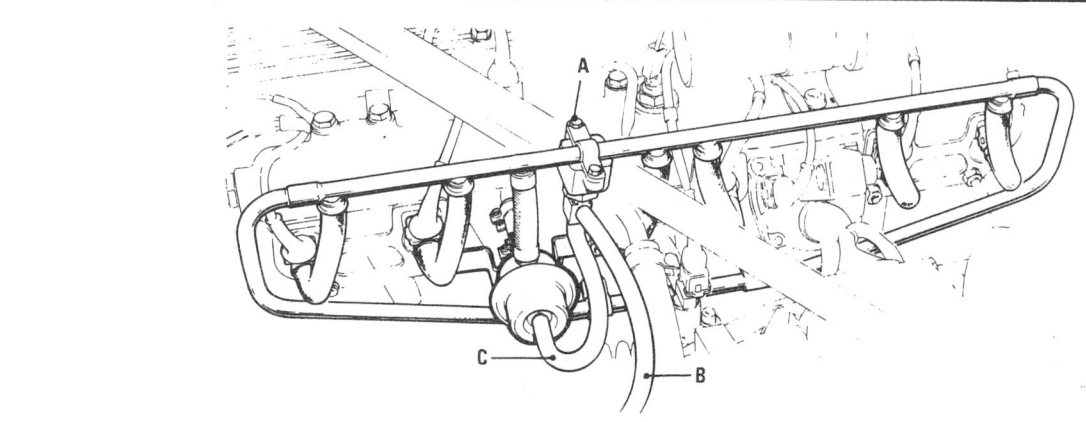

Fig. 13.40 Thermal vacuum switch mounted on fuel rail (Sec 7)

A Clamp	B Vacuum pipe from manifold	C Vacuum pipe to fuel pressure regulator

Testing procedures – fuel injection system components

151 The procedures which follow are intended to help the enthusiast check the correct functioning of some of the fuel injection system components. Testing of the complete system requires equipment and expertise beyond the scope of this book.

152 Various fuel injection components are mechanically and/or electrically fragile. Improvised or clumsy testing procedures may cause more damage than was already present.

153 The ECU should only be suspected of a fault when all other items have been proved good.

Auxiliary air valve

154 Unplug the electrical connector and use a voltmeter to check that battery voltage is present across the connector terminals when the engine is being cranked on the starter motor. If not, there is a fault in the power supply to the valve.

155 Measure the electrical resistance across the valve terminals: the correct value is 33 ohms. Open-circuit or short-circuit readings mean that the valve should be renewed.

156 Remove the valve from the coolant rail and partially immerse it in cold water. (Do not immerse the electrical terminals or the air bypass channel). The bypass channel should become fully unobstructed by the blocking plate.

157 Repeat the preceding test with hot water. The blocking plate should move gradually to close the bypass channel.

Coolant temperature sensor

158 Disconnect the battery, then unplug the temperature sensor connector.

159 Measure the resistance between each terminal of the sensor and its body. An open-circuit (infinite resistance) reading should be obtained.

160 Measure the resistance across the sensor terminals. It should vary with coolant temperature as follows:

Temperature (°F(°C))	Resistance (ohms)
+14 (-10)	9200
+32 (0)	5900
+ 68 (+20)	2500
+104 (+40)	1180
+140 (+60)	600
+176 (+80)	325

Air temperature sensor

161 Disconnect the battery and unplug the electrical connector from the airflow meter.

162 Measure the resistance between terminals 6 and 27 of the airflow meter. The reading should vary with air temperature. Refer to the table of test data for the coolant temperature sensor: the same values apply.

Thermotime switch

163 Measure the coolant temperature: it must be below the operating temperature stamped on the thermotime switch.

164 Disconnect the battery earth lead and unplug the electrical connector from the thermotime switch.

165 Measure the resistance between switch terminal 'W' and earth: a short-circuit (zero resistance) reading should be obtained.

166 Arrange a switched 12 volt supply to switch terminal 'G' (positive side of supply) and earth (negative side). Leave the ohmmeter connected between terminal 'W' and earth. Switch on the power supply and note the time taken for the thermotime switch to change state (indicated by the ohmmeter reading changing from short-circuit to open-circuit). The delay varies with coolant temperature, and should correspond to the values in the following table:

Coolant temperature (°F(°C))	Delay (sec)
-4 (-20)	8.0
+32 (0)	4.5
+50 (+10)	3.5
+95 (+35)	0

Cold start system

167 Coolant and ambient air temperatures must both be below 95°F (35°C) before the cold start system can be tested.

168 Fuel vapour will be present in the engine bay during the test. Take adequate precautions against fire or explosion.

169 Unplug the electrical connector from the cold start injector. Connect a voltmeter across the connector terminals and crank the engine on the starter motor: battery voltage should be present when cranking. If not, there is a fault in the power supply to the cold start injector.

170 Remove the injector from the manifold and refit its electrical connector. Have ready a container to catch ejected fuel and crank the engine again. Fuel should be sprayed from the injector nozzle for a few seconds until the thermotime switch opens (see previous test). No leakage should occur when the injection period is over.

Injector windings

171 Each injector should display a resistance of 2.4 ohms at 68°F (20°C) measured across its teminals. On most DIY test equipment it will not be possible to distinguish such a low resistance from a short-circuit (zero ohms) result.

172 Resistance between either injector terminal and earth should be infinite (open-circuit).

173 Note that the injectors operate at well below battery voltage, the balance being dropped across the ballast resistors. On no account apply 12 volts directly to an injector winding.

Fault diagnosis – fuel injection system

Symptom	Reason(s)
Engine will not start when warm	Fuel tank empty Vapour locks in fuel rail Clogged fuel filter Faulty fuel pump Faulty pressure regulator ECU connections loose Faulty auxiliary air valve Faulty cold start system Sticking airflow meter flaps Faulty temperature sensors
Rough idle (cold engine)	Clogged fuel filter Faulty fuel pump Loose system electrical connections Sticking airflow meter flaps Incorrect idle mixture Blocked or leaking exhaust Unequal cylinder compressions Air leaks at inlet manifold Faulty auxiliary air valve Engine oil filler cap loose or poor seal Blocked charcoal canister (when fitted) Faulty fuel injectors Faulty temperature sensors

Symptom	Reason(s)
Flat spot (hesitation)	Clogged fuel filter
	Faulty fuel pump
	Faulty pressure regulator
	Faulty throttle switch
	Loose system electrical connections
	Incorrectly adjusted throttle butterfly
	Sticking airflow meter flap
	Faulty auxiliary air valve
	Blocked or leaking exhaust system
	Air leak at inlet manifold
	Blocked charcoal canister (when fitted)
Excessive fuel consumption	General leaks
	Faulty throttle switch
	Faulty cold start system
	Air leak at inlet manifold
	Blocked exhaust system
	Engine oil filler cap loose or poor seal
	Charcoal canister blocked (when fitted)
	Faulty fuel injectors
	Faulty temperature sensors
	Faulty oxygen sensor (when fitted)
High idle speed and lack of engine braking	Air leak in inlet manifold
	Sticking throttle mechanism
	Faulty auxiliary air valve
	Incorrect idle mixture
	Leaks around throttle valve spindle
	Leaking overrun valve (when fitted)
Engine stalls at idling speed	Leaks in fuel system
	Clogged fuel line filter
	Faulty pressure regulator
	Faulty fuel pump
	Loose electrical connections
	Faulty temperature sensors
	Faulty cold start system
	Clogged air cleaner element
	Airflow meter flap sticking
	Blocked or leaking exhaust
	Air leak in inlet manifold
	Incorrect idle mixture
	Engine oil filler cap loose or poor seal
	Charcoal canister blocked (when fitted)
Running on or pinking	Incorrect fuel grade
	Blocked hoses on crankcase or fuel vent systems
	Incorrect idle speed
	Engine overheating due to cooling system fault
	Over-advanced ignition
Backfire in exhaust	Fuel starvation due to faulty fuel pump, pressure regulator or blocked fuel filter
	Loose electrical connection
	Blocked air cleaner element
	Blocked or leaking exhaust
	Air leak in inlet manifold
	Loose engine oil filler cap or poor seal
	Engine or ignition fault

8   Exhaust and emission control systems (Series 3)

Description

1   The systems described in Chapter 3 will still be found on later cars destined for territories with stringent emission control requirements. Although a fuel injection engine produces less pollutants than its carburetted counterpart, acceptable levels of exhaust emission have fallen, so emission control systems are still required.

2   At the time of writing, the positive crankcase ventilation system is the only emission-related system fitted to UK cars (photo). Elsewhere in Europe additional systems may be encountered.

Catalytic converter

General description

3   The catalytic converter (when fitted) is found in the exhaust system, upstream of the main silencers. Similar in appearance to an ordinary silencer, it contains a catalyst which promotes the conversion of unburned hydrocarbons and carbon monoxide to water and carbon dioxide.

4   Use of unleaded fuel is essential when a catalytic converter is fitted, since lead will rapidly poison the catalyst. The conversion reactions are exothermic, so the body of the converter may become extremely hot in normal use. To avoid damage to the converter, the vehicle and the environment, observe the following precautions:

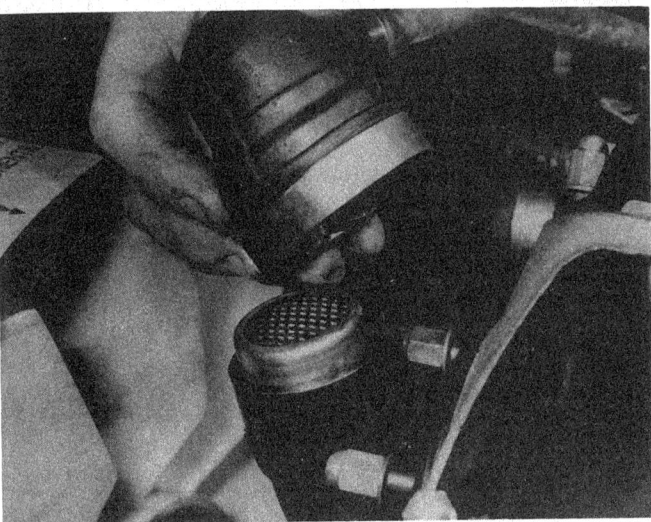

8.2 Crankcase ventilation elbow and 'thimble' filter

(a) *Do not continue to operate the car if the engine is misfiring or runs-on after switching off*

(b) *Do not park on areas of long grass or other combustible materials*

(c) *Do not overload the car or pull excessively heavy trailer loads*

(d) *Do not operate the car downhill with the engine switched off*

(e) *Do not run the engine with a spark plug removed or HT leads disconnected*

(f) *Do not use the type of tyre pump which can be screwed into a spark plug hole*

(g) *Do not push or tow-start the car, use only battery jumper leads connected to another vehicle*

(h) *Do not subject the converter casing to mechanical impact*

Checking

5 It is not possible to check the catalytic converter except by measuring its effect on exhaust emission levels. This work should be carried out by an authorised dealer.

6 If the converter casing is distorted or holed, or if the contents can be heard rattling, the converter is almost certainly defective and should be renewed.

7 At the specified intervals (usually 50 000 miles/80 000 km), or when prompted by the dashboard warning light, the catalyst must be renewed as follows.

Removal and refitting

8 Raise and support the front of the vehicle. Allow the exhaust system to cool before starting work.

9 Separate the exhaust downpipe from the intermediate pipe at the flanged joint. Support the intermediate pipe to avoid straining the mountings.

10 Remove the heat shield and the exhaust downpipes from the exhaust manifold.

11 Remove the downpipe/catalyst assembly from the car.

12 Do not attempt to dismantle the catalyst: its contents are toxic.

13 Refit in the reverse order to removal. Use exhaust jointing compound where necessary, and (preferably) new olives. Tighten the flange and manifold joint nuts progressively and in sequence to avoid distortion.

Evaporative emission control system

General description

14 The principles of the system are still as described in Chapter 3. Over the years the routing and relationships of hoses have changed, and from 1984 the charcoal canister is fitted up-side down (relative to its previous position).

Checking

15 Inspect the hoses in the system from time to time to ensure that they are secure and in good condition. Inspection should also be made if fuel smells or evidence of fuel starvation occur.

Removal and refitting

16 To remove the charcoal canister, first remove the right-hand front roadwheel.

17 Detach the pipes from the canister, noting their connections for correct refitting.

18 Release the mounting clamp and withdraw the canister.

19 Remember that fuel vapour is likely to be present in the canister and pipes. Take appropriate precautions when working on the system or when disposing of an old canister.

20 Refit the canister in the reverse order to removal.

Air injection system

21 The system described in Chapter 3 has been modified for fuel injection engines so that it only operates during the warm-up phase. At a predetermined coolant temperature, a vacuum-operated valve switches the air injection supply to atmosphere.

22 The oxygen sensor is disabled whilst the air injection system is operating, since otherwise it would try to compensate for the appearance of 'excess' oxygen by increasing fuel delivery.

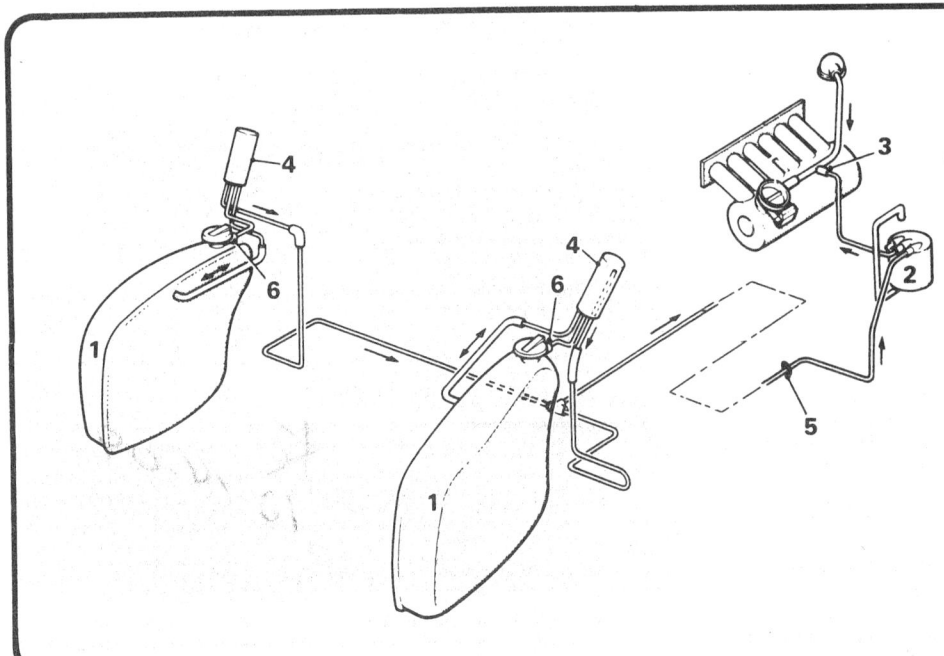

Fig. 13.41 Evaporative emission control system – schematic view (Sec 8)

1 *Fuel tanks*
2 *Charcoal canister*
3 *Restrictor*
4 *Vapour separators*
5 *Pressure relief valve*
6 *Expansion orifices*

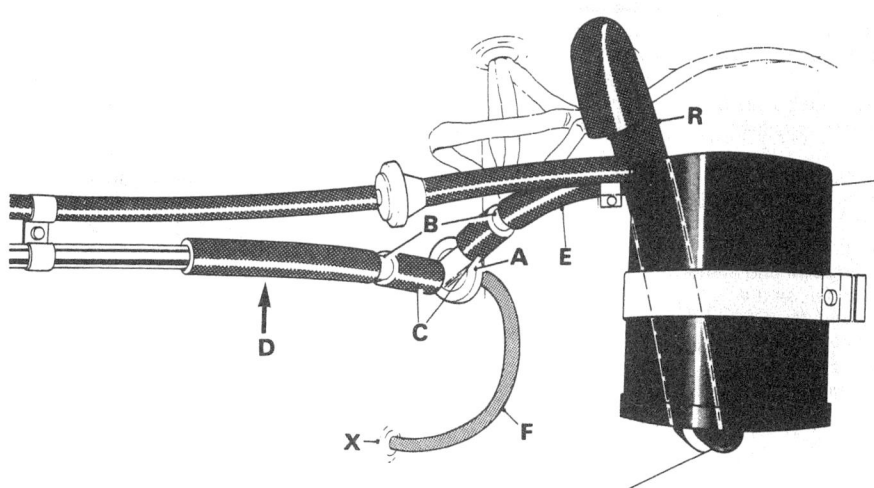

Fig. 13.42 Evaporative emission control
hoses – 1984 models (Sec 8)

A   Purge control valve
B   Connectors
C   Hoses
D   Hose
E   Hose to canister
F   Purge control valve hose
R   Breather hose
X   Grommet

9   Electronic (breakerless) ignition system (Series 2 and 3)

General description

1   The principles of operation of the breakerless ignition system fitted to certain Series 2 and Series 3 models are essentially the same as described in Chapter 4. The principal difference is that the LT circuit is interrupted not by a mechanical contact breaker but electronically, as a result of signals generated by a magnetic pick-up in the distributor and six ferrite rods mounted below the rotor arm.
2   Two systems have been used. Series 2 models are equipped with the Lucas Opus system; Series 3 models have the Lucas Constant Energy system.
3   Electronic ignition is more efficient than a contact breaker system because it is possible to use much higher current in the LT system, resulting in greater energy output on the HT side. Additionally, the gradual drifting off tune, which is unavoidable with contact breaker systems, does not occur. These two factors make for optimum engine efficiency and low emission levels.

Precautions

4   Because of the higher voltages generated on the HT side, care should be taken to avoid receiving personal electric shocks from the system. This is particularly important for people fitted with artificial cardiac pacemakers, to whom HT voltage may prove fatal.
5   Less dramatic but expensive damage can occur if the ignition system is energised with one or more HT leads disconnected. If the HT voltage cannot reach earth via the HT lead, it may do so by damaging the coil insulation.

Maintenance and adjustment

6   Periodically check that all connections are secure. Keep the HT leads and the distributor cap clean and dry.
7   At the specified intervals, remove the distributor cap, the rotor arm and the anti-flash shield. Apply a few drops of oil to the felt pad in the top of the distributor shaft, and inject a few more drops into one of the holes in the baseplate.
8   Wipe clean inside the distributor cap whilst it is removed, paying particular attention to the areas between the metal segments. Make sure that the central carbon brush is free to move. Renew the cap if its condition is in doubt.
9   Clean the rotor arm and dress the sparking tip with a fine file. Renew the arm if it is cracked or badly burnt.
10   Apart from periodic gapping and renewal of the spark plugs, as described in Chapter 4, no other routine maintenance or adjustment is required.

Pick-up air gap adjustment

11   There is no reason for the pick-up air gap to require adjustment unless it has been tampered with, or if the securing screws have worked loose.
12   A non-ferrous (eg brass or plastic) feeler gauge is best used for checking the air gap. No harm will result from using a steel gauge, but

it will be attracted by the magnetic components in the distributor and accurate measurement may in consequence be difficult.
13   The air gap is measured between the pick-up module and the rotor (Fig. 13.43 and photo). The correct gap is given in the Specifications. Adjust if necessary by releasing the pick-up securing screws, moving the pick-up and then retightening the screws.

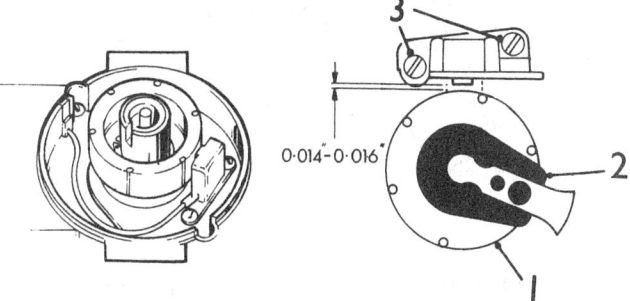

Fig. 13.43 Electronic ignition pick-up air gap adjustment –
Type 43DE6 and 45DE6 distributors (Sec 9)

1   Rotor   3   Pick-up securing screws
2   Rotor arm

9.13 Measuring the pick-up air gap

Ignition timing – static check

14 Remove the distributor cap and the anti-flash shield.

15 Turn the crankshaft until the rotor arm is just approaching the No 6 (front cylinder) HT segment in the distributor cap.

16 Continue to turn the engine very slowly until the timing scale on the crankshaft damper is aligned with the pointer at the specified mark.

17 Slacken the distributor pinch-bolt and turn the distributor body until the pick-up is in alignment with the ferrite rod or reluctor tooth in the timing rotor. The rod used should be the one which will require least movement of the distributor to achieve alignment.

18 Switch on the ignition and position the (distributor cap) end of the centre HT lead about $\frac{1}{4}$ in (6 mm) from a good earth point on the engine (eg the block). Take care to avoid electric shocks. Now turn the distributor body slowly until a spark jumps the gap between the end of the HT lead and earth. Tighten the distributor pinch-bolt.

19 Switch off the ignition and refit the anti-flash shield, cap and HT lead.

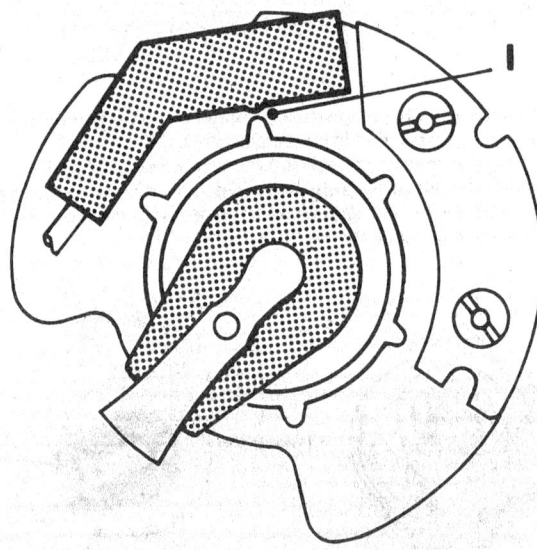

Fig. 13.44 Reluctor tooth and pick-up pip in alignment – Type 45DM6 distributor (Sec 9)

1   Air gap

Distributor – removal and refitting

20 The procedure is basically as described in Chapter 4, disregarding the references to contact breaker and condenser connections and instead attending to the distributor/amplifier LT connections.

21 After refitting, check the ignition timing as just described.

Distributor – dismantling and reassembly
Opus system

22 Remove the distributor, lift off the rotor arm and the anti-flash shield and lift out the felt lubrication pad. Do not disturb the nylon bush.

23 Extract the screws which hold the pick-up to the movable baseplate.

24 Unbolt the amplifier from the distributor body. Do this by extracting the two long screws, then holding the amplifier housing whilst the base screw is withdrawn. Carefully disengage the vacuum advance unit link from the pin in the distributor baseplate. Ease the grommet, amplifier housing and pick-up from the distributor body, taking care not to lose the spring clips.

25 Drive out the roll pin which holds the vacuum advance unit and withdraw the unit.

26 Prise off the external circlip from the distributor shaft and withdraw the timing rotor. Detach the washer and O-ring from it.

27 Lift out the baseplate (two screws) complete with movable plate.

28 The springs may be detached from the centrifugal advance unit if their differing design is first noted, but further dismantling of the distributor is not recommended. In any case it is unlikely that spares will be available.

Constant Energy system

29 Dismantling is similar to that described for the Opus system distributor, but the amplifier is not attached to the distributor body. Refer to Fig. 13.45.

30 Check that spares are available before attempting complete dismantling of the distributor.

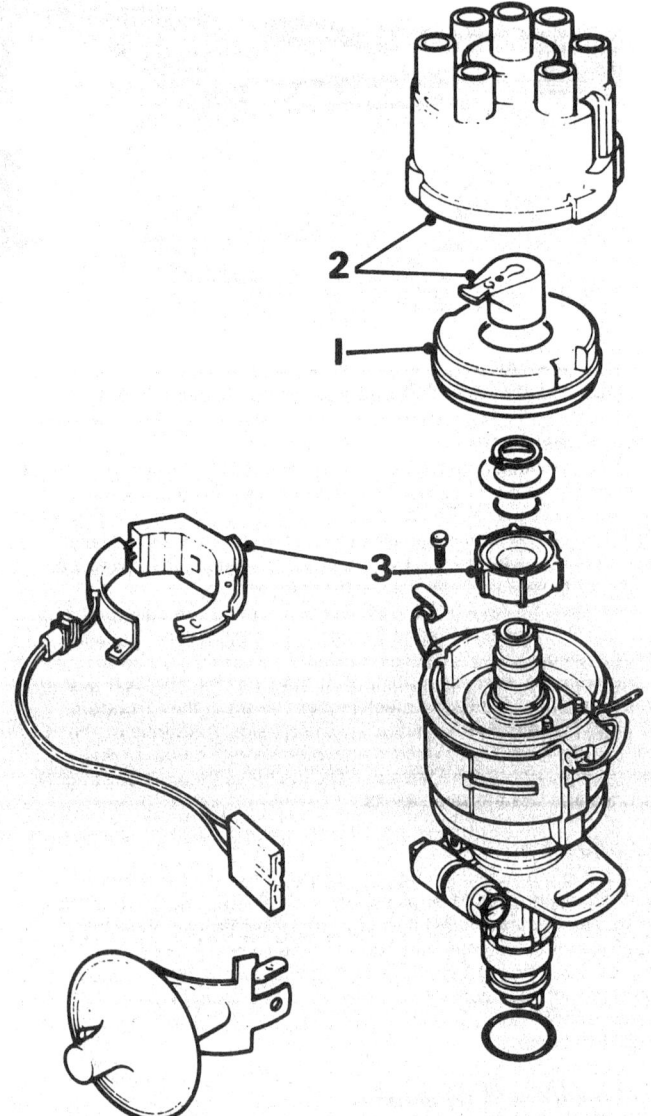

Fig. 13.45 Distributor components – Constant Energy system (Sec 9)

1   Anti-flash shield   3   Reluctor and pick-up
2   Rotor arm and distributor cap

All systems

31 Reassembly is a reversal of dismantling. Apply molybdenum type grease to the centrifugal advance mechanism and the movable plate pin.

32 When fitting the timing rotor, make sure that the master projection engages with the large slot in the shaft.

33 Adjust the pick-up air gap as previously described.

Ignition amplifier unit – removal and refitting

34 The Opus system amplifier is mounted on the distributor. Refer to the previous paragraphs dealing with distributor dismantling.

35 To remove the Constant Energy system amplifier, first disconnect the battery earth lead.

36 Remove the air cleaner.
37 Remove the coil cover and disconnect the LT leads from the coil.
38 Remove the two bolts which secure the amplifier (photo).
39 Unplug the LT connector from the distributor and remove the amplifier.
40 Refitting is a reversal of removal.

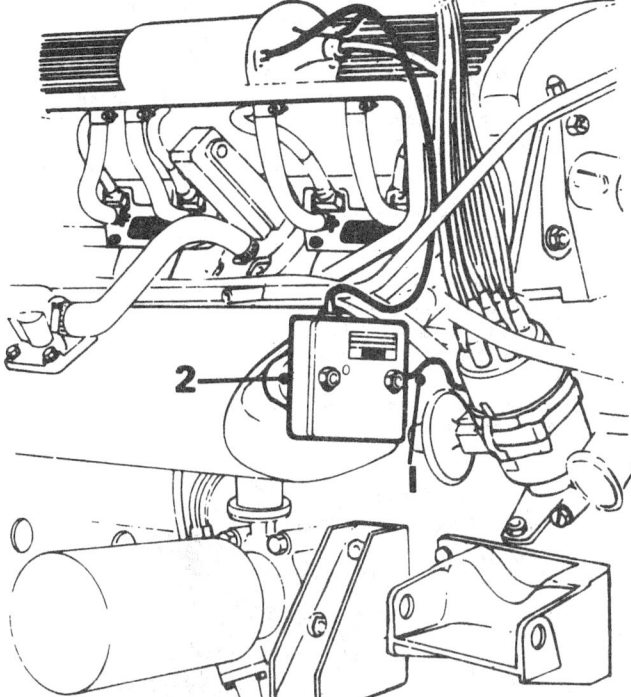

Fig. 13.46 Ignition amplifier (2) and distributor LT lead (1) – Constant Energy system (Sec 9)

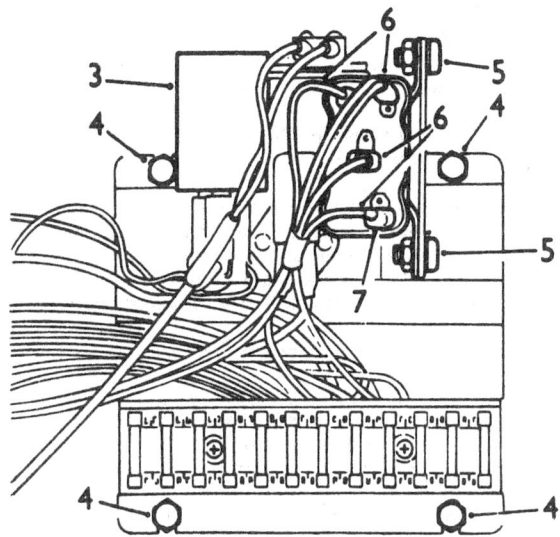

Fig. 13.47 Ignition protection relay and associated components – Opus system (Sec 9)

3 Flasher unit
4 Fuse panel mounting nuts
5 Ignition protection relay mounting bolts
6 Electrical connectors
7 Electrical connector

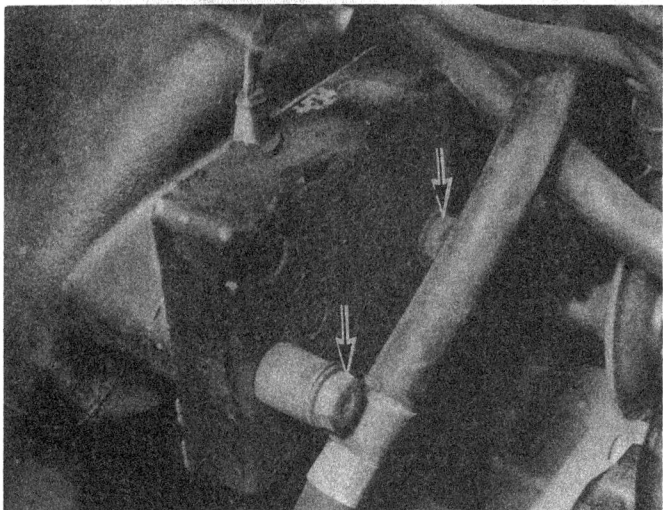

9.38 Ignition amplifier securing bolts (arrowed). Note hose clip and spacer on bolt in foreground

Ignition protection relay (Opus system) – removal and refitting

41 Disconnect the battery.
42 Remove the driver's side under scuttle casing. To do this, first unscrew the locking ring which secures the speedometer trip knob to the scuttle casing.
43 Extract the screws which hold the casing and the quarter panel to the facia support bracket.

44 Lower the casing enough to permit access to the rheostat, then detach the rheostat leads. Withdraw the casing and quarter panel.
45 Remove the direction indicator/hazard warning flasher unit by pulling it from the connector block.
46 Unscrew the four nuts which hold the fusebox mounting panel and pull the panel carefully downward.
47 Unbolt the ignition protection relay from the mounting bracket. Identify and disconnect the leads from the relay terminals. On some models the relay is of cylindrical type rather than the rectangular design usually fitted.
48 Refitting is a reversal of removal.

Ignition drive resistor (Opus system) – removal and refitting

49 Disconnect the battery, and remove the air cleaner for better access.
50 Unbolt the ignition coil mounting plate from the engine, then unbolt the ignition drive resistor from the mounting plate.
51 Note the positions of the leads and disconnect them.
52 On left-hand drive cars, better access may be obtained by reaching up from underneath the car, particularly if a pit is available.
53 Refitting is a reversal of removal.

Fault diagnosis – electronic ignition system

54 Apart from verifying the continuity of the wiring, there is little that the DIY mechanic can do to diagnose faults in the electronic ignition system. Testing by substitution of known good units is probably best, provided that components can be obtained on a 'sale or return' basis.
55 It is essential that the battery is in good condition and well charged if the ignition system is to function correctly.
56 If a good spark can be obtained when performing the ignition timing check described earlier, make sure that the distributor shaft rotates when the engine is cranked, then investigate the rotor arm, distributor cap, HT leads and spark plugs.
57 If an ohmmeter is available, the drive resistor (Opus system) can be checked. Its resistance should be approximately 10 ohms. Also check the coil ballast resistor for continuity.
58 On the Constant Energy system, the resistance of the distributor pick-up (measured across the LT plug terminals) may be measured. The correct value is 2200 to 4800 ohms.

10 Clutch (Series 3)

Removal and refitting (engine in car)

1   If it is not wished to remove the engine and gearbox in order to gain access to the clutch, the gearbox alone can be removed as described in Section 11.
2   With the gearbox removed, proceed as described in Chapter 5.
3   Refitting is a reversal of removal.

Release lever and bearing – removal and refitting

4   Remove the gearbox as described in Section 11.
5   Unscrew the clutch release lever pivot bolt. This bolt is not easy to get at: the use of a cranked spanner (Jaguar tool ST 1136, or equivalent) will make removal easier. **Do not** simply attempt to pull the release lever off the pivot bolt.
6   Remove the bearing, release lever and pivot bolt, then separate them.
7   When refitting, screw the pivot bolt into the bellhousing and tighten it to the specified torque. Place the release bearing on the gearbox input shaft, then engage the release lever with the bearing and press it onto the pivot bolt until the spring clip engages.

Clutch master cylinder – removal and refitting

8   Unclip and remove the clevis pin to disconnect the pushrod from the pedal arm.
9   Unbolt the master cylinder from the pedal box, and remove it together with any shims.
10 When refitting the original or a new master cylinder, use a suitable number of shims to ensure that the eye in the pushrod aligns with the hole in the pedal arm (pedal released).

11 Manual gearbox (Series 3)

General description

1   The manual gearbox available on Series 3 models has 5 forward gears and one reverse gear, with synchromesh on all forward gears. Fifth gear effectively takes the place of overdrive top gear on the four-speed gearbox.
2   The gearbox is generally known as the '77 mm' gearbox, the title deriving from the distance between the mainshaft and the layshaft.

Routine maintenance

3   At the specified intervals, remove the oil filler/level plug from the left-hand side of the gearbox (towards the rear). The car should be parked on level ground.
4   Top up if necessary with the specified oil until the oil is level with the bottom of the plug hole. Allow any excess to drip out, then refit the plug.
5   Regular oil changing is no longer specified by the vehicle manufacturers.
6   Note that the oil specified for filling the gearbox from dry is hypoid gear oil of SAE 75W viscosity. Oil of viscosity SAE 80W **must not** be used for refilling (although it may be used for topping-up), otherwise problems may occur with 'baulking' when changing gear, especially when cold.
7   If 'baulking' problems are experienced despite the use of the specified lubricant, the gearbox can be drained and refilled with Dexron® II automatic transmission fluid. This lubricant is used for preference in other applications of the gearbox; the gearchange problem should be solved, but some idler gear rattle may be noticed. This is not in itself harmful, and may be minimised by careful adjustment of the engine idle speed.

Removal and refitting (leaving engine in car)

8   Position the car on high ramps or over an inspection pit. Make sure that it is securely supported.
9   Disconnect the battery earth lead.
10 Inside the car, unscrew the gear lever knob.
11 Remove the cigarette lighter.
12 Remove the screws which secure the centre console. Lift the console slightly, unplug the switch connectors and remove it.
13 Remove the gear lever gaiter, then place the gear lever in 3rd gear position. It is not strictly necessary to remove the gear lever, but if it

is wished to do so, first remove the bias spring as described later in this Section. **Do not** attempt to prise the bias spring off the adjusting bolt heads, or damage may result.
14 It is now necessary to support the rear of the engine, using either a hoist or a support bar with adjustable hook engaged in the rear lifting eye. The official Jaguar support bar has the number MS 53A. If the engine is not supported, it will ultimately come to rest on the steering rack, with possible detriment both to rack and to engine front mountings.
15 Though not essential, it is advisable to unbolt the heater water valve (access through grille at base of windscreen) and move it to the top of the engine, where it will not be crushed during subsequent operations. There should be no need to disconnect the water hoses.
16 Working under the car, disconnect the exhaust intermediate pipe at the flanged joint with the downpipe. Tie the intermediate pipe out of the way.
17 Remove the exhaust heat shield.
18 Remove the stiffener plate which connects the bellhousing to the sump.
19 Use a jack and a block of wood to take the weight off the gearbox rear mounting, then remove the bolts which secure the mounting and the crossmember to the body. Make sure that the engine support is secure, then lower the jack and remove the mounting and crossmember.
20 Disconnect the speedometer cable, or unplug the connector from the speedometer transducer.

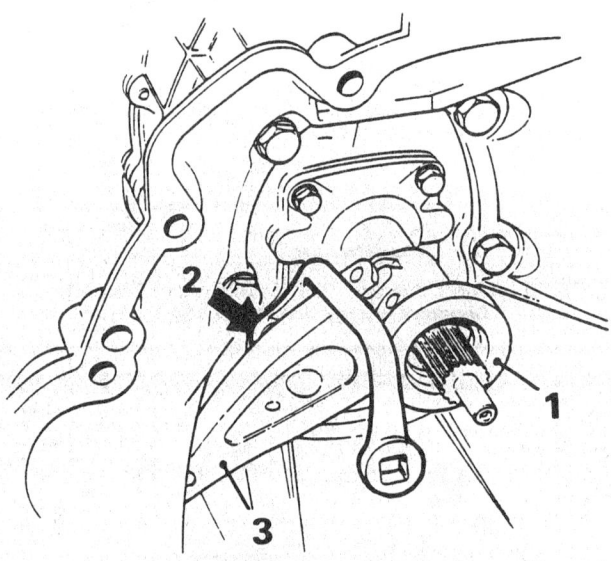

Fig. 13.48 Clutch release components – Series 3. Note use of cranked spanner to undo pivot bolt (Sec 10)

1   *Release bearing*   3   *Release lever*
2   *Pivot bolt*

Fig. 13.49 Oil filler/level plug (arrowed) on 5-speed gearbox (Sec 11)

Fig. 13.50 Supporting the rear mounting (2) with a jack (1) and some wooden blocks (Sec 11)

21 Unbolt the clutch slave cylinder from the bellhousing and tie it up out of the way. Take care not to strain the clutch hydraulic hose.
22 Unbolt the propeller shaft from the gearbox output flange, marking the flanges for correct alignment on reassembly. Move the propeller shaft out of the way.
23 Lower the rear of the engine, using the hoist or support bar, in order to improve access to some of the bellhousing bolts. Do not strain the engine mountings.
24 Unbolt the starter motor. Withdraw the motor and tie it up out of the way, taking care not to strain the electrical connections.
25 Remove the cover plate from the bottom of the gearbox.
26 Disconnect the reversing light wires from the top of the gearbox.
27 Support the gearbox securely, either with a purpose-made transmission jack or with a trolley jack and a home-made cradle.
28 Take the weight of the gearbox and remove the nuts and bolts which secure the bellhousing to the engine. Access to some of these bolts is difficult; a good selection of socket spanner drives, joints and extensions will be useful.
29 Withdraw the gearbox from the engine, taking care not to let the weight of the gearbox hang on the input shaft. When the input shaft is clear of the clutch, lower the gearbox and remove it. Recover the foam pad.
30 Refit in the reverse order to removal, noting the following points:

    (a)   If the clutch has been disturbed, the driven plate must be centralised as described in Chapter 5
    (b)   Use new self-locking nuts to secure the propeller shaft
    (c)   Use a new olive, coated with exhaust jointing compound, when reassembling the exhaust system
    (d)   If the gear lever was removed, adjust the bias spring as described later in this Section

Dismantling

31 Before deciding to dismantle the gearbox, check the price and availability of spare parts. It is not always an economically sound proposition to overhaul a gearbox when comparing the cost with that of a reconditioned or exchange unit.
32 With the gearbox removed from the car as previously described, clean away all external dirt and oil using paraffin and a stiff brush or a water-soluble solvent.
33 Drain the oil.
34 Working within the clutch bellhousing, unscrew and remove the clutch release lever pivot bolt. Refer to Section 10 for more details.
35 Withdraw the clutch release lever, bearing and slippers.
36 Unbolt the bellhousing and separate it from the gearcase.
37 Disconnect the selector shaft from the gearchange remote control rod by removing the nut and pin.
38 Unbolt the remote control housing from the rear cover of the gearcase.
39 Unbolt the output flange from the mainshaft. A length of flat steel

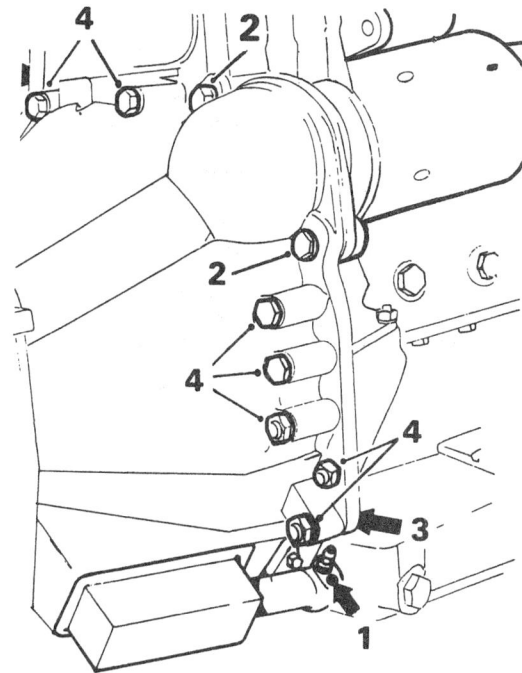

Fig. 13.51 Engine-to-gearbox attachments on the right-hand side (Sec 11)

    1   Clutch hydraulic union   3   Flywheel cover plate bolt
    2   Starter motor bolts   4   Bellhousing nuts and bolts

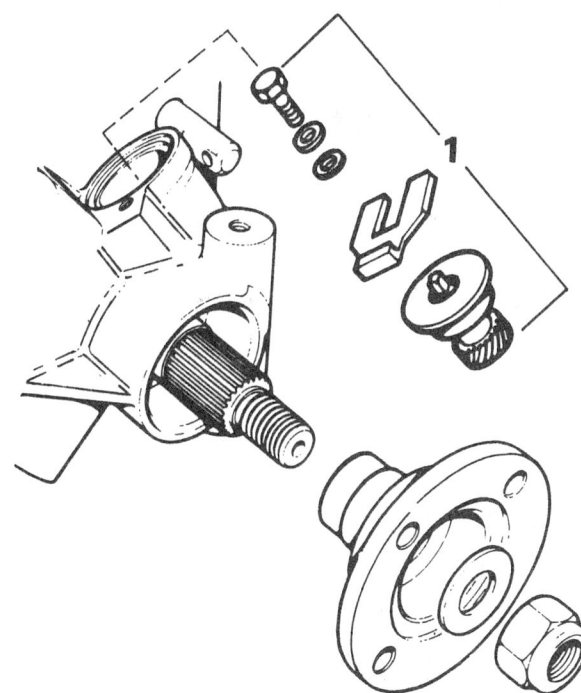

Fig. 13.52 Gearbox output flange and (1) speedometer gear components (Sec 11)

will have to be bolted to the flange and used as a lever to prevent the flange rotating as the unit is unscrewed.
40 Withdraw the flange from the mainshaft.
41 Remove the speedometer driven gear and housing. Later models with an electronic speedometer have a transducer (in place of the

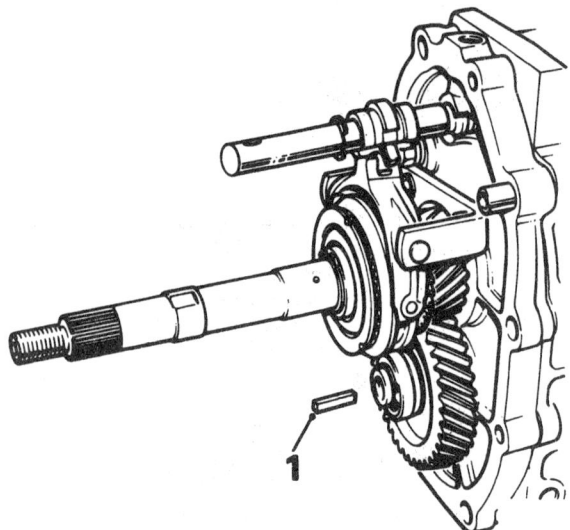

Fig. 13.53 Gearbox rear cover removed showing (1) oil pump drive key (Sec 11)

Fig. 13.55 5th gear mainshaft components and selector fork (Sec 11)

53 Unscrew the two bolts and remove the locating boss for the selector shaft front spool.
54 Unscrew the plug from the centre plate and remove the spring and ball which will be exposed.
55 Grip the centre plate in the jaws of a vice and withdraw the gearcase from the gear train.
56 Withdraw the input shaft and the synchro cone.
57 Remove the layshaft cluster.
58 Remove the reverse lever, circlip and pivot pin.
59 Remove reverse gear lever and slipper pad.
60 Slide the reverse shaft to the rear and withdraw the reverse gear spacer, mainshaft, selector shaft and fork with spool forwards to clear

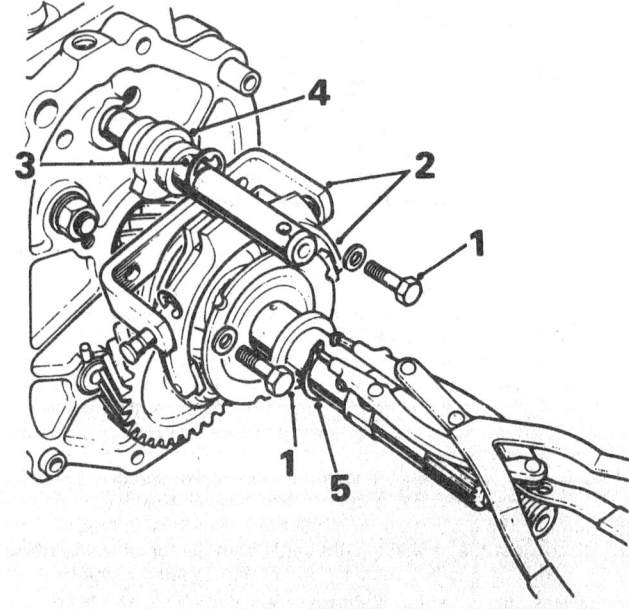

Fig. 13.54 Removing 5th gear components (Sec 11)

1	Selector fork/bracket bolts	4	Selector spool
2	Selector fork and bracket	5	Mainshaft circlip
3	Selector shaft circlip		

driven gear) without a securing clamp plate, but with a two-pin connecting plug.
42 Unbolt the locating boss for the selector rear spool and withdraw the boss.
43 Unbolt and remove the rear cover and gasket from the gearcase.
44 Withdraw the oil pump driving key.
45 Withdraw the 5th gear selector fork and bracket after extracting the two securing bolts.
46 Extract the circlip from the selector shaft.
47 Withdraw the 5th gear selector spool, noting that the longer cam of the spool is towards the bottom of the gearcase. Slide the speedometer drivegear from the mainshaft.
48 Extract the circlip which holds the 5th gear synchroniser onto the mainshaft.
49 Withdraw the 5th speed synchro and its spacer from the mainshaft.
50 Extract the circlip which holds the 5th gear onto the layshaft, then withdraw the gear and its spacer from the layshaft.
51 Unbolt and remove the front cover and its gasket from the gearcase.
52 Remove the input shaft adjustment shim and bearing track, followed by similar layshaft components, from their recesses in the gearcase.

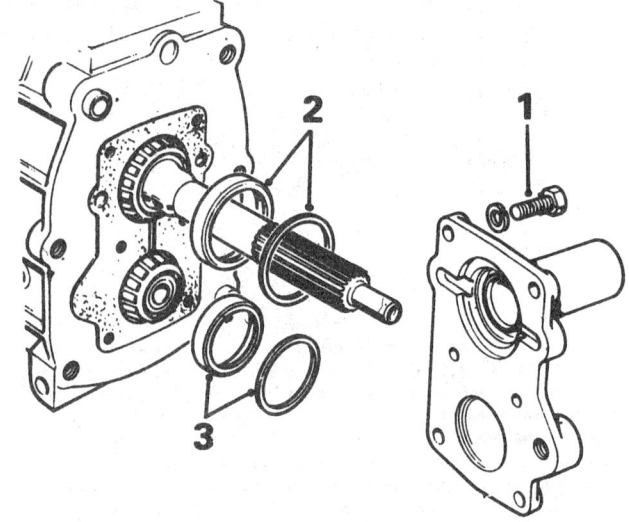

Fig. 13.56 Front cover removed from gearbox (Sec 11)

1 *Front cover bolt*
2 *Input shaft bearing track and shim*
3 *Layshaft bearing track and shim*

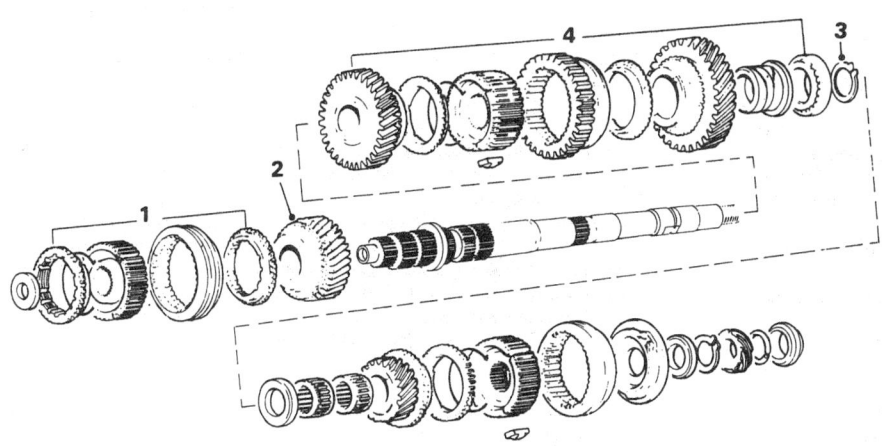

Fig. 13.57 Mainshaft components (Sec 11)

1 3rd/4th synchro unit
2 3rd speed gear
3 Circlip
4 1st/2nd gears, synchro and bearing

the centre plate. Note that the shorter cam of the spool is nearer the bottom of the gearcase.

61 If the reverse gear pivot shaft or the centre plate are to be renewed, remove the nut and spring washers which hold the shaft. The dowels should be extracted from the centre plate.

62 If the input shaft is to be dismantled, use a suitable puller to extract the bearings and tracks.

63 Also use a suitable puller to extract the layshaft bearings.

64 To dismantle the mainshaft, remove the pilot bearing and spacer from its front end.

65 Remove 3rd/4th synchro assembly.

66 Remove 3rd speed gear.

67 Extract the circlip which retains the mainshaft bearing to the rear end of the shaft.

68 Remove the mainshaft bearing, 1st gear and bush, 1st/2nd synchro assembly with cones and 2nd speed gear.

69 The rear cover can be dismantled by removing the oil seal, bearing, oil pump drive, cover and gears.

Inspection and preparation for reassembly

70 Clean all components and examine shafts and gears for wear, particularly on the teeth.

71 Examine the gearcase for cracks, especially at the bolt holes.

72 Renew the oil seals in the front and rear covers as a matter of routine.

73 The synchro assemblies may show wear in the baulk rings, teeth or cones. Also, if the synchro hub can be pushed in its outer sleeve to

overcome the spring detent with very little effort being applied, then the assemblies should be renewed complete. This action should also be taken if there has been a history of noisy gear changing or if the synchromesh could easily be 'beaten'.

74 If the synchro assemblies must be dismantled, make sure that they are not mixed up and mark the relative positions of component parts to each other. When reassembling, note that the retaining springs which engage in the sliding keys must run in opposite directions to each other, on either side of the hub, and their ends must not engage in the same grooves.

75 1st gear bush endfloat should now be checked. To do this, fit 2nd gear, 1st/2nd synchro hub and 1st gear bush onto the mainshaft.

76 A spacer should now be made up to the dimensions shown in Fig. 13.59. Slide the spacer onto the mainshaft where it will substitute for a slave bearing.

77 Fit a circlip to the shaft and using feeler blades, check the clearance between the spacer and the circlip. This should be between 0.0002 and 0.002 in (0.005 and 0.055 mm). Where adjustment is required, 1st gear bushes are available with collars of different thicknesses. Select one to suit.

78 Remove the components from the mainshaft.

79 The 5th gear endfloat must now be checked. To do this, fit 5th gear to the mainshaft together with the front spacer, synchro hub, rear plate and spacer. Install a circlip to the shaft and using feeler blades

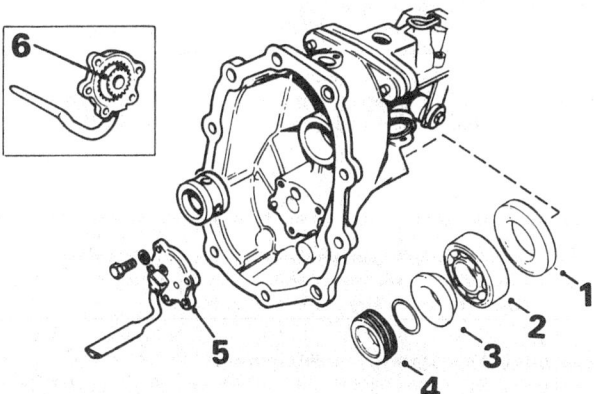

Fig. 13.58 Gearbox rear cover components (Sec 11)

1 Oil seal	4 Speedometer gear
2 Bearing	5 Oil pump cover
3 Oil seal	6 Oil pump gears

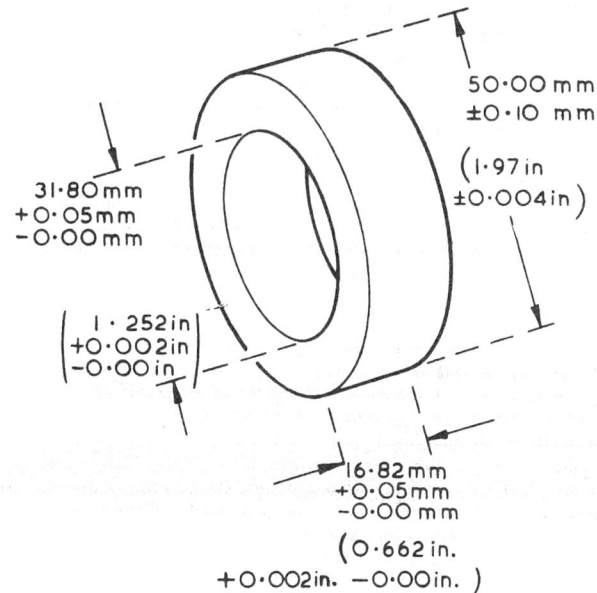

50·00 mm
±0·10 mm

(1·97 in
±0·004 in)

31·80 mm
+0·05 mm
-0·00 mm

1·252 in
+0·002 in
-0·00 in

16·82 mm
+0·05 mm
-0·00 mm

(0·662 in.
+0·002 in. -0·00 in.)

Fig. 13.59 Dimensions of spacer used for determining 1st gear bush endfloat (Sec 11)

check the endfloat of the gear. This should be between 0.0002 and 0.002 in (0.005 and 0.055 mm). If adjustment is required, select a rear spacer from the range of different lengths available.
80 Remove the components from the mainshaft.

Reassembly

81 To the rear end of the mainshaft, fit 2nd gear, the baulk ring and the 1st/2nd synchro assembly. Make sure that the shorter projecting boss of the synchro hub is towards 2nd gear. In this position, the selector fork groove in the synchro sleeve must be nearer the rear of the gearbox. If it is not, then the synchro unit has been incorrectly assembled.
82 Fit the next baulk ring, 1st gear and the selective bush (see previous paragraphs).
83 Fit the mainshaft bearing and use a new circlip. Make sure that the circlip is not over-expanded during fitting.
84 Fit 3rd gear, the baulk ring and synchro assembly to the mainshaft. Make sure that the longer projecting boss of the synchro hub is nearer the front of the gearbox.
85 To the front end of the mainshaft, fit the bearing and spacer.
86 Press the layshaft bearing track into the centre plate.
87 Fit the layshaft to the centre plate and to it fit 5th gear, the spacer and circlip. Take care not to over-expand the circlip when fitting it.
88 Press the mainshaft bearing track into the centre plate.
89 Grip the centre plate in the jaws of a vice, suitably protected with pieces of soft metal.
90 Offer the selector shaft complete with 1st/2nd selector fork, front spool and 3rd/4th selector fork to the synchro sleeves on the mainshaft so that both forks engage with their grooves.
91 Install the mainshaft gear train and selector shaft simultaneously to the centre plate in the vice.
92 To the front end of the mainshaft, now fit the spacer, 5th gear, the baulk ring synchro assembly, endplate and selective spacer (as determined previously).
93 Fit a new circlip to the mainshaft, taking care not to over-expand it during fitting.
94 Hold the reverse idler gear so that its lip for the slipper pad is towards the front of the gearbox, locate the front and rear spacers and install the reverse idler shaft.
95 Fit the reverse lever, the slipper pad, pivot pin and a new retaining circlip. If a new reverse idler shaft has been fitted, it will be necessary to adjust its radial clearance to ensure positive engagement of the slipper pad without binding.
96 Tighten the reverse components securing nuts, making sure to fit the spring lockwashers.
97 Check the movement of the reverse lever and make sure that the slipper pad is properly engaged.
98 Remove the centre plate from the vice and support the assembly so that the front end of the mainshaft is pointing directly upwards. Do not allow the reverse idler shaft to slide out of position.
99 Fit a new gasket to the front face of the centre plate.
100 To the input shaft fit the external bearing and the track for the internal (pilot) bearing.
101 Fit the input shaft to the gearcase.
102 Slide the gearcase complete with input shaft over the gear train, making sure that the dowels in the centre plate, the selector shaft and the input shaft (to mainshaft front end) all engage correctly.
103 Using a plastic faced hammer, tap the layshaft and input shaft bearing tracks into their recesses in the front face of the gearcase.
104 Again using a plastic faced hammer, tap the gearcase fully home on the centre plate. If it is particularly tight, do not apply excessive force but use some spare bolts, nuts and washers to draw the gearcase and centre plate together.
105 Place a layshaft spacer of nominal thickness 0.040 in (1.02 mm) onto the layshaft bearing track. Fit the front cover with a new gasket and secure with six bolts.
106 Using a dial gauge, check the layshaft endfloat. This should be between 0.0002 and 0.002 in (0.005 and 0.055 mm). If adjustment is required, change the spacer for one of suitable thickness to bring the endfloat within the specified tolerance.
107 Recheck the endfloat with the cover and gasket bolted into position.
108 The mainshaft/input shaft endfloat must now be checked in a similar way, with the front cover and gasket bolted in position. A more accurate reading will be obtained if a ball-bearing is located in the dimple on the front end of the input shaft with the stylus of the dial

gauge resting on the ball. The endfloat must be within the same limits as for the layshaft. Make sure that it is only endfloat you are measuring and that you are not including any side-to-side movement of the input shaft.
109 Select a suitable spacer to provide the correct endfloat.
110 It is possible to measure the endfloat using feeler blades between the ends of the shafts and a fixed point (bridge piece or bracket temporarily bolted to gearcase), but obviously the use of a dial gauge is to be preferred in the interest of accuracy.
111 When endfloat adjustments are complete, remove the front cover and fit a new oil seal.
112 Lubricate the oil seal lips and cover the input shaft splines with tape to protect the oil seal. Refit the front cover and remove the tape.
113 Place the gearbox on the bench and withdraw the spare centre plate bolts without disturbing the gearcase.
114 Fit the 5th gear spool and a new circlip to the selector shaft.
115 Fit the 5th gear selector fork and bracket.
116 Renew the O-ring seal for the selector shaft in the rear cover. Fit the oil ring bush.
117 Fit the rear gasket to the centre plate and engage the drive key for the oil pump in the layshaft.
118 Fit the oil pump gears and cover to the gearbox rear cover.
119 Fit the rear cover, ensuring that the oil pump drive key engages with the oil pump.
120 Fit the selector shaft ball, spring and plug to the centre plate.
121 Fit the two spool locating bosses to the 1st/2nd spool and 5th gear spool.
122 Fit the speedometer drivegear to the mainshaft, making sure that it engages correctly with the flats on the shaft. On early models, fit the retaining clamp plate; on later models, connect the transducer two-pin plug.
123 To the mainshaft rear end fit the spacer and ball race.
124 Lubricate the new oil seal and tap it into the rear cover.
125 Fit the output flange, washer and nut.
126 Fit the speedometer driven gear and housing.
127 Install the clutch bellhousing, using the six bolts that join the bellhousing, centre plate and gearcase together.
128 Fit the clutch release components into the bellhousing.
129 Bolt the remote control housing into position.
130 The gearbox may be filled with oil now or after installation in the car.

Gear lever bias spring – removal and refitting

131 Disconnect the battery earth lead.
132 Unscrew the gear lever knob.
133 Remove the cigarette lighter.
134 Remove the screws which secure the centre console, then lift the console and disconnect the wiring connectors.
135 Remove the gaiter from the base of the gear lever.
136 Support the gearbox with a jack and a block of wood. Take the weight of the gearbox and remove the rear mounting.
137 Disconnect the exhaust system at the junction between the downpipe and the intermediate pipe.
138 Carefully lower the jack until the bias spring securing and adjusting bolts are accessible. Take care not to damage the heater water valve or the clutch hydraulic hose. Strictly speaking an engine support bar (MS 53A or equivalent) should be used to support the rear of the engine, but provided care is taken, the jack under the gearbox will suffice.
139 Select 4th gear, then remove the bias spring securing bolt. The spring itself can now be removed.
140 Refit in the reverse order to removal, noting the following points:

  (a) Adjust the spring as described later in this Section
  (b) Use a new olive, coated with exhaust jointing compound, when reassembling the exhaust system

Gear lever bias spring – adjustment

141 Gain access to the bias spring by following the procedure in paragraphs 131 to 138.
142 Engage 1st gear and move the gear lever as far as possible to the left.
143 Measure the gap between the abutment bracket and the gear lever pad (Fig. 13.60). The desired gap is 0.014 to 0.030 in (0.35 to 0.75 mm). If necessary, release the abutment bracket bolts and move the bracket to achieve this dimension. Tighten the bolts on completion.

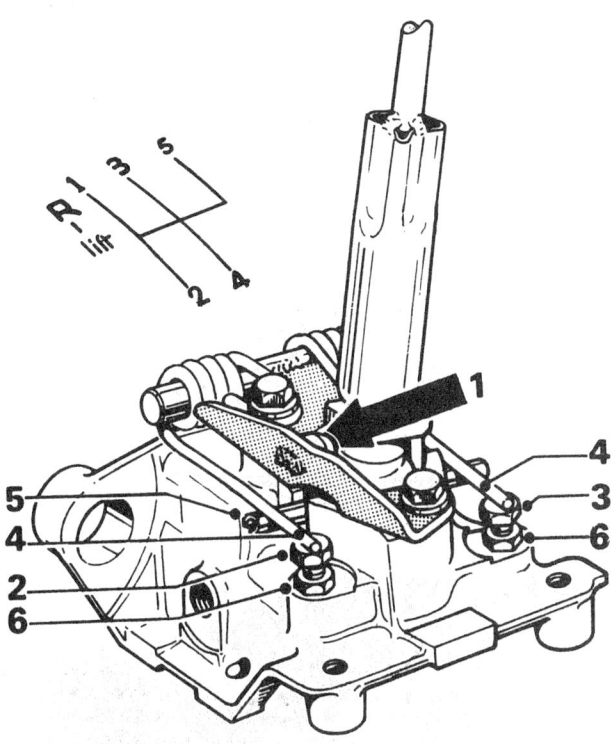

Fig. 13.60 Gear lever bias spring adjustment (Sec 11)

1	Desired gap (see text)	4	Spring legs
2	LH adjusting screw	5	Cross-pins
3	RH adjusting screw	6	Locknut

144 When the above adjustment is correct, slacken the locknuts on the spring end adjusting screws.

145 Select 3rd gear and move the end adjusting screws until each spring leg is clear of the cross-pin by 0.02 in (0.5 mm).

146 Using light hand pressure only, hold the gear lever to the left. Lower the left-hand end adjusting screw until the left-hand side of the spring *just* touches the cross-pin.

147 Move the gear lever to the right and repeat the above procedure on the right-hand side.

148 Lower both adjusting screws equally until all radial movement of the gear lever is eliminated.

149 Move the gear lever to the neutral position and push it across the gate several times: it should return to the 3rd/4th plane unaided.

150 Tighten the end adjusting screw locknuts when adjustment is complete.

151 Reverse the preliminary dismantling operations, using a new olive and exhaust jointing compound when reassembling the exhaust system.

Reversing lamp switch – adjustment

152 Disconnect the battery earth lead.

153 Gain access to the switch by freeing the centre console and removing the gear lever gaiter as previously described. Disconnect the reversing light switch.

154 Connect a continuity tester (ohmmeter or self-powered test lamp) to the switch terminals.

155 Select reverse gear, slacken the switch locknut and screw the switch in until the switch contacts close (zero resistance, or test lamp lights up). Screw the switch in a further half turn (180°) and tighten the locknut.

156 Engage the forward gears and check that the switch contacts are open; engage reverse gear and check that the contacts are closed again.

157 Remove the continuity tester, reconnect the reversing lamp switch and refit the remaining components.

Rear oil seal renewal

158 Disconnect the exhaust downpipe from the intermediate pipe. Tie the intermediate pipe out of the way. Unbolt and lower the gearbox crash bracket.

159 Take the weight of the gearbox on a jack with a piece of wood interposed, then remove the gearbox rear mounting and intermediate heat shield.

160 Remove the propeller shaft flange nuts and bolts at the gearbox end. It will be necessary to turn the shaft during this operation, so at least one rear wheel will need to be clear of the ground. Move the shaft out of the way.

161 Restrain the output flange from turning and remove the flange securing nut. Draw the flange off the gearbox output shaft.

162 Carefully prise out the old oil seal.

163 Coat the new oil seal with gearbox oil and press it into position, making sure that it is fully home.

164 Refit the remaining components in the reverse order to removal, noting the following points:

> (a) Use new self-locking nuts for the propeller shaft flange
> (b) Use a new exhaust olive, coated with exhaust jointing compound
> (c) Top up the gearbox oil level if necessary

Front oil seal renewal

165 Remove the gearbox as previously described.

166 Remove the clutch release lever and release bearing.

167 Unbolt and remove the front cover plate from the gearbox. Retrieve the gasket.

168 Note the identities of the input shaft and layshaft bearing spacers. They may appear similar but they are not necessarily identical – **do not** interchange them.

169 Carefully prise the old oil seal out of the front cover and press in the new one.

170 Cover the input shaft splines with adhesive tape to protect the seal lips. Coat the seal with gearbox oil and refit the front cover, using a new gasket. Tighten the bolts to the specified torque.

171 Refit the clutch release components as described in Section 10.

172 Refit the gearbox as previously described.

173 Check the gearbox oil level and top up if necessary.

---

12 Automatic transmission

Note: *With the exception of the fluid level checking details given for Model 12 and 35F transmissions, the information in this Section applies to Series 3 models only.*

General description

1 The BW type 66 automatic transmission was introduced on Series 3 models. Some of the improvements found in this new transmission will also be made to service replacement parts and reconditioned assemblies for the earlier Type 65 transmission.

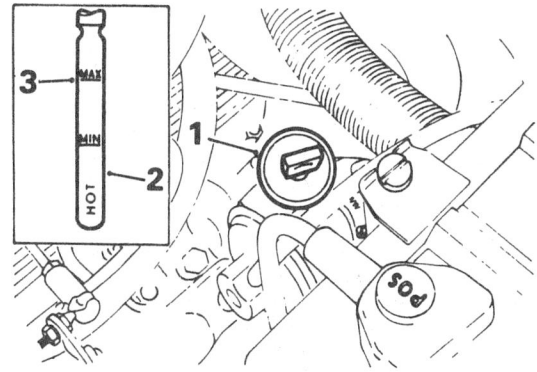

Fig. 13.61 Dipstick markings on BW 66 automatic transmission (Sec 12)

1	Dipstick	3	Max mark
2	Hot side		

2   Among the modifications is a strengthened torque converter impeller and oil pump. Improved oil flow to the rear clutch and front drum assemblies, and also to the reverse sun gear, has been provided for. A deeper oil pan is now used and a modified pump suction tube is fitted to ensure that oil starvation cannot occur under any operating conditions.

3   The dipstick markings have been changed with hot and cold sides, but the level checking procedure is as for the Type 65 described below.

Fluid level checking
Models 12 and 35F

4   With the engine idling and the transmission fluid hot (after at least 15 miles/25 km road use), move the selector lever slowly through all positions to prime the system, finally setting it in 'P'.

5   With the engine still idling, withdraw the dipstick, wipe it clean on a non-fluffy rag, re-insert it fully and then withdraw it for a second time and read off the fluid level. Top up if necessary with the specified fluid to bring the level to the full mark (Fig. 6.24).

Models 65 and 66

6   The transmission fluid level should be checked in the following way. With the fluid cold, run the engine at 750 rpm for several minutes and then move the selector lever through all positions, slowly, to prime the systm. Set the lever in 'P'.

7   With the engine still idling, withdraw the dipstick, wipe it clean on a non-fluffy cloth, re-insert it fully and then withdraw it for a second time and read off the level on the 'COLD' section. Top up if necessary to bring the level to the 'HIGH' mark on re-checking.

8   If the transmission fluid level is being checked hot (after at least 15 miles/25 km road use) use the 'HOT' section of the dipstick (Fig. 6.23), again checking with the engine idling.

Removal and refitting (leaving engine in car)

9   Before attempting to remove the transmission from below, read through the procedure and satisfy yourself that adequate equipment and manpower are available. Problems particularly likely to trouble the DIY operator are the inacessibility and tightness of some of the engine-to-transmission bolts, and the need for a transmission jack or some other safe means of lowering and raising the transmission. Depending on the equipment available, removing engine and transmission complete may still be preferable.

10 Substantial vehicle lifting tackle will be needed, preferably a commerical ramp, or failing that, an inspection pit.

11 Disconnect the battery earth lead.

12 Remove the transmission dipstick and store it safely, then unbolt the dipstick tube from the manifold.

13 Remove the bolts which secure the fan cowl. There is no need to remove the cowl completely, but it must be free to move when the engine it tilted.

14 Unbolt the kickdown cable bracket. Disconnect the cable inner at its clevis pin. Do not disturb the cable adjuster unless facilities exist for readjustment on completion.

15 Unbolt the heater water valve from the bulkhead. (Access to the nuts is via the grille at the base of the windscreen). Secure the valve to the top of the engine, where it will not be crushed during subsequent operations. There should be no need to disconnect the water hoses.

16 If an engine support bar (Jaguar tool MS 53A or equivalent) is to be used, fit it loosely now. If such a bar is not available, alternative means of support must be used. A hoist connected to the rear lifting eye, or a jack and suitable packing beneath the sump, are both suitable. Whatever support is used must be capable of being moved in a controlled fashion. An unsupported engine will come to rest on the steering rack, possibly with undesirable consequences.

17 Raise and securely support the vehicle, unless a pit is being used. Drain the transmission fluid by removing the dipstick tube from the oil pan (photo). Remember that the fluid may be very hot.

18 Disconnect the exhaust downpipe at its junction with the intermediate pipe. Tie the intermediate pipe out of the way.

19 Remove the heat shields from the floor pan.

20 Take the weight of the transmission on a suitably protected jack. Remove the crash plate (undershield) if fitted, then unbolt the transmission rear mounting from the floor pan (photo).

21 Remove the propellor shaft tunnel spreader plate. Note that two of the securing bolts are inside the tunnel, and easily overlooked.

22 Make alignment marks, then disconnect the propeller shaft flange from the transmission output flange. It will be necessary to have the rear wheels free to turn in order to rotate the propeller shaft and gain access to the flange nuts and bolts. Remember to check the front wheels when raising the rear of the car.

23 Lower the jack under the transmission to roughly the position required for transmission removal. Support the engine in this position (see paragraph 16).

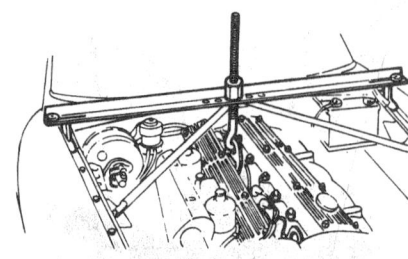

Fig. 13.62 Engine support bar engaged with rear lifting eye (Sec 12)

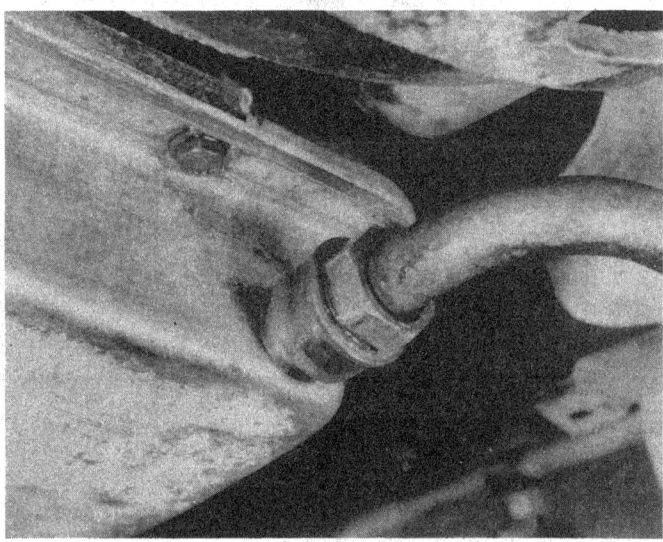

12.17 Dipstick tube union on automatic transmission oil pan

12.20 Transmission rear mounting bolt and spacer

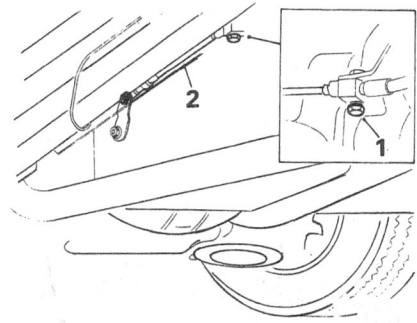

Fig. 13.63 Selector mechanism trunnion bolt (1) and cable (2) (Sec 12)

24 Unbolt the selector lever bellcrank from the cross-shaft.

25 Unbolt the selector cable trunnion from its mounting bracket.

26 Unbolt the stiffener plate from the transmission and from the engine sump.

27 Remove the cover plate from the bottom of the torque converter housing.

28 Remove the four bolts which secure the torque converter to the driveplate. It will be necessary to turn the engine to gain access to each bolt in turn. Relieve the lockwashers, on vehicles so equipped, before attempting to undo the bolts. The engine can be turned by pressing on the starter ring gear with a large screwdriver.

29 Disconnect the breather and oil cooler pipes from the transmission (photo). Either remove the pipes completely, or secure them out of the way. Plug open ends to prevent the entry of dirt.

30 Disconnect the speedometer cable (photo), or unplug the transducer connection.

31 Unbolt the starter motor and either remove it completely or tie it out of the way.

32 Slacken, but do not remove yet, the nuts and bolts which secure the torque converter housing to the engine. Access to some of these bolts is difficult; a good selection of socket spanner drives, joints and extensions will be useful.

33 Position the transmission support cradle securely, then remove the engine-to-bellhousing nuts and bolts. Note the earth strap.

34 Move the transmission jack rearwards, or push the car forwards, until the transmission is clear of the rear of the engine. Either way, make sure that the transmission leaves the engine without fouling and falling off its support. Retrieve the starter motor spacer if it falls out.

35 Lower the transmission and remove it from under the car.

36 Recover the rubber pad from the top of the transmission.

37 Remove the torque converter from the output shaft, noting how the drive dogs engage. Be prepared for ATF spillage.

38 If wished, unbolt the torque converter housing from the transmission case.

39 Refit in the reverse order to removal, noting the following points:

 (a) Make sure the torque converter drive dogs are properly engaged

 (b) Do not fully tighten the torque converter-to-driveplate bolts until all four have been fitted and tightened lightly

 (c) Use new self-locking nuts to secure the propeller shaft flange

 (d) Use a new exhaust olive, coated with exhaust jointing compound

 (e) Make any necessary adjustments as described later in this Section

40 Where a new or reconditioned transmission is being fitted, the oil cooler and its pipes **must** be flushed as subsequently described (unless they too are being renewed).

Oil cooler flushing

41 When contamination of the transmission fluid has occurred, or whenever a new or reconditioned transmission has been fitted, the oil cooler and its pipes must be flushed with clean fluid.

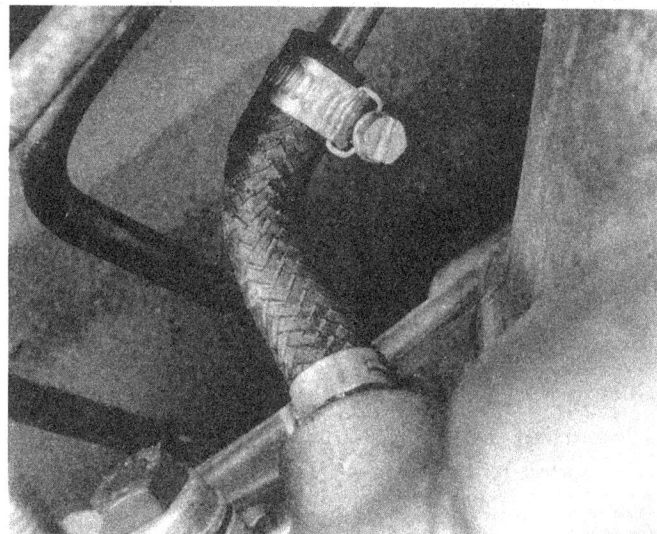

12.29 Transmission breather pipe union

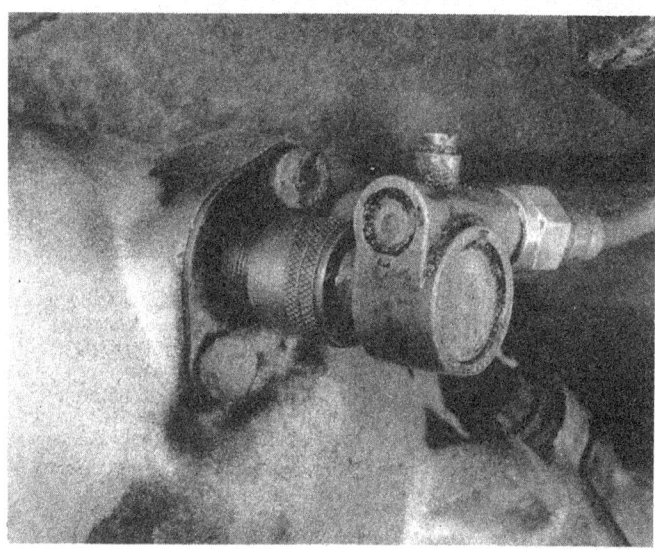

12.30 Speedometer cable connection (mechanical speedo)

42 The easiest way of flushing the cooler is to use the transmission's own pump. Proceed as follows.

43 Fill the transmission with clean fluid to the appropriate level, then add an extra quart (1.2 litres approx) of fluid.

44 Disconnect the oil cooler return pipe at the transmission. Temporarily blank the return pipe union in the transmission case; direct the pipe itself into a container of adequate capacity.

45 Place the gear selector in 'P'. Start the engine and allow it to idle until one quart (1.2 litres approx) of ATF has been discharged from the cooler return pipe. Stop the engine.

46 Reconnect the oil cooler pipe to the transmission and discard the flushing fluid.

47 Check the transmission oil level and top up if necessary.

Kickdown cable – pressure check and adjustment

48 Adjustment of the kickdown cable is only necessary when a new cable or transmission has been fitted, or if the correct adjustment has been disturbed.

49 A pressure gauge and a suitable adaptor will be required when making the pressure check. If this equipment is not available, the adjustment should be done by an authorised dealer or automatic transmission specialist. Incorrect line pressure can rapidly ruin the

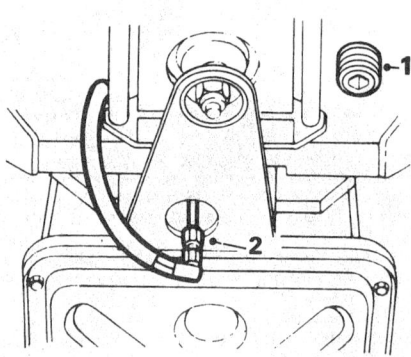

Fig. 13.64 Plug (1) is removed and pressure gauge connected using adaptor (2) (Sec 12)

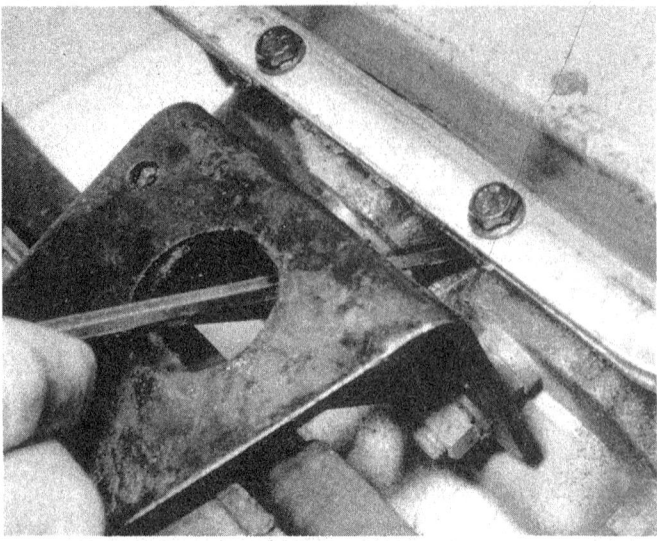

12.51 The oil pressure take-off plug is at the far end of the Allen key. Transmission is removed and inverted for clarity

transmission; it is desirable therefore that the adjustment be performed competently.

50 Make sure that the engine is in good tune.

51 Use an Allen key to remove the pressure take-off plug from the transmission case. **Do not** remove the bracket which goes from the case to the rear mounting, but work through the holes in the bracket. The plug is located at an awkward angle (photo).

52 Connect the pressure gauge to the take-off point and position it so that it can be seen from the driver's seat.

53 With the engine warmed up and idling, wheels chocked, brakes applied and 'D' engaged, read the pressure on the gauge. It should be between 55 and 75 lbf/in² (3.9 to 5.3 kgf/cm²).

54 Increase the engine speed by 500 rpm and read the pressure again. There should be an increase of 20 to 25 lbf/in² (1.4 to 1.8 kgf/cm²).

55 If the pressure readings are outside the above limits, alter the cable length at the threaded adjuster. Switch off the engine and select 'N' or 'P' before making the adjustment. Increasing the length of the cable increases the line pressure, and *vice versa*.

56 When adjustment is complete, the crimped stop on the inner cable should be approximately 0.015 in (0.4 mm) from the threaded outer (Fig. 13.65). Where a new cable is being fitted and the stop is loose, crimp it in the correct position. Remove the pressure gauge and refit the plug.

57 If correct pressures cannot be achieved by adjusting the cable, adjust the kickdown cam bracket as described later in this Section.

Kickdown cam bracket – adjustment

58 Drain the transmission fluid. Use a clean container and avoid contamination if the fluid is fit for re-use.

59 Remove the transmission oil pan.

60 Disconnect the cable from the kickdown cam. Make sure that the throttle valve moves freely in its block.

61 Slacken the two screws which secure the kickdown cam bracket.

62 Place a feeler gauge of thickness 0.040 in (1.0 mm) between the heel of the cam and the kickdown valve (photo). Move the bracket until the throttle valve exhaust port is just blanked off, then tighten the securing screws.

63 Remove the feeler gauge and reconnect the kickdown cable. With the cable connected, the cam should be in contact with its valve. Make a preliminary adjustment of the kickdown cable if necessary to achieve this.

64 Refit the sump, using a new gasket, and refill the transmission with clean ATF.

65 Adjust the kickdown cable and check the line pressure as previously described.

Oil filter – removal

66 The transmission oil filter should be renewed at the same time as the fluid change specified in the maintenance schedule.

67 Drain the fluid by unscrewing the dipstick tube union from the

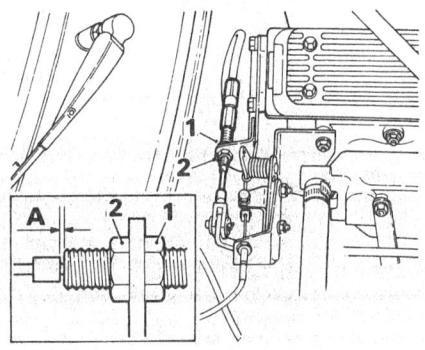

Fig. 13.65 Kickdown cable adjustment. For gap 'A' see text (Sec 12)

1 Locknut   2 Locknut

12.62 Feeler gauge inserted under heel of kickdown cam

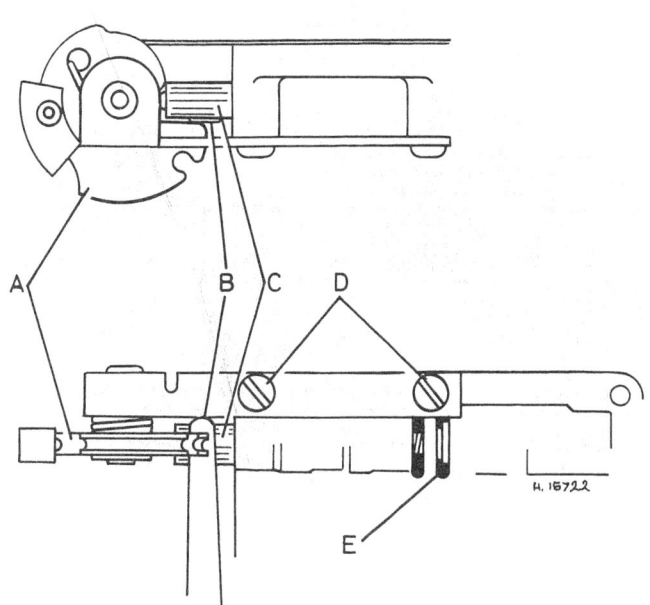

Fig. 13.66 Kickdown cam bracket adjustment (Sec 12)

A Cam   D Screws
B Feeler gauge   E Throttle valve port
C Kickdown valve

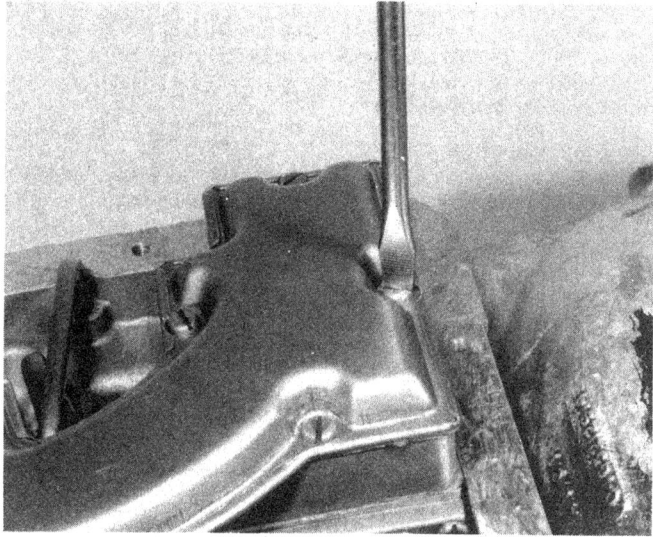

12.69A Remove the filter securing screws

12.69B Remove the automatic transmission oil filter

oil pan. Take care to avoid scalding if the fluid is hot. Remove the oil pan and recover the gasket (photo).

68 If there is magnet attached to the inside of the oil pan, remove and clean it, noting its approximate location for reference when refitting.

69 Remove the screws which secure the filter to the valve block. Remove the filter, spacer and gaskets (photos).

70 Smear the new gaskets with a little grease or clean ATF. Fit the spacer and the filter, using new gaskets, and secure with the screws.

71 Refit the oil pan, using a new gasket smeared lightly with grease. Make sure that the magnet (when fitted) is not fouling any internal projections. Tighten the oil pan bolts progressively and in a diagonal sequence, then refit the dipstick tube.

72 Refill the transmission with the correct grade and quantity of fresh ATF.

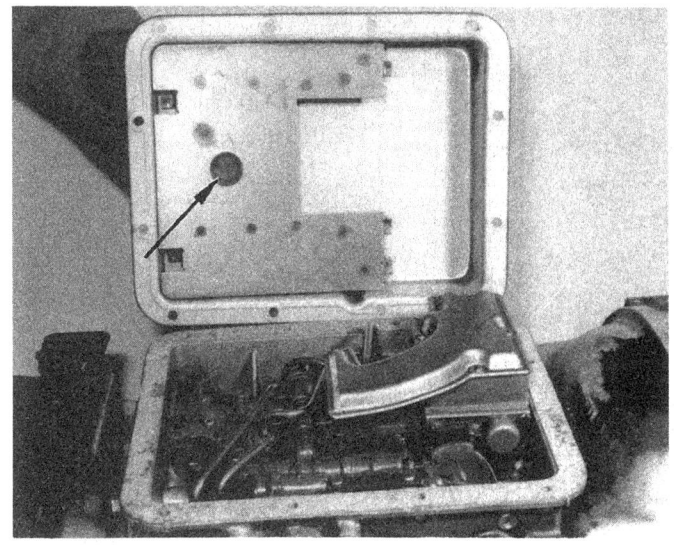

12.67 Transmission oil pan removal. Note magnet (arrowed)

12.69C Remove the spacer and gasket

Brake bands – adjustment

73 Refer to Chapter 6, Section 20. The procedure is as described for the Model 65 transmission, except that to improve access to the front brake band adjusting screw, the selector lever should be removed from the selector shaft.

Rear oil seal – removal

74 Refer to Chapter 6, Section 22; additionally, use thread locking compound when refitting the output flange securing bolt.

Front oil seal – renewal

75 Remove the transmission and remove the torque converter from the input shaft.
76 Carefully prise out the old oil seal from its location (photo).
77 Coat the new seal with ATF and carefully press it home using a piece of pipe or tube. Make sure that the seal enters its location squarely.
78 Refit the torque converter, then refit the transmission.

13 Propeller shaft (Series 3)

Description

1 The basic design of the propeller shaft remains unchanged from that described in Chapter 7. However, the flanged joint at the centre bearing has been superseded by a simple spider.
2 The propeller shaft is balanced as a single unit; renewal of individual sections is not recommended. The end flanges, universal joints, the centre bearing and the gaiter can still be renewed as necessary.

Removal and refitting

3 Raise and securely support the vehicle, making due allowance for the need to rotate the rear wheels during subsequent work.
4 Remove the exhaust heat shields. Separate the exhaust system at the junction of the downpipe and the intermediate pipe; tie the intermediate pipe to one side.
5 Mark the relationship between the propeller shaft and final drive flanges, then remove their securing nuts and bolts.
6 Unbolt and remove the centre bearing support plate, retrieving the spacers from the two front bolts.

12.76 Front oil seal removal

7 Use a suitably protected jack, a hoist or an engine support bar to take the weight off the engine/transmission rear mounting. Remove the mounting plate by unbolting it from the tunnel and releasing the nut from the transmission. Retrieve the spacers, spring and washers.
8 Remove any plates which impede access to the front flanged joint.
9 Mark the relationship of the front flanges, then remove their securing nuts and bolts.
10 Remove the propeller shaft from the rear of the vehicle.
11 When refitting, use new self-locking nuts and tighten all nuts and bolts to the specified torque. Position the centre bearing carrier as far to the right as it will go; if subsequent road testing reveals undue vibration, progressively move the centre bearing leftwards until the vibration is just eliminated. Do not attempt to alter the vertical location of the bearing.

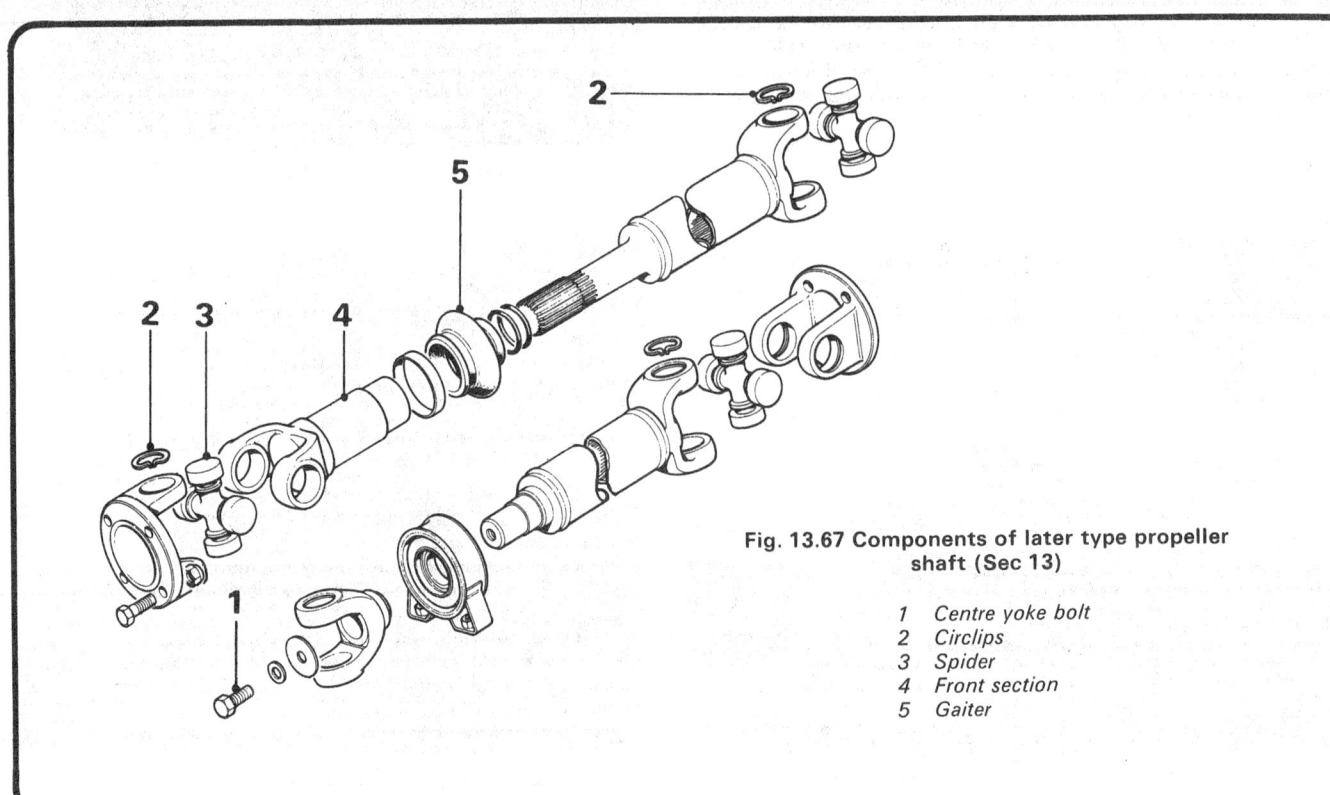

Fig. 13.67 Components of later type propeller shaft (Sec 13)

1 Centre yoke bolt
2 Circlips
3 Spider
4 Front section
5 Gaiter

Dismantling and reassembly

12 If not already present, make alignment marks establishing the relationship of all three sections of the shaft and the flanges.

13 Place a spacer (eg an old nut) between the head of the centre yoke securing bolt and its spider. Unscrew the bolt to separate the rear section of the shaft from its yoke.

14 If wished, use a puller to remove the centre bearing. The puller legs should engage in the inner reinforcing ring of the rubber mounting.

15 Overhaul of the universal joints is described in Chapter 7.

16 On reassembly, make sure the sliding splines are well greased, and take care not to damage the gaiter and O-rings which cover it.

17 Use thread locking compound on the splines which key the rear section to its yoke.

18 Make sure the alignment marks made before dismantling are correctly lined up before refitting the shaft.

Elimination of vibration

19 Remove the shaft as previously described and check all the universal joints for freedom of movement. A stiff UJ will cause vibration.

20 When satisfied with the condition of the joints, refit the shaft, paying particular attention to the instructions in paragraph 11 with regard to the positioning of the centre bearing carrier.

---

14 Final drive

Driveshaft (Series 2 on) – removal and refitting

1 Jack up the rear of the car and support it securely on stands.

2 Remove the roadwheel.

3 Working at the inner end of the driveshaft, slacken the shroud clip and slide the shroud away to expose the nuts which hold the driveshaft flange to the final drive output shaft flange. Unscrew the nuts.

4 Withdraw the split pin and remove the castellated driveshaft nut from the hub end of the driveshaft.

5 Remove the grease nipple from the hub carrier.

6 Using a suitable extractor, push the splined section of the driveshaft out of the hub assembly.

7 Pivot the hub assembly on its fulcrum bolt.

8 Remove the nut from the shock absorber lower mounting (nearest the front of the car), detach the lash-down bracket and then disconnect the lower end of the shock absorber.

9 Withdraw the driveshaft, noting carefully any camber control shims which are located between the driveshaft inner flange and the brake disc.

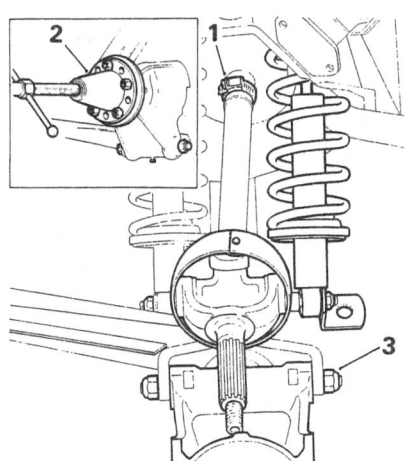

Fig. 13.68 Driveshaft removal – Series 2 on (Sec 14)

1 Shroud clip	3 Fulcrum bolt
2 Hub extractor	

10 If a new driveshaft is being installed, then the old shrouds, oil seal track and spacer will be required from the old shaft. The shroud rivets will require drilling out. Pop rivet them to the new shaft. Note which way round the chamfer on the oil track faces before removing it.

11 To fit the driveshaft, clean and locate the camber shims. Connect the inner end of the driveshaft to the final drive output flange and screw the nuts on a few threads.

12 Reconnect the shock absorber and lash-down bracket.

13 Smear thread locking compound on the driveshaft splines. Check that the spacer and the oil seal track are correctly fitted, raise the hub assembly and enter the splined end of the driveshaft into the hub.

14 Draw or tap the driveshaft fully into the hub, fit the plain washer and tighten the castellated nut to the specified torque (see Chapter 8 Specifications).

15 Check the hub bearing endfloat by inserting two levers between the hub and the hub carrier and observing any movement on a dial gauge. If necessary, the spacer will have to be changed for one of different thickness to bring the endfloat within the specified tolerance.

16 Refit the grease nipple to the hub carrier.

17 Tighten the nuts at the inner end of the driveshaft. Slide the inner shroud into position and then seal the shroud joints with mastic.

18 Refit the roadwheel and lower the car to the ground.

19 It is recommended that the rear wheel camber is checked by your dealer.

Output shaft (late Series 2 and Series 3) – removal and refitting

20 Jack up the rear of the car, support it securely and remove the roadwheel.

21 Remove the brake caliper as described in Chapter 9.

22 Drive out the shock absorber lower mounting pivot pin.

23 Cut the locking wire from the radius arm locking bolt.

24 Remove the hub pivot shaft grease nipple.

25 Support the hub and then lower the radius arm from the spigot anchor point.

26 Withdraw the driveshaft inner joint shroud and unscrew the nuts which hold the joint to the brake disc. Tap the disc mounting bolts towards the final drive unit.

27 Disconnect the inner end of the driveshaft, noting carefully the number and location of the camber control shims. Shims may also be found behind the brake disc once it is withdrawn – do not disturb these.

28 Unlock and remove the five setscrews which hold the caliper mounting bracket to the final drive housing.

29 Withdraw the output shaft from the final drive unit. Discard the O-ring seal.

30 If a new output shaft is being fitted, always check its length against the original.

31 Fit a new O-ring into the groove in the bearing housing of the output shaft.

32 Oil the output shaft splines and install the shaft into the final drive housing.

33 Reverse the rest of the removal operations. Have the rear wheel camber checked on completion.

Output shaft oil seal (late Series 2 and Series 3) – renewal

34 Remove the output shaft as described above.

35 Grip the caliper mounting bracket in the jaws of a vice fitted with jaw protectors.

36 Unlock and remove the nut from the output shaft.

37 Withdraw the output shaft from the caliper mounting bracket. Remove the inner bearing race and discard the collapsible spacer. Do not mix up the inner and outer bearing assemblies.

38 Prise the oil seal from the caliper mounting bracket and discard it. Remove the outer bearing race. Clear the caliper bracket internally.

39 Take the opportunity to examine the bearings and renew if necessary as described later.

40 Before reassembling, lightly grease the bearings, and then locate the outer bearing race.

41 Fit the oil seal, having packed the space between its lips with petroleum jelly.

42 Clamp the caliper mounting bracket between the jaws of a vice fitted with jaw protectors.

43 Check that the four special bolts for the brake disc are in position in the output shaft flange.

44 Pass the shaft carefully through the oil seal and draw the outer bearing into position.

45 Smear oil on the oil seal contact area of the shaft.

46 Fit the new spacer and fill the space between the bearings with clean gear oil. Fit the inner bearing race and a new nut lockwasher, then screw on the nut finger tight.

47 Using a spring balance or suitable torque wrench, check the torque required to just start the shaft turning in the caliper mounting bracket. Record this figure.

48 Tighten the shaft nut to just eliminate bearing endfloat. The shaft turning torque should still be as previously recorded.

49 Now tighten the nut a fraction at a time until on rechecking the turning torque, it has increased by between 1 and 5 lbf in (0.1 and 0.6 Nm) above the previously recorded figure. This indicates the correct bearing preload. If the increase is found to exceed 5 lbf in (0.6 Nm) then the shaft nut has been overtightened and a new collapsible spacer must be fitted and the adjustment repeated. It will be seen that great care is needed to prevent overtightening the nut. *Once the spacer has been overcompressed, backing off the nut will not restore it to its previous length.*

Output shaft bearings (late Series 2 and Series 3) – renewal

50 The operations are almost completely covered in the preceding sub-Section (oil seal renewal), except that the bearing tracks should be driven from the housing using a brass drift.

51 When fitting new tracks, clean out their housing recesses first and preferably press or draw them into position rather than drive them home. The tracks must seat fully.

52 Never be tempted to fit new bearing races to the old outer tracks. Never mix up the races and tracks of new inner and outer bearing assemblies, they are matched during production.

15 Braking system

Metrication

1 On later models, partial metrication of the brake hydraulic components has been implemented. On the following components, UNF threads will still be encountered until such time as full metric conversion takes place:

Rear calipers
Handbrake calipers
Fluid supply pipes from rear three-way connector to rear calipers
Three-way connector

2 It will be realised that this arrangement can prove dangerous when fitting new components or pipes unless thread compatability is first established by connecting parts initially using the fingers only.

Front disc shields – removal and refitting

3 Jack up the front roadwheel and remove it.

4 Slacken the upper bolt which holds the steering arm to the stub axle carrier.

5 Cut the locking wire and remove the caliper upper mounting bolt.

6 Remove all the clips which hold the disc shield to the stub axle carrier. Withdraw the lower and main disc shield sections.

7 Remove the brake hydraulic pipe which runs between the flexible hose and the caliper.

8 Release the locknut which retains the brake hose union to the remaining disc shield section, withdraw the hose from the shield and remove the shield.

9 Refitting is a reversal of removal. Bleed the brakes upon completion.

Master cylinder reservoir (late Series 2 and Series 3)

10 The fluid reservoir on these models is mounted directly on top of

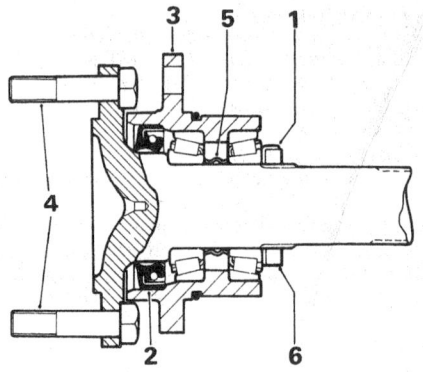

Fig. 13.69 Sectional view of output shaft (Sec 14)

1 Lockwasher tab	4 Disc bolts
2 Oil seal	5 Collapsible spacer
3 Caliper bracket	6 Nut

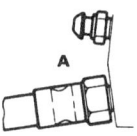
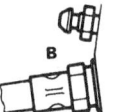
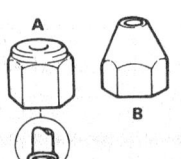
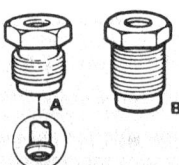
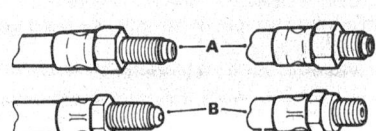

Fig. 13.70 Identification of metric (A) and UNF (B) brake hydraulic unions (Sec 15)

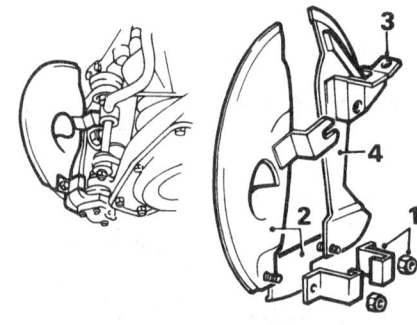

Fig. 13.71 Front disc shield attachments (Sec 15)

1 Clips	3 Brake hose bracket
2 Lower and main shields	4 Secondary shield

the master cylinder and the cap incorporates a fluid level indicator switch (photo).

11 To remove the reservoir, disconnect the battery and then remove the cap/switch assembly.

12 Detach the reservoir retaining clips and withdraw the two securing pins.

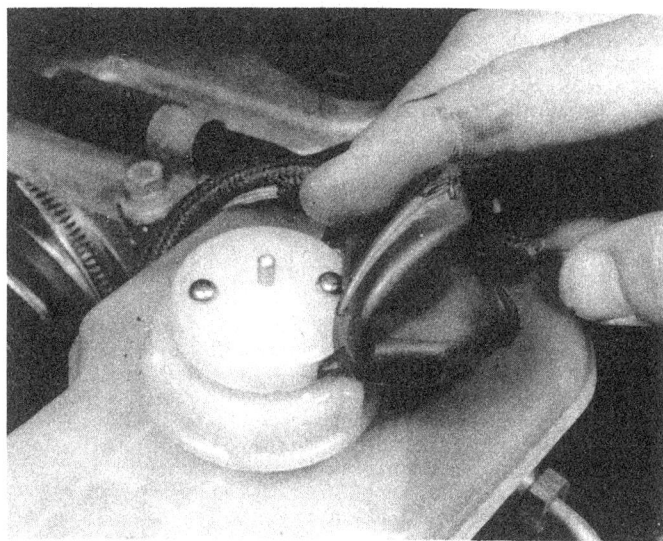

15.10 Brake fluid reservoir low level warning switch. Press centre button to test

13 Hold a container ready to catch spilled fluid and pull the reservoir directly upward from the master cylinder. Plug the open ports on the master cylinder.

14 Refit by reversing the removal operations. Fill the reservoir to the bottom of the filler neck with the specified fluid and then bleed the brakes.

Disc brake renewal

15 Commencing in 1980, front discs with a higher chrome content were fitted. These discs have an identification code cast into the hub location face.

16 Due to the different friction characteristics of these brake discs, they may only be fitted in pairs, and the pairs **must** carry the same identification code.

Brake pad material change

17 During 1983 a semi-metallic friction material was introduced on front and rear brake pads. The pads can be identified by the code FER 3401 printed on them.

18 The new pads may be fitted retrospectively to any vehicle having four-piston front calipers, but only in complete vehicle sets, ie front and rear. *On no account may conventional and metallic pads be mixed, either side to side or front to rear.* (The handbrake pads are not affected).

Handbrake pads – inspection and renewal

19 Despite the suggestion in Chapter 9 that they will not wear out, the handbrake pads should be inspected at the intervals specified in Section 3 of this Chapter.

20 The easiest way of inspecting the handbrake pads is by using a mirror and an inspection light (photo). No minimum lining thickness is specified, but common sense will enable the owner to decide when the pads are sufficiently worn to justify renewal.

21 Whenever the handbrake pads are renewed, the retraction fingers **must** be renewed also.

Pressure differential warning actuator deleted

22 The pressure differential warning actuator is not fitted to 1983 and later vehicles.

23 Warning of brake hydraulic malfunction is still provided, albeit at a later stage, by the low fluid level warning switch in the master cylinder reservoir.

Servo non-return valve location

24 During 1983 the location of the servo non-return valve was standardized for all vehicles. The valve will be found in the servo vacuum hose.

Pedal box/vacuum servo – removal and refitting

25 On cars fitted with a remotely mounted brake master cylinder fluid reservoir, the cap of which incorporates a fluid level switch, carry out the following operations to remove the pedal box/vacuum servo/master cylinder all together as one assembly.

26 Disconnect the battery.

27 Disconnect the hydraulic circuit pipes from the master cylinder, also the reservoir feed hoses.

28 Remove the fluid reservoir cap and disconnect the switch leads.

29 Unbolt the fluid reservoir and remove it from its bracket.

30 Disconnect the vacuum servo hose.

31 On left-hand drive cars with manual gearbox, disconnect the hose (banjo bolt) which connects the clutch master cylinder to the slave cylinder. Release the clutch slave cylinder hose from the pedal box.

32 On right-hand drive cars with manual gearbox, remove the clutch master cylinder to slave cylinder hose completely. Remove the self-locking nut which is adjacent to the clutch pedal housing and secures the steering column lower mounting bracket to the pedal box.

33 Remove the bolt which holds the upper part of the pedal box to the bulkhead.

15.20 Using a mirror to inspect the handbrake pads

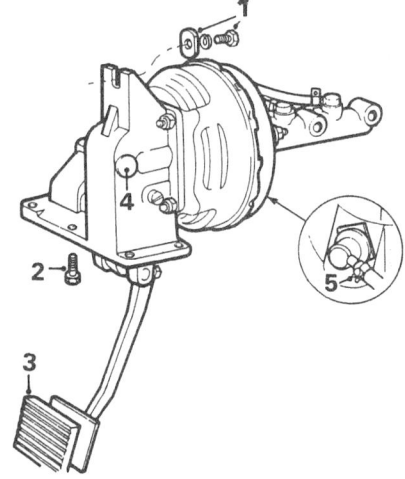

Fig. 13.72 Brake pedal, pedal box and servo (Sec 15)

1   Bolt, washer and spacer
2   Base bolt
3   Pedal rubber

4   Plug
5   Vacuum connection

34 Push the driver's seat as far as possible to the rear. Remove the seat cushion and the footwell carpets.
35 Remove the stop-lamp switch.
36 Remove the bolts which hold the base of the pedal box to the bulkhead. Retain the clips which hold the sound deadening mats.
37 On cars with manual transmission, remove the nut and spring washer which hold the clutch pedal to the operating lever and lift the pedal from the lever.
38 Raise the servo/pedal box/master cylinder assembly, draw it forwards and lift it from the car.
39 Refitting is a reversal of removal. On completion, bleed the brake (and clutch – manual transmission) hydraulic systems.

16 Electrical system – battery and alternator

Battery maintenance
1   A modern lead-acid battery, subject to a properly regulated charging regime will not need to have its electrolyte inspected so frequently as suggested earlier in the manual. Unless experience shows otherwise, inspection at monthly intervals will certainly suffice.
2   Batteries are increasingly designated 'low maintenance' or 'maintenance-free'. These terms are relative, and depend on the correct function of the rest of the charging system. Instructions for such maintenance as may still be necessary will normally be found printed on the battery case.
3   The 'sealed-for-life' battery is truly maintenance-free (except for its terminals) in that the electrolyte cannot be topped up. A built-in hydrometer shows the state of charge of the battery. Follow the instructions on the battery case when off-vehicle charging is necessary; normally, boost chaging is forbidden or subject to strict precautions.

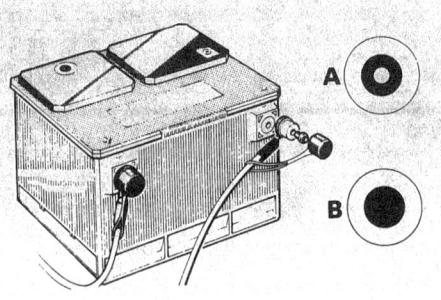

Fig. 13.73 Sealed-for-life battery with built-in hydrometer – insets show charged (A) and discharged (B) appearance (Sec 16)

Lucas 25 ACR alternator – description and testing
4   For all practical purposes, the information given in Chapter 10 for the 20 ACR alternator applies.

Lucas A133 alternator – description and testing
5   The A133 alternator is a modern development of the ACR series, which it is superseding. As would be expected, an integral solid state voltage regulator is fitted.
6   Testing on the vehicle requires a voltmeter (0 to 20V) and an ammeter (0 to 100 A).
7   Begin testing by disconnecting the leads from the rear of the alternator and measuring the voltage at each of the three disconnected leads in turn (ignition switched on). Battery voltage should be present at each lead. A zero reading at the '+' or 'S' leads means that the wiring between the alternator and the battery or starter solenoid is suspect. A zero reading at the 'IND' lead indicates a fault in the warning light circuit.
8   If the above test is satisfactory, reconnect the alternator leads and measure the voltage between the 'IND' terminal and earth (ignition on). A reading of approximately 2 volts should be

obtained. A zero reading suggests a short-circuit in the surge protection diode; a reading of 12 volts suggests a defect in the brushes, rotor or regulator. Proceed to investigate as follows.
9   Measure the voltage between the regulator metal link and earth (Fig. 13.74). The desired reading is 0.5 volts; a reading of 12 volts shows that the regulator is faulty.
10 Start the engine and run it at a steady 2500 rpm. Measure the voltage at the 'IND' and '+' terminals; they should be the same (around 14 volts). A difference of more than 0.5 volts suggests that the diode pack is defective.
11 Another sympton of a failed diode pack is that the warning light illuminates with the ignition off, but goes out when the ignition is switched on.
12 Again with the engine running at 2500 rpm, measure the voltage between the '+' terminal of the alternator and the battery positive terminal. A difference of 0.5 volts or greater is unacceptable, and means that the battery and alternator connections must be checked for security and cleanliness. A fault in this area can cause the warning light to glow at idle speed.
13 Stop the engine, disconnect the battery and connect the ammeter in the alternator output lead (between the alternator and the starter motor solenoid). Reconnect the battery and switch on as many electrical loads as possible (headlights, heated rear window etc) for a minute or two, then start the engine and run it at 2500 rpm. The ammeter should indicate the alternator's maximum rated output (see Specifications).
14 If the output is lower than specified, temporarily short the regulator link (pharagraph 9) to earth. If output now improves, the regulator is faulty; if not, the stator windings are probably faulty.
15 If the correct output in the preceding test is satisfactory, switch off the electrical loads and continue to run the engine until the charging current falls below 10 amps. Connect the voltmeter across the battery terminals: it should read 13.6 to 14.4 volts. A reading outside these limits suggests a fault in the regulator.

Motorola 9AR alternator – description and testing
16 The 9AR series alternators are high output machines, still with integral regulators. The principles of operation are the same as for the Lucas alternators, but some testing and overhaul procedures differ.
17 Before carrying out the tests, make sure that the battery is fully charged. An accurate voltmeter and ammeter will be required.
18 Switch off the ignition. Check the voltage on one of the three phases of the stator windings by passing a probe of the voltmeter through the ventilation hole as shown (Fig. 13.75).
19 Connect the voltmeter between one phase and earth, then between the windings and the positive terminal. Observe the correct polarity. If the voltmeter reading is annything but zero, there is a defective positive rectifier diode. Renew the diode bridge in that case.
20 Switch on the ignition but do not start the engine, Carry out a check of the field circuit. Do this by extracting the regulator securing screws and touching the voltmeter negative probe on the field terminal 'EX'. (The voltmeter positive probe should be on the alternator positive terminal). If the voltmeter reading exceeds 2 volts

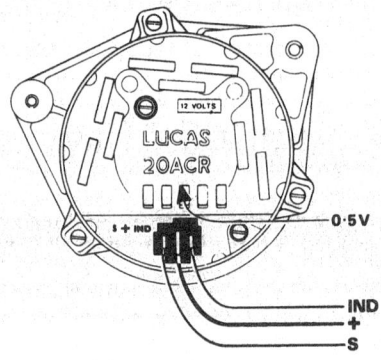

Fig. 13.74 Alternator – regulator link is accessible through rear of cover (arrowed). 20 ACR shown, others similar (Sec 16)

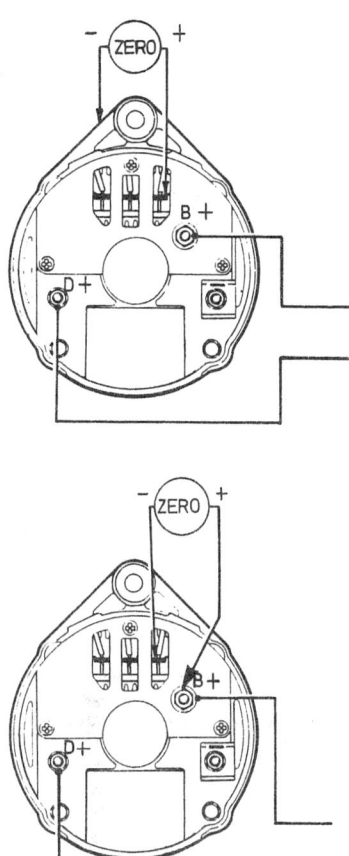

Fig. 13.75 Checking the voltage on the stator windings –
Motorola alternator (Sec 16)

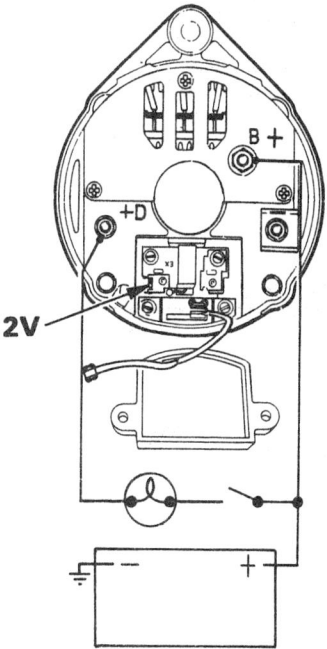

Fig. 13.76 Checking the regulator circuit – Motorola
alternator (Sec 16)

then the field circuit is defective. First check the movement of the
brushes in their holders and examine them for wear. Check that the
brush leads are not frayed, also that the slip rings are clean. If the
voltmeter reads zero, check the security of connections to the
regulator, ignition switch and the ignition indicator lamp.
21 Now check the regulator circuit by detaching its green wire from
the field EX terminal and again measuring the voltage across the
field windings (Fig. 13.76). This should again not exceed 2 volts. If
it is between 8 and 12 volts then the alternator is faulty. If the
voltage is correct, switch on the ignition and start the engine. Have
the engine speed faster than specified idle. Check the output
voltage at the alternator B + terminal and then at the battery
positive terminal. The correct reading at both checking points is
14.2V ± 0.5V at an ambient temperature of 77°F (25°C). If the
difference in voltage between the two readings is more than 0.3V,
check all wiring connections for security and absence of corrosion.
22 With the field lead disconnected, the regulator disconnected and
the output terminal shorted to the field terminal, run the engine at
fast idle. Check the voltage between the output terminal B + and
earth. If the voltage rises to between 14 and 16V but did not attain
14V in the test described in paragraph 21, then the regulator is
defective and should be renewed.
23 If the voltage does not rise but the field circuit has been tested
and found to be satisfactory (paragraph 20) then either the
alternator stator or the rectifier diodes are defective.

Alternator drivebelt (Series 3) – adjusting tension
24 Slacken the alternator pivot bolt(s) and trunnion bolt.
25 Slacken the adjuster locknut, adjuster nut and pivot bolt. On air
conditioned cars, access to the adjuster is from below.
26 Act on the adjuster nut to move the alternator about its pivot
until the drivebelt can be deflected by the specified amount.
27 Tighten the adjuster locknut and all pivot bolts.

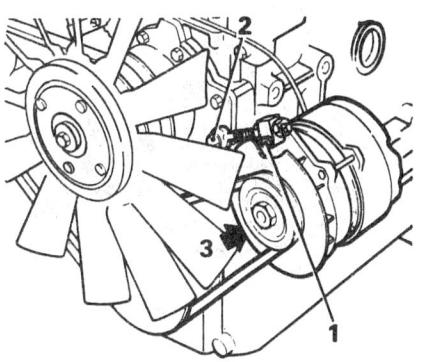

Fig. 13.77 Alternator drivebelt adjustment – Series 3
(Sec 16)

1   Trunnion bolt   3   Alternator pivot bolt
2   Adjuster pivot bolt

Alternator drivebelt (Series 3) – removal and refitting
28 Remove the water pump/steering pump drivebelt (Section 5).
29 Remove the air conditioning compressor drivebelt, on models so
equipped.
30 Slacken the alternator drivebelt as just described until it can be
slipped off its pulleys.
31 Refit in the reverse order to removal. Take the opportunity to
renew any other drivebelts if their condition is in doubt, and tension
them all correctly.
32 Recheck the tension of a new drivebelt after it has been in use
for a short period.

Alternator (Series 3) – removal and refitting
33 Disconnect the battery earth lead.
34 Slacken the alternator drivebelt as previously described until the
drivebelt can be slipped off the alternator pulley.
35 Unbolt the adjuster link from the alternator and move it out of
the way.

36 Unplug the cables from the alternator.
37 Pivot the alternator away from the engine and remove the pivot bolt(s).
38 Withdraw the alternator from its mountings.
39 Refit in the reverse order to removal. Adjust the drivebelt tension on completion.

Lucas 25 ACR alternator – overhaul
40 Proceed as described in Chapter 10 for the other ACR series alternators.

Lucas A133 alternator – overhaul
41 With the alternator removed from the car, first disconnect and unscrew the radio interference suppressor capacitor.
42 Remove the two cover securing screws and lift off the rear cover.
43 Disconnect and dismount the anti-surge diode.
44 Remove the voltage regulator, labelling the leads if there is any possibility of confusion on reassembly.
45 Undo its two securing screws and remove the brush box.
46 Further dismantling should only be undertaken by electrically competent owners. Proceed by unsoldering the stator leads from the diode pack, taking care not to damage the diodes.
47 Remove the remaining securing screws to release the diode pack.
48 Remove the through-bolts and separate the slip ring end bracket from the stator.

49 Note the orientation of the stator relative to the lugs on the bracket, then remove the stator from the drive end bracket.
50 Restrain the alternator pulley by clamping an old fanbelt round it, then undo and remove the pulley securing nut. Retrieve the washer, then draw the pulley, fan and spacers from the shaft. Remove the Woodruff key.
51 Press the shaft out of the drive end bearing.
52 To renew the slip ring end bearing, first unsolder the slip rings and carefully remove them from the rotor shaft. The old bearing can then be drawn off using a puller, and the new one pressed on using a piece of tube.
53 Reassemble in the reverse order to dismantling, noting the following points:

    (a) Take care when resoldering the slip rings that no deposit is left on the faces which bear on the brushes
    (b) Do not attempt to renew individual diodes
    (c) Make sure that the brushes move freely in their holders

Motorola 9AR alternator – overhaul
54 With the alternator removed from the car, remove the B + terminal from the end cover.
55 Detach the capacitor from the alternator casing.
56 Remove the rear cover (three screws).
57 Detach the regulator (two screws)
58 Lift out the brush holder (two setscrews).

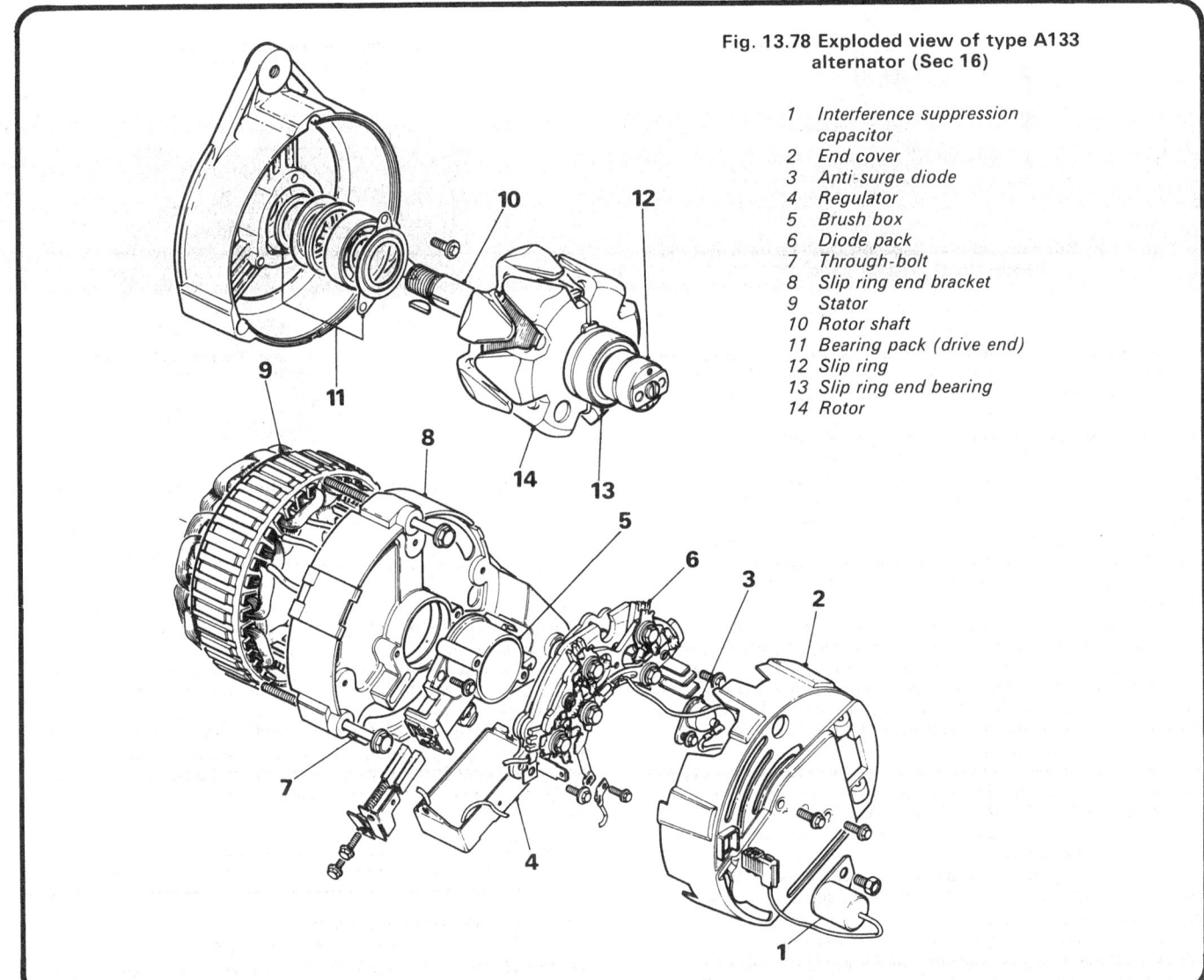

Fig. 13.78 Exploded view of type A133 alternator (Sec 16)

1   Interference suppression capacitor
2   End cover
3   Anti-surge diode
4   Regulator
5   Brush box
6   Diode pack
7   Through-bolt
8   Slip ring end bracket
9   Stator
10 Rotor shaft
11 Bearing pack (drive end)
12 Slip ring
13 Slip ring end bearing
14 Rotor

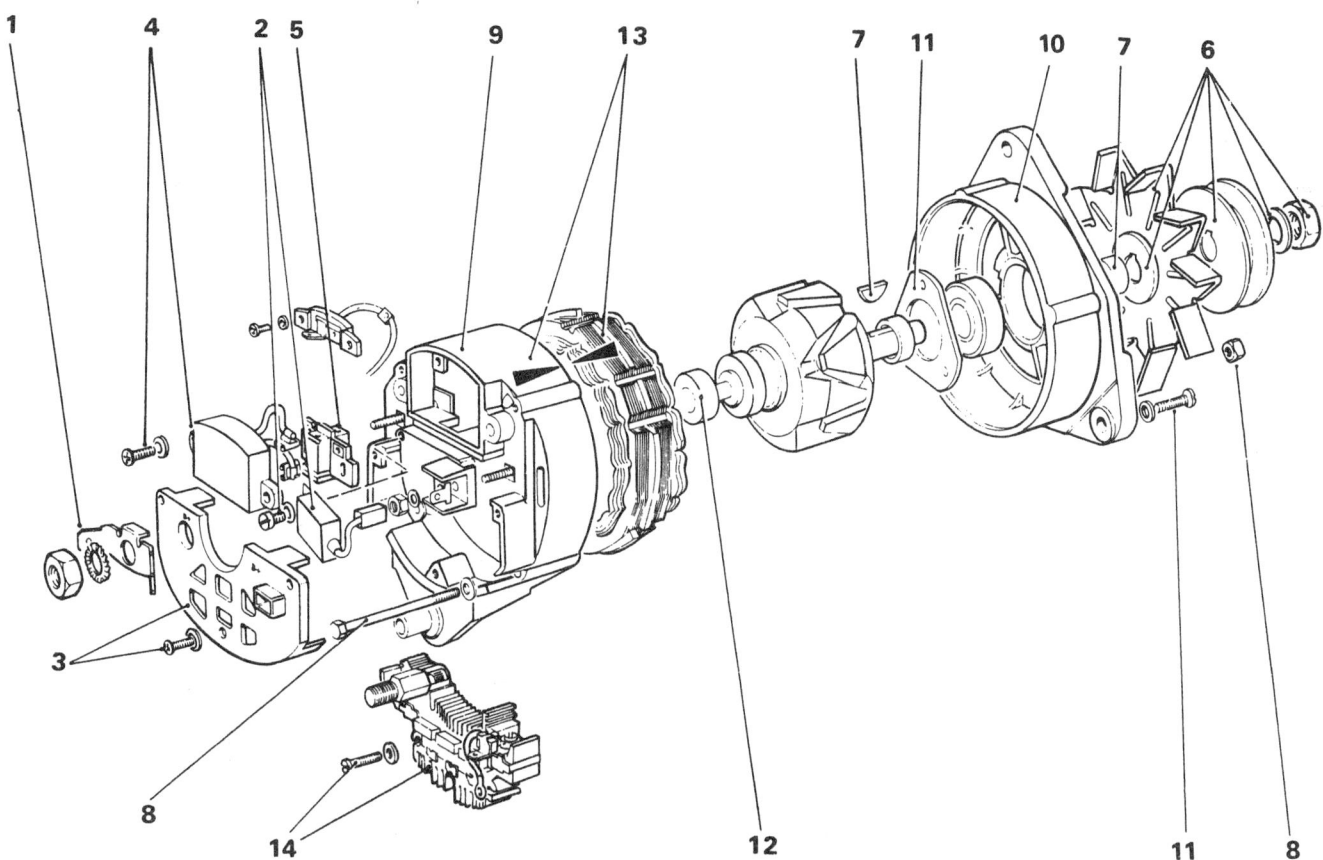

Fig. 13.79 Exploded view of Motorola 9AR alternator (Sec 16)

1	Connector	5	Brush holder
2	Capacitor and screw	6	Fan, pulley and fastenings
3	Cover and screw	7	Spacer and Woodruff key
4	Regulator and screw	8	Through-bolt and nut

9	Rear housing	13	Stator/rear housing
10	Front housing		alignment marks
11	Bearing retainer plate	14	Diode pack and screw
12	Rear bearing		

59 Unscrew the pulley nut and draw off the pulley. An old drivebelt engaged in the pulley groove and gripped in the jaws of a vice close to the pulley will stop the pulley turning as the pulley nut is unscrewed. Remove the Woodruff key and spacer.
60 Remove the four tie-bolts and retain the captive nuts.
61 Pull off the rear housing complete with the stator and the diode bridge. The rear bearing will remain on the rotor spindle.
62 Draw off the front housing and take off the short spacer next to the rotor.
63 If necessary, the front bearing can be removed if the retaining plate (3 screws) is removed and the bearing pressed out.
64 The rear bearing can be withdrawn from the rotor spindle using a suitable puller.
65 Mark the relationship of the stator ring to the rear housing to make sure that it is refitted during reassembly in its original position.
66 Unsolder the leads of the three phase windings and the D + lead from the diode bridge. Use a pair of long nosed pliers as a heat sink when unsoldering the leads, otherwise the heat may be transmitted to the diodes and damage them.
67 Lift out the diode bridge (two setscrews).
68 Withdraw the alternator housing from the stator, detach the two terminals and remove the D + lead complete.
69 Extract the O-ring from the bearing housing.
70 Commence reassembly by fitting a new O-ring into the recess in the rear bearing housing.
71 Fit the D + red lead assembly into the rear housing. Bolt it into position and pass the loose end of the lead through the hole below the D + terminal.
72 Align the stator with the housing in the previously marked position so that the three leads pass through the housing. Place the stator, with the housing resting on top of it, on a clean surface.

73 Lower the diode bridge (with the terminals and the capacitor fitted) into position in the housing so that the three leads pass through the gaps between the fins. Secure with the two setscrews, trapping the capacitor connector under the right-hand one.
74 Solder the three phase winding leads and the D + lead to the diode bridge, again using pliers to grip each terminal in turn to act as a heat sink.
75 If the rear bearing was removed, press a new one onto the rotor spindle and then press the spindle/bearing into the rear housing.
76 Place the short spacer over the front end of the spindle, making sure that the larger inside diameter is next to the rotor.
77 If the front bearing was removed, press a new one into the front housing and secure with a retaining plate. The retaining plate screws should have their threads smeared with thread locking compound.
78 Fit the alternator front housing. Apply locking compound to the tie-bolt threads and tighten them to secure the assembly, but do not overtighten.
79 Fit the plain washer to the rotor spindle and insert the Woodruff key. Fit the large washer, the fan, pulley, small washer and nut in that order. Tighten the pulley nut to 29 lbf ft (39 Nm).
80 Refit the brush holder, the regulator, the rear cover, the capacitor and the B + terminal components.

17 Electrical system – lighting, switches and instruments

Rear foglamp – bulb renewal
1 Unscrew the lens retaining screws and withdraw the lens. Remove the bayonet fitting bulb.
2 Fit the new bulb, then refit and secure the lens.

Rear foglamp – removal and refitting

3   Working under the rear bumper, release the nut and washer which hold the foglamp in position (photo).

4   Free the lamp unit and remove it rearwards. Some manipulation will be needed to persuade the unit to pass through the hole in the bumper (photo).

5   Disconnect the wiring either at the lamp unit, or at the harness connectors which are accessible from behind the rear light cluster (photo). In the latter case it may speed reassembly if a drawstring is attached to the old harness before removal and used to pull the new harness into position.

6   Refit in the reverse order to removal.

Instrument illumination bulbs (Series 3) – renewal

7   Disconnect the battery earth lead.

8   Remove the tachometer or speedometer, as described later, according to which side is to be worked on.

9   The bulb holder can now be withdrawn from the back of the instrument in question and the bulb renewed. In the case of the minor instruments, it may be necessary to remove the instrument for access.

10 Refit in the reverse order to removal.

Warning light cluster (Series 3) – removal and refitting

11 Disconnect the battery earth lead.

12 Remove the tachometer as described later.

13 Remove the lens from the warning lamp cluster (photo).

14 Reach through the tachometer aperture and unplug the warning lamp multi-connector. Bend back the harness securing clip.

15 Remove the securing screws and withdraw the cluster unit.

16 Refit in the reverse order to removal.

Bulb failure indicator units – description

17 Bulb failure indicator units, when fitted, are located on the luggage compartment front bulkhead (photo).

18 The units work by monitoring the balance of current drawn by paired bulbs. The fitting of bulbs of incorrect wattage, or sometimes even of a different make, can cause false alarms.

19 A bulb failure indicator unit which is defective should be renewed; no repair is possible.

Front fog/spot lamp bulb – renewal

20 Extract the two screws and remove the lens.

21 Push the bulb retaining clip aside and withdraw the bulb holder. Do not touch the new bulb with the fingers. If this is inadvertently done, clean the bulb with a cloth moistened with methylated spirit.

High level stop lamp bulb – renewal

22 Depress the two catches located on the lower face of the cover. Remove the cover.

23 Turn and twist the bulb holder to remove it and extract the bulb.

High level stop lamp – removal and refitting

24 Remove the cover as previously described, disconnect the wiring harness and then slide the holder assembly from the brackets attached to the rear screen. Refitting is a reversal of removal.

Master lighting switch (Series 3) – removal and refitting

25 Disconnect the battery earth lead.

26 Remove the driver's side dash liner trim.

27 Remove the two screws which secure the switch mounting bracket.

28 Withdraw the switch, carefully releasing the fibre optic lead and the wiring multi-plug.

29 Refit in the reverse order to removal.

Master lighting switch (Series 3) – disinhibiting

30 The front foglamp position of the master lighting switch is not obtainable when front foglamps are not fitted. If such lamps are subsequently fitted, the inhibition of the lighting switch can be cancelled as follows.

31 Remove the switch as previously described.

17.3 Rear fog lamp securing nut

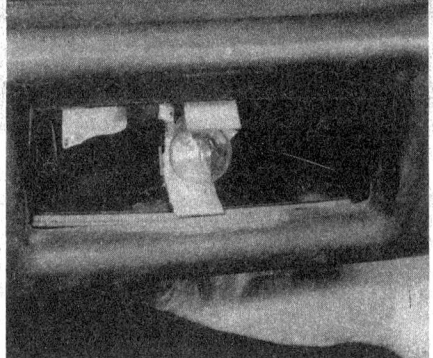
17.4 Removing rear foglamp through bumper

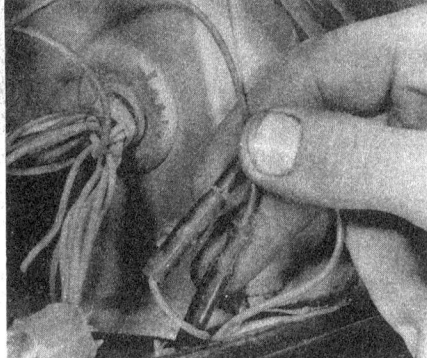
17.5 Rear foglamp harness connectors

17.13 Removing warning lamp cluster lens

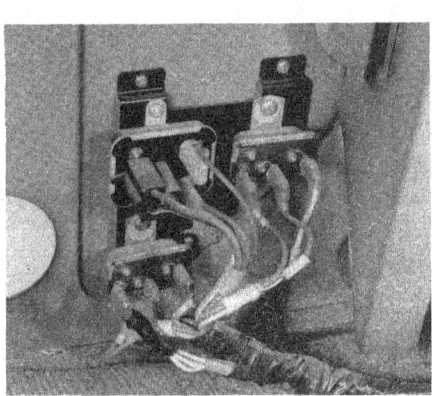
17.17 Bulb failure indicator units

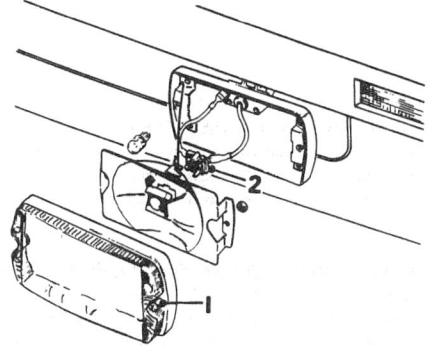

Fig. 13.80 Front foglamp (Sec 17)

1 Lens screw   2 Bulb holder

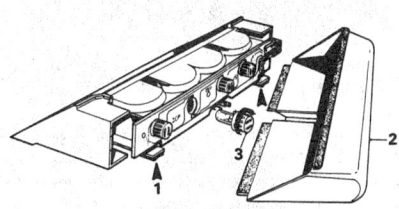

Fig. 13.81 High level stop lamp (Sec 17)

1 Cover catches   3 Bulb holder
2 Cover

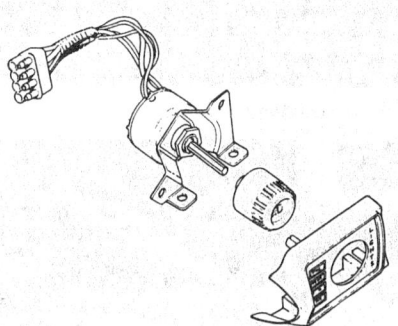

Fig. 13.82 Master lighting switch (Sec 17)

32 With the fibre optic lead withdrawn, it will be found that the switch knob can be depressed and turned to the 'front foglamp' position. With this position selected, turn the fibre optic lead holder (protruding from the back of the switch) through 90°.
33 Refit the fibre optic lead and check that all switch positions are now obtainable.
34 Refit the switch as previously described.

Steering column combination switch – removal and refitting
35 The switch arrangement will depend upon the production date of the car.
Late Series 2 models
36 Disconnect the battery.
37 Remove the steering wheel as described in Chapter 11.
38 Remove the steering column upper shrouds.
39 Remove the under scuttle panel from the driver's side.
40 Slacken the clamp pinch bolt and withdraw the switch assembly from the steering column, disconnect the wiring plugs.
41 The individual switches may be separated, but do not attempt to separate the direction indicator/headlamp/flasher switch from its bracket.
42 Refitting is a reversal of removal.
Series 3 models
43 Disconnect the battery.
44 Remove the under scuttle panel from the driver's side.
45 Disconnect the column switch wiring harness.
46 Remove the steering column lower shroud.
47 Slacken the steering wheel adjustment nut and pull the steering wheel out to its limit.
48 Turn the steering wheel for access to the grub screw. Release the locknut and remove the grubscrew.
49 Turn the steering wheel to the straight-ahead position, remove the ignition key to lock the steering column.
50 Remove the pinch bolt which holds the upper steering shaft stub to the column.
51 Remove the steering wheel and adjusting stub assembly.
52 Release the switch clamp screw and slide the switch and upper shroud from the column.
53 Separate the switch from the shroud.
54 Disconnect the wiper switch earth cable from the snap connector and disconnect the wiring harness multi-pin connector.
55 Remove the wiper switch from its mounting plate.
56 Disconnect the electrical leads and remove the hazard warning switch.
57 Do not attempt to separate the direction indicator/headlamp/flasher switch from the mounting bracket.
58 Reassembly and refitting are reversals of removal and dismantling.

Instruments (Series 2 and 3) – removal and refitting
59 Disconnect the battery earth lead.
60 To release the tachometer or speedometer, press the instrument

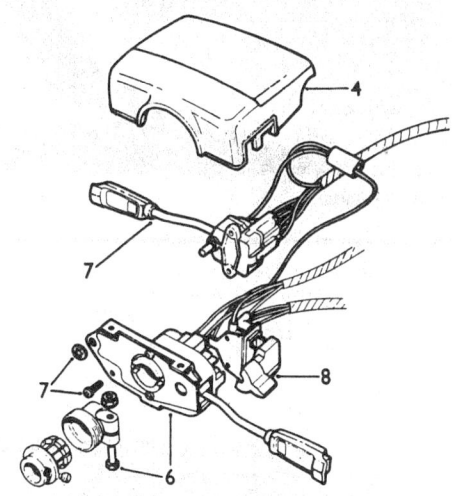

Fig. 13.83 Steering column combination switch – Series 2 (Sec 17)

4 Upper shroud   7 Wash/wipe switch and
6 Pinch bolt   fixing screws
*   8 Hazard warning switch*

inwards firmly and twist it clockwise (RHD) or anti-clockwise (LHD). Carefully pull the instrument forwards and release its electrical connections; in the case of a mechanical speedometer, disconnect the drive cable (photo).
61 To remove a minor instrument, first remove the tachometer or speedometer to provide access. The retaining bracket can then be removed from the rear of the instrument, which is withdrawn

17.60 Removing the speedometer

17.61 Removing the clock

through the front of the panel and its wires disconnected. The clock simply pulls out (photo).
62 Refit in the reverse order to removal.

Electronic speedometer (Series 3) – description

63 Later Series 3 models are fitted with electronic speedometers. A transducer, located in the same position on the transmission as the old cable take-off point, generates electrical pulses in proportion to road speed. These pulses drive the speed and distance indicators in the speedometer head. The instrument operates in the same way as an electronic tachometer.

Electronic speedometer (Series 3) – fault finding

64 Apart from checking the continuity of the wiring, there is little that the home mechanic can do when trying to locate faults in the electronic speedometer. Substitution of a known good transducer and/or speedometer head is the only course available.
65 Note that some flicker of the speedometer needle at low speeds (below 10mph/15 km/h) is normal and does not constitute a fault.

Oil pressure gauge sender (Series 2 and 3) – removal and refitting

66 Disconnect the battery earth lead.
67 Remove the air cleaner to improve access. The oil pressure gauge sender is located on top of the oil filter head.
68 Disconnect the wires from the sender unit and unscrew it, using a spanner on the flats provided.
69 Refit in the reverse order to removal, being careful not to overtighten the switch.

18 Electrical system – wipers and washers

Windscreen wiper blade fixing (later Series 3)

1 Some later models have hook fixing type wiper blades. To remove them, pull the wiper arm away from the glass until it locks.
2 Swivel the blade, squeeze the U-shaped plastic block and push the blade down the arm to release the block from the hook on the arm. Withdraw the blade from the arm by passing the hook through the blade cut-out.

Windscreen wiper blade positions (later Series 3)

3 Modified wiper arms and blades were introduced at VIN 365 950. Fig. 13.86 shows the correct parked position for these blades on a wet screen.
4 Failure to adjust the blade positions correctly may result in the blades fouling each other in some circumstances.

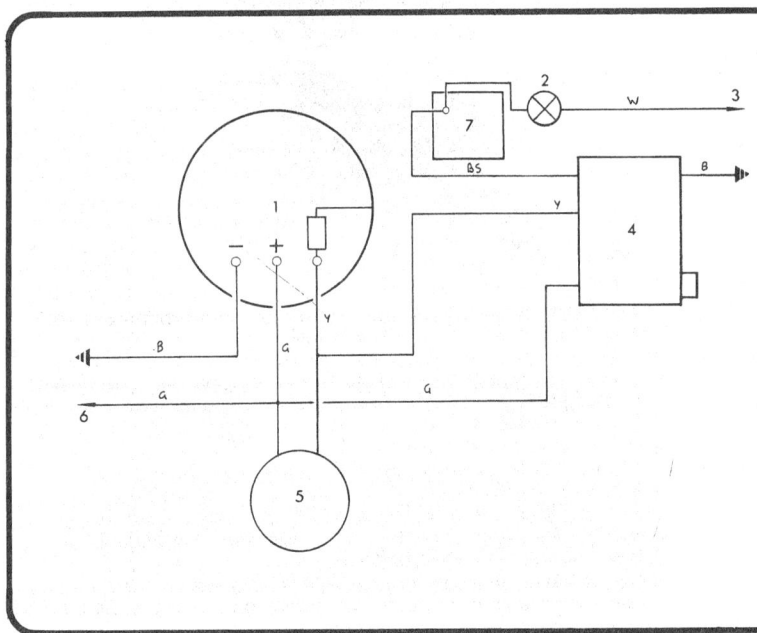

Fig. 13.84 Wiring diagram for electronic speedometer (Sec 17)

1   Speedometer
2   Oxygen sensor warning light (US only)
3   To ignition switch
4   Service interval counter (US only)
5   Speed transducer
6   To fuse
7   Bulb failure warning unit
G   Green
Y   Yellow
B   Black
BS Black/Slate
W   White

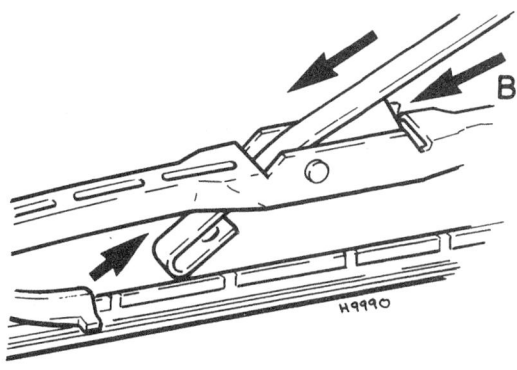

Fig. 13.85 Hook fixing type wiper blade (Sec 18)

B   Plastic block

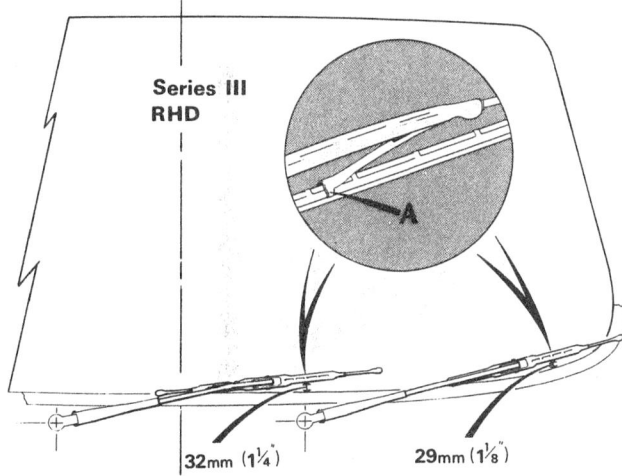

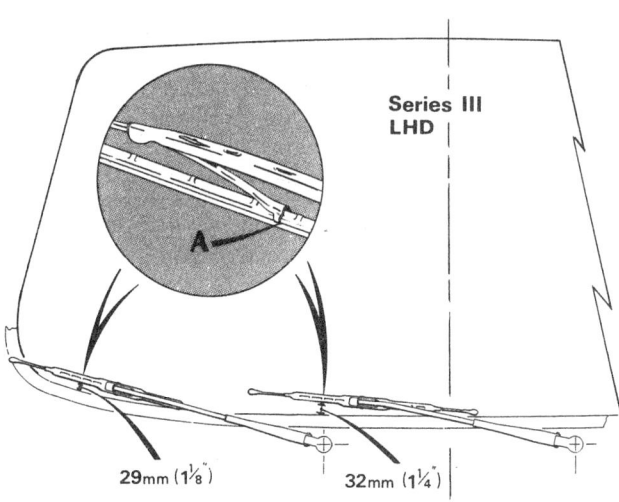

**Fig. 13.86 Windscreen wiper blade positions – later Series 3
(Sec 18)**

A   Measurement point

Windscreen wiper wheelbox – endfloat adjustment

5   If the windscreen wipers become noisy, it may be that the
wheelbox endfloat is excessive. This condition is usually caused by
the use of force when fitting the wiper arms to the splines. Correct
it as follows.

6   Remove the wiper arm from the wheelbox spindle.

7   Find a washer, or washers, of internal diameter and total
thickness both approximately 0.4 in (10 mm). Place the washers
over the wheelbox spindle.

8   Refit the wiper arm securing nut and tighten it onto the spacer
washers so that the collar is forced down the spindle. Correct
endfloat has been achieved when a feeler blade of thickness 0.003
in (0.076 mm) can just be inserted between the collar and the
wheelbox body (photo).

9   If the endfloat is accidentally reduced below that specified, back
off the nut and tap the end of the spindle smartly with a light
hammer to drive the spindle back through the collar.

10   When endfloat is correct, refit the wiper arm, being careful not
to hammer the arm onto the spindle or to overtighten the securing
nut.

*Wiper motor parking switch (Series 3) – removal and
refitting*

11   Failure of the wiper blades to park correctly, or at all, may be
due to a defective parking switch. This switch is located on the
wiper motor and may be renewed as follows.

12   Remove the battery.

13   Remove the bonnet release cable bracket and the plastic shield
to expose the wiper motor.

14   On RHD cars, unbolt the motor and slacken the rack union. Turn
the motor over to gain access to the switch. (On LHD cars the
motor is fitted the other way up so the switch is already accessible).

15   Unplug the electrical connector from the switch.

16   Release the parking switch from the motor by sliding it off,
freeing it from its spring clip.

17   Disconnect the motor feed wires from the switch.

18   Connect the motor feed wires to the new switch and slide it into
position.

19   Secure the wiper motor (RHD only). Temporarily reconnect the
battery and check for correct wiper operation before refitting the
remaining components.

*Headlamp wash/wipe components – removal and
refitting*

Washer reservoir

20   Raise and securely support the front of the vehicle. Remove the
left-hand front roadwheel.

18.8 Adjusting wiper spindle endfloat

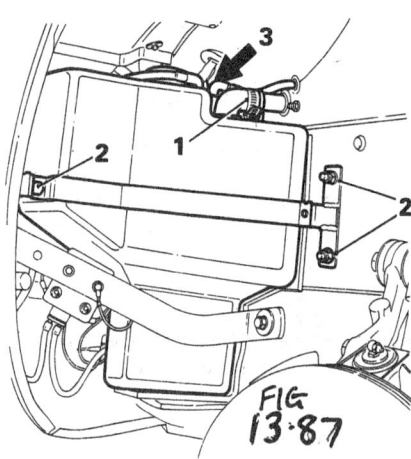

FIG
13·87

Fig. 13.87 Washer reservoir attachments (Sec 18)

1 *Filler elbow*   3 *Distribution manifold*
2 *Retaining strap*

21 Remove the stone guard (secured by three screws) and its
sealing strips.
22 Release the rubber elbow from the reservoir filler neck.
23 Remove the three nuts and bolts which retain the reservoir
retaining strap. Release the strap and lower the reservoir until the
four screws which secure the water distribution manifold are
accessible. Remove these screws and withdraw the reservoir.
24 Refit in the reverse order to removal.

Washer jets (Series 2)

25 Open the bonnet and carefully prise the supply tubes off the jet.
26 Hold the outside part of the jet still while undoing its retaining
nut behind the headlamp panel.
27 Remove the jet assembly and retrieve the rubber washers.
28 Refit in the reverse order of removal. Check the aim of the jets
on completion.

Washer pump

29 Raise and support the front of the car. Remove the left-hand
front roadwheel.
30 Carefully prise the tubes from the pump and disconnect the
electrical connectors. Note the connections for reference when
refitting.
31 Unbolt and remove the pump.
32 Refit in the reverse order to removal.

Wiper motor (Series 2)

33 Disconnect the battery earth lead.
34 Remove the four screws which secure the rack drive cover plate.
Remove the cover plate and the nylon channel, and disengage the
rack drive peg from the motor.
35 Unbolt the motor from its mountings, unplug the electrical leads
and remove the motor. Recover the mounting pad.
36 Refit in the reverse order to removal.

Wiper wheelboxes and rack tubes (Series 2)

37 Remove the headlamp outer rim finisher.
38 Remove the three screws which secure the rack tube and the
headlamp rim.
39 Draw the rim and rack tube forwards a little way and slacken the
nut at the top of the tube. Draw the rim away, allowing the wiper
blade to rotate as the rack is withdrawn from the wheelbox.
40 Refit in the reverse order to removal. Align the wiper blade in
the correct parked position, if necessary, as described in paragraph
43.

Wiper arms (Series 2)

41 Remove the central screw from the wheelbox, holding the wiper
arm to stop it turning.
42 Press the wiper arm towards the headlamp and remove it.
Recover the spacer.

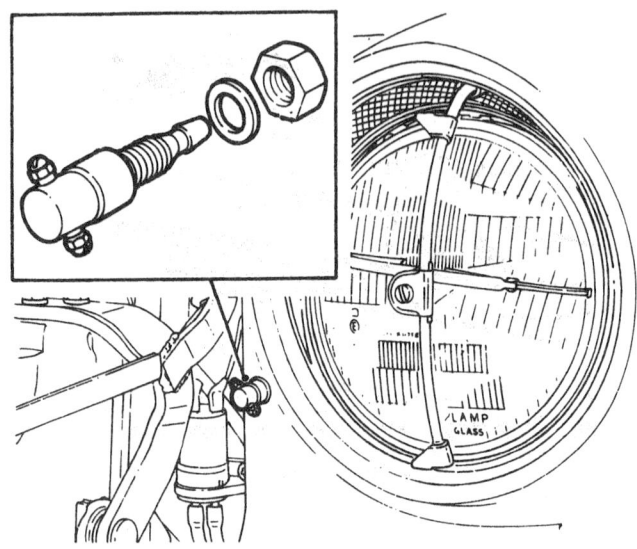

Fig. 13.88 Headlamp washer jet (Sec 18)

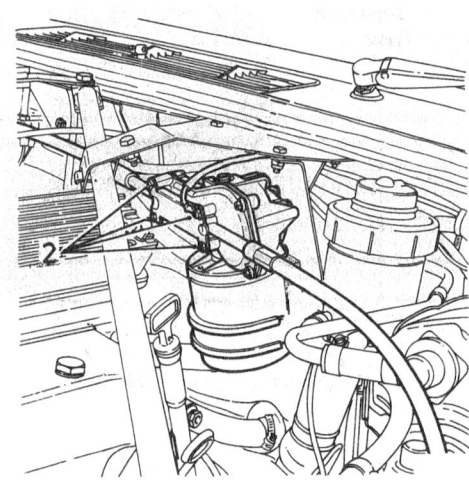

Fig. 13.89 Headlamp wiper motor – Series 2 (Sec 18)

2 *Rack cover plate screws*

43 Refit in the reverse order to removal, making sure that the O-ring
under the head of the screw is intact. Before tightening the screw
move the arm to the parked position (blades aligned with drive
tube), then tighten the central screw while holding the wiper arm in
position.

Wiper arms (Series 3)

44 Lift the cover and remove the securing nut from the base of the
wiper arm.
45 Pull the arm off its spindle and disconnect the washer tube from
it.
46 Refit in the reverse order to removal.

Wiper motors (Series 3)

47 Disconnect the battery earth lead.
48 Remove the wiper arm as just described. There is no need to
disconnect the washer tube unless the arm is to be renewed.
49 Remove the cable harness cover on the side concerned.
50 If removing the left-hand motor, release the tube from the
washer reservoir filler cap.
51 Unplug the cable connector and push the connector and the
tube through the grommets.

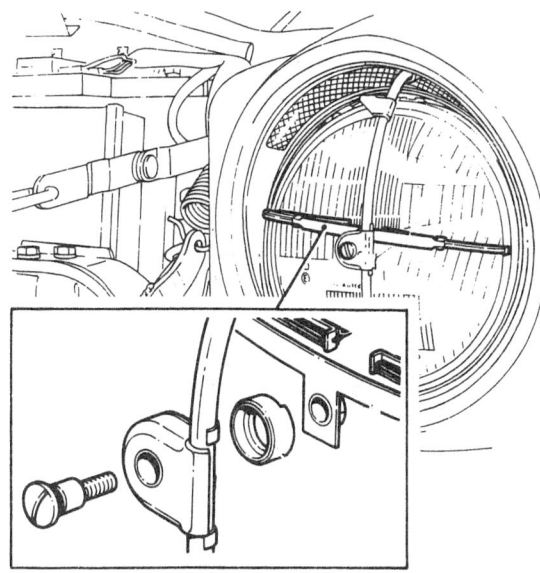

Fig. 13.90 Headlamp wiper arm fixing details – Series 2 (Sec 18)

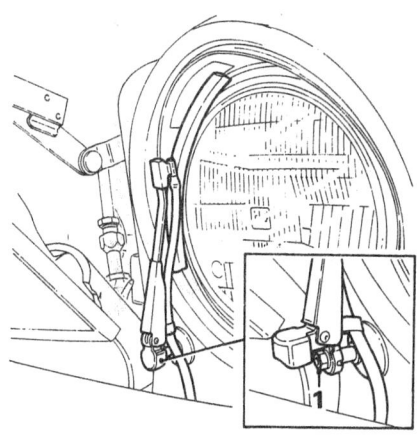

Fig. 13.91 Headlamp wiper arm fixing nut (1) – Series 3 (Sec 18)

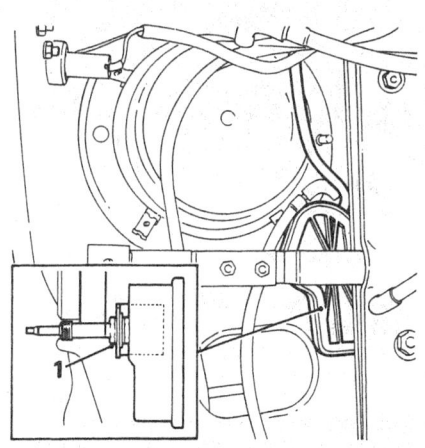

Fig. 13.92 Headlamp wiper motor securing nut (1) – Series 3 (Sec 18)

52 Turn the steering to full lock to improve access on the side in question. Remove the motor wiring harness clip.
53 If removing the left-hand motor, unbolt the washer pump and move it to one side.
54 Release the securing nut and withdraw the motor.
55 Refit in the reverse order to removal.

Headlamp wash/wipe control switch
56 Disconnect the battery earth lead.
57 Remove the three screws which secure the centre console top panel.
58 Raise the panel, disconnect the leads from the switch and remove the switch.
59 Refit in the reverse order to removal. Refer to Fig. 13.93 for the correct switch connections.

Windscreen wiper relay/delay unit
60 On models so equipped, the windscreen wiper relay and delay unit are plugged into a board located under the passenger side dash casing.
61 After removing the dash casing, the relay or delay unit can be unplugged from its socket for renewal.

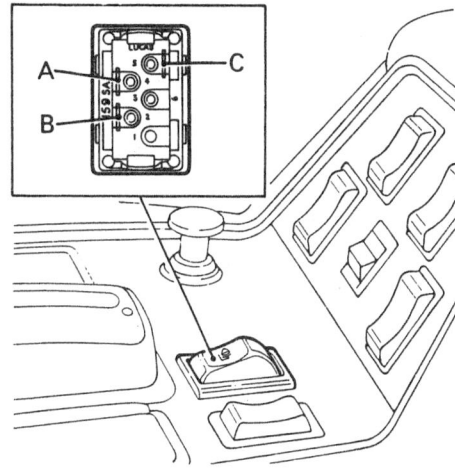

Fig. 13.93 Headlamp wash/wipe control switch – Series 2 (Sec 18)

A   Green/red   B   Green   C   Green/brown

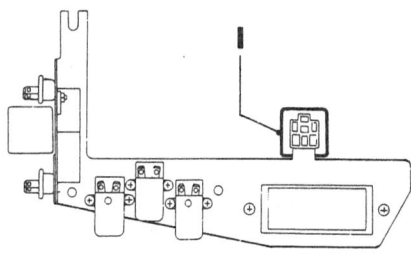

Fig. 13.94 Windscreen wiper delay unit (1) on relay board (Sec 18)

19 Electrical system – miscellaneous

Sliding roof electric motor – removal and refitting
1   Disconnect the battery earth lead.
2   Remove the rear seat cushion and squab.
3   Remove the trim from inside the boot.
4   Remove the nuts which secure the clamping plate.
5   Remove the nuts which secure the motor bracket.

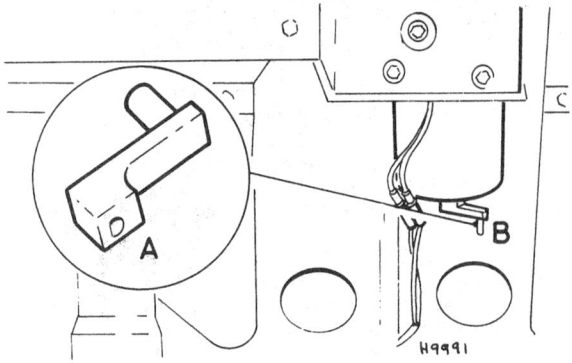

Fig. 13.95 Sliding roof handcrank (A) (Sec 19)

B   Handcrank fitted to motor

6   Disconnect the electrical leads and remove the motor. It can be separated from the bracket after removal.
7   Refit in the reverse order to removal.

Note: *A handcrank is provided for manual operation of the sunroof motor in the event of electrical failure.*

Driver's seat electric motor – removal and refitting
8   Disconnect the battery earth lead.
9   Remove the driver's seat cushion.
10 Disconnect the electrical lead beneath the cushion.
11 Remove the driver's seat (see Section 22).
12 Unbolt the rise and fall mechanism from the car floor.
13 Mark the position of the motor relative to the rest of the mechanism, then unbolt and remove the motor.
14 Refit in the reverse order to removal.

Electrically-operated radio aerial – removal and refitting
15 Disconnect the battery earth lead.
16 Empty the boot to gain access to the spare wheel well. Remove the fuel pump cover and the right-hand side trim.
17 Remove the rear lamp unit on the right-hand side.
18 Disconnect the aerial lead from the extension lead.
19 Slacken the knurled nut at the top of the aerial shaft.
20 Remove the steady bracket from the aerial shaft.
21 Remove the domed nut from the top side of the shaft.
22 Pull the aerial down into the wing. Recover the distance piece and toothed segments.
23 Remove the drive shroud from the rear of the boot.
24 Disconnect the wires from the aerial motor.
25 Unbolt the motor mounting bracket at the top. Tilt the motor and bracket away from the boot wall, pull off the drain tube and separate the motor from the bracket.
26 Withdraw the motor from the boot, guiding the drive components and the aerial itself through the body.
27 Refit in the reverse order to removal.

Electrically-operated door mirrors – general
28 Door mirrors which are electrically adjusted, and which incorporate a heater element for defrosting purposes, are fitted to some later models.
29 Refer to Section 22 of this Supplement for details of removal and refitting.
30 Both door mirrors are controlled by the driver.

Fuses (Series 3) – location and function
31 The main fuse box on Series 3 models is located below the instrument panel on the driver's side; the auxiliary fuse box is located in a similar position on the passenger side. Access to either box is obtained by turning the knurled knob to open the cover.
32 An under-bonnet fuse box, located on the left-hand side of the engine bay, contains fuses which protect the headlamps and (where applicable) the electric cooling fan(s) (photo).
33 In-line fuses, in the luggage area and elsewhere, protect components such as the electric aerial and the radio (photo). Refer

to the Specifications and to the appropriate wiring diagram for details.
34 The rating of the fuse which protects twin cooling fans has been increased to 12 amp continuous/25 amp blow. If problems are experienced with lower rated fuses blowing, fit the higher rated fuse.

Hazard warning flasher (Series 3) – removal and refitting
35 Disconnect the battery earth lead.
36 Remove the right-hand side dash casing.
37 The flasher/relay board is now accessible. As will be seen,

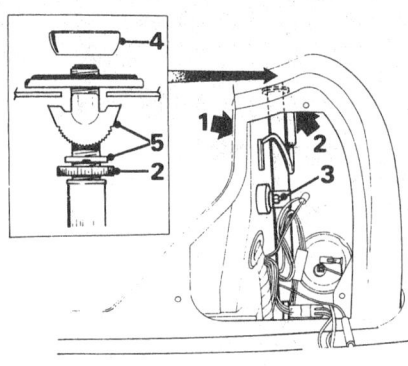

Fig. 13.96 Radio aerial fixing components (Sec 19)

1 Extension lead	4 Domed nut
2 Knurled nut	5 Distance piece and segment
3 Steady bracket	

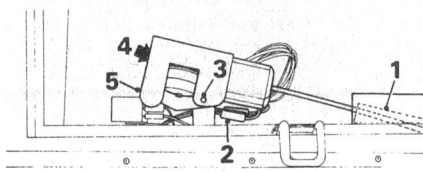

Fig. 13.97 Radio aerial drive components (Sec 19)

1 Drive cover	4 Drain tube
2 Connector	5 Bracket
3 Bracket bolt	

19.32 Under-bonnet fuse box

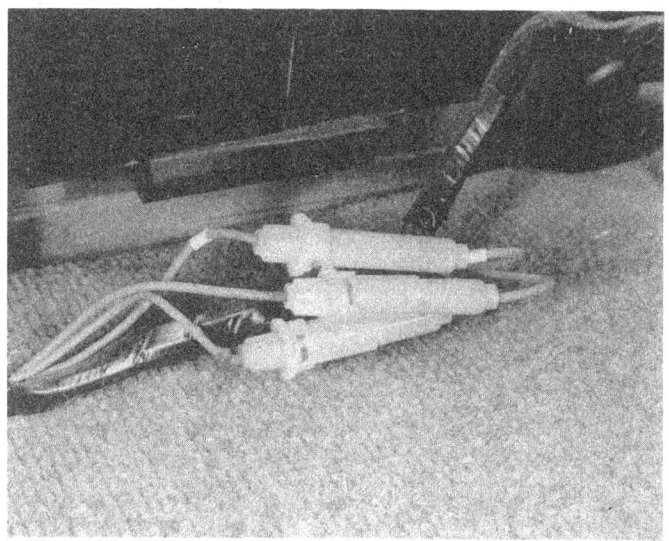

19.33 In-line fuses in luggage compartment

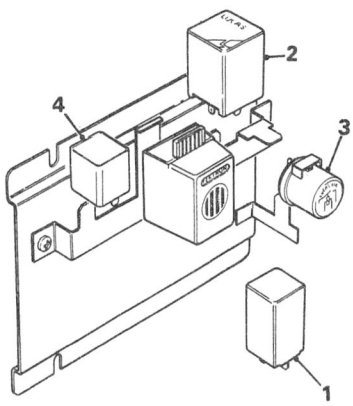

Fig. 13.98 Flasher/relay board – Series 3 (Sec 19)

1   Direction indicator flasher   3   Ignition load relay
2   Heated rear window relay   4   Hazard warning flasher

besides the hazard warning flasher it also carries other relays (Fig. 13.98).
38 The flasher unit can now be released from its bracket and unplugged from its socket.
39 Refit in the reverse order to removal.

Radio retaining panel (Series 3)

40 For security reasons, the panel which retains the factory-fitted radio is riveted in place on most Series 3 models.
41 If it is wished to remove the radio, the rivets must be drilled out and self-tapping screws used on reassembly, refer to paragraph 83 of this Section.

Trailer socket wiring (Series 3)

42 If it is wished to connect a socket for trailer lighting and signalling, it is important that the auxiliary harness provided by the makers be used. Attempts to connect the socket wiring directly to the rear lamp clusters may result in damage to the bulb failure indicator units.
43 The auxiliary wiring harness is accessible after removing the spare wheel and the fuel pump cover panel (fuel injection models). The wiring colour code is as follows.

Green/red	–	Left-hand indicator
Green/white	–	Right-hand indicator
Red/slate	–	Left-hand tail lamp
Red/orange	–	Right-hand tail lamp
Green/purple	–	Stop-lamps
Black	–	Earth

44 For other electrical connections (eg rear foglamps) and details of the latest regulations and standards relating to trailer lighting, consult an authorised dealer or other specialist.

Trip computer – general

45 Fitted to certain 1983 and later models, the trip computer receives information relating to fuel consumption and mileage covered. By storing this information and correlating it with elapsed time data, the computer can display information relating to average speed, average and instantaneous fuel consumption, and total fuel used. A digital clock display is also available.
46 This type of computer is relatively simple to understand and to operate. The speed information is derived from the electronic speedometer transducer. Fuel consumption information comes from the fuel injection ECU. Time measuring equipment is built in.
47 Reference to Fig. 13.99 will show that there are three separate

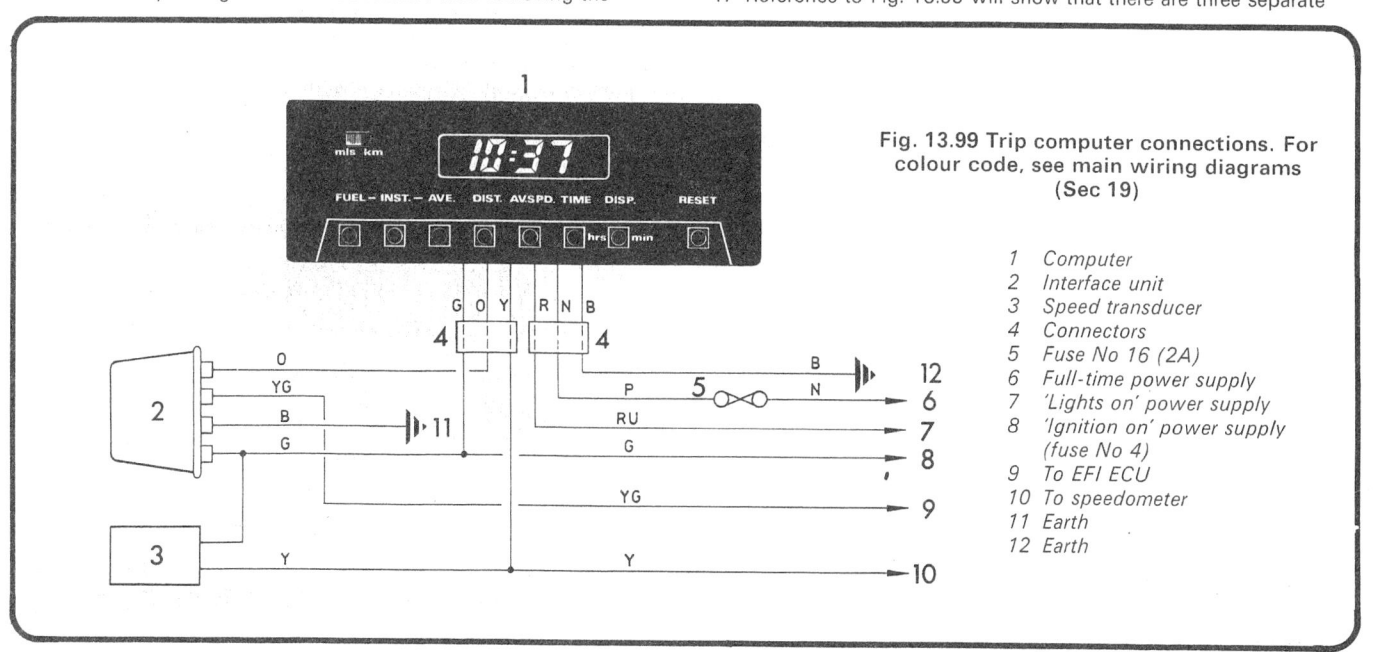

Fig. 13.99 Trip computer connections. For colour code, see main wiring diagrams (Sec 19)

1   Computer
2   Interface unit
3   Speed transducer
4   Connectors
5   Fuse No 16 (2A)
6   Full-time power supply
7   'Lights on' power supply
8   'Ignition on' power supply (fuse No 4)
9   To EFI ECU
10 To speedometer
11 Earth
12 Earth

power supplies to the computer. The full-time supply enables the clock and the memory to function continuously. The ignition-controlled supply energises the display and the control functions; the supply from the sidelights dims the display and illuminates the control legend strip.

48 No repair is possible in the event of computer malfunction. Assuming the wiring to be sound and all fuses intact, faults can be due to only three items:

(a) *Defective speedometer transducer (speedometer will also manfunction)*
(b) *Defective interface unit (fuel data will be inaccurate, speed/time data will be OK)*
(c) *Defective computer*

49 A defective ECU could be the cause of inaccurate fuel data displays, but other effects on the fuel injection system would make this obvious.

Cruise control system – description

50 This device is optionally available on Series 3 models. Its purpose is to maintain a set roadspeed with the foot released from the accelerator pedal. This is a most useful facility for long distance travel.
51 Immediate reversion to normal control is obtained once the brake pedal is operated. An inhibitor switch is incorporated to prevent the engine over-revving should the speed selector lever be moved to neutral whilst the cruise control system is in operation on automatic cars.
52 The main components of the system include the following:
Control switch
53 This controls system engagement and disengagement. Once actuated, the swtich can be moved to the 'resume' position to actuate the speed control unit memory, when the previously set roadspeed can be regained after an interruption due to braking or a temporary change of speed.
Magnetic pick-up
54 This is located on the rear axle next to the propeller shaft flange. It consists of a magnetic signal unit which indicates to the ECU the roadspeed calculated from the rotational speed of the flange.
55 On models with an electronic speedometer, the magnetic pick-up is not fitted; the ECU derives speed information from the speedometer transducer.
Set switch
56 This switch triggers the ECU to bring the cruise control system into operation.
Speed control unit
57 This is an electronic unit controlling the operation of the system. It operates solenoids which vary the vacuum used to open and close the throttle as necessary to maintain the pre-set roadspeed. 'Resume' and 'Off' modes are incorporated and the actuating vacuum is destroyed immediately the brake pedal is touched, causing the throttle to close. The control unit also includes a circuit to prevent actuation of the system below 20 mph (32 kph).

Luggage boot lid lock solenoid (Series 2) – removal and refitting

58 On Series 3 models, the luggage boot lid lock is incorporated in the central door locking system.
59 To remove the lock solenoid, disconnect the battery, open the boot and disconnect the solenoid multiplug connector (1) (Fig. 13.100).
60 Unbolt the solenoid and disconnect the earth lead.
61 Slacken the rear number plate lamp fixing nuts and withdraw the lamp until the lock operating rod and solenoid can be removed.
62 Refitting is a reversal of removal.

Central door locking system (1986 models)

63 The central door locking system on these later models incorporates a control module located in the driver's door.
64 The module is actuated through mechanical linkage from the door key or interior lock flap.
65 The luggage boot lid lock locks electrically but will only unlock using the boot lock key.
66 Access to the control module or lock motors is obtained by removing the door or boot lid trim panels. Remove the module or

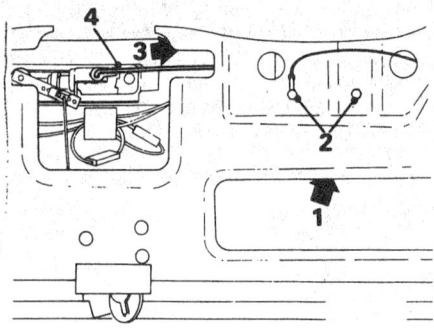

Fig. 13.100 Luggage boot lid lock solenoid attachments (Sec 19)

1 *Multi-pin connector*
2 *Solenoid fixing bolts and earth wire*
3 *Number plate fixing nuts*
4 *Lock operating rod*

motors by disconnecting the wiring and extracting the fixing screws. The door glass should be in the fully closed position.
67 When refitting the system components, carry out the following adjustment procedure.
Control module – adjustment
68 Remove the lower trim panel from the body 'A' post (windscreen pillar) on the driver's side.
69 Trace the door wiring harness multi-pin connector behind the panel. This connector has the orange/red and orange/green leads.
70 Disconnect the plug and connect a test lamp across the connector terminals on the door harness side.
71 Set the door latch to the closed position and the lock interior flap to locked.
72 Push the control module fully towards the lock assembly, then move the module very slowly away from the lock until the test lamp flashes momentarily. Tighten the module fixing screws.
73 Disconnect the test lamp, connect the multi-pin plug, refit the trim and operate the door exterior handle to release the latch.
74 Should it be necessary to connect an independent battery feed to the control module, make quite sure that the purple wire goes to the battery positive terminal and the black wire to the negative terminal.
Front passenger door lock motor – adjustment
75 Set the door latch in the closed position, then slide the lock motor towards the door lock face to eliminate all free movement. Tighten the motor fixing screws.
76 Operate the door exterior handle and close the door. Check the adjustment by operating the driver's door lock key.

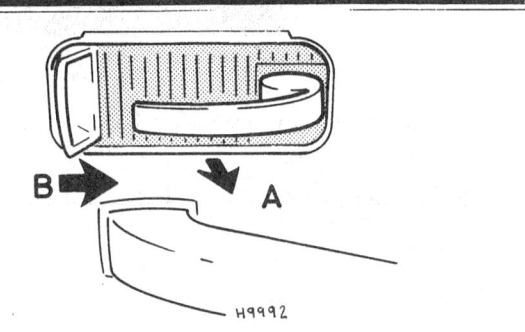

Fig. 13.101 Door interior lock handles (Sec 19)

A *Release handle*   B *Locking flap*

Rear door lock motor – adjustment

77 Set the door latch in the closed position.

78 Slide the lock motor away from the door locking edge to eliminate all free movement, then tighten the fixing screws.

79 Operate the door exterior handle to release the latch and close the door. Check the setting by operating the driver's door lock key.

Luggage boot lid lock motor – adjustment

80 Set the latch in the unlocked position.

81 Slide the lock motor towards the latch to eliminate all free movement, then tighten the fixing screws.

82 Close the lid and check the locking using the driver's door lock key.

Radio/cassette player (standard specification) – removal

83 Removal of the factory-fitted in-car entertainment equipment will vary according to the date of production of the vehicle, refer to paragraphs 40 and 41 of this Section.

84 On all models, the receiver/player is located in the upper part of the centre console.

85 On earlier models, pull off the radio control knobs, unscrew the retaining nuts and trim plate and withdraw the assembly. Disconnect the aerial, earth, power and speaker leads.

86 On later versions, inspect the front face of the radio. If there are two small holes visible at each side, two U-shaped removal tools will be required. These can be purchased or fabricated from two pieces of thin rod. Insert the tools, one into each pair of holes and depress the radio retaining springs, then withdraw the unit.

87 Some radio/cassette players incorporate two vertical slots instead of the holes, in which case insert two thin blades to depress the retaining springs.

88 The speakers are mounted in the front doors and the rear parcels shelf.

89 The aerial is power-operated and mounted on top of the right-hand rear wing.

90 After-market radio equipment may be installed as generally described in the following paragraphs. Apart from very early models, all cars have factory-fitted suppression devices for the ignition system, charging circuit and all other equipment which may cause interference whether in-car entertainment is standard specification or not.

20 Mobile radio equipment – interference-free installation

Aerials – selection and fitting

The choice of aerials is now very wide. It should be realised that the quality has a profound effect on radio performance, and a poor, inefficient aerial can make suppression difficult.

A wing-mounted aerial is regarded as probably the most efficient for signal collection, but a roof aerial is usually better for suppression purposes because it is away from most interference fields. Stick-on wire aerials are available for attachment to the inside of the windscreen, but are not always free from the interference field of the engine and some accessories.

Motorised automatic aerials rise when the equipment is switched on and retract at switch-off. They require more fitting space and supply leads, and can be a source of trouble.

There is no merit in choosing a very long aerial as, for example, the type about three metres in length which hooks or clips on to the rear of the car, since part of this aerial will inevitably be located in an interference field. For VHF/FM radios the best length of aerial is about one metre. Active aerials have a transistor amplifier mounted at the base and this serves to boost the received signal. The aerial rod is sometimes rather shorter than normal passive types.

A large loss of signal can occur in the aerial feeder cable, especially over the Very High Frequency (VHF) bands. The design of feeder cable is invariably in the co-axial form, ie a centre conductor surrounded by a flexible copper braid forming the outer (earth) conductor. Between the inner and outer conductors is an insulator material which can be in solid or stranded form. Apart from insulation, its purpose is to maintain the correct spacing and concentricity. Loss of signal occurs in this insulator, the loss usually being greater in a poor quality cable. The quality of cable used is reflected in the price of the aerial with the attached feeder cable.

The capacitance of the feeder should be within the range 65 to 75 picofarads (pF) approximately (95 to 100 pF for Japanese and American equipment), otherwise the adjustment of the car radio aerial trimmer may not be possible. An extension cable is necessary for a long run between aerial and receiver. If this adds capacitance in excess of the above limits, a connector containing a series capacitor will be required, or an extension which is labelled as 'capacity-compensated'.

Fitting the aerial will normally involve making a $7/8$ in (22 mm) diameter hole in the bodywork, but read the instructions that come with the aerial kit. Once the hole position has been selected, use a centre punch to guide the drill. Use sticky masking tape around the area for this helps with marking out and drill location, and gives protection to the paintwork should the drill slip. Three methods of making the hole are in use:

(a) Use a hole saw in the electric drill. This is, in effect, a circular hacksaw blade wrapped round a former with a centre pilot drill.

(b) Use a tank cutter which also has cutting teeth, but is made to shear the metal by tightening with an Allen key.

(c) The hard way of drilling out the circle is using a small drill, say $1/8$ in (3 mm), so that the holes overlap. The centre metal drops out and the hole is finished with round and half-round files.

Whichever method is used, the burr is removed from the body metal and paint removed from the underside. The aerial is fitted tightly ensuring that the earth fixing, usually a serrated washer, ring or clamp, is making a solid connection. *This earth connection is important in reducing interference.* Cover any bare metal with primer paint and topcoat, and follow by underseal if desired.

Aerial feeder cable routing should avoid the engine compartment and areas where stress might occur, eg under the carpet where feet will be located. Roof aerials require that the headlining be pulled back and that a path is available down the door pillar. It is wise to check with the vehicle dealer whether roof aerial fitting is recommended.

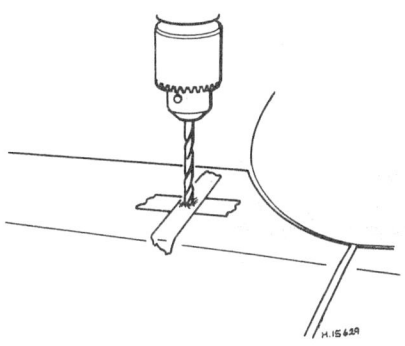

Fig. 13.102 Drilling the bodywork for aerial mounting

Loudspeakers

Speakers should be matched to the output stage of the equipment, particularly as regards the recommended impedance. Power transistors used for driving speakers are sensitive to the loading placed on them.

Before choosing a mounting position for speakers, check whether the vehicle manufacturer has provided a location for them. Generally door-mounted speakers give good stereophonic reproduction, but not all doors are able to accept them. The next best position is the rear parcel shelf, and in this case speaker apertures can be cut into the shelf, or pod units may be mounted.

For door mounting, first remove the trim, which is often held on by 'poppers' or press studs, and then select a suitable gap in the inside door assembly. Check that the speaker would not obstruct glass or winder mechanism by winding the window up and down. A template is often provided for marking out the trim panel hole, and then the four fixing holes must be drilled through. Mark out with chalk and cut cleanly with a sharp knife or keyhole saw.

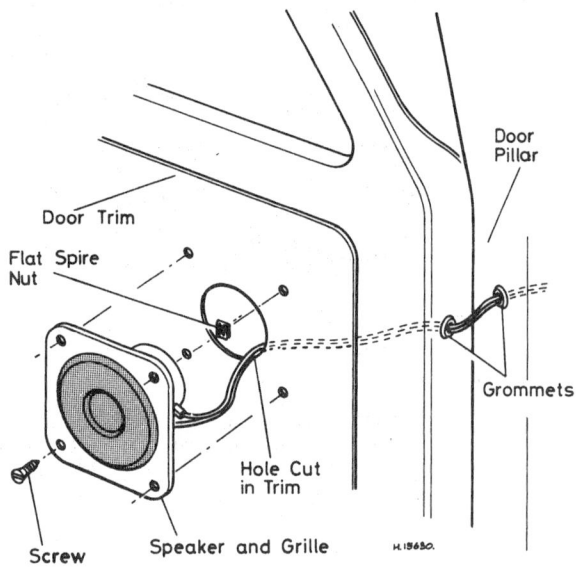

Fig. 13.103 Door-mounted speaker installation

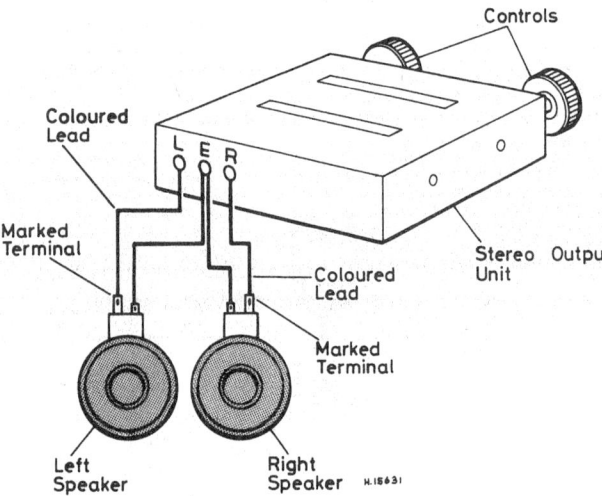

Fig. 13.104 Speaker connections must be correctly made as shown

Speaker leads are then threaded through the door and door pillar, if necessary drilling 10 mm diameter holes. Fit grommets in the holes and connect to the radio or tape unit correctly. Do not omit a waterproofing cover, usually supplied with door speakers. If the speaker has to be fixed into the metal of the door itself, use self-tapping screws, and if the fixing is to the door trim use self-tapping screws and flat spire nuts.

Rear shelf mounting is somewhat simpler but it is necessary to find gaps in the metalwork underneath the parcel shelf. However, remember that the speakers should be as far apart as possible to give a good stereo effect. Pod-mounted speakers can be screwed into position through the parcel shelf material, but it is worth testing for the best position. Sometimes good results are found by reflecting sound off the rear window.

Unit installation

Many vehicles have a dash panel aperture to take a radio/audio unit, a recognised international standard being 189.5 mm x 60 mm. Alternatively a console may be a feature of the car interior design and this, mounted below the dashboard, gives more room. If neither facility is available a unit may be mounted on the underside of the

parcel shelf; these are frequently non-metallic and an earth wire from the case to a good earth point is necessary. A three-sided cover in the form of a cradle is obtainable from car radio dealers and this gives a professional appearance to the installation; in this case choose a position where the controls can be reached by a driver with his seat belt on.

Installation of the radio/audio unit is basically the same in all cases, and consists of offering it into the aperture after removal of the knobs (not push buttons) and the trim plate. In some cases a special mounting plate is required to which the unit is attached. It is worthwhile supporting the rear end in cases where sag or strain may occur, and it is usually possible to use a length of perforated metal strip attached between the unit and a good support point nearby. In general it is recommended that tape equipment should be installed at or nearly horizontal.

Connections to the aerial socket are simply by the standard plug terminating the aerial downlead or its extension cable. Speakers for a stereo system must be matched and correctly connected, as outlined previously.

Note: *While all work is carried out on the power side, it is wise to disconnect the battery earth lead.* Before connection is made to the vehicle electrical system, check that the polarity of the unit is correct. Most vehicles use a negative earth system, but radio/audio units often have a reversible plug to convert the set to either + or − earth. *Incorrect connection may cause serious damage.*

The power lead is often permanently connected inside the unit and terminates with one half of an in-line fuse carrier. The other half is fitted with a suitable fuse (3 or 5 amperes) and a wire which should go to a power point in the electrical system. This may be the accessory terminal on the ignition switch, giving the advantage of power feed with ignition or with the ignition key at the 'accessory' position. Power to the unit stops when the ignition key is removed. Alternatively, the lead may be taken to a live point at the fusebox with the consequence of having to remember to switch off at the unit before leaving the vehicle.

Before switching on for initial test, be sure that the speaker connections have been made, for running without load can damage the output transistors. Switch on next and tune through the bands to ensure that all sections are working, and check the tape unit if applicable. The aerial trimmer should be adjusted to give the

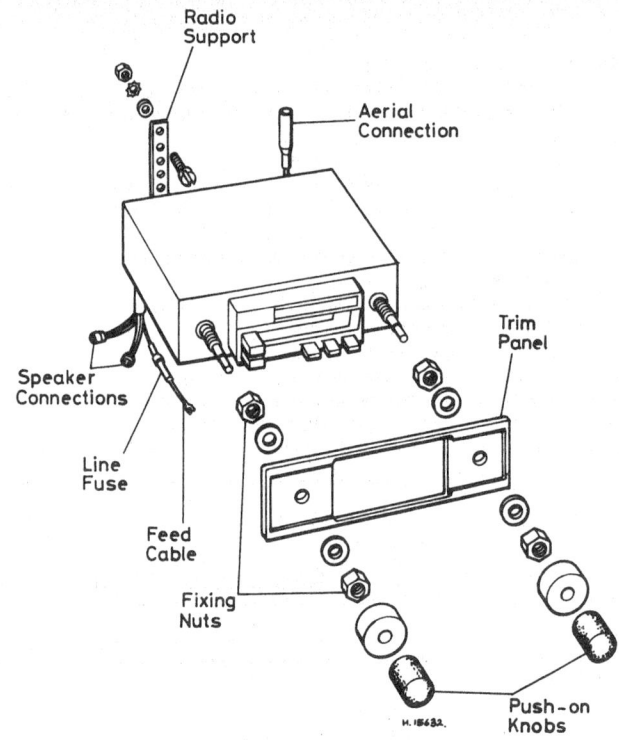

Fig. 13.105 Mounting component details for radio/cassette unit

strongest reception on a weak signal in the medium wave band, at say 200 metres.

Interference

In general, when electric current changes abruptly, unwanted electrical noise is produced. The motor vehicle is filled with electrical devices which change electric current rapidly, the most obvious being the contact breaker.

When the spark plugs operate, the sudden pulse of spark current causes the associated wiring to radiate. Since early radio transmitters used sparks as a basis of operation, it is not surprising that the car radio will pick up ignition spark noise unless steps are taken to reduce it to acceptable levels.

Interference reaches the car radio in two ways:

(a) by conduction through the wiring.
(b) by radiation to the receiving aerial.

Initial checks presuppose that the bonnet is down and fastened, the radio unit has a good earth connection (*not* through the aerial downlead outer), no fluorescent tubes are working near the car, the aerial trimmer has been adjusted, and the vehicle is in a position to receive radio signals, ie not in a metal-clad building.

Switch on the radio and tune it to the middle of the medium wave (MW) band off-station with the volume (gain) control set fairly high. Switch on the ignition (but do not start the engine) and wait to see if irregular clicks or hash noise occurs. Tapping the facia panel may also produce the effects. If so, this will be due to the voltage stabiliser, which is an on-off thermal switch to control instrument voltage. It is located usually on the back of the instrument panel, often attached to the speedometer. Correction is by attachment of a capacitor and, if still troublesome, chokes in the supply wires.

Switch on the engine and listen for interference on the MW band. Depending on the type of interference, the indications are as follows.

A harsh crackle that drops out abruptly at low engine speed or when the headlights are switched on is probably due to a voltage regulator.

A whine varying with engine speed is due to the dynamo or alternator. Try temporarily taking off the fan belt – if the noise goes this is confirmation.

Regular ticking or crackle that varies in rate with the engine speed is due to the ignition system. With this trouble in particular and others in general, check to see if the noise is entering the receiver from the wiring or by radiation. To do this, pull out the aerial plug, (preferably shorting out the input socket or connecting a 62 pF capacitor across it). If the noise disappears it is coming in through the aerial and is *radiation noise.* If the noise persists it is reaching the receiver through the wiring and is said to be *line-borne.*

Interference from wipers, washers, heater blowers, turn-indicators, stop lamps, etc is usually taken to the receiver by wiring, and simple treatment using capacitors and possibly chokes will solve the problem. Switch on each one in turn (wet the screen first for running wipers!) and listen for possible interference with the aerial plug in place and again when removed.

Electric petrol pumps are now finding application again and give rise to an irregular clicking, often giving a burst of clicks when the ignition is on but the engine has not yet been started. It is also possible to receive whining or crackling from the pump.

Note that if most of the vehicle accessories are found to be

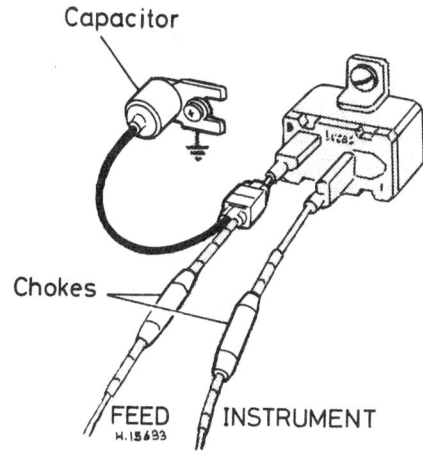

Fig. 13.106 Voltage stabiliser interference suppression

creating interference all together, the probability is that poor aerial earthing is to blame.

Component terminal markings

Throughout the following sub-sections reference will be found to various terminal markings. These will vary depending on the manufacturer of the relevant component. If terminal markings differ from those mentioned, reference should be made to the following table, where the most commonly encountered variations are listed.

Alternator	Alternator terminal (thick lead)	Exciting winding terminal
DIN/Bosch	B+	DF
Delco Remy	+	EXC
Ducellier	+	EXC
Ford (US)	+	DF
Lucas	+	F
Marelli	+B	F

Ignition coil	Ignition switch terminal	Contact breaker terminal
DIN/Bosch	15	1
Delco Remy	+	–
Ducellier	BAT	RUP
Ford (US)	B/+	CB/–
Lucas	SW/+	–
Marelli	BAT/+B	D

Voltage regulator	Voltage input terminal	Exciting winding terminal
DIN/Bosch	B+/D+	DF
Delco Remy	BAT/+	EXC
Ducellier	BOB/BAT	EXC
Ford (US)	BAT	DF
Lucas	+/A	F
Marelli		F

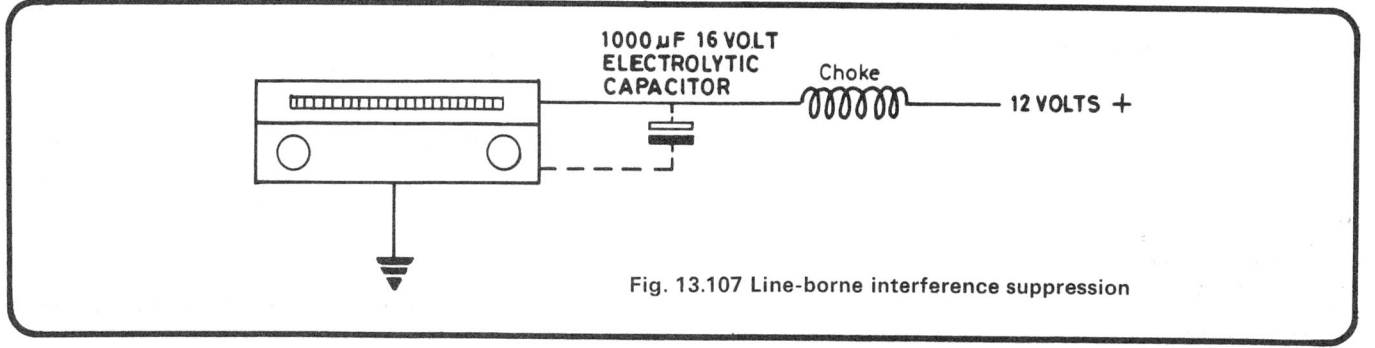

1000 µF 16 VOLT ELECTROLYTIC CAPACITOR

Choke

12 VOLTS +

Fig. 13.107 Line-borne interference suppression

Suppression methods – ignition

Suppressed HT cables are supplied as original equipment by manufacturers and will meet regulations as far as interference to neighbouring equipment is concerned. It is illegal to remove such suppression unless an alternative is provided, and this may take the form of resistive spark plug caps in conjunction with plain copper HT cable. For VHF purposes, these and 'in-line' resistors may not be effective, and resistive HT cable is preferred. Check that suppressed cables are actually fitted by observing cable identity lettering, or measuring with an ohmmeter – the value of each plug lead should be 5000 to 10 000 ohms.

A 1 microfarad capacitor connected from the LT supply side of the ignition coil to a good nearby earth point will complete basic ignition interference treatment. *NEVER fit a capacitor to the coil terminal to the contact breaker – the result would be burnt out points in a short time (mechanical breaker ignition).*

If ignition noise persists despite the treatment above, the following sequence should be followed:

(a) Check the earthing of the ignition coil; remove paint from fixing clamp.
(b) If this does not work, lift the bonnet. Should there be no change in interference level, this may indicate that the bonnet is not electrically connected to the car body. Use a proprietary braided strap across a bonnet hinge ensuring a first class electrical connection. If, however, lifting the bonnet increases the interference, then fit resistive HT cables of a higher ohms-per-metre value.
(c) If all these measures fail, it is probable that re-radiation from metallic components is taking place. Using a braided strap between metallic points, go round the vehicle systematically – try the following: engine to body, exhaust system to body, front suspension to engine and to body, steering column to body (especially French and Italian cars), gear lever to engine and to body (again especially French and Italian cars), Bowden cable to body, metal ...el shelf to body. When an offending component is ...ed it should be bonded with the strap permanently. ... next step, the fitting of distributor suppressors to each ... t the distributor end may help.
(e) Beyond this point is involved the possible screening of the distributor and fitting resistive spark plugs, but such advanced treatment is not usually required for vehicles with entertainment equipment.

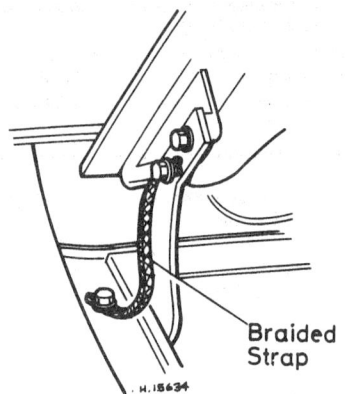

Fig. 13.108 Braided earth strap between bonnet and body

Electronic ignition systems have built-in suppression components, but this does not relieve the need for using suppressed HT leads. In some cases it is permitted to connect a capacitor on the low tension supply side of the ignition coil, but not in every case. Makers' instructions should be followed carefully, otherwise damage to the ignition semiconductors may result.

Suppression methods – generators

Alternators should be fitted with a 3 microfarad capacitor from the B+ main output terminal (thick cable) to earth. Additional suppression may be obtained by the use of a filter in the supply line to the radio receiver.

It is most important that:

(a) *Capacitors are never connected to the field terminals of an alternator.*
(b) *Alternators must not be run without connection to the battery.*

Suppression methods – voltage regulators

Voltage regulators used with DC dynamos should be suppressed by connecting a 1 microfarad capacitor from the control box D terminal to earth.

Alternator regulators come in three types:

(a) *Vibrating contact regulators separate from the alternator. Used extensively on continental vehicles.*
(b) *Electronic regulators separate from the alternator.*
(c) *Electronic regulators built-in to the alternator.*

In case (a) interference may be generated on the AM and FM (VHF) bands. For some cars a replacement suppressed regulator is available. Filter boxes may be used with non-suppressed regulators. But if not available, then for AM equipment a 2 microfarad or 3 microfarad capacitor may be mounted at the voltage terminal marked D+ or B+ of the regulator. FM bands may be treated by a feed-through capacitor of 2 or 3 microfarad.

Electronic voltage regulators are not always troublesome, but where necessary, a 1 microfarad capacitor from the regulator + terminal will help.

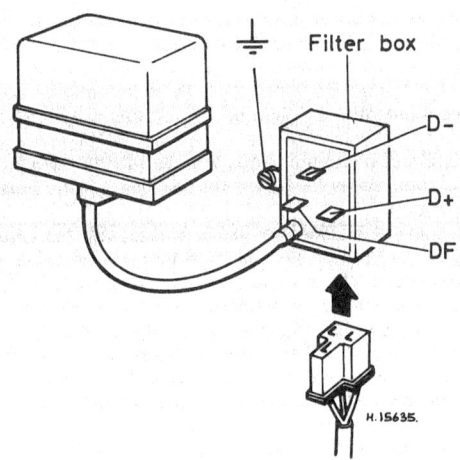

Fig. 13.109 Typical filter box for vibrating contact voltage regulator (alternator equipment)

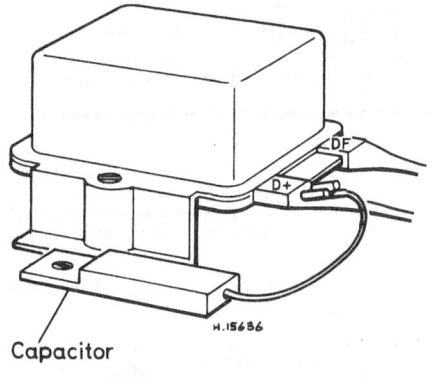

Fig. 13.110 Suppression of AM interference by vibrating contact voltage regulator (alternator equipment)

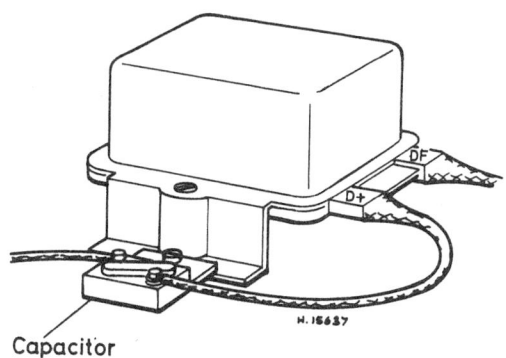

Fig. 13.111 Suppression of FM interference by vibrating contact voltage regulator (alternator equipment)

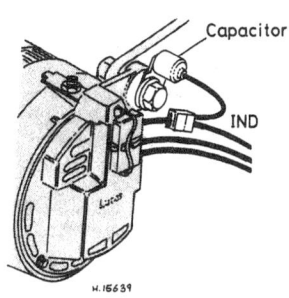

Fig. 13.113 Suppression of interference from electronic voltage regulator when integral with alternator

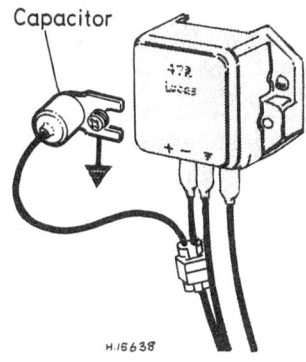

Fig. 13.112 Electronic voltage regulator suppression

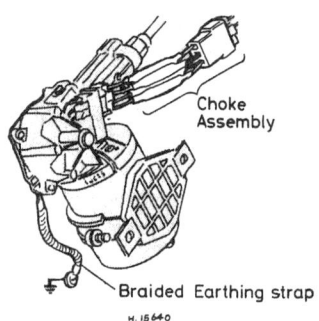

Fig. 13.114 Wiper motor suppression

Integral electronic voltage regulators do not normally generate much interference, but when encountered this is in combination with alternator noise. A 1 microfarad or 2 microfarad capacitor from the warning lamp (IND) terminal to earth for Lucas ACR alternators and Femsa, Delco and Bosch equivalents should cure the problem.

Suppression methods – other equipment

Wiper motors – Connect the wiper body to earth with a bonding strap. For all motors use a 7 ampere choke assembly inserted in the leads to the motor.

Heater motors – Fit 7 ampere line chokes in both leads, assisted if necessary by a 1 microfarad capacitor to earth from both leads.

Electronic tachometer – The tachometer is a possible source of ignition noise – check by disconnecting at the ignition coil CB terminal. It usually feeds from ignition coil LT pulses at the contact breaker terminal. A 3 ampere line choke should be fitted in the tachometer lead at the coil CB terminal.

Horn – A capacitor and choke combination is effective if the horn is directly connected to the 12 volt supply. The use of a relay is an alternative remedy, as this will reduce the length of the interference-carrying leads.

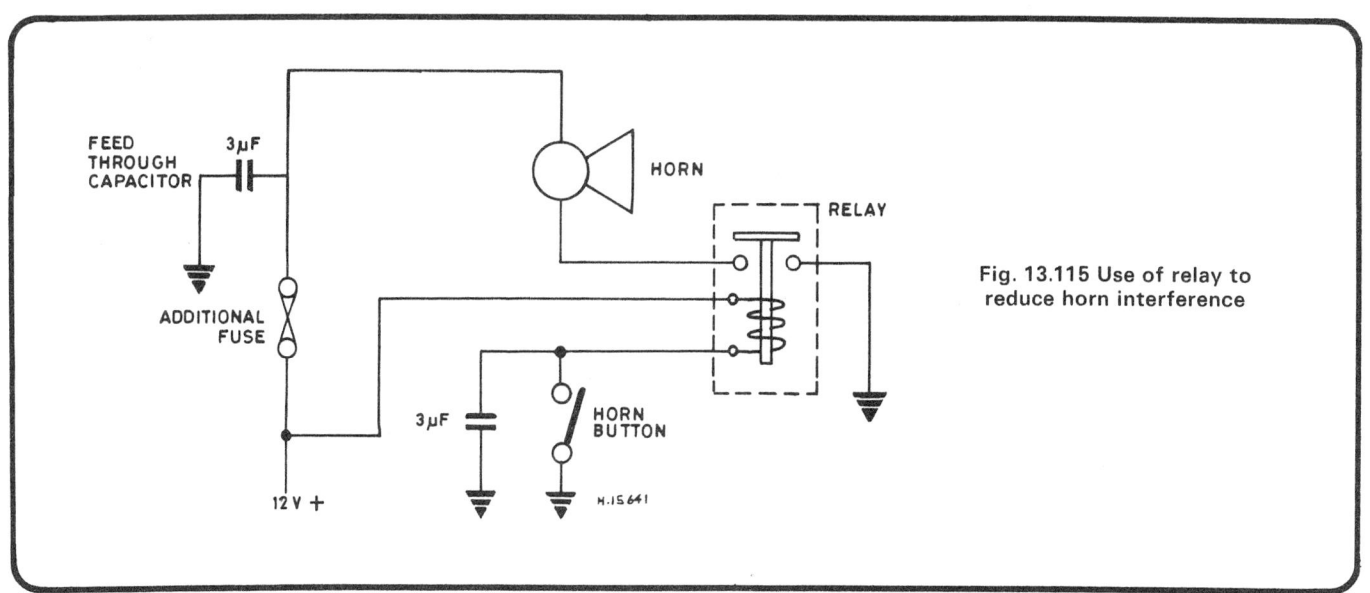

Fig. 13.115 Use of relay to reduce horn interference

Electrostatic noise – Characteristics are erratic crackling at the receiver, with disappearance of symptoms in wet weather. Often shocks may be given when touching bodywork. Part of the problem is the build-up of static electricity in non-driven wheels and the acquisition of charge on the body shell. It is possible to fit spring-loaded contacts at the wheels to give good conduction between the rotary wheel parts and the vehicle frame. Changing a tyre sometimes helps – because of tyres' varying resistances. In difficult cases a trailing flex which touches the ground will cure the problem. If this is not acceptable it is worth trying conductive paint on the tyre walls.

Fuel pump – Suppression requires a 1 microfarad capacitor between the supply wire to the pump and a nearby earth point. If this is insufficient a 7 ampere line choke connected in the supply wire near the pump is required.

Fluorescent tubes – Vehicles used for camping/caravanning frequently have fluorescent tube lighting. These tubes require a relatively high voltage for operation and this is provided by an inverter (a form of oscillator) which steps up the vehicle supply voltage. This can give rise to serious interference to radio reception, and the tubes themselves can contribute to this interference by the pulsating nature of the lamp discharge. In such situations it is important to mount the aerial as far away from a fluorescent tube as possible. The interference problem may be alleviated by screening the tube with fine wire turns spaced an inch (25 mm) apart and earthed to the chassis. Suitable chokes should be fitted in both supply wires close to the inverter.

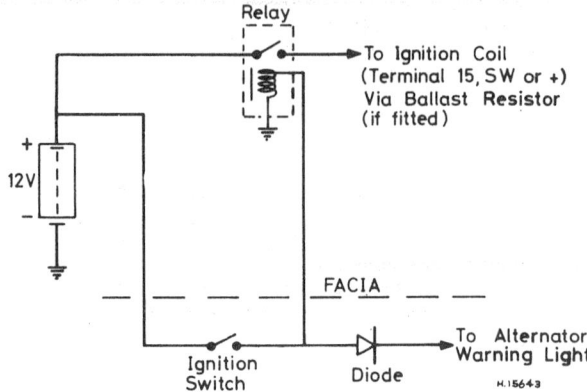

Fig. 13.117 Use of ignition coil relay to suppress case breakthrough

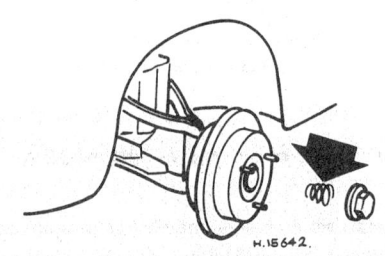

Fig. 13.116 Use of spring contacts at wheels

Radio/cassette case breakthrough

Magnetic radiation from dashboard wiring may be sufficiently intense to break through the metal case of the radio/cassette player. Often this is due to a particular cable routed too close and shows up as ignition interference on AM and cassette play and/or alternator whine on cassette play.

The first point to check is that the clips and/or screws are fixing all parts of the radio/cassette case together properly. Assuming good earthing of the case, see if it is possible to re-route the offending cable – the chances of this are not good, however, in most cars.

Next release the radio/cassette player and locate it in different positions with temporary leads. If a point of low interference is found, then if possible fix the equipment in that area. This also confirms that local radiation is causing the trouble. If re-location is not feasible, fit the radio/cassette player back in the original position.

Alternator interference on cassette play is now caused by radiation from the main charging cable which goes from the battery to the output terminal of the alternator, usually via the + terminal of the starter motor relay. In some vehicles this cable is routed under the dashboard, so the solution is to provide a direct cable route. Detach the original cable from the alternator output terminal and make up a new cable of at least 6 mm² cross-sectional area to go from alternator to battery by the shortest possible route. *Remember – do not run the engine with the alternator disconnected from the battery.*

Ignition breakthrough on AM and/or cassette play can be a difficult problem. It is worth wrapping earthed foil round the offending cable run near the equipment, or making up a deflector plate well screwed down to a good earth. Another possibility is the use of a suitable relay to switch on the ignition coil. The relay should be mounted close to the ignition coil; with this arrangement the ignition coil primary current is not taken into the dashboard area and does not flow through the ignition switch. A suitable diode should be used since it is possible that at ignition switch-off the output from the warning lamp alternator terminal could hold the relay on.

Connectors for suppression components

Capacitors are usually supplied with tags on the end of the lead, while the capacitor body has a flange with a slot or hole to fit under a nut or screw with washer.

Connections to feed wires are best achieved by self-stripping connectors. These connectors employ a blade which, when squeezed down by pliers, cuts through cable insulation and makes connection to the copper conductors beneath.

Chokes sometimes come with bullet snap-in connectors fitted to the wires, and also with just bare copper wire. With connectors, suitable female cable connectors may be purchased from an auto-accessory shop together with any extra connectors required for the cable ends after being cut for the choke insertion. For chokes with bare wires, similar connectors may be employed together with insulation sleeving as required.

VHF/FM broadcasts

Reception of VHF/FM in an automobile is more prone to problems than the medium and long wavebands. Medium/long wave transmitters are capable of covering considerable distances, but VHF transmitters are restricted to line of sight, meaning ranges of 10 to 50 miles, depending upon the terrain, the effects of buildings and the transmitter power.

Because of the limited range it is necessary to retune on a long journey, and it may be better for those habitually travelling long distances or living in areas of poor provision of transmitters to use an AM radio working on medium/long wavebands.

When conditions are poor, interference can arise, and some of the suppression devices described previously fall off in performance at very high frequencies unless specifically designed for the VHF band. Available suppression devices include reactive HT cable, resistive distributor caps, screened plug caps, screened leads and resistive spark plugs.

For VHF/FM receiver installation the following points should be particularly noted:

(a) Earthing of the receiver chassis and the aerial mounting is important. Use a separate earthing wire at the radio, and scrape paint away at the aerial mounting.

(b) If possible, use a good quality roof aerial to obtain maximum height and distance from interference generating devices on the vehicle.

(c) Use of a high quality aerial download is important, since losses in cheap cable can be significant.

(d) The polarisation of FM transmissions may be horizontal, vertical, circular or slanted. Because of this the optimum mounting angle is at 45° to the vehicle roof.

Citizens' Band radio (CB)

In the UK, CB transmitter/receivers work within the 27 MHz and 934 MHz bands, using the FM mode. At present interest is concentrated on 27 MHz where the design and manufacture of equipment is less difficult. Maximum transmitted power is 4 watts, and 40 channels spaced 10 kHz apart within the range 27.60125 to 27.99125 MHz are available.

Aerials are the key to effective transmission and reception. Regulations limit the aerial length to 1.65 metres including the loading coil and any associated circuitry, so tuning the aerial is necessary to obtain optimum results. The choice of a CB aerial is dependent on whether it is to be permanently installed or removable, and the performance will hinge on correct tuning and the location point on the vehicle. Common practice is to clip the aerial to the roof gutter or to employ wing mounting where the aerial can be rapidly unscrewed. An alternative is to use the boot rim to render the aerial theftproof, but a popular solution is to use the 'magmount' – a type of mounting having a strong magnetic base clamping to the vehicle at any point, usually the roof.

Aerial location determines the signal distribution for both transmission and reception, but it is wise to choose a point away from the engine compartment to minimise interference from vehicle electrical equipment.

The aerial is subject to considerable wind and acceleration forces. Cheaper units will whip backwards and forwards and in so doing will alter the relationship with the metal surface of the vehicle with which it forms a ground plane aerial system. The radiation pattern will change correspondingly, giving rise to break-up of both incoming and outgoing signals.

Interference problems on the vehicle carrying CB equipment fall into two categories:

(a) Interference to nearby TV and radio receivers when transmitting.
(b) Interference to CB set reception due to electrical equipment on the vehicle.

Problems of break-through to TV and radio are not frequent, but can be difficult to solve. Mostly trouble is not detected or reported because the vehicle is moving and the symptoms rapidly disappear at the TV/radio receiver, but when the CB set is used as a base station any trouble with nearby receivers will soon result in a complaint.

It must not be assumed by the CB operator that his equipment is faultless, for much depends upon the design. Harmonics (that is, multiples) of 27 MHz may be transmitted unknowingly and these can fall into other user's bands. Where trouble of this nature occurs, low pass filters in the aerial or supply leads can help, and should be fitted in base station aerials as a matter of course. In stubborn cases it may be necessary to call for assistance from the licensing authority, or, if possible, to have the equipment checked by the manufacturers.

Interference received on the CB set from the vehicle equipment is, fortunately, not usually a severe problem. The precautions outlined previously for radio/cassette units apply, but there are some extra points worth noting.

It is common practice to use a slide-mount on CB equipment enabling the set to be easily removed for use as a base station, for example. Care must be taken that the slide mount fittings are properly earthed and that first class connection occurs between the set and slide-mount.

Vehicle manufacturers in the UK are required to provide suppression of electrical equipment to cover 40 to 250 MHz to protect TV and VHF radio bands. Such suppression appears to be adequately effective at 27 MHz, but suppression of individual items such as alternators/dynamos, clocks, stabilisers, flashers, wiper motors, etc, may still be necessary. The suppression capacitors and chokes available from auto-electrical suppliers for entertainment receivers will usually give the required results with CB equipment.

Other vehicle radio transmitters

Besides CB radio already mentioned, a considerable increase in the use of transceivers (ie combined transmitter and receiver units) has taken place in the last decade. Previously this type of equipment was fitted mainly to military, fire, ambulance and police vehicles, but a large business radio and radio telephone usage has developed.

Generally the suppression techniques described previously will suffice, with only a few difficult cases arising. Suppression is carried out to satisfy the 'receive mode', but care must be taken to use heavy duty chokes in the equipment supply cables since the loading on 'transmit' is relatively high.

Wiring diagrams overleaf

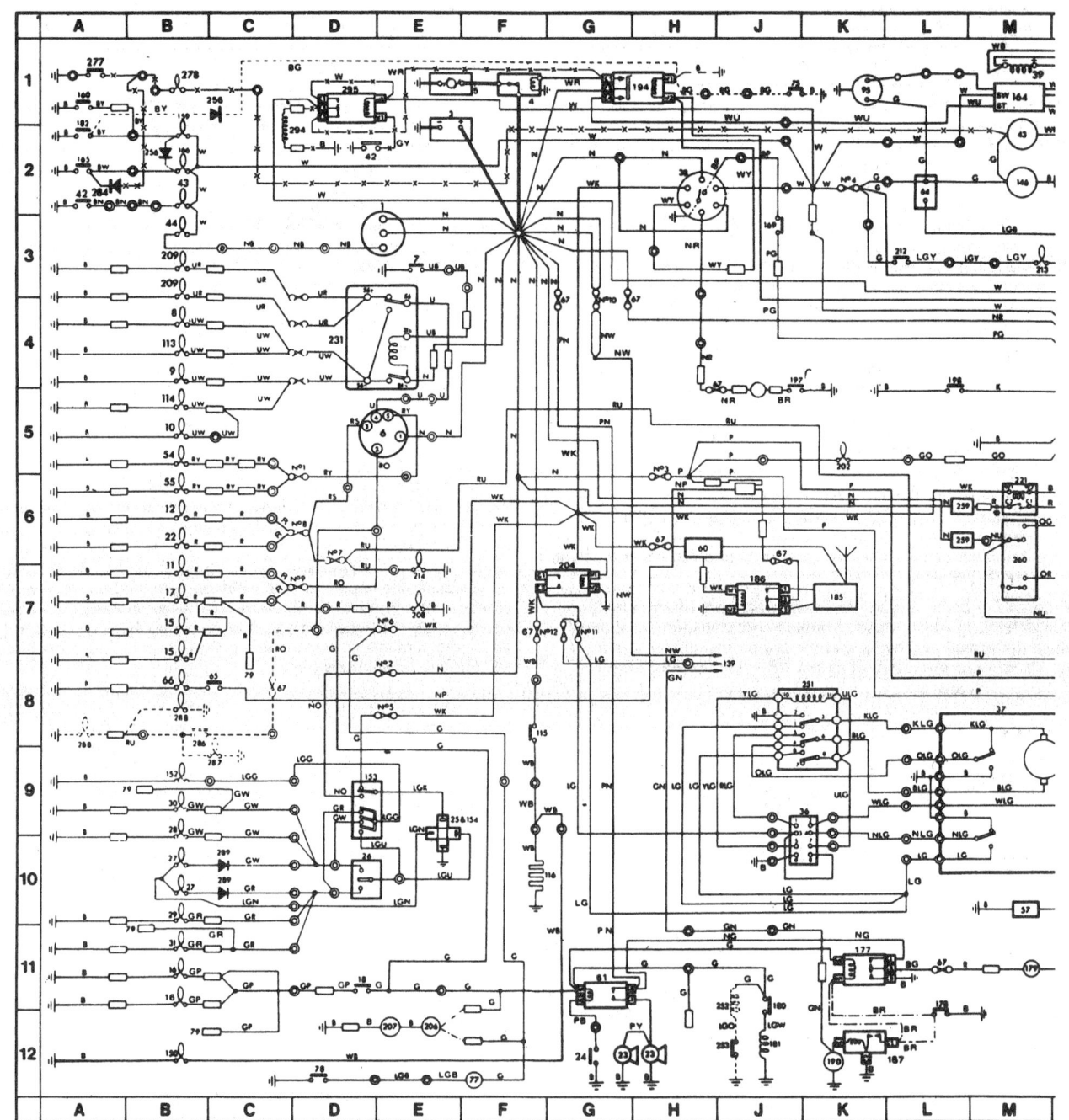

Fig. 13.118 Wiring diagram for US specification XJ6L Series 2 models, including fuel injection

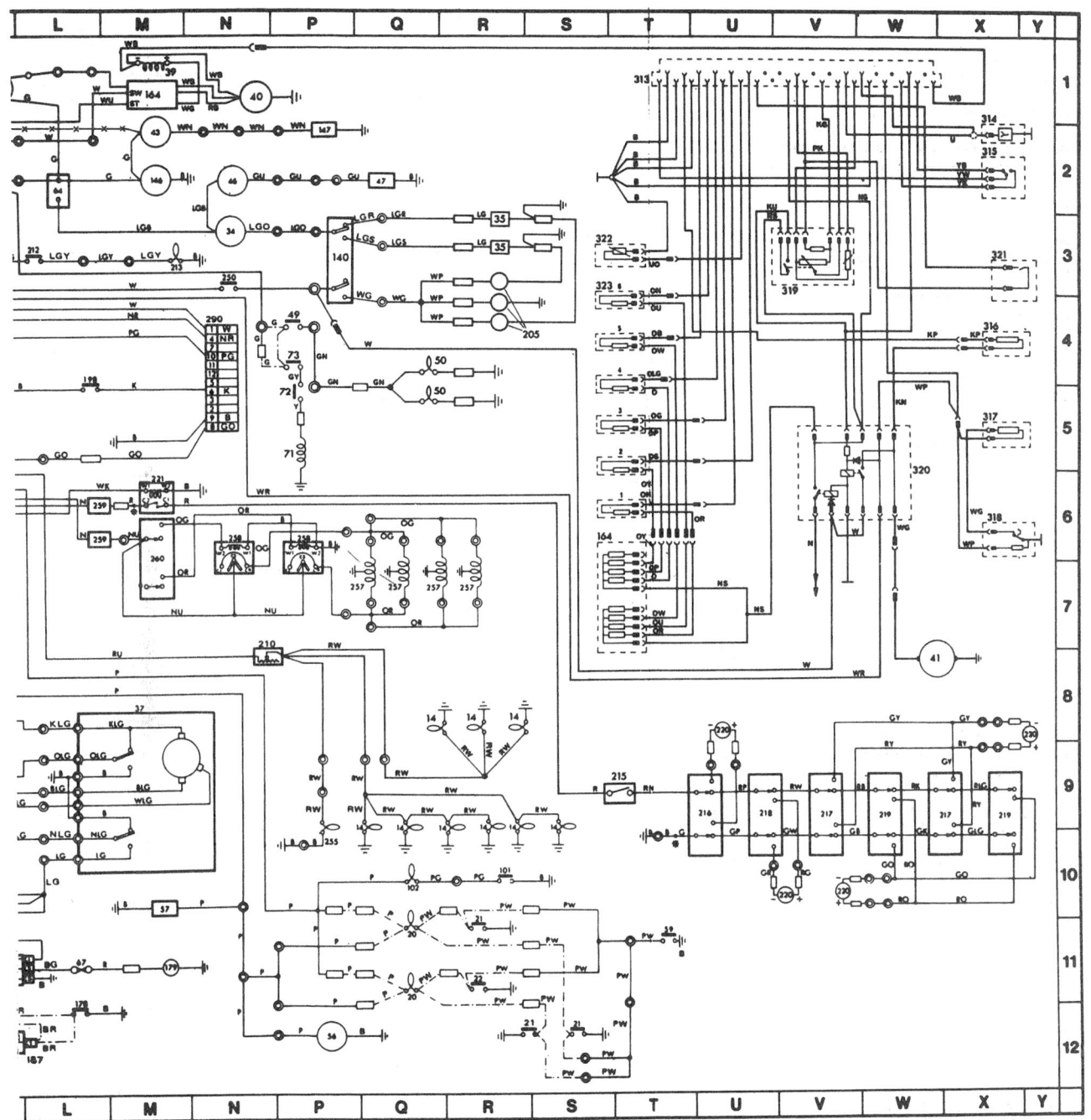

Fig. 13.118 (cont'd) Wiring diagram for US specification XJ6L Series 2 models, including fuel injection.

Key to Fig. 13.118. Not all items fitted to all models

Component	Grid ref	No
Alternator	DE3	1
Aerial motor	K7	185
Aerial motor relay	J7	186
Air conditioning compressor	K12	190
Air conditioning/heater circuit (to)	H8	139
Air conditioning relay	K12	187
Altitude switch	X3	321
Airflow meter	V3	319
Air valve	X4	316
Anti-run-on relay	D1	295
Anti-run-on valve	C2	294
Automatic transmission kickdown solenoid	J12	181
Automatic transmission kickdown switch	J11	180
Automatic transmission safety switch	J1	75
Ballast resistor	M1, T7	164
Battery	E2	3
Battery condition indicator	MN2	146
Battery cooling fan motor	E12	206
Battery cooling fan thermostat	E12	207
Bi-metal instrument voltage stabiliser	L2	64
Blocking diode – brake warning	B2	256
Blocking diodes – direction indicators	C10	289
Boot light	B8	66
Boot light switch	C8	65
Brake fluid level switch	A2	182
Buzzer alarm door switch	J3	169
Choke control illumination	E6	214
Choke warning light	M3	213
Choke warning light switch	L3	212
Cigar lighter	M10	57
Cigar lighter illumination	E7	208
Clock	P11	56
Cold start injector	X5	317
Direction indicator switch	D10	26
Direction indicator warning lamps	B10	27
Distributor	N1	40
Door lock solenoid	Q7	257
Door lock solenoid relay	N6	258
Door lock switch	M6	260
Door switch LH	R11	22
Door switch RH	R12,S12	21
Electric windscreen washer	F12	77
Electric windscreen washer switch	D12	78
Electronic control unit	T1	313
Emission control valve solenoid	J11	252
Emission control valve switch	J12	253
Fibre optics illumination lamp	P9	255
Flasher unit	E9	25
Flasher lamp, front, LH	B10	29
Flasher lamp, front, RH	B9	28
Flasher lamp, rear, LH	B11	31
Flasher lamp, rear, RH	B9	30
Fog lamp, LH	B6	55
Fog lamp, RH	B5	54
Fuel gauge	N3	34
Fuel gauge tank unit	R3	35
Fuel injection relay	V5	320
Fuel injector	T456	323
Fuel pump	R3	41
Fuel solenoid valves	R4	205
Fuel tank changeover switch	P3	140
Handbrake switch	A2	165
Handbrake warning lamp	B2	166
Hazard warning flasher unit	E9	154
Hazard warning lamp	B9	152
Hazard warning switch	D9	153
Headlamp dip switch	E3	7
Headlamp, inner, LH	B5	114
Headlamp, inner, RH	B4	113
Headlamp, outer, LH	B4	9
Headlamp, outer, RH	B4	8
Headlamp relay	D4	231

Component	Grid ref	No
Horns	H12	23
Horn push	G12	24
Horn relay	G11	61
Ignition amplifier	P1	183
Ignition coil	M1	39
Ignition protection relay	G7	204
Ignition switch	H2	38
Ignition warning lamp	B3	44
Inertia switch	N3	250
Interior lights	Q10,11	20
Interior lights switch	T11	59
Left and right-hand dipped beam lamps	B3	209
Lighting switch	E5	6
Line fuse	G3	67
Main beam warning lamp	B5	10
Map light	Q10	102
Map light switch	R10	101
Number plate lamps	B7,8	15
Oil pressure switch	D2	42
Oil pressure transmitter	P2	147
Oil pressure lamp or gauge	M2	43
Overdrive control switch	53	72
Overdrive gearbox switch	P4	73
Overdrive solenoid	P5	71
Oxygen sensor	X2	314
Panel lamps	Q,R,8,9	14
Panel lamps rheostat	N7	210
Radiator cooling fan motor	M11	179
Radiator cooling fan thermostat	L11	178
Radio	H6	60
Rear fog guard lamp	A8.B8	288
Rear fog guard switch	C8	286
Rear fog guard warning lamp	C9	287
Rear window demist switch	F8	115
Rear window demist unit	F10	116
Rear window demist warning light	B12	150
Reverse lamps	Q4	50
Reverse lamp switch	P4	49
Revolution counter	K1	95
Seat belt switch – Driver	L5	198
Seat belt warning control unit	N4	290
Service interval indicator	1A	277
Service interval w/lamp	1B	278
Side lamp LH	B6	12
Side lamp RH	B7	11
Split brake differential switch	A1	160
Split brake test switch and warning lamp	B1	159
Starter motor	E1	5
Starter solenoid	F1	4
Starter solenoid/ballast coil relay	H1	194
Stop and tail lamp LH	B11	16
Stop and tail lamp RH	B11	16
Stoplamp switch	D11	18
Thermal circuit breaker	M6	259
Throttle switch	X2	315
Thermotime switch	X6	318
Trailer socket	C8	79
Water temperature gauge	N2	46
Water temperature transmitters	T3, Q2	322, 47
Window lift master switch	N5	215
Window lift motor	V10,UY8, T4	220
Window lift safety relay	M6	221
Window lift switch, front, LH	U9	218
Window lift switch, front, RH	U9	216
Window lift switch, rear, LH	WX9	219
Window lift switch, rear, RH	VW9	217
Windscreen wiper motor	M9	37
Windscreen wiper relay	K8	251
Windscreen wiper switch	K9	36

Cable colour code

B	Black	L	Light	P	Purple	U	Blue
G	Green	N	Brown	R	Red	W	White
K	Pink	O	Orange	S	Slate	Y	Yellow

Key to Figs. 13.119 to 13.124. Not all items fitted to all models

Component	Grid ref	Circuit No
1 Alternator	A1	
3 Battery	A1	
4 Starter solenoid	A1	
5 Starter motor	A1	
6 Master lighting switch	A1	
7 Headlamp flash switch	A2	
8 Headlamp beam RH	A2	
9 Headlamp beam LH	A2	
10 Main beam warning light	A2	
11 RH side lamp	A2	
12 LH side lamp	A2	
13 Panel lamp rheostat	B1	
14 Panel lamps	B1	
15 Number plate illumination lamp(s)	A2	
16 Stop-lamp(s)	A3	
17 Tail lamp RH	A2	
18 Stop-lamp switch	A3	
19 Fuse box(es)		
20 Interior light(s)	C1	
21 Door switch	C1	
22 Tail lamp LH	A2	
23 Horn(s)	B2	
24 Horn push	B2	
25 Flasher unit (part of 154)	A3	
26 Direction indicator switch	A3	
27 Direction indicator warning lights	A3	
28 RH front flasher	A3	
29 LH front flasher	A3	
30 RH rear flasher	A3	
31 LH rear flasher	A3	
33 Blower motors	C3	
34 Fuel gauge	B1	
35 Fuel gauge tank unit	B1	
36 Windscreen wiper switch	B2	
37 Windscreen wiper motor	B2	
38 Ignition/starter switch	A1	
38A Key switch (part of 38)	A1	
39 Ignition coil	A1	
40 Distributor	A1	
41 Fuel pump		2 & 4
42 Oil pressure switch	B2	
43 Oil pressure warning light	B2	
44 Ignition warning light	A1	
46 Coolant temperature gauge	B1	
47 Water temperature transmitter	B1	
48 Oil pressure gauge	B1	
49 Reverse lamp switch	A3	
50 Reverse lamp(s)	A3	
54 Fog lamp RH	A2	
55 Fog lamp LH	A2	
56 Clock	C1	
57 Cigar lighter socket	C1	
59 Interior light switch	C1	
60 Radio	C1	
61 Horn relay	B2	
65 Boot light switch	C1	
66 Boot light	C1	
67 Line fuse		
75 Automatic gearbox safety switch	A1	
76 Automatic gearbox selector lamp	B1	
77 Windscreen washer pump	B2	
78 Windscreen washer switch	B2	
93 Charging and inspection lamp socket	C2	
95 Tachometer	B1	
101 Map light switch	C1	
102 Map light	C1	
113 Headlamp inner RH	A2	
114 Headlamp inner LH	A2	
115 Rear window demist switch	B2	
116 Rear window demist unit	B2	
140 Fuel changeover switch	B1	
146 Battery condition indicator	B1	
147 Oil pressure transmitter	B1	
150 Rear window demister warning light	B2	
152 Hazard warning light	A3	

Component	Grid ref	Circuit No
153 Hazard warning switch	A3	
154 Hazard warning flasher unit	A3	
159 Brake fluid level warning light	B1	
160 Brake differential pressure switch	B1	
164 Ballast resistor	A1	
165 Handbrake switch	A3	
166 Handbrake warning light	B1	
170 Side markers RH front	A2	
171 Side markers LH front	A2	
172 Side markers RH rear	A3	
173 Side markers LH rear	A3	
174 Radiator cooling fan diode(s)	C3	
177 Radiator cooling fan relay	C3	
178 Radiator cooling fan thermostat (in radiator)	C3	
179 Radiator cooling fan motor	C3	
182 Brake fluid level switch	B1	
183 Ignition amplifier	A1	
185 Aerial motor	C1	
186 Aerial motor relay	C1	
188 Resistor	C3	
189 Blower speed relay	C3	
190 Compressor clutch		3
191 Thermostat		3
192 Control switch		3
194 Starter solenoid ballast coil relay	A1	
195 Anti-run-on solenoid valve	3.4 only	
197 Anti-run-on oil pressure switch	3.4 only	
198 Seat belt switch – driver	C1	
199 Seat belt switch – passenger	C1	
200 Seat switch – passenger	C1	
202 Seat belt warning light	C1	
204 Ignition protection relay	A1	
205 Fuel solenoid valves	B1	
206 Battery cooling fan	B2	
207 Battery cooling fan otterstat	B2	
208 Cigar lighter illumination	B1	
209 Headlamp dip beam RH & LH	A2	
215 Window lift master switch	B3	
216 Window lift switch RH front	B3	
217 Window lift switch LH front	B3	
218 Window lift switch RH rear	B3	
219 Window lift switch LH rear	B3	
220 Window lift motor(s)	B3	
221 Window lift relay	B3	
231 Headlamp relay	A2	
250 Inertia switch	B1	
255 Fibre optics illumination bulb	B1	
257 Door lock solenoid	B3	
258 Door lock solenoid relay	B3	
259 Thermal circuit breaker	B3	
260 Door lock switch	B3	
261 Amplifier		3
262 Servo		3
263 Vacuum valve		3
264 In-car sensor		3
265 Ambient sensor		3
266 Headlamp wiper motor	B2	
267 Headlamp wash motor	B2	
277 Service Interval counter		
278 Oxygen sensor warning light		
287 Fog guard warning light	A2	
288 Fog guard lamp	A2	
289 Direction indicator blocking diode	A3	
290 Seat belt logic unit (Federal)	C1	
293 Fuel injection control unit (ECU)		
295 Fuel safety relay		
296 Fuel injectors		
297 Air temperature sensor		
298 Thermotime switch		
299 Cold start relay		
300 Cold start injector		
301 Stop lamp failure sensor	A3	
303 Low coolant control unit	B1	
304 Park lamp failure sensor	A2	

Non Federal — 198, 199, 200

Key to Figs. 13.119 to 13.124 (cont'd). Not all items fitted to all models

Component	Grid ref	Circuit No	Component	Grid ref	Circuit No
305 Coolant temperature sensor			332 Sliding roof switch	B3	
309 Low coolant sensor	B1		333 Sliding roof motor	B3	
310 Throttle switch		2 & 4	334 Electric door motor	C2	
311 Airflow meter			335 Interior lamp delay	C1	
312 Main relay		2 & 4	336 Aerial adjusting switch	C1	
313 Power resistor		4	339 Headlamp wiper relay	B2	
314 Fuel pump relay		2 & 4	340 Heated rear window delay	B2	
315 Blocking diode – inhibit incorrect polarity		2 & 4	341 Boot lock solenoid	B3	
316 Oxygen sensor		4	342 Speed control unit	C2	
317 Extra air valve			343 Magnet pick-up	C2	
320 Low coolant warning light	B1		344 Inhibit switch	C2	
323 Lamp failure warning light	A3		345 Set switch	C2	
324 Invertor	B1		346 Switch control unit	C2	
326 Full throttle switch		4	347 Actuator	C2	
327 Temperature selector		3	349 Throttle micro-switch		4
329 Time relay wipers	B2		350 Overtemperature switch		3
330 Seat adjuster motor	C2		351 Thermal fuse		3
331 Seat adjuster switch	C2		352 Speed control brake switch	C2	

Cable colour code

B	Black	L	Light	P	Purple	U	Blue
G	Green	N	Brown	R	Red	W	White
K	Pink	O	Orange	S	Slate	Y	Yellow

	A	B	C
1	Ignition Charging Starting	Instruments Panel lamps Warning lamps Fuel switch	Seat belt logic Interior/map lamp Clock/Cigar lighter Boot lamp
2	Side lamps Tail lamps Headlamps Stop lamps Lamp failure units	Windscreen/wipe Headlamp wash/wipe Heated rear window Horn Battery cooling fan	Electric Mirror Seat adjusting motor Speed Control
3	Direction indicators Hazard flashers	Window lift motors Door lock solenoids Sliding roof motor	Radiator cooling fan Heater circuit (Alternative to Air conditioning) (Circuit 3)

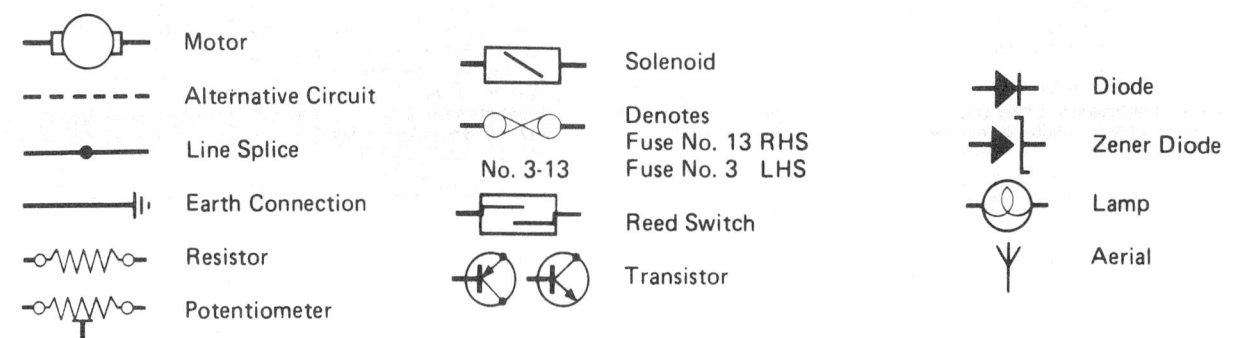

Motor

Alternative Circuit

Line Splice

Earth Connection

Resistor

Potentiometer

Solenoid

Denotes
Fuse No. 13 RHS
No. 3-13   Fuse No. 3   LHS

Reed Switch

Transistor

Diode

Zener Diode

Lamp

Aerial

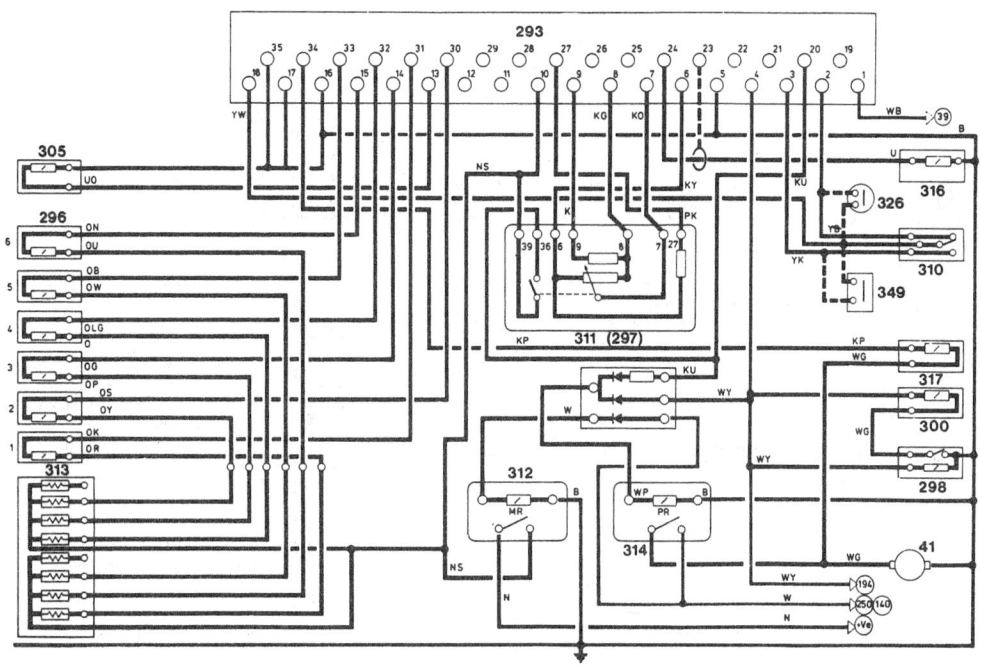

Fig. 13.119 Supplementary wiring diagram for Series 3 models. Circuit No. 2 – fuel injection (later models).

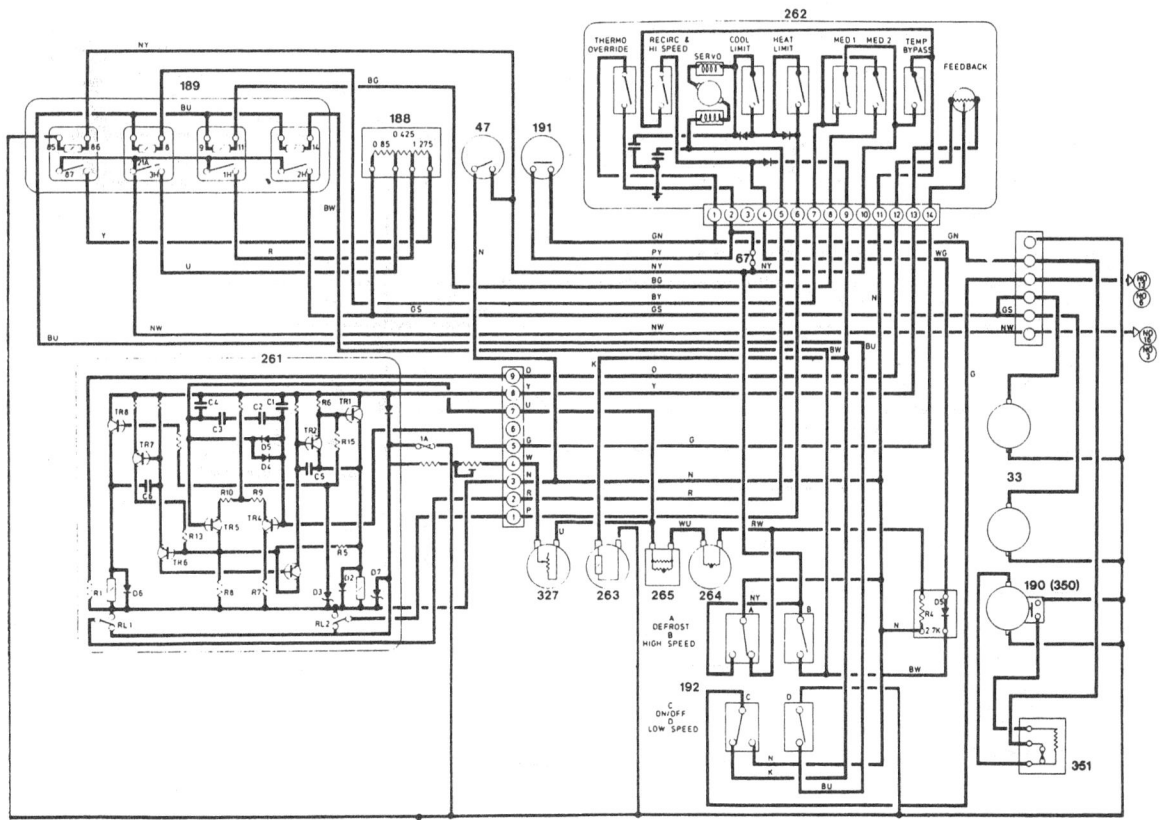

Fig. 13.120 Supplementary wiring diagram for Series 3 models. Circuit No. 3 – air conditioning.

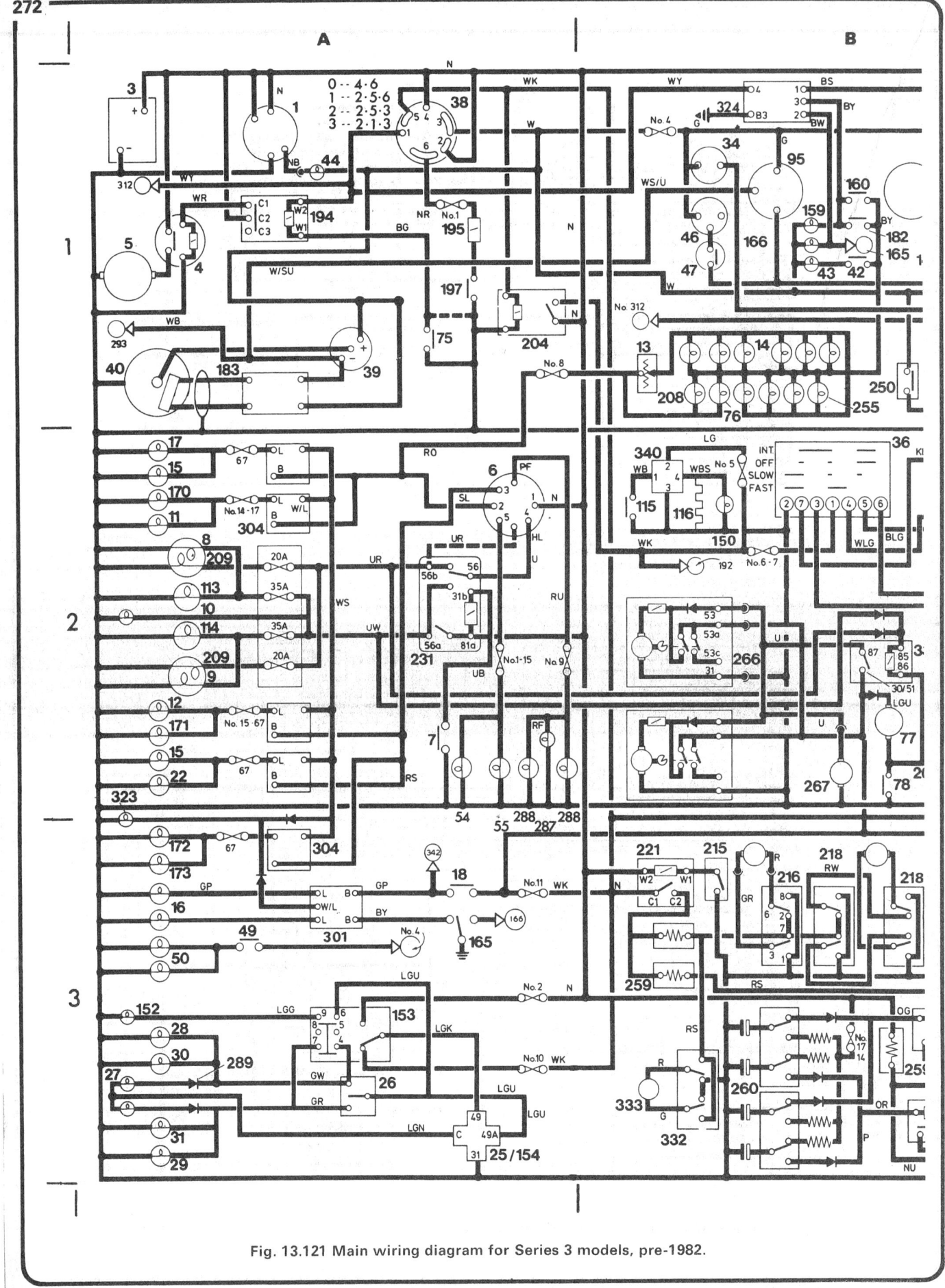

Fig. 13.121 Main wiring diagram for Series 3 models, pre-1982.

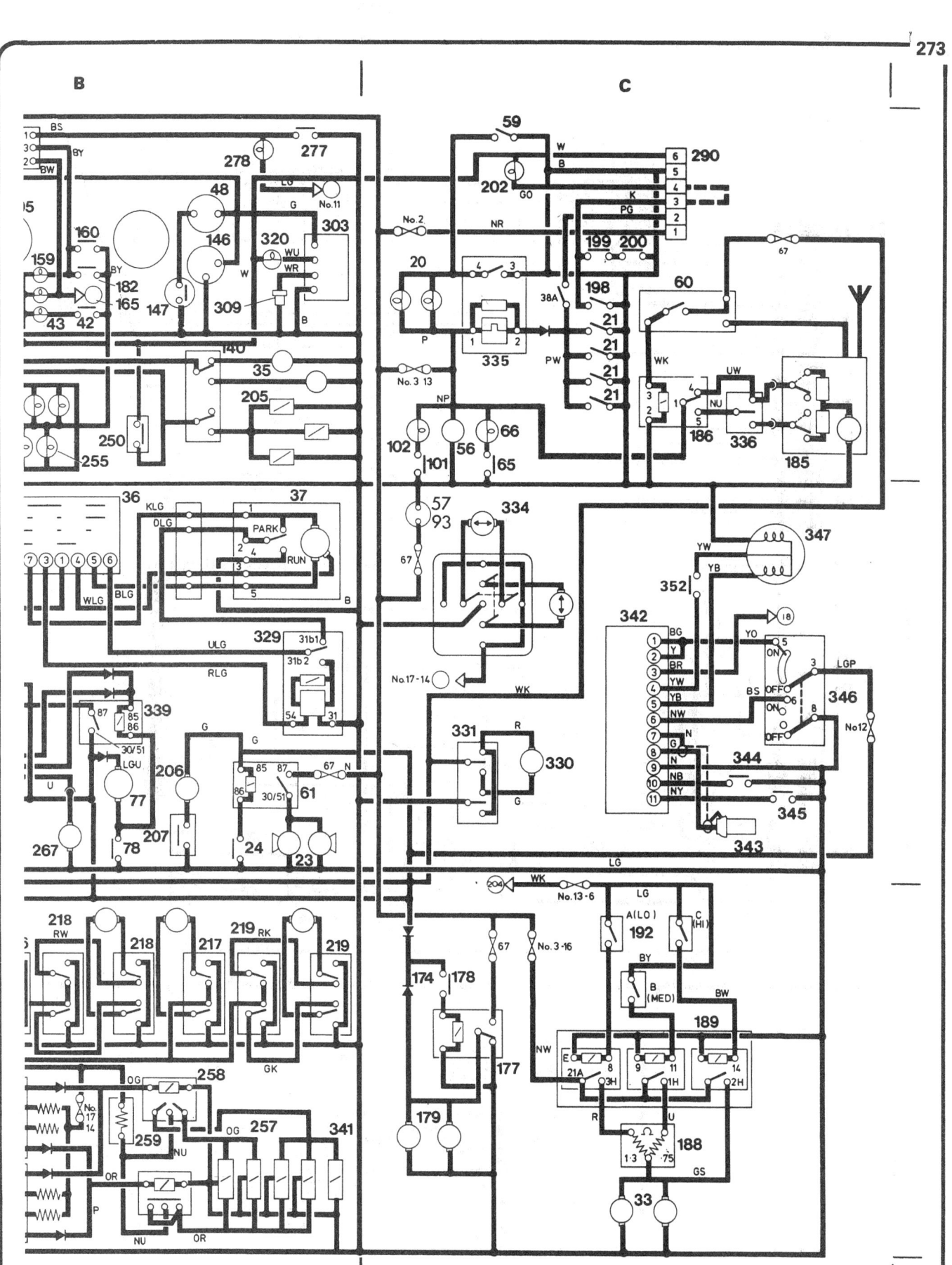

Fig. 13.121 (cont'd) Main wiring diagram for Series 3 models, pre-1982.

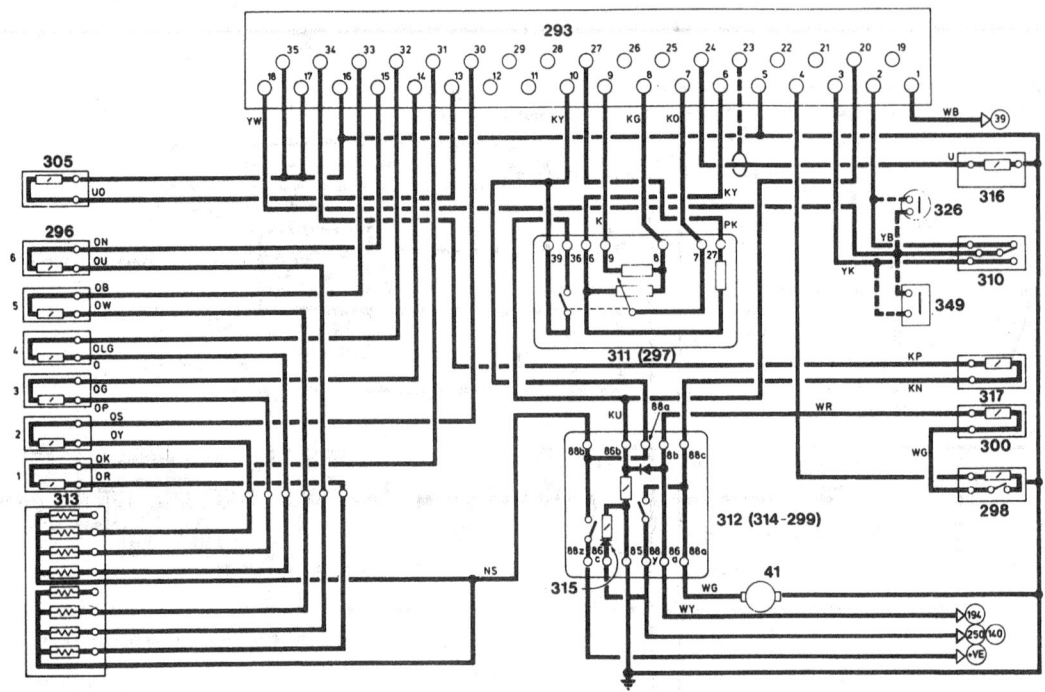

Fig. 13.122 Supplementary wiring diagram for Series 3 models. Circuit No. 4 – fuel injection (early models).

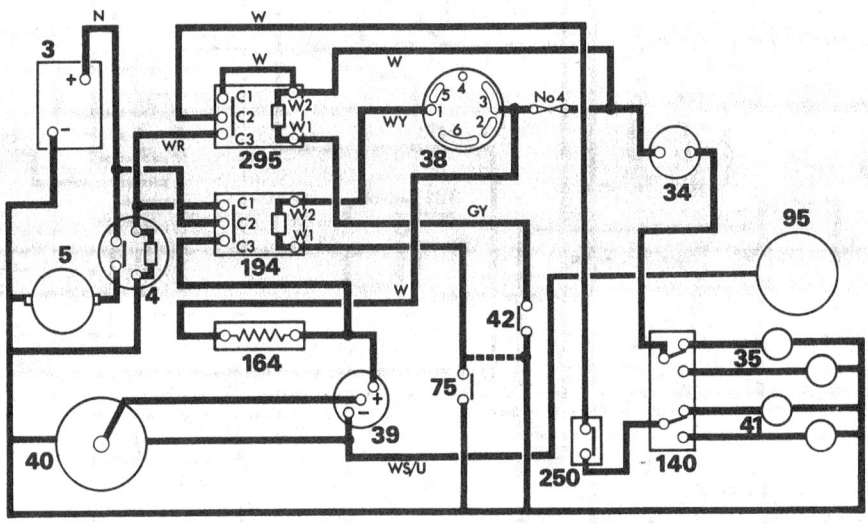

Fig. 13.123 Supplementary wiring diagram for Series 3 models. Circuit No. 5 – ignition and fuel systems for 3.4 litre models.

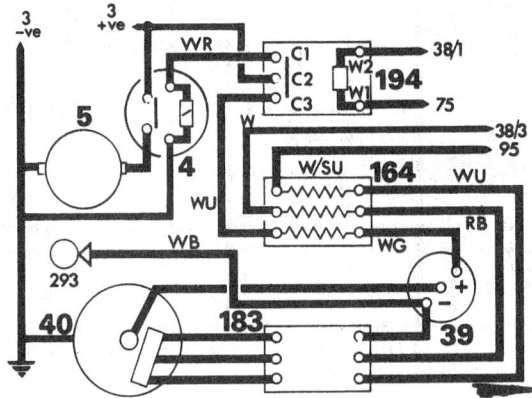

Fig. 13.124 Supplementary wiring diagram for Series 3 models. Circuit No. 6 – ignition system (early 4.2 litre models).

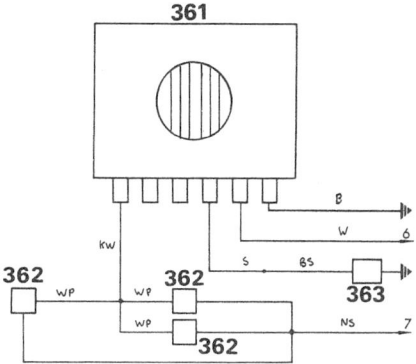

Fig. 13.125 Supplementary wiring diagram for Series 2 models. Vacuum timer delay – North American models.

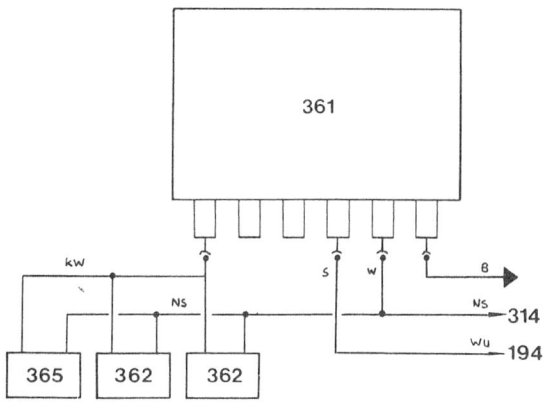

Fig. 13.126 Supplementary wiring diagram for Series 3 models. Vacuum timer delay – except North American models.

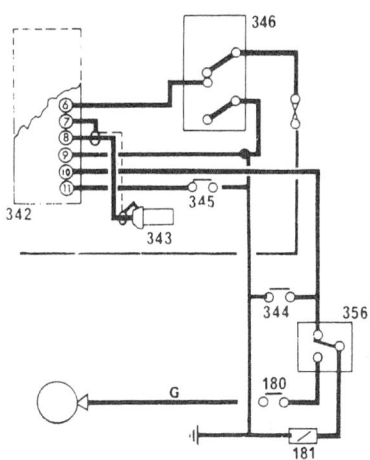

Fig. 13.127 Supplementary wiring diagram for Series 3 models (alternative circuit). Kickdown inhibitor/speed control.

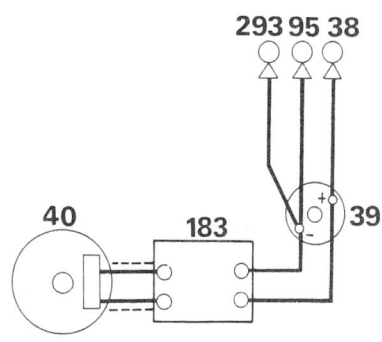

Fig. 13.128 Supplementary wiring diagram for Series 3 models. Ignition system – 1980-on models.

Key to Figs 13.125 to 13.129. Not all items fitted to all models

	Component	Grid ref.			Component	Grid ref.
1	Alternator	A1		56	Clock (where fitted)	C1
2	Battery	A1		57	Cigar lighter socket	C1
4	Starter solenoid	A1		59	Interior light switch	C1
5	Starter motor	A1		60	Radio	C1
6	Master lighting switch	A1		61	Horn relay	B2
7	Headlamp flash switch	A2		65	Boot light switch	C1
8	Hedlamp beam RH	A2		66	Boot light	C1
9	Headlamp beam LH	A2		67	Line fuse	–
10	Main beam warning light	A2		75	Automatic gearbox safety switch	A1
11	RD side lamp	A2		76	Automatic gearbox selector lamp	B1
12	LH side lamp	A2		77	Windscreen washer pump	B2
13	Panel lamp rheostat	B1		78	Windscreen washer switch	B2
14	Panel lamps	B1		93	Charging and inspection lamp socket	C2
15	Number plate illumination lamp(s)	A2		95	Tachometer	B1
16	Stop lamp(s)	A3		101	Map light switch	C1
17	Tail lamp RH	A2		102	Map light	C1
18	Stop lamp switch	A3		111	Rear passenger lamps	
19	Fuse box(es) (not shown)			112	Drivers lamp	
20	Step illumination light(s)	C1		113	Headlamp inner RH	A2
21	Door switch	C1		114	Headlamp inner LH	A2
22	Tail lamp RH	A2		115	Rear window demist switch	B2
23	Horns	B2		116	Rear window demist unit	B2
24	Horn push	B2		140	Fuel changeover switch	B1
25	Flasher unit (part of 154)	A3		146	Battery condition indicator	B1
26	Direction indicator switch	A3		147	Oil pressure transmitter	B1
27	Direction indicator warning lights	A3		150	Rear window demister warning light	B2
28	RH front flasher	A3		152	Hazard warning light	A3
29	LH front flasher	A3		153	Hazard warning switch	A3
30	RH rear flasher	A3		154	Hazard warning flasher unit	A3
31	LH rear flasher	A3		159	Brake fluid level warning light	B1
33	Blower motors	C3		160	Brake differential pressure switch	B1
34	Fuel gauge	B1		164	Ballast resistor	A1
35	Fuel gauge tank unit	B1		165	Handbrake switch	A3
36	Windscreen wiper switch	B2		166	Handbrake warning light	B1
37	Windscreen wiper motor	B2		170	Side markers RH front	A2
38	Ignition/starter switch	A1		171	Side markers LH front	A2
38A	Key switch (part of 38)	A1		172	Side markers RH rear	A3
39	Ignition coil	A1		173	Side markers LH rear	A3
39A	Auxiliary coil 12 cyl.			174	Radiator cooling fan diode(s)	C3
40	Distributor	A1		177	Radiator cooling fan relay	C3
41	Fuel pump	–		178	Radiator cooling thermostat (in pump)	C3
42	Oil pressure switch	B2		179	Radiator cooling fan motor	C3
43	Oil pressure warning light	B2		180	Kickdown switch	B2
44	Ignition warning light	A1		181	Kickdown solenoid	B2
46	Coolant temperature gauge	B1		182	Brake fluid level switch	B1
47	Water temperature transmitter	B1		183	Ignition amplifier	A1
48	Oil pressure gauge	B1		185	Aerial motor	C1
49	Reverse lamp switch	A3		186	Aerial motor relay	C1
50	Reverse lamp(s)	A3		188	Resistor	C3
54	Fog lamp RH	A2		189	Blower speed relay	C3
55	Fog lamp LH	A2		190	Compressor clutch	

Key to Figs. 13.125 to 13.129 (Cont'd). Not all items fitted to all models

	Component		Grid ref.
191	Thermostat		
192	Control switch		
194	Starter solenoid/ballast coil relay		A1
198	Seat belt switch-driver		C1
199	Seat belt switch-passenger	Non	C1
200	Seat switch-passenger	Fed.	C1
202	Seat belt warning light		C1
204	Ignition protection relay		A1
205	Fuel solenoid valves		B1
206	Battery cooling fan		B2
207	Battery cooling fan otterstat		B2
208	Cigar lighter illumination		B1
209	Headlamp dip beam RH and LH		A2
215	Window lift master switch		B3
216	Window lift switch RH front		B3
217	Window lift switch LH front		B3
218	Window lift switch RH rear		B3
219	Window lift switch LH rear		B3
220	Window lift motor(s)		B3
221	Window lift relay		B3
231	Headlamp relay		A2
231A	Headlamp inhibit relay (XJS only)		
250	Inertia switch		B1
255	Fibre optics illumination bulb		B1
257	Door lock solenoid		B3
257A	Rear door lock solenoid		
258	Door lock solenoid relay		B3
259	Thermal circuit breaker		B3
260	Door lock switch		B3
261	Amplifier		
262	Servo		
263	Vacuum valve		
264	In car sensor		
265	Ambient sensor		
266	Headlamp wiper motor		B2
267	Headlamp washer motor		B2
280	Roof lamps		
287	Fog guard warning light		A2
288	Fog guard lamp		A2
289	Direction indicator blocking diode		A3
290	Seat belt logic unit (Federal)		C1
291	EGR control unit		
292	Fuel injection amplifier		
293	Fuel injection control unit (ECU)		
296	Fuel injectors		
297	Air temperature sensor		
298	Thermotime switch		
299	Cold start relay		
300	Cold start injector		
301	Stop lamp failure sensor		A3
303	Low coolant control unit		B1

	Component	Grid ref.
304	Park lamp failure sensor	A2
305	Coolant temperature sensor	
306	Trigger unit	
307	EGR valve	
308	EGR thermo switch	
309	Low coolant sensor	B1
310	Throttle switch	
312	Main relay	
313	Power resistor	
314	Fuel pump relay	
315	Blocking diode (part of 312)	
316	Oxygen sensor	
318	Manifold pressure sensor	
320	Low coolant warning light	B1
323	Lamp failure warning light	A3
324	Invertor	B1
326	Full throttle switch	
327	Temperature selector	
329	Timer Relay – wipers	B2
330	Seat adjust motor	C2
331	Seat adjuster switch	C2
332	Sliding roof switch	B3
333	Sliding roof motor	B3
334	Electric door mirror	C2
335	Interior lamp delay up to 1983	C1
339	Headlamp wiper relay	B2
340	Heated back-light delay (XJS only)	B2
341	Boot lock solenoid (not applicable to XJS)	
342	Speed control unit	C2
344	Inhibit switch (see 356)	C2
345	Set switch	C2
346	Switch control unit	C2
347	Actuator	C2
349	Throttle micro-switch	
350	Over-temperature switch	
351	Thermal fuse	
352	Speed control brake switch	C2
353	Feedback monitor socket	
354	Feedback disable socket	
355	Feedback relay	
356	Kickdown/Speed control inhibit switch	C2
357	Trip computer	C1
358	Interface unit (where fitted)	C1
359	Pulse generator	C2
360	Speedometer (electronic)	B1
361	Vacuum timer relay	
362	Solenoid valves	
363	Coolant temperature switch	
364	Service interval counter (NAS)	
365	Purge valve	

Cable colour code as Fig. 13.118

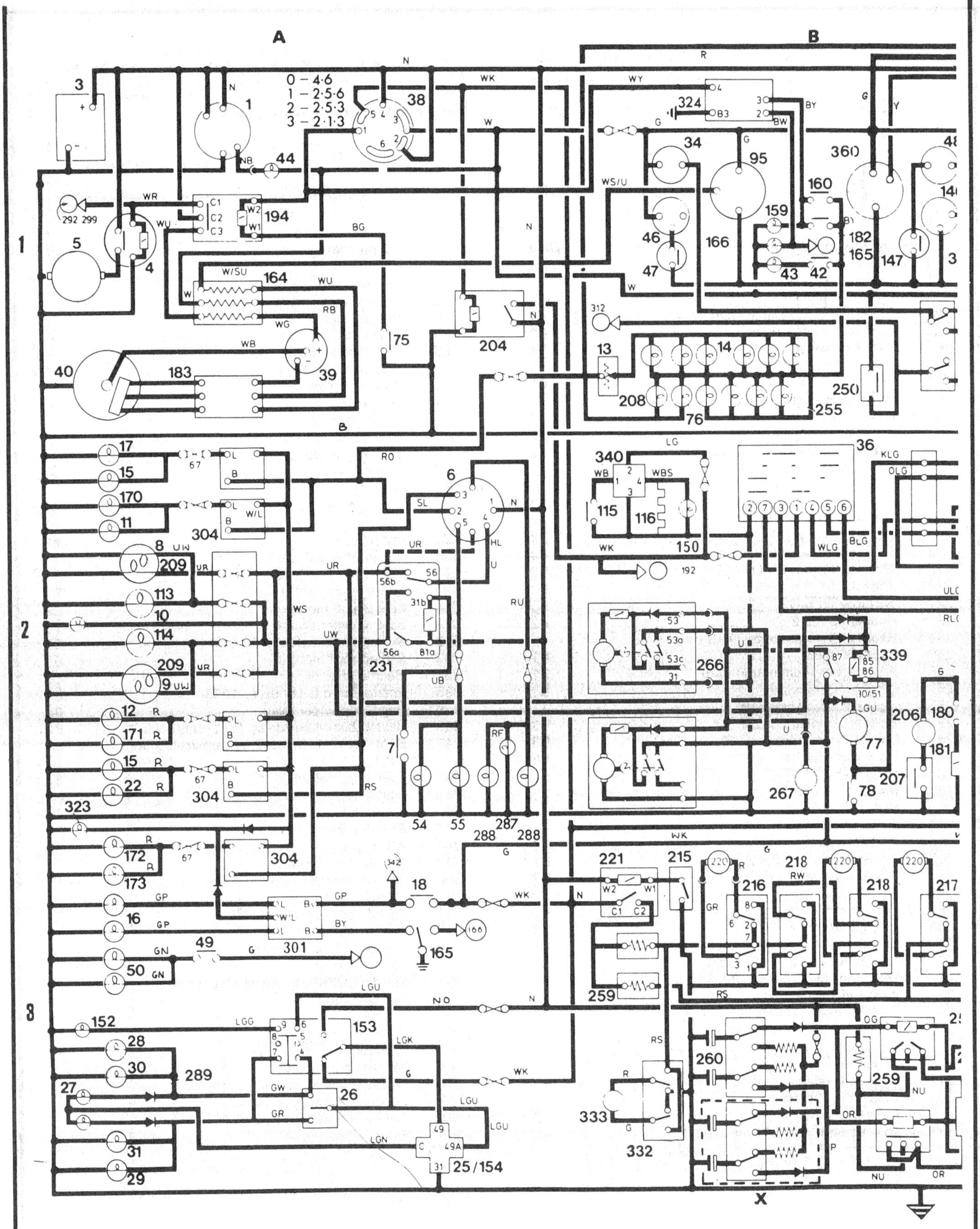

Fig. 13.129 Main wiring diagram for Series 3 models, 1982 to 1986.

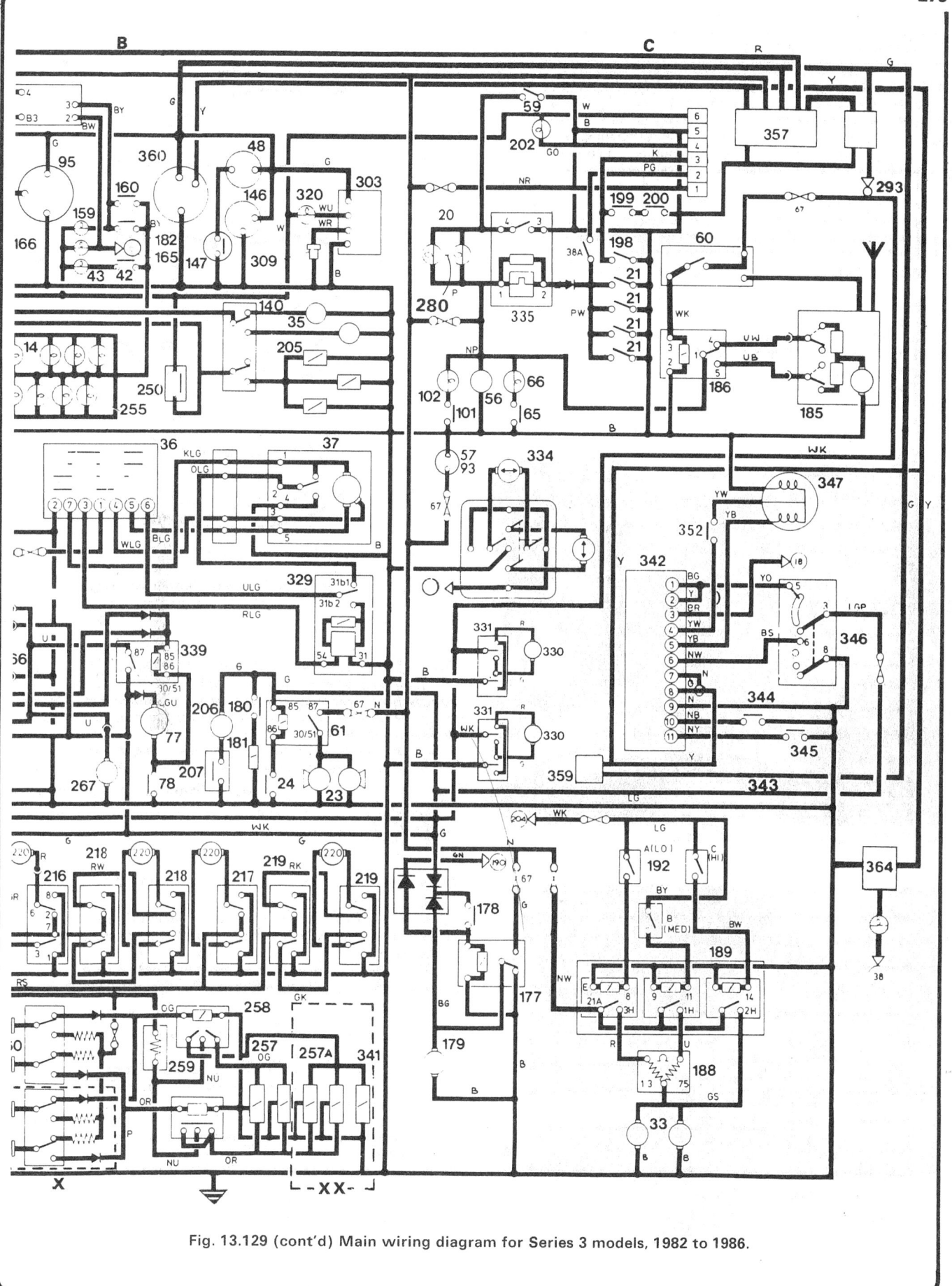

Fig. 13.129 (cont'd) Main wiring diagram for Series 3 models, 1982 to 1986.

21 Suspension and steering

Maintenance tasks (all models)

1 When inspecting the rear suspension mountings, use a lever between the angled sections of the mounting to detect cracks or failure in the rubber and in the rubber-to-metal bonding (photo).

2 Later type track rod end balljoints do not have grease nipples, but are sealed for life. Lubrication in service is not possible.

Front hub – removal and refitting

3 In order to avoid having to remove the front disc brake caliper prior to withdrawing the hub/disc assembly, later models have a modified disc shield which incorporates an aperture.

4 With the front of the car jacked up and the roadwheel removed, pass a socket wrench through the aperture in the disc shield and unscrew in turn the five bolts which secure the brake disc to the hub (photo).

5 Tap off the hub grease cap, extract the split pin and remove the nut and thrust washer from the end of the stub axle.

6 Withdraw the hub by hand, leaving the disc in position.

7 Refitting is a reversal of removal. Refer to Chapter 11, Section 5 for the adjustment procedure.

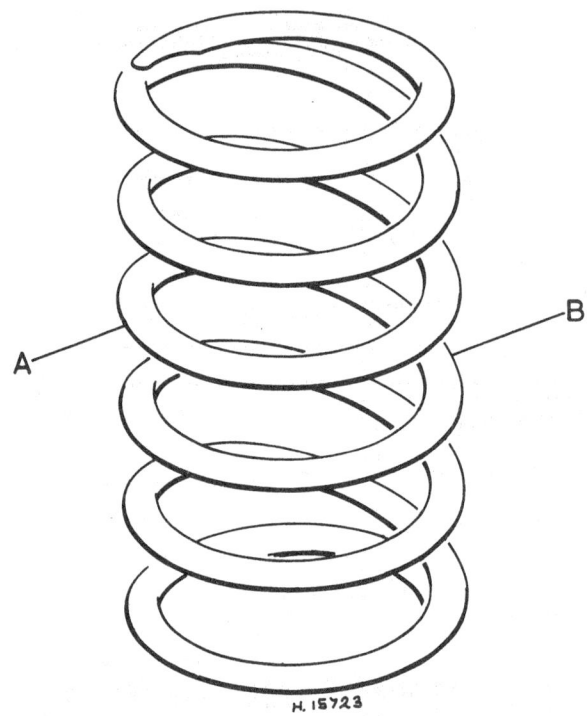

Fig. 13.130 Front coil spring identification (Sec 20)

A   Paint stripe   B   Paint spot

21.1 Using a lever to check a rear suspension mounting

21.4 Unscrewing a front hub/disc fixing bolt

Front spring and spacer identification (Series 3)

8 Two grades of front spring are used on the cars covered by this manual. Springs fitted to cars without air conditioning are identified by a green paint stripe; on cars with air conditioning, the spring stripe is coloured blue.

9 A paint spot on the centre coil of the spring gives information on the number of packing pieces used with the spring, as follows:

	Red	Yellow	Purple	White
3.4 litre	2	1	0	0
4.2 litre (UK)	4	3	2	1
4.2 litre (US)	–	4	3	2

Lower swivel balljoint – setscrew identification (all models)

10 When removing the setscrews which retain the lower swivel balljoint, it may be found that the heads of the inboard screws are thicker than those of the outboard screws.

11 Where this difference in screw head thickness is found, it is important that the bolts are refitted in the same positions as just described.

Front suspension unit mounting bushes – removal

12 These flexible bushes should always be renewed in pairs (two front or two rear) even if only one appears to be worn.

13 Place a trolley jack under the suspension crossbeam and raise the front of the car.

14 Place axle stands under the car jacking points, and then lower the jack slightly to relieve the suspension bushes of any load.

Front bushes

15 Unscrew the self-locking nut (2) shown in Fig. 13.131 and drive the bolt out of the bush. Note the location of the washers and fixing bracket.

16 Slacken the bush eye clamp bolt and tap the bush out of its eye. Remove the bush sleeve.

17 Fit the new bush and associated components and tighten the nut to specified torque, see Chapter 11, Specifications.

18 Renew the opposite front bush in a similar way.

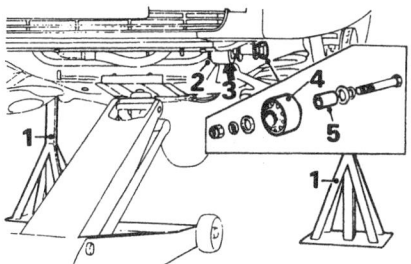

Fig. 13.131 Front suspension unit front mounting bushes
(Sec 20)

1   *Axle stands*
2   *Self-locking nut*
3   *Clamp nut*
4   *Mounting bush*
5   *Sleeve*

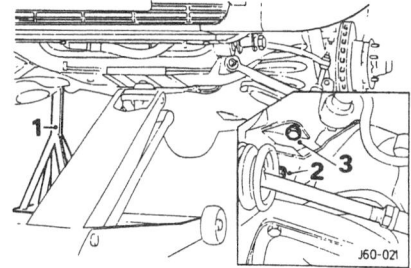

Fig. 13.132 Front suspension unit rear mounting bushes
(Sec 21)

1   *Axle stands*   2   *Self-locking nuts*   3   *Special set screws*

Rear bushes

19 Refer to Chapter 3 and remove the front section of the exhaust system.
20 Slacken the self-locking nuts on the suspension mounting bolts.
21 Raise the front of the car and support it on axle stands placed under the jacking points.
22 Remove both front roadwheels.
23 Using a trolley jack, support the front suspension crossmember.
24 Unbolt the suspension from the mountings and lower the rear of the suspension just enough to provide room to be able to unscrew the two setscrews and lockwashers which hold the mountings to the body subframe.
25 When fitting the new mountings, note that they are offset. Tighten all fixings to the specified torque, see Chapter 11, Specifications.

Rear suspension wishbone inner pivot mounting bracket – removal and refitting

26 Raise the rear of the car and support it securely on stands placed just forward of the radius arms.
27 Remove the roadwheels.
28 Remove the fourteen bolts and setscrews which hold the bottom tie plate to the crossmember and inner pivot brackets.
29 Disconnect the forward end of the radius arm from the body.
30 Disconnect the anti-roll bar link from the radius arm.
31 Disconnect the shock absorber from the wishbone.
32 Suspend the hub/driveshaft assembly from the crossmember using wire or string. Remove the rear nut from the inner pivot shaft, then tap the shaft forward to free the wishbone from the inner pivot. Tap the spacer tube from between the lugs of the pivot bracket.
33 Cut the locking wire from the two setscrews which hold the pivot bracket to the final drive unit. Unscrew and remove the securing setscrews and lift away the pivot bracket. Note carefully the location and number of shims.

34 Refitting is a reversal of removal, but make sure that all shims are replaced exactly as originally fitted.
35 The use of two dummy shafts when offering up the wishbone to the pivot bracket lugs will greatly assist installation and prevent displacement of the various components.

Rear suspension wishbone – removal and refitting

36 Raise the rear of the car and support it on axle stands placed just forward of the radius arms.
37 Remove the roadwheel.
38 Remove the self-locking nut from the outer pivot shaft and drive out the shaft.
39 Fit a suitable rod to the hub carrier in place of the shaft and use adhesive tape to retain the shims and oil seal washers.
40 Raise the hub/driveshaft and tie it to the crossmember with string or wire.
41 Unbolt the tie plate from the crossmember (six bolts).
42 Cut the locking wire and unbolt the radius arm from the body.
43 Unbolt the tie plate from the inner pivot brackets.
44 Disconnect the shock absorbers from the wishbone.

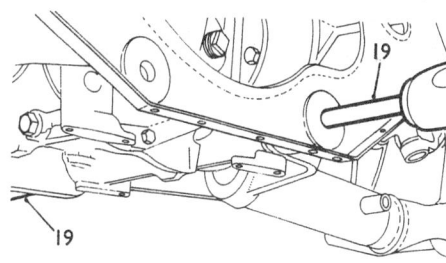

Fig. 13.134 Using dummy shafts (19) to locate rear
suspension wishbone on pivot bracket (Sec 21)

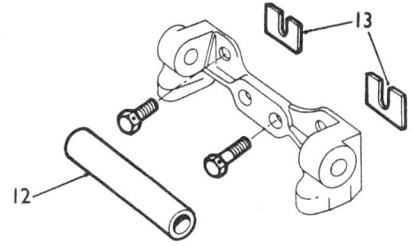

Fig. 13.133 Rear suspension inner pivot bracket (Sec 21)

12   *Spacer tube*   13   *Shims*

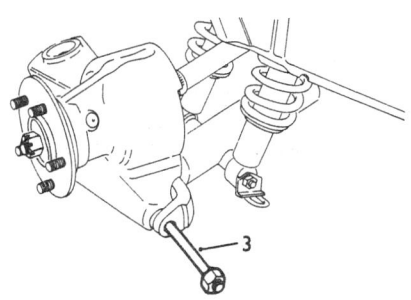

Fig. 13.135 Rear suspension outer pivot shaft (3) (Sec 21)

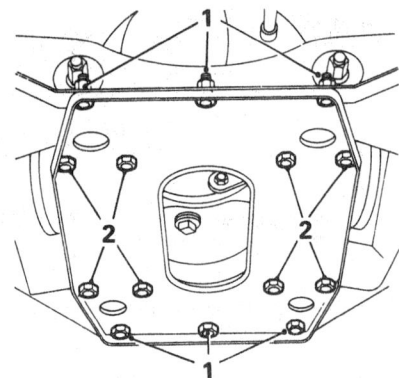

Fig. 13.136 Rear suspension tie-plate nuts and bolts (Sec 21)

1   Crossmember   2   To inner pivot bracket

45 Unscrew the rear nut from the inner pivot shaft, and then drive the shaft forward to free the wishbone from the inner pivot.
46 Remove the wishbone and the radius arm.
47 Refitting is a reversal of removal, but apply grease to the needle bearing cages. The wishbone inner pivot boss must have its engraved face pointing outwards.
48 Use the dummy shafts when offering up the wishbone to the inner pivot mounting bracket to prevent displacement of the pivot bearing components. The radius arm should be towards the front of the suspension assembly.
49 Tighten all bolts to the specified torque (Chapter 11 Specifications) and on completion apply grease to the bearing nipples.

Steering gear (Alford and Alder type) – overhaul
50 This type of power steering gear is fitted as alternative equipment on RHD cars built after 1974.
51 With the gear removed from the car and cleaned externally (see Chapter 11), eject the oil from the rack by moving the rack slowly through its full stroke in both directions.
52 Mark the position of the valve housing porting face in relation to the pinion housing, also the position of the two valve-to-cylinder pipes.
53 Grip the unit at the pinion end in a vice fitted with soft jaw protectors.
54 Cut the lockwires and slide the gaiters along the tie-rods to expose the inner balljoints.
55 Extend the rack and grip it in a soft-jawed vice.
56 Disconnect the inner balljoints, then remove the air transfer and the fluid pipes.
57 Slacken the rack housing ring nut using a C-spanner.
58 Release the locknut on the plunger housing and unscrew the threaded plug to ease the tension exerted by the spring.
59 Remove the three locknuts and withdraw the valve assembly without separating the pinion from the valve housing.
60 Unscrew the rack housing ring nut completely and withdraw the end housing. Pull out the rack assembly.
61 Remove the porting adaptor and slide the porting ring along the cylinder to expose the feed hole.
62 Extract the seal and expander ring by inserting a pointed tool through the feed hole, without damaging the seating, to turn the seal across the cylinder bore and then pull it out with a hooked length of wire.
63 Remove the locknut, plug, spring and plunger from the pinion housing.
64 Clean the rack and cylinder but do not remove the piston ring.
65 Extract the O-ring and abutment washer from the end housing. Clean the end housing, but do not apply any degreasing agent to the sintered iron rack bush as it may wash out its lubricant impregnation. Inspect and renew components as necessary. Obtain the appropriate repair kit of seals and gaskets.

66 Lubricate the rack housing end seal and then fit the narrower expander ring from the repair kit into the seal.
67 Locate the anti-extrusion ring in the end housing and fit the seal so that it is pressed fully against the expander ring and engages with the anti-extrusion ring.
68 Fit an O-ring (lubricated) into its groove in the housing.
69 Fit a centre feed porting adaptor into the porting ring. Position the ring to allow the conical seating on the adaptor to engage with the cylinder seating. Tighten to 25 lbf ft (34 Nm).
70 Oil the rubber part of the rack seal and then fit the wider expander ring from the repair kit into the seal.
71 Using a suitable protective sleeve over the rack teeth, pass the rack seal over the rack to bring it up to the piston. Oil the anti-extrusion ring and engage it in the recess in the back of the seal.
72 Apply oil to the open end of the cylinder bore and grease the rack on its plunger contact area.
73 Enter the rack and piston assembly into the cylinder using firm even pressure, pushing the seal down the cylinder until it contacts the abutment face. As the piston ring enters the bore it must contract.
74 Fit a new gasket to the valve mounting face of the pinion housing.
75 Apply plenty of grease to the pinion and bearing components and install the control valve to the pinion housing with the valve port correctly located. Screw on the three locknuts and tighten to 14 lbf ft (19 Nm).

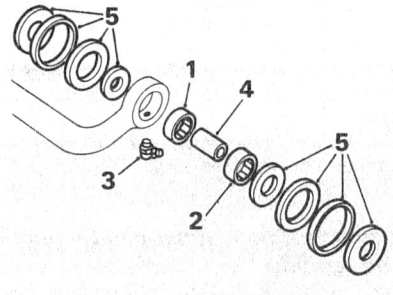

Fig. 13.137 Rear suspension wishbone pivot bearing components (Sec 21)

1   Cage   4   Tube
2   Cage   5   Thrust washers, seals and
3   Grease nipple   retainers

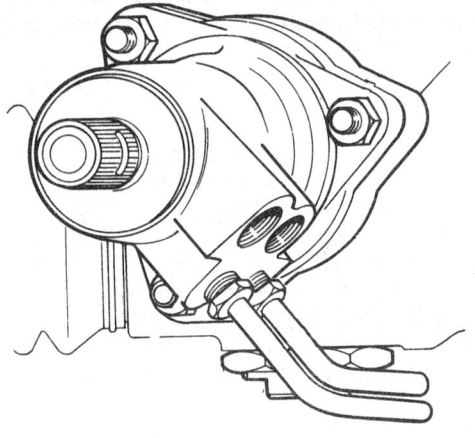

Fig. 13.138 Steering control valve and pinion housing (Alford and Alder type) (Sec 21)

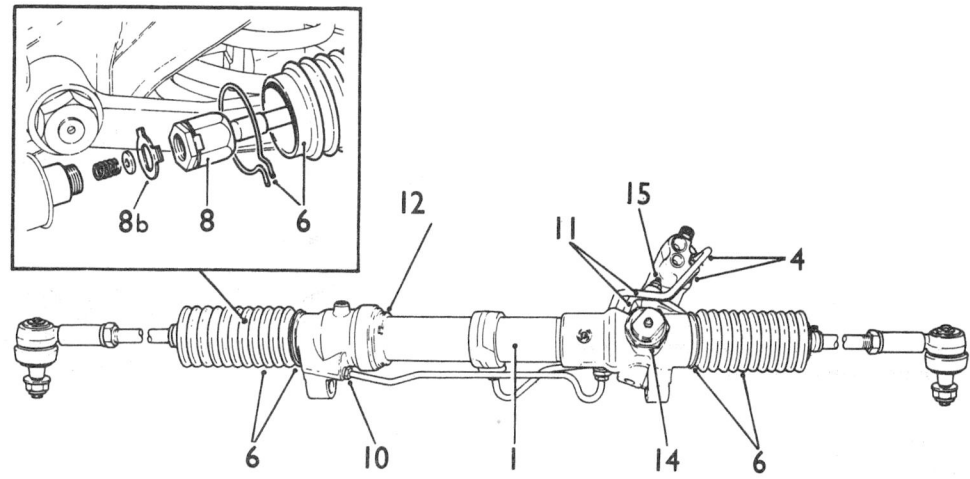

Fig. 13.139 External view of Alford and Alder steering gear (Sec 21)

1	Rack housing	8	Inner balljoint assemblies
4	Valve housing	8b	Lockplates
6	Bellows and clip	10	Air transfer pipe

11	Valve-to-cylinder connecting pipes	
12	Rack housing ring nut	

14	Rack damper assembly
15	Valve assembly locknuts

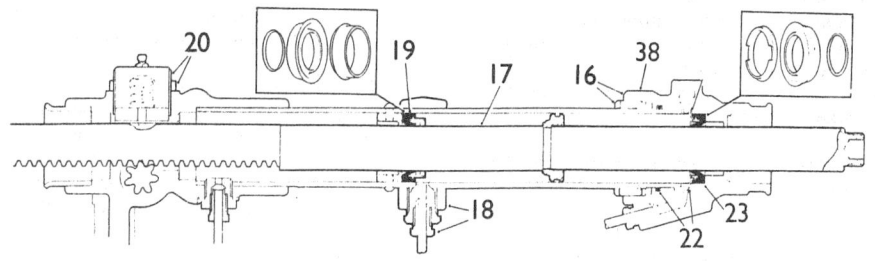

Fig. 13.140 Sectional view of Alford and Alder steering gear (Sec 21)

16	Rack housing ring nut	18	Porting ring and adaptor
17	Rack	19	Seal

20	Rack damper assembly	23	End housing seal
22	O-ring and abutment washer	38	End housing

76 Apply grease to the end housing bush and seal and to the abutment washer. Fit the abutment washer into the housing.

77 Align and fit the end housing, screw on the ring nut just tight enough to hold the gear housing mounting feet in alignment.

78 Support the assembly in a soft-jawed vice so that the cylinder is vertical and tighten the ring nut to 90 lbf ft (122 Nm). Use a C-spanner with a spring balance attached if a suitable torque wrench is not available. Do not disturb the alignment of the mounting feet.

79 Fit the spring plunger components. Tighten the plug while the rack is being moved through its full stroke until the movement becomes stiff, then unscrew the plug about 1/8 of a turn to achieve smooth action. Tighten the plug locknut.

80 Fit the air transfer and fluid pipes.

81 Using new lockplates, fit and tighten the inner balljoints to 80 lbf ft (109 Nm). Do not grip the pinion housing when tightening the inner balljoints.

82 Bend down all six locking tabs onto the six flats of each ball housing.

83 Extend the rack at the end housing section and smear it with grease.

84 Pack each rack gaiter with two ounces (56g) of grease and secure with wire.

85 Fit a grease nipple into the hole in the plunger threaded plug and apply 5 or 6 strokes of the grease gun, not more. Remove the grease nipple and refit the blanking plug.

Steering gear (Series 2 and 3) – pinion oil seal renewal

86 It is possible to renew the pinion seal without removing the steering rack from the car. Great care must be taken to avoid contamination of the rack internal components, however.

87 Begin operations by emptying the steering pump fluid reservoir with an old poultry baster or similar item.

88 Inside the car, remove the pinch-bolts from the coupling which joins the upper end and lower steering columns. Mark the relationship of the coupling to the upper column, then slide it down the lower column until the two column sections are separate. Do not turn the steering wheel or move the roadwheels from now on.

89 Raise and securely support the front of the vehicle.

90 Remove the pinch-bolt and nut which secure the lower steering column to the pinion. Mark the relationship of the column to the pinion housing, then separate the column from the pinion shaft and move it aside. Clean the area round the seal.

91 Have ready a drain pan to catch escaping fluid. Remove the wave washer and the weathersill from the pinion shaft, then remove the circlip and washer and prise out the oil seal. Take care not to damage the seal housing or pinion shaft.

92 Clean the seal housing and the pinion shaft, taking care not to introduce foreign matter. Lubricate the new seal with ATF and fit it into the housing, using a wooden wedge to press it home.

93 Refit the washer, circlip, weathershield and wave washer.

94 Reconnect the steering column joints, observing the alignment marks made previously. Tighten the pinch-bolts.

95 Lower the car, then refill and bleed the power steering system.

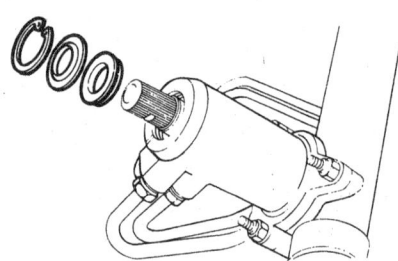

Fig. 13.141 Steering gear pinion oil seal and retaining components (Sec 21)

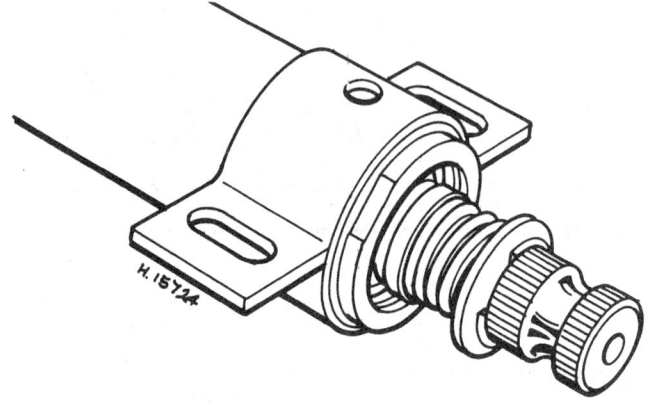

Fig. 13.143 Spring-loaded upper steering column bearing (Sec 21)

Steering rack modifications – Series 3
96 During 1980, various modifications were made to the steering rack, mainly concerned with improving the oil-tightness of the unit.
97 The new rack is fully interchangeable with the old one as a complete unit, but the seals and O-rings from one **cannot** be fitted to the other. It is therefore important to specify the type of rack when obtaining seals. The new rack (known as the 1980 PTFE Unit) can be identified by the natural zinc coated finish on the centre rack tube. An identification plate is attached to the pinion housing.

Steering pump modifications – Series 3
98 Coincident with the steering rack modifications just noted, the steering pump has been modified by changing to metric threads on the mounting bracket and at the pressure pipe outlet.
99 Provided that new pressure pipes and mountings are used, a new type pump can be fitted in place of an old one.

Steering column lock (Series 3) – removal and refitting
100 Disconnect the battery, then remove the lower cowl from the steering column.
101 Move the steering wheel to its fully extended position, disconnect the fibre optic filament and remove the ignition switch/ steering lock cover.
102 Remove the two shear bolts which secure the lock, either by drilling their centres and inserting a stud extractor, or by tapping their heads anti-clockwise with a hammer and a small chisel or punch. These bolts are not meant to be easily removed.
103 Remove the screw which secures the lock to the switch and separate the two.
104 When refitting, insert the new shear bolts finger tight at first. Check for correct operation of the lock and the ignition switch, then tighten the bolts until their heads break off.

Upper steering column bearing modificaton (Series 3)
105 A redesigned upper steering column, incorporating a spring-loaded top bearing, was introduced during the 1982 model year. The new column is less likely to rattle or to transmit noise from elsewhere.

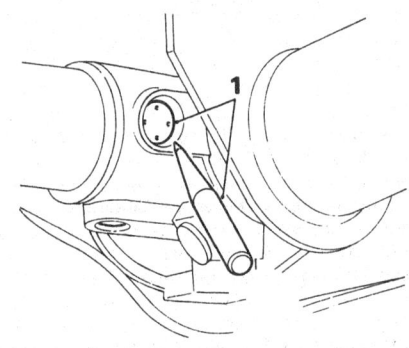

Fig. 13.142 Removal of steering column lock shear bolts using a centre punch (1) (Sec 21)

106 The new type upper column is interchangeable, as a complete unit, with the old type.

Steering gear (Series 3) – removal and installation
107 On these models, the operations are similar to those described in Chapter 11, Section 26 except that the steering column need not be removed, simply release the steering shaft lower coupling.

Steering wheel (Series 2 and 3) – removal and refitting
108 Centralise the steering so that the front roadwheels are in the straight-ahead position. The steering rack can be centralised by removing the grease nipple from the rack damper plug and inserting a pointed rod. Apply slight pressure on the rod at the same time turning the pinion shaft until the rod is felt to drop into an indentation.
109 Extract the three screws and remove the column lower switch cover.
110 Working from under the steering wheel, remove the clamp bolt which holds the collet adaptor to the steering column.
111 Slacken the locknut of the grubscrew in the collet adaptor. Unscrew the grubscrew two turns.
112 Withdraw the steering wheel, complete with hand locknut, inspect rubber, collet adaptor and shaft.
113 If the steering wheel must be dismantled, extract the two self-tapping screws from the rear face of the steering wheel boss and lift off the padded horn contact.
114 Unscrew the nylon nut from the top of the steering wheel shaft and remove it together with the horn contact tube.
115 Remove the self-locking nut and plain washer which secure the steering wheel. Withdraw the steering wheel from its splined shaft, retain the split collets.
116 When reassembling and refitting, smear the components with engine oil.
117 Tighten the grub screw only finger tight before tightening its locknut.

Alloy roadwheels – precautions
118 When cast alloy roadwheels are fitted, they must be inspected regularly for freedom from cracks and corrosion. The protective coating on the alloy, which prevents corrosion, must be undamaged.
119 Tyre removal and refitting must **not** be performed using tyre levers or any form of leverage on the wheel. Only entrust such work to experts.
120 When refitting a wheel, always tighen the wheel nuts evenly and in sequence, making sure that they are properly seated. Do not exceed the specified tightening torque.

Snow tyres – precautions
121 The snow tyres listed in the Specifications are the only ones recommended by the makers. They may be fitted only as a complete set.

122 The correct type of inner tubes (marked with the words 'Weathermaster only') must be used with the snow tyres.
123 Snow tyres may be fitted with studs, where not prohibited by law, providing that the car is not driven at more than 75 mph (120 km/h).

Wheels and tyres – general care and maintenance

Wheels and tyres should give no real problems in use provided that a close eye is kept on them with regard to excessive wear or damage. To this end, the following points should be noted.

Ensure that tyre pressures are checked regularly and maintained correctly. Checking should be carried out with the tyres cold and not immediately after the vehicle has been in use. If the pressures are checked with the tyres hot, an apparently high reading will be obtained owing to heat expansion. Under no circumstances should an attempt be made to reduce the pressures to the quoted cold reading in this instance, or effective underinflation will result.

Underinflation will cause overheating of the tyre owing to excessive flexing of the casing, and the tread will not sit correctly on the road surface. This will cause a consequent loss of adhesion and excessive wear, not to mention the danger of sudden tyre failure due to heat build-up.

Overinflation will cause rapid wear of the centre part of the tyre tread coupled with reduced adhesion, harsher ride, and the danger of shock damage occurring in the tyre casing.

Regularly check the tyres for damage in the form of cuts or bulges, especially in the sidewalls. Remove any nails or stones embedded in the tread before they penetrate the tyre to cause deflation. If removal of a nail *does* reveal that the tyre has been punctured, refit the nail so that its point of penetration is marked. Then immediately change the wheel and have the tyre repaired by a tyre dealer. Do *not* drive on a tyre in such a condition. In many cases a puncture can be simply repaired by the use of an inner tube of the correct size and type. If in any doubt as to the possible consequences of any damage found, consult your local tyre dealer for advice.

Periodically remove the wheels and clean any dirt or mud from the inside and outside surfaces. Examine the wheel rims for signs of rusting, corrosion or other damage. Light alloy wheels are easily damaged by 'kerbing' whilst parking, and similarly steel wheels may become dented or buckled. Renewal of the wheel is very often the only course of remedial action possible.

The balance of each wheel and tyre assembly should be maintained to avoid excessive wear, not only to the tyres but also to the steering and suspension components. Wheel imbalance is normally signified by vibration through the vehicle's bodyshell, although in many cases it is particularly noticeable through the steering wheel. Conversely, it should be noted that wear or damage in suspension or steering components may cause excessive tyre wear. Out-of-round or out-of-true tyres, damaged wheels and wheel bearing wear/maladjustment also fall into this category. Balancing will not usually cure vibration caused by such wear.

Wheel balancing may be carried out with the wheel either on or off the vehicle. If balanced on the vehicle, ensure that the wheel-to-hub relationship is marked in some way prior to subsequent wheel removal so that it may be refitted in its original position.

General tyre wear is influenced to a large degree by driving style – harsh braking and acceleration or fast cornering will all produce more rapid tyre wear. Interchanging of tyres may result in more even wear, but this should only be carried out where there is no mix of tyre types on the vehicle. However, it is worth bearing in mind that if this is completely effective, the added expense of replacing a complete set of tyres simultaneously is incurred, which may prove financially restrictive for many owners.

Front tyres may wear unevenly as a result of wheel misalignment. The front wheels should always be correctly aligned according to the settings specified by the vehicle manufacturer.

Legal restrictions apply to the mixing of tyre types on a vehicle. Basically this means that a vehicle must not have tyres of differing construction on the same axle. Although it is not recommended to mix tyre types between front axle and rear axle, the only legally permissible combination is crossply at the front and radial at the rear. When mixing radial ply tyres, textile braced radials must always go on the front axle, with steel braced radials at the rear. An obvious disadvantage of such mixing is the necessity to carry two spare tyres to avoid contravening the law in the event of a puncture.

In the UK, the Motor Vehicles Construction and Use Regulations apply to many aspects of tyre fitting and usage. It is suggested that a copy of these regulations is obtained from your local police if in doubt as to the current legal requirements with regard to tyre condition, minimum tread depth, etc.

22 Bodywork and fittings

Bonnet lock cables – adjustment

1 Open the bonnet and locate the catches, one on each side.
2 Slacken the cable clamp bolt and push the release lever forwards as far as possible. Hold the lever in this position and tighten the clamp bolt.
3 Repeat the operation on the other side.
4 With the aid of an assistant, check that both catches are operating before closing the bonnet.

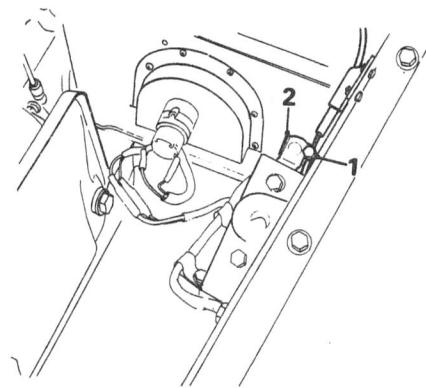

Fig. 13.144 Bonnet lock cable clamp bolt (1) and release lever (2) (Sec 22)

Bonnet lock cables – removal and refitting

5 Open the bonnet and release the cable clamp bolts. Pull the cable ends out of the clamps.
6 Unbolt the bracket which supports the longer cable.
7 Inside the car, pull the cables through the grommet and free them from the operating lever.
8 Refit in the reverse order to removal, then adjust the cables as just described.

Bonnet counterbalance springs – removal and refitting

9 Open the bonnet and insert thick washers or coins between the spring coils until they are no longer under tension.
10 Unbolt the spring upper retaining brackets. Remove the upper brackets and unhook the springs from the lower brackets.
11 Leave the washers or coins in place, unless new springs are to be fitted, in which case they may be carefully transferred to the new springs.
12 Refit in the reverse order to removal.

Luggage compartment lid (Series 3) – removal and refitting

13 Proceed as described in Chapter 12, Section 12, but additionally disconnect the wiring harness behind the boot side panel and draw it up through the hinges with string attached to the end. The string can then be used to pull the harness back into position when refitting.

Luggage compartment lid seal (Series 3) – removal and refitting

14 Remove the screws which secure the bottom trim plate and ease the seal off its flange in this area.

15 Remove the tape which holds the ends of the seal together.
16 Ease the seal off the rest of the flange.
17 When refitting, start by fitting the ends of the seal and taping them together, then work outwards from the join. Be careful not to stretch the seal, and make sure it is well fitted in the corners.
18 Check for fit by dusting the seal with French chalk or talc, then closing and opening the boot lid and observing the transfer of chalk. Adjust the hinges or lock striker if necessary.

Front door trim (Series 3) – removal and refitting
19 Remove the armrest. On Vanden Plas models, disconnect the battery before doing this, and note that the lamp in the rear of the armrest must be partly dismantled to gain access to the rear retaining screw; disconnect the wiring harness as the armrest is withdrawn. On other models, free the armrest from its 'keyhole' slots by thumping it upwards with the heel of the hand.
20 Release the bottom edge and the sides of the trim panel from the door by prising outwards. Be careful not to break the clips.
21 Pull the panel downwards to free it from the crash roll.
22 Refit in the reverse order to removal.

Door locks and exterior handles (Series 3)
23 Door lock adjustment is as described in Chapter 12, Section 14 or 15 but note the different design of the link rod adjusters (photo). The new design of exterior door handle is shown in Fig. 13.146. The handle can be removed after withdrawing the door trim panel and retaining bracket (3).

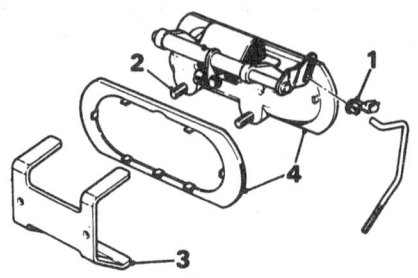

Fig. 13.146 Door exterior handle components (Sec 22)

1	Spring clip	4	Gasket and handle
2	Fixing stud		assembly
3	Retainer		

Front door glass and lift motor (Series 3) – removal and refitting
24 Disconnect the battery earth lead.
25 Remove the door trim panel as previously described.
26 Remove the mirror remote control surround. Separate the control assembly from the surround (except on electrically-operated mirrors) and unclip and remove the crash roll.
27 Remove the outer weatherstrip from the window channel.
28 Remove the loudspeaker from the door.
29 Remove the securing screws and the stop peg from the lift motor mounting plate.
30 Remove the securing bolts from the window lower channel.
31 Remove the spacer from the rear of the motor mounting plate.
32 Remove the bolts which secure the outer slide channel, then remove the channel.
33 Remove the motor from its mounting plate, disconnect the cables and lower it to the bottom of the door.
34 Slide the glass forwards and free the lift arm from the guide channel.
35 Remove the glass from the door and take from it the guide channel and seal.
36 The motor and regulator may now be removed from the door, if wished. Mark their relationship before separating them.
37 When refitting, use a new guide channel seal. Position the seal on the glass and offer the channel to it; seat the channel by tapping it gently with a mallet.
38 Refit the remaining components in the reverse order to removal. If wished, temporarily reconnect the battery and check the window for correct operation before refitting the door trim.

Rear door glass (Series 3) – removal and refitting
39 Remove the door trim casing. This is done in the same way as already described for the front door.

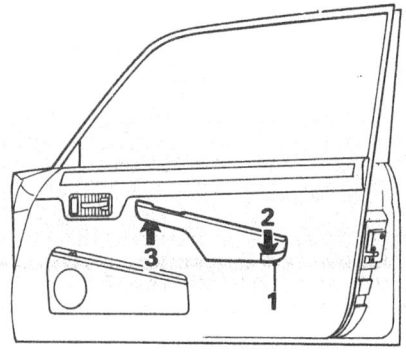

Fig. 13.145 Armrest fixing points – Vanden Plas (Sec 22)

1	Lamp	2	Screw	3	Screw

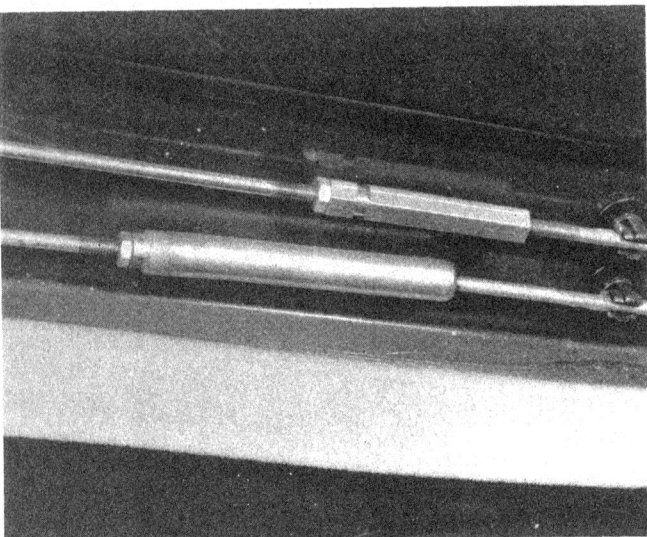

22.23 Typical door link rod adjusters

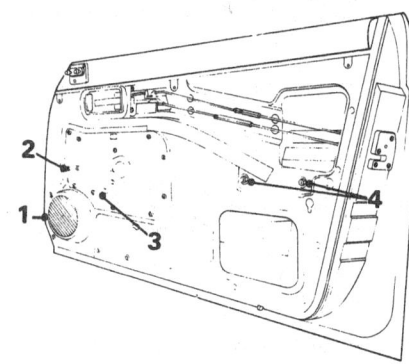

Fig. 13.147 Front door, trim panel removed (Sec 22)

1	Loudspeaker	3	Stop peg
2	Window lift motor	4	Outer slide channel bolts
	mounting plate		

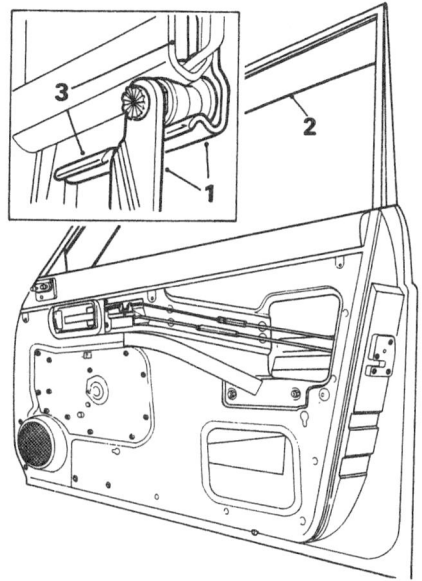

Fig. 13.148 Front door glass lift arm (1), glass (2) and guide channel (3) (Sec 22)

40 Prise the chrome trim from the glass frame. Part of the trim is retained by a screw (1) which should be removed (Fig. 13.149).
41 Free the rubber seal from the glass frame.
42 Lower the glass and extract the upper part of the felt channel from the quarterlight end of the frame. Remove the screws exposed by the removal of the felt.
43 Remove the screws which secure the top of the glass frame to the vertical part. Carefully tap the top of the frame free and remove it.
44 Unscrew and remove the buffer stop from the bottom of the door.
45 Remove the four screws which secure the lift mechanism to the door.

46 Unhook the lift arm from the glass guide bracket, support the glass and remove it from the door.
47 Separate the guide bracket and the seal from the glass.
48 The motor and regulator may now be removed if wished. Mark their relationship before separating them.
49 Refit in the reverse order to removal. Use new sealing components where possible, and fill the ends of the bottom channel with a silicone sealant.

Windscreen and rear window (Series 3) – removal and refitting
50 Both the windscreen and the rear window are 'direct glazed' on Series 3 vehicles. Special equipment and techniques are required to remove and (more particularly) refit such glass; the operation must be left to professionals.

Rear view mirrors – removal and refitting
Interior mirror
51 Grip the mirror stem and jerk it rearwards to disengage the stem from the base.
52 Refit by engaging the front of the stem in the mounting cut-out and strike the underside of the stem sharply to engage the clip.
Exterior mirror (manually-operated)
53 Extract the two screws from the mirror control knob trim plate.
54 Partially withdraw the trim plate complete with operating control knob, and then extract the setscrews which hold the control to the trim plate.

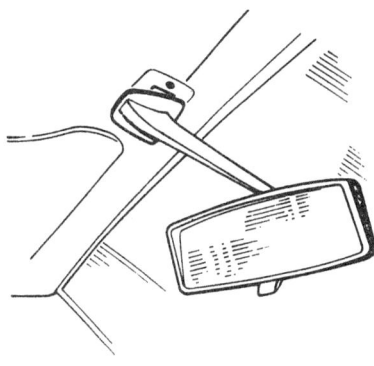

Fig. 13.150 Interior rear view mirror (Sec 22)

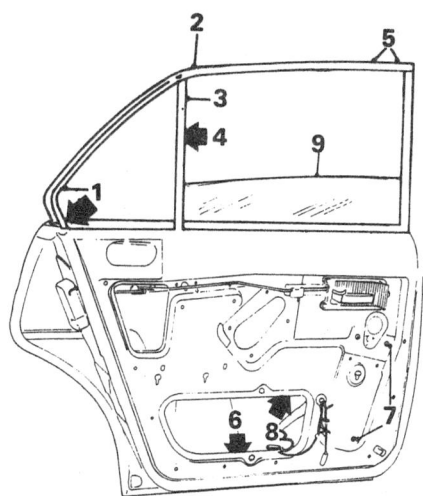

Fig. 13.149 Rear door with trim panel removed (Sec 22)

1	Trim retaining screw	6	Buffer
2	Seal	7	Light mechanism screws
3	Felt channel		(2 of 4)
4	Screws	8	Lift arm
5	Screws	9	Glass

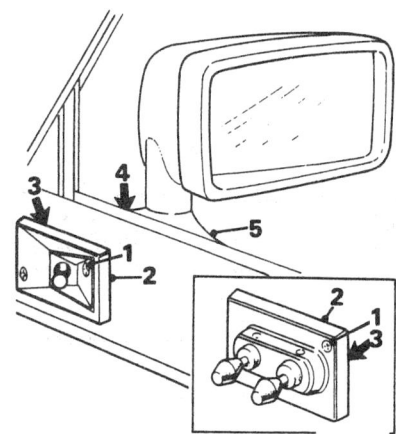

Fig. 13.151 Exterior rear view mirror (Sec 22)

1	Trim plate screws	4	Mirror fixing screws
2	Trim plate	5	Mirror mounting base
3	Set screws		

Inset – electrically-operated controls

55 Extract the two mirror fixing screws.
56 Refitting is a reversal of removal.
Exterior mirror (electrically-operated)
57 On Vanden Plas models, first remove the door armrest and door trim panel.
58 Disconnect the battery and extract the two screws which hold the mirror control trim panel to the door (or pocket, Vanden Plas).
59 The remaining operations are as for the manually-operated type, carefully feed the wiring harness and levers through the door panel.

Front bumper – removal and refitting
60 Disconnect the battery.
61 Unbolt the chrome finisher, (1) in Fig. 13.152, from the side mounting brackets.
62 Prise up the plastic covers (2) which are located under each inner headlamp and unbolt the finisher from the inner mounting brackets. Remove the upper apron.
63 Unclip the rubber finishers (4) and remove them.
64 Disconnect the bumper-mounted lamps by turning the connector (5) anti-clockwise.
65 Unbolt and remove the bumper beam (6).
66 Refitting is a reversal of removal.
67 On North American models fitted with impact-absorbing struts, these can be removed as described in Chapter 12 Section 30.

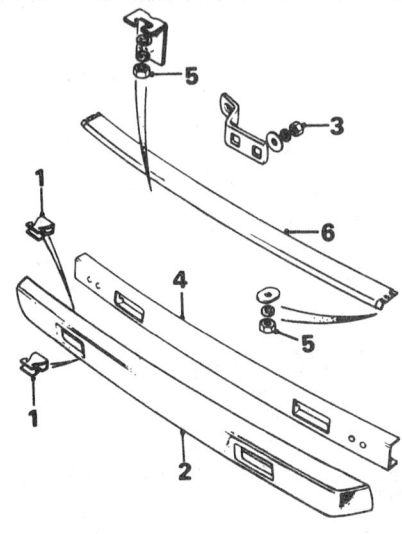

Fig. 13.153 Rear bumper centre section (Sec 22)

1	Clip	4	Bumper beam
2	Rubber finisher	5	Fixing nuts
3	Fixing nuts	6	Blade

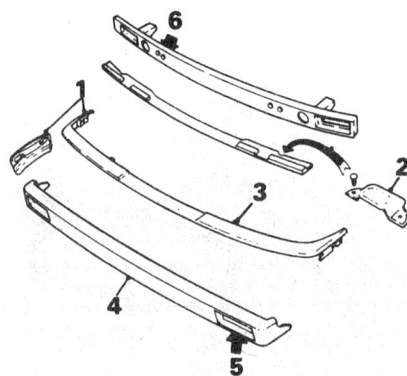

Fig. 13.152 Front bumper (Sec 22)

1	Chrome finisher and side bracket	4	Rubber finisher
2	Plastic covers	5	Lamp unit
3	Finisher	6	Bumper beam

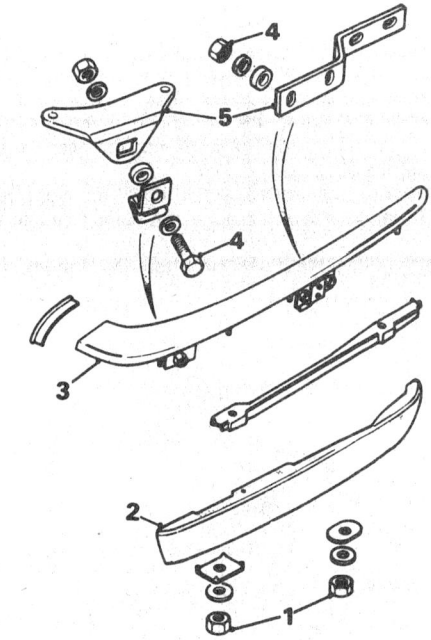

Fig. 13.154 Rear bumper side section (Sec 22)

1	Fixing nuts	4	Fixing nuts
2	Rubber finisher	5	Mounting brackets
3	Blade		

Rear bumper – removal and refitting
Centre section
68 Disconnect the battery and rear fog lamps.
69 Unclip the rubber buffer (2) shown in Fig. 13.153.
70 Unbolt the bumper beam (4) from the body mounting brackets.
71 Unbolt and remove the bumper blade (6) and retain the sealing strips.
Side section
72 Remove the bumper beam as described in the preceding paragraphs.
73 Unbolt the rubber buffer, (2) in Fig. 13.154, from the quarter blade (3).
74 Unbolt the quarter blade from the body mounting brackets.
75 Refitting of the centre and side sections is a reversal of removal.

Glovebox lid and lock – removal and refitting
76 Disconnect the glovebox sliding stay.
77 Extract the lid hinge screws.
78 Extract the screws and remove the lid liner.
79 Remove the lock retaining plate and ring.
80 Refitting is a reversal of removal, but make sure that the lock key slot is vertical before tightening the ring.

81 Slight adjustment of the glovebox lid within its aperture is possible by moving the hinges on the facia.

Glovebox – removal and refitting
82 Remove the underscuttle (Chapter 12, Section 51).
83 Extract the six fixing screws and withdraw the glovebox from the rear of the facia in a downward direction.
84 Refit in the reverse direction to removal, remember to connect the lid sliding stay with one screw.

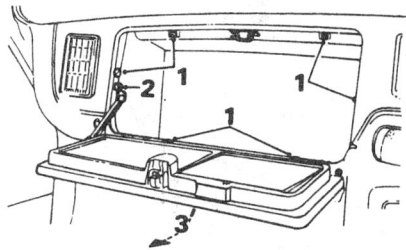

Fig. 13.155 Glovebox (Sec 22)

1	Fixing screws	3	Glovebox lid
2	Sliding stay screw		

22.96 Rear seat squab retaining clip

Front seat (Series 3) – removal and refitting

35 On cars equipped with electric motors for seat adjustment, and/or seat belt warning systems, disconnect the battery earth lead.
86 Remove the cross-head screw which secures the front of the cushion to the bracket. Remove the bracket from below the cushion.
87 Place the seat in the fully reclining position, then lift the front of the cushion and draw it forwards. Disconnect any electrical leads from the base of the cushion, then remove it.
88 Unhook the return springs from the front runner supports.
89 Remove the nuts which secure the front runners to the mounting brackets. Recover the washers and spacers.
90 Slide the remains of the seat forwards and remove the nuts and washers which secure the rear rubbers. Remove the seat.
91 Refit in the reverse order to removal.

Rear seat – removal and refitting

92 Move the front seats forwards as far as possible.
93 Remove the two screws, one each side of the prop shaft tunnel, which secure the cushion to the pan.
94 Pull the cushion forwards and remove it.
95 Remove the two bolts and shakeproof washers which secure the seat squab to the pan (photo).
96 Lift the squab upwards until it is free of the retaining clips and remove it (photo).
97 Refit in the reverse order to removal.

Rear seat armrest – removal and refitting

98 Remove the rear seat as described in the preceding paragraphs.
99 The armrest is held by four bolts to the frame of the seat squab. Also release the armrest trim clips before removing the armrest.
100 Refitting is a reversal of removal.

Seat belts – maintenance, removal and refitting

101 The seat belts should be regularly checked for cuts or fraying and renewed if any such problems are seen. If the belts have been subjected to strain due to a front end collision, they should be renewed. A belt can only be renewed as an assembly complete with inertia reel.
102 If the belts require cleaning use only warm water and liquid detergent, never use solvent of any kind.
Front belt – removal
103 To remove a front belt, unbolt the anchor plate from the body pillar, and then unbolt the reel from the bottom of the pillar.

22.95 Rear seat squab retaining bolt

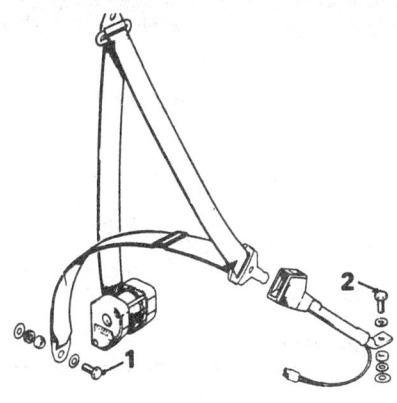

Fig. 13.156 Front seat belt (Sec 22)

1	Lower anchor plate bolt	
2	Stalk bolt	

104 The stalk can be unbolted from the floor pan remembering to disconnect the warning circuit connector plug.

Rear belt – removal

105 Slide the front seats fully forward.

106 Remove the rear seat as described in earlier paragraphs.

107 Prise off the plastic cover from the inertia reel. Do this gently to avoid breaking the retaining lugs.

108 Unbolt the reel and the belt anchor plates..

Front and rear belts – refitting

109 Refitting is a reversal of the removal operations, but observe the following points.

110 Make sure that the sequence of components at the anchor plates (spacer, washer, wave washer) is exactly as originally fitted otherwise the anchor plate will not swivel.

111 The front belt inertia reel must be set in the vertical attitude.

112 Smear the rear belt anchor plate bolts (seat pan) with suitable sealant to prevent the ingress of water.

Rear parcel shelf – removal and refitting

113 Remove the rear seat as described previously.

114 If rear seat belts are fitted, carefully prise the covers off the inertia reel units and unbolt the units. Note the positions of spacers and washers.

115 Remove the plastic screws, then free the parcel shelf from its clips by prising (photo). Remove the shelf.

116 Refit in the reverse order to removal.

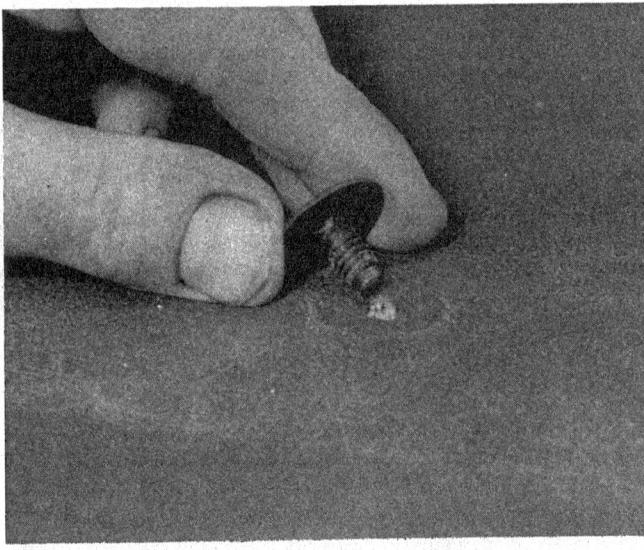

22.115 Rear parcels shelf retaining screw

Sliding roof panel – removal and refitting

117 Open the panel by about 6 to 9 in (15 to 23 cm).

118 Remove the four screws from the front flange of the panel.

119 Close the panel and lift the front edge.

120 Pull the panel forward and upwards so releasing the spring clips at the rear of the panel.

Sliding roof – adjustment

121 Should wind noise or other misalignment be a problem, proceed as follows.

122 Open the sliding roof as far as possible.

123 Remove the black nylon wedges, one on each side of the roof opening, by sliding them rearwards.

124 On the underside of each wedge is a screw. Turn the screw anti-clockwise to raise the rear of the roof, or clockwise to lower it. Beware of excessive upward adjustment, which may cause the roof to jam.

125 Refit the wedges to check the adjustment; proceed as necessary on a trial and error basis.

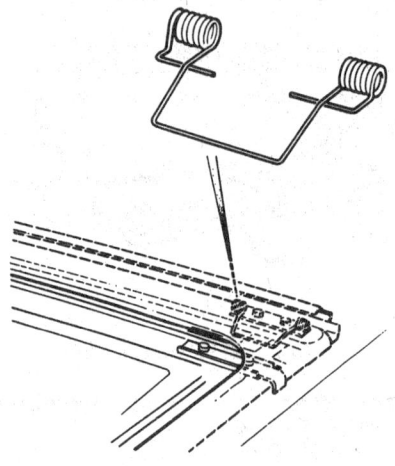

Fig. 13.157 Sliding roof panel clips (Sec 22)

Sliding roof operating rack – renewal

126 If wear occurs in the rack, it should be renewed in the following way after first having removed the sliding panel (see paragraph 117).

127 Fully close the under panel.

128 Remove the rear seat (see paragraph 92).

129 Unscrew the nuts and remove the wheelbox cover, then move the racks away from the housing.

130 Remove the plastic block (A) in Fig. 13.158, bend back the lock tab (B) and take off the nuts, lockplates, spring plate and rack mounting plate.

131 Mark the position of the rack stop (C), unscrew the nuts and remove the stop from the rack tube. Withdraw the rack from its tube, wiping away any thick grease.

132 To refit the rack, grease it liberally and insert it into its tube. Make sure that the rack enters the second tube adjacent to the motor wheelbox.

133 Refit the rack stop and all the other components.

134 Fully close the panel by hand, making sure that full travel is obtained.

135 Refit the racks to the wheelbox housing and then fit the cover.

136 Check that the roof operates electrically, refit the roof panel and the rear seat.

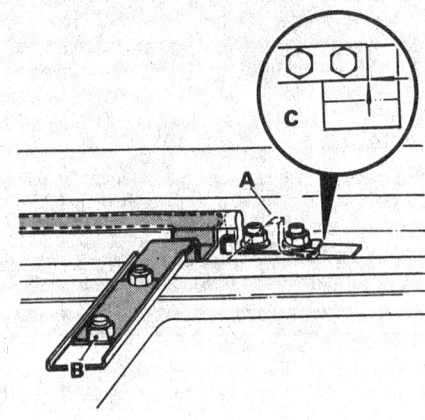

Fig. 13.158 Sliding roof operating rack (Sec 22)

A	Plastic block	C Rack stop location
B	Lock tab	

Sliding roof motor/wheelbox/drivegear – removal and refitting

137 Remove the rear seat (see paragraph 92).
138 Unscrew the nuts and remove the wheelbox cover.
139 Remove the racks from the housing.
140 Unbolt the motor mounting bracket from the rear bulkhead.
141 Open the luggage boot and remove the front trim panel to gain access to the motor. Disconnect the electrical leads.
142 Withdraw the motor and bracket.
143 The motor and wheelbox with drivegear can be renewed after unbolting and separating them.

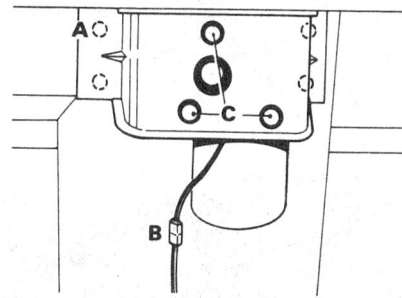

Fig. 13.159 Sliding roof panel motor mounting bracket (A), electrical wiring plug (B) and motor mounting screws (C) (Sec 22)

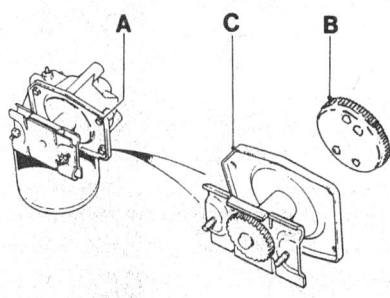

Fig. 13.160 Sliding roof motor (A), drivegear (B) and wheelbox (C) (Sec 22)

Front wings – removal and refitting

144 Disconnect the battery.
145 Remove the direction indicator lamps.
146 Remove the horns, front bumper and apron.
147 Remove the outer headlamp bezel, wiring loom cover and fusebox on LHD models.
148 Remove the headlamp inner casing and tension spring, also the flasher repeater lamp.
149 Raise the front of the car and remove the appropriate roadwheel.
150 Remove the underwiring protective covers, also the bonnet counterbalance spring.
151 Unscrew the row of fixing bolts at the top edge of the wing, also those which hold the wing to the sill and the body 'A' pillar.
152 The mastic joints at the wing flanges will have to be cut through with a sharp knife before the wing can be removed.
153 To refit a wing: clean the wing mating flanges on the bodyshell and apply a thick bead of sealing mastic. Offer up the wing and bolt it into position.
154 Apply underseal to the lower wing surface and spray the top surface to match the body colour.
155 Refit all removed components, and reconnect the battery.

Headlining – renewal

156 A damaged headlining can be renewed in the following way, but note that the fibreglass content can cause skin irritation or a rash, so wear protective clothing.
157 The use of a strip of Velcro (12 x 2 in 304 x 51 mm) will make operations easier.

158 Remove the cant rail trim, (1), Fig. 13.161, from the door apertures.
159 Remove the interior mirror and sun visors, also the grab handles. The screws for the latter are accessible after removal of the end covers.
160 Prise the windscreen and rear screen trim panels clear of the roof rail (3).
161 Attach the Velcro strip to the headlining and pull forward to disengage the rear of the headlining from the locating recess.
162 Disengage the left-hand and then the right-hand edges of the headlining and withdraw it from the car interior.
163 Before fitting the new headlining, trim any thick sections of the outer edge so that it is all of equal thickness.
164 Engage the right-hand corner and the right-hand side of the headlining in the recesses and then using the Velcro strip engage the remaining edges and corners.
165 Refit all the removed components and trim.

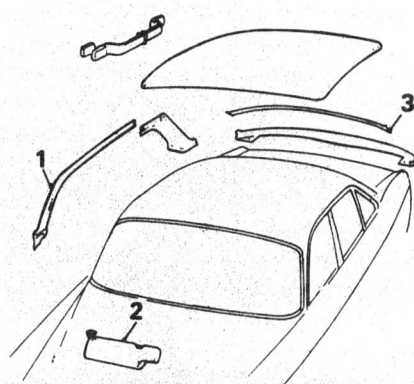

Fig. 13.161 Headlining components (Sec 22)

1 Cant rail trim	3 Trim strip
2 Sun visor	

Plastic components

166 With the use of more and more plastic body components by the vehicle manufacturers (eg bumpers, spoilers, and in some cases major body panels), rectification of more serious damage to such items has become a matter of either entrusting repair work to a specialist in this field, or renewing complete components. Repair of such damage by the DIY owner is not really feasible owing to the cost of the equipment and materials required for effecting such repairs. The basic technique involves making a groove along the line of the crack in the plastic using a rotary burr in a power drill. The damaged part is then welded back together by using a hot air gun to heat up and fuse a plastic filler rod into the groove. Any excess plastic is then removed and the area rubbed down to a smooth finish. It is important that a filler rod of the correct plastic is used, as body components can be made of a variety of different types (eg polycarbonate, ABS, polypropylene).
167 Damage of a less serious nature (abrasions, minor cracks etc) can be repaired by the DIY owner using a two-part epoxy filler repair material, like Holts Body + Plus or Holts No Mix which can be used directly from the tube. Once mixed in equal proportions (or applied direct from the tube in the case of Holts No Mix), this is used in similar fashion to the bodywork filler used on metal panels. The filler is usually cured in twenty to thirty minutes, ready for sanding and painting.
168 If the owner is renewing a complete component himself, or if he has repaired it with epoxy filler, he will be left with the problem of finding a suitable paint for finishing which is compatible with the type of plastic used. At one time the use of a universal paint was not possible owing to the complex range of plastics encountered in body component applications. Standard paints, generally speaking, will not bond to plastic or rubber satisfactorily, but Holts Professional Spraymatch paints to match any plastic or rubber finish can be obtained from dealers. However, it is now possible to obtain a plastic body parts finishing kit which consists of a pre-primer treatment, a primer and coloured top coat. Full instructions are normally supplied with a kit, but basically the method of use is to

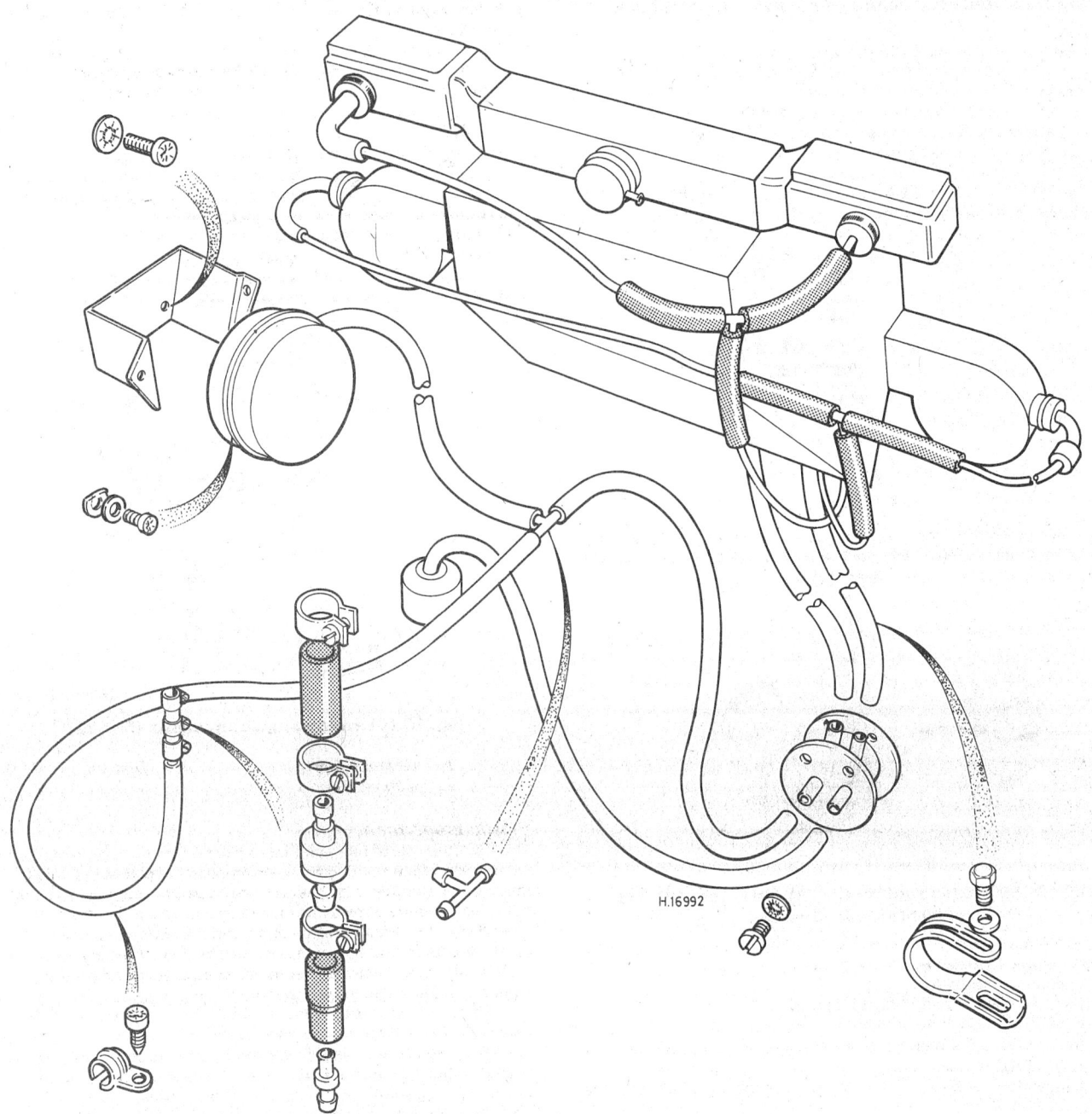

Fig. 13.162 Heater vacuum servo system – Series 2 and 3 models (Sec 22)

first apply the pre-primer to the component concerned and allow it to dry for up to 30 minutes. Then the primer is applied and left to dry for about an hour before finally applying the special coloured top coat. The result is a correctly coloured component where the paint will flex with the plastic or rubber, a property that standard paint does not normally possess.

Heater (Series 2 and 3) – vacuum servo system
168 The layout of the heater vacuum servo system for Series 2 and 3 models is shown in Fig. 13.162.

Heater (Series 3) – flap linkage adjustment
169 Disconnect the battery.
170 Remove the right-hand console casing and underscuttle casing.

Note the position of the electrical leads to the panel light rheostat on right-hand drive models.
171 Turn the temperature control knob to the 'vent' position.
172 Slacken the rod locking screw (1) – Fig. 13.163.
173 Set the adjuster (2) towards the top of the slot in the lever (3). Tighten the lock screw (1).
174 Slacken the upper heater flap link adjuster (4) and release the lower flap link adjuster (8).
175 Using finger pressure, rotate the link (6) fully clockwise and then tighten screw (4).
176 Rotate the flap lever (7) fully clockwise to extend the link (8), then tighten screw (5).
177 Select 'DEF' on the right-hand heater control knob. Slacken the screw (9) and move the link (10) to fully extend the rod (11).

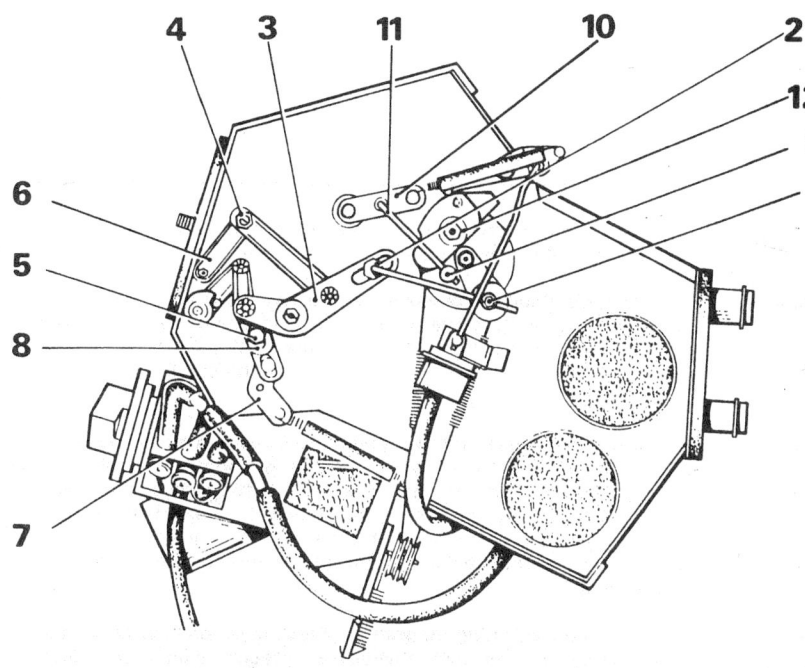

Fig. 13.163 Flap linkage adjustment diagram (Sec 22)

1   Main drive rod locking screw
2   Adjuster
3   Lever
4   Flap link adjuster (upper)
5   Lockscrew
6   Link
7   Cooling flap lever
8   Flap link adjuster (lower)
9   Locking screw
10 Link
11 Drive rod
12 Eccentric pivot

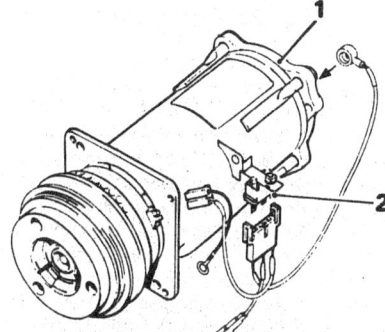

Fig. 13.164 Air conditioning compressor (1) showing thermal fuse (2) (Sec 22)

Tighten the screw.

178 The eccentric pivot (12) on the flap cam is adjustable through 180°. This varies the upper level air temperature. Turning the nut clockwise increases the upper air temperature anti-clockwise reduces it.

179 Refit the console casing panels and reconnect the battery.

Air conditioning system (Series 3) – general

180 The remarks in Section 44 of Chapter 12 are generally applicable to the air conditioning system fitted to later models.

181 If the system is discharged with a view to removing particular components, whether for access or for renewal, the open refrigerant unions must be plugged or capped **at once**. The absorption of atmospheric moisture is harmful to the system. The receiver/dryer must be renewed whenever the system has been opened.

182 The compressor fitted to Series 3 cars incorporates an overload protection device known as a superheat switch. In the event of refrigerant temperature becoming excessive, due perhaps to a leak reducing the quantity in circulation, the superheat switch will close and cause a thermal fuse to blow. The fuse is easily renewed (Fig. 13.164) but this should **not** be done until the reason for the superheat switch operation has been established and corrected.

183 Repair of the automatic temperature regulation system should be left to a specialist.

Fault diagnosis

Introduction

The vehicle owner who does his or her own maintenance according to the recommended schedules should not have to use this section of the manual very often. Modern component reliability is such that, provided those items subject to wear or deterioration are inspected or renewed at the specified intervals, sudden failure is comparatively rare. Faults do not usually just happen as a result of sudden failure, but develop over a period of time. Major mechanical failures in particular are usually preceded by characteristic symptoms over hundreds or even thousands of miles. Those components which do occasionally fail without warning are often small and easily carried in the vehicle.

With any fault finding, the first step is to decide where to begin investigations. Sometimes this is obvious, but on other occasions a little detective work will be necessary. The owner who makes half a dozen haphazard adjustments or replacements may be successful in curing a fault (or its symptoms), but he will be none the wiser if the fault recurs and he may well have spent more time and money than was necessary. A calm and logical approach will be found to be more satisfactory in the long run. Always take into account any warning signs or abnormalities that may have been noticed in the period preceding the fault – power loss, high or low gauge readings, unusual noises or smells, etc – and remember that failure of components such as fuses or spark plugs may only be pointers to some underlying fault.

The pages which follow here are intended to help in cases of failure to start or breakdown on the road. There is also a Fault Diagnosis Section at the end of each Chapter which should be consulted if the preliminary checks prove unfruitful. Whatever the fault, certain basic principles apply. These are as follows:

Verify the fault. This is simply a matter of being sure that you know what the symptoms are before starting work. This is particularly important if you are investigating a fault for someone else who may not have described it very accurately.

Don't overlook the obvious. For example, if the vehicle won't start, is there petrol in the tank? (Don't take anyone else's word on this particular point, and don't trust the fuel gauge either!) If an electrical fault is indicated, look for loose or broken wires before digging out the test gear.

Cure the disease, not the symptom. Substituting a flat battery with a fully charged one will get you off the hard shoulder, but if the underlying cause is not attended to, the new battery will go the same way. Similarly, changing oil-fouled spark plugs for a new set will get you moving again, but remember that the reason for the fouling (if it wasn't simply an incorrect grade of plug) will have to be established and corrected.

Don't take anything for granted. Particularly, don't forget that a 'new' component may itself be defective (especially if it's been rattling round in the boot for months), and don't leave components out of a fault diagnosis sequence just because they are new or recently fitted. When you do finally diagnose a difficult fault, you'll probably realise that all the evidence was there from the start.

Electrical faults

Electrical faults can be more puzzling than straightforward mechanical failures, but they are no less susceptible to logical analysis if the basic principles of operation are understood. Vehicle electrical wiring exists in extremely unfavourable conditions – heat, vibration and chemical attack – and the first things to look for are loose or corroded connections and broken or chafed wires, especially where the wires pass through holes in the bodywork or are subject to vibration.

Carrying a selection of spares and equipment is a wise precaution

All metal-bodied vehicles in current production have one pole of the battery 'earthed', ie connected to the vehicle bodywork, and in nearly all modern vehicles it is the negative (–) terminal. The various electrical components – motors, bulb holders etc – are also connected to earth, either by means of a lead or directly by their mountings. Electric current flows through the component and then back to the battery via the bodywork. If the component mounting is loose or corroded, or if a good path back to the battery is not available, the circuit will be incomplete and malfunction will result. The engine and/or gearbox are also earthed by means of flexible metal straps to the body or subframe; if these straps are loose or missing, starter motor, generator and ignition trouble may result.

Assuming the earth return to be satisfactory, electrical faults will be due either to component malfunction or to defects in the current supply. Individual components are dealt with in Chapter 10. If supply wires are broken or cracked internally this results in an open-circuit, and the easiest way to check for this is to bypass the suspect wire temporarily with a length of wire having a crocodile clip or suitable connector at each end. Alternatively, a 12V test lamp can be used to verify the presence of supply voltage at various points along the wire and the break can be thus isolated.

If a bare portion of a live wire touches the bodywork or other earthed metal part, the electricity will take the low-resistance path thus formed back to the battery: this is known as a short-circuit. Hopefully a short-circuit will blow a fuse, but otherwise it may cause burning of the insulation (and possibly further short-circuits) or even a fire. This is why it is inadvisable to bypass persistently blowing fuses with silver foil or wire.

Spares and tool kit

Most vehicles are supplied only with sufficient tools for wheel changing; the *Maintenance and minor repair* tool kit detailed in *Tools and working facilities,* with the addition of a hammer, is probably sufficient for those repairs that most motorists would consider attempting at the roadside. In addition a few items which can be fitted without too much trouble in the event of a breakdown should be carried. Experience and available space will modify the list below, but the following may save having to call on professional assistance:

Spark plugs, clean and correctly gapped
HT lead and plug cap – long enough to reach the plug furthest from the distributor
Distributor rotor, condenser and contact breaker points (as applicable)
Drivebelt(s) – emergency type may suffice
Spare fuses
Set of principal light bulbs
Tin of radiator sealer and hose bandage
Exhaust bandage
Roll of insulating tape
Length of soft iron wire
Length of electrical flex
Torch or inspection lamp (can double as test lamp)
Battery jump leads
Tow-rope
Ignition water dispersing aerosol
Litre of engine oil
Sealed can of hydraulic fluid
Emergency windscreen
'Worm drive' clips

If spare fuel is carried, a can designed for the purpose should be used to minimise risks of leakage and collision damage. A first aid kit and a warning triangle, whilst not at present compulsory in the UK, are obviously sensible items to carry in addition to the above.

When touring abroad it may be advisable to carry additional spares which, even if you cannot fit them yourself, could save having to wait while parts are obtained. The items below may be worth considering:

Throttle cables
Cylinder head gasket
Alternator brushes
Fuel injector(s) and set of O-rings (as applicable)

One of the motoring organisations will be able to advise on availability of fuel etc in foreign countries.

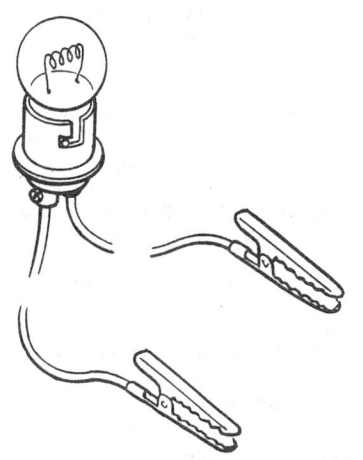

A simple test lamp is useful for tracing electrical faults

Engine will not start

Engine fails to turn when starter operated

Flat battery (recharge, use jump leads, or push start)
Battery terminals loose or corroded
Battery earth to body defective
Engine earth strap loose or broken
Starter motor (or solenoid) wiring loose or broken
Automatic transmission selector in wrong position, or inhibitor switch faulty
Ignition/starter switch faulty
Major mechanical failure (seizure)
Starter or solenoid internal fault (see Chapter 10)

Starter motor turns engine slowly

Partially discharged battery (recharge, use jump leads, or push start)
Battery terminals loose or corroded
Battery earth to body defective
Engine earth strap loose
Starter motor (or solenoid) wiring loose
Starter motor internal fault (see Chapter 10)

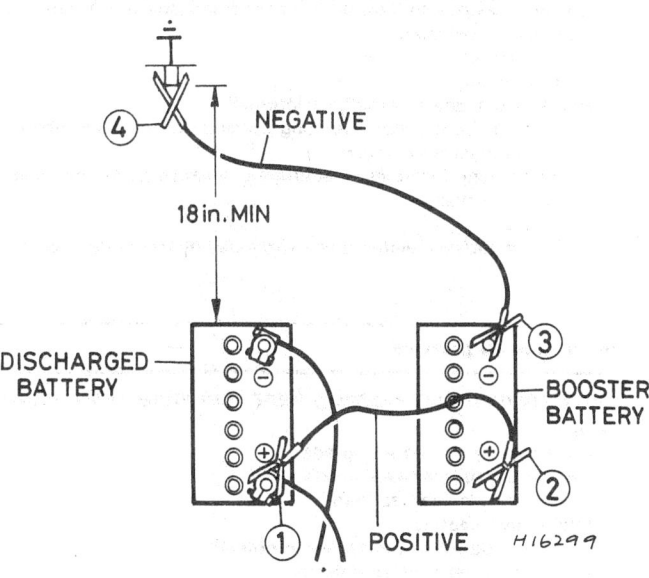

Jump start lead connections for negative earth vehicles – connect leads in order shown

Starter motor spins without turning engine
Flywheel gear teeth damaged or worn
Starter motor mounting bolts loose

Engine turns normally but fails to start
Damp or dirty HT leads and distributor cap (crank engine and
check for spark) – try moisture dispersant such as Holts Wet Start
Dirty or incorrectly gapped distributor points (if applicable)
No fuel in tank (check for delivery at carburettor)
Fouled or incorrectly gapped spark plugs (remove, clean and
regap)
Other ignition system fault (see Chapter 4)
Other fuel system fault (see Chapter 3)
Poor compression (see Chapter 1)
Major mechanical failure (eg camshaft drive)

Engine fires but will not run
Air leaks at carburettor or inlet manifold
Fuel starvation (see Chapter 3)
Ballast resistor defective, or other ignition fault (see Chapter 4)

Engine cuts out and will not restart

Engine cuts out suddenly – ignition fault
Loose or disconnected LT wires
Wet HT leads or distributor cap (after traversing water splash)
Coil or condenser failure (check for spark)
Other ignition fault (see Chapter 4)

Engine misfires before cutting out – fuel fault
Fuel tank empty
Fuel pump defective or filter blocked (check for delivery)
Fuel tank filler vent blocked (suction will be evident on releasing
cap)
Carburettor needle valve sticking
Carburettor jets blocked (fuel contaminated)
Other fuel system fault (see Chapter 3)

Engine cuts out – other causes
Serious overheating
Major mechanical failure (eg camshaft drive)

Engine overheats

Slack or broken drivebelt – retension or renew (Chapter 2)
Coolant loss due to internal or external leakage (see Chapter 2)
Thermostat defective
Low oil level
Brakes binding
Radiator clogged externally or internally
Electric cooling fan not operating correctly (when applicable)
Engine waterways clogged
Ignition timing incorrect or automatic advance malfunctioning
Mixture too weak

Note: *Do not add cold water to an overheated engine or damage may
result*

Low engine oil pressure

Gauge reads low or warning light illuminated with engine running
Oil level low or incorrect grade
Defective gauge or sender unit
Wire to sender unit earthed
Engine overheating
Oil filter clogged or bypass valve defective
Oil pressure relief valve defective

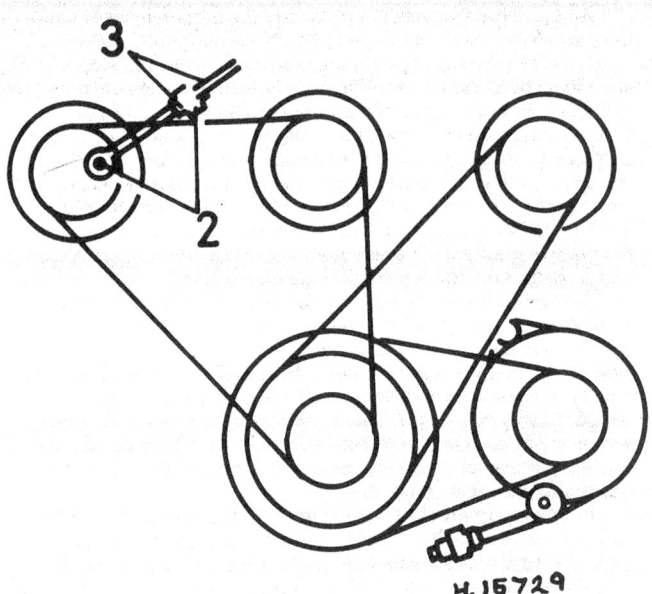

H.15729

**Drivebelt tensioning arrangements. Slack belts can cause
overheating or battery charging problems**

2   *Adjuster eye-bolt and trunnion bolt*
3   *Adjuster nut and locknut*

Oil pick-up strainer clogged
Oil pump worn or mountings loose
Worn main or big-end bearings
Note: *Low oil pressure in a high-mileage engine at tickover is not
necessarily a cause for concern. Sudden pressure loss at speed is far
more significant. In any event, check the gauge or warning light sender
before condemning the engine.*

Engine noises

Pre-ignition (pinking) on acceleration
Incorrect grade of fuel
Ignition timing incorrect
Distributor faulty or worn
Worn or maladjusted carburettor
Excessive carbon build-up in engine

Whistling or wheezing noises
Leaking vacuum hose
Leaking carburettor or manifold gasket
Blowing head gasket

Tapping or rattling
Incorrect valve clearances
Worn valve gear
Worn timing chain
Broken piston ring (ticking noise)

Knocking or thumping
Unintentional mechanical contact (eg fan blades)
Worn fanbelt
Peripheral component fault (generator, water pump etc)
Worn big-end bearings (regular heavy knocking, perhaps less
under load)
Worn main bearings (rumbling and knocking, perhaps worsening
under load)
Piston slap (most noticeable when cold)

Jacking and towing

Jacking

Use the jack supplied with the car only for roadside wheel changing. The head of the jack must engage positively with the appropriate spigot on the underside of the car. Apply the handbrake, select 'P' (or engage 1st gear on manual transmission models), and chock the wheel diagonally opposite that being removed before raising the jack.

To raise one wheel off the ground using a scissor or 'bottle' jack, place the head of the jack under the outer wishbone fork, using a block of wood between the jack head and the wishbone. Make sure that the block of wood does not foul the hub carrier or the grease nipple as the jack is raised.

A trolley jack of adequate lifting capacity, is satisfactory for raising one end or other of the car when servicing or repair work is to be carried out. Position the head of the jack under the centre of the front crossmember or under the plate below the final drive unit, in each case using a suitably shaped block of wood between the head of the jack and the vehicle.

Never venture under the car when it is supported only by a jack — always use axle stands, of adequate rating and properly positioned. Ideally the stands should engage in the service jack spigots so that they are positively located.

Towing

Front towing eyes are provided for recovery purposes. They are located next to the forward attachment points of the front crossmember. The eyes near the rear shock absorber lower mountings are lash-down points — they are **not** intended for towing.

Vehicles with automatic transmission may be towed no further than 30 miles (50 km) and no faster than 30 mph (50 km/h), provided that an extra 3 pints (1.7 litres) of ATF is added to the transmission before towing. If these conditions cannot be met, or if transmission damage is the reason for seeking a tow, the car must be towed with the rear wheels suspended or with the propeller shaft disconnected.

Vehicles with four-speed manual transmission can be towed without restriction on speed or distance, at least as far as the transmission is concerned.

Vehicles with five-speed manual transmission **must not** be towed with the rear wheels on the ground unless the propeller shaft is first disconnected. Failure to observe this point can result in transmission damage due to lack of lubrication.

On all vehicles, remember to unlock the steering before being towed. Bear in mind that power steering and brake servo assistance will not be available when the engine is not running.

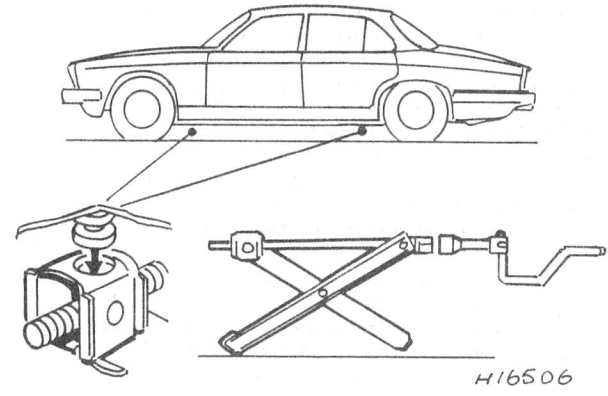

Jacking points for use with wheel changing jack

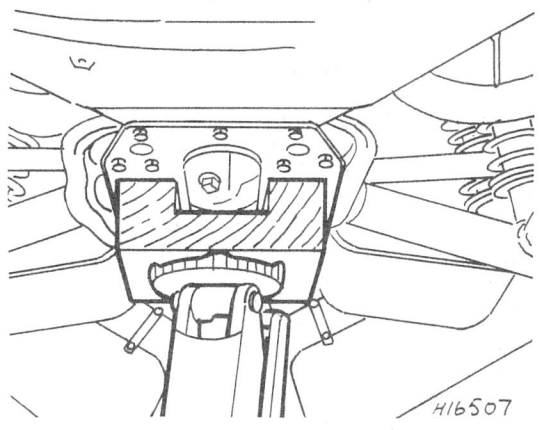

Jacking point for use with trolley jack at rear – note block of wood

Tools and working facilities

Introduction

A selection of good tools is a fundamental requirement for anyone contemplating the maintenance and repair of a motor vehicle. For the owner who does not possess any, their purchase will prove a considerable expense, offsetting some of the savings made by doing-it-yourself. However, provided that the tools purchased meet the relevant national safety standards and are of good quality, they will last for many years and prove an extremely worthwhile investment.

To help the average owner to decide which tools are needed to carry out the various tasks detailed in this manual, we have compiled three lists of tools under the following headings: *Maintenance and minor repair*, *Repair and overhaul*, and *Special*. The newcomer to practical mechanics should start off with the *Maintenance and minor repair* tool kit and confine himself to the simpler jobs around the vehicle. Then, as his confidence and experience grow, he can undertake more difficult tasks, buying extra tools as, and when, they are needed. In this way, a *Maintenance and minor repair* tool kit can be built-up into a *Repair and overhaul* tool kit over a considerable period of time without any major cash outlays. The experienced do-it-yourselfer will have a tool kit good enough for most repair and overhaul procedures and will add tools from the *Special* category when he feels the expense is justified by the amount of use to which these tools will be put.

It is obviously not possible to cover the subject of tools fully here. For those who wish to learn more about tools and their use there is a book entitled *How to Choose and Use Car Tools* available from the publishers of this manual.

Maintenance and minor repair tool kit

The tools given in this list should be considered as a minimum requirement if routine maintenance, servicing and minor repair operations are to be undertaken. We recommend the purchase of combination spanners (ring one end, open-ended the other); although more expensive than open-ended ones, they do give the advantages of both types of spanner.

> *Combination spanners covering the range $\frac{3}{8}$ in to 1 in AF (Series 1 and 2) and/or 10 to 17 mm (Series 3)*
> *Adjustable spanner - 9 inch*
> *Engine sump/gearbox/rear axle drain plug key*
> *Spark plug spanner (with rubber insert)*
> *Spark plug gap adjustment tool*
> *Set of feeler gauges*
> *Brake bleed nipple spanner*
> *Screwdriver - 4 in long x $\frac{1}{4}$ in dia (flat blade)*
> *Screwdriver - 4 in long x $\frac{1}{4}$ in dia (cross blade)*
> *Combination pliers - 6 inch*
> *Hacksaw (junior)*
> *Tyre pump*
> *Tyre pressure gauge*
> *Grease gun*
> *Oil can*
> *Fine emery cloth (1 sheet)*
> *Wire brush (small)*
> *Funnel (medium size)*

Repair and overhaul tool kit

These tools are virtually essential for anyone undertaking any major repairs to a motor vehicle, and are additional to those given in the *Maintenance and minor repair* list. Included in this list is a comprehensive set of sockets. Although these are expensive they will be found invaluable as they are so versatile - particularly if various drives are included in the set. We recommend the $\frac{1}{2}$ in square-drive type, as this can be used with most proprietary torque wrenches. If you cannot afford a socket set, even bought piecemeal, then inexpensive tubular box spanners are a useful alternative.

The tools in this list will occasionally need to be supplemented by tools from the *Special* list.

> *Sockets (or box spanners) to cover range in previous list*
> *Reversible ratchet drive (for use with sockets)*
> *Extension piece, 10 inch (for use with sockets)*
> *Universal joint (for use with sockets)*
> *Torque wrench (for use with sockets)*
> *'Mole' wrench - 8 inch*
> *Ball pein hammer*
> *Soft-faced hammer, plastic or rubber*
> *Screwdriver - 6 in long x $\frac{5}{16}$ in dia (flat blade)*
> *Screwdriver - 2 in long x $\frac{5}{16}$ in square (flat blade)*
> *Screwdriver - 1$\frac{1}{2}$ in long x $\frac{1}{4}$ in dia (cross blade)*
> *Screwdriver - 3 in long x $\frac{1}{8}$ in dia (electricians)*
> *Pliers - electricians side cutters*
> *Pliers - needle nosed*
> *Pliers - circlip (internal and external)*
> *Cold chisel - $\frac{1}{2}$ inch*
> *Scriber*
> *Scraper*
> *Centre punch*
> *Pin punch*
> *Hacksaw*
> *Valve grinding tool*
> *Steel rule/straight-edge*
> *Allen keys*
> *Selection of files*
> *Wire brush (large)*
> *Axle-stands*
> *Jack (strong scissor or hydraulic type)*

Special tools

The tools in this list are those which are not used regularly, are expensive to buy, or which need to be used in accordance with their manufacturers' instructions. Unless relatively difficult mechanical jobs are undertaken frequently, it will not be economic to buy many of these tools. Where this is the case, you could consider clubbing together with friends (or joining a motorists' club) to make a joint purchase, or borrowing the tools against a deposit from a local garage or tool hire specialist.

The following list contains only those tools and instruments freely available to the public, and not those special tools produced by the vehicle manufacturer specifically for its dealer network. You will find occasional references to these manufacturers' special tools in the text of this manual. Generally, an alternative method of doing the job without the vehicle manufacturers' special tool is given. However, sometimes, there is no alternative to using them. Where this is the case and the relevant tool cannot be bought or borrowed, you will have to entrust the work to a franchised garage.

Valve spring compressor
Piston ring compressor
Balljoint separator
Universal hub/bearing puller
Impact screwdriver
Micrometer and/or vernier gauge
Dial gauge
Stroboscopic timing light
Dwell angle meter/tachometer
Universal electrical multi-meter
Cylinder compression gauge
Lifting tackle
Trolley jack
Light with extension lead

Buying tools

For practically all tools, a tool factor is the best source since he will have a very comprehensive range compared with the average garage or accessory shop. Having said that, accessory shops often offer excellent quality tools at discount prices, so it pays to shop around.

There are plenty of good tools around at reasonable prices, but always aim to purchase items which meet the relevant national safety standards. If in doubt, ask the proprietor or manager of the shop for advice before making a purchase.

Care and maintenance of tools

Having purchased a reasonable tool kit, it is necessary to keep the tools in a clean serviceable condition. After use, always wipe off any dirt, grease and metal particles using a clean, dry cloth, before putting the tools away. Never leave them lying around after they have been used. A simple tool rack on the garage or workshop wall, for items such as screwdrivers and pliers is a good idea. Store all normal wrenches and sockets in a metal box. Any measuring instruments, gauges, meters, etc, must be carefully stored where they cannot be damaged or become rusty.

Take a little care when tools are used. Hammer heads inevitably become marked and screwdrivers lose the keen edge on their blades from time to time. A little timely attention with emery cloth or a file will soon restore items like this to a good serviceable finish.

Working facilities

Not to be forgotten when discussing tools, is the workshop itself. If anything more than routine maintenance is to be carried out, some form of suitable working area becomes essential.

It is appreciated that many an owner mechanic is forced by circumstances to remove an engine or similar item, without the benefit of a garage or workshop. Having done this, any repairs should always be done under the cover of a roof.

Wherever possible, any dismantling should be done on a clean, flat workbench or table at a suitable working height.

Any workbench needs a vice: one with a jaw opening of 4 in (100 mm) is suitable for most jobs. As mentioned previously, some clean dry storage space is also required for tools, as well as for lubricants, cleaning fluids, touch-up paints and so on, which become necessary.

Another item which may be required, and which has a much more general usage, is an electric drill with a chuck capacity of at least $\frac{5}{16}$ in (8 mm). This, together with a good range of twist drills, is virtually essential for fitting accessories such as mirrors and reversing lights.

Last, but not least, always keep a supply of old newspapers and clean, lint-free rags available, and try to keep any working area as clean as possible.

Spanner jaw gap comparison table

Jaw gap (in)	Spanner size
0.250	$\frac{1}{4}$ in AF
0.276	7 mm
0.313	$\frac{5}{16}$ in AF
0.315	8 mm
0.344	$\frac{11}{32}$ in AF; $\frac{1}{8}$ in Whitworth
0.354	9 mm
0.375	$\frac{3}{8}$ in AF
0.394	10 mm
0.433	11 mm
0.438	$\frac{7}{16}$ in AF
0.445	$\frac{3}{16}$ in Whitworth; $\frac{1}{4}$ in BSF
0.472	12 mm
0.500	$\frac{1}{2}$ in AF
0.512	13 mm
0.525	$\frac{1}{4}$ in Whitworth; $\frac{5}{16}$ in BSF
0.551	14 mm
0.563	$\frac{9}{16}$ in AF
0.591	15 mm
0.600	$\frac{5}{16}$ in Whitworth; $\frac{3}{8}$ in BSF
0.625	$\frac{5}{8}$ in AF
0.630	16 mm
0.669	17 mm
0.686	$\frac{11}{16}$ in AF
0.709	18 mm
0.710	$\frac{3}{8}$ in Whitworth; $\frac{7}{16}$ in BSF
0.748	19 mm
0.750	$\frac{3}{4}$ in AF
0.813	$\frac{13}{16}$ in AF
0.820	$\frac{7}{16}$ in Whitworth; $\frac{1}{2}$ in BSF
0.866	22 mm
0.875	$\frac{7}{8}$ in AF
0.920	$\frac{1}{2}$ in Whitworth; $\frac{9}{16}$ in BSF
0.938	$\frac{15}{16}$ in AF
0.945	24 mm
1.000	1 in AF
1.010	$\frac{9}{16}$ in Whitworth; $\frac{5}{8}$ in BSF
1.024	26 mm
1.063	$1\frac{1}{16}$ in AF; 27 mm
1.100	$\frac{5}{8}$ in Whitworth; $\frac{11}{16}$ in BSF
1.125	$1\frac{1}{8}$ in AF
1.181	30 mm
1.200	$\frac{11}{16}$ in Whitworth; $\frac{3}{4}$ in BSF
1.250	$1\frac{1}{4}$ in AF
1.260	32 mm
1.300	$\frac{3}{4}$ in Whitworth; $\frac{7}{8}$ in BSF
1.313	$1\frac{5}{16}$ in AF
1.390	$\frac{13}{16}$ in Whitworth; $\frac{15}{16}$ in BSF
1.417	36 mm
1.438	$1\frac{7}{16}$ in AF
1.480	$\frac{7}{8}$ in Whitworth; 1 in BSF
1.500	$1\frac{1}{2}$ in AF
1.575	40 mm; $\frac{15}{16}$ in Whitworth
1.614	41 mm
1.625	$1\frac{5}{8}$ in AF
1.670	1 in Whitworth; $1\frac{1}{8}$ in BSF
1.688	$1\frac{11}{16}$ in AF
1.811	46 mm
1.813	$1\frac{13}{16}$ in AF
1.860	$1\frac{1}{8}$ in Whitworth; $1\frac{1}{4}$ in BSF
1.875	$1\frac{7}{8}$ in AF
1.969	50 mm
2.000	2 in AF
2.050	$1\frac{1}{4}$ in Whitworth; $1\frac{3}{8}$ in BSF
2.165	55 mm
2.362	60 mm

General repair procedures

Whenever servicing, repair or overhaul work is carried out on the car or its components, it is necessary to observe the following procedures and instructions. This will assist in carrying out the operation efficiently and to a professional standard of workmanship.

Joint mating faces and gaskets

Where a gasket is used between the mating faces of two components, ensure that it is renewed on reassembly, and fit it dry unless otherwise stated in the repair procedure. Make sure that the mating faces are clean and dry with all traces of old gasket removed. When cleaning a joint face, use a tool which is not likely to score or damage the face, and remove any burrs or nicks with an oilstone or fine file.

Make sure that tapped holes are cleaned with a pipe cleaner, and keep them free of jointing compound if this is being used unless specifically instructed otherwise.

Ensure that all orifices, channels or pipes are clear and blow through them, preferably using compressed air.

Oil seals

Whenever an oil seal is removed from its working location, either individually or as part of an assembly, it should be renewed.

The very fine sealing lip of the seal is easily damaged and will not seal if the surface it contacts is not completely clean and free from scratches, nicks or grooves. If the original sealing surface of the component cannot be restored, the component should be renewed.

Protect the lips of the seal from any surface which may damage them in the course of fitting. Use tape or a conical sleeve where possible. Lubricate the seal lips with oil before fitting and, on dual lipped seals, fill the space between the lips with grease.

Unless otherwise stated, oil seals must be fitted with their sealing lips toward the lubricant to be sealed.

Use a tubular drift or block of wood of the appropriate size to install the seal and, if the seal housing is shouldered, drive the seal down to the shoulder. If the seal housing is unshouldered, the seal should be fitted with its face flush with the housing top face.

Screw threads and fastenings

Always ensure that a blind tapped hole is completely free from oil, grease, water or other fluid before installing the bolt or stud. Failure to do this could cause the housing to crack due to the hydraulic action of the bolt or stud as it is screwed in.

When tightening a castellated nut to accept a split pin, tighten the nut to the specified torque, where applicable, and then tighten further to the next split pin hole. Never slacken the nut to align a split pin hole unless stated in the repair procedure.

When checking or retightening a nut or bolt to a specified torque setting, slacken the nut or bolt by a quarter of a turn, and then retighten to the specified setting.

Locknuts, locktabs and washers

Any fastening which will rotate against a component or housing in the course of tightening should always have a washer between it and the relevant component or housing.

Spring or split washers should always be renewed when they are used to lock a critical component such as a big-end bearing retaining nut or bolt.

Locktabs which are folded over to retain a nut or bolt should always be renewed.

Self-locking nuts can be reused in non-critical areas, providing resistance can be felt when the locking portion passes over the bolt or stud thread.

Split pins must always be replaced with new ones of the correct size for the hole.

Special tools

Some repair procedures in this manual entail the use of special tools such as a press, two or three-legged pullers, spring compressors etc. Wherever possible, suitable readily available alternatives to the manufacturer's special tools are described, and are shown in use. In some instances, where no alternative is possible, it has been necessary to resort to the use of a manufacturer's tool and this has been done for reasons of safety as well as the efficient completion of the repair operation. Unless you are highly skilled and have a thorough understanding of the procedure described, never attempt to bypass the use of any special tool when the procedure described specifies its use. Not only is there a very great risk of personal injury, but expensive damage could be caused to the components involved.

Use of English

As this book has been written in England, it uses the appropriate English component names, phrases, and spelling. Some of these differ from those used in America. Normally, these cause no difficulty, but to make sure, a glossary is printed below. In ordering spare parts remember the parts list may use some of these words:

English	American	English	American
Accelerator	Gas pedal	Locks	Latches
Aerial	Antenna	Methylated spirit	Denatured alcohol
Anti-roll bar	Stabiliser or sway bar	Motorway	Freeway, turnpike etc
Big-end bearing	Rod bearing	Number plate	License plate
Bonnet (engine cover)	Hood	Paraffin	Kerosene
Boot (luggage compartment)	Trunk	Petrol	Gasoline (gas)
Bulkhead	Firewall	Petrol tank	Gas tank
Bush	Bushing	'Pinking'	'Pinging'
Cam follower or tappet	Valve lifter or tappet	Prise (force apart)	Pry
Carburettor	Carburetor	Propeller shaft	Driveshaft
Catch	Latch	Quarterlight	Quarter window
Choke/venturi	Barrel	Retread	Recap
Circlip	Snap-ring	Reverse	Back-up
Clearance	Lash	Rocker cover	Valve cover
Crownwheel	Ring gear (of differential)	Saloon	Sedan
Damper	Shock absorber, shock	Seized	Frozen
Disc (brake)	Rotor/disk	Sidelight	Parking light
Distance piece	Spacer	Silencer	Muffler
Drop arm	Pitman arm	Sill panel (beneath doors)	Rocker panel
Drop head coupe	Convertible	Small end, little end	Piston pin or wrist pin
Dynamo	Generator (DC)	Spanner	Wrench
Earth (electrical)	Ground	Split cotter (for valve spring cap)	Lock (for valve spring retainer)
Engineer's blue	Prussian blue	Split pin	Cotter pin
Estate car	Station wagon	Steering arm	Spindle arm
Exhaust manifold	Header	Sump	Oil pan
Fault finding/diagnosis	Troubleshooting	Swarf	Metal chips or debris
Float chamber	Float bowl	Tab washer	Tang or lock
Free-play	Lash	Tappet	Valve lifter
Freewheel	Coast	Thrust bearing	Throw-out bearing
Gearbox	Transmission	Top gear	High
Gearchange	Shift	Torch	Flashlight
Grub screw	Setscrew, Allen screw	Trackrod (of steering)	Tie-rod (or connecting rod)
Gudgeon pin	Piston pin or wrist pin	Trailing shoe (of brake)	Secondary shoe
Halfshaft	Axleshaft	Transmission	Whole drive line
Handbrake	Parking brake	Tyre	Tire
Hood	Soft top	Van	Panel wagon/van
Hot spot	Heat riser	Vice	Vise
Indicator	Turn signal	Wheel nut	Lug nut
Interior light	Dome lamp	Windscreen	Windshield
Layshaft (of gearbox)	Countershaft	Wing/mudguard	Fender
Leading shoe (of brake)	Primary shoe		

Conversion factors

Length (distance)

	X		=		X		=	
Inches (in)	X	25.4	=	Millimetres (mm)	X	0.0394	=	Inches (in)
Feet (ft)	X	0.305	=	Metres (m)	X	3.281	=	Feet (ft)
Miles	X	1.609	=	Kilometres (km)	X	0.621	=	Miles

Volume (capacity)

	X		=		X		=	
Cubic inches (cu in; in³)	X	16.387	=	Cubic centimetres (cc; cm³)	X	0.061	=	Cubic inches (cu in; in³)
Imperial pints (Imp pt)	X	0.568	=	Litres (l)	X	1.76	=	Imperial pints (Imp pt)
Imperial quarts (Imp qt)	X	1.137	=	Litres (l)	X	0.88	=	Imperial quarts (Imp qt)
Imperial quarts (Imp qt)	X	1.201	=	US quarts (US qt)	X	0.833	=	Imperial quarts (Imp qt)
US quarts (US qt)	X	0.946	=	Litres (l)	X	1.057	=	US quarts (US qt)
Imperial gallons (Imp gal)	X	4.546	=	Litres (l)	X	0.22	=	Imperial gallons (Imp gal)
Imperial gallons (Imp gal)	X	1.201	=	US gallons (US gal)	X	0.833	=	Imperial gallons (Imp gal)
US gallons (US gal)	X	3.785	=	Litres (l)	X	0.264	=	US gallons (US gal)

Mass (weight)

	X		=		X		=	
Ounces (oz)	X	28.35	=	Grams (g)	X	0.035	=	Ounces (oz)
Pounds (lb)	X	0.454	=	Kilograms (kg)	X	2.205	=	Pounds (lb)

Force

	X		=		X		=	
Ounces-force (ozf; oz)	X	0.278	=	Newtons (N)	X	3.6	=	Ounces-force (ozf; oz)
Pounds-force (lbf; lb)	X	4.448	=	Newtons (N)	X	0.225	=	Pounds-force (lbf; lb)
Newtons (N)	X	0.1	=	Kilograms-force (kgf; kg)	X	9.81	=	Newtons (N)

Pressure

	X		=		X		=	
Pounds-force per square inch (psi; lbf/in²; lb/in²)	X	0.070	=	Kilograms-force per square centimetre (kgf/cm²; kg/cm²)	X	14.223	=	Pounds-force per square inch (psi; lbf/in²; lb/in²)
Pounds-force per square inch (psi; lbf/in²; lb/in²)	X	0.068	=	Atmospheres (atm)	X	14.696	=	Pounds-force per square inch (psi; lbf/in²; lb/in²)
Pounds-force per square inch (psi; lbf/in²; lb/in²)	X	0.069	=	Bars	X	14.5	=	Pounds-force per square inch (psi; lbf/in²; lb/in²)
Pounds-force per square inch (psi; lbf/in²; lb/in²)	X	6.895	=	Kilopascals (kPa)	X	0.145	=	Pounds-force per square inch (psi; lbf/in²; lb/in²)
Kilopascals (kPa)	X	0.01	=	Kilograms-force per square centimetre (kgf/cm²; kg/cm²)	X	98.1	=	Kilopascals (kPa)
Millibar (mbar)	X	100	=	Pascals (Pa)	X	0.01	=	Millibar (mbar)
Millibar (mbar)	X	0.0145	=	Pounds-force per square inch (psi; lbf/in²; lb/in²)	X	68.947	=	Millibar (mbar)
Millibar (mbar)	X	0.75	=	Millimetres of mercury (mmHg)	X	1.333	=	Millibar (mbar)
Millibar (mbar)	X	0.401	=	Inches of water (inH₂O)	X	2.491	=	Millibar (mbar)
Millimetres of mercury (mmHg)	X	0.535	=	Inches of water (inH₂O)	X	1.868	=	Millimetres of mercury (mmHg)
Inches of water (inH₂O)	X	0.036	=	Pounds-force per square inch (psi; lbf/in²; lb/in²)	X	27.68	=	Inches of water (inH₂O)

Torque (moment of force)

	X		=		X		=	
Pounds-force inches (lbf in; lb in)	X	1.152	=	Kilograms-force centimetre (kgf cm; kg cm)	X	0.868	=	Pounds-force inches (lbf in; lb in)
Pounds-force inches (lbf in; lb in)	X	0.113	=	Newton metres (Nm)	X	8.85	=	Pounds-force inches (lbf in; lb in)
Pounds-force inches (lbf in; lb in)	X	0.083	=	Pounds-force feet (lbf ft; lb ft)	X	12	=	Pounds-force inches (lbf in; lb in)
Pounds-force feet (lbf ft; lb ft)	X	0.138	=	Kilograms-force metres (kgf m; kg m)	X	7.233	=	Pounds-force feet (lbf ft; lb ft)
Pounds-force feet (lbf ft; lb ft)	X	1.356	=	Newton metres (Nm)	X	0.738	=	Pounds-force feet (lbf ft; lb ft)
Newton metres (Nm)	X	0.102	=	Kilograms-force metres (kgf m; kg m)	X	9.804	=	Newton metres (Nm)

Power

	X		=		X		=	
Horsepower (hp)	X	745.7	=	Watts (W)	X	0.0013	=	Horsepower (hp)

Velocity (speed)

	X		=		X		=	
Miles per hour (miles/hr; mph)	X	1.609	=	Kilometres per hour (km/hr; kph)	X	0.621	=	Miles per hour (miles/hr; mph)

Fuel consumption*

	X		=		X		=	
Miles per gallon, Imperial (mpg)	X	0.354	=	Kilometres per litre (km/l)	X	2.825	=	Miles per gallon, Imperial (mpg)
Miles per gallon, US (mpg)	X	0.425	=	Kilometres per litre (km/l)	X	2.352	=	Miles per gallon, US (mpg)

Temperature

Degrees Fahrenheit = (°C x 1.8) + 32

Degrees Celsius (Degrees Centigrade; °C) = (°F - 32) x 0.56

*It is common practice to convert from miles per gallon (mpg) to litres/100 kilometres (l/100km), where mpg (Imperial) x l/100 km = 282 and mpg (US) x l/100 km = 235

Index

Zeitfracht Medien GmbH
Ferdinand-Jühlke-Straße 7
99095 Erfurt, Deutschland
produktsicherheit@kolibri360.de